CARL H. KLAUS
UNIVERSITY OF IOWA

CHRIS ANDERSON
OREGON STATE UNIVERSITY

REBECCA BLEVINS FAERY
MOUNT HOLYOKE COLLEGE

In DEPTH

ESSAYISTS FOR OUR TIME

SECOND EDITION

Harcourt Brace College Publishers

FORT WORTH   PHILADELPHIA   SAN DIEGO   NEW YORK   ORLANDO   AUSTIN   SAN ANTONIO
TORONTO   MONTREAL   LONDON   SYDNEY   TOKYO

PUBLISHER	Ted Buchholz
ACQUISITIONS EDITOR	Stephen T. Jordan
DEVELOPMENTAL EDITOR	Laurie Runion
PROJECT EDITOR	Mike Hinshaw
PRODUCTION MANAGER	Debra A. Jenkin
BOOK DESIGNER	Peggy Young

ISBN: 0-15-500172-8

Library of Congress Number: 92-72058

PRINTED IN THE UNITED STATES OF AMERICA

3 4 5 6 7 8 9 0 1 2 016 9 8 7 6 5 4 3 2

Acknowledgments of permission begin on page 806.

PREFACE

In Depth: Essayists for Our Time, Second Edition, offers writing instructors a wide-ranging collection of outstanding essayists and essays. Twenty-six essayists make up this collection: Woody Allen, Francis Bacon, Russell Baker, James Baldwin, Bruno Bettelheim, Joan Didion, Annie Dillard, Loren Eiseley, Ellen Goodman, Stephen Jay Gould, Edward Hoagland, Martin Luther King, Jr., Nancy Mairs, Margaret Mead, N. Scott Momaday, Michel de Montaigne, Joyce Carol Oates, George Orwell, Cynthia Ozick, Lewis Thomas, Henry David Thoreau, Mark Twain, Alice Walker, E.B. White, Tom Wolfe, and Virginia Woolf. Five of the authors—Mairs, Momaday, Montaigne, Oates, and Ozick—are new to this edition. Each essayist is represented by four, five, or six pieces, resulting in a collection of 110 essays, 35 of which are new to this edition and 51 of which are by minority or women writers.

This culturally varied anthology includes current essayists as well as writers from earlier periods whose work continues to speak to the interests and issues of our time. It provides essays by notable literary figures as well as by authors best known for their achievements in the natural sciences, social sciences, and public affairs. Taken as a whole, this anthology offers students the opportunity to read the essays of distinguished writers and thinkers whose interests cover a broad spectrum of subjects and fields of study.

Because the material is organized alphabetically by author, this collection leaves instructors free to approach the essays as they wish— by author, by culture, by gender, by mode, by structure, by theme, or by field of interest. To facilitate these and other approaches, a topical guide to the essays immediately follows the table of contents, and both a rhetorical index and an author-title index appear at the back of the book.

To provide students with a framework for thinking about the essay as a form of reading and writing, the general introduction focuses on distinctive aspects of the essay as defined or commented on by essayists. Though essays can be understood in and of themselves, they are also directly related to the culture, experience, and outlook of their authors. Accordingly, the introduction to each essayist provides a richly detailed body of information about their lives, careers, accomplishments, interests and ideas, as well as their thoughts about writing.

To encourage a careful study of the essays, questions that follow each selection explore a sequence of interrelated issues. These "Lines of Inquiry" are grouped into paragraphs not only because they are closely related but also because they are intended to stimulate lines of thought or investigation bearing on important aspects of each essay. In each case, the Lines of Inquiry contain three sets of questions: the first ordinarily focuses on aspects of form; the second on aspects of content; and the third on the relationship of the piece to personal experience and ideas, to contemporary culture and thought, or to other essays in the collection. So, the Lines of Inquiry, like the instructions, are meant to stimulate thoughtful reading, discussion, and writing—to lead students, in depth, through essays and essayists for our time.

For their detailed reactions to the first edition of *In Depth* and for their knowledgeable suggestions as to authors and titles to include in the second edition, we are grateful to the following instructors: Paul Baender of the University of Iowa, Robin Bourjaily of Suffolk Community College, Victoria Boynton of the State University of New York at Cortland, Rachel Carnell of Boston University, Jeffrey D. Clapp of Dutchess Community College, Barbara Guenther of the School of the Art Institute of Chicago, Henry Hahn of Modesto Junior College, Donald J. Hammar of Ricks College, Robbie C. Pinter of Belmont University, and James R. Scrimgeour of Western Connecticut State University. For their expert work in bringing this book into print, we are grateful to the staff of Harcourt Brace Jovanovich, especially Stephen T. Jordan, Acquisitions Editor, Laurie Runion, Developmental Editor, Michael Hinshaw, Project Editor, Debra Jenkin, Production Manager, and Peggy Young, Designer.

C.H.K.
C.A.
R.B.F.

CONTENTS

TOPICAL GUIDE TO THE ESSAYS

AUTOBIOGRAPHY AND PERSONAL EXPERIENCE

BIOGRAPHY AND PORTRAITURE

POLITICS AND GOVERNMENT

PSYCHOLOGY AND HUMAN BEHAVIOR

INTRODUCTION: ON THE ESSAY

The principle which controls it is simply that it give pleasure; the desire which impels us when we take it from the shelf is simply to receive pleasure. Everything in an essay must be subdued to that end.

In this uncompromising statement from "The Modern Essay," Virginia Woolf reminds us that before essays became the solemn business of English courses, people read them "simply to receive pleasure." People have also written them for pleasure, as E. B. White makes clear by describing the essayist as someone "who thoroughly enjoys his work." In citing these passages from essays and essayists in this collection, we don't mean to suggest that the essay is a trivial kind of writing—far from it. Indeed, if you look at Woolf's "The Death of the Moth" or White's "The Age of Dust," you'll see that in these very short pieces, as in their longer essays, they engage quite serious aspects of experience. Yet they do so in a way that people have often found pleasurable to read and that they evidently found pleasurable to write. So, it seems useful to begin by considering what essayists mean by the pleasure of the essay and how it can go hand in hand with a serious approach to experience and ideas.

By looking into the way that essayists describe the pleasure of the essay, you can also discover something about the nature of the essay. For example, in writing about what "delights him" as an essayist, White alludes to the origin of the word "essay," which comes from the French verb *essayer,* meaning literally to attempt or to try.

Each new excursion of the essayist, each new "attempt," differs from the last and takes him into new country.

In keeping with the root meanings of the word, many essayists have looked upon the essay as a means of trying things out or attempting something new in writing. So, too, it has often come to be regarded as a type of writing that is particularly amenable to exploration, to "excursion," to a kind of mental journeying that takes the writer—and the reader—"into new country." If you look, for example, at Joan Didion's "On the Road," you'll see that while it seems to focus primarily on her experiences and impressions during a cross-country series of radio and television interviews, it also takes account of her mental journey during that trip as she tried to answer a single question—"Where are we heading?"—a question that echoes hauntingly from the first to the last line of the essay.

In some sense, of course, every kind of writing—essay, sonnet, or scientific report—is an adventure, if only because a writer never knows exactly what a piece is going to say or exactly how it's going to work out until it is completely written. So, you're far from being alone whenever you wonder exactly how you're going to finish a piece of writing. The uncertainty and the discovery that come from writing are probably best captured in the well-known question that has been attributed to many writers: "How do I know what I think until I see what I've said?" But some kinds of writing involve more foreknowledge or prestructuring than others. The author of a scientific article knows exactly what data it will include before the writing begins, just as the author of a sonnet knows the fourteen line structure that it will follow before the writing begins. Essayists usually prefer to take a less predetermined, more venturesome, approach to writing.

to risk being in uncertainty

The adventurous impulse of most essayists has led the essay, in turn, to become an unusually varied kind of writing, as you can see just by looking at the work of the first two writers in this collection—at the deadpan comic wit of Woody Allen and the epigrammatic wisdom of Francis Bacon. Throughout this collection, in fact, you will find equally striking contrasts as you move from one author to the next, or one piece to the next. In her first piece, for example, Margaret Mead offers a vivid and evocatively detailed description of a typical day in a primitive Samoan fishing village; in her second, by contrast, she offers a closely reasoned argument against the inevitability of war. In short, the essay is an open form. It gives a writer the freedom to travel in any direction, even on occasion to reverse direction in midcourse, or to make some very surprising turns, as Eiseley does in "The Bird and the Machine." So, too, it gives a reader the pleasure of being taken on an engaging, and often surprising, mental journey.

Given such freedom, it's hardly surprising that essayists celebrate "the extraordinary flexibility" of the essay, as Edward Hoagland does in "What I Think, What I Am." Flexibility, according to Hoagland, is what has enabled the essay "to ride out rough weather and hybridize into forms that suit the times." So you will find that the essays in this collection embody a wide range of forms: stories, parodies, meditations, impersonations, parables, portraits, and interviews. They rely, too, upon numerous ways of explaining and defending ideas, from straightforward description and illustration to elaborate modes of argument and logic. And they are written in every possible style, from casual to formal, from earthy to airy, from plain and simple to ornate and highly oratorical. The essay is an open invitation to you to "hybridize into forms that suit the times."

change of form

A successful hybrid is the product of careful cross-breeding. So, essayists have always faced a special challenge—not just to run rampant, like an unchecked weed, but to flourish and flower and bear fruit in ways that are disciplined, yet not mechanically predictable. Lacking preset or prescribed structures, such as the who, what, when, where, and why of a news report, essayists feel compelled to develop their own structures, their own means of achieving coherence. As White puts it, "the essay, although a relaxed form, imposes its own disciplines, raises its own problems, and these disciplines and problems soon become apparent . . . to anyone wielding a pen merely because he entertains random thoughts or is in a happy or wandering mood." In a similar vein, Hoagland observes that "though more wayward or informal than an article or treatise, somewhere it contains a point which is its real center, even if the point couldn't be uttered in fewer words than the essayist has used."

pointed, somehow

Pointedness, as Hoagland implies, is perhaps the essayist's most important source of discipline, the quality that gives an essay "its real center," its authentic sense of coherence, even when it may lack most conventional forms of surface continuity. For example, George Orwell's "Marrakech" may at first glance appear to consist of five completely separate and unrelated segments, each of which offers a snapshot-like description of a different scene in and around Marrakech. But if you look at the essay closely, you'll see that those snapshots provide a progressively more disturbing picture of the colonial world at work at Marrakech. Similarly, Russell Baker's "Completely Different" at first glance seems to be a disconnected sequence of sentences, but a close examination of those sentences reveals that they are connected to each other by their critique of contemporary American society. Without such a clear sense of purpose, of pointedness, even the most carefully organized piece of prose would be a hollow bit of writing. So, while affirming the importance of pleasure, Woolf also takes pains to note that the art of the essay "has for backbone some fierce attachment to an idea."

coherence

If pointedness were the hallmark of the essay, however, it would be difficult to distinguish from a newspaper editorial or a scholarly article, both of which are also attached to issues and ideas. So, you might wonder exactly what it is that sets the essay apart from these other forms of writing. Hoagland suggests some of its most important distinguishing qualities in this contrast of the essay and the article:

Q:

> Essays don't usually boil down to a summary, as articles do, and the style of the writer has a "nap" to it, a combination of personality and originality and energetic loose ends that stand up like the nap of a piece of wool and can't be brushed flat. Essays belong to the animal kingdom, with a surface that generates sparks, like a coat of fur, compared with the flat, conventional cotton of the magazine article writer, who works in the vegetable kingdom, instead.

loose ends

By putting his contrast in terms of an extended and richly suggestive metaphor, rather than in terms of a straightforwardly literal statement, Hoagland clearly echoes the qualities of the essay that he defines in this passage. As an essayist, Hoagland seeks to display the very "original-ity" and energy that distinguish the essay, as he sees it, from the "con-ventional" and methodical ways of the article.

What Hoagland calls originality, others might refer to as artfulness, and still others might define as a concern for the craft of writing, or the "magic of writing," as Woolf puts it in "The Modern Essay." What-ever terms they use to talk about this aspect of the essay, essayists clearly see it as a means of conveying their ideas in striking, evocative, and engaging ways. In some pieces, such as Hoagland's, this special quality may show itself in a vivid and suggestive metaphor; in others, such as Didion's "On the Road," it may come from variations upon a haunting and evocative question or statement; in others, such as Mead's "A Day in Samoa," it may result from a richly detailed description; in others, such as Eiseley's "The Bird and the Machine," it may come from a well-turned story of personal experience; and in others it may come just from "the impact of one sound on another" or "the firmness of good prose," as Orwell says in "Why I Write." Wherever it comes from, this special quality must be responsible for at least part of the pleasure that Woolf attributes to the essay and part of the power that she claims it has to "lay us under a spell," "to fix us in a trance which is not sleep but rather an intensification of life."

Still, the magic of good writing alone, while it might be capable of laying us under a spell, is surely not sufficient in and of itself to produce what Woolf refers to as "an intensification of life." Something else about the essay must be responsible for that, much as something else about it must be responsible for Hoagland's assertion that "essays belong to the animal kingdom" rather than "the vegetable kingdom" of the article. The only thing that could, in fact, account for both of their claims is what both of them refer to as "personality" in the essay—the sense of a human presence that you can hear and feel and see at work whenever you are reading an essay and giving it your sole attention. Listen, for example, to this sentence from Alice Walker's essay on the civil rights movement, in which she tries to convey how it affected her, and you will get a sense of what we mean by talking about a human presence in the essay:

> I have fought and kicked and fasted and prayed and cursed and cried myself to the point of existing.

That single sentence conveys both the intensity of her past experi-ence and the continuing intensity of her feelings about it. Walker pro-duced the intensity in part by piling up all those plain and simple but forceful verbs, each of which denotes a quite different yet equally in-tense kind of activity. You can feel the intensity, too, in the way she moves from one verb, one action, to the next by means of the conjunction "and," which gives each of those verbs much more emphasis than if she had strung them out in the more usual way with commas:

> I have fought, kicked, fasted, prayed, cursed, and cried myself to the point of existing.

You can also sense how extraordinary she considers the outcome of all those actions by the surprising way in which she ends the sentence, not by crying herself to sleep but by crying herself "to the point of existing." That, surely, is what Woolf means by "an intensification of life" in the essay, or what Hoagland means when he speaks of essays as having "a surface that generates sparks, like a coat of fur. . . ."

The essay, as you can see, allows for the presence of personality in a way that technical articles do not. Indeed, personality is so important an aspect of the essay that Woolf considers it "the essayist's most proper . . . tool." Yet she also considers it a "most dangerous and delicate tool." It is dangerous, because it can be overdone to the point of being self-conscious, and delicate because it entails perhaps the most difficult of all balancing acts in writing: "Never to be yourself and yet always [to be yourself]." How is it possible, you might wonder, both to be yourself and not be yourself? If you think about the matter, you'll realize soon enough that whatever you write can never fully convey yourself in all its flesh-and-blood complexity. Because an essay consists of words, it embodies an essentially fictional version of yourself. Besides, some aspects of yourself you'd probably just as soon not display in writing. The best you can hope for, then, in any piece of writing is to be true to some aspect of yourself that bears on whatever you are writing about at that moment.

Just to see how an essayist's mood or outlook can change from one essay to the next (or one passage to the next), look at this sentence from "Beauty: When the Other Dancer Is the Self," an essay in which Walker writes about the experience of having lost the sight in one of her eyes and at this moment is trying to convey the worry and embarrassment she has felt about the possibility of people detecting her damaged eye:

> At night in bed with my lover I think up reasons why I should not appear on the cover of a magazine.

This sentence is just as frank as the other, indeed is much more personal and intimate in the details that it reveals. Yet it is by no means as intense as the other, if only because it does not engage in any kind of stylistic heightening. It seems by contrast to be a coolly matter-of-fact statement, in which Walker almost seems to be poking fun at herself for worrying about how her eye might look on the cover of a magazine when she is not at all worried about how it looks when she is in bed with her lover. And now to hear yet another side of Walker, a more formal, intellectual, and culturally critical aspect of her self, listen to this stylistically complex sentence from "The Black Writer and the Southern Experience":

> Outcasts to be used and humiliated by the larger society, the Southern black sharecropper and poor farmer clung to his own kind and to a religion that had been given to pacify him as a slave but which he soon transformed into an antidote against bitterness.

The play of personality that you have witnessed in these few sentences by Walker typifies what you will find within the writing of virtually every essayist in this collection. As E. B. White says, "The essayist . . . can pull on any sort of shirt, be any sort of person, according to his mood or his subject matter—philosopher, scold, jester, raconteur, confidant, pundit, devil's advocate, enthusiast." In that long list of possible roles, White suggests what may ultimately account for the special pleasure and power of the essay. To the writer, it offers an inexhaustible set of possibilities for giving voice to experience, thought, and belief in an artful and authentically human way. To the reader, it offers equally rich possibilities for witnessing other minds, other personalities, in action. By enabling such a humane give and take of ideas, the essay satisfies one of the most enduring and significantly human desires. So it is that people continue to get pleasure from the essay.

many voices of Walker – a useful tool for starting the course

assign a Tribune column?

do 350 students want to write essays on these terms, or what sort of writing do they want to do, and why?

WOODY ALLEN

1935 –

Not only is there no God, but try getting a plumber on the weekends.

The universe is merely a fleeting idea in God's mind—a pretty uncomfortable thought, particularly if you've just made a down payment on a house.

In these one-liners from an essay entitled "My Philosophy," Woody Allen demonstrates why he has been called the "cerebral comedian," "Camus with a sense of humor." In his essays as in his movies, he reflects on philosophical questions, speculating about the existence of God and the identity of modern man. But in the next breath he undercuts his own abstractions, reducing the philosophical to the physical, the serious to the ridiculous, or rather, he holds the serious and the ridiculous in tension, so that even while we're laughing at the joke we're thinking about its larger context.

The son of a jewelry engraver, Allen was born in Brooklyn, New York, named Allen Stewart Konigsberg, and raised as "a religious Jew." He legally changed his name to Heywood Allen as a young man. (According to his father he got the nickname of "Woody" because he always brought the stick to the stickball game.) Not particularly bookish or intellectual at first, he graduated from high school with a C− average, then went to New York University, where he was expelled for bad grades, and then to the City College of New York, where he dropped out after a few classes. "I loathed every day and regret every day I spent in school," he said in an interview. "I never had a good teacher who made the least impression on me." Yet at some point in his youth Allen became "a voracious reader," delving into philosophy and literature on his own. "You have to read to stay alive," he said in another interview. Early on, he also showed such talent as a writer that his teachers frequently read his essays aloud as examples of grace and organization.

While still in high school, Allen began exploiting his way with words, selling gags and one-liners to New York columnists and celebrities. At 17 he went to work as a regular staff writer for the National Broadcasting Company, creating jokes and comic routines for such popular comedians of the time as Sid Caesar, Art Carney, Buddy Hackett, and

Gary Moore. When he was just 22, he won the Sylvania Award for the best comedy script of 1957. Dissatisfied with the way other people were reading his lines, he then went on the road himself as a stand-up comic, and after several years of learning and struggle was also writing and starring in his own plays and movies.

During the last twenty years he has made more than a dozen widely praised, as well as widely criticized, films, and has become one of the most successful and influential filmmakers in America. His early movies, like *Take the Money and Run* or *Play It Again Sam* (1972), are antic, slapstick stories about a hapless "schlemiel" or dolt victimized by the physical world and inept with women. In *Love and Death* (1975), Allen began exploiting more serious themes for his comedy, parodying Russian literature and the films of Ingmar Bergman. In 1977 he wrote, directed, and starred in *Annie Hall,* a partly autobiographical film examining the relationship between a neurotic intellectual and a beautiful young woman who finally grows beyond him. It won Academy Awards for best picture, best director, and best screenplay. Since *Annie Hall* Allen has often experimented with darker themes and more innovative cinematic techniques in movies like *Interiors* (1978), *Manhattan* (1979), *Stardust Memories* (1980), *Radio Days* (1987), and *September* (1988). He has also continued to display his comic vision of experience in such films as *A Midsummer Night's Sex Comedy* (1982), *Zelig* (1983), and *Hannah and Her Sisters* (1986).

Varied though his films have been, the heroes of Allen's movies are often pessimistic and guilt-ridden, often uneasy about their Jewishness, always obsessed with sex and death, rarely able to find fulfillment, compulsively sharing with us and with their filmic companions the intimate details of their personal lives. Underneath the humor is anxiety; underneath the farce, confessional. Some cultural observers, such as Joan Didion, have attacked Allen for being excessively self-absorbed, convinced that "adolescence can extend to middle age." Others have defended him as a satirist who turns the clichés and preoccupations of contemporary life back onto themselves, subtly making fun of his own characters and the narcissism of our culture.

These tensions also characterize Allen's essays and short stories, which he has been publishing from the beginning of his career in the *New Yorker, Playboy,* and other magazines. They are collected in three books: *Getting Even* (1971), *Without Feathers* (1975), and *Side Effects* (1980). Some of these short pieces, like the early movies and the stand-up routines, are loose narratives laced with one-liners, a stitching together of gags and what Allen calls "verbal cartoons," in which he describes his reactions to absurd physical situations or juxtaposes concrete images in surrealistic ways. Yet many of the short stories have a tight narrative structure. For example, "The Kuglemass Episodes" won the O. Henry

Award for the best short story of 1976–77. And his essays often balance humor and reflection with the sophistication of his finest movies.

In his essays as in his movies, Allen tries to amuse us while also exploring the frustrations and anxieties of contemporary life, to depict both our human incapacity and our intellectual drive:

> Once again I tried committing suicide—this time by wetting my nose and inserting it into the light socket. Unfortunately, there was a short in the wiring, and I merely caromed off the icebox. Still obsessed by thoughts of death, I brood constantly. I keep wondering if there is an afterlife, and if there is will they be able to break a twenty?

Here, as in many of his prose pieces, he combines comic improbability with philosophic anxiety, the humor of the wet nose in the light socket with the "brooding" and the "wondering," and the thoughts of death. Allen's strategy is to put these levels of meaning together, not so much in one-liners as in what we might think of as two-liners: first the serious ("I keep wondering if there is an afterlife"), then the absurd undercutting ("and if there is will they be able to break a twenty?"). So he portrays himself as a bumbler and incompetent yet at the same time parodies intellectual pretention. He makes us laugh but in the same instant helps us to see ourselves more clearly.

However casual or spontaneous he might sometimes seem, Allen has "absolutely Prussian self-discipline when it comes to writing." He is "driven"—as a writer of screenplays, fiction, and essays—to get the words right, to sharpen his commentary on American culture. "If I don't write every minute," he says, "I have this terrible guilt. It's like— I don't know—if I don't write, I'll be sorry someday."

SPRING BULLETIN

The number of college bulletins and adult-education come-ons that keep turning up in my mailbox convinces me that I must be on a special mailing list for dropouts. Not that I'm complaining; there is something about a list of extension courses that piques my interest with a fascination hitherto reserved for a catalogue of Hong Kong honeymoon accessories, sent to me once by mistake. Each time I read through the latest bulletin of extension courses, I make immediate plans to drop everything and return to school. (I was ejected from college many years ago, the victim of unproved accusations not unlike those once attached to Yellow Kid Weil.) So far, however, I am still an uneducated, unextended adult, and I have fallen into the habit of browsing through an imaginary, handsomely printed course bulletin that is more or less typical of them all:

Summer Session

Economic Theory: A systematic application and critical evaluation of the basic analytic concepts of economic theory, with an emphasis on money and why it's good. Fixed coefficient production functions, cost and supply curves, and nonconvexity comprise the first semester, with the second semester concentrating on spending, making change, and keeping a neat wallet. The Federal Reserve System is analyzed, and advanced students are coached in the proper method of filling out a deposit slip. Other topics include: Inflation and Depression—how to dress for each. Loans, interest, welching.

History of European Civilization: Ever since the discovery of a fossilized eohippus in the men's washroom at Siddon's Cafeteria in East Rutherford, New Jersey, it has been suspected that at one time Europe and America were connected by a strip of land that later sank or became East Rutherford, New Jersey, or both. This throws a new perspective on the formation of European society and enables historians to conjecture about why it sprang up in an area that would have made a much better Asia. Also studied in the course is the decision to hold the Renaissance in Italy.

Introduction to Psychology: The theory of human behavior. Why some men are called "lovely individuals" and why there are others you just want to pinch. Is there a split between mind and body, and, if so, which is better to have? Aggression and rebellion are discussed. (Students particularly interested in these aspects of psychology are advised to take one of these Winter Term courses: Introduction to Hostility; Intermediate Hostility; Advanced Hatred; Theoretical Foundations of Loathing.) Special consideration is given to a study of consciousness as opposed to unconsciousness, with many helpful hints on how to remain conscious.

Psychopathology: Aimed at understanding obsessions and phobias, including the fear of being suddenly captured and stuffed with crab-meat, reluctance to return a volleyball serve, and the inability to say the word "mackinaw" in the presence of women. The compulsion to seek out the company of beavers is analyzed.

Philosophy I: Everyone from Plato to Camus is read, and the follow- 5
ing topics are covered:
    Ethics: The categorical imperative, and six ways to make it work for you.
    Aesthetics: Is art the mirror of life, or what?
    Metaphysics: What happens to the soul after death? How does it manage?
    Epistemology: Is knowledge knowable? If not, how do we know this?
    The Absurd: Why existence is often considered silly, particularly for 10
men who wear brown-and-white shoes. Manyness and oneness are studied as they relate to otherness. (Students achieving oneness will move ahead to twoness.)

Philosophy XXIX-B: Introduction to God. Confrontation with the Creator of the universe through informal lectures and field trips.

The New Mathematics: Standard mathematics has recently been rendered obsolete by the discovery that for years we have been writing the numeral five backward. This has led to a reëvaluation of counting as a method of getting from one to ten. Students are taught advanced concepts of Boolean Algebra, and formerly unsolvable equations are dealt with by threats of reprisals.

Fundamental Astronomy: A detailed study of the universe and its care and cleaning. The sun, which is made of gas, can explode at any moment, sending our entire planetary system hurtling to destruction; students are advised what the average citizen can do in such a case. They are also taught to identify various constellations, such as the Big Dipper, Cygnus the Swan, Sagittarius the Archer, and the twelve stars that form Lumides the Pants Salesman.

Modern Biology: How the body functions, and where it can usually be found. Blood is analyzed, and it is learned why it is the best possible thing to have coursing through one's veins. A frog is dissected by students and its digestive tract is compared with man's, with the frog giving a good account of itself except on curries.

Rapid Reading: This course will increase reading speed a little each day until the end of the term, by which time the student will be required to read *The Brothers Karamazov* in fifteen minutes. The method is to scan the page and eliminate everything except pronouns from one's field of vision. Soon the pronouns are eliminated. Gradually the student is encouraged to nap. A frog is dissected. Spring comes. People marry and die. Pinkerton does not return.

Musicology III: The Recorder. The student is taught how to play "Yankee Doodle" on this end-blown wooden flute, and progresses rapidly to the Brandenburg Concertos. Then slowly back to "Yankee Doodle."

Music Appreciation: In order to "hear" a great piece of music correctly, one must: (1) know the birthplace of the composer, (2) be able to tell a rondo from a scherzo, and back it up with action. Attitude is important. Smiling is bad form unless the composer has intended the music to be funny, as in *Till Eulenspiegel,* which abounds in musical jokes (although the trombone has the best lines.) The ear, too, must be trained, for it is our most easily deceived organ and can be made to think it is a nose by bad placement of stereo speakers. Other topics include: The four-bar rest and its potential as a political weapon. The Gregorian Chant: Which monks kept the beat.

Writing for the Stage: All drama is conflict. Character development is also very important. Also what they say. Students learn that long, dull speeches are not so effective, while short, "funny" ones seem to go over well. Simplified audience psychology is explored: Why is a play about a lovable old character named Gramps often not as interesting in the theatre as staring at the back of someone's head and trying to make him turn around? Interesting aspects of stage history are also examined. For example, before the invention of italics, stage directions were often mistaken for dialogue, and great actors frequently found themselves saying, "John rises, crosses left." This naturally led to embarrassment and, on some occasions, dreadful notices. The phenomenon is analyzed in detail, and students are guided in avoiding mistakes. Required text: A. F. Shulte's *Shakespeare: Was He Four Women?*

Introduction to Social Work: A course designed to instruct the social worker who is interested in going out "in the field." Topics covered include: how to organize street gangs into basketball teams, and vice versa; playgrounds as a means of preventing juvenile crime, and how to get potentially homicidal cases to try the sliding pond; discrimination; the broken home; what to do if you are hit with a bicycle chain.

Yeats and Hygiene, A Comparative Study: The poetry of William   20
Butler Yeats is analyzed against a background of proper dental care. (Course open to a limited number of students.)

LINES OF INQUIRY
"Spring Bulletin"

In the opening paragraph of this piece, Allen claims that his "imaginary . . . course bulletin" is "more or less typical of them all." What aspects of its visual layout, its organization, and its prose style seem typical to you? What aspects of its content do you think typical? In what respects are its form and content exaggeratedly typical? In what respects are its form and content atypical? Examine one or two of the course descriptions closely to see how the interplay among typical, exaggeratedly typical, and atypical elements of form and content produce its humorous effects.

The target of a satiric essay may or may not be the same as its nominal subject. For example, to what extent do you think this piece is intended to poke fun at college bulletins? To what extent does it seem instead to be mocking "adult-education come-ons"? To what extent does it seem to be ridiculing college education itself? Does Allen's humor have a potentially serious side to it? Based on this "imaginary" but "typical" bulletin, how does Allen seem to be portraying and evaluating the purposes, contents, and methods of college courses?

How do you think your response to this piece was affected by the fact that you are presently enrolled in college courses? How do you suppose someone who has been out of college for several years might respond to this piece? How do you suppose someone who had never been to college might respond to it? In other words, what kind of experience and knowledge does a reader have to bring to this piece in order to understand it and enjoy it?

MY SPEECH TO THE GRADUATES

More than any other time in history, mankind faces a crossroads. One path leads to despair and utter hopelessness. The other, to total extinction. Let us pray we have the wisdom to choose correctly. I speak, by the way, not with any sense of futility, but with a panicky conviction of the absolute meaninglessness of existence which could easily be misinterpreted as pessimism. It is not. It is merely a healthy concern for the predicament of modern man. (Modern man is here defined as any person born after Nietzsche's edict that "God is dead," but before the hit recording "I Wanna Hold Your Hand.") This "predicament" can be stated one of two ways, though certain linguistic philosophers prefer to reduce it to a mathematical equation where it can be easily solved and even carried around in the wallet.

Put in its simplest form, the problem is: How is it possible to find meaning in a finite world given my waist and shirt size? This is a very difficult question when we realize that science has failed us. True, it has conquered many diseases, broken the genetic code, and even placed human beings on the moon, and yet when a man of eighty is left in a room with two eighteen-year-old cocktail waitresses nothing happens. Because the real problems never change. After all, can the human soul be glimpsed through a microscope? Maybe—but you'd definitely need one of those very good ones with two eyepieces. We know that the most advanced computer in the world does not have a brain as sophisticated as that of an ant. True, we could say that of many of our relatives but we only have to put up with them at weddings or special occasions. Science is something we depend on all the time. If I develop a pain in the chest I must take an X-ray. But what if the radiation from the X-ray causes me deeper problems? Before I know it, I'm going in for surgery. Naturally, while they're giving me oxygen an intern decides to light up a cigarette. The next thing you know I'm rocketing over the World Trade Center in bed clothes. Is this science? True, science has taught us how to pasteurize cheese. And true, this can be fun in mixed company—but what of the H-bomb? Have you ever seen what happens when one of those things falls off a desk accidentally? And where is science when one ponders the eternal riddles? How did the cosmos originate? How long has it been around? Did matter begin with an explosion or by the word of God? And if by the latter, could He not have begun it just two weeks earlier to take advantage of some of the warmer weather? Exactly what do we mean when we say, man is mortal? Obviously it's not a compliment.

Religion too has unfortunately let us down. Miguel de Unamuno writes blithely of the "eternal persistence of consciousness," but this is no easy feat. Particularly when reading Thackeray. I often think how comforting life must have been for early man because he believed in a powerful, benevolent Creator who looked after all things. Imagine his disappointment when he saw his wife putting on weight. Contemporary man, of course, has no such peace of mind. He finds himself in the midst of a crisis of faith. He is what we fashionably call "alienated." He has seen the ravages of war, he has known natural catastrophes, he has been to singles bars. My good friend Jacques Monod spoke often of the randomness of the cosmos. He believed everything in existence occurred by pure chance with the possible exception of his breakfast, which he felt certain was made by his housekeeper. Naturally belief in a divine intelligence inspires tranquillity. But this does not free us from our human responsibilities. Am I my brother's keeper? Yes. Interestingly, in my case I share that honor with the Prospect Park Zoo. Feeling godless then, what we have done is made technology God. And yet can technology really be the answer when a brand new Buick, driven by my close associate, Nat Zipsky, winds up in the window of Chicken Delight causing hundreds of customers to scatter? My toaster has never once worked properly in four years. I follow the instructions and push two slices of bread down in the slots and seconds later they rifle upward. Once they broke the nose of a woman I loved very dearly. Are we counting on nuts and bolts and electricity to solve our problems? Yes, the telephone is a good thing—and the refrigerator—and the air conditioner. But not every air conditioner. Not my sister Henny's, for instance. Hers makes a loud noise and still doesn't cool. When the man comes over to fix it, it gets worse. Either that or he tells her she needs a new one. When she complains, he says not to bother him. This man is truly alienated. Not only is he alienated but he can't stop smiling.

The trouble is, our leaders have not adequately prepared us for a mechanized society. Unfortunately our politicians are either incompetent or corrupt. Sometimes both on the same day. The Government is unresponsive to the needs of the little man. Under five-seven, it is impossible to get your Congressman on the phone. I am not denying that democracy is still the finest form of government. In a democracy at least, civil liberties are upheld. No citizen can be wantonly tortured, imprisoned, or made to sit through certain Broadway shows. And yet this is a far cry from what goes on in the Soviet Union. Under their form of totalitarianism, a person merely caught whistling is sentenced to thirty years in a labor camp. If, after fifteen years, he still will not stop whistling, they shoot him. Along with this brutal fascism we find its handmaiden, terrorism. At no other time in history has man been so afraid to cut into his veal chop for fear that it will explode. Violence breeds more violence and it is predicted that by 1990 kidnapping will be the dominant mode of social interaction. Overpopulation will exacerbate problems to the breaking point. Figures tell us there are already more people on earth than we need to move even the heaviest piano. If we do not call a halt to breeding, by the year 2000 there will be no room to serve dinner unless one is willing to set the table on the heads of strangers. Then they must not move for an hour while we eat. Of course energy will be in short supply and each car owner will be allowed only enough gasoline to back up a few inches.

Instead of facing these challenges we turn instead to distractions like   5
drugs and sex. We live in far too permissive a society. Never before has pornography been this rampant. And those films are lit so badly! We are a people who lack leaders and coherent programs. We have no spiritual center. We are adrift alone in the cosmos wreaking monstrous violence on one another out of frustration and pain. Fortunately, we have not lost our sense of proportion. Summing up, it is clear the future holds great opportunities. It also holds pitfalls. The trick will be to avoid the pitfalls, seize the opportunities, and get back home by six o'clock.

LINES OF INQUIRY
"My Speech to the Graduates"

In writing this imaginary speech, Allen relies on a number of playful stylistic maneuvers, which you can see by examining a segment of it in detail. For example, make a list of the clichés and trite expressions that he uses in the first paragraph. Then make a list of the nonsequiturs that appear in the first paragraph. Then make a list of the other disjunctive and surprising passages that appear in the first paragraph. To what extent does this humorous blend of elements seem to prevail in each of the subsequent paragraphs?

The title of this piece suggests a parody of a typical graduation speech. In what respects might it also be understood as a playful engagement with some very disturbing aspects of contemporary culture? In what respects might it even be considered as expressing a genuine sense of the absurd in the contemporary world? In other words, how seriously do you take Allen's discussion of science in the second paragraph, religion in the third paragraph, and government in the fourth?

You've probably sat through a long-winded graduation speech or sermon at some point in your life, so you know how boring it can be for listeners when a speaker runs on too long. But Allen is clearly poking fun at something more than just the length of such talks. What is it about such talks that leaves them open to the kind of mockery that is at work in this piece?

A BRIEF, YET HELPFUL, GUIDE TO CIVIL DISOBEDIENCE

In perpetrating a revolution, there are two requirements: someone or something to revolt against and someone to actually show up and do the revolting. Dress is usually casual and both parties may be flexible about time and place but if either faction fails to attend, the whole enterprise is likely to come off badly. In the Chinese Revolution of 1650 neither party showed up and the deposit on the hall was forfeited.

The people or parties revolted against are called the "oppressors" and are easily recognized as they seem to be the ones having all the fun. The "oppressors" generally get to wear suits, own land, and play their radios late at night without being yelled at. Their job is to maintain the "status quo," a condition where everything remains the same although they may be willing to paint every two years.

When the "oppressors" become too strict, we have what is known as a police state, wherein all dissent is forbidden, as is chuckling, showing up in a bow tie, or referring to the mayor as "Fats." Civil liberties are greatly curtailed in a police state, and freedom of speech is unheard of, although one is allowed to mime to a record. Opinions critical of the government are not tolerated, particularly about their dancing. Freedom of the press is also curtailed and the ruling party "manages" the news, permitting the citizens to hear only acceptable political ideas and ball scores that will not cause unrest.

The groups who revolt are called the "oppressed" and can generally be seen milling about and grumbling or claiming to have headaches. (It should be noted that the oppressors never revolt and attempt to become the oppressed as that would entail a change of underwear.)

Some famous examples of revolutions are: 5

The French Revolution, in which the peasants seized power by force and quickly changed all locks on the palace doors so the nobles could not get back in. Then they had a large party and gorged themselves. When the nobles finally recaptured the palace they were forced to clean up and found many stains and cigarette burns.

The Russian Revolution, which simmered for years and suddenly erupted when the serfs finally realized that the Czar and the Tsar were the same person.

It should be noted that after a revolution is over, the "oppressed" frequently take over and begin acting like the "oppressors." Of course by then it is very hard to get them on the phone and money lent for cigarettes and gum during the fighting may as well be forgotten about.

Methods of Civil Disobedience:

Hunger Strike. Here the oppressed goes without food until his demands are met. Insidious politicians will often leave biscuits within easy reach or perhaps some cheddar cheese, but they must be resisted. If the party in power can get the striker to eat, they usually have little trouble putting down the insurrection. If they can get him to eat and also lift the check, they have won for sure. In Pakistan, a hunger strike was broken when the government produced an exceptionally fine veal cordon bleu which the masses found was too appealing to turn down, but such gourmet dishes are rare.

The problem with the hunger strike is that after several days one   10
can get quite hungry, particularly since sound trucks are paid to go through the street saying, "Um . . . what nice chicken—umm . . . some peas . . . umm . . ."

A modified form of the Hunger Strike for those whose political convictions are not quite so radical is giving up chives. This small gesture, when used properly, can greatly influence a government, and it is well known that Mahatma Gandhi's insistence on eating his salads untossed shamed the British government into many concessions. Other things besides food one can give up are: whist, smiling, and standing on one foot and imitating a crane.

Sit-down Strike. Proceed to a designated spot and then sit down, but sit all the way down. Otherwise you are squatting, a position that makes no political point unless the government is also squatting. (This is rare, although a government will occasionally crouch in cold weather.) The trick is to remain seated until concessions are made, but as in the Hunger Strike, the government will try subtle means of making the striker rise. They may say, "Okay, everybody up, we're closing." Or, "Can you get up for a minute, we'd just like to see how tall you are?"

Demonstration and Marches. The key point about a demonstration is that it must be seen. Hence the term "demonstration." If a person demonstrates privately in his own home, this is not technically a demonstration but merely "acting silly" or "behaving like an ass."

A fine example of a demonstration was the Boston Tea Party, where outraged Americans disguised as Indians dumped British tea into the harbor. Later, Indians disguised as outraged Americans dumped actual British into the harbor. Following that, the British disguised as tea, dumped each other into the harbor. Finally, German mercenaries clad only in costumes from *The Trojan Women* leapt into the harbor for no apparent reason.

When demonstrating, it is good to carry a placard stating one's po-   15
sition. Some suggested positions are: (1) lower taxes, (2) raise taxes, and (3) stop grinning at Persians.

Miscellaneous methods of Civil Disobedience:

Standing in front of City Hall and chanting the word "pudding" until one's demands are met.

Tying up traffic by leading a flock of sheep into the shopping area.

Phoning members of "the establishment" and singing "Bess, You Is My Woman Now" into the phone.

Dressing as a policeman and then skipping.

Pretending to be an artichoke but punching people as they pass.

LINES OF INQUIRY
"A Brief, Yet Helpful, Guide to Civil Disobedience"

Look closely at the first paragraph and try to figure out the source(s) of humor, if any, in each sentence. How do you react, for example, to the notion of trying to identify a fixed number of "requirements" for "perpetrating a revolution," to the specific requirements that Allen defines, and to the style in which he defines those requirements? Does the second sentence, about "dress . . . time and place," work in a similar or different way? And how about the third sentence? Compare the second paragraph to the first to see if you can discern a similarly comic process at work. Can you discern a pattern of humor at work in these and subsequent paragraphs, or does it arise unpredictably?

Here, as in his other pieces, Allen challenges us to pinpoint the object(s) of his ridicule. In what respects do you think this piece intends to mock the idea of civil disobedience? In what respects does it seem to be mocking revolutionaries themselves? In what respects does it seem to be mocking the methodical format of guidebooks, handbooks, textbooks, and the like? To what extent does it seem to be having fun for the sake of fun itself? To what extent does the humor have a serious side to it, as in the observation that "after a revolution is over, the 'oppressed' frequently take over and begin acting like the 'oppressors' "?

How do you suppose the timing of this piece, which was first published in 1972, affected the initial response of readers? Consider, for example, how it might have been received by readers during the civil rights marches of the mid-sixties, or the campus demonstrations of the late sixties? How are your understanding of this piece and your response to it affected by a reading of Thoreau's "Civil Disobedience" or King's "An Experiment in Love: Nonviolent Resistance"?

RANDOM REFLECTIONS
OF A SECOND-RATE MIND

Dining at a fashionable restaurant on New York's chic Upper East Side, I noticed a Holocaust survivor at the next table. A man of sixty or so was showing his companions a number tattooed on his arm while I overheard him say he had gotten it at Auschwitz. He was graying and distinguished-looking with a sad, handsome face, and behind his eyes there was the predictable haunted look. Clearly he had suffered and gleaned deep lessons from his anguish. I heard him describe how he had been beaten and had watched his fellow inmates being hanged and gassed, and how he had scrounged around in the camp garbage for anything—a discarded potato peel—to keep his corpse-thin body from giving in to disease. As I eavesdropped I wondered: If an angel had come to him then, when he was scheming desperately not to be among those chosen for annihilation, and told him that one day he'd be sitting on Second Avenue in Manhattan in a trendy Italian restaurant amongst lovely young women in designer jeans, and that he'd be wearing a fine suit and ordering lobster salad and baked salmon, would he have grabbed the angel around the throat and throttled him in a sudden fit of insanity?

Talk about cognitive dissonance! All I could see as I hunched over my pasta were truncheons raining blows on his head as second after second dragged on in unrelieved agony and terror. I saw him weak and freezing—sick, bewildered, thirsty, and in tears, an emaciated zombie in stripes. Yet now here he was, portly and jocular, sending back the wine and telling the waiter it seemed to him slightly too tannic. I knew without a doubt then and there that no philosopher ever to come along, no matter how profound, could even begin to understand the world.

Later that night I recalled that at the end of Elie Wiesel's fine book, *Night,* he said that when his concentration camp was liberated he and others thought first and foremost of food. Then of their families and next of sleeping with women, but not of revenge. He made the point several times that the inmates didn't think of revenge. I find it odd that I, who was a small boy during World War II and who lived in America, unmindful of any of the horror Nazi victims were undergoing, and who never missed a good meal with meat and potatoes and sweet desserts, and who had a soft, safe, warm bed to sleep in at night, and whose memories of those years are only blissful and full of good times and good music—that I think of nothing but revenge.

.   .   .

Confessions of a hustler. At ten I hustled dreidel. I practiced end-lessly spinning the little lead top and could make the letters come up in my favor more often than not. After that I mercilessly contrived to play dreidel with kids and took their money.

"Let's play for two cents," I'd say, my eyes waxing wide and inno-   5
cent like a big-time pool shark's. Then I'd lose the first game deliber-ately. After, I'd move the stakes up. Four cents, maybe six, maybe a dime. Soon the other kid would find himself en route home, gutted and mut-tering. Dreidel hustling got me through the fifth grade. I often had visions of myself turning pro. I wondered if when I got older I could play my generation's equivalent of Legs Diamond or Dutch Schultz for a hundred thousand a game. I saw myself bathed in won money, sitting around a green felt table or getting off great trains, my best dreidel in a smart carrying case as I went from city to city looking for action, always cleaning up, always drinking bourbon, always taking care of my pre-cious manicured spinning hand.

.   .   .

On the cover of this magazine, under the title, is printed the line: A Bimonthly Jewish Critique of Politics, Culture & Society. But why a Jewish critique? Or a gentile critique? Or any limiting perspective? Why not simply a magazine with articles written by human beings for other humans to read? Aren't there enough real demarcations without creating artificial ones? After all, there's no biological difference be-tween a Jew and a gentile despite what my Uncle Max says. We're talking here about exclusive clubs that serve no good purpose; they exist only to form barriers, trade commercially on human misery, and provide additional differences amongst people so they can further ra-tionalize their natural distrust and aggression.

After all, you know by ten years old there's nothing bloodier or more phony than the world's religious history. What could be more awful than, say, Protestant versus Catholic in Northern Ireland? Or the late Ayatollah? Or the expensive cost of tickets to my local syna-gogue so my parents can pray on the high holidays? (In the end they could only afford to be seated downstairs, not in the main room, and the service was piped in to them. The smart money sat ringside, of course.) Is there anything uglier than families that don't want their children to marry loved ones because they're of the wrong religion? Or professional clergy whose pitch is as follows: "There is a God. Take my word for it. And I pretty much know what He wants and how to get on with Him and I'll try to help you to get and remain in His good graces, because that way your life won't be so fraught with terror. Of course, it's going to cost you a little for my time and stationery. . . ."

Incidentally, I'm well aware that one day I may have to fight because I'm a Jew, or even die because of it, and no amount of professed apathy to religion will save me. On the other hand, those who say they want to kill me because I'm Jewish would find other reasons if I were not Jewish. I mean, think if there were no Jews or Catholics, or if everyone were white or German or American, if the earth was one country, one color; then endless new, creative rationalizations would emerge to kill "other people"—the left-handed, those who prefer vanilla to strawberry, all baritones, any person who wears saddle shoes.

So what was my point before I digressed? Oh—do I really want to contribute to a magazine that subtly helps promulgate phony and harmful differences? (Here I must say that *Tikkun*[1] appears to me as a generally wonderful journal—politically astute, insightful, and courageously correct on the Israeli-Palestinian issue.)

I experienced this type of ambivalence before when a group wanted   10 me to front and raise money for the establishment of a strong pro-Israel political action committee. I don't approve of PACs, but I've always been a big rooter for Israel. I agonized over the decision and in the end I did front the PAC and helped them raise money and get going. Then, after they were off and running, I quietly slipped out. This was the compromise I made which I've never regretted. Still, I'd be happier contributing to *Tikkun* if it had a different line, or no line, under the title. After all, what if other magazines felt the need to employ their own religious perspectives? You might have: *Field and Stream: A Catholic Critique of Fishing and Hunting.* This month: "Angling for Salmon as You Baptize."

. . .

I was amazed at how many intellectuals took issue with me over a piece I wrote a while back for the *New York Times* saying I was against the practice of Israeli soldiers going door-to-door and randomly breaking the hands of Palestinians as a method of combating the intifada. I said also I was against the too-quick use of real bullets before other riot control methods were tried. I was for a more flexible attitude on negotiating land for peace. All things I felt to be not only more in keeping with Israel's high moral stature but also in its own best interest. I never doubted the correctness of my feelings and I expected all who read it to agree. Visions of a Nobel danced in my head and, in truth, I had even formulated the first part of my acceptance speech. Now, I have frequently been accused of being a self-hating Jew, and while it's true I am Jewish and I don't like myself very much, it's not because of my persuasion. The reasons lie in totally other areas—like the way I look when I get up in the morning, or that I can never read a road map. In retrospect, the fact that I did not win a peace prize but became an object of some derision was what I should have expected.

---

[1] This essay first appeared in the journal *Tikkun.*

"How can you criticize a place you've never been to?" a cabbie asked me. I pointed out I'd never been many places whose politics I took issue with, like Cuba for instance. But this line of reasoning cut no ice.

"Who are you to speak up?" was a frequent question in my hate mail. I replied I was an American citizen and a human being, but neither of these affiliations carried enough weight with the outraged.

The most outlandish cut of all was from the Jewish Defense League, which voted me Pig of the Month. How they misunderstood me! If only they knew how close some of my inner rages have been to theirs. (In my movie *Manhattan,* for example, I suggested breaking up a Nazi rally not with anything the ACLU would approve, but with baseball bats.)

But it was the intellectuals, some of them close friends, who hated   15
most of all that I had made my opinions public on such a touchy subject. And yet, despite all their evasions and circumlocutions, the central point seemed to me inescapable: Israel was not responding correctly to this new problem.

"The Arabs are guilty for the Middle East mess, the bloodshed, the terrorism, with no leader to even try to negotiate with," reasoned the typical thinker.

"True," I agreed, with Socratic simplicity.

"Victims of the Holocaust deserve a homeland, a place to be free and safe."

"Absolutely." I was totally in accord.

"We can't afford disunity. Israel is in a precarious situation." Here   20
I began to feel uneasy, because we can afford disunity.

"Do you want the soldiers going door-to-door and breaking hands?" I asked, cutting to the kernel of my complaint.

"Of course not."

"So?"

"I'd still rather you hadn't written that piece." Now I'd be fidgeting in my chair, waiting for a cogent rebuttal to the breaking-of-hands issue. "Besides," my opponent argued, "the *Times* prints only one side."

"But even the Israeli press—"   25

"You shouldn't have spoken out," he interrupted.

"Many Israelis agree," I said, "and moral issues apart, why hand the Arabs a needless propaganda victory?"

"Yes, yes, but still you shouldn't have said anything. I was disappointed in you." Much talk followed by both of us about the origins of Israel, the culpability of Arab terrorists, the fact there's no one in charge of the enemy to negotiate with, but in the end it always came down to them saying, "You shouldn't have spoken up," and me saying, "But do you think they should randomly break hands?" and them adding, "Certainly not—but I'd still feel better if you had just not written that piece."

My mother was the final straw. She cut me out of her will and then tried to kill herself just to hasten my realization that I was getting no inheritance.

·   ·   ·

At fifteen I received as a gift a pair of cuff links with a William   30 Steig cartoon on them. A man with a spear through his body was pictured and the accompanying caption read, "People are no damn good." A generalization, an oversimplification, and yet it was the only way I ever could get my mind around the Holocaust. Even at fifteen I used to read Anne Frank's line about people being basically good and place it on a par with Will Rogers's pandering nonsense, "I never met a man I didn't like."

The questions for me were not: How could a civilized people, and especially the people of Goethe and Mozart, do what they did to another people? And how could the world remain silent? Remain silent and indeed close their doors to millions who could have, with relative simplicity, been plucked from the jaws of agonizing death? At fifteen I felt I knew the answers. If you went with the Anne Frank idea or the Will Rogers line, I reasoned as an adolescent, of course the Nazi horrors became unfathomable. But if you paid more attention to the line on the cuff links, no matter how unpleasant that caption was to swallow, things were not so mysterious.

After all, I had read about all those supposedly wonderful neighbors throughout Europe who lived beside Jews lovingly and amiably. They shared laughter and fun and the same experiences I shared with my community and friends. And I read, also, how they turned their backs on the Jews instantly when it became the fashion and even looted their homes when they were left empty by sudden departure to the camps. This mystery that had confounded all my relatives since World War II was not such a puzzle if I understood that inside every heart lived the worm of self-preservation, of fear, greed, and an animal will to power. And the way I saw it, it was nondiscriminating. It abided in gentile or Jew, black, white, Arab, European, or American. It was part of who we all were, and that the Holocaust could occur was not at all so strange. History had been filled with unending examples of equal bestiality, differing only cosmetically.

The real mystery that got me through my teen years was that every once in a while one found an act of astonishing decency and sacrifice. One heard of people who risked their lives and their family's lives to save lives of people they didn't even know. But these were the rare exceptions and in the end there were not enough humane acts to keep six million from being murdered.

I still own those cuff links. They're in a shoe box along with a lot of memorabilia from my teens. Recently I took them out and looked at them and all these thoughts returned to me. Perhaps I'm not quite as sure of all I was sure of at fifteen, but the waffling may come from just being middle-aged and not as virile. Certainly little has occurred since then to show me much different.

LINES OF INQUIRY
"Random Reflections of a Second-Rate Mind"

Allen's title for this essay, "random reflections," suggests that he composed it without any definite plan or structure or purpose for the piece, simply putting down the thoughts that came to his mind after looking at "those cuff links" he refers to in his concluding paragraph. What signs of randomness do you see in the piece? What signs of planning or purposefulness do you see in the piece? What aspects of the piece suggest that Allen is just letting his mind ramble on reflectively? What aspects of the piece suggest that he might have edited his reflections?

Each of the six segments in Allen's essay focuses on a distinctly different experience, memory, topic, or concern. How do you account for the selection and arrangement of the changing subject matter in these segments? For example, what connections, if any, do you see between his opening reflections on a Holocaust survivor, his immediately following "confessions" of being a childhood "hustler," his subsequent attack on the cultural bias of the magazine in which his essay appeared, and so on? Consider some different ways of arranging the six segments— how does each of your rearrangements affect the overall development and significance of the piece?

Like Allen's other pieces in this collection, "Random Reflections" might be considered a parody of a particular kind of writing—a parody in this case of reflective personal writing that purports to be "random," free-flowing, and emotionally frank. Yet this piece often seems to be much more straightforwardly serious than the others. In what places, if any, does this essay seem to verge on the comic or parodic techniques of the others? In what places does it seem most unlike the others by virtue of being directly and uninterruptedly serious?

FRANCIS BACON

1561 – 1626

The inquiry of truth which is the love-making or wooing of it, the knowledge of truth which is the presence of it, and the belief of truth, which is the enjoying of it, is the sovereign good of mankind.

So Bacon wrote in 1625, shortly before his death, and throughout his life he did, in fact, work on an elaborate plan to reform existing methods for the discovery of truth in every area of learning. But for most of his life he dedicated himself to the acquisition of political influence and power—first in the court of Queen Elizabeth I, then in the court of her successor King James I. So he lived a divided existence, continually engaged in the public affairs of a lawyer and statesman, while also pursuing his private interests as a philosopher and essayist.

The youngest of eight children, he was born in London to a well-connected family, attended Cambridge University from 1573 to 1575, turned to the study of law in 1579, and was formally qualified as a barrister in 1582. By 1584 he had taken a seat in Parliament, by 1585 he was writing letters of political advice to the queen, and by 1591 he had allied himself with the Earl of Essex, a young favorite of the queen. Like any aspiring statesman of his time, Bacon knew that only by gaining access to the court could he hope to win political appointments and to influence the course of his country's affairs. But neither his perenially good advice, nor his friendship with Essex, nor even his hand in prosecuting Essex for an attempted revolt against the queen in 1601 was sufficient to help Bacon gain advancement during Elizabeth's reign. Though she respected his mind and trusted his allegiance, she rarely acted on his advice, and apparently never forgave him for once having voted against a special military tax that she had requested from Parliament.

Not until the accession of James in 1603 did Bacon's services and connections begin to pay off, though somewhat more slowly than he expected. Still, despite thinking in 1605 that he was "fitter to hold a book than play a part," he had evidently learned the statesman's part well enough to acquire positions and titles of increasing influence and status—King's Counsel in 1604, Solicitor-General in 1607, Attorney-General in 1613, Privy Councillor in 1616, Lord Keeper in 1617, Lord Chancellor in 1618, Baron Verulam in 1618, and Viscount St. Albans in 1621. But by 1621, Bacon's close connection with the court had made him a suspect figure in the eyes of Parliament which was then fiercely at odds with the King. Parliament, therefore, was delighted to receive petitions against Bacon charging him with bribery—in particular, with accepting gifts from persons whose cases he was adjudicating. Though Bacon claimed that he had not ever allowed such gifts "to pervert justice," he did "confess that in the points charged against me . . . there is a great deal of corruption and neglect." Accordingly, he was fined, imprisoned briefly, dismissed from the office of Chancellor, and declared ineligible ever to hold public office again. So he retired to his family home and turned full time to the philosophic and literary projects that he had been working at for more than twenty years.

Chief among these projects was Bacon's ambitious plan to create a new philosophy of scientific investigation. At the opening of the seventeenth century, when Bacon was working on this project, science still relied very heavily upon abstract reasoning, ancient authority, *a priori* assumptions, and occult beliefs. Bacon, by contrast, believed that scientifically reliable truths could only be derived from repeated observation, systematic investigation, and coordinated experimentation. Bacon, in short, anticipated modern scientific research by recognizing the need to establish and sustain a careful inductive method. So, he set himself the task of preparing an elaborate treatise that would survey existing sciences, expose all the errors and sources of error in human knowledge, expound a new method of interpreting nature, and provide a comprehensive record of natural phenomena to be interpreted by this method. Though he could not possibly have completed this extraordinary project, he did write a number of works related to it, most notably *The Advancement of Learning,* 1605, *Novum Organum* (literally, the new method), 1620, and *The New Atlantis,* 1624, a piece of utopian fiction in which he envisioned an ideal state based on the principles of his new philosophy.

Of all Bacon's literary works, the most carefully wrought are unquestionably his *Essays,* three different editions of which were published during his lifetime—in 1597, 1612, and 1625—each successive edition reflecting a marked growth in the range of Bacon's interests and experience. So, the collection of essays grew from ten in the first edition, to thirty-eight in the second edition, to fifty-eight in the third edition. The breadth of their subject matter gradually increased to focus not only on such worldly topics as "Of Counsel," "Of Ceremonies and Respects," "Of Expense," "Of Negotiating," and "Of Regiment of Health," but also to engage a rich array of psychological, social, and ethical topics, such as "Of Anger," "Of Boldness," "Of Envy," "Of Friendship," "Of Goodness and Goodness of Nature," and "Of Marriage and Single Life." So whereas the title of the first and second editions refers to the pieces as simply *Essays,* the title of the third edition quite appropriately gives them the much more expansive name of *Essays or Counsels, Civil and Moral.* Not only did Bacon add new essays to each edition, but he also revised the essays that he carried over from one edition to the next, making them successively more cohesive, detailed, and weighty.

As the first essayist in English, the ever-ambitious Bacon unquestionably wanted to leave his mark on the form, and he did so by writing essays that clearly differed from those of his predecessor in France, Michel de Montaigne (1533–92). Whereas Montaigne made himself the centerpiece of his essays, and thus is usually regarded as the creator of the personal essay, Bacon carefully worked to exclude any appearance of himself from his essays, and thus scholars often regard him as originating a formal tradition in the essay. Whereas Montaigne thought of the essay as a tentative form of writing, a means of exploring his thoughts and feelings, in keeping with the meaning of the French verb *essayer* (literally, to try out, or to test), Bacon conceived of his essays as "counsels," "as grains of salt," as aphorisms that would contain "some good quantity of observation," and thus "come home to men's business and bosoms."

Given his background as a lawyer and statesman and his desire to give good counsel, Bacon's essays often convey a markedly cautious, prudential, and even calculating view of experience, especially when he is dealing with subjects that touch upon the world of public affairs and business:

> It is generally better to deal by speech than by letter, and by the mediation of a third than by a man's self. Letters are good when a man would draw an answer by letter back again, or when it may serve for a man's justification afterwards to produce his own letter, or where it may be danger to be interrupted or heard by pieces.

But given his enduring commitment to the advancement of truth, Bacon's essays just as often cut to the heart of a matter in memorably pointed prose:

> If you would work any man, you must either know his nature and fashions, and so lead him; or his ends, and so persuade him; or his weakness and disadvantages, and so awe him; or those that have interest in him, and so govern him.

NARCISSUS; OR SELF-LOVE

Narcissus is said to have been a young man of wonderful beauty, but intolerably proud, fastidious, and disdainful. Pleased with himself and despising all others, he led a solitary life in the woods and hunting grounds; with a few companions to whom he was all in all; followed also wherever he went by a nymph called Echo. Living thus, he came by chance one day to a clear fountain, and (being in the heat of noon) lay down by it; when beholding in the water his own image, he fell into such a study and then into such a rapturous admiration of himself, that he could not be drawn away from gazing at the shadowy picture, but remained rooted to the spot till sense left him; and at last he was changed into the flower that bears his name; a flower which appears in the early spring; and is sacred to the infernal deities,—Pluto, Proserpine, and the Furies.

In this fable are represented the dispositions, and the fortunes too, of those persons who from consciousness either of beauty or some other gift with which nature unaided by any industry of their own has graced them, fall in love as it were with themselves. For with this state of mind there is commonly joined an indisposition to appear much in public or engage in business; because business would expose them to many neglects and scorns, by which their minds would be dejected and troubled. Therefore they commonly live a solitary, private, and shadowed life; with a small circle of chosen companions, all devoted admirers, who assent like an echo to everything they say, and entertain them with mouth-homage; till being by such habits gradually depraved and puffed up, and besotted at last with self-admiration, they fall into such a sloth and listlessness that they grow utterly stupid, and lose all vigour and alacrity. And it was a beautiful thought to choose the flower of spring as an emblem of characters like this: characters which in the opening of their career flourish and are talked of, but disappoint in maturity the promise of their youth. The fact too that this flower is sacred to the infernal deities contains an allusion to the same thing. For men of this disposition turn out utterly useless and good for nothing whatever; and anything that yields no fruit, but like the way of a ship in the sea passes and leaves no trace, was by the ancients held sacred to the shades and infernal gods.

LINES OF INQUIRY
"Narcissus; or Self-Love"

Bacon structured this essay like Aesop's fables or Christ's parables: it begins with a story that is followed by a moral interpretation of it. How did you react to this basic structure? How might you have reacted to the story of Narcissus had Bacon not provided any commentary on it? How might you have reacted to an essay on the dangers of self-love without the story of Narcissus? What do you consider to be the benefits and the limitations of combining story and commentary in this basic two-part structure?

The full story of Narcissus is much longer than Bacon's version of it—five pages of verse rather than one brief paragraph of prose, as you can see by looking it up in a translation of Ovid's *Metamorphoses*. What details has Bacon omitted? What details has he changed? How has he altered the story to fit the purposes of his moral point? How would you alter Ovid's story to make it suit a moral point of your own about the dangers of narcissism in our own time?

Bacon is not the only essayist in this collection to combine story and commentary in a morally pointed way, as you can see by looking at Baldwin's "Stranger in the Village," Bettelheim's "The Ignored Lesson of Anne Frank," Dillard's "Living Like Weasels," Orwell's "A Hanging," Walker's "Am I Blue?" or Woolf's "The Death of the Moth." Read one or two of these essays on your own, and then consider how—and why—they differ from Bacon's in their use of story and commentary.

OF MARRIAGE AND
SINGLE LIFE

He that hath wife and children hath given hostages to fortune;[1] for they are impediments to great enterprises, either of virtue or mischief. Certainly the best works, and of greatest merit for the public, have proceeded from the unmarried or childless men, which both in affection and means have married and endowed the public. Yet it were great reason that those that have children should have greatest care of future times, unto which they know they must transmit their dearest pledges. Some there are who, though they lead a single life, yet their thoughts do end with themselves, and account future times impertinences.[2] Nay, there are some other that account wife and children but as bills of charges. Nay more, there are some foolish rich covetous men that take a pride in having no children, because they may be thought so much the richer. For perhaps they have heard some talk, "Such an one is a great rich man," and another except to it, "Yea, but he hath a great charge for children"; as if it were an abatement to his riches. But the most ordinary cause of a single life is liberty, especially in certain self-pleasing and humorous[3] minds, which are so sensible of every restraint, as they will go near to think their girdles and garters to be bonds and shackles. Unmarried men are best friends, best masters, best servants, but not always best subjects, for they are light[4] to run away, and almost all fugitives are of that condition. A single life doth well with churchmen, for charity will hardly water the ground where it must first fill a pool. It is indifferent[5] for judges and magistrates, for if they be facile[6] and corrupt, you shall have a servant five times worse than a wife. For soldiers, I find the generals commonly in their hortatives[7] put men in mind of their wives and children; and I think the despising of marriage amongst the Turks maketh the vulgar[8] soldier more base. Certainly wife and children are a kind of discipline

---

[1] That is, has put himself in a disadvantageous position, because he cannot make any decision or take any action without considering its potential effect upon the well-being of his family
[2] Irrelevant; that is, of no interest to them
[3] Eccentric
[4] Unencumbered by any responsibilities; that is, ready
[5] Of no interest to
[6] Easily influenced
[7] Exhortations
[8] Common

of humanity; and single men, though they be many times more charitable, because their means are less exhaust,[9] yet, on the other side, they are more cruel and hard-hearted (good to make severe inquisitors), because their tenderness is not so oft called upon. Grave natures, led by custom, and therefore constant, are commonly loving husbands, as was said of Ulysses, *Vetulam suam proetulit immortalitati.*[10] Chaste women are often proud and forward, as presuming upon the merit of their chastity. It is one of the best bonds, both of chastity and obedience, in the wife if she think her husband wise, which she will never do if she find him jealous. Wives are young men's mistresses, companions for middle age, and old men's nurses, so as a man may have a quarrel[11] to marry when he will. But yet he was reputed one of the wise men[12] that made answer to the question when a man should marry: "A young man not yet, an elder man not at all." It is often seen that bad husbands have very good wives; whether it be that it raiseth the price of their husbands' kindness when it comes, or that the wives take a pride in their patience. But this never fails, if the bad husbands were of their own choosing, against their friends' consent; for then they will be sure to make good their own folly.

LINES OF INQUIRY
"Of Marriage and Single Life"

The title of this essay suggests that it is a comparison and contrast. In what respects is it organized like a comparison and contrast "of marriage and single life"? In what respects is it organized, instead, like a string of associated thoughts that have to do with "marriage and single life"? In what respects is it organized, instead, like a meditation on "marriage" with references as necessary to "single life"? In what respects is it organized, instead, like a meditation on "single life" with references as necessary to "marriage"? Exactly how would you describe the organization of this essay?

In the opening third of his essay, Bacon seems to be as much concerned with the difference between a marriage with or without children as he is with the difference between marriage and single life. Why do you suppose he is so preoccupied with the question of children? What do you take to be his basis for implying in his second sentence that the status of "unmarried" and "childless men" is essentially identical? What issues appear to be most important to Bacon in his discussion of marriage and single life? What issues seem least important to him? What relevant topics do you think he ignores? Which of the two

---

[9] Exhausted

[10] He preferred his old wife to immortality.

[11] A reason for marrying

[12] Thales of Miletus, a sage of ancient Greece, reportedly attempted to explain his decision not to marry, first by saying he was too young, later by saying he was too old.

conditions does Bacon appear to favor? Or does he seem instead to be a detached observer, impartially weighing the benefits and deficiencies of each?

When you think about choosing between "marriage and single life," what issues are uppermost in your mind? What differences between the two do you consider to be most important? What do you believe to be the benefits and limitations of each condition for yourself? For the society at large? How does your thinking on this subject compare with Bacon's?

handwritten annotations:

* experience vs study

Study's traits
① experience's relation to study
② proper traits of reading
③ various types of study—traits

1's, 2's, 3's chronology

formality via parallel structure

suppressed verbs or other parts of the sent.

Title Style

OF STUDIES

Articulation

occasion

rhythm? sound etc

± 480 words

(3)

Studies serve for delight, for ornament, and for ability.[1] Their chief use for delight, is in privateness and retiring;[2] for ornament, is in discourse; and for ability, is in the judgement and disposition of business. For expert men[3] can execute, and perhaps judge of particulars, one by one; but the general counsels, and the plots and marshalling of affairs come best from those that are learned. To spend too much time in studies is sloth; to use them too much for ornament is affection; to make judgement wholly by their rules is the humour of a scholar. They perfect nature, and are perfected by experience, for natural abilities are like natural plants that need proyning[4] by study; and studies themselves do give forth directions too much at large, except they be bounded in by experience. Crafty[5] men condemn studies, simple men admire them, and wise men use them; for they teach not their own use; but that is a wisdom without them and above them, won by observation. Read not to contradict and confute; nor to believe and take for granted; nor to find talk and discourse; but to weigh and consider. Some books are to be tasted, others to be swallowed, and some few to be chewed and digested: that is, some books are to be read only in parts; others to be read, but not curiously;[6] and some few to be read wholly and with diligence and attention. Some books also may be read by deputy, and extracts made of them by others, but that would be only in the less important arguments, and the meaner sort of books; else distilled books are like common distilled waters, flashy[7] things. Reading maketh a full man; conference a ready man; and writing an exact man. And therefore, if a man write little, he had need have a great memory; if he confer little, he had need have a present wit;[8] and if he read little, he had need have much cunning, to seem to know that he doth not. Histories make men wise, poets witty,[9] the mathematics subtle, natural philosophy deep, moral grave, logic and rhetoric able to contend. (*Abeunt studia in mores.*[10])

---

[1] To make men able.
[2] Seclusion.
[3] Men who have learned only from experience, not study.
[4] Cultivating.
[5] Practical (but also, cunning).
[6] With great care.
[7] Insipid.
[8] Ready mind.
[9] Ingenious.
[10] Studies go to make up a man's character (Ovid, *Heroides,* XV.83).

topic + lists of 3's + 2's for �"⌐ + quotes for π.
find a sentence to imitate   (Eng. is okay)

Nay, there is no stond[11] or impediment in the wit[12] but may be wrought out by fit studies, like as diseases of the body may have appropriate exercises. Bowling is good for the stone and reins;[13] shooting[14] for the lungs and breast; gentle walking for the stomach; riding for the head; and the like. So if a man's wit be wandering, let him study the mathematics; for in demonstrations, if his wit be called away never so little, he must begin again. If his wit be not apt to distinguish or find differences, let him study the Schoolmen,[15] for they are *cymini sectores*.[16] If he be not apt to beat over matters,[17] and to call up one thing to prove and illustrate another, let him study the lawyers' cases. So every defect of the mind may have a special receipt.[18]

LINES OF INQUIRY
"Of Studies"

Throughout this essay, Bacon tends to break down topics into three parallel parts, as in his opening sentence—"Studies serve for delight, for ornament, and for ability." What benefits and what drawbacks do you find in this form of writing? As a means of evaluating the form, try out a few different ways of revising Bacon's opening sentence: drop one of the three parallel phrases, add a fourth of your own choosing; rearrange the three, rewrite the sentence completely to put Bacon's ideas in your own words. How does each of your revisions affect the coherence, development, meaning, and rhythm of the sentence? How would you have to revise the second sentence to make it fit your revisions of the first?

Judging from the various uses of studies that Bacon discusses, what do you suppose he considers to be the most important purpose of education? Judging from the various methods of learning he discusses, what do you suppose he considers to be the most effective method of education? How do you suppose he would react to the educational ideas that Eiseley discusses in "The Hidden Teacher"?

In what respects do Bacon's educational ideas strike you as being out of date? In what respects do they appear to be up to date? How does the range of subjects that he surveys in his essay compare to the range of coursework in your own academic experience? In Woody Allen's "Spring Bulletin"? In what respects do you agree, in what respects do you disagree, with Bacon's ideas of education?

---

[11] Obstacle.
[12] Mind.
[13] Playing bowls is good for the bladder and kidneys.
[14] Archery.
[15] Medieval theologians and academics.
[16] Hair-splitters.
[17] Cover the ground thoroughly.
[18] Prescription (for remedy).

OF NEGOTIATING

It is generally better to deal by speech than by letter, and by the mediation of a third than by a man's self. Letters are good when a man would draw an answer by letter back again, or when it may serve for a man's justification afterwards to produce his own letter, or where it may be danger to be interrupted or heard by pieces. To deal in person is good when a man's face breedeth regard, as commonly with inferiors, or in tender[1] cases, where a man's eye upon the countenance of him with whom he speaketh may give him a direction how far to go; and generally, where a man will reserve to himself liberty either to disavow or to expound. In choice of instruments, it is better to choose men of a plainer sort, that are like to do that that is committed to them, and to report back again faithfully the success,[2] than those that are cunning[3] to contrive out of other men's business somewhat to grace themselves, and will help the matter in report for satisfaction sake.[4] Use also such persons as affect[5] the business wherein they are employed, for that quickeneth much; and such as are fit for the matter, as bold men for expostulation, fair-spoken men for persuasion, crafty men for inquiry and observation, forward and absurd[6] men for business that doth not well bear out itself. Use also such as have been lucky and prevailed before in things wherein you have employed them; for that breeds confidence, and they will strive to maintain their prescription.[7] It is better to sound a person with whom one deals afar off, than to fall upon the point at first, except you mean to surprise him by some short question. It is better dealing with men in appetite,[8] than with those that are where they would be. If a man deal with another upon conditions, the start or first performance is all;[9] which a man cannot reasonably demand, except either the nature of the thing be such which must go before; or else a man can persuade the other party that he shall still need him in some other thing; or else that

---

[1] Delicate.
[2] Outcome.
[3] Who know how.
[4] Report the outcome as better than it really is (in order to please their employer).
[5] Like.
[6] Unyielding.
[7] Their claim to be considered lucky.
[8] Keen for advancement.
[9] All-important.

he be counted the honester man. All practice is to discover, or to work.[10] Men discover themselves in trust, in passion, at unawares, and of necessity, when they would have somewhat done and cannot find an apt pretext. If you would work any man, you must either know his nature and fashions,[11] and so lead him; or his ends, and so persuade him; or his weakness and disadvantages, and so awe him; or those that have interest in him, and so govern him. In dealing with cunning persons, we must ever consider their ends, to interpret their speeches; and it is good to say little to them, and that which they least look for. In all negotiations of difficulty, a man may not look to sow and reap at once, but must prepare business, and so ripen it by degrees.

---

[10]The purpose of all smart dealing is to find out things about men, or to manipulate them.

[11]Habits.

LINES OF INQUIRY
"Of Negotiating"

In this essay, unlike his others in this collection, Bacon uses both the indicative and imperative mode—sometimes making assertions that "it is better" to do this or do that, sometimes making commands. What tone of voice and personality do you associate with each mode? How do you account for the frequency and location of each mode? Bacon also combines different forms of address in this essay—sometimes using the third person indirect address, sometimes using the second person direct address (you), and sometimes using the first person plural (we). Again, what effects do you associate with each form of address, and how do you account for the points at which he uses each form? What connections, if any, do you see between his shifting mode, shifting form of address, and his overall subject and purpose in this piece?

What kinds of negotiations do you suppose that Bacon is referring to in this essay? Why do you suppose he considers it better in these situations "to deal by . . . the mediation of a third than by a man's self"? What criteria does he seem to be using in his choice of persons to do the negotiating? Given his advice about choosing negotiators and carrying on negotiations, what do you infer about Bacon's idea of negotiating? About his view of human nature? About his ethical standards?

Think about a recent negotiating experience of your own. Did you do the negotiating yourself or did you use someone else to do it for you? Was the negotiating carried on by letter, in person, or in some other form? What issues did you take into account in deciding how to carry on your negotiations? How did your method of negotiating compare with Bacon's? How was your method of negotiating influenced, if at all, by your views of human nature? By your ethical standards? By contemporary styles of negotiating? By twentieth-century technologies that influence the process of negotiating?

RUSSELL BAKER

1925 –

I don't suppose that anybody can make it through a whole lifetime here in the twentieth century twilight zone without an occasional suspicion that he is living in a global booby hatch.

For over twenty years, writing in his thrice weekly "Observer" column for *The New York Times,* Russell Baker has been voicing his suspicions about the "booby hatch" of contemporary American life. His stance in these columns is that of a simple, down-to-earth man trying to hold onto his sanity in the face of technological progress, social change, and the pressures of the big city, someone longing for the family values of the past. The world has become too complex, he said in an interview, and "no individual really controls his own destiny." Baker responds to this situation, not with despair or nostalgia, but with humor. Week after week he parodies contemporary excesses and his own frustrated yearnings, describing with dry, understated wit "the ironies of the public condition."

Baker was born in Morrisville, Virginia, during the Depression, and in early childhood lived the simple, rural life of another time. After his father died he moved from relative to relative with his mother and sister, living in New Jersey and finally Baltimore while his mother struggled both to make a living and to make "a good man" out of his passive, dreamy son. She was a strong-willed woman, as Baker describes her in his autobiography *Growing Up* (1982), determined to give him the "gumption" he needed to make it in the world. As a schoolboy, he dreamed of becoming a writer because he envied "the ease of the writer's life." "What writers did," he thought then, "couldn't even be classified as work." His first real experience of the pleasure, and the hard work, of writing came in high school when he wrote a theme on "The Art of Eating Spaghetti." The idea of writing an essay didn't interest him at all at first—"of all forms of writing, none seemed so boring as the essay"—but suddenly, sitting sprawled on the sofa, he recalled "the warmth and good feeling" of his family eating spaghetti around the kitchen table. "Suddenly I wanted to write about that," he recalls. "I wanted to put it down simply for my own joy," not for the teacher. The result was an A$^+$ and the beginning of Baker's characteristically personal, engaged prose style.

After earning a B.A. in English at Johns Hopkins University in Baltimore, with a brief interruption in the Navy, Baker went to work as a reporter for the *Baltimore Sun*. He had wanted to write a novel, to become the next Hemingway, but his experience as a journalist convinced him that "the world I was living in was so much more interesting than the world I was capable of conceiving." Eventually he became the *Sun*'s London reporter and then in 1954 went to work for the *New York Times* in Washington, D.C., covering congressional politics. Political reporting challenged Baker at first, but he became disillusioned and bored after a few years. Congress was a "pocket of tedium." All he seemed to do was "sit in the lobby and listen to the older reporters breathe." Besides, people and events interested him most, not ideas or policies. "I've always been weak on political theory," he admits.

In 1962 he was given the chance to refurbish the "Observer" column for the *New York Times* and began writing more open-ended, informal pieces, developing his gift for humor. He continued to deal with political subjects at first, but gradually shifted to more personal, domestic topics and more literary forms, particularly after moving from Washington to New York. Over the last two decades, writing three times a week—140 pieces a year, nearly 100,000 words a year—Baker has become one of America's most respected columnists, essayists, and humorists. His columns have been collected in a number of books, including *All Things Considered* (1965), *So This Is Depravity* (1980), and *The Rescue of Miss Yaskell and Other Pipe Dreams* (1983). In 1979 he won the Pulitzer Prize for commentary, and in 1982 won the Pulitzer again for his autobiography, *Growing Up,* regarded by many as a classic of the genre. His subsequent memoir, *The Good Times* (1989) focuses on his remarkably successful career in journalism.

In his political columns Baker writes about the pretentions and absurdities of big government, from waste and fraud in the Pentagon to self-delusion in the imperial presidency to the "fat" and deliberate vagueness of bureaucratic rhetoric. One of his favorite strategies is to invent absurd hypothetical situations—the Pentagon delivering a state-of-the-art tank on his doorstep, a disgruntled scientist appearing in his office carrying an atomic bomb. He also likes to take shots at the hypocrisies of Congress. "There's a natural affinity," he says, "between a used car salesman and a congressman. Neither one wants you to know what's under the hood." As he moved away from strictly political themes Baker continued to draw upon the basic forms of satire: as he puts it, "dialogues, fantasies, hoaxes, parodies, burlesques." He imagines the Lone Ranger in a lawyer's office being stripped of his hero's status. He imagines watching contemporary movies with Gary Cooper at his side, fantasizing about Cooper's angry responses to the modern anti-hero.

More recently Baker has gone from satire "back to the essay form," writing more directly about his concerns. In what might be called his "city essays," he describes the rudeness of cab drivers in New York, the impossibility of finding a parking place, the ceaseless noise, portraying himself as an ordinary man victimized by a society that has become too big for any individual to change. "As things become bigger and bigger," he says, "the results become smaller and smaller." He is especially interested in the anxieties of the middle-class consumer, and often writes about the implications of television and television commercials. "I am shaving and it worries me," he says in one essay. "It has become too complicated. . . . Nowadays you don't have a razor anymore. You have a shaving system. I am always nervous in the presence of systems."

In his "country essays," by contrast, Baker describes his early childhood in rural Virginia, growing up in a large family without the burden of material wealth, as well as his visits to Virginia as an adult and his recent purchase of a farm outside the town where he was born. In the simple, natural world of the country—lying in bed at night with the window open, watching "a fattening moon glide imperceptibly toward the mountain behind the raspberry patch"—he has the time and the quiet "to pause and try to make sense of things." In these pieces, too, Baker worries that the pace of modern life has taken us away from basic values. As he said in an interview, "I tend to be very strongly in favor of family, continuity of family relationships, like things the way they are, am very slow to accept change." It was his belief in the importance of family and tradition that led him to write his acclaimed autobiography. He wanted his children "to know that they were a part of a long chain of humanity extending deep into the past and that they had some responsibility for extending it into the future."

Understatement, concreteness, and compactness characterize Baker's prose. Convinced that most readers of the *Times* were bored or intimidated by the paper's polysyllabic, Latinate style, he set out in his columns to "simplify the diction," to evolve a more "casual," conversational style that would "hook people and get them to read." He sees humor as the most effective of these "devices" for communicating a moral, but his humor is not slapstick, nor dependent upon one-liners. It develops more from the subtle ironies of the situations he describes— a blending, in a sense, of Woody Allen's sharpness and sense of the ridiculous with the whimsy and descriptiveness of E. B. White. He causes us to chuckle, not to laugh. "My aim," he says, "is really to sneak up on some pretty dense skulls and just insert a little needle in and let in a little daylight."

THE CRUELEST MONTH

The third week of September has always been a grisly time for schoolchildren. It is then that the romance of education, sparked by the back-to-school excitement of fresh books, new teachers, virginal fountain pens and notebooks unstained by ink blots and baffling mathematical formulas, begins to yield to reality.

And what is that reality? It is knowledge. Knowledge that it will be nine long months before summer vacation rolls around again. Knowledge that the geography teacher dislikes you. Knowledge that the gym instructor finds your physique absurd. Knowledge that you are never going to understand at least three of the subjects with which you are saddled and are going to suffer horribly for months as you sink into the quagmire of F's recording the progress of your ignorance.

It was Jean Shepherd, I believe, who said that after three weeks in chemistry he was six months behind the class. This is a common experience, this sensation of being locked forever in the starting gate while the rest of the class is galloping for the back stretch, and it leaves many people scarred for life.

A woman I know, though financially well-heeled, still refuses to set foot in Italy because in seventh-grade Latin she became aware, after three weeks in the classroom, that she would never be able to conjugate the verb *esse* to Cicero's satisfaction. Assurances that Cicero is no longer to be encountered in Rome do not comfort her. She associates the Italian peninsula with personal humiliation.

I myself have always avoided Germany since discovering in 10th grade that German has two dozen ways of saying "the." I could be wrong about this, since I was wrong about everything else in German. Nevertheless, there is the fact. That memory of a third week in September when classmates began hooting about my tendency to use the dative feminine singular form of "the" when the accusative neuter plural was called for—this memory has created a lifelong barrier between Germany and me.

Schools do not concede that it is ridiculous to require every student to learn at the same pace. They operate on the assumption that every brain in the classroom will achieve a firm grasp of the binomial theorem at the same instant and be ready to move on simultaneously to those many cheerful facts about the square of the hypotenuse waiting at the next hitching post.

Readers who met the educators' expectations in mathematics may deduce from the above that my own pace in math was decidedly slow if, as I suspect, you have to master the hypotenuse before proceeding on to the binomial theorem. The truth is that, never understanding either one, I was utterly lost and made a terrible mess of things when I reached the cosine and the secant.

All of this probably resulted because some teacher during the third week of some long-ago September assumed, wrongly, that I understood that 9 times 6 is 54, and rushed on to impress me with the realization that 9 times 8 is 77, or whatever it may be.

Almost all of us have dreadful third weeks of September in our backgrounds somewhere. If psychoanalysts would let up a bit on our libidinal childhood experiences, they might discover a rich new source of adult neurosis here.

The third week of September that mutilated my own life is the reason I am not a brilliant nuclear physicist today. Here let me confess that in youth it was not my intent to become a typewriter pounder hacking out material for Sunday supplements. Hooked on the romance of science, I yearned to take up the torch from Einstein and carry it forward.

Thus I came to physics class. The first week of September was thrilling, as textbooks were issued and the teacher discoursed on Isaac Newton and apples and introduced us to the lab, that frontier of human progress. In the second week, he introduced us to the erg. I was quite happy with the erg, without which blocks of wood could not be made to overcome the villainous friction of inclined ramps and moved upward, triumphantly ascending those ramps.

At the end of the week, he introduced the dyne, which seemed excessive. It was not that I couldn't understand the dyne. I could have. What I could not understand was why, since we already had the erg, it was also necessary to have the dyne.

I was still puzzling over this philosophical question the following Monday when the teacher, assuming that everybody now had a firm grip on the dyne, plunged ahead into the centimeter. Perhaps it was only the millimeter. I am hazy here because reality was fading rapidly.

It was disconcerting to have the dyne taken utterly for granted when I still had profound doubts about it and to be asked to cope with the centimeter. The next day was worse. That was the day of the milligram. The following day there was a test.

I was astonished that the rest of the class took it without a roar of protest that it was outrageous to ask us to cope with ergs, dynes, centimeters and milligrams while we were still baffled about the dyne. The rest of the class did not protest. Most passed easily. I failed every question not devoted exclusively to the erg. The rest of that year was a nightmare, and the world still awaits a worthy successor to Einstein.

LINES OF INQUIRY
"The Cruelest Month"

The organization of this essay seems casual at first, offhand, as if Baker is talking off the top of his head, going from point to point in no particular order. Why do you think Baker tries to create this impression? Study the selection and arrangement of his material from paragraph to paragraph. What would happen if you put these paragraphs in a different order? Do any paragraphs function together as a group? In what respects do you find a design here? In what respects is the piece as casual as it seemed at first?

"The Cruelest Month" is a good example of Baker's unique style of humor. How would you characterize this humor? Is it light or heavy, amusing or slapstick? How is he different from a stand-up comedian? How is he different from Woody Allen? Do you think Baker's purpose is simply to poke fun at himself, to make us laugh—to entertain us—or could there be a serious, darker theme underneath—for example, an attack on American public schools? If so, what aspect(s) of school do you think he is attacking?

Baker says that "almost all of us have a dreadful third week of September in our backgrounds somewhere." Have you ever had a dreadful third week? Have you ever been six months behind after three weeks? Was it in physics and chemistry, or literature and composition? Baker doesn't finally seem too upset about his failures as a student. Are you able to look back on your own failures with the same detachment and equanimity? Why or why not?

A VISIT WITH THE FOLKS *)— seemingly very ordinary title*

(— setting, topic, very direct

Periodically I go back to a churchyard cemetery on the side of an Appalachian hill in northern Virginia to call on family elders. *(a sort of summary)* It slows the juices down something marvelous. *}— slangy*

M They are all situated right behind an imposing brick church with a tall square brick bell-tower best described as honest but not flossy. Some of the family elders did construction repair work on that church and some of them, the real old timers, may even have helped build it, but I couldn't swear to that because it's been there a long, long time. *history / setting, context*

The view, especially in early summer, is so pleasing that it's a pity they can't enjoy it. Wild roses blooming on fieldstone fences, fields white with daisies, that soft languorous air turning the mountains pastel blue out toward the West. *Rich scene-writing* */fragment (free mood?)*

The tombstones are not much to look at. Tombstones never are in my book, but they do help in keeping track of the family and, unlike a family, they have the virtue of never chafing at you. */a small joke*

This is not to say they don't talk after a fashion. Every time I pass Uncle Lewis's I can hear it say, "Come around to the barber shop, boy, and I'll cut that hair." Uncle Lewis was a barber. He left up here for a while and went to the city. Baltimore. But he came back after the end. Almost all of them came back finally, those that left, but most stayed right here all along.

a catalog of them

Well, not right here in the churchyard, but out there over the fields, two, three, four miles away. Grandmother was born just over that rolling field out there near the woods the year the Civil War ended, lived most of her life about three miles out the other way there near the mountain, and has been right here near this old shade tree for the past 50 years. *5 talky*

✳

We weren't people who went very far. Uncle Harry, her second child, is right beside her. A carpenter. He lived 87 years in these parts without ever complaining about not seeing Paris. To get Uncle Harry to say anything, you have to ask for directions. *6 Thesis*

"Which way is the schoolhouse?" I ask, though not aloud of course.

"Up the road that way a right good piece," he replies, still the master of indefinite navigation whom I remember from my boyhood.

It's good to call on Uncle Lewis, grandmother and Uncle Harry like this. It improves your perspective to commune with people who are not alarmed about the condition of NATO or whining about the flabbiness of the dollar. *)— echo of para 1.*

The elders take the long view. Of course, you don't want to indulge too extensively in that long a view, but it's useful to absorb it in */implied c + e of this world with their world*

✳ mini-portraits with dialogue implying character

short doses. It corrects the blood pressure and puts things in a more *echo of para 1* sensible light.

C+C

After a healthy dose of it, you realize that having your shins kicked 10 in the subway is not the gravest insult to dignity ever suffered by common humanity. *a corrective*

catalog continues

Somewhere in the vicinity is my great-grandfather who used to live back there against the mountain and make guns, but I could never find him. He was born out that way in 1817—James Monroe was President then—and I'd like to find him to commune a bit with somebody of blood kin who was around when Andrew Jackson was in his heyday.

After Jackson and Abraham Lincoln and the Civil War, he would probably not be very impressed about much that goes on nowadays, and I would like to get a few resonances off his tombstone, a cool *frisson* of contempt maybe for a great-grandchild who had missed all the really perilous times.

Unfortunately, I am never able to find him, but there is Uncle Irvey, grandmother's oldest boy. An unabashed Hoover Republican. "Eat all those string beans, boy," I hear as I nod at his tombstone.

a little scene

And here is a surprise: Uncle Edgar. He has been here for years, but I have never bumped into him before. I don't dare disturb him, for he is an important man, the manager of the baseball team, and his two pitchers, my Uncle Harold and my Cousin-in-law Howard, have both been shelled on the mound and Uncle Edgar has to decide whether to ask the shortstop if he knows anything about pitching.

death is a leveler

My great-grandfather who made guns is again not to be found, but 15 on the way out I pass the tombstone of another great-grandfather whose distinction was that he left an estate of $3.87. It is the first time I have passed this way since I learned of this, and I smile his way, but something says, "In the long run, boy, we all end up as rich as Rockefeller," *in a sentence* and I get into the car and drive out onto the main road, gliding through fields white with daisies, past fences perfumed with roses, and am rather more content with the world. *vivid scene*

LINES OF INQUIRY
"A Visit with the Folks"

Baker uses a good deal of colloquial, folksy language here—"out that way," "blood kin," "nowadays." Yet he also uses words like "resonances" and phrases like "cool *frisson* of contempt." How would you characterize the style of these words and phrases? What kind of personality do they suggest? Often he mixes these two styles, these two ways of talking, in the same paragraph, even the same sentence. How do you react to this mixing? Do you find it inconsistent? What does it suggest about Baker as a person? How does Baker's style compare with that of his relatives? What do you make of the similarities and differences?

"A Visit with the Folks" is in part about a big city man returning to the small country community where he was raised. How does Baker evoke the feel, the sensation, the atmosphere of the country? What does the country represent for him? What do you infer about his attitude toward city life from what he says about this quiet rural place? What do you infer about his attitude toward the country from the fact that all the people he's talking with are dead? What are the implications of this fantasy?

We all have places to escape or return to now and then to get a better perspective on our lives. What places do you return to? What people do you talk to? Do you ever wish you could talk again with a dead family member? Do the dead speak to you in some real ways?

Catalog of portraits to fill the space

brief portraits, vivid scenes & little events } a natural for free modifier work

MARRIAGE À LA MODE

In our third year of marriage my wife telephoned to ask if I would like to meet her. I did not want to meet her or anyone else. It had been seven years since I had met anybody at all, and though I had recently thought it might do me good to meet somebody—if only to see whether people still looked the way they used to—I did not want to start by meeting my wife.

One of the advantages of electronic living was that you never had to meet your wife. The man who installed my computer and television cables had harped on that. "One of its big advantages," he said, "is that you'll never have to meet your wife."

At the time, of course, I did not intend to marry. I changed my mind only after setting up my tax picture in the computer and discovering that a wife of a certain income profile would cut my tax bill by nearly 2 percent.

It was a simple matter to plug into the central information bank, obtain the names of several thousand single women in the same tax predicament and, for a small fee, have the engagement and marriage arranged by the bank.

The ceremony was performed by a minister of the Ecumenical   5
Computer Church while I was reading the sports news in the electronic newspaper on my video terminal in New York and my bride, who lived in Oregon, was monitoring a Phil Donahue interview with three well-adjusted transsexuals on her cable TV.

At the appropriate moment I punched "I do" and "I will" into my computer, and after she did likewise I switched the computer into "check-account shopping mode" and ordered my bank to authorize an Oregon jeweler to deliver her a wedding ring.

It was exhilarating being married. To celebrate, I put on a video cassette of the Super Bowl game of 1995 and spent half the night watching the Chattanooga Data trounce the Fargo Inputs by a score of 35 to 3.

After that I forgot about being married except at tax time, when it was mighty convenient. Naturally, it was a surprise when she telephoned to propose a meeting.

I should point out that I did not answer the phone myself. I had not answered a telephone for years. I had a machine that not only answered for me, but also made calls for me. My machine, speaking in a voice entirely unlike my own, said, "I am very busy now scanning my display terminal to select a meal to be delivered to my food slot so that I will not have to be interrupted while watching the cricket test match from Pakistan on my cable television during the evening. Please state your message at the sound of the beep and my machine will process your call."

On this evening the machine said, "Your wife has telephoned to   10
ask if you would like to meet her."

"Tell her," I told the machine, "I have not met anybody in seven years and do not propose to start now."

While the machine was transmitting the message, a noise at the door indicated that the central restaurant bank was having my dinner delivered at the food slot. Since the restaurant bank had not yet replaced all its delivery people with robots, I waited a safe interval before opening the slot, so as not to risk catching a glimpse of a human being.

This irritated my telephone machine. "You may not want to see a human being," said the machine, "but I'd like to, once in a while."

"Nonsense," I said, "you see me 24 hours a day."

"People ought to see people, ought to talk to people," said the   15
machine.

"If God had meant people to see people, he wouldn't have created electronic living," I said. "If God wanted people to talk to people, he wouldn't have given us the telephone-answering machine."

I went to the slot to collect my dinner. Instead of a steak, I found a small electronic device. "So," I said, "they have finally succeeded in inventing the electronic steak. This ought to teach the beef trust a little humility."

I put my computer in "dining mode." Instantly the TV set activated a 1968 video cassette of "Bowling for Dollars" and presented me with a fork and a steak knife. The small electronic device spoke up. "Do not carve me," it said. "Kiss me. I am your wife and I am dying for love. At the sound of the beep, place your computer in 'osculation mode' and activate my 'input' key by framing your lips in the pursed position."

It was my telephone machine that replied. "Don't waste your time, baby," it said. "That bird has been dead for years." It uttered a highly suggestive "beep." My wife beeped back.

My wife? But I was married to a tax shelter, not to a flirting beeper.   20
Or was I? It had been so long since I had met anybody. I thought of going to the window, raising the blinds, but I didn't. It is better not to know some things.

I sat back to enjoy "Bowling for Dollars." The telephone machine said, "If you'd turn off that tube, machines could have a little privacy around here." I turned it off and sat in the dark. The beeping became intense.

LINES OF INQUIRY
"Marriage à la Mode"

This piece is obviously ironic and satirical from the very beginning, yet the point of the fantasy isn't immediately clear. When did you figure out the situation? Why do you suppose that Baker develops the story obliquely, indirectly, even somewhat misleadingly at first? After a while, it becomes clear, too, that Baker is simply inventing a possible future world. Is this kind of fictionalizing legitimate in a nonfiction piece?

Baker's concern here is evidently the problematic relationship of humans and machines, particularly computers. But rather than voice his concerns directly, Baker implies them through the imaginary story, told by the imaginary speaker in the piece. What do you suppose is Baker's attitude towards the computer, and how does it differ from the attitude of his imagined speaker? What do you suppose is Baker's attitude towards marriage, and how does it differ from the attitude of his imagined speaker? How do you know that Baker doesn't agree with the speaker on these issues?

Look at Eiseley's "The Bird and the Machine" and compare Baker's thoughts about machines with those of Eiseley. In what respect(s) are they similar? In what respect(s) different? Also consider the different ways in which they voice their concerns. Do you think Baker and Eiseley are just old curmudgeons, blindly resistant to progress? Or do you think they have raised legitimate questions about humanity and high technology?

COMPLETELY DIFFERENT

This is all new.

It is completely different.

You have never experienced anything like it.

Now that you are experiencing it you will never be the same again.

You will be all new.   5

You will be completely different.

You will never want to experience the old experiences again.

Everything that is old has been discarded to create a completely different experience.

Long sentences have been.

Discarded.   10

Everything has been completely miniaturized.

Thought. Soap. "King Lear." Liver spots on the backs of hands. Travel time. Sunsets. Spin-dry cycles. Headaches.

All are now reduced to their absolute essentials.

All miniaturized.

This is a revolutionary new concept.   15

It will give you twice as much time as your old unrevolutionary new concept.

You will be twice as dynamic.

You will enjoy endless hours.

You will stay younger twice as fast.

Here is what the critics say: 20

"Since experiencing the revolutionary new concept I have become twice as irresistible to women"—Mr. B. T. of Houma, La.

"—a dynamic new route to newness. . . . I never knew what 'King Lear' could be until I saw it performed without commas or punctuation marks"—Mrs. C. J. of Rochester, N.Y.

You will also smell newer.

Why is this extraordinary advance in newness vital to success?

Because we live in today's world.   25

Today's world is completely different.

Today's world is all new.

Today's world requires people who are completely different.

It requires people who are all new.

We have all seen people who live in yesterday's world.   30

Are those people fun people?

Dynamic people?

When you open their doors do you smell an exciting new fresh-from-the-factory new-people smell?

With a hidden camera we interviewed a typical scrubwoman.

Note that these pictures show her seated before two boxes.   35

She cannot see the labels visible to you.

Note that one box is labeled "New Completely Different Person."

The other is labeled "Old Unchanged Person."

We will now run the tape.

"Mrs. Hummell, you are a weary 67-year-old scrubwoman who   40
spends long nights alone on her knees in this empty building. We ask
you to study these two boxes and tell us which box contains the sort
of person you would prefer to keep you company through the night."

"Easy. That box right there."

"Now, you, Mrs. Hummel, have chosen the box labeled—unbeknownst to you—'New Completely Different Person.' Tell me why
you did not pick this other box labeled 'Old Unchanged Person.' "

"Because it looked too heavy to carry around all night."

"Let's open both boxes and look."

Notice Mrs. Hummel's expression as the "Old Unchanged Person"   45
box is opened and a 135-pound woman emerges and asks her to spend
an hour walking on the beach watching a sunset.

Notice that Mrs. Hummel recoils.

Mrs. Hummel recoils because the woman is not new.

She does not have new-woman smell.

She has not miniaturized the liver spots on the backs of her hands.

She does not propose living dynamically, but instead speaks in the   50
exhausting rhythms of this particular sentence, with its antiquated commas and cumbersomely involuted grammatical structure, thereby making it all too evident that she is incapable of living dynamically by getting
right to the point, a fact which is driven home by her suggestion that
they spend an entire hour watching a sunset, thus consuming precious
time that could be used to have her wrinkles surgically removed and
the dull soap glaze banished from her hair by application of a new,
completely different shampoo.

Note, by contrast, how delighted Mrs. Hummel looks when the
box labeled "New Completely Different Person" is opened.

Yes, the figure emerging is a 10-ounce man.

He has been reduced to the absolute essentials of newness.

Mrs. Hummel can keep him in her apron pocket throughout the
night. She can remove him when she wishes to inhale his exciting new
smell.

He will tell her without commas how to have twice as much time   55
for dynamic living by watching a sunset in 15 seconds.

Mrs. Hummel will never be the same again.

LINES OF INQUIRY
"Completely Different"

The most striking aspects of this essay's beginning are its short sentences and extremely short paragraphs. How do you react to these features? Are the short sentences easy to read, or hard? How long before you identify the issue, and how do you feel about being forced to solve the puzzle? How does repetition of key words and phrases work to hold this section together?

Despite the compactness and economy of his phrasing, Baker explores a very complex set of interrelated problems here. Try to sort out and define the problems that concern him here. What does Baker mean by "miniaturization"? What things are being reduced, diminished, in contemporary society? Baker has said elsewhere that "the bigger things get, the smaller the results." How does this statement apply to "Completely Different"? How does it apply to that very long sentence that comes near the end of the essay? What do you suppose that Baker is suggesting about language, society, and values through the contrast between that sentence and the others in the piece?

Across these four essays Baker displays a range of different voices and attitudes. Try to define these voices. How do they vary? Yet, how would you know even without the by-line that whatever the style, whatever the tone, each is still a piece by Russell Baker?

JAMES BALDWIN
1924 – 87

It began to seem that one would have to hold in the mind forever two sides which seemed to be in opposition. The first idea was acceptance, the acceptance, totally and without rancor, of life as it is, and men as they are: in the light of this idea, it goes without saying that injustice is a commonplace. But this did not mean that one could be complacent, for the second idea was of equal power: that one must never, in one's own life, accept these injustices as commonplace but must fight them with all one's strength.

In this passage from "Notes of a Native Son," the title piece from his first collection of essays, Baldwin describes his coming to understand what would be his mission as a black writer in white America. Through his writing he waged his war against those commonplace injustices, relentlessly stripping away, often with anger but always with love, the fictions which have clothed race relations in this country. But the "Negro question," as it was called in the days of Baldwin's early writing, was only the point of entry for his cultural criticism, which, while it kept issues of race at its center, always reached beyond them to a critique of Americans' understanding of their history, their national identity, and their place in a shifting global culture.

James Baldwin was born in Harlem in 1924, the child of an unmarried mother who had come north as part of the Great Migration of blacks from the South in the years during and following World War I, making him, as he put it, "but one generation removed from the South." When he was three his mother married David Baldwin, a preacher and laborer who had come to New York from New Orleans, and the couple had eight more children. Baldwin was raised, said one biographer, "under the twin disciplines of poverty and the store-front church." As the eldest child, he took on much of the responsibility for caring for his younger siblings. "As they were born, I took them over with one hand and held a book with the other"; by the time he was thirteen, he claims, he had read nearly all the books in Harlem's two public libraries. Baldwin graduated in 1942 from DeWitt Clinton High School in the Bronx, a mostly white school to which his early writing abilities had won him admittance, but it was his extensive and eclectic reading combined with his firsthand experience of life on the streets and in the hallways and back alleys of Harlem which constituted his real education.

Baldwin's relationship with his stepfather was an intense and complicated one, a confusion of hatred and love. That paradoxical mixture of emotions, combined with his struggle as the stepchild to find his place in a large family of half-brothers and half-sisters, prefigured the lifelong ambivalence of his relationship with his native land and his efforts to claim a place for himself in its culture. When he was fourteen, he experienced a profound religious conversion and, following in his stepfather's footsteps, became a preacher in a store-front pentecostal church in his Harlem neighborhood. Three years later he left the church; some critics have observed, though, that he never really abandoned the role of preacher, continuing to sermonize with the pen rather than from the pulpit.

In 1948, encouraged by novelist Richard Wright, Baldwin left the United States for Paris. There he was able to complete *Go Tell It on the Mountain* (1952), a fictionalized rendering of his own teenage experience of conversion and the call to preach, which received wide critical acclaim. Though he returned many times to the United States, often for lengthy visits to observe, report, speak, write, and teach, he lived abroad, mostly in France, for the remainder of his life. Europe gave him a place distant enough to develop a necessary perspective on the country of his birth and from which to view with penetrating clarity the fabric of American life. He insisted that Europe was not a "haven" for him from the racial strife in the United States and that he was *"not* in exile," claiming instead that ". . . the world is very small, and it is no longer possible for an American, and certainly not an American black man, and certainly not James Baldwin, to leave America." In Europe Baldwin recognized himself to be "as American as any Texas GI"; it was not possible for him to leave America because wherever he went, he took America with him. Still the distance was necessary for him to work, and while the frequent visits to the United States fueled his writing, it was mostly in Europe that he got the writing done.

In the course of his thirty-five years of professional life, Baldwin published prolifically—novels, plays, short stories, and newspaper articles. It was in the essay form, however, that he achieved his greatest success. Collected in *Notes of a Native Son, Nobody Knows My Name, The Fire Next Time,* and *The Price of the Ticket,* Baldwin's essays moved readers to re-examine what it means to be an American. Calling him "strongest as an essayist," one critic said of his essays that they "probe, deeper than anyone has dared, the psychic history of this nation." When Baldwin died in 1987, the novelist and essayist Norman Mailer praised him by saying, "Nobody has more elegance than Baldwin as an essayist; not one of us hasn't learned something about the art of the essay from him." It was the essay form that could best accommodate the urgency of Baldwin's prophetic voice, the stark realities of his personal narratives, the exhortatory power of his pleas for Americans to rise up and meet the challenge to "end the racial nightmare, and achieve our country, and change the history of the world."

It was at the level of the word that Baldwin worked his changes. "We live in a country in which words are mostly used to cover the sleeper, not to wake him up," he wrote. "For the horrors of the American Negro's life there has been almost no language." Inventing that language in a cadence powerful enough to wake the sleeping country was the charge that he laid himself:

> It is, alas, the truth that to be an American writer today means mounting an unending attack on all that Americans believe themselves to hold sacred. It means fighting an astute and agile guerrilla warfare with that American complacency which so inadequately masks the American panic.

While he was committed to the idea that "one must really do great violence to language, one must somehow disrupt the comforting beat, in order to be heard," the eloquence, rhetoric, and rhythm of his prose arise largely from the traditions of the King James Bible and the great masters of nineteenth-century fiction such as Charles Dickens and Henry James. It was perhaps that precise combination which made Baldwin, of all the black polemicists of his generation, so widely read by whites and blacks alike.

The breadth of his vision never failed; he wrote to and for a whole nation, insisting always that the fate of whites and blacks in America was inextricably bound together. Like Orwell before him, Baldwin stressed that injustice wounds the oppressor as well as the oppressed: "It is a terrible, an inexorable, law that one cannot deny the humanity of another without diminishing one's own: in the face of one's victim, one sees oneself." As an alternative to racial conflict, Baldwin repeatedly offers the haunting vision of black America and white America locked together in the regenerative embrace of love. The future is the awaited fruit of that union, an offspring anticipated with alternating fear and hope:

> For nothing is fixed, forever and forever and forever, it is not fixed; the earth is always shifting, the light is always changing, the sea does not cease to grind down rock. Generations do not cease to be born, and we are responsible to them because we are the only witnesses they have. The sea rises, the light fails, lovers cling to each other, and children cling to us. The moment we cease to hold each other, the moment we break faith with one another, the sea engulfs us and the light goes out.

Like that haunting vision, the trajectory of Baldwin's life was itself remarkable, beginning in the Harlem ghetto and rising to the heights of fame and wealth and achievement. At his death, one eulogist praised him for having possessed to a great degree "that quality of his people that he loved most . . . their ability to turn annihilating hostility into a strength that lifted rather than buried the human spirit." Baldwin once described himself this way: "I am a very tight, tense, lean, abnormally ambitious, abnormally intelligent and hungry black cat. I'm not a nigger. I'm a man." To be a man, he insisted, was to possess a moral vision and the courage to press that vision on the world. "If there is not a moral question, there is no reason to write," he said. "I'm an old-fashioned writer and, despite the odds, I want to change the world. What I hope to convey? Well, joy, love, the passion to feel how our choices affect the world . . . that's all."

AUTOBIOGRAPHICAL NOTES

I was born in Harlem thirty-one years ago. I began plotting novels at about the time I learned to read. The story of my childhood is the usual bleak fantasy, and we can dismiss it with the restrained observation that I certainly would not consider living it again. In those days my mother was given to the exasperating and mysterious habit of having babies. As they were born, I took them over with one hand and held a book with the other. The children probably suffered, though they have since been kind enough to deny it, and in this way I read *Uncle Tom's Cabin* and *A Tale of Two Cities* over and over and over again; in this way, in fact, I read just about everything I could get my hands on—except the Bible, probably because it was the only book I was encouraged to read. I must also confess that I wrote—a great deal—and my first professional triumph, in any case, the first effort of mine to be seen in print, occurred at the age of twelve or thereabouts, when a short story I had written about the Spanish revolution won some sort of prize in an extremely short-lived church newspaper. I remember the story was censored by the lady editor, though I don't remember why, and I was outraged.

Also wrote plays, and songs, for one of which I received a letter of congratulations from Mayor La Guardia, and poetry, about which the less said, the better. My mother was delighted by all these goings-on, but my father wasn't; he wanted me to be a preacher. When I was fourteen I became a preacher, and when I was seventeen I stopped. Very shortly thereafter I left home. For God knows how long I struggled with the world of commerce and industry—I guess they would say they struggled with *me*—and when I was about twenty-one I had enough done of a novel to get a Saxton Fellowship. When I was twenty-two the fellowship was over, the novel turned out to be unsalable, and I started waiting on tables in a Village restaurant and writing book reviews—mostly, as it turned out, about the Negro problem, concerning which the color of my skin made me automatically an expert. Did another book, in company with photographer Theodore Pelatowski, about the store-front churches in Harlem. This book met exactly the same fate as my first—fellowship, but no sale. (It was a Rosenwald Fellowship.) By the time I was twenty-four I had decided to stop reviewing books about the Negro problem—which, by this time, was only slightly less horrible in print than it was in life—and I packed my bags and went to France, where I finished, God knows how, *Go Tell It on the Mountain*.

Any writer, I suppose, feels that the world into which he was born is nothing less than a conspiracy against the cultivation of his talent—

which attitude certainly has a great deal to support it. On the other hand, it is only because the world looks on his talent with such a frightening indifference that the artist is compelled to make his talent important. So that any writer, looking back over even so short a span of time as I am here forced to assess, finds that the things which hurt him and the things which helped him cannot be divorced from each other; he could be helped in a certain way only because he was hurt in a certain way; and his help is simply to be enabled to move from one conundrum to the next—one is tempted to say that he moves from one disaster to the next. When one begins looking for influences one finds them by the score. I haven't thought much about my own, not enough anyway; I hazard that the King James Bible, the rhetoric of the store-front church, something ironic and violent and perpetually understated in Negro speech—and something of Dickens' love for bravura—have something to do with me today; but I wouldn't stake my life on it. Likewise, innumerable people have helped me in many ways; but finally, I suppose, the most difficult (and most rewarding) thing in my life has been the fact that I was born a Negro and was forced, therefore, to effect some kind of truce with this reality. (Truce, by the way, is the best one can hope for.)

One of the difficulties about being a Negro writer (and this is not special pleading, since I don't mean to suggest that he has it worse than anybody else) is that the Negro problem is written about so widely. The bookshelves groan under the weight of information, and everyone therefore considers himself informed. And this information, furthermore, operates usually (generally, popularly) to reinforce traditional attitudes. Of traditional attitudes there are only two—For or Against—and I, personally, find it difficult to say which attitude has caused me the most pain. I am speaking as a writer; from a social point of view I am perfectly aware that the change from ill-will to good-will, however motivated, however imperfect, however expressed, is better than no change at all.

But it is part of the business of the writer—as I see it—to examine   5 attitudes, to go beneath the surface, to tap the source. From this point of view the Negro problem is nearly inaccessible. It is not only written about so widely; it is written about so badly. It is quite possible to say that the price a Negro pays for becoming articulate is to find himself, at length, with nothing to be articulate about. ("You taught me language," says Caliban to Prospero, "and my profit on't is I know how to curse.") Consider: the tremendous social activity that this problem generates imposes on whites and Negroes alike the necessity of looking forward, of working to bring about a better day. This is fine, it keeps the waters troubled; it is all, indeed, that has made possible the Negro's progress. Nevertheless, social affairs are not generally speaking the writer's prime concern, whether they ought to be or not; it is absolutely necessary that he establish between himself and these affairs a distance which will allow, at least, for clarity, so that before he can look forward in any meaningful sense, he must first be allowed to take a long look back. In the context of the Negro problem neither whites nor blacks, for excellent reasons of their own, have the faintest desire to look back; but I think that the past is all that makes the present coherent, and further, that the past will remain horrible for exactly as long as we refuse to assess it honestly.

I know, in any case, that the most crucial time in my own development came when I was forced to recognize that I was a kind of bastard of the West; when I followed the line of my past I did not find myself in Europe but in Africa. And this meant that in some subtle way, in a really profound way, I brought to Shakespeare, Bach, Rembrandt, to the stones of Paris, to the cathedral at Chartres, and to the Empire State Building, a special attitude. These were not really my creations, they did not contain my history; I might search in them in vain forever for any reflection of myself. I was an interloper; this was not my heritage. At the same time I had no other heritage which I could possibly hope to use—I had certainly been unfitted for the jungle or the tribe. I would have to appropriate these white centuries, I would have to make them mine—I would have to accept my special attitude, my special place in this scheme—otherwise I would have no place in *any* scheme. What was the most difficult was the fact that I was forced to admit something I had always hidden from myself, which the American Negro has had to hide from himself as the price of his public progress; that I hated and feared white people. This did not mean that I loved black people; on the contrary, I despised them, possibly because they failed to produce Rembrandt. In effect, I hated and feared the world. And this meant, not only that I thus gave the world an altogether murderous power over me, but also that in such a self-destroying limbo I could never hope to write.

One writes out of one thing only—one's own experience. Everything depends on how relentlessly one forces from this experience the last drop, sweet or bitter, it can possibly give. This is the only real concern of the artist, to recreate out of the disorder of life that order which is art. The difficulty then, for me, of being a Negro writer was the fact that I was, in effect, prohibited from examining my own experience too closely by the tremendous demands and the very real dangers of my social situation.

I don't think the dilemma outlined above is uncommon. I do think, since writers work in the disastrously explicit medium of language, that it goes a little way towards explaining why, out of the enormous resources of Negro speech and life, and despite the example of Negro music, prose written by Negroes has been generally speaking so pallid and so harsh. I have not written about being a Negro at such length because I expect that to be my only subject, but only because it was the gate I had to unlock before I could hope to write about anything else. I don't think that the Negro problem in America can be even discussed coherently without bearing in mind its context; its context being the history, traditions, customs, the moral assumptions and preoccupations of the country; in short, the general social fabric. Appearances to the contrary, no one in America escapes its effects and everyone in America bears some responsibility for it. I believe this the more firmly because it is the overwhelming tendency to speak of this problem as though it were a thing apart. But in the work of Faulkner, in the general attitude and certain specific passages in Robert Penn Warren, and, most significantly, in the advent of Ralph Ellison, one sees the beginnings—at least—of a more genuinely penetrating search. Mr. Ellison, by the way, is the first Negro novelist I have ever read to utilize in language, and brilliantly, some of the ambiguity and irony of Negro life.

About my interests: I don't know if I have any, unless the morbid desire to own a sixteen-millimeter camera and make experimental movies can be so classified. Otherwise, I love to eat and drink—it's my melancholy conviction that I've scarcely ever had enough to eat (this is because it's *impossible* to eat enough if you're worried about the next meal)—and I love to argue with people who do not disagree with me too profoundly, and I love to laugh. I do *not* like bohemia, or bohemians, I do not like people whose principal aim is pleasure, and I do not like people who are *earnest* about anything. I don't like people who like me because I'm a Negro; neither do I like people who find in the same accident grounds for contempt. I love America more than any other country in the world, and exactly for this reason, I insist on the right to criticize her perpetually. I think all theories are suspect, that the finest principles may have to be modified, or may even be pulverized by the demands of life, and that one must find, therefore, one's own moral center and move through the world hoping that this center will guide one aright. I consider that I have many responsibilities, but none greater than this: to last, as Hemingway says, and get my work done.

I want to be an honest man and a good writer.   10

LINES OF INQUIRY
"Autobiographical Notes"

The title of this piece suggests that it might be as casual in its style and as random in its structure as notes or jottings. In what respects does it seem to have the random order that might be expected of someone remembering, free-associating, and thinking to himself about aspects of his past? In what respects does it seem to follow a systematic procedure, as might be expected of someone providing autobiographical information? In what respects does it seem to be guided neither by a desire to remember, nor by a desire to inform, but by an intent to express a personal set of beliefs?

Baldwin makes a striking and paradoxical assertion in the third paragraph when he claims that "any writer . . . finds that the things which hurt him and the things which helped him cannot be divorced from each other." On what basis does he make this seemingly paradoxical assertion? For example, how does he show that being "born a Negro" was "the most difficult (and most rewarding) thing" in his personal life"? In his life as a writer?

How broadly applicable do you consider Baldwin's paradoxical assertion to be? For example, what has been "the most difficult" thing in your life? In what respects, if any, has it also been the "most rewarding"? What has been the most difficult thing for you as a writer? In what respects, if any, has it also been the most rewarding for you as a writer?

STRANGER IN THE VILLAGE

From all available evidence no black man had ever set foot in this tiny Swiss village before I came. I was told before arriving that I would probably be a "sight" for the village; I took this to mean that people of my complexion were rarely seen in Switzerland, and also that city people are always something of a "sight" outside of the city. It did not occur to me—possibly because I am an American—that there could be people anywhere who had never seen a Negro.

It is a fact that cannot be explained on the basis of the inaccessibility of the village. The village is very high, but it is only four hours from Milan and three hours from Lausanne. It is true that it is virtually unknown. Few people making plans for a holiday would elect to come here. On the other hand, the villagers are able, presumably, to come and go as they please—which they do: to another town at the foot of the mountain, with a population of approximately five thousand, the nearest place to see a movie or go to the bank. In the village there is no movie house, no bank, no library, no theater; very few radios, one jeep, one station wagon; and, at the moment, one typewriter, mine, an invention which the woman next door to me here had never seen. There are about six hundred people living here, all Catholic—I conclude this from the fact that the Catholic church is open all year round, whereas the Protestant chapel, set off on a hill a little removed from the village, is open only in the summertime when the tourists arrive. There are four or five hotels, all closed now, and four or five *bistros,* of which, however, only two do any business during the winter. These two do not do a great deal, for life in the village seems to end around nine or ten o'clock. There are a few stores, butcher, baker, *épicerie,* a hardware store, and a money-changer—who cannot change travelers' checks, but must send them down to the bank, an operation which takes two or three days. There is something called the *Ballet Haus,* closed in the winter and used for God knows what, certainly not ballet, during the summer. There seems to be only one schoolhouse in the village, and this for the quite young children; I suppose this to mean that their older brothers and sisters at some point descend from these mountains in order to complete their education—possibly, again, to the town just below. The landscape is absolutely forbidding, mountains towering on all four sides, ice and snow as far as the eye can reach. In this white wilderness, men and women and children move all day, carrying washing, wood, buckets of milk or water, sometimes skiing on Sunday afternoons. All week long boys and young men are to be seen shoveling snow off the rooftops, or dragging wood down from the forest in sleds.

The village's only real attraction, which explains the tourist season, is the hot spring water. A disquietingly high proportion of these tourists are cripples, or semi-cripples, who come year after year—from other parts of Switzerland, usually—to take the waters. This lends the village, at the height of the season, a rather terrifying air of sanctity, as though it were a lesser Lourdes. There is often something beautiful, there is always something awful, in the spectacle of a person who has lost one of his faculties, a faculty he never questioned until it was gone, and who struggles to recover it. Yet people remain people, on crutches or indeed on deathbeds; and wherever I passed, the first summer I was here, among the native villagers or among the lame, a wind passed with me—of astonishment, curiosity, amusement, and outrage. That first summer I stayed two weeks and never intended to return. But I did return in the winter, to work; the village offers, obviously, no distractions whatever and has the further advantage of being extremely cheap. Now it is winter again, a year later, and I am here again. Everyone in the village knows my name, though they scarcely ever use it, knows that I come from America—though, this, apparently, they will never really believe: black men come from Africa—and everyone knows that I am the friend of the son of a woman who was born here, and that I am staying in their chalet. But I remain as much a stranger today as I was the first day I arrived, and the children shout *Neger! Neger!* as I walk along the streets.

It must be admitted that in the beginning I was far too shocked to have any real reaction. In so far as I reacted at all, I reacted by trying to be pleasant—it being a great part of the American Negro's education (long before he goes to school) that he must make people "like" him. This smile-and-the-world-smiles-with-you routine worked about as well in this situation as it had in the situation for which it was designed, which is to say that it did not work at all. No one, after all, can be liked whose human weight and complexity cannot be, or has not been, admitted. My smile was simply another unheard-of phenomenon which allowed them to see my teeth—they did not, really, see my smile and I began to think that, should I take to snarling, no one would notice any difference. All of the physical characteristics of the Negro which had caused me, in America, a very different and almost forgotten pain were nothing less than miraculous—or infernal—in the eyes of the village people. Some thought my hair was the color of tar, that it had the texture of wire, or the texture of cotton. It was jocularly suggested that I might let it all grow long and make myself a winter coat. If I sat in the sun for more than five minutes some daring creature was certain to come along and gingerly put his fingers on my hair, as though he were afraid of an electric shock, or put his hand on my hand, astonished that the color did not rub off. In all of this, in which it must be conceded there was the charm of genuine wonder and in which there was certainly no element of intentional unkindness, there was yet no suggestion that I was human: I was simply a living wonder.

I knew that they did not mean to be unkind, and I know it now; it is necessary, nevertheless, for me to repeat this to myself each time that I walk out of the chalet. The children who shout *Neger!* have no way of knowing the echoes this sound raises in me. They are brimming with good humor and the more daring swell with pride when I stop to speak with them. Just the same, there are days when I cannot pause and smile, when I have no heart to play with them; when, indeed, I mutter sourly to myself, exactly as I muttered on the streets of a city these children have never seen, when I was no bigger than these children are now: *Your* mother *was a nigger*. Joyce is right about history being a nightmare—but it may be the nightmare from which no one *can* awaken. People are trapped in history and history is trapped in them.

There is a custom in the village—I am told it is repeated in many villages—of "buying" African natives for the purpose of converting them to Christianity. There stands in the church all year round a small box with a slot for money, decorated with a black figurine, and into this box the villagers drop their francs. During the *carnaval* which precedes Lent, two village children have their faces blackened—out of which bloodless darkness their blue eyes shine like ice—and fantastic horsehair wigs are placed on their blond heads; thus disguised, they solicit among the villagers for money for the missionaries in Africa. Between the box in the church and the blackened children, the village "bought" last year six or eight African natives. This was reported to me with pride by the wife of one of the *bistro* owners and I was careful to express astonishment and pleasure at the solicitude shown by the village for the souls of black folk. The *bistro* owner's wife beamed with a pleasure far more genuine than my own and seemed to feel that I might now breathe more easily concerning the souls of at least six of my kinsmen.

I tried not to think of these so lately baptized kinsmen, of the price paid for them, or the peculiar price they themselves would pay, and said nothing about my father, who having taken his own conversion too literally never, at bottom, forgave the white world (which he described as heathen) for having saddled him with a Christ in whom, to judge at least from their treatment of him, they themselves no longer believed. I thought of white men arriving for the first time in an African village, strangers there, as I am a stranger here, and tried to imagine the astounded populace touching their hair and marveling at the color of their skin. But there is a great difference between being the first white man to be seen by Africans and being the first black man to be seen by whites. The white man takes the astonishment as tribute, for he arrives to conquer and to convert the natives, whose inferiority in relation to himself is not even to be questioned; whereas I, without a thought of conquest, find myself among a people whose culture controls me, has even, in a sense, created me, people who have cost me more in anguish and rage than they will ever know, who yet do not even know of my existence. The astonishment with which I might have greeted them, should they have stumbled into my African village a few hundred years ago, might have rejoiced their hearts. But the astonishment with which they greet me today can only poison mine.

And this is so despite everything I may do to feel differently, despite my friendly conversations with the *bistro* owner's wife, despite their three-year-old son who has at last become my friend, despite the *saluts* and *bonsoirs* which I exchange with people as I walk, despite the fact that I know that no individual can be taken to task for what history is doing, or has done. I say that the culture of these people controls me—but they can scarcely be held responsible for European culture. America comes out of Europe, but these people have never seen America, nor have most of them seen more of Europe than the hamlet at the foot of their mountain. Yet they move with an authority which I shall never have; and they regard me, quite rightly, not only as a stranger in their village but as a suspect latecomer, bearing no credentials, to everything they have—however unconsciously—inherited.

For this village, even were it incomparably more remote and incredibly more primitive, is the West, the West onto which I have been so strangely grafted. These people cannot be, from the point of view of power, strangers anywhere in the world; they have made the modern world, in effect, even if they do not know it. The most illiterate among them is related, in a way that I am not, to Dante, Shakespeare, Michelangelo, Aeschylus, Da Vinci, Rembrandt, and Racine; the cathedral at Chartres says something to them which it cannot say to me, as indeed would New York's Empire State Building, should anyone here ever see it. Out of their hymns and dances come Beethoven and Bach. Go back a few centuries and they are in their full glory—but I am in Africa, watching the conquerors arrive.

The rage of the disesteemed is personally fruitless, but it is also absolutely inevitable; this rage, so generally discounted, so little understood even among the people whose daily bread it is, is one of the things that makes history. Rage can only with difficulty, and never entirely, be brought under the domination of the intelligence and is therefore not susceptible to any arguments whatever. This is a fact which ordinary representatives of the *Herrenvolk,* having never felt this rage and being unable to imagine it, quite fail to understand. Also, rage cannot be hidden, it can only be dissembled. This dissembling deludes the thoughtless, and strengthens rage and adds, to rage, contempt. There are, no doubt, as many ways of coping with the resulting complex of tensions as there are black men in the world, but no black man can hope ever to be entirely liberated from this internal warfare—rage, dissembling, and contempt having inevitably accompanied his first realization of the power of white men. What is crucial here is that, since white men represent in the black man's world so heavy a weight, white men have for black men a reality which is far from being reciprocal; and hence all black men have toward all white men an attitude which is designed, really, either to rob the white man of the jewel of his naïveté, or else to make it cost him dear.

The black man insists, by whatever means he finds at his disposal,   10
that the white man cease to regard him as an exotic rarity and recognize him as a human being. This is a very charged and difficult moment, for there is a great deal of will power involved in the white man's naïveté. Most people are not naturally reflective any more than they are naturally malicious, and the white man prefers to keep the black man at a certain human remove because it is easier for him thus to preserve his simplicity and avoid being called to account for crimes committed by his forefathers, or his neighbors. He is inescapably aware, nevertheless, that he is in a better position in the world than black men are, nor can he quite put to death the suspicion that he is hated by black men therefore. He does not wish to be hated, neither does he wish to change places, and at this point in his uneasiness he can scarcely avoid having recourse to those legends which white men have created about black men, the most usual effect of which is that the white man finds himself enmeshed, so to speak, in his own language which describes hell, as well as the attributes which lead one to hell, as being as black as night.

Every legend, moreover, contains its residuum of truth, and the root function of language is to control the universe by describing it. It is of quite considerable significance that black men remain, in the imagination, and in overwhelming numbers in fact, beyond the disciplines of salvation; and this despite the fact that the West has been "buying" African natives for centuries. There is, I should hazard, an instantaneous necessity to be divorced from this so visibly unsaved stranger, in whose heart, moreover, one cannot guess what dreams of vengeance are being nourished; and, at the same time, there are few things on earth more attractive than the idea of the unspeakable liberty which is allowed the unredeemed. When, beneath the black mask, a human being begins to make himself felt one cannot escape a certain awful wonder as to what kind of human being it is. What one's imagination makes of other people is dictated, of course, by the laws of one's own personality and it is one of the ironies of black-white relations that, by means of what the white man imagines the black man to be, the black man is enabled to know who the white man is.

I have said, for example, that I am as much a stranger in this village today as I was the first summer I arrived, but this is not quite true. The villagers wonder less about the texture of my hair than they did then, and wonder rather more about me. And the fact that their wonder now exists on another level is reflected in their attitudes and in their eyes. There are the children who make those delightful, hilarious, sometimes astonishingly grave overtures of friendship in the unpredictable fashion of children; other children, having been taught that the devil is a black man, scream in genuine anguish as I approach. Some of the older women never pass without a friendly greeting, never pass, indeed, if it seems that they will be able to engage me in conversation; other women look down or look away or rather contemptuously smirk. Some of the men drink with me and suggest that I learn how to ski—partly, I gather, because they cannot imagine what I would look like on skis—and want to know if I am married, and ask questions about my *métier*. But some of the men have accused *le sale nègre*—behind my back—of stealing wood and there is already in the eyes of some of them that peculiar, intent, paranoiac malevolence which one sometimes surprises in the eyes of American white men when, out walking with their Sunday girl, they see a Negro male approach.

There is a dreadful abyss between the streets of this village and the streets of the city in which I was born, between the children who shout *Neger!* today and those who shouted *Nigger!* yesterday—the abyss is experience, the American experience. The syllable hurled behind me today expresses, above all, wonder: I am a stranger here. But I am not a stranger in America and the same syllable riding on the American air expresses the war my presence has occasioned in the American soul.

For this village brings home to me this fact: that there was a day, and not really a very distant day, when Americans were scarcely Americans at all but discontented Europeans, facing a great unconquered continent and strolling, say, into a marketplace and seeing black men for the first time. The shock this spectacle afforded is suggested, surely, by the promptness with which they decided that these black men were not really men but cattle. It is true that the necessity on the part of the settlers of the New World of reconciling their moral assumptions with the fact—and the necessity—of slavery enhanced immensely the charm of this idea, and it is also true that this idea expresses, with a truly American bluntness, the attitude which to varying extents all masters have had toward all slaves.

But between all former slaves and slave-owners and the drama which begins for Americans over three hundred years ago at Jamestown, there are at least two differences to be observed. The American Negro slave could not suppose, for one thing, as slaves in past epochs had supposed and often done, that he would ever be able to wrest the power from his master's hands. This was a supposition which the modern era, which was to bring about such vast changes in the aims and dimensions of power, put to death; it only begins, in unprecedented fashion, and with dreadful implications, to be resurrected today. But even had this supposition persisted with undiminished force, the American Negro slave could not have used it to lend his condition dignity, for the reason that this supposition rests on another: that the slave in exile yet remains related to his past, has some means—if only in memory—of revering and sustaining the forms of his former life, is able, in short, to maintain his identity.

This was not the case with the American Negro slave. He is unique   15 among the black men of the world in that his past was taken from him, almost literally, at one blow. One wonders what on earth the first slave found to say to the first dark child he bore. I am told that there are Haitians able to trace their ancestry back to African kings, but any American Negro wishing to go back so far will find his journey through time abruptly arrested by the signature on the bill of sale which served as the entrance paper for his ancestor. At the time—to say nothing of the circumstances—of the enslavement of the captive black man who was to become the American Negro, there was not the remotest possibility that he would ever take power from his master's hands. There was no reason to suppose that his situation would ever change, nor was there, shortly, anything to indicate that his situation had ever been different. It was his necessity, in the words of E. Franklin Frazier, to find a "motive for living under American culture or die." The identity of the American Negro comes out of this extreme situation, and the evolution of this identity was a source of the most intolerable anxiety in the minds and the lives of his masters.

For the history of the American Negro is unique also in this: that the question of his humanity, and of his rights therefore as a human being, became a burning one for several generations of Americans, so burning a question that it ultimately became one of those used to divide the nation. It is out of this argument that the venom of the epithet *Nigger!* is derived. It is an argument which Europe has never had, and hence Europe quite sincerely fails to understand how or why the argument arose in the first place, why its effects are so frequently disastrous and always so unpredictable, why it refuses until today to be entirely settled. Europe's black possessions remained—and do remain—in Europe's colonies, at which remove they represented no threat whatever to European identity. If they posed any problem at all for the European conscience, it was a problem which remained comfortingly abstract: in effect, the black man, *as a man,* did not exist for Europe. But in America, even as a slave, he was an inescapable part of the general social fabric and no American could escape having an attitude toward him. Americans attempt until today to make an abstraction of the Negro, but the very nature of these abstractions reveals the tremendous effects the presence of the Negro has had on the American character.

When one considers the history of the Negro in America it is of the greatest importance to recognize that the moral beliefs of a person, or a people, are never really as tenuous as life—which is not moral—very often causes them to appear; these create for them a frame of reference and a necessary hope, the hope being that when life has done its worst they will be enabled to rise above themselves and to triumph over life. Life would scarcely be bearable if this hope did not exist. Again, even when the worst has been said, to betray a belief is not by any means to have put oneself beyond its power; the betrayal of a belief is not the same thing as ceasing to believe. If this were not so there would be no moral standards in the world at all. Yet one must also recognize that morality is based on ideas and that all ideas are dangerous—dangerous because ideas can only lead to action and where the action leads no man can say. And dangerous in this respect: that confronted with the impossibility of remaining faithful to one's beliefs, and the equal impossibility of becoming free of them, one can be driven to the most inhuman excesses. The ideas on which American beliefs are based are not, though Americans often seem to think so, ideas which originated in America. They came out of Europe. And the establishment of democracy on the American continent was scarcely as radical a break with the past as was the necessity, which Americans faced, of broadening this concept to include black men.

This was, literally, a hard necessity. It was impossible, for one thing, for Americans to abandon their beliefs, not only because these beliefs alone seemed able to justify the sacrifices they had endured and the blood that they had spilled, but also because these beliefs afforded them their own bulwark against a moral chaos as absolute as the physical chaos of the continent it was their destiny to conquer. But in the situation in which Americans found themselves, these beliefs threatened an idea which, whether or not one likes to think so, is the very warp and woof of the heritage of the West, the idea of white supremacy.

Americans have made themselves notorious by the shrillness and the brutality with which they have insisted on this idea, but they did not invent it; and it has escaped the world's notice that those very excesses of which Americans have been guilty imply a certain, unprecedented uneasiness over the idea's life and power, if not, indeed, the idea's validity. The idea of white supremacy rests simply on the fact that white men are the creators of civilization (the present civilization, which is the only one that matters; all previous civilizations are simply "contributions" to our own) and are therefore civilization's guardians and defenders. Thus it was impossible for Americans to accept the black man as one of themselves, for to do so was to jeopardize their status as white men. But not so to accept him was to deny his human reality, his human weight and complexity, and the strain of denying the overwhelmingly undeniable forced Americans into rationalizations so fantastic that they approached the pathological.

At the root of the American Negro problem is the necessity of the American white man to find a way of living with the Negro in order to be able to live with himself. And the history of this problem can be reduced to the means used by Americans—lynch law and law, segregation and legal acceptance, terrorization and concession—either to come to terms with this necessity, or to find a way around it, or (most usually) to find a way of doing both these things at once. The resulting spectacle, at once foolish and dreadful, led someone to make the quite accurate observation that "the Negro-in-America is a form of insanity which overtakes white men."

In this long battle, a battle by no means finished, the unforeseeable effects of which will be felt by many future generations, the white man's motive was the protection of his identity; the black man was motivated by the need to establish an identity. And despite the terrorization which the Negro in America endured and endures sporadically until today, despite the cruel and totally inescapable ambivalence of his status in his country, the battle for his identity has long ago been won. He is not a visitor to the West, but a citizen there, an American; as American as the Americans who despise him, the Americans who fear him, the Americans who love him—the Americans who became less than themselves, or rose to be greater than themselves by virtue of the fact that the challenge he represented was inescapable. He is perhaps the only black man in the world whose relationship to white men is more terrible, more subtle, and more meaningful than the relationship of bitter possessed to uncertain possessor. His survival depended, and his development depends, on his ability to turn his peculiar status in the Western world to his own advantage and, it may be, to the very great advantage of that world. It remains for him to fashion out of his experience that which will give him sustenance, and a voice.

The cathedral at Chartres, I have said, says something to the people of this village which it cannot say to me; but it is important to understand that this cathedral says something to me which it cannot say to them. Perhaps they are struck by the power of the spires, the glory of the windows; but they have known God, after all, longer than I have known him, and in a different way, and I am terrified by the slippery bottomless well to be found in the crypt, down which heretics were hurled to death, and by the obscene, inescapable gargoyles jutting out of the stone and seeming to say that God and the devil can never be divorced. I doubt that the villagers think of the devil when they face a cathedral because they have never been identified with the devil. But I must accept the status which myth, if nothing else, gives me in the West before I can hope to change the myth.

Yet, if the American Negro has arrived at his identity by virtue of the absoluteness of his estrangement from his past, American white men still nourish the illusion that there is some means of recovering the European innocence, of returning to a state in which black men do not exist. This is one of the greatest errors Americans can make. The identity they fought so hard to protect has, by virtue of that battle, undergone a change: Americans are as unlike any other white people in the world as it is possible to be. I do not think, for example, that it is too much to suggest that the American vision of the world—which allows so little reality, generally speaking, for any of the darker forces in human life, which tends until today to paint moral issues in glaring black and white—owes a great deal to the battle waged by Americans to maintain between themselves and black men a human separation which could not be bridged. It is only now beginning to be borne in on us— very faintly, it must be admitted, very slowly, and very much against our will—that this vision of the world is dangerously inaccurate, and perfectly useless. For it protects our moral high-mindedness at the terrible expense of weakening our grasp of reality. People who shut their eyes to reality simply invite their own destruction, and anyone who insists on remaining in a state of innocence long after that innocence is dead turns himself into a monster.

The time has come to realize that the interracial drama acted out on the American continent has not only created a new black man, it has created a new white man, too. No road whatever will lead Americans back to the simplicity of this European village where white men still have the luxury of looking on me as a stranger. I am not, really, a stranger any longer for any American alive. One of the things that distinguishes Americans from other people is that no other people has ever been so deeply involved in the lives of black men, and vice versa. This fact faced, with all its implications, it can be seen that the history of the American Negro problem is not merely shameful, it is also something of an achievement. For even when the worst has been said, it must also be added that the perpetual challenge posed by this problem was always, somehow, perpetually met. It is precisely this black-white experience which may prove of indispensable value to us in the world we face today. This world is white no longer, and it will never be white again.

LINES OF INQUIRY
"Stranger in the Village"

Baldwin depicts the Swiss mountain village as being so small, so geographically and culturally isolated, and so thoroughly white as to make it seem completely unrelated to any place in modern America, Europe, or Africa. Why, then, does he devote the first quarter of his piece to describing so strange and atypical a place? How does he manage to keep the village in mind during the last three quarters of the essay when he no longer focuses on his experience there? How does he use his experience in the village to illuminate the "black-white experience" in America? In Europe? In Africa? In the world?

In his final paragraph, Baldwin asserts that "the interracial drama acted out on the American continent has not only created a new black man, it has created a new white man, too." What do you suppose he means by "a new black man" and "a new white man"? How do the "new black man" and the "new white man" differ from their old counterparts? From their counterparts in Europe? In Africa? How does "the interracial drama" of these new persons differ from the interracial drama of their old counterparts?

How does Baldwin's depiction of the black-white experience in Africa compare to Orwell's depiction of that experience at the end of "Marrakech"? How does Baldwin's depiction of the black-white experience in America compare to Walker's depiction of it in "The Black Writer and the Southern Experience"? How does Baldwin's depiction of it compare to your own experience and understanding of it? How do you account for any differences between his perception and yours?

A FLY IN BUTTERMILK

"**Y**ou can take the child out of the country," my elders were fond of saying, "but you can't take the country out of the child." They were speaking of their own antecedents, I supposed; it didn't, anyway, seem possible that they could be warning me; I took myself out of the country and went to Paris. It was there I discovered that the old folks knew what they had been talking about: I found myself, willy-nilly, alchemized into an American the moment I touched French soil.

Now, back again after nearly nine years, it was ironical to reflect that if I had not lived in France for so long I would never have found it necessary—or possible— to visit the American South. The South had always frightened me. How deeply it had frightened me—though I had never seen it—and how soon, was one of the things my dreams revealed to me while I was there. And this made me think of the privacy and mystery of childhood all over again, in a new way. I wondered where children got their strength—the strength, in this case, to walk through mobs to get to school.

"You've got to remember," said an older Negro friend to me in Washington, "that no matter what you see or how it makes you feel, it can't be compared to twenty-five, thirty years ago—you remember those photographs of Negroes hanging from trees?" I looked at him differently. *I* had seen the photographs—but *he* might have been one of them. "I remember," he said, "when conductors on streetcars wore pistols and had police powers." And he remembered a great deal more. He remembered, for example, hearing Booker T. Washington speak, and the day-to-day progress of the Scottsboro case, and the rise and bloody fall of Bessie Smith. These had been books and headlines and music for me but it now developed that they were also a part of my identity.

"You're just one generation away from the South, you know. You'll find," he added, kindly, "that people will be willing to talk to you . . . if they don't feel that you look down on them just because you're from the North."

The first Negro I encountered, an educator, didn't give me any opportunity to look down. He forced me to admit, at once, that I had never been to college; that northern Negroes lived herded together, like pigs in a pen; that the campus on which we met was a tribute to the industry and determination of southern Negroes. "Negroes in the South form a *community*." My humiliation was complete with his discovery that I couldn't even drive a car. I couldn't ask him anything. He made

5

me feel so hopeless an example of the general northern spinelessness that it would have seemed a spiteful counterattack to have asked him to discuss the integration problem which had placed his city in the headlines.

At the same time, I felt that there was nothing which bothered him more; but perhaps he did not really know what he thought about it; or thought too many things at once. His campus risked being very different twenty years from now. Its special function would be gone—and so would his position, arrived at with such pain. The new day a-coming was not for him. I don't think this fact made him bitter but I think it frightened him and made him sad; for the future is like heaven—everyone exalts it but no one wants to go there now. And I imagine that he shared the attitude, which I was to encounter so often later, toward the children who were helping to bring this future about: admiration before the general spectacle and a skepticism before the individual case.

That evening I went to visit G., one of the "integrated" children, a boy of about fifteen. I had already heard something of his first day in school, the peculiar problems his presence caused, and his own extraordinary bearing.

He seemed extraordinary at first mainly by his silence. He was tall for his age and, typically, seemed to be constructed mainly of sharp angles, such as elbows and knees. Dark gingerbread sort of coloring, with ordinary hair, and a face disquietingly impassive, save for his very dark, very large eyes. I got the impression, each time that he raised them, not so much that they spoke but that they registered volumes; each time he dropped them it was as though he had retired into the library.

We sat in the living room, his mother, younger brother and sister, and I, while G. sat on the sofa, doing his homework. The father was at work and the older sister had not yet come home. The boy had looked up once, as I came in, to say, "Good evening, sir," and then left all the rest to his mother.

Mrs. R. was a very strong-willed woman, handsome, quiet-looking, dressed in black. Nothing, she told me, beyond name-calling, had marked G.'s first day at school; but on the second day she received the last of several threatening phone calls. She was told that if she didn't want her son "cut to ribbons" she had better keep him at home. She heeded this warning to the extent of calling the chief of police.

"He told me to go on and send him. He said he'd be there when the cutting started. So I sent him." Even more remarkably, perhaps, G. went.

No one cut him, in fact no one touched him. The students formed a wall between G. and the entrances, saying only enough, apparently, to make their intention clearly understood, watching him, and keeping him outside. (I asked him, "What did you feel when they blocked your way?" G. looked up at me, very briefly, with no expression on his face, and told me, "Nothing, sir.") At last the principal appeared and took him by the hand and they entered the school, while the children shouted behind them, "Nigger-lover!"

G. was alone all day at school.

"But I thought you already knew some of the kids there," I said. I had been told that he had friends among the white students because of their previous competition in a Soapbox Derby.

"Well, none of them are in his classes," his mother told me—a shade   15 too quickly, as though she did not want to dwell on the idea of G.'s daily isolation.

"We don't have the same schedule," G. said. It was as though he were coming to his mother's rescue. Then, unwillingly, with a kind of interior shrug, "Some of the guys had lunch with me but then the other kids called them names." He went back to his homework.

I began to realize that there were not only a great many things G. would not tell me, there was much that he would never tell his mother.

"But nobody bothers you, anyway?'

"No," he said. "They just—call names. I don't let it bother me."

Nevertheless, the principal frequently escorts him through the halls.   20 One day, when G. was alone, a boy tripped him and knocked him down and G. reported this to the principal. The white boy denied it but a few days later, while G. and the principal were together, he came over and said, "I'm sorry I tripped you; I won't do it again," and they shook hands. But it doesn't seem that this boy has as yet developed into a friend. And it is clear that G. will not allow himself to expect this.

I asked Mrs. R. what had prompted her to have her son reassigned to a previously all-white high school. She sighed, paused; then, sharply, "Well, it's not because I'm so anxious to have him around white people." Then she laughed. "I really don't know how I'd feel if I was to carry a white baby around who was calling me Grandma." G. laughed, too, for the first time. "White people say," the mother went on, "that that's all a Negro wants. I don't think they believe that themselves."

Then we switched from the mysterious question of what white folks believe to the relatively solid ground of what she, herself, knows and fears.

"You see that boy? Well, he's always been a straight-A student. He didn't hardly have to work at it. You see the way he's so quiet now on the sofa, with his books? Well, when he was going to———High School, he didn't have no homework or if he did, he could get it done in five minutes. Then, there he was, out in the streets, getting into mischief, and all he did all day in school was just keep clowning to make the other boys laugh. He wasn't learning nothing and didn't nobody care if he *never* learned nothing and I could just see what was going to happen to him if he kept on like that."

The boy was very quiet.

"What were you learning in——High?" I asked him.   25

"Nothing!" he exploded, with a very un-boyish laugh. I asked him to tell me about it.

"Well, the teacher comes in," he said, "and she gives you something to read and she goes out. She leaves some other student in charge . . . ." ("You can just imagine how much reading gets done," Mrs. R. interposed.) "At the end of the period," G. continued, "she comes back and tells you something to read for the next day."

So, having nothing else to do, G. began amusing his classmates and his mother began to be afraid. G. is just about at the age when boys begin dropping out of school. Perhaps they get a girl into trouble; she also drops out; the boy gets work for a time or gets into trouble for a long time. I was told that forty-five girls had left school for the maternity ward the year before. A week or ten days before I arrived in the city eighteen boys from G.'s former high school had been sentenced to the chain gang.

"My boy's a good boy," said Mrs. R., "and I wanted to see him have a chance."

"Don't the teachers care about the students?" I asked. This brought   30
forth more laughter. How could they care? How much could they do if they *did* care? There were too many children, from shaky homes and worn-out parents, in aging, inadequate plants. They could be considered, most of them, as already doomed. Besides, the teachers' jobs were safe. They were responsible only to the principal, an appointed official, whose judgment, apparently, was never questioned by his (white) superiors or confreres.

The principal of G.'s former high school was about seventy-five when he was finally retired and his idea of discipline was to have two boys beat each other—"under his supervision"—with leather belts. This once happened with G., with no other results than that his parents gave the principal a tongue-lashing. It happened with two boys of G.'s acquaintance with the result that, after school, one boy beat the other so badly that he had to be sent to the hospital. The teachers have themselves arrived at a dead end, for in a segregated school system they cannot rise any higher, and the students are aware of this. Both students and teachers soon cease to struggle.

"If a boy can wash a blackboard," a teacher was heard to say, "I'll promote him."

I asked Mrs. R. how other Negroes felt about her having had G. reassigned.

"Well, a lot of them didn't like it," she said—though I gathered that they did not say so to her. As school time approached, more and more people asked her, "Are you going to send him?" "Well," she told them, "the man says the door is open and I feel like, yes, I'm going to go on and send him."

Out of a population of some fifty thousand Negroes, there had been only forty-five applications. People had said that they would send their children, had talked about it, had made plans; but, as the time drew near, when the application blanks were actually in their hands, they said, "I don't believe I'll sign this right now. I'll sign it later." Or, "I been thinking about this. I don't believe I'll send him right now."

"Why?" I asked. But to this she couldn't, or wouldn't, give me any   35
answer.

I asked if there had been any reprisals taken against herself or her husband, if she was worried while G. was at school all day. She said that, no, there had been no reprisals, though some white people, under the pretext of giving her good advice, had expressed disapproval of her action. But she herself doesn't have a job and so doesn't risk losing one. Nor, she told me, had anyone said anything to her husband, who, however, by her own proud suggestion, is extremely closemouthed. And it developed later that he was not working at his regular trade but at something else.

As to whether she was worried, "No," she told me; in much the same way that G., when asked about the blockade, had said, "Nothing, sir." In her case it was easier to see what she meant: she hoped for the best and would not allow herself, in the meantime, to lose her head. "I don't feel like nothing's going to happen," she said, soberly. "I *hope* not. But I know if anybody tries to harm me or any of my children, I'm going to strike back with all my strength. I'm going to strike them in God's name."

G., in the meantime, on the sofa with his books, was preparing himself for the next school day. His face was as impassive as ever and I found myself wondering—again—how he managed to face what must surely have been the worst moment of his day—the morning, when he opened his eyes and realized that it was all to be gone through again. Insults, and incipient violence, teachers, and—exams.

"One among so many," his mother said, "that's kind of rough."

"Do you think you'll make it?" I asked him. "Would you rather go   40
back to———High?"

"No," he said, "I'll make it. I ain't going back."

"He ain't thinking about going back," said his mother—proudly and sadly. I began to suspect that the boy managed to support the extreme tension of his situation by means of a nearly fanatical concentration on his schoolwork; by holding in the center of his mind the issue on which, when the deal went down, others would be *forced* to judge him. Pride and silence were his weapons. Pride comes naturally, and soon, to a Negro, but even his mother, I felt, was worried about G.'s silence, though she was too wise to break it. For what was all this doing to him really?

"It's hard enough," the boy said later, still in control but with flashing eyes, "to keep quiet and keep walking when they call you nigger. But if anybody ever spits on me, I *know* I'll have to fight."

His mother laughs, laughs to ease them both, then looks at me and says, "I wonder sometimes what makes white folks so mean."

This is a recurring question among Negroes, even among the most   45
"liberated"—which epithet is meant, of course, to describe the writer. The next day, with this question (more elegantly phrased) still beating in my mind, I visited the principal of G.'s new high school. But he didn't look "mean" and he wasn't "mean": he was a thin, young man of about my age, bewildered and in trouble. I asked him how things were working out, what he thought about it, what he thought would happen—in the long run, or the short.

"Well, I've got a job to do," he told me, "and I'm going to do it." He said that there hadn't been any trouble and that he didn't expect any. "Many students, after all, never see G. at all." None of the children have harmed him and the teachers are, apparently, carrying out their rather tall orders, which are to be kind to G. and, at the same time, to treat him like any other student.

I asked him to describe to me the incident, on the second day of school, when G.'s entrance had been blocked by the students. He told me that it was nothing at all—"It was a gesture more than anything else." He had simply walked out and spoken to the students and brought G. inside. "I've seen them do the same thing to other kids when they were kidding," he said. I imagine that he would like to be able to place this incident in the same cheerful if rowdy category, despite the shouts (which he does not mention) of "nigger-lover!"

Which epithet does not, in any case, describe him at all.

"Why," I asked, "is G. the only Negro student here?" According to this city's pupil-assignment plan, a plan designed to allow the least possible integration over the longest period of time, G. was the only Negro student who qualified.

"And, anyway," he said, "I don't think it's right for colored chil-   50
dren to come to white schools just *because* they're white."

"Well," I began, "even if you don't like it . . ."

"Oh," he said quickly, raising his head and looking at me sideways, "I never said I didn't like it."

And then he explained to me, with difficulty, that it was simply contrary to everything he'd ever seen or believed. He'd never dreamed of a mingling of the races; had never lived that way himself and didn't suppose that he ever would; in the same way, he added, perhaps a trifle defensively, that he only associated with a certain stratum of white people. But, "I've never seen a colored person toward whom I had any hatred or ill-will."

His eyes searched mine as he said this and I knew that he was wondering if I believed him.

I certainly did believe him; he impressed me as being a very gentle   55
and honorable man. But I could not avoid wondering if he had ever really *looked* at a Negro and wondered about the life, the aspirations, the universal humanity hidden behind the dark skin. As I wondered, when he told me that race relations in his city were "excellent" and had not been strained by recent developments, how on earth he managed to hold on to this delusion.

I later got back to my interrupted question, which I phrased more tactfully.

"Even though it's very difficult for all concerned—this situation— doesn't it occur to you that the reason colored children wish to come to white schools isn't because they want to be with white people but simply because they want a better education?"

"Oh, I don't know," he replied, "it seems to me that colored schools are just as good as white schools." I wanted to ask him on what evidence he had arrived at this conclusion and also how they could possibly be "as good" in view of the kind of life they came out of, and perpetuated, and the dim prospects faced by all but the most exceptional or ruthless Negro students. But I only suggested that G. and his family, who certainly should have known, so thoroughly disagreed with him that they had been willing to risk G.'s present well-being and his future psychological and mental health in order to bring about a change in his environment. Nor did I mention the lack of enthusiasm evinced by G.'s mother when musing on the prospect of a fair grandchild. There seemed no point in making this man any more a victim of his heritage than he so gallantly was already.

"Still," I said at last, after a rather painful pause, "I should think that the trouble in this situation is that it's very hard for *you* to face a child and treat him unjustly because of something for which he is no more responsible than—than *you* are."

The eyes came to life then, or a veil fell, and I found myself staring   60
at a man in anguish. The eyes were full of pain and bewilderment and he nodded his head. This was the impossibility which he faced every day. And I imagined that his tribe would increase, in sudden leaps and bounds was already increasing.

For segregation has worked brilliantly in the South, and, in fact, in the nation, to this extent: it has allowed white people, with scarcely any pangs of conscience whatever, to *create*, in every generation, only the Negro they wished to see. As the walls come down they will be forced to take another, harder look at the shiftless and the menial and will be forced into a wonder concerning them which cannot fail to be agonizing. It is not an easy thing to be forced to reexamine a way of life and to speculate, in a personal way, on the general injustice.

"What do you think," I asked him, "will happen? What do you think the future holds?"

He gave a strained laugh and said he didn't know. "I don't want to think about it." Then, "I'm a religious man," he said, "and I believe the Creator will always help us find a way to solve our problems. If a man loses that, he's lost everything he had." I agreed, struck by the look in his eyes.

"You're from the North?" he asked me, abruptly.

"Yes," I said.   65

"Well," he said, "you've got your troubles too."

"Ah, yes, we certainly do," I admitted and shook hands and left him. I did not say what I was thinking, that our troubles were the same trouble and that, unless we were very swift and honest, what is happening in the South today will be happening in the North tomorrow.

LINES OF INQUIRY
"A Fly in Buttermilk"

The spotlight in this piece focuses clearly on G., yet Baldwin's evening with G. is not the only incident that he tells about in this piece. Why do you suppose that he precedes G.'s story by telling about his conversations with an older Negro friend in Washington and a southern Negro educator? Why do you suppose that he follows G.'s story by giving such a detailed description of his meeting with the principal of G.'s new school? Imagine how you might have reacted to G.'s situation if Baldwin had confined himself only to telling about his evening with G. and G.'s mother.

This essay might well be understood as having several important themes: the inexplicable cruelty of racism ("what makes white folks so mean?"); the heroism of lonely black children, such as G., who challenge segregation in the schools; the mixed attitudes of both blacks and whites towards segregation, as well as towards the prospect of integration; the tensions between Northerners and Southerners precipitated by governmental enforcement of integration. Why do you suppose that Baldwin tries to address all of these issues in this piece? How are they interrelated? Which of these themes do you think is Baldwin's primary concern?

Just as this piece deals with the experience of G. as the only black student in an all white high school, so "Stranger in the Village" deals with the experience of Baldwin as the only black in an all white community. Have you ever experienced such extreme racial isolation, or observed others experiencing it? Have you ever experienced, or observed others experiencing, extreme isolation on any other account—cultural, religious, or sexual? What similarities, what differences, do you think are at work in these varied forms of extreme human isolation?

IF BLACK ENGLISH ISN'T A LANGUAGE, THEN TELL ME, WHAT IS?

The argument concerning the use, or the status, or the reality, of black English is rooted in American history and has absolutely nothing to do with the question the argument supposes itself to be posing. The argument has nothing to do with language itself but with the role of language. Language, incontestably, reveals the speaker. Language, also, far more dubiously, is meant to define the other—and, in this case, the other is refusing to be defined by a language that has never been able to recognize him.

People evolve a language in order to describe and thus control their circumstances or in order not to be submerged by a situation that they cannot articulate. (And if they cannot articulate it, they are submerged.) A Frenchman living in Paris speaks a subtly and crucially different language from that of the man living in Marseilles; neither sounds very much like a man living in Quebec; and they would all have great difficulty in apprehending what the man from Guadeloupe, or Martinique, is saying, to say nothing of the man from Senegal—although the "common" language of all these areas is French. But each has paid, and is paying, a different price for this "common" language, in which, as it turns out, they are not saying, and cannot be saying, the same things: They each have very different realities to articulate, or control.

What joins all languages, and all men, is the necessity to confront life, in order, not inconceivably, to outwit death: The price for this is the acceptance, and achievement, of one's temporal identity. So that, for example, though it is not taught in the schools (and this has the potential of becoming a political issue) the south of France still clings to its ancient and musical Provençal, which resists being described as a "dialect." And much of the tension in the Basque countries, and in Wales, is due to the Basque and Welsh determination not to allow their languages to be destroyed. This determination also feeds the flames in Ireland for among the many indignities the Irish have been forced to undergo at English hands is the English contempt for their language.

It goes without saying, then, that language is also a political instrument, means, and proof of power. It is the most vivid and crucial key to identity: It reveals the private identity, and connects one with, or divorces one from, the larger, public, or communal identity. There have been, and are, times and places, when to speak a certain language could be dangerous, even fatal. Or, one may speak the same language, but in such a way that one's antecedents are revealed, or (one hopes) hidden. This is true in France, and is absolutely true in England: The range (and reign) of accents on that damp little island make England coherent for the English and totally incomprehensible for everyone else. To open your mouth in England is (if I may use black English) to "put your business in the street." You have confessed your parents, your youth, your school, your salary, your self-esteem, and, alas, your future.

Now, I do not know what white Americans would sound like if   5
there had never been any black people in the United States, but they would not sound the way they sound. *Jazz,* for example, is a very specific sexual term, as in *jazz me, baby,* but white people purified it into the Jazz Age. *Sock it to me,* which means, roughly, the same thing, has been adopted by Nathaniel Hawthorne's descendants with no qualms or hesitations at all, along with *let it all hang out* and *right on! Beat to his socks,* which was once the black's most total and despairing image of poverty, was transformed into a thing called the Beat Generation, which phenomenon was, largely, composed of *uptight,* middle-class white people, imitating poverty, trying to *get down,* to get *with it,* doing their *thing,* doing their despairing best to be *funky,* which we, the blacks, never dreamed of doing—we were funky, baby, like *funk* was going out of style.

Now, no one can eat his cake, and have it, too, and it is late in the day to attempt to penalize black people for having created a language that permits the nation its only glimpse of reality, a language without which the nation would be even more *whipped* than it is.

I say that the present skirmish is rooted in American history, and it is. Black English is the creation of the black diaspora. Blacks came to the United States chained to each other, but from different tribes. Neither could speak the other's language. If two black people, at that bitter hour of the world's history, had been able to speak to each other, the institution of chattel slavery could never have lasted as long as it did. Subsequently, the slave was given, under the eye, and the gun, of his master, Congo Square, and the Bible—or, in other words, and under those conditions, the slave began the formation of the black church, and it is within this unprecedented tabernacle that black English began to be formed. This was not, merely, as in the European example, the adoption of a foreign tongue, but an alchemy that transformed ancient elements into a new language: *A language comes into existence by means of brutal necessity, and the rules of the language are dictated by what the language must convey.*

There was a moment, in time, and in this place, when my brother, or my mother, or my father, or my sister, had to convey to me, for example, the danger in which I was standing from the white man standing just behind me, and to convey this with a speed and in a language, that the white man could not possibly understand, and that, indeed, he cannot understand, until today. He cannot afford to understand it. This understanding would reveal to him too much about himself and smash that mirror before which he has been frozen for so long.

Now, if this passion, this skill, this (to quote Toni Morrison) "sheer intelligence," this incredible music, the mighty achievement of having brought a people utterly unknown to, or despised by "history"—to have brought this people to their present, troubled, troubling, and unassailable and unanswerable place—if this absolutely unprecedented journey does not indicate that black English is a language, I am curious to know what definition of languages is to be trusted.

A people at the center of the western world, and in the midst of so   10
hostile a population, has not endured and transcended by means of what is patronizingly called a "dialect." We, the blacks, are in trouble, certainly, but we are not inarticulate because we are not compelled to defend a morality that we know to be a lie.

The brutal truth is that the bulk of the white people in America never had any interest in educating black people, except as this could serve white purposes. It is not the black child's language that is despised. It is his experience. A child cannot be taught by anyone who despises him, and a child cannot afford to be fooled. A child cannot be taught by anyone whose demand, essentially, is that the child repudiate his experience, and all that gives him sustenance, and enter a limbo in which he will no longer be black, and in which he knows that he can never become white. Black people have lost too many black children that way.

And, after all, finally, in a country with standards so untrustworthy, a country that makes heroes of so many criminal mediocrities, a country unable to face why so many of the nonwhite are in prison, or on the needle, or standing, futureless, in the streets—it may very well be that both the child, and his elder, have concluded that they have nothing whatever to learn from the people of a country that has managed to learn so little.

LINES OF INQUIRY
"If Black English Isn't a Language, Then Tell Me, What Is?"

As his title indicates, Baldwin's purpose in this piece is to argue that black English is a language rather than a dialect. Given this intention, why does he devote his second, third, and fourth paragraphs to discussing languages other than black English? What, in turn, is the point of his showing in paragraph 5 that numerous American words and phrases were originated by black people? What is the point of his concluding comments on the education of black children? In other words, what is the relevance of the material he discusses to the point he is trying to make?

Having considered the relevance of his discussion, you might explore the nature of his assumptions. For example, what assumptions about the nature of language does Baldwin bring to his argument that black English is a language rather than a dialect? Why, for example, does he claim that the issue as a whole is "rooted in American history?" What does he mean by his assertion in the ninth paragraph that "if this absolutely unprecedented journey does not indicate that black English is a language, I am curious to know what definition of language is to be trusted"?

Why do you suppose that Baldwin is so angered over the question of whether black English is referred to as a language or a dialect? What grounds do you think he has for considering language in such a charged social and political context?

BRUNO BETTELHEIM

1903 — 1990

While we are scarcely able to believe any longer that life has a specific goal, but must be satisfied with striving in what seems the right direction, still we must continue to struggle to integrate our personality and master difficult experiences.

A survivor of Nazi concentration camps, an expert in the behavior of emotionally disturbed children, psychoanalyst Bruno Bettelheim was concerned from the beginning of his long career with the traumatizing effects of what he here calls, in an essay entitled "The Ultimate Limit," the "extreme situations" of modern life. Like his teacher Sigmund Freud, Bettelheim believed that our task as individuals is to "integrate" our personality and achieve "autonomy" in response to life's crucial experiences. But in his view the horrors of the twentieth century—the two world wars, the atomic bomb, and especially the near extermination of European Jews—made this task even more difficult, breaking down our defenses against the "death anxiety." Over the last forty years, in a distinguished series of books, articles, and essays, Bettelheim attempted to show that integration and mastery are still possible even in the absence of "specific goals," but only if we face our traumas rather than deny them, and only if we are willing to accept that some questions are finally not answerable.

Bettelheim was born in Vienna, where he studied under Freud, and before the war had begun working with autistic children. But in 1938, the year he received his PhD in psychology from the University of Vienna, he was arrested by the Nazis and imprisoned in concentration camps at Dachau and Buchenwald, where, along with other prisoners, he was beaten and tortured. He was released a year later, emigrated to the United States, and began in earnest his career as a child psychologist. In 1944 he became professor of psychology at the University of Chicago and director of the Orthogenic School for autistic children, positions he held until his retirement in 1973. He wrote more than a dozen books, most of them concerning the education and upbringing of children, including *Love Is Not Enough, Truants from Life, The Empty Fortress,* and *A Home for the Heart*—all based on his work with emotionally disturbed children at the Orthogenic School—*The Children of the Dream,* a study of how children are raised on kibbutzes in Israel, and *The Uses of Enchantment,* a study of the psychological value of fairy tales that won him the National Book Award.

But as Bettelheim himself acknowledged, the central preoccupation of his career, and his underlying motivation as a writer, was an effort to work out the implications of his experience in the Nazi concentration camps. His first important published article, written immediately after his escape from Germany, was "Individual and Mass Behavior in Extreme Situations," a detailed and lengthy exploration, based on personal experience, of how prisoners in the concentration camps succeeded or failed in maintaining their identity in the face of torture and deprivation, living with "an existential predicament which does not permit of any solution." Though rejected at first by a number of scholarly journals—so resistant was the American public to believing that the camps even existed—the essay was finally published and became extremely influential. "I was so full of the experience that it would not be contained," Bettelheim said. He wanted to "bear witness" to the atrocity of the camps, making it possible for others to "grasp" what happened. But he also wrote the essay for his own benefit, out of a need "to comprehend better what had happened to me while in the camps, so I could gain intellectual mastery over the experience." The rigidly objective style of the essay, he realized even then, its careful abstractions and measured sequence of observations, were part of his "intellectual defense against being overwhelmed" by the memories of "the terrible things done by average people to average persons."

In subsequent essays, the most important of which are collected in *Surviving,* in *Freud's Vienna and Other Essays,* and in a book-length study of the Holocaust, *The Informed Heart: Autonomy in a Mass Age,* Bettelheim continued to develop his argument—that to deal with the death camps and what they represent about human nature we must first admit how horrible they were, not deny their evil. Denial, he believed, is "the earliest, most primitive, most inappropriate and ineffective of all psychological defenses used by man" because "it does not permit taking appropriate actions which might safeguard against the real dangers." Only if we face the reality of extreme situations can we then begin the slow, careful, step-by-step process of "adjusting" our personality in "accordance" with our new awareness. There are no simple answers. The task never ends. Somehow, not deluding ourselves about the "death principle" inside of us, we must labor to establish the priority of the "life principle" that also exists in the psyche, saying in effect, "I am trying to make the best of my life, limited as it must be by my shortcomings." As for questions about the ultimate meaning of life, they are "unanswerable," and we must simply do the best we can without a knowable truth.

This model of trauma and reintegration, extremity and response, underlies all of Bettelheim's theories. As his research and writing developed, he began to realize that there was a "parallel" between the personality disintegration caused by the Holocaust and "psychotic collapses" caused by a variety of psychological problems. He realized, for example, that the behavior of autistic children can be seen as a struggle for integration in response to extreme situations, though those situations are more often imagined than real. The therapies and routines he developed at the Orthogenic School were designed to give disturbed children exactly the kind of freedom and dignity that prisoners had been denied in the concentration camps. Indeed, Bettelheim came to believe that technology, affluence, and the complexity of modern life are in themselves kinds of extremities that healthy personalities must somehow assimilate—that in a sense all of us are forced to integrate our personalities in response to the traumas of contemporary existence.

With this view of human development as his framework, Bettelheim wrote about a variety of topics. He argued that elementary and secondary education should teach children how to postpone pleasure for the sake of greater future gains, instilling in them a sense of "the reality principle"; that parents should give children as much freedom as is appropriate for their age level, but also establish limits and demand moral behavior; that urban planners must create environments ensuring privacy without isolating the individual; that the value of art is not its unleashing of the unconscious but the examples it gives of a "disciplined working-over of unconscious material"; that the value of fairy tales is the safe outlet they provide for the violence instinctive in children. All of his writing, Bettelheim said, deals "with what can be done in society, and in persons' life experiences, to promote the achievement of self-respect, integration, and the ability to form meaningful and lasting relations."

Integration characterizes Bettelheim's prose style as well. This passage from "The Ultimate Limit," the full context for our opening epigraph, exemplifies his effort to integrate ideas in balanced clauses and phrases, carefully assimilating a complex set of issues:

> While we are scarcely able to believe any longer that life has a specific goal, but must be satisfied with striving in what seems the right direction, still we must continue to struggle to integrate our personality and master difficult experiences. We can never hope to achieve these elusive goals once and for all. This is true in general, but it is much more pressingly so for the crucial experiences of our lives, especially an extreme experience. Even more unsolvable are extreme experiences that also pose the central problem of our times: the potentially destructive aspects of progress.

In this sequence of assertions, each statement qualified and related to the next, we glimpse something of Bettelheim's desire to "objectify" his experience through academic prose. We see here someone who, as he put it, tried to "conform in his writing to the requirements of an acceptable objectivity—the consequences of having lived his life in academe, and of having in large part embraced its values." But at the same time Bettelheim's personal engagement shows through in his deep concern for human values. "The underlying motif" of his writing is "to give words to one man's struggle against the destructive tendency in society and in individual man—which very much includes himself." So, Bettelheim's writing reflects "a very personal effort to extract meaning from life."

RETURNING TO DACHAU*

Off and on for many years, beginning long before my own experience made them a very personal and immediate issue, the problems posed by totalitarian societies have occupied my mind. A year (1938–39) of incarceration in the concentration camps at Dachau and Buchenwald made me realize what a central role the concentration camp (or prison) plays as an instrument of control under totalitarianism, and how essential it is in shaping the individual's personality into the type such a society requires. Originally, therefore, it was the psychology and the sociology of the concentration camp that interested me most.

The first article I wrote about the camps was a monograph published during World War II when information about the camps was still meager. It was met with skepticism from the American audience. In it I described the ways in which the integrity of the human being was undermined by the camp regimen and how one's personality radically changes. That was a beginning, but a more important study remained to be written, one dealing with the problem of reviving, restoring, and reintegrating the personality that had undergone the experience of the concentration camps. That problem, the rehabilitation of traumatized or "destroyed" individuals, has been my vocation for many years, and I have written a number of books on the subject.

Among the reasons I accepted an invitation to spend several months at the University of Frankfurt in 1955 was the knowledge that I would be working with a group of sociologists who might help me to understand the process of rehabilitation. Originally my plan of research was simple: I would interview Germans who had been in concentration

---

* This essay appeared in *Commentary, XXI,* 2 (February 1956). In the many years since it was written, things have changed radically in West Germany. There are no longer any displaced persons living in the barracks of the Dachau camp, nor any American soldiers in what had been the SS quarters. Most important, while at the time this essay was written most adult Germans had lived during the Hitler period, by now the vast majority of adult Germans were either born after Hitler or were small children during the Hitler years.

However, the problem of how to react to what happened in Germany under Hitler is still a real one, not just for the survivors of this period but also for many of their children. So it seemed worthwhile to reprint this article in a revised form. Although more than a generation—some fifty years—has passed since I was a prisoner at Dachau and more than thirty years have passed since I wrote this piece, and despite the several visits I have paid to West Germany in the meantime, on rereading it now I find that it accurately states my present views.

camps in order to try to fathom the ways in which they had dealt with their experiences. But a few weeks of careful observation made me realize that I had seen my problem too simplistically.

Although I myself had already said in print that no person who had passed through a Nazi concentration camp could be immune to the effect of its institutions on their personality, I had not realized the overwhelming significance the Nazi experience had for the German population. After a few weeks of talking to natives in all walks of life, and observing the present-day forms of that life—in universities, on the street, or in the workplace—the conclusion became inescapable that every German had in some way or other been an inmate of that wider concentration camp which was the Third Reich. Every German who had lived under the Nazi regime, whether he accepted it or fought it, had been through a concentration camp in a sense. Some, the actual camp inmates, had gone through it as tortured slaves; others, the majority of Germans, had gone through it as trustees, so to speak.

Basically the German citizen had only two stances available to him   5
under Hitler: to preserve his inner integrity by fighting all aspects of the Nazi state—which a small minority did—or to accept it to a large degree and shape his personality in accordance with its demands, which was what the vast majority did. This difference between minority and majority still exists in Adenauer's Germany, and in all probability in the East Zone too. There are those who still cannot extricate themselves from their struggle against the concentration-camp society, and those who still cannot extricate themselves from having assented or been resigned to it.

Psychologically speaking, one might say that both groups were severely traumatized. But since the nature of the traumas was antithetical, they have reacted differently. Those who more or less accepted the concentration-camp society deny the nature of the camps and their horrors; in their case it is obvious that defensive amnesia has set in. When broken through, such amnesia tries to reestablish itself by frantic denials, by alibis and by reaction formations (complaints about what the Americans and Russians did to Germans, what Americans still do to Negroes, and so on). Such a repertory of defensive mechanisms is set in motion when the amnesia needed by an individual in order to continue functioning is attacked from the outside.

But those who fought the Nazi regime are not better equipped to live in tranquility. They do not deny, or block out by amnesia, the fact of the concentration-camp society; on the contrary, they seem to go on reliving that trauma in an "unintegrated" way. I met a man who wanted, most devotedly, to build a better Germany; he was not an isolated individual but an active leader of German intellectual life. After a while our conversation turned to the concentration camps, whereupon he took a two-year-old newspaper clipping out of his wallet and showed it to me. It reported that a visitor to Dachau had been told by his German guide that none but criminals were confined in the camps, that torture was never practiced in them, and that what most people said about them was all lies—no decent citizen had ever been sent to a concentration camp. He was obviously so shocked that such lies found common acceptance, and were published by a respectable newspaper, that he could not discard this evidence of blatant denial of the facts. What struck me was that this man had carried the clipping in his breast pocket for two years—over his heart, as it were—which suggested that he, too, was unable to forget the concentration camps, not for a moment.

On this trip I had been told Dachau was being preserved as a kind of memorial; and I had been considering revisiting it. The newspaper clipping and the dramatic way it had been brought to my attention made me decide to do so.

I had spent the spring and summer of 1938 in Dachau, before being transferred to Buchenwald. In a way, I wanted to have the guide who would take me around deny the horror of the camp; this would confirm my conviction that today's Germans prefer to deny wholly the Nazi experience. But reality, as so often happens, turned out to be entirely different.

On my way to Dachau I stayed at one of the best hotels in Munich, registering as an American citizen and deliberately speaking nothing but English. When I asked how to make arrangements to visit the site of the concentration camp at Dachau, the desk clerk, who until then had been most polite and helpful, suddenly busied himself with another guest. Pressed, he told me that he didn't know if one could visit Dachau or how, and that there was nothing of interest left there anyway. I insisted nevertheless, and again he turned away from me, with the indication this time that I was showing very bad taste. After waiting awhile, I turned to another desk clerk with the same question, and got more or less the same response.

Finally, in the face of my persistence, they said they didn't know how the camp could be reached since it was quite far from the train station, and hiring a car and driving there from Munich would be very expensive. I answered that I would take the train and try to get a ride from the Dachau station. This, they said, might be possible, but they were not at all sure I would be able to get a taxi there. I said I was willing to risk it. Was it not a memorable, though sinister, place that might be interesting to see? Icy silence was the response. Then I asked for the train schedule, and was told that trains ran often to Dachau. When was the next one? I was shown a huge timetable giving all the trains leaving Munich in all directions. It was fastened to the desk facing the clerks, so I had to scan it upside down.

Until then I had not felt very strongly about visiting Dachau, but these hotel clerks gradually awoke a cold anger in me, first at their implicit denial of the importance of the camp, and then at the attitude of disapproval they manifested toward one who seemed interested in it. Once aboard the suburban train from Munich to Dachau, I let myself relive some of the feelings I had known while in the camp itself. I felt the stark contrast between this easy, comfortable half-hour ride and my trip of seventeen years before, with all its brutality involving the murder of good friends and the maiming of others. By the time I walked out of the sleepy Dachau station to one of the several waiting taxis, I was ready for an emotional experience.

I had planned the trip in the spirit of the newspaper clipping that had partly motivated it. I had decided to act like a skeptical Austrian. In my best Viennese dialect I asked the taxi driver how far it was to the camp, whether there was anything to see there, and how much time it would take to visit it. His friendliness and eagerness to do business with a sightseer disarmed me; he encouraged me to visit the place and offered to point out all the interesting sights, claiming to be thoroughly familiar with them.

I then mentioned casually that I had heard a lot of contradictory stories and, having some time on my hands, had felt the impulse to find out the truth about Dachau's camp. I added that people seemed to exaggerate and dramatize things—whereupon he told me it was hardly possible to exaggerate Dachau's horrors. He began to tell me about incidents some of which, curiously enough, I had witnessed myself. He spoke of the petty difficulties he had experienced with the SS men guarding the camp, and of the greater difficulties with them experienced by peasants in the neighborhood. He described to me the killing of prisoners in 1938 and 1939, and the incredibly callous attitude of the SS men involved—exactly what I myself had witnessed so many times. I was just beginning to wonder how it was that this man could accept the truth about the concentration camps with so much equanimity when he gave me the answer, or the clue to it. Suddenly he left his tale of Dachau to reminisce about his four years in a prisoner-of-war camp in Siberia; how he had lived in fear of his life between the Russian guards and the cold, dirt, and hunger. It was as if a story about one prison camp naturally led to one about another.

Here, then, was my answer. This German felt he had suffered under Hitler just as much as those in Hitler's concentration camps had. So he felt free of guilt. As a resident of the village of Dachau, he had not only known of the existence of the camp, but had feared its presence more than most other Germans. True, he had been happy about German military successes as long as they continued, and he commended the greater equality in the distribution of earthly goods (particularly food) under the Nazis as compared with the years immediately after 1945, when some had plenty while he had starved. Nonetheless, he was full of hatred for Hitler; it was, however, mainly for very personal reasons.

15

Before the war, the SS men from the Dachau camp had filled the taverns in town and monopolized the free girls. Even worse, they had interfered with one of the great pleasures of this man's youth, which was to sit in the tavern with his friends and sound off about everything that displeased him. The constant presence of the SS men had prevented them from talking freely to one another. The cab driver became even more heated when describing to me how that scoundrel Hitler, by locating the camp outside this nice hometown of his, had given it a bad name to the world. Whenever this man traveled elsewhere, he preferred not to say where he lived, since that invariably led to an unpleasant discussion.

If anything could be learned from this little incident, it was that a man like this one, who had had firsthand experience of the proximity of the Dachau concentration camp, could never be made to view it in a favorable light. Nor, unlike most other Germans today, could he put it out of his mind, living as he still did near its site. The camp could not be regarded as a unique experience, a nightmare that could be pushed out of memory; for him, it was a reality he had been forced to learn to live with over the years. Although the Dachau camp had not originally turned him against the Nazi regime, which had, he felt, done a great deal of good for people like himself, he could never accept the camp itself. At the same time, since this same regime had brought him suffering that he could liken to that of the prisoners at Dachau, he did not need to feel guilty or to deny anything. His constant contact with the fact of the camp, so that its horror had impressed itself on him slowly, not suddenly, deprived it of the nightmarish qualities of a trauma that overshadowed all of life or needed to be denied. In his own simple way, he had worked through the reality of Dachau and what it stood for, and his attitude was therefore a matter-of-fact one.

As the driver showed me around Dachau I felt quite comfortable in my role of naive visitor. He pointed out what he could, calmly, neither omitting nor hiding anything he might have been expected to know.

He told me about the tower over the camp's entrance gate. He pointed it out from a distance, regretting the fact that we could not get closer because it was, as I could see, now part of an American army installation, and in a restricted area. Had I addressed myself to the commanding officer, I could probably have obtained permission to go inside, but it seemed pointless. I was not trying to revisit specific sites or buildings; I wanted to receive impressions. And the fact that the dreadful tower was now part of an American army installation removed all its dread. What we prisoners had not dared hope for, and had hardly dared to dream—that the Stars and Stripes would fly over the tower— had become an everyday reality. This being so, what use was there in looking at a collection of stones close up?

We drove along outside the stockade, the electric fence, the watch-   20
towers, the ditch that used to be filled with water. But the logs of the
once formidable stockade were weathered, rotting, and askew; the
cruel wire was torn and dangling; the bottom of the ditch was dry, its
steep sides slowly caving in and overgrown with grass, weeds, and
wildflowers. It was the same place, and yet it was not. Only by a
deliberate act of memory could I re-create the past, which at every step
was belied by the appearance of the towers, the stockade walls, and the
grass-covered moat, all looking like ancient ruins—and, most of all, by
the presence of American soldiers and armor.

We drove through what had once been the main street of the camp,
which was lined with a double row of barracks. Slowly, we approached
the one in which I had lived. For a moment I was tempted to ask the
driver to stop and let me out, but children were playing in front of it,
and I thought better of disturbing their play and privacy for the sake of
what by now was empty curiosity.

The camp now houses refugees from the German East Zone, and
its administration has tried to improve the looks of the place. The
windows—through which rotating floodlights had glared all night
into the eyes of the prisoners, men trying to catch a moment of sleep or
rest against the next day's torture and threat of death—were now softened by curtains, by the efforts of women to make homes behind them.
It was just like any other DP camp, dreary in the main, but at least its
inmates had some hope of getting out.

This was not Dachau. It was as if the concentration camp had never
existed. It was neither a monument by which to remember a terrible
past, nor one that could promise a better future. It simply represented
the practical utilization of available facilities, just as the American
troops, for utilitarian reasons, are now making use of the excellent facilities the prisoners once built under the whip for the use of SS troops.

I do not believe this erasing of the past was deliberate. The military
occupation, and indeed the whole postwar history of Germany, have
lent themselves exceedingly well to the obliteration of the Nazi past—
or rather, the deepest wishes of the Germans themselves combine with
history to do just that. In those surroundings and at that moment, it
seemed as if only the cab driver and I remembered Dachau's past, if for
very different reasons and perhaps with different feelings.

What about the memorial? We drove into a conspicuously marked-   25
off enclosure, where two American soldiers on guard waved us on in
friendly fashion. There was a small space in which three cars were
parked, clearly marked by their license plates as belonging to the American occupation forces. The omnipresence of U.S. Army symbols, while
most reassuring, in a way took the edge off one's experience of the spirit
of the place. The reaction of the clerks at the hotel in Munich to my

inquiries had reawakened my old anger; the displaced persons living in the camp and the presence of the American military had once again subdued it. It was no use beating a dead dog, even though when alive it had mauled, maimed, and killed.

The memorial covered only a small area, and included the old place of execution, the gallows, the gas chamber, the crematorium, and two or three (my cab driver was not quite sure) places of mass burial. In the center of all this stood the statue of a concentration-camp prisoner in typical uniform, his face and figure showing the ravages of physical and mental suffering. It was true to life, yet at the same time idealized. Not a great piece of art, but decent and well meant. Perhaps we are still too close to what happened in the camps to express it more symbolically, and hence in a way that would be more aesthetically valid.

In this pleasant grove, interspersed with well-kept flower beds, only the statue of the prisoner and my own conscious effort brought to mind what the memorial was there to commemorate. Of course, I saw signs explaining what each place of horror had been used for. It was hard to imagine, looking at the neatness of everything, that tens of thousands of people had over many years suffered incredible degradation and pain here, had been viciously murdered. True, in a way the orderliness and dispatch with which bureaucratic transactions in human lives were once effected here had been one of the supreme horrors of the place. But this, too, no longer came through from the present neatness and orderliness.

Maybe what oppressed me was the smallness of it all. The little box that had been the death chamber could not have held very many prisoners at once. There were only two openings, each admitting but a single corpse at a time, to the oven of the crematorium. The two burial places, one marked with a wooden cross, the other with a Jewish star—pits into which the ashes of thousands of human beings had been dumped—were each not much larger than an individual grave.

The wilted wreaths, with their faded inscriptions, added to the illusion that everything belonged to a remote past. The walls of the death chamber and the crematorium were covered with graffiti, the names and remarks of visitors—all so typical of the historical monument—but not even these emblems of the tourist aroused more than a mild disgust in me. After all, most of the visitors had been Jewish and American. Why be angry at those who had defaced the walls of the memorial if they were in deep sympathy with those who had suffered here? That they inscribed their names and the dates of their visits meant only that they, too, felt they had been in a historical place, and one with so little connection to their immediate lives that, far from being overawed by the spirit of it, they had tried to establish a connection with it by leaving signs of their presence on its walls. Some inscriptions included angry remarks, but they too seemed out of place if not childish, because of the abyss between what they were meant to express and what they actually said.

If my experience in the camp had been a single event, I could per-   30
haps have recaptured the old feeling of the place. But what made Dachau
memorable to me was innumerable experiences: the day I and hundreds
of my comrades suddenly went blind, caused by a temporary edema of
the eyelids; the shooting of a friend; the suicide of another, who deliberately ran into charged wire; and, most of all, the constant, continuous
petty suffering and degradation, and the frantic and desperate way one
tried to maintain oneself in the face of all this.

A small group was going around at the same time as we: an American major, a captain, and two or three ladies with them; probably they
had come in the cars I saw in the parking lot. The major looked grim
and angry as he inspected the gas chamber and the crematorium, but
the others seemed indifferent, even slightly bored, if I read their faces
right. Also, a teacher was leading a group of German schoolchildren
through the place, boys and girls of about ten or eleven, some twenty-
five in all. They seemed neither interested nor impressed. The teacher
told them something about the number of those who had died here.
The children joked, hardly glancing at the small building or the inscriptions. My impression was that they were enjoying their escape
from the classroom, but that the place itself meant nothing to them,
despite the teacher's objective explanations, which amounted to no
more than a flat recital of facts. He, too, seemed uninterested, and after
a quick tour left with his charges.

I do not know how others feel when something once a terrible part
of their lives becomes a monument to be visited by sightseers. For
myself, it was not the right way to reexperience the past. My reaction
was similar to the schoolchildren's. I have avoided mass graves all my
life because they call up no meaning for me. The tomb of the Unknown
Soldier affects me; the mass tomb at Verdun does not. As I stood there
in Dachau, the concentration camp was more over and done with for
me than when I had thought of it in faraway Chicago. The mass com-
memoration of the tens of thousands of Dachau's victims gave the
remoteness of chronicle to their deaths, as to their lives. I felt stronger
emotion when, a few days later, relatives in Vienna pointed out where,
to escape the Gestapo, one person had jumped from a window and
another had hanged himself. These were single human fates, and there
was a great sense of immediacy in their loss.

Driving back to the station, the driver unburdened his heart, and
thereby reduced Dachau once more to the human experience it was for
him. Why had the camp been located at Dachau, his hometown, not
somewhere else? It was all because of an old farmer and his good-
for-nothing sons, who did not know how to till the soil. The site of
the camp had once been a large farm; then it had been sold to the
government, which before the First World War had built a munitions
or arms factory on it. When the Nazis came to power, they used it for a

concentration camp because it already had barracks on it, and a stockade and barbedwire fence. It had just been a matter of utilitarian convenience, as it now was for the American authorities to use part of the camp, and for the Bonn government to use the remainder to quarter DPs.

Leaving Dachau, we again passed the barracks, and then came my last view of the camp and of its awful gate, through which some jeeps were now rolling. A large U.S. Army installation, a large DP camp, and a few small buildings as a memorial to the past—I could not quite accept it. For my own reasons, I wished they had preserved the camp just as it had been when it was liberated. Then I probably would have been able to recapture my memories better; then Dachau might have come to life on the tide of old feelings of anger, degradation, and despair. But history (and the crematorium) had been relegated to a small area located, as if symbolically, at the farthest corner of the camp, away from the business of the present.

Waiting at the train station, I listened to German DPs who   35
sipped beer and talked of how they had lost everything. On the ride back to Munich I looked out of the train window over bombed-out areas. I realized, when I left the station at Munich and saw the utter destruction still around me, that unconsciously I had wanted the Germans to dedicate the old Dachau for all time as a monument to my sufferings and those of my fellow Jews and antifascists, but had not wanted them to dedicate any monuments to their own suffering, which were almost equally a result of Nazism.

Of course, the inmates of Dachau had been helpless victims of the Hitler regime, whereas the Germans, or nearly half of them, had embraced it of their own free will. Might it not be, then, that I had hoped unconsciously for the dedication of an unchanged Dachau more as a monument to the vileness of the torturers who established and ran it than as a memorial to its victims?

So this was one lesson I learned: that one cannot dedicate monuments to the depravity of a system by tending carefully the graves of its victims. After all, it is the Christian martyrs themselves who symbolized their faith and religious creed; it was not the cruelty of their torturers, which was only incidental, or seems so to us now, that really counted. I realized that I had gone to Dachau in the wrong spirit. Dachau, to me, was now a symbol more of the cruelty that took human beings and converted them into ciphers to be processed in a gas chamber than of suffering mankind. One simply cannot look at the statue of a concentration-camp prisoner in stone or bronze when one has been a prisoner oneself; the survivor cannot look at the graves of his fellows in suffering and say: Behold the greatness of my suffering, and admire it! One can do something about one's own suffering, and that of others, only by living and acting.

And then I realized that the present state of Dachau was more in keeping with reality, present-day reality, than it would be if it had been preserved as it was at its liberation—as, I am told, Buchenwald is. Preserving a site intact removes it from the stream of history, makes it a monument that is no longer of this time and this place.

Actually, the presence of these refugees commemorates, far better than does the monument, the sufferings of human beings at the hands of their fellows. The extreme misery of Dachau belongs to the past, but misery in general survives; people are still being driven from their homes by fear and terror. The victims of the moment were German, but I did not find any historical justice in that fact. If one believes, as I do, that our first concern must be for the living, it becomes understandable that for the Germans, too, the horrors of the concentration-camp regime fade before the misery of the DPs who have taken it over.

This, then, was what I learned from revisiting Dachau: that I   40
could best preserve it in my mind. Other camp survivors who, like myself, had left Germany could do the same, because our lives did not need to continue in and around Dachau. We had radically separated ourselves from the country of which it had once been a central institution. I could keep the old Dachau intact as an emotional experience. I could digest its impact by working it out emotionally and psychologically, and it would remain the impact of a Dachau that preserved its old physical reality unchanged because I was no longer attached to the physical reality of Germany itself. For me, Dachau had become a problem of human nature and a personal experience, but it was not a particular place in the country that was my home.

The Germans, however, have had to live more closely than I with the memory of their concentration camps. During the war and most of the time since then, they have lived with it every day. They could not detach themselves from the suffering brought about by Nazism by crossing an ocean and entering upon a new way of life. If they wanted to go on living as more than mere survivors of Nazism and defeat, the Germans had to deal with the place Dachau, as well as with Dachau the crime. If they had preserved Dachau in its entirety as a monument to the shame of Nazism, and to the immense suffering it inflicted, it would follow that they should have preserved their ruined cities as a monument to the suffering they themselves had experienced.

So probably the Germans did the right thing when they set aside only a small enclosure at Dachau to the memory of the victims, while using the largest part of the place for DPs, and letting the Americans use the rest of it for an army installation. "Letting," I write, as though it were all their choice. Then I remember seeing vehicles roll by with license plates marked "U.S. Forces in Germany." One sees these license plates everywhere in West Germany, and so I asked myself: Suppose the unthinkable had happened, and the Japanese had overrun the

United States? How would Americans have met, dealt with, and worked through ten years of life with the symbols all around them of utter defeat, and with the victors everywhere on their streets? Would they have made a memorial of anything that reminded them of their defeat? I do not know. But I do know that the only way to live with such a past is not to keep it alive unchanged, encapsulated—but to confine it to an ever smaller place, as had been done with the memorial at Dachau.

Sad as this is in view of my own experience and those of the friends and relatives of the millions murdered by the Nazis, we cannot expect present-day Germans to have a much different attitude toward their victims than they have toward their own devastated cities. Since they are much more matter-of-fact about the ruins of their own homes than I am, I must accept their being more matter-of-fact about Dachau. As if with a vengeance, present-day Germany is turning away from the destruction of the past toward the building of the present and the future. Yes, they do it all with a will and a vengeance, as if they had a need to cover up, forget, and undo the past, including Dachau. So far only the frantic activity is obvious. Will it lead to a better future? This as yet is hard to say, but much will depend on their and our attitudes toward their past.

LINES OF INQUIRY
"Returning to Dachau"

Although Bettelheim is nominally concerned in this essay with his return to Dachau, he seems to devote as much attention to the hotel clerks, the taxi driver, the American soldiers, the East German refugees, and the various tourists he met on his trip back as he does to the concentration camp and its remains. How does Bettelheim organize the story of his return so as strike a balance between telling about the people and telling about the camp? How does each of the people affect his perceptions of Dachau, his feelings about Dachau, his reactions to Dachau? How, by comparison, does the state of the concentration camp, together with his memories of it, affect his reactions to the place?

When he is not focusing on the camp or the people he met along the way, Bettelheim tells about the insights he gained and the lessons he learned as a result of his return to Dachau. Make a list of all his realizations. Given these realizations, what aspects or implications of Dachau seem uppermost in his mind? In what respects do Bettelheim's lessons seem applicable only to the specific historical situation of the Nazi concentration camps? In what respects do they seem to be more broadly applicable to other historical situations?

Bettelheim is not the only essayist in this collection to write about the Holocaust, as you can see by looking at the opening and closing segments in Woody Allen's "Random Reflections of a Second-Rate Mind." In what respect(s) are Bettelheim and Allen concerned with similar aspects of the Holocaust? In what respect(s) are they concerned with different aspects of it? What aspects of it do you consider to be of utmost concern?

JOEY: A "MECHANICAL BOY"

Joey, when we began to work with him, was a mechanical boy. He functioned as if by remote control, run by machines of his own powerfully creative fantasy. Not only did he himself believe that he was a machine but, more remarkably, he created this impression in others. Even while he performed actions that are intrinsically human, they never appeared to be other than machine-started and executed. On the other hand, when the machine was not working we had to concentrate on recollecting his presence, for he seemed not to exist. A human body that functions as if it were a machine and a machine that duplicates human functions are equally fascinating and frightening. Perhaps they are so uncanny because they remind us that the human body can operate without a human spirit, that body can exist without soul. And Joey was a child who had been robbed of his humanity.

Not every child who possesses a fantasy world is possessed by it. Normal children may retreat into realms of imaginary glory or magic powers, but they are easily recalled from these excursions. Disturbed children are not always able to make the return trip; they remain withdrawn, prisoners of the inner world of delusion and fantasy. In many ways Joey presented a classic example of this state of infantile autism.

At the Sonia Shankman Orthogenic School of the University of Chicago it is our function to provide a therapeutic environment in which such children may start life over again. I have previously described in this magazine the rehabilitation of another of our patients ["Schizophrenic Art: A Case Study"; SCIENTIFIC AMERICAN, April, 1952]. This time I shall concentrate upon the illness, rather than the treatment. In any age, when the individual has escaped into a delusional world, he has usually fashioned it from bits and pieces of the world at hand. Joey, in his time and world, chose the machine and froze himself in its image. His story has a general relevance to the understanding of emotional development in a machine age.

Joey's delusion is not uncommon among schizophrenic children today. He wanted to be rid of his unbearable humanity, to become completely automatic. He so nearly succeeded in attaining this goal that he could almost convince others, as well as himself, of his mechanical character. The descriptions of autistic children in the literature take for their point of departure and comparison the normal or abnormal human being. To do justice to Joey I would have to compare him simultaneously to a most inept infant and a highly complex piece of machinery. Often we had to force ourselves by a conscious act of will to realize that Joey was a child. Again and again his acting-out of his delusions froze our own ability to respond as human beings.

During Joey's first weeks with us we would watch absorbedly as   5
this at once fragile-looking and imperious nine-year-old went about his mechanical existence. Entering the dining room, for example, he would string an imaginary wire from his "energy source"—an imaginary electric outlet—to the table. There he "insulated" himself with paper napkins and finally plugged himself in. Only then could Joey eat, for he firmly believed that the "current" ran his ingestive apparatus. So skillful was the pantomime that one had to look twice to be sure there was neither wire nor outlet nor plug. Children and members of our staff spontaneously avoided stepping on the "wires" for fear of interrupting what seemed the source of his very life.

For long periods of time, when his "machinery" was idle, he would sit so quietly that he would disappear from the focus of most conscientious observation. Yet in the next moment he might be "working" and the center of our captivated attention. Many times a day he would turn himself on and shift noisily through a sequence of higher and higher gears until he "exploded," screaming "Crash, crash!" and hurling items from his ever present apparatus—radio tubes, light bulbs, even motors or, lacking these, any handy breakable object. (Joey had an astonishing knack for snatching bulbs and tubes unobserved.) As soon as the object thrown had shattered, he would cease his screaming and wild jumping and retire to mute, motionless nonexistence.

Our maids, inured to difficult children, were exceptionally attentive to Joey; they were apparently moved by his extreme infantile fragility, so strangely coupled with megalomaniacal superiority. Occasionally some of the apparatus he fixed to his bed to "live him" during his sleep would fall down in disarray. This machinery he contrived from masking tape, cardboard, wire and other paraphernalia. Usually the maids would pick up such things and leave them on a table for the children to find, or disregard them entirely. But Joey's machine they carefully restored: "Joey must have the carburetor so he can breathe." Similarly they were on the alert to pick up and preserve the motors that ran him during the day and the exhaust pipes through which he exhaled.

How had Joey become a human machine? From intensive interviews with his parents we learned that the process had begun even before birth. Schizophrenia often results from parental rejection, sometimes combined ambivalently with love. Joey, on the other hand, had been completely ignored.

"I never knew I was pregnant," his mother said, meaning that she had already excluded Joey from her consciousness. His birth, she said, "did not make any difference." Joey's father, a rootless draftee in the wartime civilian army, was equally unready for parenthood. So, of course, are many young couples. Fortunately most such parents lose their indifference upon the baby's birth. But not Joey's parents. "I did not want to see or nurse him," his mother declared. "I had no feeling of actual dislike—I simply didn't want to take care of him." For the first three months of his life Joey "cried most of the time." A colicky baby, he was kept on a rigid four-hour feeding schedule, was not touched unless necessary and was never cuddled or played with. The mother, preoccupied with herself, usually left Joey alone in the crib or playpen during the day. The father discharged his frustration by punishing Joey when the child cried at night.

Soon the father left for overseas duty, and the mother took Joey, now a year and a half old, to live with her at her parents' home. On his arrival the grandparents noticed that ominous changes had occurred in the child. Strong and healthy at birth, he had become frail and irritable; a responsive baby, he had become remote and inaccessible. When he began to master speech, he talked only to himself. At an early date he became preoccupied with machinery, including an old electric fan which he could take apart and put together again with surprising deftness.

Joey's mother impressed us with a fey quality that expressed her insecurity, her detachment from the world and her low physical vitality. We were struck especially by her total indifference as she talked about Joey. This seemed much more remarkable than the actual mistakes she made in handling him. Certainly he was left to cry for hours when hungry, because she fed him on a rigid schedule; he was toilet-trained with great rigidity so that he would give no trouble. These things happen to many children. But Joey's existence never registered with his mother. In her recollections he was fused at one moment with one event or person; at another, with something or somebody else. When she told us about his birth and infancy, it was as if she were talking about some vague acquaintance, and soon her thoughts would wander off to another person or to herself.

When Joey was not yet four, his nursery school suggested that he enter a special school for disturbed children. At the new school his autism was immediately recognized. During his three years there he experienced a slow improvement. Unfortunately a subsequent two years in a parochial school destroyed this progress. He began to develop compulsive defenses, which he called his "preventions." He could not drink, for example, except through elaborate piping systems built of straws. Liquids had to be "pumped" into him, in his fantasy, or he could not suck. Eventually his behavior became so upsetting that he could not be kept in the parochial school. At home things did not improve. Three months before entering the Orthogenic School he made a serious attempt at suicide.

To us Joey's pathological behavior seemed the external expression of an overwhelming effort to remain almost nonexistent as a person.

For weeks Joey's only reply when addressed was "Bam." Unless he thus neutralized whatever we said, there would be an explosion, for Joey plainly wished to close off every form of contact not mediated by machinery. Even when he was bathed he rocked back and forth with mute, engine-like regularity, flooding the bathroom. If he stopped rocking, he did this like a machine too; suddenly he went completely rigid. Only once, after months of being lifted from his bath and carried to bed, did a small expression of puzzled pleasure appear on his face as he said very softly: "They even carry you to your bed here."

For a long time after he began to talk he would never refer to anyone by name, but only as "that person" or "the little person" or "the big person." He was unable to designate by its true name anything to which he attached feelings. Nor could he name his anxieties except through neologisms or word contaminations. For a long time he spoke about "master paintings" and "a master painting room" (i.e., masturbating and masturbating room). One of his machines, the "criticizer," prevented him from "saying words which have unpleasant feelings." Yet he gave personal names to the tubes and motors in his collection of machinery. Moreover, these dead things had feelings; the tubes bled when hurt and sometimes got sick. He consistently maintained this reversal between animate and inanimate objects.

In Joey's machine world everything, on pain of instant destruction, obeyed inhibitory laws much more stringent than those of physics. When we came to know him better, it was plain that in his moments of silent withdrawal, with his machine switched off, Joey was absorbed in pondering the compulsive laws of his private universe. His preoccupation with machinery made it difficult to establish even practical contacts with him. If he wanted to do something with a counselor, such as play with a toy that had caught his vague attention, he could not do so: "I'd like this very much, but first I have to turn off the machine." But by the time he had fulfilled all the requirements of his preventions, he had lost interest. When a toy was offered to him, he could not touch it because his motors and his tubes did not leave him a hand free. Even certain colors were dangerous and had to be strictly avoided in toys and clothing, because "some colors turn off the current, and I can't touch them because I can't live without the current."

Joey was convinced that machines were better than people. Once when he bumped into one of the pipes on our jungle gym he kicked it so violently that his teacher had to restrain him to keep him from injuring himself. When she explained that the pipe was much harder than his foot, Joey replied: "That proves it. Machines are better than the body. They don't break; they're much harder and stronger." If he lost or forgot something, it merely proved that his brain ought to be thrown away and replaced by machinery. If he spilled something, his arm should be broken and twisted off because it did not work properly. When his head or arm failed to work as it should, he tried to punish it by hitting it. Even Joey's feelings were mechanical. Much later in his therapy, when he had formed a timid attachment to another child and had been rebuffed, Joey cried: "He broke my feelings."

Gradually, we began to understand what had seemed to be contradictory in Joey's behavior—why he held on to the motors and tubes, then suddenly destroyed them in a fury, then set out immediately and urgently to equip himself with new and larger tubes. Joey had created these machines to run his body and mind because it was too painful to be human. But again and again he became dissatisfied with their failure to meet his need and rebellious at the way they frustrated his will. In a recurrent frenzy he "exploded" his light bulbs and tubes, and for a moment became a human being—for one crowning instant he came alive. But as soon as he had asserted his dominance through the self-created explosion, he felt his life ebbing away. To keep on existing he had immediately to restore his machines and replenish the electricity that supplied his life energy.

What deep-seated fears and needs underlay Joey's delusional system? We were long in finding out, for Joey's preventions effectively concealed the secret of his autistic behavior. In the meantime we dealt with his peripheral problems one by one.

During his first year with us Joey's most trying problem was toilet behavior. This surprised us, for Joey's personality was not "anal" in the Freudian sense; his original personality damage had antedated the period of his toilet-training. Rigid and early toilet-training, however, had certainly contributed to his anxieties. It was our effort to help Joey with this problem that led to his first recognition of us as human beings.

Going to the toilet, like everything else in Joey's life, was sur-   20
rounded by elaborate preventions. We had to accompany him; he had to take off all his clothes; he could only squat, not sit, on the toilet seat; he had to touch the wall with one hand, in which he also clutched frantically the vacuum tubes that powered his elimination. He was terrified lest his whole body be sucked down.

To counteract this fear we gave him a metal wastebasket in lieu of a toilet. Eventually, when eliminating into the wastebasket, he no longer needed to take off all his clothes, nor to hold on to the wall. He still needed the tubes and motors which, he believed, moved his bowels for him. But here again the all-important machinery was itself a source of new terrors. In Joey's world the gadgets had to move their bowels, too. He was terribly concerned that they should, but since they were so much more powerful than men, he was also terrified that if his tubes moved their bowels, their feces would fill all of space and leave him no room to live. He was thus always caught in some fearful contradiction.

Our readiness to accept his toilet habits, which obviously entailed some hardship for his counselors, gave Joey the confidence to express

Elaborate sewage system in Joey's drawing of a house reflects his long preoccupation with excretion. His obsession with sewage reflected intense anxieties produced by his early toilet-training, which was not only rigid but also completely impersonal.

his obsessions in drawings. Drawing these fantasies was a first step toward letting us in, however distantly, to what concerned him most deeply. It was the first step in a yearlong process of externalizing his anal preoccupations. As a result he began seeing feces everywhere; the whole world became to him a mire of excrement. At the same time he began to eliminate wherever he happened to be. But with this release from his infantile imprisonment in compulsive rules, the toilet and the whole process of elimination became less dangerous. Thus far it had been beyond Joey's comprehension that anybody could possibly move his bowels without mechanical aid. Now Joey took a further step forward; defecation became the first physiological process he could perform without the help of vacuum tubes. It must not be thought that he was proud of this ability. Taking pride in an achievement presupposes that one accomplishes it of one's own free will. He still did not feel himself an autonomous person who could do things on his own. To Joey defecation still seemed enslaved to some incomprehensible but utterly binding cosmic law, perhaps the law his parents had imposed on him when he was being toilet-trained.

It was not simply that his parents had subjected him to rigid, early training. Many children are so trained. But in most cases the parents have a deep emotional investment in the child's performance. The child's response in turn makes training an occasion for interaction between them and for the building of genuine relationships. Joey's parents had no emotional investment in him. His obedience gave them no satisfaction and won him no affection or approval. As a toilet-trained child he saved his mother labor, just as household machines saved her labor. As a machine he was not loved for his performance, nor could he love himself.

So it had been with all other aspects of Joey's existence with his parents. Their reactions to his eating or noneating, sleeping or wakening, urinating or defecating, being dressed or undressed, washed or bathed did not flow from any unitary interest in him, deeply embedded in their personalities. By treating him mechanically his parents made him a machine. The various functions of life—even the parts of his body—bore no integrating relationship to one another or to any sense of self that was acknowledged and confirmed by others. Though he had acquired mastery over some functions, such as toilet-training and speech, he had acquired them separately and kept them isolated from each other. Toilet-training had thus not gained him a pleasant feeling of body mastery; speech had not led to communication of thought or feeling. On the contrary, each achievement only steered him away from self-mastery and integration. Toilet-training had enslaved him. Speech left him talking in neologisms that obstructed his and our ability to relate to each other. In Joey's development the normal process of growth had been made to run backward. Whatever he had learned put him not at the end of his infantile development toward integration but, on the contrary, farther behind than he was at its very beginning. Had we understood this sooner, his first years with us would have been less baffling.

It is unlikely that Joey's calamity could befall a child in any time and culture but our own. He suffered no physical deprivation; he starved for human contact. Just to be taken care of is not enough for relating. It is a necessary but not a sufficient condition. At the extreme where utter scarcity reigns, the forming of relationships is certainly hampered. But our society of mechanized plenty often makes for equal difficulties in a child's learning to relate. Where parents can provide the simple creature-comforts for their children only at the cost of significant effort, it is likely that they will feel pleasure in being able to provide for them; it is this, the parents' pleasure, that gives children a sense of personal worth and sets the process of relating in motion. But if comfort is so readily available that the parents feel no particular pleasure in winning it for their children, then the children cannot develop the feeling of being worthwhile around the satisfaction of their basic needs. Of course parents and children can and do develop relationships around other situations. But matters are then no longer so simple and direct. The child must be on the receiving end of care and concern given with pleasure

25

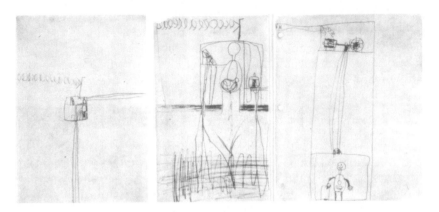

Growing self-esteem is shown in this sequence of drawings. At left Joey portrays himself as an electrical "papoose," completely enclosed, suspended in empty space and operated by wireless signals. In center drawing his figure is much larger, though still under wireless control. At right he is able to picture the machine which controls him, and he has acquired hands with which he can manipulate his immediate environment.

and without the exaction of return if he is to feel loved and worthy of respect and consideration. This feeling gives him the ability to trust; he can entrust his well-being to persons to whom he is so important. Out of such trust the child learns to form close and stable relationships.

For Joey, a relationship with his parents was empty of pleasure in comfort giving as in all other situations. His was an extreme instance of a plight that sends many schizophrenic children to our clinics and hospitals. Many months passed before he could relate to us; his despair that anybody could like him made contact impossible.

When Joey could finally trust us enough to let himself become more infantile, he began to play at being a papoose. There was a corresponding change in his fantasies. He drew endless pictures of himself as an electrical papoose. Totally enclosed, suspended in empty space, he is run by unknown, unseen powers through wireless electricity.

As we eventually came to understand, the heart of Joey's delusional system was the artificial, mechanical womb he had created and into which he had locked himself. In his papoose fantasies lay the wish to be entirely reborn in a womb. His new experiences in the school suggested that life, after all, might be worth living. Now he was searching for a way to be reborn in a better way. Since machines were better than men, what was more natural than to try rebirth through them? This was the deeper meaning of his electrical papoose.

As Joey made progress, his pictures of himself became more dominant in his drawings. Though still machine-operated, he has grown in self-importance. *(See illustration above.)* Another great step forward is represented in the picture above. Now he has acquired hands that do

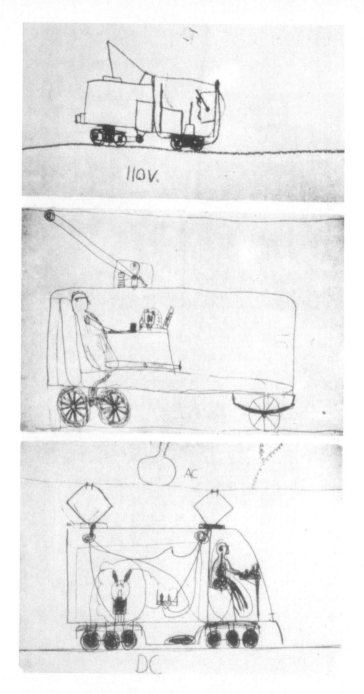

Growing autonomy is shown in Joey's drawings of the imaginary "Carr" (car) family. Top drawing shows a machine which can move but is unoccupied. Machine in center is occupied, but by a passive figure. In bottom drawing figure has gained control of machine.

Gentle landscape painted by Joey after his recovery symbolizes the human emotions he had regained. At 12, having learned to express his feelings, he was no longer a machine.

something, and he has had the courage to make a picture of the machine that runs him. Later still the papoose became a person, rather than a robot encased in glass.

Eventually Joey began to create an imaginary family at the school: 30 the "Carr" family. Why the Carr family? In the car he was enclosed as he had been in his papoose, but at least the car was not stationary; it could move. More important, in a car one was not only driven but also could drive. The Carr family was Joey's way of exploring the possibility of leaving the school, of living with a good family in a safe, protecting car. (*See illustration on page 115.*)

Joey at last broke through his prison. In this brief account it has not been possible to trace the painfully slow process of his first true relations with other human beings. Suffice it to say that he ceased to be a mechanical boy and became a human child. This newborn child was, however, nearly 12 years old. To recover the lost time is a tremendous task. That work has occupied Joey and us ever since. Sometimes he sets to it with a will; at other times the difficulty of real life makes him regret that he ever came out of his shell. But he has never wanted to return to his mechanical life.

One last detail and this fragment of Joey's story has been told. When Joey was 12, he made a float for our Memorial Day parade. It carried the slogan: "Feelings are more important than anything under the sun." Feelings, Joey had learned, are what make for humanity; their absence, for a mechanical existence. With this knowledge Joey entered the human condition.

LINES OF INQUIRY
"Joey: A 'Mechanical Boy'"

Bettelheim tells several stories during the course of his essay: he tells how Joey came to be a "mechanical boy"; how Joey's problems were diagnosed and treated at the Orthogenic School; how Joey's behavior gradually changed from being mechanical to being human. How does Bettelheim organize his material to develop each story clearly? How does Bettelheim organize his material to show the significant relationships among these stories? How do Joey's drawings contribute to Bettelheim's storytelling?

From the beginning to the end of this essay, Bettelheim discusses Joey in terms of his being a mechanical boy. In what senses does this term serve to describe Joey's behavior, to explain the origin of his condition, and to imply an appropriate mode of helping him to deal with his problems? Why is Bettelheim especially interested in telling us about Joey and his mechanical existence? What aspect of Joey's mechanical condition do you find most fascinating? Most disturbing? Most puzzling? Most illuminating?

Though you may not have known anyone so disturbed as Joey, you probably have known someone—a friend or relative—who has gone through a very troubled and difficult period. What do you suppose to have been the nature of this person's problems? What conditions do you think led to the problems? Do you perceive this person to be a unique psychological case? Or do you perceive this person's situation to be in some sense typical of significant problems in his or her culture, much as Bettelheim regards Joey's story as being relevant "to the understanding of emotional development in a machine age"? Can you think of a single adjective, such as mechanical, that would accurately and evocatively explain the condition of this person?

THE IGNORED LESSON
OF ANNE FRANK

When the world first learned about the Nazi concentration and death camps, most civilized people felt the horrors committed in them to be so uncanny as to be unbelievable. It came as a severe shock that supposedly civilized nations could stoop to such inhuman acts. The implication that modern man has such inadequate control over his cruel and destructive proclivities was felt as a threat to our views of ourselves and our humanity. Three different psychological mechanisms were most frequently used for dealing with the appalling revelation of what had gone on in the camps:

(1) its applicability to man in general was denied by asserting—contrary to evidence—that the acts of torture and mass murder were committed by a small group of insane or perverted persons;

(2) the truth of the reports was denied by declaring them vastly exaggerated and ascribing them to propaganda (this originated with the German government, which called all reports on terror in the camps "horror propaganda"—*Greuelpropaganda*);

(3) the reports were believed, but the knowledge of the horror repressed as soon as possible.

All three mechanisms could be seen at work after liberation of those prisoners remaining. At first, after the discovery of the camps and their death-dealing, a wave of extreme outrage swept the Allied nations. It was soon followed by a general repression of the discovery in people's minds. Possibly this reaction was due to something more than the blow dealt to modern man's narcissism by the realization that cruelty is still rampant among men. Also present may have been the dim but extremely threatening realization that the modern state now has available the means for changing personality, and for destroying millions it deems undesirable. The ideas that in our day a people's personalities might be changed against their will by the state, and that other populations might be wholly or partially exterminated, are so fearful that one tries to free oneself of them and their impact by defensive denial, or by repression.

The extraordinary world-wide success of the book, play, and movie *The Diary of Anne Frank* suggests the power of the desire to counteract the realization of the personality-destroying and murderous nature of the camps by concentrating all attention on what is experienced as a demonstration that private and intimate life can continue to flourish even under the direct persecution by the most ruthless totalitarian system. And this although Anne Frank's fate demonstrates how efforts at disregarding in private life what goes on around one in society can hasten one's own destruction.

What concerns me here is not what actually happened to the Frank family, how they tried—and failed—to survive their terrible ordeal. It would be very wrong to take apart so humane and moving a story, which aroused so much well-merited compassion for gentle Anne Frank and her tragic fate. What is at issue is the universal and uncritical response to her diary and to the play and movie based on it, and what this reaction tells about our attempts to cope with the feelings her fate—used by us to serve as a symbol of a most human reaction to Nazi terror—arouses in us. I believe that the world-wide acclaim given her story cannot be explained unless we recognize in it our wish to forget the gas chambers, and our effort to do so by glorifying the ability to retreat into an extremely private, gentle, sensitive world, and there to cling as much as possible to what have been one's usual daily attitudes and activities, although surrounded by a maelstrom apt to engulf one at any moment.

The Frank family's attitude that life could be carried on as before may well have been what led to their destruction. By eulogizing how they lived in their hiding place while neglecting to examine first whether it was a reasonable or an effective choice, we are able to ignore the crucial lesson of their story—that such an attitude can be fatal in extreme circumstances.

While the Franks were making their preparations for going passively into hiding, thousands of other Jews in Holland (as elsewhere in Europe) were trying to escape to the free world, in order to survive and/or fight. Others who could not escape went underground—into hiding—each family member with, for example, a different gentile family. We gather from the diary, however, that the chief desire of the Frank family was to continue living as nearly as possible in the same fashion to which they had been accustomed in happier times.

Little Anne, too, wanted only to go on with life as usual, and what 10
else could she have done but fall in with the pattern her parents created for her existence? But hers was not a necessary fate, much less a heroic one; it was a terrible but also a senseless fate. Anne had a good chance to survive, as did many Jewish children in Holland. But she would have had to leave her parents and go to live with a gentile Dutch family, posing as their own child, something her parents would have had to arrange for her.

Everyone who recognized the obvious knew that the hardest way to go underground was to do it as a family; to hide out together made detection by the SS most likely; and when detected, everybody was doomed. By hiding singly, even when one got caught, the others had a chance to survive. The Franks, with their excellent connections among gentile Dutch families, might well have been able to hide out singly, each with a different family. But instead, the main principle of their planning was continuing their beloved family life—an understandable desire, but highly unrealistic in those times. Choosing any other course would have meant not merely giving up living together, but also realizing the full measure of the danger to their lives.

The Franks were unable to accept that going on living as a family as they had done before the Nazi invasion of Holland was no longer a desirable way of life, much as they loved each other; in fact, for them and others like them, it was most dangerous behavior. But even given their wish not to separate, they failed to make appropriate preparations for what was likely to happen.

There is little doubt that the Franks, who were able to provide themselves with so much while arranging for going into hiding, and even while hiding, could have provided themselves with some weapons had they wished. Had they had a gun, Mr. Frank could have shot down at least one or two of the "green police" who came for them. There was no surplus of such police, and the loss of an SS with every Jew arrested would have noticeably hindered the functioning of the police state. Even a butcher knife, which they certainly could have taken with them into hiding, could have been used by them in self-defense. The fate of the Franks wouldn't have been very different, because they all died anyway except for Anne's father. But they could have sold their lives for a high price, instead of walking to their death. Still, although one must assume that Mr. Frank would have fought courageously, as we know he did when a soldier in the first World War, it is not everybody who can plan to kill those who are bent on killing him, although many who would not be ready to contemplate doing so would be willing to kill those who are bent on murdering not only them but also their wives and little daughters.

An entirely different matter would have been planning for escape in case of discovery. The Franks' hiding place had only one entrance; it did not have any other exit. Despite this fact, during their many months of hiding, they did not try to devise one. Nor did they make other plans for escape, such as that one of the family members— as likely as not Mr. Frank—would try to detain the police in the narrow entrance way—maybe even fight them, as suggested above—thus giving other members of the family a chance to escape, either by reaching the roofs of adjacent houses, or down a ladder into the alley behind the house in which they were living.

Any of this would have required recognizing and accepting the des- 15 perate straits in which they found themselves, and concentrating on how best to cope with them. This was quite possible to do, even under the terrible conditions in which the Jews found themselves after the Nazi occupation of Holland. It can be seen from many other accounts, for example from the story of Marga Minco, a girl of about Anne Frank's age who lived to tell about it. Her parents had planned that when the police should come for them, the father would try to detain them by arguing and fighting with them, to give the wife and daughter a chance to escape through a rear door. Unfortunately it did not quite work out this way, and both parents got killed. But their short-lived resistance permitted their daughter to make her escape as planned and to reach a Dutch family who saved her.[1]

This is not mentioned as a criticism that the Frank family did not plan or behave along similar lines. A family has every right to arrange their life as they wish or think best, and to take the risks they want to take. My point is not to criticize what the Franks did, but only the universal admiration of their way of coping, or rather of not coping. The story of little Marga who survived, every bit as touching, remains totally neglected by comparison.

Many Jews—unlike the Franks, who through listening to British radio news were better informed than most—had no detailed knowledge of the extermination camps. Thus it was easier for them to make themselves believe that complete compliance with even the most outrageously debilitating and degrading Nazi orders might offer a chance for survival. But neither tremendous anxiety that inhibits clear thinking and with it well-planned and determined action, nor ignorance about what happened to those who responded with passive waiting for being rounded up for their extermination, can explain the reaction of audiences to the play and movie retelling Anne's story, which are all about such waiting that results finally in destruction.

I think it is the fictitious ending that explains the enormous success of this play and movie. At the conclusion we hear Anne's voice from the beyond, saying, "In spite of everything, I still believe that people are really good at heart." This improbable sentiment is supposedly from a girl who had been starved to death, had watched her sister meet the same fate before she did, knew that her mother had been murdered, and had watched untold thousands of adults and children being killed. This statement is not justified by anything Anne actually told her diary.

Going on with intimate family living, no matter how dangerous it might be to survival, was fatal to all too many during the Nazi regime. And if all men are good, then indeed we can all go on with living our lives as we have been accustomed to in times of undisturbed safety and can afford to forget about Auschwitz. But Anne, her sister, her mother, may well have died because her parents could not get themselves to believe in Auschwitz.

While play and movie are ostensibly about Nazi persecution and destruction, in actuality what we watch is the way that, despite this terror, lovable people manage to continue living their satisfying inti-

20

---

[1] Marga Minco, *Bitter Herbs* (New York: Oxford University Press), 1960.

mate lives with each other. The heroine grows from a child into a young adult as normally as any other girl would, despite the most abnormal conditions of all other aspects of her existence, and that of her family. Thus the play reassures us that despite the destructiveness of Nazi racism and tyranny in general, it is possible to disregard it in one's private life much of the time, even if one is Jewish.

True, the ending happens just as the Franks and their friends had feared all along; their hiding place is discovered, and they are carried away to their doom. But the fictitious declaration of faith in the goodness of all men which concludes the play falsely reassures us since it impresses on us that in the combat between Nazi terror and continuance of intimate family living the latter wins out, since Anne has the last word. This is simply contrary to fact, because it was she who got killed. Her seeming survival through her moving statement about the goodness of men releases us effectively of the need to cope with the problems Auschwitz presents. That is why we are so relieved by her statement. It explains why millions loved play and movie, because while it confronts us with the fact that Auschwitz existed, it encourages us at the same time to ignore any of its implications. If all men are good at heart, there never really was an Auschwitz; nor is there any possibility that it may recur.

The desire of Anne Frank's parents not to interrupt their intimate family living, and their inability to plan more effectively for their survival, reflect the failure of all too many others faced with the threat of Nazi terror. It is a failure that deserves close examination because of the inherent warnings it contains for us, the living.

Submission to the threatening power of the Nazi state often led both to the disintegration of what had once seemed well-integrated personalities and to a return to an immature disregard for the dangers of reality. Those Jews who submitted passively to Nazi persecution came to depend on primitive and infantile thought processes: wishful thinking and disregard for the possibility of death. Many persuaded themselves that they, out of all the others, would be spared. Many more simply disbelieved in the possibility of their own death. Not believing in it, they did not take what seemed to them desperate precautions, such as giving up everything to hide out singly; or trying to escape even if it meant risking their lives in doing so; or preparing to fight for their lives when no escape was possible and death had become an immediate possibility. It is true that defending their lives in active combat before they were rounded up to be transported into the camps might have hastened their deaths, and so, up to a point, they were protecting themselves by "rolling with the punches" of the enemy.

But the longer one rolls with the punches dealt not by the normal vagaries of life, but by one's eventual executioner, the more likely it becomes that one will no longer have the strength to resist when death becomes imminent. This is particularly true if yielding to the enemy is accompanied not by a commensurate strengthening of the personality, but by an inner disintegration. We can observe such a process among the Franks, who bickered with each other over trifles, instead of supporting each other's ability to resist the demoralizing impact of their living conditions.

Those who faced up to the announced intentions of the Nazis prepared for the worst as a real and imminent possibility. It meant risking one's life for a self-chosen purpose, but in doing so, creating at least a small chance for saving one's own life or those of others, or both. When Jews in Germany were restricted to their homes, those who did not succumb to inertia took the new restrictions as a warning that it was high time to go underground, join the resistance movement, provide themselves with forged papers, and so on, if they had not done so long ago. Many of them survived.

Some distant relatives of mine may furnish an example. Early in the war, a young man living in a small Hungarian town banded together with a number of other Jews to prepare against a German invasion. As soon as the Nazis imposed curfews on the Jews, his group left for Budapest—because the bigger capital city with its greater anonymity offered chances for escaping detection. Similar groups from other towns converged in Budapest and joined forces. From among themselves they selected typically "Aryan"-looking men who equipped themselves with false papers and immediately joined the Hungarian SS. These spies were then able to warn of impending persecution and raids.

Many of these groups survived intact. Furthermore, they had also equipped themselves with small arms, so that if they were detected, they could put up enough of a fight for the majority to escape while a few would die fighting to make the escape possible. A few of the Jews who had joined the SS were discovered and immediately shot, probably a death preferable to one in the gas chambers. But most of even these Jews survived, hiding within the SS until liberation.

Compare these arrangements not just to the Franks' selection of a hiding place that was basically a trap without an outlet but with Mr. Frank's teaching typically academic high-school subjects to his children rather than how to make a getaway: a token of his inability to face the seriousness of the threat of death. Teaching high-school subjects had, of course, its constructive aspects. It relieved the ever-present anxiety about their fate to some degree by concentrating on different matters, and by implication it encouraged hope for a future in which such knowledge would be useful. In this sense such teaching was purposeful, but it was erroneous in that it took the place of much more pertinent teaching and planning: how best to try to escape when detected.

Unfortunately the Franks were by no means the only ones who, out of anxiety, became unable to contemplate their true situation and with it to plan accordingly. Anxiety, and the wish to counteract it by clinging to each other, and to reduce its sting by continuing as much as possible with their usual way of life incapacitated many, particularly when survival plans required changing radically old ways of living that they cherished, and which had become their only source of satisfaction.

My young relative, for example, was unable to persuade other members of his family to go with him when he left the small town where he had lived with them. Three times, at tremendous risk to himself, he returned to plead with his relatives, pointing out first the growing persecution of the Jews, and later the fact that transport to the gas chambers had already begun. He could not convince these Jews to leave their homes and break up their families to go singly into hiding.

As their desperation mounted, they clung more determinedly to their old living arrangements and to each other, became less able to consider giving up the possessions they had accumulated through hard work over a lifetime. The more severely their freedom to act was reduced, and what little they were still permitted to do restricted by insensible and degrading regulations imposed by the Nazis, the more did they become unable to contemplate independent action. Their life energies drained out of them, sapped by their ever-greater anxiety. The less they found strength in themselves, the more they held on to the little that was left of what had given them security in the past—their old surroundings, their customary way of life, their possessions—all these seemed to give their lives some permanency, offer some symbols of security. Only what had once been symbols of security now endangered life, since they were excuses for avoiding change. On each successive visit the young man found his relatives more incapacitated, less willing or able to take his advice, more frozen into inactivity, and with it further along the way to the crematoria where, in fact, they all died.

Levin renders a detailed account of the desperate but fruitless efforts made by small Jewish groups determined to survive to try to save the rest. She tells how messengers were "sent into the provinces to warn Jews that deportation meant death, but their warnings were ignored because most Jews refused to contemplate their own annihilation."[2] I believe the reason for such refusal has to be found in their inability to take action. If we are certain that we are helpless to protect ourselves against the danger of destruction, we cannot contemplate it. We can consider the danger only as long as we believe there are ways to protect ourselves, to fight back, to escape. If we are convinced none of this is possible for us, then there is no point in thinking about the danger; on the contrary, it is best to refuse to do so.

---

[2]Nora Levin, *The Holocaust* (New York: Thomas Y. Crowell, 1968).

As a prisoner in Buchenwald, I talked to hundreds of German Jewish prisoners who were brought there as part of the huge pogrom in the wake of the murder of vom Rath in the fall of 1938. I asked them why they had not left Germany, given the utterly degrading conditions they had been subjected to. Their answer was: How could we leave? It would have meant giving up our homes, our work, our sources of income. Having been deprived by Nazi persecution and degradation of much of their self-respect, they had become unable to give up what still gave them a semblance of it: their earthly belongings. But instead of using possessions, they became captivated by them, and this possession by earthly goods became the fatal mask for their possession by anxiety, fear, and denial.

How the investment of personal property with one's life energy could make people die bit by bit was illustrated throughout the Nazi persecution of the Jews. At the time of the first boycott of Jewish stores, the chief external goal of the Nazis was to acquire the possessions of the Jews. They even let Jews take some things out of the country at that time if they would leave the bulk of their property behind. For a long time the intention of the Nazis, and the goal of their first discriminatory laws, was to force undesirable minorities, including Jews, into emigration.

Although the extermination policy was in line with the inner logic of Nazi racial ideology, one may wonder whether the idea that millions of Jews (and other foreign nationals) could be submitted to extermination did not partially result from seeing the degree of degradation Jews accepted without fighting back. When no violent resistance occurred, persecution of the Jews worsened, slow step by slow step.

Many Jews who on the invasion of Poland were able to survey their situation and draw the right conclusions survived the Second World War. As the Germans approached, they left everything behind and fled to Russia, much as they distrusted and disliked the Soviet system. But there, while badly treated, they could at least survive. Those who stayed on in Poland believing they could go on with life-as-before sealed their fate. Thus in the deepest sense the walk to the gas chamber was only the last consequence of these Jews' inability to comprehend what was in store; it was the final step of surrender to the death instinct, which might also be called the principle of inertia. The first step was taken long before arrival at the death camp.

We can find a dramatic demonstration of how far the surrender to inertia can be carried, and the wish not to know because knowing would create unbearable anxiety, in an experience of Olga Lengyel.[3] She re-

---

[3]Olga Lengyel, *Five Chimneys: The Story of Auschwitz* (Chicago: Ziff-Davis, 1947).

ports that although she and her fellow prisoners lived just a few hundred yards from the crematoria and the gas chambers and knew what they were for, most prisoners denied knowledge of them for months. If they had grasped their true situation, it might have helped them save either the lives they themselves were fated to lose, or the lives of others.

When Mrs. Lengyel's fellow prisoners were selected to be sent to the gas chambers, they did not try to break away from the group, as she successfully did. Worse, the first time she tried to escape the gas chambers, some of the other selected prisoners told the supervisors that she was trying to get away. Mrs. Lengyel desperately asks the question: How was it possible that people denied the existence of the gas chambers when all day long they saw the crematoria burning and smelled the odor of burning flesh? Why did they prefer ignoring the exterminations to fighting for their very own lives? She can offer no explanation, only the observation that they resented anyone who tried to save himself from the common fate, because they lacked enough courage to risk action themselves. I believe they did it because they had given up their will to live and permitted their death tendencies to engulf them. As a result, such prisoners were in the thrall of the murdering SS not only physically but also psychologically, while this was not true for those prisoners who still had a grip on life.

Some prisoners even began to serve their executioners, to help speed   40
the death of their own kind. Then things had progressed beyond simple inertia to the death instinct running rampant. Those who tried to serve their executioners in what were once their civilian capacities were merely continuing life as usual and thereby opening the door to their death.

For example, Mrs. Lengyel speaks of Dr. Mengele, SS physician at Auschwitz, as a typical example of the "business as usual" attitude that enabled some prisoners, and certainly the SS, to retain whatever balance they could despite what they were doing. She describes how Dr. Mengele took all correct medical precautions during childbirth, rigorously observing all aseptic principles, cutting the umbilical cord with greatest care, etc. But only half an hour later he sent mother and infant to be burned in the crematorium.

Having made his choice, Dr. Mengele and others like him had to delude themselves to be able to live with themselves and their experience. Only one personal document on the subject has come to my attention, that of Dr. Nyiszli, a prisoner serving as "research physician" at Auschwitz.[4] How Dr. Nyiszli deluded himself can be seen, for example, in the way he repeatedly refers to himself as working in Auschwitz as a physician, although he worked as the assistant of a criminal

---

[4] Miklos Nyiszli, *Auschwitz: A Doctor's Eyewitness Account* (New York: Frederick Fell, 1960).

murderer. He speaks of the Institute for Race, Biological, and Anthropological Investigation as "one of the most qualified medical centers of the Third Reich," although it was devoted to proving falsehoods. That Nyiszli was a doctor didn't alter the fact that he—like any of the prisoner foremen who served the SS better than some SS were willing to serve it—was a participant in the crimes of the SS. How could he do it and live with himself?

The answer is: by taking pride in his professional skills, irrespective of the purpose they served. Dr. Nyiszli and Dr. Mengele were only two among hundreds of other—and far more prominent—physicians who participated in the Nazis' murderous pseudo-scientific human experiments. It was the peculiar pride of these men in their professional skill and knowledge, without regard for moral implications, that made them so dangerous. Although the concentration camps and crematoria are no longer here, this kind of pride still remains with us; it is characteristic of a modern society in which fascination with technical competence has dulled concern for human feelings. Auschwitz is gone, but so long as this attitude persists, we shall not be safe from cruel indifference to life at the core.

I have met many Jews as well as gentile anti-Nazis, similar to the activist group in Hungary described earlier, who survived in Nazi Germany and in the occupied countries. These people realized that when a world goes to pieces and inhumanity reigns supreme, man cannot go on living his private life as he was wont to do, and would like to do; he cannot, as the loving head of a family, keep the family living together peacefully, undisturbed by the surrounding world; nor can he continue to take pride in his profession or possessions, when either will deprive him of his humanity, if not also of his life. In such times, one must radically reevaluate all of what one has done, believed in, and stood for in order to know how to act. In short, one has to take a stand on the new reality—a firm stand, not one of retirement into an even more private world.

If today, Negroes in Africa march against the guns of a police that defends *apartheid*—even if hundreds of dissenters are shot down and tens of thousands rounded up in camps—their fight will sooner or later assure them of a chance for liberty and equality. Millions of the Jews of Europe who did not or could not escape in time or go underground as many thousands did, could at least have died fighting as some did in the Warsaw ghetto at the end, instead of passively waiting to be rounded up for their own extermination.

LINES OF INQUIRY
"The Ignored Lesson of Anne Frank"

Though Bettelheim focuses on the story of the Frank family, he also refers to stories of other families and persons, some drawn from his own experience and that of his distant Hungarian relative, others from the published accounts of Minco, Levin, Lengyel, and Nyiszli. Why does Bettelheim tell about these other families and persons? How does each of their experiences reflect on the story of the Frank family? Why does he arrange their stories in a sequence beginning with Minco's and ending with Nyiszli's?

As his title indicates, Bettelheim believes that the experience of Anne Frank and her family embodies an important lesson that most people have overlooked. What is "the ignored lesson of Anne Frank"? In what respects is the ignored lesson of her experience at odds with other interpretations of it? What beliefs or values or ways of living are called into question by the ignored lesson? What beliefs or values or ways of living are implicitly affirmed by the ignored lesson? In what respects does Bettelheim consider the ignored lesson to have universal implications?

In this essay, as in "Joey: A 'Mechanical Boy,' " Bettelheim focuses on the experience of a single young person and that person's family, yet he approaches them in completely different ways. What is most distinctive about his analysis of each case? What is most distinctive about his presentation of each case? Despite these important differences, do you see any recurrent beliefs and ideas that Bettelheim conveys in these two pieces?

SOME COMMENTS ON PRIVACY

When contemplating the issues raised by an ever more frequent, pervasive, and intrusive invasion of privacy by governmental agencies, private organizations, and the mass media—aggravated by requests from researchers for all kinds of detailed information on one's activities, opinions, and preferences—I am motivated by my considerable personal need and liking for privacy, and my resentment when it is infringed upon. I even dislike intensely what appear to be quite innocuous invasions of my private domain, unless I happen to be momentarily in the mood where it makes no difference to me. For example, there are times when I am quite annoyed if I have to listen to some music in an elevator or airplane, because it may jar with my mood of the moment, stop me from pursuing private thoughts, or interfere with a conversation. While petty, such incidents are indicative of a much larger issue: the usurpation of my right to decide whether, and if so, where I should listen to music, and what kind of music this should be. The fact that it is an anonymous organization which has made these decisions for me only makes it worse; while I am involved as an individual, there is no other individual to whom I can complain about the music, or ask for redress.

What I resent is not the music per se; even as I am disturbed by it, I recognize that it was arranged with the good intention of entertaining me while I am forced to spend time in a dull place. What bothers me is the tacit assumption either that I have no private thoughts I wish to pursue without interruption, or that these thoughts can easily be fitted to the mood of the music, or most offensive of all, that my wish to engage in thoughts of my own need not be respected.

I cite a trivial example because I believe privacy to be an unqualified right. The same principle that one's privacy should be respected and inviolate should apply in minor areas like elevators as well as in major ones such as one's professional life. As a psychoanalyst I am the recipient of highly confidential information about people's most intimate affairs, and not just from patients suffering from severe psychological disturbances. I am frequently subjected to the demand that I divulge this information. Although I reject such requests, to do so is often made very difficult. With all this, I would make a forceful case that privacy must be safeguarded under all circumstances, especially against any infringements by the power of the state. This conviction has been strengthened by my experiences with totalitarian systems.

However, I recognize how much my attitudes were formed in a particular era—the late- and post-Victorian one—and how much things have changed since that time. Reflecting on how things are now, I began to feel not just old, but outright archaic. I have had to accept that privacy is not universally desired, nor an absolute good, as I wished to believe. Instead, its high valuation belongs very much to a particular style of life and historical period, is further characteristic of certain social classes, and thus is culture-bound.

The troublesome nature of this divergence of attitudes began to dawn upon me as I was typing the first draft of these remarks, in solitude, the door of my room closed, in the stillness of the night—the time when I prefer working and when I work best, because no unexpected interruptions interfere with my concentration. As I was typing away, my eyes strayed to a favorite picture hung on the wall over the desk, and I had to laugh at myself. The picture was a copy of a famous painting by Pieter Breughel the Elder, a master I greatly admire. I particularly like this painting of his because it seems to me to be a celebration of life as it really is, not as it pretends to be, as is often rendered in pictures. It shows a world teeming with people, doing all sorts of things. A crowd is depicted who, singly or in groups, are unconcernedly, even happily, going about in public what I, from my very different perspective, would have called their private business. Only for them, such affairs were not at all private—on the contrary. They were fully aware that they transacted their interactions in public; they wanted all to be seen and known by neighbors and strangers; and they did things with more gusto because they did them in the presence of others who reacted to the events being carried on in their presence. I had enjoyed and admired this and other paintings of the Dutch masters, many of which depicted the most "private" aspects of life as being transacted in the public domain, without recognizing that my admiration was incompatible with my feelings about the desirability of privacy. These paintings and many others from later periods indicate how recently our need for privacy has developed; and as I reflected on it, I also realized that this need may already be passing out of our life.

When I studied as a youngster, the door to my room had to be closed; all had to be quiet, and was quiet. Only then could I concentrate on my thoughts and my work, to the exclusion of all other distractions. But my own children—the generation born during and after World War II—studied best with the door open and the record player or the radio going full blast; in this radically different setting they learned as much and as well as I had. Why then do I still need a high degree of privacy and have to work—or at least much prefer to work—only in quiet concentration; and why do they—like the people in the Breughel painting—need to be in continuous close touch with their age-mates, or at least symbolically through a shared musical interest, when they want to concentrate on a mentally demanding task?

Maybe the answer is that we all function best when we feel in communion with what seems to symbolize our highest personal value. I, as a child of the Victorian age, had to create for myself a setting that emphasized privacy, personal uniqueness, and individual development before I could concentrate on a learning task whose ultimate goal— whether or not I was consciously aware of it—was to attain the highest possible degree of individuation. My children, in order to work best, needed to feel that they had not lost touch with their peer group. Nothing and nobody forced them to accept the intrusion of the music into the privacy of their thoughts. If anything, their parents, who were the "authorities" in the home, were most dubious about their studying with the songs of the Beatles distracting them—or at least we thought that this loud music must distract them.

Actually, far from distracting, the music helped my children to concentrate by comforting and reassuring them that they had not lost contact with what they needed most. It gave them the feeling that even when immersed in their studies, they were still somehow in touch with what counted for much in their lives: the connection to their age group. This connection heightened life for them in all of their doings, including the effort to study.

The more lonely they felt, the more these children needed to deny their isolation, to drown it out by the loudness of the music. It expressed for them their angers, their longings, even their loneliness. In doing so, the loud music did for them what they felt unable to do for themselves: to bring their emotions into some semblance of order, put them into a frame which would make them manageable enough to be expressed; emotions which otherwise would be much too chaotic to be coped with in any way. This vicarious expression of their feelings by the music permitted the children—who hardly listened to it but let themselves be enveloped by it—to continue with their studies; otherwise the pressure of these feelings might have prevented them from doing so. The music did this for them because they knew their age-mates who suffered from overpowering parallel emotions listened to the same music. Thus even in their anger, their alienation, their loneliness, it established an invisible—I am tempted to say, an audible— imaginary bond between them and those others with whom, alas, no real bonds existed.

When I came to this country about thirty years ago, among the many customs which struck me as different and thus strange was having the window shades pulled down halfway, more or less all the time. The lowered shade signified a wish for privacy, while leaving half of the window unobstructed expressed that there was no desire, nor any

10

need, to hide from inspection what went on in the room behind the window. This seemed to me to bespeak a strange ambivalence about the wish for privacy. Now the picture window, which exposes so much more of what goes on in the inside to outside scrutiny, while at the same time permitting insiders to observe so much of what is going on in front of the window, has more or less done away with half-pulled-down shades.

In comparison, I remembered how the same problem of seeing and being seen through a window was often dealt with in my native Vienna, and in many other European countries. In the generation of my grandparents, many homes had one window of the living room fitted with an outside mirror that was angled so that a person sitting inside, in a window seat specially fitted for this purpose, could spy on all the comings and goings in the street by watching the mirror without being observed.

I could not help reflecting that a situation where one person would sit hidden in semi-obscurity while observing the behavior of others had its similarities with the psychoanalytic setting, where things go on in utter privacy and confidentiality. If so, the semi-private and semi-public nature of the partly pulled-down shade, and the more public exposure inherent in the picture window, might then be likened to group therapeutic settings or encounter groups, where a mixed group of patients and therapist are equally exposed to each other and things can barely be kept private or confidential. Maybe there were some deeper reasons why a setting that was typically Victorian in its insistence on maintaining total privacy and confidentiality was conducive to the invention of psychoanalysis, and with this to the liberation from Victorian hypocrisy.

How things have changed since Freud explained his reasons for developing the particular psychoanalytic setting! He created it because people, he felt, could not be expected to talk about sexual or other "private" matters while they were aware that somebody was observing their face. But the setting protected the analyst equally: sitting behind the couch where the patient could not observe him was absolutely necessary for the analyst, if he was to be able to concentrate on the patient and what he was saying without worrying about any expressions which might appear on *his* face as he listened to the patient's revelations.

But since Freud's time, and to a considerable degree because of his influence, what used to be eminently private has become quite public— often, I feel defensively, with a vengeance. Feelings and actions a patient could talk about only to the trusted analyst in the carefully guarded privacy of the treatment room are now freely discussed in public, with relative strangers and in the most casual settings. Questions which once a patient broached to his analyst only with great anxiety are now asked in widely and indiscriminately disseminated questionnaires and are readily answered, although they pertain to matters which I still believe ought best to be kept private. What used to be considered most intimate matters are now discussed in great detail in family magazines or shown on the TV or movie screen.

This greater openness, as concerning sexual matters for example, has not altered the fact that today, as in Freud's time, there is much a person will not disclose unless he is absolutely certain that his confidences will be kept secret; but the content of what needs to be kept private has changed. For example, it used to be that the revelation of a person's sexual predilections—ordinary or deviant—had to be protected by complete confidentiality before he dared open up about them. Today many people speak freely about such matters in public. What now is kept secret is often a person's true feelings about behavior which he openly flaunts; feelings which may be the opposite of those he claims to have, for he may secretly be ashamed of what he so openly admits to, or, contrary to his assertions, he may not be able to feel at all.

Thus today, as much as in Freud's time, people insist on confidentiality and on keeping things private, whenever they are ashamed of what they have to reveal. What people may be ashamed of can and does change radically from place to place, and over time. This poses the psychological problem of whether such shame—and with it the demand for confidentiality and privacy—is desirable and beneficial, or rather lessens our well-being as individuals, or that of man in society. Do we benefit more when we are able to hide, keep private and secret, that of which we are ashamed, or is it preferable that this should be made public and openly accepted?

Here the psychoanalyst is caught in his own contradictions, like the rest of us. He tells his patients that there is nothing to be ashamed of in fantasies or feelings, not to mention dreams and daydreams. All these flow of necessity from one's total life history, from the vagaries of experiences and one's reactions to them. Most of all, they reflect early childhood events and reactions, and how one then immaturely interpreted the world; there is no reason for anybody to feel shame about such things. Yet when the same patient behaves in society too openly by acting on the basis of these fantasies, when he thus makes public things he has been told not to shrink from, then as likely as not, the psychoanalyst will consider such openness as acting-out on the part of the patient, viewing it as irresponsible and self-destructive behavior—which indeed it may be.

We all seem caught between our own morality and society's clamor about what should be kept private, and what not. So we all end up functioning by a double standard of morality. But as Freud has shown, keeping a double moral standard—maintaining one for public show and another for private and somehow shameful action—leads only to neurosis and hysteria. Maybe our present dilemma regarding what belongs in the private domain and what in the public, although different from

15

the double standard of Freud's day, is caused by equally severe unresolved inner conflicts about what is right and what wrong.

As a Freudian psychoanalyst I cannot help one further reflection: that the genitals are called a person's private parts, and that the place where one defecates is called a privy. Behind these two "private" designations lies a discomfort with natural functions, a distrust concerning basic parts of oneself, and an uneasiness about how others feel about such things—in short, a deep inner conflict.[1] Maybe these are the emotions behind many demands for privacy.

Lewis Mumford writes: "Today the degradation of the inner life is   20 symbolized by the fact that the only place sacred from intrusion is the private toilet."[2] In this connection it might be mentioned that organizations which wish to de-individualize the individual insist on the use of common toilets, such as in the army, or in summer camps, where the desire is to make everybody feel like "one of the boys." This underlines the relation between individualism and privacy on the one hand, and on the other that between feelings of communality and absence of privacy. (Deliberate deprivation of all privacy can be used not only for purposes of de-individualization, but also of degradation and depersonalization, as happened in the concentration camps.)

Now the degradation Mumford talks of can be interpreted in two ways. One is the thought Mumford had in mind: that unfortunately too little in our lives is as private, as safe from intrusion, as we are while we are on the toilet. But is it not also degrading that functions so natural to our bodies, eliminatory functions we cannot live without, are considered so shameful that they have to be carefully hidden from others, and avoided through lingual circumlocution even with ourselves?

It is precisely the feelings we experience around toilet training, or what is called anality, that often become the greatest source of neurotic anxieties; our inherited shame about elimination sometimes forces us to keep shameful guilty feelings private and hidden from others, causing tremendous unhappiness. At the same time, this very shame is one of the foundations on which our Western civilization rests, although along with it came the discomfort Freud wrote about which bedevils modern man.

Nevertheless in other areas, when and where we crave privacy has undergone great change. My Victorian parents, when they went out to

---

[1] As openly as many people now talk about sexual matters, when it comes to elimination we still talk about "going to the bathroom," or washroom. Elimination is still "dirty." The shame about this finds expression in our circumlocution as we refer not to elimination, but instead to that which will free us from having been engaged in something we consider "dirty"—washing and cleaning ourselves.

[2] Lewis Mumford, *The City in History* (New York: Harcourt, Brace & World, 1961).

dinner, preferred a spacious restaurant with their table set off by an ample distance from the next one. Conversation would then not be overheard, nor their attention imposed on or distracted by too immediate an awareness of others. Nowadays our young people seem to prefer to crowd together in small discotheques, not to speak of the hippies who sleep many to a room. Many of the latter feel so desperately alone and out of contact with others that bodily closeness is sought avidly to bridge the gap. This raises the problem of whether parents have not gone too far in their demand for and in their imposition of privacy.

One need not go as far back as when whole families lived in one room. Nobody had privacy then. One couldn't effectively hide certain skeletons in the closet then because there were no closets. Reconstructions of what life was like in colonial days, even among the affluent, show that parents and children alike lived not only physically close, but with hardly any privacy. A family had to be quite well off to afford separate bedrooms—that is, one for the parents, and one for all the children together. Nowadays the ideal seems to be for each child to have his own room and own bathroom. But the children raised in this spacious isolation are often those who, when they finally come into their own, crowd together into one tiny room.

Our Western society has gone far in seeking privacy and avoiding   25
the pains of closeness; at least as an ideal, although many poor people cannot afford the luxury of privacy, which they desire. On the other hand, many who can afford privacy in consequence suffer from too much distance, from isolation. Maybe what we view as the infringement of privacy today has to do with human efforts at rectifying the balance.

Mumford writes that

> the first radical change which was to alter the form of the Medieval house, was the development of a sense of privacy. This means in effect withdrawal at will from the common life and the common interests of one's fellows. Privacy in sleep, privacy in eating, privacy in religious and social rituals, finally privacy in thought. . . . The desire for privacy marked the beginning of that new alignment of classes which was to usher in the merciless class competition and individual self-assertion of a later day. . . . In the castles of the thirteenth century, one notes the existence of a private bedroom for the noble owners; and one also finds, not far from it, perched over the moat, a private toilet. . . . Privacy in bed came first in Italy among the upper classes only, but the desire for it seems to have developed almost as slowly as the means. Michelangelo, for example, on occasion slept with his workmen four to a bed.

From these remarks it seems obvious that an absence of privacy in living conditions did not and need not interfere with creative achievements, which even we moderns regard as the reflection of rarest uniqueness. But it also appears that as long as all the bodily functions, including sex and elimination, were more or less public, no great shame attached to them. Only as they became more and more relegated to a private room which became the privy, did we learn to feel shame about our bodies and bodily functions. The tragedy is that alienation from one's body leads to alienation from oneself and from others. And once we no longer feel comfortable with others, we crave privacy. Maybe what is missing is the right balance between closeness and distance, between public and private.

When we think about privacy we think of the wish for privacy in thought, feeling and experience; these should be exclusively our own. No one should have the right to intrude on these inner processes; they should be open to others only when we wish to give of them. Otherwise they should be and remain our private "business."

The desire for privacy is closely linked to the increased insistence on private property in ever-larger aspects of life. My home ought to be the castle where I am protected from anyone's intruding on my privacy. But my home is my castle only when it is my private possession. Understandably, it was the lord of the castle who first claimed privacy for himself and his doings. Thus from the very beginning, demands for privacy were closely connected with private property. Whoever owned no place of his own, owned no privacy either, and he has very little even today. And private property is virtually inseparable from class structure.

Only in the seventeenth century, for example, did the common dinner table stop being common to all members of the household, servants and masters alike; no private conversations were held at the dinner table then. In short, the more class-structured a society becomes, the more privacy do its privileged members demand. How understandable, then, that a society which tries to do away with class structure should also try to do away with privacy, and demand that ever larger areas of life should be public.

What comes as harder to realize is that as long as everyone knew everything about everyone else there was no need for informers, for elaborate spy systems, or for bugging in order to know what people did, said, and thought. This brings to mind the absence of crime, delinquency, and other asocial behavior in the Israeli kibbutzim. There are no police there, because there is no need for policing. Everyone lives much more collectively and openly with everyone else than among us, and with this, in essence everybody polices everybody else. There is very little privacy and everyone knows just about everything about everyone else. I personally felt suffocated by the lack of privacy, when I lived there for a time. But I could not blind myself to what to me was an astonishing absence of all asocial behavior in this society, as follows from the absence of privacy—or from having everything in the public domain.

Servan-Schreiber, in comparing Americans to the French, remarks that "France is a country where distrust of one's neighbor still prevails.

30

This is due to the conviction that men are by nature hostile and ego-tistical. Therefore each protects himself from the other through a complex network of laws, which complexity conforms to the French tendency of carefully limiting and defining all aspects of human existence. The straitjacket which results, quite naturally, prevents all change."[3] And it is true that the demand for privacy implies a distrust of others.

Where does all this leave me? Despite all of my realizations I do not cherish privacy less, and I still resent deeply any intrusion upon it.

I recognize that modern anomy and alienation, even much of modern *tedium vitae,* result from how distantly people live from each other. Most of our social problems, whether distrust by one group in the population of the other—call it racial discrimination, or class hatred—or the prevalence of crime and delinquency, merely reflect this alienation. The best way to do away with them, perhaps the only one, would be to create true communities. But one cannot live in true communality and also keep much of life private to oneself. Many of our laws telling us what to do and what not to do, which even invade our private lives, are intended to make our society more equitable.

If consensus does not arise from communal living, from everyone's sharing the same values and having much the same concerns, then it has to be imposed from the outside. But what suffers then is the individualism my own rearing forces me to cherish so highly. So I am caught in my own contradictions, truly a child of our age of transition. At present I see no way to achieve all these good things together: a true community of living, and an individualism safeguarded by privacy. So let me close with some thoughts on the psychological dimensions of the problem.

Professionally I am confronted daily with the suffering of emotionally disturbed children who were raised in situations where great privacy deteriorated into complete isolation from others, and with it from themselves. As a result they became desperately fearful and ashamed of any relations with others, or any familiarity with their bodies. It remains for the next generation to see if it can design a model of privacy which is not founded on repression—on feelings of shame about one's body, its function in elimination, its desire for various forms of sexual satisfaction. Maybe the solution is in a much better balance between those areas that should remain private and those we are better off assigning to the public domain. What is certainly needed is a privacy which does not dwarf but enhances our capacity for true intimacy with those who ought to be closest to us.

Among the unresolved problems of modern city life today is the prevalence of fear in our streets. I would like to suggest something far removed from reconstructing our cities, or an incredible enlarging of

35

---

[3]J. J. Servan-Schreiber, *Le Défi américain* (Paris: Denoel, 1967).

the police force and law-enforcing agents within them. What we need, in my opinion, is a return to much smaller, more self-contained communities where a great deal of what is now private can become public; where we would share and know much more about each other, and care about each other, even to the degree of protecting each other's well-being and property. After all, much crime is prevented, and criminals apprehended, when neighbors pay attention and report their observations to the police. In short, what we need is a desire for privacy that is based not on shame or the fear of what others might do to or think of us, but solely on a wish for simple solitude.

Maybe what we must strive for is a way of life where we would wish to share far more with each other because we can trust others more than we presently can, but without the community imposing any rules on how one must think, feel, and shape one's life, as was typical before the anonymity of big city life offered protection against such restraints on the individual's chance to find self-realization in his own ways. What would then be kept private would be kept that way not because it was shameful, but because it was valuable. And if there were less emphasis on private property, as in the kibbutz, there would be less need to protect private property, but only private emotions and experiences. If private property were less valued, it would require less protection and would arouse less desire to grab it away on the part of those who do not own it; and then we might come to value the private experience much more highly. Out of the high value we would then place on our own private experience we would come to respect the privacy of others.

While the millennium is not about to arrive, there is at least reasonable hope that modern technology will make the necessary types of property so readily available that they will no longer need to be anxiously guarded. Certainly our attitudes toward our bodies and what is shameful about them, needing to be hidden, are changing. We are a long way from accepting the body and its functions freely, but there is hope that the time may come when the desire for privacy will no longer be based on the need to hide what is experienced as the shameful functions of the body. The less we feel ashamed of, the less we feel curiosity about the private life of others. After all, it is the Peeping Tom who knows so little about his own body and emotions, is so afraid and confused about his own sexuality that he is sneakily trying to find out about that of others; it is he who is so embarrassed about his own instinctual desires that he tries to gain satisfaction from embarrassing others.

If we all became more secure about our own bodies, more secure economically, socially, and sexually, we would be able to grant others great individual freedom both out of a desire for such freedom for ourselves, and out of a lack of interest in their private lives, because any morbid interest in the other is always the consequence of a felt inadequacy in ourselves. That is why we are dying to know how others manage things. If we all were able to manage our own lives, we would have little reason to try to manage the lives of others.

Neither a medieval absence of privacy, nor a big brother's spying that makes all of our life public, will do. What we must strive for, as so often and in so many other matters, is the right balance between what should be respected and protected as private in our life, and what should be part of our more or less public communal life. Then the home will be just that—neither a castle, nor a public place.

LINES OF INQUIRY
"Some Comments on Privacy"

In developing and illustrating his ideas, Bettelheim discusses numerous examples of privacy, of intrusions upon privacy, and of communality. Why do you suppose that he uses so many examples? Why doesn't he limit himself instead to just a few closely related ones, such as those dealing with background music, or those dealing with windows and shades, or those dealing with living rooms and bedrooms, or those dealing with bathroom and bodily functions, or those dealing with psychoanalysis, or those dealing with sexuality? How do you account for his selection and arrangement of these varied examples? Why does he begin by talking about background music, then move on to windows and shades, then to psychoanalysis, and so on?

Though Bettelheim begins by complaining about the intrusiveness of background music on his privacy, he ends by envisioning a time "when the desire for privacy will no longer be based on the need to hide what is experienced as the shameful functions of the body." Given these apparently differing attitudes towards privacy, where do you think he really stands on the matter? What kinds of privacy do you think are most important to him? What kinds do you think are least important to him? What aspects of privacy raise the most perplexing and significant problems for him?

Bettelheim wrote this piece in 1966, when communal activities and communal living were prominent aspects of the nationwide counter-cultural movement. Now, twenty-five years later, how far do you think the country has come towards achieving what Bettelheim considers to be "the right balance between what should be respected and protected as private in our life, and what should be part of our more or less public communal life"? How far have you come toward achieving what you consider to be the right balance of privacy and communality in your own life?

JOAN DIDION

1934 –

If I could believe that going to a barricade would affect man's fate in the slightest I would go to that barricade, and quite often I wish that I could, but it would be less than honest to say that I expect to happen upon such a happy ending.

In this frank passage from the *The White Album,* Joan Didion acknowledges that the endings of the stories she tells as novelist and essayist are rarely happy. Relentlessly candid, broodingly perceptive, with a haunting attentiveness to the absurdities in contemporary life, Didion has become a high priestess of postmodern malaise, tracking the dissolution of meaning in the forms of modern culture with the tenacity of a bloodhound and lamenting the loss in essays so beautifully crafted as to earn her a solid reputation as one of the most accomplished prose stylists of her generation.

Didion was born in Sacramento, California, in 1934, a fifth-generation Californian. She grew up in a comfortably well-off family with a strong sense of her pioneer heritage and a passionate attachment to the Sacramento Valley landscape which was her home, running "over the same flat fields that our great-great-grandfather had found virgin and had planted" and swimming in "the same rivers we had swum for a century." That deep sense of generational familiarity, though, was doomed to be short-lived, for before Didion reached adulthood, California experienced the postwar economic boom that transformed it into "the golden land," the last frontier, the final toehold of American culture on the continent, the place where the American Dream, if it was ever to be realized, had to come true. This urgency precipitated change so rapid as to be drastically disorienting, instilling in Didion a presentiment of loss and a nostalgia for what is lost that still infuses her writing. "All that is constant about the California of my childhood is the rate at which it disappears," she wrote in 1965. In that sense, California epitomizes for Didion all "the things we lose and the promises we break as we grow older."

In 1952 Didion entered the University of California at Berkeley and graduated with a degree in English literature in 1956. She describes her undergraduate days this way:

> I read Camus and Henry James and I watched a flowering plum come in
> and out of blossom and at night, most nights, I walked outside and looked
> up to where the cyclotron and the bevatron glowed on the dark hillside,
> unspeakable mysteries which engaged me, in the style of my time, only
> personally.

This passage captures the dilemma which Didion explores in all her work: suspended between the cyclical time of the blossoming plum tree and the fragmenting of time and matter in the accelerators, between the balanced order of James' prose and Camus' exploration of a disintegrating social order, Didion records the sensibilities of the new era, in which cyclotrons rather than stars glow against the night sky, while mourning the loss of the old.

When she was still an undergraduate, Didion won an essay contest sponsored by *Vogue* magazine which secured her a job with the magazine after her graduation. She lived in New York for eight years, moving from copywriter to associate features editor at *Vogue*. During this time she fell "into the habit of writing fiction" and completed a novel, *Run River,* published in 1963. That same year she married John Gregory Dunne, also a writer, and the following year the couple moved to southern California, where they and their daughter still live. Over the years Didion and Dunne have been frequent collaborators on a number of writing projects, from magazine columns to Hollywood screenplays, while continuing to publish individually both fiction and non-fiction. Like her contemporary James Baldwin, Didion set out to be a novelist, and she has written two novels that portray women struggling to survive the painful circumstances of their lives, *Play It As It Lays* (1970) and *A Book of Common Prayer* (1977). But it is her essays that have earned the highest praise of readers and critics.

Didion's first collection of essays, *Slouching Towards Bethlehem,* appeared in 1968 and was an instant success. She took her title from W. B. Yeats' poem "The Second Coming," printing the entire poem as an epigraph to the book and repeatedly evoking the line "Things fall apart; the center cannot hold," as when she describes the experience of writing the title essay, a report on the drug subculture in San Francisco's Haight-Ashbury district, as "the first time I had dealt directly and flatly with the evidence of atomization, the proof that things fall apart." Of herself at the time she wrote the essay she says, "I . . . had been paralyzed by the conviction that writing was an irrelevant act, that the world as I had understood it no longer existed." Didion's mental landscape was, in other words, a mirror of the disintegration she felt herself surrounded by and described so vividly in the essays. She was, as one critic said of her, a "prescient witness" to the character of the time, as was the book itself, which appeared during the same year that Martin Luther King, Jr., and Robert Kennedy were assassinated, violence erupted at the Democratic National Convention in Chicago, and the My Lai massacre brought the blurred backdrop of the Vietnam war into sharp and bitter focus. That same year Didion was named a Los Angeles Times Woman of the Year and suffered a mental breakdown. Later she wrote that "the attack of vertigo and nausea" which first evidenced her breakdown "does not now seem to me an inappropriate response to the summer of 1968."

"I can recall," Didion has said, "always thinking there was more to be had from the dark journey. The dark journey engaged me more." Her preoccupation with that "dark journey" has caused one critic to observe, "One just wishes the woman wasn't in so much pain." But Didion is unapologetic about the refined subjectivity of her work: "I write entirely to find out what I'm thinking, what I'm looking at, what I see and what it means," she says. She has been criticized for being too self-revelatory in her essays—inserting excerpts from her psychiatric evaluation, discussing the possibility of a divorce from her husband, reporting on being diagnosed as having multiple sclerosis (the disease later went into remission). Recording the ways a fragmenting culture has impressed itself on her own consciousness has been her persistent concern; but as one critic has said, "her personality does not self-indulgently intrude itself on her subjects"; it "informs and illuminates them."

Didion's second collection of essays, *The White Album* (1979), is in many ways a return to the earlier terrain—life in California during the chaos of the sixties, replete with senseless mass murders, campus riots, and racial warfare—but it offers a retrospective view and thus in some sense is an awakening from the nightmare of that era. "I remember a time when the dogs barked every night and the moon was always full," she writes, and when the Manson murders occurred, "I also remember this, and wish I did not: *I remember that no one was surprised.*" But it is a memory, and Didion has survived. That is not to say that the essays in *The White Album* are healing or hopeful; Didion persists in detailing the progressive loss of coherence, which she sees as characterizing America in the late twentieth century, pursuing traces of that loss into the realm of language itself. The period from the mid-sixties to the early seventies was for Didion

> a time when I began to doubt the premises of all the stories I had ever told myself, a common condition but one I found troubling. . . . I was supposed to have a script, and had mislaid it. I was supposed to hear cues, and no longer did. I was meant to know the plot, but all I knew was what I saw: flash pictures in variable sequence, images with no "meaning" beyond their temporary arrangement. . . .

This "common condition" of inability "to believe in the narrative and in the narrative's intelligibility" is for her the loss at the heart of the postmodern world.

Her recent non-fiction consists of two book-length essays, *Salvador* (1983) and *Miami* (1987), both of which report the resulting chaos in regions of cultural collapse or confrontation. In *Salvador,* the fragmentation characteristic of the contemporary world extends itself into the very flesh of the inhabitants: "The dead and pieces of the dead turn up in El Salvador everywhere, every day, as taken for granted as in a nightmare, or a horror movie."

In such a world, how is a writer—"a person whose most absorbed and passionate hours are spent arranging words on pieces of paper"—to keep working? For Didion, arranging words and structuring sentences enables her to knit up the ravelling edges of her world:

> To shift the structure of a sentence alters the meaning of that sentence, as definitely and inflexibly as the position of a camera alters the meaning of the object photographed. Many people know about camera angles now but not so many know about sentences. The arrangement of the words matters, and the arrangement you want can be found in the picture in your mind. The picture dictates the arrangement. . . . The picture tells you how to arrange the words and the arrangement of the words tells you, or tells me, what's going on in the picture.

So, in the grammar of her sentences as in the structure of her essays, Didion achieves at least a measure of control in a world she finds largely out of control.

ON GOING HOME

I am home for my daugh-
ter's first birthday. By "home" I do not mean the house in Los Angeles
where my husband and I and the baby live, but the place where my
family is, in the Central Valley of California. It is a vital although
troublesome distinction. My husband likes my family but is uneasy in
their house, because once there I fall into their ways, which are difficult, oblique, deliberately inarticulate, not my husband's ways. We live
in dusty houses ("D-U-S-T," he once wrote with his finger on surfaces
all over the house, but no one noticed it) filled with mementos quite
without value to him (what could the Canton dessert plates mean to
him? how could he have known about the assay scales, why should he
care if he did know?), and we appear to talk exclusively about people we
know who have been committed to mental hospitals, about people
we know who have been booked on drunk-driving charges, and about
property, particularly about property, land, price per acre and C-2
zoning and assessments and freeway access. My brother does not understand my husband's inability to perceive the advantage in the rather
common real-estate transaction known as "sale-leaseback," and my
husband in turn does not understand why so many of the people he
hears about in my father's house have recently been committed to
mental hospitals or booked on drunk-driving charges. Nor does he
understand that when we talk about sale-leasebacks and right-of-way
condemnations we are talking in code about the things we like best, the
yellow fields and the cottonwoods and the rivers rising and falling and
the mountain roads closing when the heavy snow comes in. We miss
each other's points, have another drink and regard the fire. My brother
refers to my husband, in his presence, as "Joan's husband." Marriage is
the classic betrayal.

Or perhaps it is not any more. Sometimes I think that those of us who
are now in our thirties were born into the last generation to carry the
burden of "home," to find in family life the source of all tension and
drama. I had by all objective accounts a "normal" and a "happy" family
situation, and yet I was almost thirty years old before I could talk to my
family on the telephone without crying after I had hung up. We did not
fight. Nothing was wrong. And yet some nameless anxiety colored
the emotional charges between me and the place that I came from. The
question of whether or not you could go home again was a very real part
of the sentimental and largely literary baggage with which we left home
in the fifties; I suspect that it is irrelevant to the children born of the
fragmentation after World War II. A few weeks ago in a San Francisco

bar I saw a pretty young girl on crystal take off her clothes and dance for the cash prize in an "amateur-topless" contest. There was no particular sense of moment about this, none of the effect of romantic degradation, of "dark journey," for which my generation strived so assiduously. What sense could that girl possibly make of, say, *Long Day's Journey into Night?* Who is beside the point?

That I am trapped in this particular irrelevancy is never more apparent to me than when I am home. Paralyzed by the neurotic lassitude engendered by meeting one's past at every turn, around every corner, inside every cupboard, I go aimlessly from room to room. I decide to meet it head-on and clean out a drawer, and I spread the contents on the bed. A bathing suit I wore the summer I was seventeen. A letter of rejection from *The Nation,* an aerial photograph of the site for a shopping center my father did not build in 1954. Three teacups hand-painted with cabbage roses and signed "E.M.," my grandmother's initials. There is no final solution for letters of rejection from *The Nation* and teacups hand-painted in 1900. Nor is there any answer to snapshots of one's grandfather as a young man on skis, surveying around Donner Pass in the year 1910. I smooth out the snapshot and look into his face, and do and do not see my own. I close the drawer, and have another cup of coffee with my mother. We get along very well, veterans of a guerrilla war we never understood.

Days pass. I see no one. I come to dread my husband's evening call, not only because he is full of news of what by now seems to me our remote life in Los Angeles, people he has seen, letters which require attention, but because he asks what I have been doing, suggests uneasily that I get out, drive to San Francisco or Berkeley. Instead I drive across the river to a family graveyard. It has been vandalized since my last visit and the monuments are broken, overturned in the dry grass. Because I once saw a rattlesnake in the grass I stay in the car and listen to a country-and-Western station. Later I drive with my father to a ranch he has in the foothills. The man who runs his cattle on it asks us to the roundup, a week from Sunday, and although I know that I will be in Los Angeles I say, in the oblique way my family talks, that I will come. Once home I mention the broken monuments in the graveyard. My mother shrugs.

I go to visit my great-aunts. A few of them think now that I am   5
my cousin, or their daughter who died young. We recall an anecdote about a relative last seen in 1948, and they ask if I still like living in New York City. I have lived in Los Angeles for three years, but I say that I do. The baby is offered a horehound drop, and I am slipped a dollar bill "to buy a treat." Questions trail off, answers are abandoned, the baby plays with the dust motes in a shaft of afternoon sun.

It is time for the baby's birthday party: a white cake, strawberry-marshmallow ice cream, a bottle of champagne saved from another party. In the evening, after she has gone to sleep, I kneel beside the crib and touch her face, where it is pressed against the slats, with mine. She is an open and trusting child, unprepared for and unaccustomed to the ambushes of family life, and perhaps it is just as well that I can offer her little of that life. I would like to give her more. I would like to promise her that she will grow up with a sense of her cousins and of rivers and of her great-grandmother's teacups, would like to pledge her a picnic on a river with fried chicken and her hair uncombed, would like to give her *home* for her birthday, but we live differently now and I can promise her nothing like that. I give her a xylophone and a sundress from Madeira, and promise to tell her a funny story.

[1967]

LINES OF INQUIRY
"On Going Home"

Though Didion opens this essay with the announcement that "I am home for my daughter's first birthday," she doesn't say anything more about her daughter or her daughter's birthday party until the last two paragraphs of the piece. Why do you suppose she tells about her daughter only at the end? Why do you suppose she devotes so much space to telling about other visits home and about her other activities during this particular visit, such as cleaning out a drawer, driving to a family graveyard, and visiting her great aunts? And what is the effect of her telling about all these experiences in present rather than past tense?

In the concluding paragraph of her essay, Didion says that she would like to give her daughter "home for her birthday, but we live differently now and I can promise her nothing like that." What exactly does Didion mean by "home"? In what sense(s) does she think "we live differently now"? And why does this different way of living lead Didion to say that she can "promise" her daughter "nothing like that"? As a means of trying to answer these questions, examine all of Didion's references to "home" and "house," and take special note of how she depicts the way people live in her parents' home and community.

Consider your own experiences and understandings of "home." What particular place, if any, do you think of as most truly embodying your idea of "home"? What do you and others do at home that you consider to be most distinctive of the way you live when you are at home? If you no longer go home anymore, what experiences do you remember as being most distinctive of your life at home? What exactly does "home" mean to you, and do you think you could promise to give something like it to someone else?

ON THE ROAD

Where are we heading, they asked in all the television and radio studios. They asked it in New York and Los Angeles and they asked it in Boston and Washington and they asked it in Dallas and Houston and Chicago and San Francisco. Sometimes they made eye contact as they asked it. Sometimes they closed their eyes as they asked it. Quite often they wondered not just where we were heading but where we were heading "as Americans," or "as concerned Americans," or "as American women," or, on one occasion, "as the American guy and the American woman." I never learned the answer, nor did the answer matter, for one of the eerie and liberating aspects of broadcast discourse is that nothing one says will alter in the slightest either the form or the length of the conversation. Our voices in the studios were those of manic actors assigned to do three-minute, four-minute, seven-minute improvs. Our faces on the monitors were those of concerned Americans. On my way to one of those studios in Boston I had seen the magnolias bursting white down Marlborough Street. On my way to another in Dallas I had watched the highway lights blazing and dimming pink against the big dawn sky. Outside one studio in Houston the afternoon heat was sinking into the deep primeval green of the place and outside the next, that night in Chicago, snow fell and glittered in the lights along the lake. Outside all these studios America lay in all its exhilaratingly volatile weather and eccentricity and specificity, but inside the studios we shed the specific and rocketed on to the general, for they were The Interviewers and I was The Author and the single question we seemed able to address together was *where are we heading*.

> *"8:30 A.M. to 9:30 A.M.: LIVE on WFSB TV/THIS MORNING.*
> *"10 A.M. to 10:30 A.M.: LIVE on WINF AM/THE WORLD TODAY.*
> *"10:45 A.M. to 11:45 A.M.: PRESS INTERVIEW with HARTFORD COURANT.*
> *"12 noon to 1:30 P.M.: AUTOGRAPHING at BARNES AND NOBLE.*
> *"2 P.M. to 2:30 P.M.: TAPE at WDRC AM/FM.*
> *"3 P.M. to 3:30 P.M.: PRESS INTERVIEW with THE HILL INK.*
> *"7:30 P.M. to 9 P.M.: TAPE at WHNB TV/WHAT ABOUT WOMEN."*

From 12 noon to 1:30 P.M., that first day in Hartford, I talked to a man who had cut a picture of me from a magazine in 1970 and had come round to Barnes and Noble to see what I looked like in 1977. From 2 P.M. to 2:30 P.M., that first day in Hartford, I listened to the receptionists at WDRC AM/FM talk about the new records and I watched snow drop from the pine boughs in the cemetery across the street. The name of the cemetery was Mt. St. Benedict and my husband's father had been buried there. "Any Steely Dan come in?" the receptionists kept asking. From 8:30 A.M. until 9 P.M., that first day in Hartford, I neglected to mention the name of the book I was supposed to be promoting. It was my fourth book but I had never before done what is called in the trade a book tour. I was not sure what I was doing or why I was doing it. I had left California equipped with two "good" suits, a box of unanswered mail, Elizabeth Hardwick's *Seduction and Betrayal,* Edmund Wilson's *To the Finland Station,* six Judy Blume books and my eleven-year-old daughter. The Judy Blume books were along to divert my daughter. My daughter was along to divert me. Three days into the tour I sent home the box of unanswered mail to make room for a packet of Simon and Schuster press releases describing me in favorable terms. Four days into the tour I sent home *Seduction and Betrayal* and *To the Finland Station* to make room for a thousand-watt hair blower. By the time I reached Boston, ten days into the tour, I knew that I had never before heard and would possibly never again hear America singing at precisely this pitch: ethereal, speedy, an angel choir on Dexamyl.

Where were we heading. The set for this discussion was always the same: a cozy oasis of wicker and ferns in the wilderness of cables and cameras and Styrofoam coffee cups that was the actual studio. On wicker settees across the nation I expressed my conviction that we were heading "into an era" of whatever the clock seemed to demand. In green rooms across the nation I listened to other people talk about where we were heading, and also about their vocations, avocations, and secret interests. I discussed L-dopa and biorhythm with a woman whose father invented prayer breakfasts. I exchanged makeup tips with a former Mouseketeer. I stopped reading newspapers and started relying on bulletins from limo drivers, from Mouseketeers, from the callers-in on call-in shows and from the closed-circuit screens in airports that flashed random stories off the wire ("CARTER URGES BARBITURATE BAN" is one that got my attention at La Guardia) between advertisements for *Shenandoah.* I gravitated to the random. I swung with the non-sequential.

I began to see America as my own, a child's map over which my child and I could skim and light at will. We spoke not of cities but of airports. If rain fell at Logan we could find sun at Dulles. Bags lost at O'Hare could be found at Dallas/Fort Worth. In the first-class cabins of the planes on which we traveled we were often, my child and I, the only female passengers, and I apprehended for the first time those particular illusions of mobility which power American business. Time was money. Motion was progress. Decisions were snap and the ministrations of other people were constant. Room service, for example, assumed paramount importance. We needed, my eleven-year-old and I, instant but erratically timed infusions of consommé, oatmeal, crab salad and asparagus vinaigrette. We needed Perrier water and tea to drink when we were working. We needed bourbon on the rocks and Shirley Temples to drink when we were not. A kind of irritable panic came over us when room service went off, and also when no one answered in the housekeeping department. In short we had fallen into the peculiar hormonal momentum of business travel, and I had begun to understand the habituation many men and a few women have to planes and telephones and schedules. I had begun to regard my own schedule—a sheaf of thick cream-colored pages printed with the words "SIMON & SCHUSTER/A DIVISION OF GULF & WESTERN CORPORATION"—with a reverence approaching the mystical. We wanted 24-hour room service. We wanted direct-dial telephones. We wanted to stay on the road forever.

We saw air as our element. In Houston the air was warm and rich   5 and suggestive of fossil fuel and we pretended we owned a house in River Oaks. In Chicago the air was brilliant and thin and we pretended we owned the 27th floor of the Ritz. In New York the air was charged and crackling and shorting out with opinions, and we pretended we had some. Everyone in New York had opinions. Opinions were demanded in return. The absence of opinion was construed as opinion. Even my daughter was developing opinions. "Had an interesting talk with Carl Bernstein," she noted in the log she had been assigned to keep for her fifth-grade teacher in Malibu, California. Many of these New York opinions seemed intended as tonic revisions, bold corrections to opinions in vogue during the previous week, but since I had just dropped from the sky it was difficult for me to distinguish those opinions which were "bold" and "revisionist" from those which were merely "weary" and "rote." At the time I left New York many people were expressing a bold belief in "joy"—joy in children, joy in wedlock, joy in the dailiness of life—but joy was trickling down fast to show-business personalities. Mike Nichols, for example, was expressing his joy in the pages of *Newsweek,* and also his weariness with "lapidary bleakness." Lapidary bleakness was definitely rote.

We were rethinking the Sixties that week, or Morris Dickstein was.

We were taking another look at the Fifties that week, or Hilton Kramer was.

I agreed passionately. I disagreed passionately. I called room service on one phone and listened attentively on the other to people who seemed convinced that the "texture" of their lives had been agreeably or adversely affected by conversion to the politics of joy, by regression to lapidary bleakness, by the Sixties, by the Fifties, by the recent change in administrations and by the sale of *The Thorn Birds* to paper for one-million-nine.

I lost track of information.

I was blitzed by opinion.   10

I began to see opinions arcing in the air, intersecting flight patterns. The Eastern shuttle was cleared for landing and so was lapidary bleakness. John Leonard and joy were on converging vectors. I began to see the country itself as a projection on air, a kind of hologram, an invisible grid of image and opinion and electronic impulse. There were opinions in the air and there were planes in the air and there were even people in the air: one afternoon in New York my husband saw a man jump from a window and fall to the sidewalk outside the Yale Club. I mentioned this to a *Daily News* photographer who was taking my picture. "You have to catch a jumper in the act to make the paper," he advised me. He had caught two in the act but only the first had made the paper. The second was a better picture but coincided with the crash of a DC-10 at Orly. "They're all over town," the photographer said. "Jumpers. A lot of them aren't even jumpers. They're window washers. Who fall."

What does that say about us as a nation, I was asked the next day when I mentioned the jumpers and window washers on the air. *Where are we headed.* On the 27the floor of the Ritz in Chicago my daughter and I sat frozen at the breakfast table until the window washers glided safely out of sight. At a call-in station in Los Angeles I was told by the guard that there would be a delay because they had a jumper on the line. "I say let him jump," the guard said to me. I imagined a sky dense with jumpers and fallers and DC-10s. I held my daughter's hand at takeoff and landing and watched for antennae on the drive into town. The big antennae with the pulsing red lights had been for a month our landmarks. The big antennae with the pulsing red lights had in fact been for a month our destinations. "Out I-10 to the antenna" was the kind of direction we had come to understand, for we were on the road, on the grid, on the air and also in it. *Where were we heading.* I don't know where you're heading, I said in the studio attached to the last of these antennae, my eyes fixed on still another of the neon FLEETWOOD MAC signs that flickered that spring in radio stations from coast to coast, but I'm heading home.

1977

LINES OF INQUIRY
"On the Road"

Throughout this piece, Didion relies quite heavily on the repetition or echoing of particular words, phrases, or clauses, as in the opening question, "Where are we headed," which appears several times in various forms later in the piece. What are the effects of these repetitions and echoes? As a way of beginning to answer this question, underline all of the echoes and repetitions you can find in the first paragraph, and then consider their effect in this particular context. How does Didion come across and how does her point come across as a result of these echoes? Then for purposes of comparison, identify and analyze the echoes and repetitions in the final paragraph.

Between the beginning and end of this piece, Didion touches on quite a few subjects, but she keeps veering back to the experience of being "on the road" and to the question of "where are we heading." What does she convey about the experience of her cross-country tour? What does she suggest about where America is headed? What do these two subjects have to do with each other?

Fifteen years have passed since Didion made the trip on which this piece is based, so it might be interesting to consider whether or not her experiences and observations are up-to-date. Do you think her piece is consistent with the impressions of America that you get nowadays from reading the newspaper, watching TV, and traveling on your own? Or do you have a significantly different set of perceptions from hers? In what respects do you consider her portrait of America to be up-to-date? In what respects do you consider it out-of-date?

JOHN WAYNE: A LOVE SONG

In the summer of 1943 I was eight, and my father and mother and small brother and I were at Peterson Field in Colorado Springs. A hot wind blew through that summer, blew until it seemed that before August broke, all the dust in Kansas would be in Colorado, would have drifted over the tar-paper barracks and the temporary strip and stopped only when it hit Pikes Peak. There was not much to do, a summer like that: there was the day they brought in the first B-29, an event to remember but scarcely a vacation program. There was an Officers' Club, but no swimming pool; all the Officers' Club had of interest was artificial blue rain behind the bar. The rain interested me a good deal, but I could not spend the summer watching it, and so we went, my brother and I, to the movies.

We went three and four afternoons a week, sat on folding chairs in the darkened Quonset hut which served as a theater, and it was there, that summer of 1943 while the hot wind blew outside, that I first saw John Wayne. Saw the walk, heard the voice. Heard him tell the girl in a picture called *War of the Wildcats* that he would build her a house, "at the bend in the river where the cottonwoods grow." As it happened I did not grow up to be the kind of woman who is the heroine in a Western, and although the men I have known have had many virtues and have taken me to live in many places I have come to love, they have never been John Wayne, and they have never taken me to that bend in the river where the cottonwoods grow. Deep in that part of my heart where the artificial rain forever falls, that is still the line I wait to hear.

I tell you this neither in a spirit of self-revelation nor as an exercise in total recall, but simply to demonstrate that when John Wayne rode through my childhood, and perhaps through yours, he determined forever the shape of certain of our dreams. It did not seem possible that such a man could fall ill, could carry within him that most inexplicable and ungovernable of diseases. The rumor struck some obscure anxiety, threw our very childhoods into question. In John Wayne's world, John Wayne was supposed to give the orders. "Let's ride," he said, and "Saddle up." "Forward *ho,*" and "A man's gotta do what he's got to do." "Hello, there," he said when he first saw the girl, in a construction camp or on a train or just standing around on the front porch waiting for somebody to ride up through the tall grass. When John Wayne spoke, there was no mistaking his intentions; he had a sexual authority so strong that even a child could perceive it. And in a world we understood early to be characterized by venality and doubt and paralyzing ambigüities, he suggested another world, one which may or may not have existed ever but in any case existed no more: a place where a man could move free, could make his own code and live by it; a world in which, if a man did what he had to do, he could one day take the girl and go riding through the draw and find himself home free, not in a hospital with something going wrong inside, not in a high bed with the flowers and the drugs and the forced smiles, but there at the bend in the bright river, the cottonwoods shimmering in the early morning sun.

"Hello, there." Where did he come from, before the tall grass? Even his history seemed right, for it was no history at all, nothing to intrude upon the dream. Born Marion Morrison in Winterset, Iowa, the son of a druggist. Moved as a child to Lancaster, California, part of the migration to that promised land sometimes called "the west coast of Iowa." Not that Lancaster was the promise fulfilled; Lancaster was a town on the Mojave where the dust blew through. But Lancaster was still California, and it was only a year from there to Glendale, where desolation had a different flavor: antimacassars among the orange groves, a middle-class prelude to Forest Lawn. Imagine Marion Morrison in Glendale. A Boy Scout, then a student at Glendale High. A tackle for U.S.C., a Sigma Chi. Summer vacations, a job moving props on the old Fox lot. There, a meeting with John Ford, one of the several directors who were to sense that into this perfect mold might be poured the inarticulate longings of a nation wondering at just what pass the trail had been lost. "Dammit," said Raoul Walsh later, "the son of a bitch looked like a man." And so after a while the boy from Glendale became a star. He did not become an actor, as he has always been careful to point out to interviewers ("How many times do I gotta tell you, I don't act at all, I *re*-act"), but a star, and the star called John Wayne would spend most of the rest of his life with one or another of those directors, out on some forsaken location, in search of the dream.

> *Out where the skies are a trifle bluer*
> *Out where friendship's a little truer*
> *That's where the West begins.*

Nothing very bad could happen in the dream, nothing a man could not face down. But something did. There it was, the rumor, and after a while the headlines. "I licked the Big C," John Wayne announced, as John Wayne would, reducing those outlaw cells to the level of any other outlaws, but even so we all sensed that this would be the one unpredictable confrontation, the one shoot-out Wayne could lose. I have as much trouble as the next person with illusion and reality, and I did not much want to see John Wayne when he must be (or so I thought) having some trouble with it himself, but I did, and it was down in Mexico when he was making the picture his illness had so long delayed, down in the very country of the dream.

It was John Wayne's 165th picture. It was Henry Hathaway's 84th. It was number 34 for Dean Martin, who was working off an old contract to Hal Wallis, for whom it was independent production number 65. It was called *The Sons of Katie Elder,* and it was a Western, and after the three-month delay they had finally shot the exteriors up in Durango, and now they were in the waning days of interior shooting at Estudio Churubusco outside Mexico City, and the sun was hot and the air was clear and it was lunchtime. Out under the pepper trees the boys from the Mexican crew sat around sucking caramels, and down the road some of the technical men sat around a place which served a stuffed lobster and a glass of tequila for one dollar American, but it was inside the cavernous empty commissary where the talent sat around, the reasons for the exercise, all sitting around the big table picking at *huevos con queso* and Carta Blanca beer. Dean Martin, unshaven. Mack Gray, who goes where Martin goes. Bob Goodfried, who was in charge of Paramount publicity and who had flown down to arrange for a trailer and who had a delicate stomach. "Tea and toast," he warned repeatedly. "That's the ticket. You can't trust the lettuce." And Henry Hathaway, the director, who did not seem to be listening to Goodfried. And John Wayne, who did not seem to be listening to anyone.

"This week's gone slow," Dean Martin said, for the third time.

"How can you say that?" Mack Gray demanded.

"This . . . week's . . . gone . . . slow, that's how I can say it."

"You don't mean you want it to end."   10

"I'll say it right out, Mack, I want it to *end.* Tomorrow night I shave this beard, I head for the airport, I say *adios amigos!* Bye-bye *muchachos!"*

Henry Hathaway lit a cigar and patted Martin's arm fondly. "Not tomorrow, Dino."

"Henry, what are you planning to add? A World War?"

Hathaway patted Martin's arm again and gazed into the middle distance. At the end of the table someone mentioned a man who, some years before, had tried unsuccessfully to blow up an airplane.

"He's still in jail," Hathaway said suddenly.   15

"In jail?" Martin was momentarily distracted from the question whether to send his golf clubs back with Bob Goodfried or consign them to Mack Gray. "What's he in jail for if nobody got killed?"

"Attempted murder, Dino," Hathaway said gently. "A felony."

"You mean some guy just *tried* to kill me he'd end up in jail?"

Hathaway removed the cigar from his mouth and looked across the table. "Some guy just tried to kill *me* he wouldn't end up in jail. How about you, Duke?"

Very slowly, the object of Hathaway's query wiped his mouth, 20 pushed back his chair, and stood up. It was the real thing, the authentic article, the move which had climaxed a thousand scenes on 165 flickering frontiers and phantasmagoric battlefields before, and it was about to climax this one, in the commissary at Estudio Churubusco outside Mexico City. "Right," John Wayne drawled. "I'd kill him."

Almost all the cast of *Katie Elder* had gone home, that last week; only the principals were left, Wayne, and Martin, and Earl Holliman, and Michael Anderson, Jr., and Martha Hyer. Martha Hyer was not around much, but every now and then someone referred to her, usually as "the girl." They had all been together nine weeks, six of them in Durango. Mexico City was not quite Durango; wives like to come along to places like Mexico City, like to shop for handbags, go to parties at Merle Oberon Pagliai's, like to look at her paintings. But Durango. The very name hallucinates. Man's country. Out where the West begins. There had been ahuehuete trees in Durango; a waterfall, rattlesnakes. There had been weather, nights so cold that they had postponed one or two exteriors until they could shoot inside at Churubusco. "It was the girl," they explained. "You couldn't keep the girl out in cold like that." Henry Hathaway had cooked in Durango, *gazpacho* and ribs and the steaks that Dean Martin had ordered flown down from the Sands; he had wanted to cook in Mexico City, but the management of the Hotel Bamer refused to let him set up a brick barbecue in his room. "You really missed something, *Durango,*" they would say, sometimes joking and sometimes not, until it became a refrain, Eden lost.

But if Mexico City was not Durango, neither was it Beverly Hills. No one else was using Churubusco that week, and there inside the big sound stage that said LOS HIJOS DE KATIE ELDER on the door, there with the pepper trees and the bright sun outside, they could still, for just so long as the picture lasted, maintain a world peculiar to men who liked to make Westerns, a world of loyalties and fond raillery, of sentiment and shared cigars, of interminable desultory recollections; campfire talk, its only point to keep a human voice raised against the night, the wind, the rustlings in the brush.

"Stuntman got hit accidentally on a picture of mine once," Hathaway would say between takes of an elaborately choreographed fight scene. "What was his name, married Estelle Taylor, met her down in Arizona."

The circle would close around him, the cigars would be fingered. The delicate art of the staged fight was to be contemplated.

"I only hit one guy in my life," Wayne would say. "Accidentally, 25 I mean. That was Mike Mazurki."

"Some guy. Hey, Duke says he only hit one guy in his life, Mike Mazurki."

"Some choice." Murmurings, assent.

"It wasn't a choice, it was an accident."

"I can believe it."

"You bet."   30

"Oh boy. Mike Mazurki."

And so it would go. There was Web Overlander, Wayne's makeup man for twenty years, hunched in a blue Windbreaker, passing out sticks of Juicy Fruit. *"Insect* spray," he would say. "Don't tell us about insect spray. We saw insect spray in Africa, all right. Remember Africa?" Or, *"Steamer* clams. Don't tell us about steamer clams. We got our fill of steamer clams all right, on the *Hatari!* appearance tour. Remember Bookbinder's?" There was Ralph Volkie, Wayne's trainer for eleven years, wearing a red baseball cap and carrying around a clipping from Hedda Hopper, a tribute to Wayne. "This Hopper's some lady," he would say again and again. "Not like some of these guys, all they write is sick, sick, sick, how can you call that guy *sick,* when he's got pains, coughs, works all day, *never complains.* That guy's got the best hook since Dempsey, not *sick."*

And there was Wayne himself, fighting through number 165. There was Wayne, in his thirty-three-year-old spurs, his dusty neckerchief, his blue shirt. "You don't have too many worries about what to wear in these things," he said. "You can wear a blue shirt, or, if you're down in Monument Valley, you can wear a yellow shirt." There was Wayne, in a relatively new hat, a hat which made him look curiously like William S. Hart. "I had this old cavalry hat I loved, but I lent it to Sammy Davis. I got it back, it was unwearable. I think they all pushed it down on his head and said *O.K., John Wayne*—you know, a joke."

There was Wayne, working too soon, finishing the picture with a bad cold and a racking cough, so tired by late afternoon that he kept an oxygen inhalator on the set. And still nothing mattered but the Code. "That guy," he muttered of a reporter who had incurred his displeasure. "I admit I'm balding. I admit I got a tire around my middle. What man fifty-seven doesn't? Big news. Anyway, that guy."

He paused, about to expose the heart of the matter, the root of the   35
distaste, the fracture of the rules that bothered him more than the alleged misquotations, more than the intimation that he was no longer the Ringo Kid. "He comes down, uninvited, but I ask him over anyway. So we're sitting around drinking mescal out of a water jug."

He paused again and looked meaningfully at Hathaway, readying him for the unthinkable denouement. "He had to be *assisted* to his room."

They argued about the virtues of various prizefighters, they argued about the price of J & B in pesos. They argued about dialogue.

"As rough a guy as he is, Henry, I still don't think he'd raffle off his mother's *Bible*."

"I like a shocker, Duke."

They exchanged endless training-table jokes. "You know why they call this memory sauce?" Martin asked, holding up a bowl of chili.   40

"Why?"

"Because you *remember it in the morning.*"

"Hear that Duke? Hear why they call this memory sauce?"

They delighted one another by blocking out minute variations in the free-for-all fight which is a set piece in Wayne pictures; motivated or totally gratuitous, the fight sequence has to be in the picture, because they so enjoy making it. "Listen—this'll really be funny. Duke picks up the kid, see, and then it takes both Dino and Earl to throw him out the door—*how's that?*"

They communicated by sharing old jokes; they sealed their cama-   45
raderie by making gentle, old-fashioned fun of wives, those civilizers, those tamers. "So Señora Wayne takes it into her head to stay up and have one brandy. So for the rest of the night it's 'Yes, Pilar, you're right, dear. I'm a bully, Pilar, you're right, I'm impossible.' "

"You hear that? Duke says Pilar threw a table at him."

"Hey, Duke, here's something funny. That finger you hurt today, get the Doc to bandage it up, go home tonight, show it to Pilar, tell her she did it when she threw the table. You know, make her think she was really cutting up."

They treated the oldest among them respectfully; they treated the youngest fondly. "You see that kid?" they said of Michael Anderson, Jr. "What a kid."

"He don't act, it's right from the heart," said Hathaway, patting his heart.

"Hey kid," Martin said. "You're gonna be in my next picture. We'll   50
have the whole thing, no beards. The striped shirts, the girls, the hi-fi, the eye lights."

They ordered Michael Anderson his own chair, with "BIG MIKE" tooled on the back. When it arrived on the set, Hathaway hugged him. "You see that?" Anderson asked Wayne, suddenly too shy to look him in the eye. Wayne gave him the smile, the nod, the final accolade. "I saw it, kid."

On the morning of the day they were to finish *Katie Elder,* Web Overlander showed up not in his Windbreaker but in a blue blazer. "Home, Mama," he said, passing out the last of his Juicy Fruit. "I got on my getaway clothes." But he was subdued. At noon, Henry Hathaway's wife dropped by the commissary to tell him that she might fly over to Acapulco. "Go ahead," he told her. "I get through here, all I'm gonna do is take Seconal to a point just this side of suicide." They were all subdued. After Mrs. Hathaway left, there were desultory attempts at reminiscing, but man's country was receding fast; they were already halfway home, and all they could call up was the 1961 Bel Air fire, during which Henry Hathaway had ordered the Los Angeles Fire Department off his property and saved the place himself by, among other measures, throwing everything flammable into the swimming pool. "Those fire guys might've just given it up," Wayne said. "Just let it burn." In fact this was a good story, and one incorporating several of their favorite themes, but a Bel Air story was still not a Durango story.

In the early afternoon they began the last scene, and although they spent as much time as possible setting it up, the moment finally came when there was nothing to do but shoot it. "Second team out, first team in, *doors closed,*" the assistant director shouted one last time. The stand-ins walked off the set, John Wayne and Martha Hyer walked on. "All right, boys, *silencio,* this is a picture." They took it twice. Twice the girl offered John Wayne the tattered Bible. Twice John Wayne told her that "there's a lot of places I go where that wouldn't fit in." Everyone was very still. And at 2:30 that Friday afternoon Henry Hathaway turned away from the camera, and in the hush that followed he ground out his cigar in a sand bucket. "O.K.," he said. "That's it."

Since that summer of 1943 I had thought of John Wayne in a number of ways. I had thought of him driving cattle up from Texas, and bringing airplanes in on a single engine, thought of him telling the girl at the Alamo that "Republic is a beautiful word." I had never thought of him having dinner with his family and with me and my husband in an expensive restaurant in Chapultepec Park, but time brings odd mutations, and there we were, one night that last week in Mexico. For a while it was only a nice evening, an evening anywhere. We had a lot of drinks and I lost the sense that the face across the table was in certain ways more familiar than my husband's.

And then something happened. Suddenly the room seemed suffused with the dream, and I could not think why. Three men appeared out of nowhere, playing guitars. Pilar Wayne leaned slightly forward, and John Wayne lifted his glass almost imperceptibly toward her. "We'll need some Pouilly-Fuissé for the rest of the table," he said "and some red Bordeaux for the Duke." We all smiled, and drank the Pouilly-Fuissé for the rest of the table and the red Bordeaux for the Duke, and all the while the men with the guitars kept playing, until finally I realized what they were playing, what they had been playing all along: "The Red River Valley" and the theme from *The High and the Mighty.* They did not quite get the beat right, but even now I can hear them, in another country and a long time later, even as I tell you this.

1965

LINES OF INQUIRY
"John Wayne: A Love Song"

Didion tells three stories in this essay: about the time in her childhood when she first saw John Wayne; about the early life and movie career of John Wayne; and about the final week in the filming of *The Sons of Katie Elder*. Rather than beginning with a story about her own childhood, why doesn't Didion begin with the story of Wayne's early life? What relevance does her story have to the stories about Wayne? Why, in turn, does she devote so little time to the story of Wayne's overall career and so much time to the story of one week in the filming of 1 of his 165 movies? In other words, how do you account for her selection, arrangement, and proportioning of these stories?

In paragraph 3, Didion claims that "when John Wayne rode through my childhood, and perhaps through yours, he determined forever the shape of certain of our dreams." What kinds of dreams is she referring to here? In what sense(s) are those dreams related to the dream (in paragraph 4) that she claims John Wayne was "in search of" for most of his life? How, in turn, are Didion's dreams and Wayne's dream related to the dream that "the room seemed suffused with" in the final paragraph of the essay? What can you infer about Didion's attitudes towards all of the dreams and dreamers that she writes about in her essay? Have you ever had any such dreams yourself?

Didion's essay on Wayne is not her only effort at portraiture, as you can see by looking at her essay on the artist, Georgia O'Keeffe, which also appears in this collection. In what respects does she use similar techniques in portraying these two persons? In what respects does she not? How do you account for the similarities and differences?

GEORGIA O'KEEFFE

"**W**here I was born and where and how I have lived is unimportant," Georgia O'Keeffe told us in the book of paintings and words published in her ninetieth year on earth. She seemed to be advising us to forget the beautiful face in the Stieglitz photographs. She appeared to be dismissing the rather condescending romance that had attached to her by then, the romance of extreme good looks and advanced age and deliberate isolation. "It is what I have done with where I have been that should be of interest." I recall an August afternoon in Chicago in 1973 when I took my daughter, then seven, to see what Georgia O'Keeffe had done with where she had been. One of the vast O'Keeffe "Sky Above Clouds" canvases floated over the back stairs in the Chicago Art Institute that day, dominating what seemed to be several stories of empty light, and my daughter looked at it once, ran to the landing, and kept on looking. "Who drew it," she whispered after a while. I told her. "I need to talk to her," she said finally.

My daughter was making, that day in Chicago, an entirely unconscious but quite basic assumption about people and the work they do. She was assuming that the glory she saw in the work reflected a glory in its maker, that the painting was the painter as the poem is the poet, that every choice one made alone—every word chosen or rejected, every brush stroke laid or not laid down—betrayed one's character. *Style is character*. It seemed to me that afternoon that I had rarely seen so instinctive an application of this familiar principle, and I recall being pleased not only that my daughter responded to style as character but that it was Georgia O'Keeffe's particular style to which she responded: this was a hard woman who had imposed her 192 square feet of clouds on Chicago.

"Hardness" has not been in our century a quality much admired in women, nor in the past twenty years has it even been in official favor for men. When hardness surfaces in the very old we tend to transform it into "crustiness" or eccentricity, some tonic pepperiness to be indulged at a distance. On the evidence of her work and what she has said about it, Georgia O'Keeffe is neither "crusty" nor eccentric. She is simply hard, a straight shooter, a woman clean of received wisdom and open to what she sees. This is a woman who could early on dismiss most of her contemporaries as "dreamy," and would later single out one she liked as "a very poor painter." (And then add, apparently by way of softening the judgment: "I guess he wasn't a painter at all. He had no courage and I believe that to create one's own world in any of the arts takes courage.") This is a woman who in 1939 could advise her admirers that they were missing her point, that their appreciation of her famous flowers was merely sentimental. "When I paint a red hill," she observed coolly in the catalogue for an exhibition that year, "you say it is too bad that I don't always paint flowers. A flower touches almost everyone's heart. A red hill doesn't touch everyone's heart." This is a woman who could describe the genesis of one of her most well-known paintings—the "Cow's Skull: Red, White and Blue" owned by the Metropolitan—as an act of quite deliberate and derisive orneriness. "I thought of the city men I had been seeing in the East," she wrote. "They talked so often of writing the Great American Novel—the Great American Play—the Great American Poetry. . . . So as I was painting my cow's head on blue I thought to myself, 'I'll make it an American painting. They will not think it great with the red stripes down the sides—Red, White and Blue—but they will notice it.' "

The city men. The men. They. The words crop up again and again as this astonishingly aggressive woman tells us what was on her mind when she was making her astonishingly aggressive paintings. It was those city men who stood accused of sentimentalizing her flowers: "I made you take time to look at what I saw and when you took time to really notice my flower you hung all your associations with flowers on my flower and you write about my flower as if I think and see what you think and see—and I don't." *And I don't.* Imagine those words spoken, and the sound you hear is *don't tread on me.* "The men" believed it impossible to paint New York, so Georgia O'Keeffe painted New York. "The men" didn't think much of her bright color, so she made it brighter. The men yearned toward Europe so she went to Texas, and then New Mexico. The men talked about Cézanne, "long involved remarks about the 'plastic quality' of his form and color," and took one another's long involved remarks, in the view of this angelic rattlesnake in their midst, altogether too seriously. "I can paint one of those dismal-colored paintings like the men," the woman who regarded herself always as an outsider remembers thinking one day in 1922, and she did: a painting of a shed "all low-toned and dreary with the tree beside the door." She called this act of rancor "The Shanty" and hung it in her next show. "The men seemed to approve of it," she reported fifty-four years later, her contempt undimmed. "They seemed to think that maybe I was beginning to paint. That was my only low-toned dismal-colored painting."

Some women fight and others do not. Like so many successful 5 guerrillas in the war between the sexes, Georgia O'Keeffe seems to have been equipped early with an immutable sense of who she was and a fairly clear understanding that she would be required to prove it. On the surface her upbringing was conventional. She was a child on the Wisconsin prairie who played with china dolls and painted watercolors with cloudy skies because sunlight was too hard to paint and, with her brother and sisters, listened every night to her mother read stories of the Wild West, of Texas, of Kit Carson and Billy the Kid. She told adults that she wanted to be an artist and was embarrassed when they asked what kind of artist she wanted to be: she had no idea "what kind." She had no idea what artists did. She had never seen a picture that interested her, other than a pen-and-ink Maid of Athens in one of her mother's books, some Mother Goose illustrations printed on cloth, a tablet cover that showed a little girl with pink roses, and the painting of Arabs on horseback that hung in her grandmother's parlor. At thirteen, in a Dominican convent, she was mortified when the sister corrected her drawing. At Chatham Episcopal Institute in Virginia she painted lilacs and sneaked time alone to walk out to where she could see the line of the Blue Ridge Mountains on the horizon. At the Art Institute in Chicago she was shocked by the presence of live models and wanted to abandon anatomy lessons. At the Art Students League in New York one of her fellow students advised her that, since he would be a great painter and she would end up teaching painting in a girls' school, any work of hers was less important than modeling for him. Another painted over her work to show her how the Impressionists did trees. She had not before heard how the Impressionists did trees and she did not much care.

At twenty-four she left all those opinions behind and went for the first time to live in Texas, where there were no trees to paint and no one to tell her how not to paint them. In Texas there was only the horizon she craved. In Texas she had her sister Claudia with her for a while, and in the late afternoons they would walk away from town and toward the horizon and watch the evening star come out. "That evening star fascinated me," she wrote. "It was in some way very exciting to me. My sister had a gun, and as we walked she would throw bottles into the air and shoot as many as she could before they hit the ground. I had nothing but to walk into nowhere and the wide sunset space with the star. Ten watercolors were made from that star." In a way one's interest is compelled as much by the sister Claudia with the gun as by the painter Georgia with the star, but only the painter left us this shining record. Ten watercolors were made from that star.

1976

LINES OF INQUIRY
"Georgia O'Keeffe"

Rather than beginning this piece with a statement of her own, Didion opens it with a quotation from O'Keeffe, and at several other points Didion refers to statements by O'Keeffe. What impression of O'Keeffe did you get from these quotations? What purpose do you suppose that Didion had in mind for repeating and echoing bits and pieces of O'Keeffe's remarks as she does in paragraphs 3 and 4?

Given the title of this piece, consider exactly what you learned about O'Keeffe from reading it. What are the most notable things that you learned about O'Keeffe's life? About her personality? About her art? Which of these topics do you think was uppermost in Didion's mind? What do you think is the single most important point about O'Keeffe that Didion is trying to make in this essay?

Now that you know what Didion and some other people have thought and said about O'Keefe's art, take a look at it yourself to decide what you think of it. For example, locate a book in the library that reproduces some of her paintings, or see if you can find any of her work at a nearby museum. What qualities do you find in her work? Do her paintings seem "astonishingly aggressive" to you? Aside from this phrase of Didion, what other words would you use to describe O'Keefe's painting?

ON KEEPING A NOTEBOOK

" 'That woman Estelle,' " the note reads, " 'is partly the reason why George Sharp and I are separated today.' *Dirty crepe-de-Chine wrapper, hotel bar, Wilmington RR, 9:45 a.m. August Monday morning."*

Since the note is in my notebook, it presumably has some meaning to me. I study it for a long while. At first I have only the most general notion of what I was doing on an August Monday morning in the bar of the hotel across from the Pennsylvania Railroad station in Wilmington, Delaware (waiting for a train? missing one? 1960? 1961? why Wilmington?), but I do remember being there. The woman in the dirty crepe-de-Chine wrapper had come down from her room for a beer, and the bartender had heard before the reason why George Sharp and she were separated today. "Sure," he said, and went on mopping the floor. "You told me." At the other end of the bar is a girl. She is talking, pointedly, not to the man beside her but to a cat lying in the triangle of sunlight cast through the open door. She is wearing a plaid silk dress from Peck & Peck, and the hem is coming down.

Here is what it is: the girl has been on the Eastern Shore, and now she is going back to the city, leaving the man beside her, and all she can see ahead are the viscous summer sidewalks and the 3 a.m. long-distance calls that will make her lie awake and then sleep drugged through all the steaming mornings left in August (1960? 1961?). Because she must go directly from the train to lunch in New York, she wishes that she had a safety pin for the hem of the plaid silk dress, and she also wishes that she could forget about the hem and the lunch and stay in the cool bar that smells of disinfectant and malt and make friends with the woman in the crepe-de-Chine wrapper. She is afflicted by a little self-pity, and she wants to compare Estelles. That is what that was all about.

Why did I write it down? In order to remember, of course, but exactly what was it I wanted to remember? How much of it actually happened? Did any of it? Why do I keep a notebook at all? It is easy to deceive oneself on all those scores. The impulse to write things down is a peculiarly compulsive one, inexplicable to those who do not share it, useful only accidentally, only secondarily, in the way that any compulsion tries to justify itself. I suppose that it begins or does not begin in the cradle. Although I have felt compelled to write things down since I was five years old, I doubt that my daughter ever will, for she is a singularly blessed and accepting child, delighted with life exactly as life presents itself to her, unafraid to go to sleep and unafraid to wake up.

Keepers of private notebooks are a different breed altogether, lonely and resistant rearrangers of things, anxious malcontents, children afflicted apparently at birth with some presentiment of loss.

My first notebook was a Big Five tablet, given to me by my mother   5
with the sensible suggestion that I stop whining and learn to amuse myself by writing down my thoughts., She returned the tablet to me a few years ago; the first entry is an account of a woman who believed herself to be freezing to death in the Arctic night, only to find, when day broke, that she had stumbled onto the Sahara Desert, where she would die of the heat before lunch. I have no idea what turn of a five-year-old's mind could have prompted so insistently "ironic" and exotic a story, but it does reveal a certain predilection for the extreme which has dogged me into adult life; perhaps if I were analytically inclined I would find it a truer story than any I might have told about Donald Johnson's birthday party or the day my cousin Brenda put Kitty Litter in the aquarium.

So the point of my keeping a notebook has never been, nor is it now, to have an accurate factual record of what I have been doing or thinking. That would be a different impulse entirely, an instinct for reality which I sometimes envy but do not possess. At no point have I ever been able successfully to keep a diary; my approach to daily life ranges from the grossly negligent to the merely absent, and on those few occasions when I have tried dutifully to record a day's events, boredom has so overcome me that the results are mysterious at best. What is this business about "shopping, typing piece, dinner with E, depressed"? Shopping for what? Typing what piece? Who is E? Was this "E" depressed, or was I depressed? Who cares?

In fact I have abandoned altogether that kind of pointless entry; instead I tell what some would call lies. "That's simply not true," the members of my family frequently tell me when they come up against my memory of a shared event. "The party was *not* for you, the spider was *not* a black widow, *it wasn't that way at all.*" Very likely they are right, for not only have I always had trouble distinguishing between what happened and what merely might have happened, but I remain unconvinced that the distinction, for my purposes, matters. The cracked crab that I recall having for lunch the day my father came home from Detroit in 1945 must certainly be embroidery, worked into the day's pattern to lend verisimilitude; I was ten years old and would not now remember the cracked crab. The day's events did not turn on cracked crab. And yet it is precisely that fictitious crab that makes me see the afternoon all over again, a home movie run all too often, the father bearing gifts, the child weeping, an exercise in family love and guilt. Or that is what it was to me. Similarly, perhaps it never did snow that

August in Vermont; perhaps there never were flurries in the night wind, and maybe no one else felt the ground hardening and summer already dead even as we pretended to bask in it, but that was how it felt to me, and it might as well have snowed, could have snowed, did snow.

How it felt to me: that is getting closer to the truth about a notebook. I sometimes delude myself about why I keep a notebook, imagine that some thrifty virtue derives from preserving everything observed. See enough and write it down, I tell myself, and then some morning when the world seems drained of wonder, some day when I am only going through the motions of doing what I am supposed to do, which is write—on that bankrupt morning I will simply open my notebook and there it will all be, a forgotten account with accumulated interest, paid passage back to the world out there: dialogue overheard in hotels and elevators and at the hat-check counter in Pavillon (one middle-aged man shows his hat check to another and says, "That's my old football number"); impressions of Bettina Apthekcr and Benjamin Sonnenberg and Teddy ("Mr. Acapulco") Stauffer; careful *aperçus* about tennis bums and failed fashion models and Greek shipping heiresses, one of whom taught me a significant lesson (a lesson I could have learned from F. Scott Fitzgerald, but perhaps we all must meet the very rich for ourselves) by asking, when I arrived to interview her in her orchid-filled sitting room on the second day of a paralyzing New York blizzard, whether it was snowing outside.

I imagine, in other words, that the notebook is about other people. But of course it is not. I have no real business with what one stranger said to another at the hat-check counter in Pavillon; in fact I suspect that the line "That's my old football number" touched not my own imagination at all, but merely some memory of something once read, probably "The Eighty-Yard Run." Nor is my concern with a woman in a dirty crepe-de-Chine wrapper in a Wilmington bar. My stake is always, of course, in the unmentioned girl in the plaid silk dress. *Remember what it was to be me:* that is always the point.

It is a difficult point to admit. We are brought up in the ethic that others, any others, all others, are by definition more interesting than ourselves; taught to be diffident, just this side of self-effacing. ("You're the least important person in the room and don't forget it," Jessica Mitford's governess would hiss in her ear on the advent of any social occasion; I copied that into my notebook because it is only recently that I have been able to enter a room without hearing some such phrase in my inner ear.) Only the very young and the very old may recount their dreams at breakfast, dwell upon self, interrupt with memories of beach picnics and favorite Liberty lawn dresses and the rainbow trout in a creek near Colorado Springs. The rest of us are expected, rightly, to

10

affect absorption in other people's favorite dresses, other people's trout.

And so we do. But our notebooks give us away, for however dutifully we record what we see around us, the common denominator of all we see is always, transparently, shamelessly, the implacable "I." We are not talking here about the kind of notebook that is patently for public consumption, a structural conceit for binding together a series of graceful *pensées;* we are talking about something private, about bits of t'ie mind's string too short to use, an indiscriminate and erratic assemblage with meaning only for its maker.

And sometimes even the maker has difficulty with the meaning. There does not seem to be, for example, any point in my knowing for the rest of my life that, during 1964, 720 tons of soot fell on every square mile of New York City, yet there it is in my notebook, labeled "FACT". Nor do I really need to remember that Ambrose Bierce liked to spell Leland Stanford's name "£eland $tanford" or that "smart women almost always wear black in Cuba," a fashion hint without much potential for practical application. And does not the relevance of these notes seem marginal at best?:

In the basement museum of the Inyo County Courthouse in Independence, California, sign pinned to a mandarin coat: "This MANDARIN COAT was often worn by Mrs. Minnie S. Brooks when giving lectures on her TEAPOT COLLECTION."

Redhead getting out of car in front of Beverly Wilshire Hotel, chinchilla stole, Vuitton bags with tags reading:

MRS LOU FOX
HOTEL SAHARA
VEGAS

Well, perhaps not entirely marginal. As a matter of fact, Mrs. Minnie S. Brooks and her MANDARIN COAT pull me back into my own childhood, for although I never knew Mrs. Brooks and did not visit Inyo County until I was thirty, I grew up in just such a world, in houses cluttered with Indian relics and bits of gold ore and ambergris and the souvenirs my Aunt Mercy Farnsworth brought back from the Orient. It is a long way from that world to Mrs. Lou Fox's world, where we all live now, and is it not just as well to remember that? Might not Mrs. Minnie S. Brooks help me to remember what I am? Might not Mrs. Lou Fox help me to remember what I am not?

But sometimes the point is harder to discern. What exactly did I have in mind when I noted down that it cost the father of someone I know $650 a month to light the place on the Hudson in which he lived before the Crash? What use was I planning to make of this line by

Jimmy Hoffa: "I may have my faults, but being wrong ain't one of them"? And although I think it interesting to know where the girls who travel with the Syndicate have their hair done when they find themselves on the West Coast, will I ever make suitable use of it? Might I not be better off just passing it on to John O'Hara? What is a recipe for sauerkraut doing in my notebook? What kind of magpie keeps this notebook? *"He was born the night the Titanic went down."* That seems a nice enough line, and I even recall who said it, but is it not really a better line in life than it could ever be in fiction?

But of course that is exactly it: not that I should ever use the line,   15 but that I should remember the woman who said it and the afternoon I heard it. We were on her terrace by the sea, and we were finishing the wine left from lunch, trying to get what sun there was, a California winter sun. The woman whose husband was born the night the *Titanic* went down wanted to rent her house, wanted to go back to her children in Paris. I remember wishing that I could afford the house, which cost $1,000 a month. "Someday you will," she said lazily. "Someday it all comes." There in the sun on her terrace it seemed easy to believe in someday, but later I had a low-grade afternoon hangover and ran over a black snake on the way to the supermarket and was flooded with inexplicable fear when I heard the checkout clerk explaining to the man ahead of me why she was finally divorcing her husband. "He left me no choice," she said over and over as she punched the register. "He has a little seven-month-old baby by her, he left me no choice." I would like to believe that my dread then was for the human condition, but of course it was for me, because I wanted a baby and did not then have one and because I wanted to own the house that cost $1,000 a month to rent and because I had a hangover.

It all comes back. Perhaps it is difficult to see the value in having one's self back in that kind of mood, but I do see it; I think we are well advised to keep on nodding terms with the people we used to be, whether we find them attractive company or not. Otherwise they turn up unannounced and surprise us, come hammering on the mind's door at 4 a.m. of a bad night and demand to know who deserted them, who betrayed them, who is going to make amends. We forget all too soon the things we thought we could never forget. We forget the loves and the betrayals alike, forget what we whispered and what we screamed, forget who we were. I have already lost touch with a couple of people I used to be; one of them, a seventeen-year-old, presents little threat, although it would be of some interest to me to know again what it feels like to sit on a river levee drinking vodka-and-orange-juice and listening to Les Paul and Mary Ford and their echoes sing "How High the Moon" on the car radio. (You see I still have the scenes, but I no longer perceive myself among those present, no longer could even improvise the dialogue.) The other one, a twenty-three-year-old, bothers me more.

She was always a good deal of trouble, and I suspect she will reappear when I least want to see her, skirts too long, shy to the point of aggravation, always the injured party, full of recriminations and little hurts and stories I do not want to hear again, at once saddening me and angering me with her vulnerability and ignorance, an apparition all the more insistent for being so long banished.

It is a good idea, then, to keep in touch, and I suppose that keeping in touch is what notebooks are all about. And we are all on our own when it comes to keeping those lines open to ourselves: your notebook will never help me, nor mine you. *"So what's new in the whiskey business?"* What could that possibly mean to you? To me it means a blonde in a Pucci bathing suit sitting with a couple of fat men by the pool at the Beverly Hills Hotel. Another man approaches, and they all regard one another in silence for a while. "So what's new in the whiskey business?" one of the fat men finally says by way of welcome, and the blonde stands up, arches one foot and dips it in the pool, looking all the while at the cabaña where Baby Pignatari is talking on the telephone. That is all there is to that, except that several years later I saw the blonde coming out of Saks Fifth Avenue in New York with her California complexion and a voluminous mink coat. In the harsh wind that day she looked old and irrevocably tired to me, and even the skins in the mink coat were not worked the way they were doing them that year, not the way she would have wanted them done, and there is the point of the story. For a while after that I did not like to look in the mirror, and my eyes would skim the newspapers and pick out only the deaths, the cancer victims, the premature coronaries, the suicides, and I stopped riding the Lexington Avenue IRT because I noticed for the first time that all the strangers I had seen for years—the man with the seeing-eye dog, the spinster who read the classified pages every day, the fat girl who always got off with me at Grand Central—looked older than they once had.

It all comes back. Even that recipe for sauerkraut: even that brings it back. I was on Fire Island when I first made that sauerkraut, and it was raining, and we drank a lot of bourbon and ate the sauerkraut and went to bed at ten, and I listened to the rain and the Atlantic and felt safe. I made the sauerkraut again last night and it did not make me feel any safer, but that is, as they say, another story.

1966

LINES OF INQUIRY
"On Keeping a Notebook"

From the beginning to the end of her essay, Didion gives us short, sample excerpts from her notebook, but none of the passages that she cites refers to her own past activities, thoughts, or feelings. What is her purpose in citing these passages? How, exactly, do they fit into her rationale for keeping a notebook? If such passages are meant to keep her in touch with her former selves, why does she tell us that she often has trouble in making sense of these notes?

Near the end of her essay (in paragraph 16), Didion advises us "to keep on nodding terms with the people we used to be." Else, she warns us, "they turn up unannounced and surprise us." What do you think she means by the people we used to be? And how can they possibly turn up unannounced and surprise us? why does she believe that keeping a notebook is the best way of "keeping those lines open to ourselves"? Why mightn't an album of personal snapshots do just as well?

Near the end of her essay (again in paragraph 16), Didion says that she has "already lost touch with a couple of people I used to be." According to this statement and others like it, she evidently looks upon her self as a changeable person. How changeable—how unchangeable—a person does she seem to be in her essays that appear in this collection? What kind of person does she seem to be in each piece? What aspect of her self does she seem most concerned with in each piece? In what respects does she seem to change—in what respects does she seem to remain the same—from one essay to the next?

WHY I WRITE

Of course I stole the title for this talk from George Orwell. One reason I stole it was that I like the sound of the words: *Why I Write.* There you have three short unambiguous words that share a sound, and the sound they share is this:

I

I

I

In many ways writing is the act of saying *I,* of imposing oneself upon other people, of saying *listen to me, see it my way, change your mind.* It's an aggressive, even a hostile act. You can disguise its aggressiveness all you want with veils of subordinate clauses and qualifiers and tentative subjunctives, with ellipses and evasions—with the whole manner of intimating rather than claiming, of alluding rather than stating—but there's no getting around the fact that setting words on paper is the tactic of a secret bully, an invasion, an imposition of the writer's sensibility on the reader's most private space.

I stole the title not only because the words sounded right but because they seemed to sum up, in a no-nonsense way, all I have to tell you. Like many writers I have only this one "subject," this one "area": the act of writing. I can bring you no reports from any other front. I may have other interests: I am "interested," for example, in marine biology, but I don't flatter myself that you would come out to hear me talk about it. I am not a scholar. I am not in the least an intellectual, which is not to say that when I hear the word "intellectual" I reach for my gun, but only to say that I do not think in abstracts. During the years when I was an undergraduate at Berkeley I tried, with a kind of hopeless late-adolescent energy, to buy some temporary visa into the world of ideas, to forge for myself a mind that could deal with the abstract.

In short I tried to think. I failed. My attention veered inexorably back to the specific, to the tangible, to what was generally considered, by everyone I knew then and for that matter have known since, the peripheral. I would try to contemplate the Hegelian dialectic and would find myself concentrating instead on a flowering pear tree outside my window and the particular way the petals fell on my floor. I would try to read linguistic theory and would find myself wondering instead if the lights were on in the bevatron up the hill. When I say that I was wondering if the lights were on in the bevatron you might immediately suspect, if you deal in ideas at all, that I was registering the bevatron as a political symbol, thinking in shorthand about the military-industrial complex and its role in the university community, but you would be wrong. I was only wondering if the lights were on in the bevatron, and how they looked. A physical fact.

I had trouble graduating from Berkeley, not because of this inability to deal with ideas—I was majoring in English, and I could locate the house-and-garden imagery in *The Portrait of a Lady* as well as the next person, "imagery" being by definition the kind of specific that got my attention—but simply because I had neglected to take a course in Milton. For reasons which now sound baroque I needed a degree by the end of that summer, and the English department finally agreed, if I would come down from Sacramento every Friday and talk about the cosmology of *Paradise Lost,* to certify me proficient in Milton. I did this. Some Fridays I took the Greyhound bus, other Fridays I caught the Southern Pacific's City of San Francisco on the last leg of its transcontinental trip. I can no longer tell you whether Milton put the sun or the earth at the center of his universe in *Paradise Lost,* the central question of at least one century and a topic about which I wrote 10,000 words that summer, but I can still recall the exact rancidity of the butter in the City of San Francisco's dining car, and the way the tinted windows on the Greyhound bus cast the oil refineries around Carquinez Straits into a grayed and obscurely sinister light. In short my attention was always on the periphery, on what I would see and taste and touch, on the butter, and the Greyhound bus. During those years I was traveling on what I knew to be a very shaky passport, forged papers: I knew that I was no legitimate resident in any world of ideas. I knew I couldn't think. All I knew then was what I couldn't do. All I knew then was what I wasn't, and it took me some years to discover what I was.

Which was a writer.

By which I mean not a "good" writer or a "bad" writer but simply a writer, a person whose most absorbed and passionate hours are spent arranging words on pieces of paper. Had my credentials been in order I would never have become a writer. Had I been blessed with even limited access to my own mind there would have been no reason to write. I write entirely to find out what I'm thinking, what I'm looking at, what I see and what it means. What I want and what I fear. Why did the oil refineries around Carquinez Straits seem sinister to me in the summer of 1956? Why have the night lights in the bevatron burned in my mind for twenty years? *What is going on in these pictures in my mind?*

When I talk about pictures in my mind I am talking, quite specifically, about images that shimmer around the edges. There used to be an illustration in every elementary psychology book showing a cat drawn by a patient in varying stages of schizophrenia. This cat had a shimmer around it. You could see the molecular structure breaking down at the very edges of the cat: the cat became the background and the background the cat, everything interacting, exchanging ions. People on hallucinogens describe the same perception of objects. I'm not a schizophrenic, nor do I take hallucinogens, but certain images do shimmer for me. Look hard enough, and you can't miss the shimmer. It's there. You can't think too much about these pictures that shimmer. You just lie low and let them develop. You stay quiet. You don't talk to many people and you keep your nervous system from shorting out and try to locate the cat in the shimmer, the grammar in the picture.

Just as I meant "shimmer" literally I mean "grammar" literally. Grammar is a piano I play by ear, since I seem to have been out of school the year the rules were mentioned. All I know about grammar is its infinite power. To shift the structure of a sentence alters the meaning of that sentence, as definitely and inflexibly as the position of a camera alters the meaning of the object photographed. Many people know about camera angles now, but not so many know about sentences. The arrangement of the words matters, and the arrangement you want can be found in the picture in your mind. The picture dictates the arrangement. The picture dictates whether this will be a sentence with or without clauses, a sentence that ends hard or a dying-fall sentence, long or short, active or passive. The picture tells you how to arrange the words and the arrangement of the words tells you, or tells me, what's going on in the picture. *Nota bene:*

It tells you.

You don't tell it.

Let me show you what I mean by pictures in the mind. I began *Play It as It Lays* just as I have begun each of my novels, with no notion of "character" or "plot" or even "incident." I had only two pictures in my mind, more about which later, and a technical intention, which was to write a novel so elliptical and fast that it would be over before you noticed it, a novel so fast that it would scarcely exist on the page at all. About the pictures: the first was of white space. Empty space. This was clearly the picture that dictated the narrative intention of the book—a book in which anything that happened would happen off the page, a "white" book to which the reader would have to bring his or her own bad dreams—and yet this picture told me no "story," suggested no situation. The second picture did. This second picture was of something actually witnessed. A young woman with long hair and a short white halter dress walks through the casino at the Riviera in Las Vegas at one in the morning. She crosses the casino alone and picks up a house telephone. I watch her because I have heard her paged, and recognize her name: she is a minor actress I see around Los Angeles from time to time, in places like Jax and once in a gynecologist's office in the Beverly Hills Clinic, but have never met. I know nothing about her. Who is paging her? Why is she here to be paged? How exactly did she come to this? It was precisely this moment in Las Vegas that made *Play It as It Lays* begin

10

to tell itself to me, but the moment appears in the novel only obliquely, in a chapter which begins:

> Maria made a list of things she would never do. She would never: walk through the Sands or Caesar's alone after midnight. She would never: ball at a party, do S-M unless she wanted to, borrow furs from Abe Lipsey, deal. She would never: carry a Yorkshire in Beverly Hills.

That is the beginning of the chapter and that is also the end of the chapter, which may suggest what I meant by "white space."

I recall having a number of pictures in my mind when I began the novel I just finished, *A Book of Common Prayer.* As a matter of fact one of these pictures was of that bevatron I mentioned, although I would be hard put to tell you a story in which nuclear energy figured. Another was a newspaper photograph of a hijacked 707 burning on the desert in the Middle East. Another was the night view from a room in which I once spent a week with paratyphoid, a hotel room on the Colombian coast. My husband and I seemed to be on the Colombian coast representing the United States of America at a film festival (I recall invoking the name "Jack Valenti" a lot, as if its reiteration could make me well), and it was a bad place to have fever, not only because my indisposition offended our hosts but because every night in this hotel the generator failed. The lights went out. The elevator stopped. My husband would go to the event of the evening and make excuses for me and I would stay alone in this hotel room, in the dark. I remember standing at the window trying to call Bogotá (the telephone seemed to work on the same principle as the generator) and watching the night wind come up and wondering what I was doing eleven degrees off the equator with a fever of 103. The view from that window definitely figures in *A Book of Common Prayer,* as does the burning 707, and yet none of these pictures told me the story I needed.

The picture that did, the picture that shimmered and made these other images coalesce, was the Panama airport at 6 A.M. I was in this airport only once, on a plane to Bogotá that stopped for an hour to refuel, but the way it looked that morning remained superimposed on everything I saw until the day I finished *A Book of Common Prayer.* I lived in that airport for several years. I can still feel the hot air when I step off the plane, can see the heat already rising off the tarmac at 6 A.M. I can feel my skirt damp and wrinkled on my legs. I can feel the asphalt stick to my sandals. I remember the big tail of a Pan American plane floating motionless down at the end of the tarmac. I remember the sound of a slot machine in the waiting room. I could tell you that I remember a particular woman in the airport, an American woman, a *norteamericana,* a thin *norteamericana* about 40 who wore a big square emerald in lieu of a wedding ring, but there was no such woman there.

15

I put this woman in the airport later. I made this woman up, just as I later made up a country to put the airport in, and a family to run the country. This woman in the airport is neither catching a plane nor meeting one. She is ordering tea in the airport coffee shop. In fact she is not simply "ordering" tea but insisting that the water be boiled, in front of her, for twenty minutes. Why is this woman in this airport? Why is she going nowhere, where has she been? Where did she get that big emerald? What derangement, or disassociation, makes her believe that her will to see the water boiled can possibly prevail?

> She had been going to one airport or another for four months, one could see it, looking at the visas on her passport. All those airports where Charlotte Douglas's passport had been stamped would have looked alike. Sometimes the sign on the tower would say "Bienvenidos" and sometimes the sign on the tower would say "Bienvenue," some places were wet and hot and others dry and hot, but at each of these airports the pastel concrete walls would rust and stain and the swamp off the runway would be littered with the fuselages of cannibalized Fairchild F-227's and the water would need boiling.
> I knew why Charlotte went to the airport even if Victor did not.
> I knew about airports.

These lines appear about halfway through *A Book of Common Prayer,* but I wrote them during the second week I worked on the book, long before I had any idea where Charlotte Douglas had been or why she went to airports. Until I wrote these lines I had no character called "Victor" in mind: the necessity for mentioning a name, and the name "Victor," occurred to me as I wrote the sentence. *I knew why Charlotte went to the airport* sounded incomplete. *I knew why Charlotte went to the airport even if Victor did not* carried a little more narrative drive. Most important of all, until I wrote these lines I did not know who "I" was, who was telling the story. I had intended until that moment that the "I" be no more than the voice of the author, a 19th-century omniscient narrator. But there it was:

> I knew why Charlotte went to the airport even if Victor did not.
> I knew about airports.

This "I" was the voice of no author in my house. This "I" was someone who not only knew why Charlotte went to the airport but also knew someone called "Victor." Who was Victor? Who was this narrator? Why was this narrator telling me this story? Let me tell you one thing about why writers write: had I known the answer to any of these questions I would never have needed to write a novel.

[1976]

LINES OF INQUIRY
"Why I Write"

Although the title of this essay leads one to expect that Didion will offer a detailed definition and explanation of her motive(s) for writing, she directly discusses her reasons only in paragraph 7. Why does she spend so much time instead telling stories to illustrate her undergraduate "attention . . . to the specific, to the tangible" and her subsequent preoccupation with "pictures in my mind"? Given her undergraduate attention to things she could "see and taste and touch," how do you account for her later preoccupation as a novelist with "pictures in my mind"? In other words, what reason(s), if any, does she offer for her apparent shift of attention from tangible things to mental pictures, from actual to imaginary experience?

Didion begins and ends her essay not by talking about tangible things or about mental pictures, but about "I." What does she mean by saying that "In many respects writing is the act of saying I"? How does her conviction about the I-ness of writing square with her commitment to tangible things and mental pictures? And how, in turn, do these apparently different commitments square with the belief she expresses in paragraph 9 in the "infinite power" of "grammar"? In other words, what, if any, is the unifying principle in her convictions about writing?

"Why I Write" is not the only essay in which Didion discusses her writing, as you can see by looking at her previous piece in this collection, "On Keeping a Notebook." What similarities, what differences, do you see in her ideas about writing, her reasons for writing, and her way of conveying what she has to say about writing in these two essays? How do you account for the differences?

ANNIE DILLARD

1945 –

I am a frayed and nibbled survivor in a fallen world, and I am getting along. I am aging and eaten and have done my share of eating too. I am not washed and beautiful, in control of a shining world in which everything fits, but instead am wandering awed about on a splintered wreck I've come to care for, whose gnawed trees breathe a delicate air, whose bloodied and scarred creatures are my dearest companions, and whose beauty beats and shines not in its imperfections but overwhelmingly in spite of them, under the wind-rent clouds, upstream and down.

Thus does Annie Dillard characterize herself, the world she inhabits, and her relationship to that world in her best-selling *Pilgrim at Tinker Creek* (1974). That book won Dillard, then only twenty-nine, a Pulitzer Prize and a lasting place in the ranks of contemporary writers of creative nonfiction. Echoing Thoreau's *Walden,* it chronicles a year's sojourn on the banks and in the environs of Tinker Creek in the Roanoke Valley of Virginia by a "wanderer with a background in theology and a penchant for quirky facts," a year of walking, watching, and writing with breath-stopping precision about what she sees—and what she learns to see. Here as in her subsequent works, she sees both sides of the world, dark along with light, and insists on confounding their traditional associations: "If we are blinded by darkness, we are also blinded by light." The effect in her writing is a kind of *chiaroscuro,* light and darkness intensifying each other by juxtaposition with their opposite. And while the world might be "fallen," a "splintered wreck," it is still filled with a "beauty" that "beats and shines," inspiring Dillard to register her response in richly poetic language filled with surprise and delight.

Dillard was born in 1945 in Pittsburgh, the eldest of three daughters in a well-to-do family. She has written of her early years in her most recent book, *An American Childhood* (1987), "I grew up in Pittsburgh in the 1950s, in a house full of comedians, reading books." She attended private girls' schools, spent summers at the lake or the country club pool, took dancing lessons, planned to be an architect, and "began a life of reading books, and drawing, and playing at the sciences." Above all, she read books, "to delirium," and her memoir of childhood is more than anything else the record of an emerging consciousness shaped by reading. Despite the privileged conformity in which she was raised, she thought of herself as fierce, odd, and difficult, and one of her high-school teachers described her this way: "Here, alas, is a child of the twentieth century."

She began writing poetry while she was still in high school, and at Hollins College in Virginia's Blue Ridge Mountains she continued reading and writing, but with more seriousness and discipline. After completing her undergraduate degree in English in 1967, she continued her apprenticeship in the Hollins graduate writing program, earning a master's degree in 1968. Her first book was a collection of poems, *Tickets for a Prayer Wheel* (1973), which appeared while she was still living in the Roanoke Valley. In 1975 she traveled west to teach writing at Western Washington State College on the Puget Sound, and in 1979 she crossed the country again, returning to the east coast to accept a position at Wesleyan College in Connecticut, where she still makes her home.

In her early published prose work, Dillard staked out for herself a distinctive combination of form and content—essays which focus on a personal experience of the natural world and which employ to an elaborate degree the techniques of poetry. Her attention to the sounds and rhythms of language, her evident pleasure in precise and suggestive words, are hallmarks of her style. Readers of her prose have become accustomed to finding sentences or whole passages which are lyric, even rhapsodic, and which, in their use of metaphor, rhyme, and repetition of sound and syntactic structure, would be equally at home in a poem, as would this one: "There are no events but thoughts and the heart's hard turning, the heart's slow learning where to love and whom."

Dillard herself, though, has insisted that "any art, including an art of surface, must do more than dazzle." Her own subject, as she has expressed it, is "the paradoxical nature of all our days, the curious way we bump up against the unexpected everywhere," and that description of her subject applies equally to her style. Beauty is a serious enough motive for writing, to be sure, but other serious impulses are at work in Dillard's writing—in particular the quest for spiritual enlightenment, for knowledge of who made such a world as that in which she finds herself, and why. "What's going on here? Who's in charge?" are the questions which constitute her refrain. She is in bold terms "a seeker, a pilgrim in the religious sense of the word," as one critic puts it, pressing always toward a definition of what it means to be a believer.

Persistently she seeks to know the world in all its minute detail, not to blink at the horror which is the twin of joy, to find in what she sees a key to what it all might mean. Always for Dillard it is language which transforms sight into insight, which opens the door to significance:

> Seeing is of course very much a matter of verbalization. Unless I call my attention to what passes before my eyes, I simply won't see it. It is, as Ruskin says, "not merely unnoticed, but in the full clear sense of the word, unseen." . . . I have to say the words, describe what I'm

seeing. . . . Otherwise, especially in a strange place, I'll never know what's happening.

One critic has said Dillard is "a connoisseur of spirit, who knows that seeing, if intense enough, becomes vision."

Dillard seeks vision, though, in often homely sources: the ways of cats, the wastes of violent weather, a mockingbird's flight, a flash of light from the side of swimming fish, the grotesqueries of the insect world, the profligacy of nature. Far from refusing to acknowledge what is awful about the intricate texture of creation, she confronts it in its most gruesome details—a praying mantis devouring her mate in the act of coition, a giant water bug sucking a frog dry of its liquid life. Yet, even as the emptied frog skin rumples and sinks, it is beauty and grace that Dillard insistently seeks and celebrates:

> As a thinker I keep discovering that beauty itself is as much a fact, and a mystery, as the most gruesome parastic roundworm. I consider nature's facts—its beautiful and grotesque forms and events—in terms of their import to thought and their impetus to the spirit. In nature I find grace tangled in a rapture with violence; I find an intricate landscape whose forms are fringed with death; I find mystery, newness, and a kind of exuberant, spendthrift energy.

The rapturous tangle of grace with violence is for Dillard not an obstacle to faith but the central mystery of being, the paradox which is the doorway to the satisfaction of spiritual longing for contact with a creator who is anything but tame:

> The texture of the world, its filigree and scrollwork, means that there is the possibility for beauty here, a beauty inexhaustible in its complexity, which opens to my knock, which answers in me a call I do not remember calling, and which trains me to the wild and extravagant nature of the spirit I seek.

Her recent essays, collected in *Teaching a Stone to Talk* (1982), continue to press that vision, but in contrast with *Pilgrim at Tinker Creek* their settings are sometimes far-flung and often exotic—an imaginary polar expedition, the Galapagos Islands, the rivers and jungles and villages of South America. "Possibly because Father had loaded his boat one day and gone down the Ohio River, I confused leaving with living, and vowed that when I got my freedom, I would be the one to do both." Always, though, however broad or narrow her setting, the record of the human spirit impressing itself on the world is the central fact of her work. She sees "the mind and the world as inextricably fitted twin puzzles. The mind fits the world and shapes it as a river fits and shapes its own banks." The essay form is particularly well-suited to such a project, and in keeping with her vision Dillard's essays repeatedly confound the distinctions between factual narrative and story, just as in their style they blur the boundaries between poetry and prose:

> What interests me here, and elsewhere, is the possibility for a purified nonfiction narration—a kind of Chekhovian storytelling which might illuminate the actual world with a delicate light—coupled with humor in the American tradition and no comment.

Dillard's preoccupations, finally, are not new ones; she worries in all her work the questions about time, change, mortality, and the presence of evil which have obsessed the race since the dawn of history. Her contributions are to the style and form of the essay, and they have been significant. She has made her mark as a storyteller with a gift for depicting her vision of the world in writing that delights as much as it reveals:

> I intend only to tell some small stories, and to depict precise moments precisely, in the hope that a collection of such moments might give an impression of many sharp points going in different directions—might give a vivid sense of complexity.

THE DEATH OF A MOTH

Transfiguration in a Candle Flame

I live alone with two cats, who sleep on my legs. There is a yellow one, and a black one whose name is Small. In the morning I joke to the black one, Do you remember last night? Do you remember? I throw them both out before breakfast, so I can eat.

There is a spider, too, in the bathroom, of uncertain lineage, bulbous at the abdomen and drab, whose six-inch mess of web works, works somehow, works miraculously, to keep her alive and me amazed. The web is in a corner behind the toilet, connecting tile wall to tile wall. The house is new, the bathroom immaculate, save for the spider, her web, and the sixteen or so corpses she's tossed to the floor.

The corpses appear to be mostly sow bugs, those little armadillo creatures who live to travel flat out in houses, and die round. In addition to sow-bug husks, hollow and sipped empty of color, there are what seem to be two or three wingless moth bodies, one new flake of earwig, and three spider carcasses crinkled and clenched.

I wonder on what fool's errand an earwig, or a moth, or a sow bug, would visit that clean corner of the house behind the toilet; I have not noticed any blind parades of sow bugs blundering into corners. Yet they do hazard there, at a rate of more than one a week, and the spider thrives. Yesterday she was working on the earwig, mouth on gut; today he's on the floor. It must take a certain genius to throw things away from there, to find a straight line through that sticky tangle to the floor.

Today the earwig shines darkly, and gleams, what there is of him: 5
a dorsal curve of thorax and abdomen, and a smooth pair of pincers by which I knew his name. Next week, if the other bodies are any indication, he'll be shrunk and gray, webbed to the floor with dust. The sow bugs beside him are curled and empty, fragile, a breath away from brittle fluff. The spiders lie on their sides, translucent and ragged, their legs drying in knots. The moths stagger against each other, headless, in a confusion of arcing strips of chitin like peeling varnish, like a jumble of buttresses for cathedral vaults, like nothing resembling moths, so that I would hesitate to call them moths, except that I have had some experience with the figure Moth reduced to a nub.

Two summers ago I was camped alone in the Blue Ridge Mountains of Virginia. I had hauled myself and gear up there to read, among other things, *The Day on Fire,* by James Ullman, a novel about Rimbaud that had made me want to be a writer when I was sixteen; I was hoping it would do it again. So I read every day sitting under a tree by my tent, while warblers sang in the leaves overhead and bristle worms trailed their inches over the twiggy dirt at my feet; and I read every night by candlelight, while barred owls called in the forest and pale moths seeking mates massed round my head in the clearing, where my light made a ring.

Moths kept flying into the candle. They would hiss and recoil, reeling upside down in the shadows among my cooking pans. Or they would singe their wings and fall, and their hot wings, as if melted, would stick to the first thing they touched—a pan, a lid, a spoon—so that the snagged moths could struggle only in tiny arcs, unable to flutter free. These I could release by a quick flip with a stick; in the morning I would find my cooking stuff decorated with torn flecks of moth wings, ghostly triangles of shiny dust here and there on the aluminum. So I read, and boiled water, and replenished candles, and read on.

One night a moth flew into the candle, was caught, burnt dry, and held. I must have been staring at the candle, or maybe I looked up where a shadow crossed my page; at any rate, I saw it all. A golden female moth, a biggish one with a two-inch wingspread, flapped into the fire, dropped abdomen into the wet wax, stuck, flamed, and frazzled in a second. Her moving wings ignited like tissue paper, like angels' wings, enlarging the circle of light in the clearing and creating out of the darkness the sudden blue sleeves of my sweater, the green leaves of jewelweed by my side, the ragged red trunk of a pine; at once the light contracted again and the moth's wings vanished in a fine, foul smoke. At the same time, her six legs clawed, curled, blackened, and ceased, disappearing utterly. And her head jerked in spasms, making a spattering noise; her antennae crisped and burnt away and her heaving mouthparts cracked like pistol fire. When it was all over, her head was, so far as I could determine, gone, gone the long way of her wings and legs. Her head was a hole lost to time. All that was left was the glowing horn shell of her abdomen and thorax—a fraying, partially collapsed gold tube jammed upright in the candle's round pool.

And then this moth-essence, this spectacular skeleton, began to act as a wick. She kept burning. The wax rose in the moth's body from her soaking abdomen to her thorax to the shattered hole where her head should have been, and widened into flame, a saffron-yellow flame that robed her to the ground like an immolating monk. That candle had two wicks, two winding flames of identical light, side by side. The moth's head was fire. She burned for two hours, until I blew her out.

She burned for two hours without changing, without swaying or   10
kneeling—only glowing within, like a building fire glimpsed through silhouetted walls, like a hollow saint, like a flame-faced virgin gone to God, while I read by her light, kindled, while Rimbaud in Paris burnt out his brain in a thousand poems, while night pooled wetly at my feet.

So. That is why I think those hollow shreds on the bathroom floor are moths. I believe I know what moths look like, in any state.

I have three candles here on the table which I disentangle from the plants and light when visitors come. The cats avoid them, although Small's tail caught fire once; I rubbed it out before she noticed. I don't mind living alone. I like eating alone and reading. I don't mind sleeping alone. The only time I mind being alone is when something is funny; then, when I am laughing at something funny, I wish someone were around. Sometimes I think it is pretty funny that I sleep alone.

LINES OF INQUIRY
"The Death of a Moth"

The second section of this piece, in which Dillard vividly describes the striking spectacle of a moth burning to death in a candle flame, could easily stand alone, for like a well-told story it contains a clear-cut beginning, middle, and end. What, then, is the purpose of the first and third sections? Why does Dillard go to so much trouble in the first section to describe all of the insect carcasses littering the corner of her bathroom, and why in the third section does she give so much attention to her feelings about living alone?

Given the fact that she combines details about the moth with details about her own existence, it seems appropriate to consider what they have to do with each other. What does the death of a moth have to do with the life of Dillard? In particular, what does the spectacle of the moth burning for two hours have to do with Dillard's living alone? What does that spectacle have to do with her aspirations as a writer? Why in her subtitle does she refer to that spectacle as a "transfiguration"?

In this piece, as in "Living Like Weasels," Dillard uses the existence or experience of another creature as a metaphor for a way of living that she wishes to emulate. What similarities, what differences, do you see in the way she develops her metaphor in each piece? What similarities, what differences, do you see in the way of living that Dillard is concerned with in each case?

LIVING LIKE WEASELS

A weasel is wild. Who knows what he thinks? He sleeps in his underground den, his tail draped over his nose. Sometimes he lives in his den for two days without leaving. Outside, he stalks rabbits, mice, muskrats, and birds, killing more bodies than he can eat warm, and often dragging the carcasses home. Obedient to instinct, he bites his prey at the neck, either splitting the jugular vein at the throat or crunching the brain at the base of the skull, and he does not let go. One naturalist refused to kill a weasel who was socketed into his hand deeply as a rattlesnake. The man could in no way pry the tiny weasel off, and he had to walk half a mile to water, the weasel dangling from his palm, and soak him off like a stubborn label.

And once, says Ernest Thompson Seton—once, a man shot an eagle out of the sky. He examined the eagle and found the dry skull of a weasel fixed by the jaws to his throat. The supposition is that the eagle had pounced on the weasel and the weasel swiveled and bit as instinct taught him, tooth to neck, and nearly won. I would like to have seen that eagle from the air a few weeks or months before he was shot: was the whole weasel still attached to his feathered throat, a fur pendant? Or did the eagle eat what he could reach, gutting the living weasel with his talons before his breast, bending his beak, cleaning the beautiful airborne bones?

I have been reading about weasels because I saw one last week. I startled a weasel who startled me, and we exchanged a long glance.

Twenty minutes from my house, through the woods by the quarry and across the highway, is Hollins Pond, a remarkable piece of shallow-ness, where I like to go at sunset and sit on a tree trunk. Hollins Pond is also called Murray's Pond; it covers two acres of bottomland near Tinker Creek with six inches of water and six thousand lily pads. In winter, brown-and-white steers stand in the middle of it, merely damp-ening their hooves; from the distant shore they look like miracle itself, complete with miracle's nonchalance. Now, in summer, the steers are gone. The water lilies have blossomed and spread to a green horizontal plane that is terra firma to plodding blackbirds, and tremulous ceiling to black leeches, crayfish, and carp.

This is, mind you, suburbia. It is a five-minute walk in three direc-tions to rows of houses, though none is visible here. There's a 55 mph highway at one end of the pond, and a nesting pair of wood ducks at the other. Under every bush is a muskrat hole or a beer can. The far end is an alternating series of fields and woods, fields and woods, threaded everywhere with motorcycle tracks—in whose bare clay wild turtles lay eggs.

So. I had crossed the highway, stepped over two low barbed-wire fences, and traced the motorcycle path in all gratitude through the wild rose and poison ivy of the pond's shoreline up into high grassy fields. Then I cut down through the woods to the mossy fallen tree where I sit. This tree is excellent. It makes a dry, upholstered bench at the upper, marshy end of the pond, a plush jetty raised from the thorny shore between a shallow blue body of water and a deep blue body of sky.

The sun had just set. I was relaxed on the tree trunk, ensconced in the lap of lichen, watching the lily pads at my feet tremble and part dreamily over the thrusting path of a carp. A yellow bird appeared to my right and flew behind me. It caught my eye; I swiveled around— and the next instant, inexplicably, I was looking down at a weasel, who was looking up at me.

Weasel! I'd never seen one wild before. He was ten inches long, thin as a curve, a muscled ribbon, brown as fruitwood, soft-furred, alert. His face was fierce, small and pointed as a lizard's; he would have made a good arrowhead. There was just a dot of chin, maybe two brown hairs' worth, and then the pure white fur began that spread down his underside. He had two black eyes I didn't see, any more than you see a window.

The weasel was stunned into stillness as he was emerging from beneath an enormous shaggy wild rose bush four feet away. I was stunned into stillness twisted backward on the tree trunk. Our eyes locked, and someone threw away the key.

Our look was as if two lovers, or deadly enemies, met unexpectedly on an overgrown path when each had been thinking of something else: a clearing blow to the gut. It was also a bright blow to the brain, or a sudden beating of brains, with all the charge and intimate grate of rubbed balloons. It emptied our lungs. It felled the forest, moved the fields, and drained the pond; the world dismantled and tumbled into that black hole of eyes. If you and I looked at each other that way, our skulls would split and drop to our shoulders. But we don't. We keep our skulls. So.

He disappeared. This was only last week, and already I don't remember what shattered the enchantment. I think I blinked, I think I retrieved my brain from the weasel's brain, and tried to memorize what I was seeing, and the weasel felt the yank of separation, the careening splashdown into real life and the urgent current of instinct. He vanished under the wild rose. I waited motionless, my mind suddenly full of data and my spirit with pleadings, but he didn't return.

Please do not tell me about "approach-avoidance conflicts." I tell you I've been in that weasel's brain for sixty seconds, and he was in mine. Brains are private places, muttering through unique and secret tapes—but the weasel and I both plugged into another tape simultaneously, for a sweet and shocking time. Can I help it if it was a blank?

What goes on in his brain the rest of the time? What does a weasel think about? He won't say. His journal is tracks in clay, a spray of feathers, mouse blood and bone, uncollected, unconnected, loose-leaf, and blown.

I would like to learn, or remember, how to live. I come to Hollins Pond not so much to learn how to live as, frankly, to forget about it. That is, I don't think I can learn from a wild animal how to live in particular—shall I suck warm blood, hold my tail high, walk with my footprints precisely over the prints of my hands?—but I might learn something of mindlessness, something of the purity of living in the physical senses and the dignity of living without bias or motive. The weasel lives in necessity and we live in choice, hating necessity and dying at the last ignobly in its talons. I would like to live as I should, as the weasel lives as he should. And I suspect that for me the way is like the weasel's: open to time and death painlessly, noticing everything, remembering nothing, choosing the given with a fierce and pointed will.

I missed my chance. I should have gone for the throat. I should have lunged for that streak of white under the weasel's chin and held on, held on through mud and into the wild rose, held on for a dearer life. We could live under the wild rose wild as weasels, mute and uncomprehending. I could very calmly go wild. I could live two days in the den, curled, leaning on mouse fur, sniffing bird bones, blinking, licking, breathing musk, my hair tangled in the roots of grasses. Down is a good place to go, where the mind is single. Down is out, out of your ever-loving mind and back to your careless senses. I remember muteness as a prolonged and giddy fast, where every moment is a feast of utterance received. Time and events are merely poured, unremarked, and ingested directly, like blood pulsed into my gut through a jugular vein. Could two live that way? Could two live under the wild rose, and explore by the pond, so that the smooth mind of each is as everywhere present to the other, and as received and as unchallenged, as falling snow?

We could, you know. We can live any way we want. People take vows of poverty, chastity, and obedience—even of silence—by choice. The thing is to stalk your calling in a certain skilled and supple way, to locate the most tender and live spot and plug into that pulse. This is yielding, not fighting. A weasel doesn't "attack" anything; a weasel

lives as he's meant to, yielding at every moment to the perfect freedom
of single necessity.

I think it would be well, and proper, and obedient, and pure, to
grasp your one necessity and not let it go, to dangle from it limp wherever it takes you. Then even death, where you're going no matter how
you live, cannot you part. Seize it and let it seize you up aloft even, till
your eyes burn out and drop; let your musky flesh fall off in shreds,
and let your very bones unhinge and scatter, loosened over fields, over
fields and woods, lightly, thoughtless, from any height at all, from as
high as eagles.

commas for emphasis.

catalog

*echo of
Previous
Section*

framing image – Red herred by new context.

LINES OF INQUIRY
"Living Like Weasels"

From the beginning to the end of this essay, Dillard covers quite a bit of
territory. How does she manage to get from her opening description of weasels
to her concluding meditation on how to live? How does she organize and develop her essay to show what she perceives to be the relationship between the
two? Exactly how does each of the six sections in the piece contribute to Dillard's ideas about "living like weasels"? What would be lost—what gained,
perhaps—by omitting most of the second section, except for the first paragraph
of it? What would be the effect(s) of omitting the entire fifth section?

Given the importance of weasels in this essay it seems appropriate to consider exactly what information Dillard conveys about them. What aspects of
weasel life does she report in this piece? What aspects of their behavior are
most important to her? Exactly what does Dillard see in their way of living that
applies to the lives of human beings? What do you suppose would be some of the
consequences—both beneficial and detrimental—of living like weasels?

Think of an animal whose way of living is especially interesting and appealing to you, and do some reading about the animal, much as Dillard read
about weasels, to learn about its most distinctive behavior. What aspect of this
animal's behavior is most striking and most fraught with implications for the
lives of human beings? What would it be like for human beings to live like
this animal?

sections

*1 Introducing his powerful force of instinct + Q
2 setting of the encounter
3 the encounter + Q
4 C+C human + weasel (answer Q)
5 ∴ what it adds up to, what we should do
6 Summary – repair image in new context*

THE DEER AT PROVIDENCIA

There were four of us North Americans in the jungle, in the Ecuadorian jungle on the banks of the Napo River in the Amazon watershed. The other three North Americans were metropolitan men. We stayed in tents in one riverside village, and visited others. At the village called Providencia we saw a sight which moved us, and which shocked the men.

The first thing we saw when we climbed the riverbank to the village of Providencia was the deer. It was roped to a tree on the grass clearing near the thatch shelter where we would eat lunch.

The deer was small, about the size of a whitetail fawn, but apparently full-grown. It had a rope around its neck and three feet caught in the rope. Someone said that the dogs had caught it that morning and the villagers were going to cook and eat it that night.

This clearing lay at the edge of the little thatched-hut village. We could see the villagers going about their business, scattering feed corn for hens about their houses, and wandering down paths to the river to bathe. The village headman was our host; he stood beside us as we watched the deer struggle. Several village boys were interested in the deer; they formed part of the circle we made around it in the clearing. So also did four businessmen from Quito who were attempting to guide us around the jungle. Few of the very different people standing in this circle had a common language. We watched the deer, and no one said much.

The deer lay on its side at the rope's very end, so the rope lacked   5
slack to let it rest its head in the dust. It was "pretty," delicate of bone like all deer, and thin-skinned for the tropics. Its skin looked virtually hairless, in fact, and almost translucent, like a membrane. Its neck was no thicker than my wrist; it was rubbed open on the rope, and gashed. Trying to paw itself free of the rope, the deer had scratched its own neck with its hooves. The raw underside of its neck showed red stripes and some bruises bleeding inside the muscles. Now three of its feet were hooked in the rope under its jaw. It could not stand, of course, on one leg, so it could not move to slacken the rope and ease the pull on its throat and enable it to rest its head.

Repeatedly the deer paused, motionless, its eyes veiled, with only its rib cage in motion, and its breaths the only sound. Then, after I would think, "It has given up; now it will die," it would heave. The rope twanged; the tree leaves clattered; the deer's free foot beat the ground. We stepped back and held our breaths. It thrashed, kicking, but only one leg moved; the other three legs tightened inside the rope's loop. Its hip jerked; its spine shook. Its eyes rolled; its tongue, thick with spittle, pushed in and out. Then it would rest again. We watched this for fifteen minutes.

Once three young native boys charged in, released its trapped legs, and jumped back to the circle of people. But instantly the deer scratched up its neck with its hooves and snared its forelegs in the rope again. It was easy to imagine a third and then a fourth leg soon stuck, like Brer Rabbit and the Tar Baby.

We watched the deer from the circle, and then we drifted on to lunch. Our palm-roofed shelter stood on a grassy promontory from which we could see the deer tied to the tree, pigs and hens walking under village houses, and black-and-white cattle standing in the river. There was even a breeze.

Lunch, which was the second and better lunch we had that day, was hot and fried. There was a big fish called *doncella,* a kind of catfish, dipped whole in corn flour and beaten egg, then deep fried. With our fingers we pulled soft fragments of it from its sides to our plates, and ate; it was delicate fish-flesh, fresh and mild. Someone found the roe, and I ate of that too—it was fat and stronger, like egg yolk, naturally enough, and warm.

There was also a stew of meat in shreds with rice and pale brown gravy. I had asked what kind of deer it was tied to the tree; Pepe had answered in Spanish, *"Gama."* Now they told us this was *gama* too, stewed. I suspect the word means merely game or venison. At any rate, I heard that the village dogs had cornered another deer just yesterday, and it was this deer which we were now eating in full sight of the whole article. It was good. I was surprised at its tenderness. But it is a fact that high levels of lactic acid, which builds up in muscle tissues during exertion, tenderizes.

After the fish and meat we ate bananas fried in chunks and served on a tray; they were sweet and full of flavor. I felt terrific. My shirt was wet and cool from swimming; I had had a night's sleep, two decent walks, three meals, and a swim—everything tasted good. From time to time each of us, separately, would look beyond our shaded roof to the sunny spot where the deer was still convulsing in the dust. Our meal completed, we walked around the deer and back to the boats.

That night I learned that while we were watching the deer, the others were watching me.

We four North Americans grew close in the jungle in a way that was not the usual artificial intimacy of travelers. We liked each other. We stayed up all that night talking, murmuring, as though we rocked on hammocks slung above time. The others were from big cities: New York, Washington, Boston. They all said that I had no expression on my face when I was watching the deer—or at any rate, not the expression they expected.

They had looked to see how I, the only woman, and the youngest, was taking the sight of the deer's struggles. I looked detached, apparently, or hard, or calm, or focused, still. I don't know. I was thinking. I remember feeling very old and energetic. I could say like Thoreau that I have traveled widely in Roanoke, Virginia. I have thought a great deal about carnivorousness; I eat meat. These things are not issues; they are mysteries.

Gentlemen of the city, what surprises you? That there is suffering   15
here, or that I know it?

We lay in the tent and talked. "If it had been my wife," one man said with special vigor, amazed, "she wouldn't have cared *what* was going on; she would have dropped *everything* right at that moment and gone in the village from here to there to there, she would not have *stopped* until that animal was out of its suffering one way or another. She couldn't *bear* to see a creature in agony like that."

I nodded.

Now I am home. When I wake I comb my hair before the mirror above my dresser. Every morning for the past two years I have seen in that mirror, beside my sleep-softened face, the blackened face of a burnt man. It is a wire-service photograph clipped from a newspaper and taped to my mirror. The caption reads: "Alan McDonald in Miami hospital bed." All you can see in the photograph is a smudged triangle of face from his eyelids to his lower lip; the rest is bandages. You cannot see the expression in his eyes; the bandages shade them.

The story, headed MAN BURNED FOR SECOND TIME, begins:

"Why does God hate me?" Alan McDonald asked from his hospital bed.
"When the gunpowder went off, I couldn't believe it," he said. "I just couldn't believe it. I said, 'No, God couldn't do this to me again.' "

He was in a burn ward in Miami, in serious condition. I do not   20
even know if he lived. I wrote him a letter at the time, cringing.

He had been burned before, thirteen years previously, by flaming gasoline. For years he had been having his body restored and his face remade in dozens of operations. He had been a boy, and then a burnt boy. He had already been stunned by what could happen, by how life could veer.

Once I read that people who survive bad burns tend to go crazy; they have a very high suicide rate. Medicine cannot ease their pain;

drugs just leak away, soaking the sheets, because there is no skin to hold them in. The people just lie there and weep. Later they kill themselves. They had not known, before they were burned, that the world included such suffering, that life could permit them personally such pain.

This time a bowl of gunpowder had exploded on McDonald.

> "I didn't realize what had happened at first," he recounted. "And then I heard that sound from 13 years ago. I was burning. I rolled to put the fire out and I thought, 'Oh God, not again.'
>
> "If my friend hadn't been there, I would have jumped into a canal with a rock around my neck."

His wife concludes the piece, "Man, it just isn't fair."

I read the whole clipping again every morning. This is the Big Time here, every minute of it. Will someone please explain to Alan McDonald in his dignity, to the deer at Providencia in his dignity, what is going on? And mail me the carbon.

When we walked by the deer at Providencia for the last time, I said to Pepe, with a pitying glance at the deer, *"Pobrecito"*—"poor little thing." But I was trying out Spanish. I knew at the time it was a ridiculous thing to say.

LINES OF INQUIRY
"The Deer at Providencia"

According to her male traveling companions, Dillard "looked detached, apparently, or hard, or calm" while she was looking at "the deer's struggles." How does she come across when she is describing the deer and its struggles? What does the wording of her description suggest about her attitude? What does her choice of descriptive details suggest about her attitude? What do her remarks in the final paragraph imply about her attitude?

The story of the deer and of people's differing reactions to its struggles, which appears in sections 1–7 and 10, could easily stand on its own. Why, then, do you suppose that Dillard includes the story of Alan McDonald in this piece? What do the deer and Alan McDonald have in common? What sets them apart? How does Dillard's attitude towards McDonald compare with her apparent attitude toward the deer?

In sections 1, 6, and 7, Dillard clearly makes an issue of the difference between her reaction to the deer and the reactions of her male traveling companions, and in sections 6 and 7 she also reports on how the men too made an issue of her reaction, as if to suggest that they perceived it as being atypical of women. In what respects do you think her reaction to the deer is atypical? In what respects, for example, is the supposed reaction of one man's wife, as outlined in section 7, more typical of women? To what extent do you believe that the reaction of women (or of men) can be typified?

SINGING WITH THE FUNDAMENTALISTS

It is early spring. I have a temporary office at a state university on the West Coast. The office is on the third floor. It looks down on the Square, the enormous open courtyard at the center of campus. From my desk I see hundreds of people moving between classes. There is a large circular fountain in the Square's center.

Early one morning, on the first day of spring quarter, I hear singing. A pack of students has gathered at the fountain. They are singing something which, at this distance, and through the heavy window, sounds good.

I know who these singing students are: they are the Fundamentalists. This campus has a lot of them. Mornings they sing on the Square; it is their only perceptible activity. What are they singing? Whatever it is, I want to join them, for I like to sing; whatever it is, I want to take my stand with them, for I am drawn to their very absurdity, their innocent indifference to what people think. My colleagues and students here, and my friends everywhere, dislike and fear Christian fundamentalists. You may never have met such people, but you've heard what they do: they pile up money, vote in blocs, and elect right-wing crazies; they censor books; they carry handguns; they fight fluoride in the drinking water and evolution in the schools; probably they would lynch people if they could get away with it. I'm not sure my friends are correct. I close my pen and join the singers on the Square.

There is a clapping song in progress. I have to concentrate to follow it:

> Come on, rejoice,
> And let your heart sing,
> Come on, rejoice,
> Give power to the king.
> Singing alleluia—
> He is the king of kings;
> Singing alleluia—
> He is the king of kings.

Two song leaders are standing on the broad rim of the fountain; the water is splashing just behind them. The boy is short, hard-faced, with a moustache. He bangs his guitar with the backs of his fingers. The blonde girl, who leads the clapping, is bouncy; she wears a bit of make-up. Both are wearing blue jeans.

5

The students beside me are wearing blue jeans, too—and athletic jerseys, parkas, football jackets, turtlenecks, and hiking shoes or jogging shoes. They all have canvas or nylon book bags. They look like any random batch of seventy or eighty students at this university. They are grubby or scrubbed, mostly scrubbed; they are tall, fair, or red-headed in large proportions. Their parents are white-collar workers, blue-collar workers, farmers, loggers, orchardists, merchants, fishermen; their names are, I'll bet, Olsen, Jensen, Seversen, Hansen, Klok-ker, Sigurdsen.

Despite the vigor of the clapping song, no one seems to be giving it much effort. And no one looks at anyone else; there are no sentimental glances and smiles, no glances even of recognition. These kids don't seem to know each other. We stand at the fountain's side, out on the broad, bricked Square in front of the science building, and sing the clapping song through three times.

It is quarter to nine in the morning. Hundreds of people are crossing the Square. These passersby—faculty, staff, students—pay very little attention to us; this morning singing has gone on for years. Most of them look at us directly, then ignore us, for there is nothing to see: no animal sacrifices, no lynchings, no collection plate for Jesse Helms, no seizures, snake handling, healing, or glossolalia. There is barely anything to hear. I suspect the people glance at us to learn if we are really singing: how could so many people make so little sound? My fellow singers, who ignore each other, certainly ignore passersby as well. Within a week, most of them will have their eyes closed anyway.

We move directly to another song, a slower one.

> He is my peace
> Who has broken down every wall;
> He is my peace,
> He is my peace.
>
> Cast all your cares on him,
> For he careth for you—oo—oo
> He is my peace,
> He is my peace.

I am paying strict attention to the song leaders, for I am singing at   10
the top of my lungs and I've never heard any of these songs before. They are not the old American low-church Protestant hymns; they are not the old European high-church Protestant hymns. These hymns seem to have been written just yesterday, apparently by the same people who put out lyrical Christian greeting cards and bookmarks.

"Where do these songs come from?" I ask a girl standing next to me. She seems appalled to be addressed at all, and startled by the question. "They're from the praise albums!" she explains, and moves away.

The songs' melodies run dominant, subdominant, dominant, tonic, dominant. The pace is slow, about the pace of "Tell Laura I Love Her," and with that song's quavering, long notes. The lyrics are simple and repetitive; there are very few of them to which a devout Jew or Mohammedan could not give wholehearted assent. These songs are similar to the things Catholics sing in church these days. I don't know if any studies have been done to correlate the introduction of contemporary songs into Catholic churches with those churches' decline in membership, or with the phenomenon of Catholic converts' applying to enter cloistered monasteries directly, without passing through parish churches.

> I'm set free to worship,
> I'm set free to praise him,
> I'm set free to dance before the Lord . . .

At nine o'clock sharp we quit and scatter. I hear a few quiet "see you's." Mostly the students leave quickly, as if they didn't want to be seen. The Square empties.

The next day we show up again, at twenty to nine. The same two leaders stand on the fountain's rim; the fountain is pouring down behind them.

After the first song, the boy with the moustache hollers, "Move on   10
up! Some of you guys aren't paying attention back there! You're talking to each other. I want you to concentrate!" The students laugh, embarrassed for him. He sounds like a teacher. No one moves. The girl breaks into the next song, which we join at once:

> In my life, Lord,
> Be glorified, be glorified, be glorified;
> In my life, Lord,
> Be glorified, be glorified, today.

At the end of this singularly monotonous verse, which is straining my tolerance for singing virtually anything, the boy with the moustache startles me by shouting, "Classes!"

At once, without skipping a beat, we sing, "In my classes, Lord, be glorified, be glorified . . ." I give fleet thought to the class I'm teaching this afternoon. We're reading a little "Talk of the Town" piece called "Eggbag," about a cat in a magic store on Eighth Avenue. "Relationships!" the boy calls. The students seem to sing "In my relationships, Lord," more easily than they sang "classes." They seemed embarrassed by "classes." In fact, to my fascination, they seem embarrassed by almost everything. Why are they here? I will sing with the Fundamentalists every weekday morning all spring; I will decide, tentatively, that they come pretty much for the same reasons I do: each has a private relationship with "the Lord" and will put up with a lot of junk for it.

I have taught some Fundamentalist students here, and know a bit of what they think. They are college students above all, worried about their love lives, their grades, and finding jobs. Some support moderate Democrats; some support moderate Republicans. Like their classmates, most support nuclear freeze, ERA, and an end to the draft. I believe they are divided on abortion and busing. They are not particularly political. They read *Christianity Today* and *Campus Life* and *Eternity*— moderate, sensible magazines, I think; they read a lot of C. S. Lewis. (One such student, who seemed perfectly tolerant of me and my shoddy Christianity, introduced me to C. S. Lewis's critical book on Charles Williams.) They read the Bible. I think they all "believe in" organic evolution. The main thing about them is this; there isn't any "them." Their views vary. They don't know each other.

Their common Christianity puts them, if anywhere, to the left of their classmates. I believe they also tend to be more able than their classmates to think well in the abstract, and also to recognize the complexity of moral issues. But I may be wrong.

In 1980, the media were certainly wrong about television evange- 15 lists. Printed estimates of Jerry Falwell's television audience ranged from 18 million to 30 million people. In fact, according to Arbitron's actual counts, fewer than 1.5 million people were watching Falwell. And, according to an Emory University study, those who did watch television evangelists didn't necessarily vote with them. Emory University sociologist G. Melton Mobley reports, "When that message turns political, they cut it off." Analysis of the 1982 off-year elections turned up no Fundamentalist bloc voting. The media were wrong, but no one printed retractions.

The media were wrong, too, in a tendency to identify all fundamentalist Christians with Falwell and his ilk, and to attribute to them, across the board, conservative views.

Someone has sent me two recent issues of *Eternity: The Evangelical Monthly*. One lead article criticizes a television preacher for saying that the United States had never used military might to take land from another nation. The same article censures Newspeak, saying that government rhetoric would have us believe in a "clean bomb," would have us believe that we "defend" America by invading foreign soil, and would have us believe that the dictatorships we support are "democracies." "When the President of the United States says that one reason to support defense spending is because it creates jobs," this lead article says, "a little bit of *1984* begins to surface." Another article criticizes a "heavy-handed" opinion of Jerry Falwell Ministries—in this case a broadside attack on artificial insemination, surrogate motherhood, and lesbian motherhood. Browsing through *Eternity,* I find a double crosstic. I find an intelligent, analytical, and enthusiastic review of the new London Philharmonic recording of Mahler's second symphony—a review which stresses the "glorious truth" of the Jewish composer's magnificent work, and cites its recent performance in Jerusalem to celebrate the recapture of the Western Wall following the Six Day War. Surely, the evangelical Christians who read this magazine are not book-burners. If by chance they vote with the magazine's editors, then it looks to me as if they vote with the American Civil Liberties Union and Americans for Democratic Action.

Every few years some bold and sincere Christian student at this university disagrees with a professor in class—usually about the professor's out-of-hand dismissal of Christianity. Members of the faculty, outraged, repeat the stories of these rare and uneven encounters for years on end, as if to prove that the crazies are everywhere, and gaining ground. The notion is, apparently, that these kids can't think for themselves. Or they wouldn't disagree.

Now again the moustached leader asks us to move up. There is no harangue, so we move up. (This will be a theme all spring. The leaders want us closer together. Our instinct is to stand alone.) From behind the tall fountain comes a wind; on several gusts we get sprayed. No one seems to notice.

We have time for one more song. The leader, perhaps sensing that   20 no one likes him, blunders on. "I want you to pray this one through," he says. "We have a lot of people here from a lot of different fellowships, but we're all one body. Amen?" They don't like it. He gets a few polite Amens. We sing:

> Bind us together, Lord,
> With a bond that can't be broken;
> Bind us together, Lord,
> With love.

Everyone seems to be in a remarkably foul mood today. We don't like this song. There is no one here under seventeen, and, I think, no one here who believes that love is a bond that can't be broken. We sing the song through three times; then it is time to go.

The leader calls after our retreating backs. "Hey, have a good day! Praise Him all day!" The kids around me roll up their eyes privately. Some groan; all flee.

The next morning is very cold. I am here early. Two girls are talking on the fountain's rim; one is part Indian. She says, "I've got all the

Old Testament, but I can't get the New. I screw up the New." She takes a breath and rattles off a long list, ending with "Jonah, Micah, Nahum, Habakkuk, Zephaniah, Haggai, Zechariah, Malachi." The other girl produces a slow, sarcastic applause. I ask one of the girls to help me with the words to a song. She is agreeable, but says, "I'm sorry, I can't. I just became a Christian this year, so I don't know all the words yet."

The others are coming; we stand and separate. The boy with the moustache is gone, replaced by a big, serious fellow in a green down jacket. The bouncy girl is back with her guitar; she's wearing a skirt and wool knee socks. We begin, without any preamble, by singing a song that has so few words that we actually stretch one syllable over eleven separate notes. Then we sing a song in which the men sing one phrase and the women echo it. Everyone seems to know just what to do. In the context of our vapid songs, the lyrics of this one are extraordinary:

> I was nothing before you found me.
> Heartache! Broken people! Ruined lives
> Is why you died on Calvary.

The last line rises in a regular series of half-notes. Now at last some people are actually singing; they throw some breath into the business. There is a seriousness and urgency to it: "Heartache! Broken people! Ruined lives . . . I was nothing."

We don't look like nothing. We look like a bunch of students of every stripe, ill-shaven or well-shaven, dressed up or down, but dressed warmly against the cold: jeans and parkas, jeans and heavy sweaters, jeans and scarves and blow-dried hair. We look ordinary. But I think, quite on my own, that we are here because we know this business of nothingness, brokenness, and ruination. We sing this song over and over.

Something catches my eye. Behind us, up in the science building, professors are standing alone at opened windows.

The long brick science building has three upper floors of faculty offices, thirty-two windows. At one window stands a bearded man, about forty; his opening his window is what caught my eye. He stands full in the open window, his hands on his hips, his head cocked down toward the fountain. He is drawn to look, as I was drawn to come. Up on the building's top floor, at the far right window, there is another: an Asian-American professor, wearing a white shirt, is sitting with one hip on his desk, looking out and down. In the middle of the row of windows, another one, an old professor in a checked shirt, stands sideways to the opened window, stands stock-still, his long, old ear to the air. Now another window cranks open, another professor—or maybe a graduate student—leans out, his hands on the sill.

We are all singing, and I am watching these five still men, my colleagues, whose office doors are surely shut—for that is the custom here: five of them alone in their offices at the science building who have opened their windows on this very cold morning, who motionless hear the Fundamentalists sing, utterly unknown to each other.

We sing another four songs, including the clapping song, and one which repeats, "This is the day which the Lord hath made; rejoice and be glad in it." All the professors but one stay still by their opened windows, figures in a frieze. When after ten minutes we break off and scatter, each cranks his windows shut. Maybe they have nine o'clock classes too.

I miss a few sessions. One morning of the following week, I rejoin   30
the Fundamentalists on the Square. The wind is blowing from the north; it is sunny and cold. There are several new developments.

Someone has blown up rubber gloves and floated them in the fountain. I saw them yesterday afternoon from my high office window, and couldn't quite make them out: I seemed to see hands in the fountain waving from side to side, like those hands wagging on springs which people stick in the back windows of their cars. I saw these many years ago in Quito and Guayaquil, where they were a great fad long before they showed up here. The cardboard hands said, on their palms, HOLA GENTE, hello people. Some of them just said HOLA, hello, with a little wave to the universe at large, in case anybody happened to be looking. It is like our sending radio signals to planets in other galaxies: HOLA, if anyone is listening. Jolly folk, these Ecuadorians, I thought.

Now, waiting by the fountain for the singing, I see that these particular hands are long surgical gloves, yellow and white, ten of them, tied off at the cuff. They float upright and they wave, *hola, hola, hola;* they mill around like a crowd, bobbing under the fountain's spray and back again to the pool's rim, *hola.* It is a good prank. It is far too cold for the university's maintenance crew to retrieve them without turning off the fountain and putting on rubber boots.

From all around the Square, people are gathering for the singing. There is no way I can guess which kids, from among the masses crossing the Square, will veer off to the fountain. When they get here, I never recognize anybody except the leaders.

The singing begins without ado as usual, but there is something different about it. The students are growing prayerful, and they show it this morning with a peculiar gesture. I'm glad they weren't like this when I first joined them, or I never would have stayed.

Last night there was an educational television special, part of "Mid-   35
dletown." It was a segment called "Community of Praise," and I watched

it because it was about Fundamentalists. It showed a Jesus-loving family in the Midwest; the treatment was good and complex. This family
attended the prayer meetings, healing sessions, and church services of
an unnamed sect—a very low-church sect, whose doctrine and culture
were much more low-church than those of the kids I sing with. When
the members of this sect prayed, they held their arms over their heads
and raised their palms, as if to feel or receive a blessing or energy from
above.

Now today on the Square there is a new serious mood. The leaders
are singing with their eyes shut. I am impressed that they can bang their
guitars, keep their balance, and not fall into the pool. It is the same
bouncy girl and earnest boy. Their eyeballs are rolled back a bit. I look
around and see that almost everyone in this crowd of eighty or so has
his eyes shut and is apparently praying the words of this song or praying some other prayer.

Now as the chorus rises, as it gets louder and higher and simpler in
melody—

> I exalt thee,
> I exalt thee,
> I exalt thee,
> Thou art the Lord—

then, at this moment, hands start rising. All around me, hands are going
up—that tall girl, that blond boy with his head back, the redheaded boy
up front, the girl with the McDonald's jacket. Their arms rise as if
pulled on strings. Some few of them have raised their arms very high
over their heads and are tilting back their palms. Many, many more of
them, as inconspicuously as possible, have raised their hands to the level
of their chins.

What is going on? Why are these students today raising their palms
in this gesture, when nobody did it last week? Is it because the leaders
have set a prayerful tone this morning? Is it because this gesture always
accompanies this song, just as clapping accompanies other songs? Or is
it, as I suspect, that these kids watched the widely publicized documentary last night just as I did, and are adopting, or trying out, the gesture?

It is a sunny morning, and the sun is rising behind the leaders and
the fountain, so those students have their heads tilted, eyes closed, and
palms upraised toward the sun. I glance up at the science building and
think my own prayer: thank God no one is watching this.

The leaders cannot move around much on the fountain's rim. The 40
girl has her eyes shut; the boy opens his eyes from time to time, glances
at the neck of the guitar, and closes his eyes again.

When the song is over, the hands go down, and there is some desultory chatting in the crowd, as usual; can I borrow your library card?
And, as usual, nobody looks at anybody.

All our songs today are serious. There is a feudal theme to them, or a feudal analogue:

> I will eat from abundance of your household.
> I will dream beside your streams of righteousness.
> You are my king.
> Enter his gates
> with thanksgiving in your heart;
> come before his courts with praise.
> He is the king of kings.
> Thou art the Lord.

All around me, eyes are closed and hands are raised. There is no social pressure to do this, or anything else. I've never known any group to be less cohesive, imposing fewer controls. Since no one looks at anyone, and since passersby no longer look, everyone out here is inconspicuous and free. Perhaps the palm-raising has begun because the kids realize by now that they are not on display; they're praying in their closets, right out here on the Square. Over the course of the next weeks, I will learn that the palm-raising is here to stay.

The sun is rising higher. We are singing our last song. We are praying. We are alone together.

> He is my peace
> Who has broken down every wall . . .

When the song is over, the hands go down. The heads lower, the eyes open and blink. We stay still a second before we break up. We have been standing in a broad current; now we have stepped aside. We have dismantled the radar cups; we have closed the telescope's vault. Students gather their book bags and go. The two leaders step down from the fountain's rim and pack away their guitars. Everyone scatters. I am in no hurry, so I stay after everyone is gone. It is after nine o'clock, and the Square is deserted. The fountain is playing to an empty house. In the pool the cheerful hands are waving over the water, bobbing under the fountain's veil and out again in the current, *hola.*

45

LINES OF INQUIRY
"Singing with the Fundamentalists"

Though Dillard gives a detailed record of what she observed while singing with the Fundamentalists, she does not ever explicitly define the purpose, or state the point, of this essay. How does she manage to imply the point of this piece? How does she tell about the daily singing sessions to get her point across?

What kinds of details does she repeatedly focus on in her story of the daily singing sessions? How does she establish the significance of these details?

Though Dillard had little if anything to do with Fundamentalists prior to the experience she describes in this piece, she did evidently have some clear-cut opinions of them. What was Dillard's attitude toward Fundamentalists prior to her experience of singing with them? What other attitudes toward Fundamentalists does she discuss during the course of her essay? What does she discover about them during the process of singing with them? How is her attitude affected by her overall experience of singing with them?

What is your attitude toward Christian Fundamentalists? What do you know from firsthand observation and from reading about their beliefs and practices? As a means of checking up on your attitude and understanding of them, as well as on Dillard's, look at some recent issues of the Fundamentalist magazine she refers to in her piece, *Eternity: The Evangelical Monthly*. What impression of them do you get from this material? How does it square with your prior assumptions about them?

LOREN EISELEY

1907 – 77

No utilitarian philosophy explains a snow crystal, no doctrine of use or disuse. Water has merely leapt out of vapor and thin nothingness in the night sky to array itself in form. There is no logical reason for the existence of a snow-flake any more than there is for evolution.

Though Loren Eiseley was a distinguished physical anthropologist, one of several responsible for discovering that early man existed in America thousands of years earlier than previously thought, he came to be most fascinated, as he is in this passage, by the mysteriousness, the illogic, perhaps even the arbitrariness of the physical world and of human evolution. For him, the history of the human species is as beautiful, and as incomprehensible, as the structure of a snowflake: both are "apparition[s] from that mysterious shadow world beyond nature, that final world which contains—if anything contains—the explanation of men and catfish and green leaves." To express his sense of wonder and awe before nature's vastness, and his loneliness, his sense of man's comparative insignificance, Eiseley gradually turned away from the strictures of the scientific article to the literary forms of the personal essay. The "secret" of life, "will not yield to the kind of analysis our science is capable of making."

Eiseley's childhood in Nebraska was full of "terror, anxiety, ostracism, and shame," as he describes it in his autobiography, *All the Strange Hours*. His relationship with his deaf and mentally disturbed mother was particularly troubled, leaving deep scars that afflicted him the rest of his life. So from an early age, he sought refuge in reading and writing. Indeed, as an eighth grader he wrote an essay announcing that "I have selected Nature Writing as my vocation, because at this time it appeals to me more than any other subject." Still, he grew up rootless and unhappy, dropping in and out of college from the mid-1920s to the early 1930s, "bumming about" the West on freight trains, recuperating from tuberculosis in the Mojave desert and the mountains of Colorado—a "child of the early century," "molded of plains' dust and seed of those who came West with the wagons."

Eventually he was able to apply himself to his studies at the University of Nebraska, where he graduated in 1933 with a double major in English and anthropology. His youth and young manhood were marked by these two interests: on the one hand a passion for the history of the earth and the early Plains' people; on the other, a passion for literature and creative writing. As an undergraduate he had not only been part of a paleontological expedition that found artifacts of early man scattered among the bones of extinct bison, but he also served on the staff of the influential creative writing magazine, *The Prairie Schooner,* eventually becoming a contributing editor.

As a graduate student in anthropology at the University of Pennsylvania, he took part in an expedition to the Southwest in search of early man, and quickly proceeded to earn his MA in 1935, his PhD in 1937, as well as to publish his first professional articles. The subject of his dissertation was the usefulness of various scientific measurements of "Quaternary Time," reflecting not only his interests as a scientist but also foreshadowing his obsession in the essays with the vastness and elusiveness of time. From 1937 to 1942, he taught at the University of Kansas in Lawrence. During his first year there, he looked upon himself as "the proverbial Russian fleeing in a sleigh across the steppes before a wolf pack," yet he managed to impress his colleagues and students and to establish a solid reputation for his anthropological research and publications. From Kansas he moved to Oberlin College in Ohio as department chair, then to the University of Pennsylvania, where he succeeded his mentor as chair of the Department of Anthropology, a position he held from 1947 to 1962. He also served at various times as Curator of Early Man at the University of Pennsylvania and, briefly, as University Provost.

In 1942, while still at Kansas, Eiseley began experimenting with forms of writing that would ultimately lead him to develop what he called the "concealed essay." He wanted not only a way of channeling his ambitions and talents as a creative writer but a form of discourse capable of conveying his growing sense of man's insignificance in time. He wanted to humanize his research, both for himself and for his larger audience, writing about the experience of nature and the discoveries of science in a poetic, personal way. As he said of the great Victorian naturalists like Huxley, "even though they were not discoverers in the objective sense, one feels at times that the great nature essayists had more individual perception than their scientific contemporaries." Through the power of their language, they added a new "dimension" to our understanding of nature, "something that lies beyond the careful analysis of professional biology."

Eiseley himself added a new dimension to writing about nature in his first and most widely known imaginative book, *The Immense Journey* (1957), a collection of shorter pieces that had originally appeared in

Scientific American, Prairie Schooner, Harpers, and *The American Scholar,* unified into a coherent sequence of essays that meditate on the evolution of life from Precambrian times to the formation of the human mind. Here he sounds his central themes, his antimaterialism, his opposition to narrow scientific rationalism, his desire to recover the past through the power of the imagination, his fascination with man's physical development and genetic endowments, his awe at the vastness of time and "the enormous interlinked complexity of life." Each piece begins with a concrete, evocative personal experience which then leads to scientific or philosophical meditation—the sight of birds flying from ledges in New York, for example, leads to a meditation on Eiseley's longing for death and on man's separateness from nature. Natural history becomes metaphor for personal history, and vice versa, Eiseley's own personal experience serving as a vehicle for illustrating larger concepts, as well as a strategy for engaging the reader's intense interest. So, Eiseley developed a form that could blend the two facets of his personality, situating himself in the tradition of imaginative naturalists like Thoreau, and preparing the way for scientists turned essayists like Lewis Thomas and Stephen Jay Gould.

A number of books followed, including several more prose meditations—*The Firmament of Time* (1960), *The Unexpected Universe* (1969), and *Night Country* (1971)—several books of poems, and his final work, the disturbing and haunting autobiography, *All the Strange Hours: An Excavation of a Life* (1975), in which ecstasy and wonder give way to sadness, loneliness, even cynicism. He also wrote several more scholarly studies, including an intellectual history clarifying and disputing Darwin's theory of evolution, and an analysis of Francis Bacon's visionary approach to science as an alternative to Darwin's materialism. None of this later writing, to paraphrase *The Immense Journey,* can be regarded as a straightforward "guide," but is, rather, "a somewhat unconventional record of the prowlings of one mind which has sought to explore, to understand, and to enjoy the miracles of this world, both in and out of science."

What characterizes this record, at its best, is a poetic lyricism, as in this meditation on water from *The Immense Journey:*

Once in a lifetime, perhaps, one escapes the actual confines of the flesh. Once in a lifetime, if one is lucky, one so merges with sunlight and air and running water that whole eons, the eons that mountains and deserts know, might pass in a single afternoon without discomfort. The mind has sunk away into its beginning among old roots and the obscure tricklings and movings that stir inanimate things. Like the charmed fairy circle into which a man once stepped, and upon emergence learned that a whole century had passed in a single night, one can never quite define this secret: but it has something to do, I am sure, with common water. Its substance reaches everywhere; it touches the past and prepares the future;

it moves under the poles and wanders thinly in the heights of air. It can assume the forms of exquisite perfection in a snowflake, or strip the living to a single shining bone cast up by the sea.

Here, as elsewhere, Eiseley re-creates what he called a "natural revelation," a temporary merging of man and nature, a brief transcending of time. The language moves through repetition and balanced structure, through metaphor and patterns of sound, to the level of incantation, enabling us to see "in the flow of ordinary events" what Eiseley was always trying to help us see: "the point at which the mundane world gives way to quite another dimension."

HOW FLOWERS CHANGED
THE WORLD

If it had been possible to observe the Earth from the far side of the solar system over the long course of geological epochs, the watchers might have been able to observe a subtle change in the light emanating from our planet. That world of long ago would, like the red deserts of Mars, have reflected light from vast drifts of stone and gravel, the sands of wandering wastes, the blackness of naked basalt, the yellow dust of endlessly moving storms. Only the ceaseless marching of the clouds and the intermittent flashes from the restless surface of the sea would have told a different story, but still essentially a barren one. Then, as the millennia rolled away and age followed age, a new and greener light would, by degrees, have come to twinkle across those endless miles.

This is the only difference those far watchers, by the use of subtle instruments, might have perceived in the whole history of the planet Earth. Yet that slowly growing green twinkle would have contained the epic march of life from the tidal oozes upward across the raw and unclothed continents. Out of the vast chemical bath of the sea—not from the deeps, but from the element-rich, light-exposed platforms of the continental shelves—wandering fingers of green had crept upward along the meanderings of river systems and fringed the gravels of forgotten lakes.

In those first ages plants clung of necessity to swamps and watercourses. Their productive processes demanded direct access to water. Beyond the primitive ferns and mosses that enclosed the borders of swamps and streams the rocks still lay vast and bare, the winds still swirled the dust of a naked planet. The grass cover that holds our world secure in place was still millions of years in the future. The green marchers had gained a soggy foothold upon the land, but that was all. They did not reproduce by seeds but by microscopic swimming sperm that had to wriggle their way through water to fertilize the female cell. Such plants in their higher forms had clever adaptations for the use of rain water in their sexual phases, and survived with increasing success in a wet land environment. They now seem part of man's normal environment. The truth is, however, that there is nothing very "normal" about nature. Once upon a time there were no flowers at all.

A little while ago—about one hundred million years, as the geologist estimates time in the history of our four-billion-year-old planet—flowers were not to be found anywhere on the five continents.

Wherever one might have looked, from the poles to the equator, one would have seen only the cold dark monotonous green of a world whose plant life possessed no other color.

Somewhere, just a short time before the close of the Age of Rep-   5
tiles, there occurred a soundless, violent explosion. It lasted millions of years, but it was an explosion, nevertheless. It marked the emergence of the angiosperms—the flowering plants. Even the great evolutionist, Charles Darwin, called them "an abominable mystery," because they appeared so suddenly and spread so fast.

Flowers changed the face of the planet. Without them, the world we know—even man himself—would never have existed. Francis Thompson, the English poet, once wrote that one could not pluck a flower without troubling a star. Intuitively he had sensed like a naturalist the enormous interlinked complexity of life. Today we know that the appearance of the flowers contained also the equally mystifying emergence of man.

If we were to go back into the Age of Reptiles, its drowned swamps and birdless forests would reveal to us a warmer but, on the whole, a sleepier world than that of today. Here and there, it is true, the serpent heads of bottom-feeding dinosaurs might be upreared in suspicion of their huge flesh-eating compatriots. Tyrannosaurs, enormous bipedal caricatures of men, would stalk mindlessly across the sites of future cities and go their slow way down into the dark of geologic time.

In all that world of living things nothing saw save with the intense concentration of the hunt, nothing moved except with the grave sleep-walking intentness of the instinct-driven brain. Judged by modern standards, it was a world in slow motion, a cold-blooded world whose occupants were most active at noonday but torpid on chill nights, their brains damped by a slower metabolism than any known to even the most primitive of warm-blooded animals today.

A high metabolic rate and the maintenance of a constant body temperature are supreme achievements in the evolution of life. They enable an animal to escape, within broad limits, from the overheating or the chilling of its immediate surroundings, and at the same time to maintain a peak mental efficiency. Creatures without a high metabolic rate are slaves to weather. Insects in the first frosts of autumn all run down like little clocks. Yet if you pick one up and breathe warmly upon it, it will begin to move about once more.

In a sheltered spot such creatures may sleep away the winter, but   10
they are hopelessly immobilized. Though a few warm-blooded mammals, such as the woodchuck of our day, have evolved a way of reducing their metabolic rate in order to undergo winter hibernation, it is a survival mechanism with drawbacks, for it leaves the animal helplessly exposed if enemies discover him during his period of suspended animation. Thus bear or woodchuck, big animal or small, must seek, in

this time of descending sleep, a safe refuge in some hidden den or burrow. Hibernation is, therefore, primarily a winter refuge of small, easily concealed animals rather than of large ones.

A high metabolic rate, however, means a heavy intake of energy in order to sustain body warmth and efficiency. It is for this reason that even some of these later warm-blooded mammals existing in our day have learned to descend into a slower, unconscious rate of living during the winter months when food may be difficult to obtain. On a slightly higher plane they are following the procedure of the cold-blooded frog sleeping in the mud at the bottom of a frozen pond.

The agile brain of the warm-blooded birds and mammals demands a high oxygen consumption and food in concentrated forms, or the creatures cannot long sustain themselves. It was the rise of the flowering plants that provided that energy and changed the nature of the living world. Their appearance parallels in a quite surprising manner the rise of the birds and mammals.

Slowly, toward the dawn of the Age of Reptiles, something over two hundred and fifty million years ago, the little naked sperm cells wriggling their way through dew and raindrops had given way to a kind of pollen carried by the wind. Our present-day pine forests represent plants of a pollen-disseminating variety. Once fertilization was no longer dependent on exterior water, the march over drier regions could be extended. Instead of spores simple primitive seeds carrying some nourishment for the young plant had developed, but true flowers were still scores of millions of years away. After a long period of hesitant evolutionary groping, they exploded upon the world with truly revolutionary violence.

The event occurred in Cretaceous times in the close of the Age of Reptiles. Before the coming of the flowering plants our own ancestral stock, the warm-blooded mammals, consisted of a few mousy little creatures hidden in trees and underbrush. A few lizard-like birds with carnivorous teeth flapped awkwardly on ill-aimed flights among archaic shrubbery. None of these insignificant creatures gave evidence of any remarkable talents. The mammals in particular had been around for some millions of years, but had remained well lost in the shadow of the mighty reptiles. Truth to tell, man was still, like the genie in the bottle, encased in the body of a creature about the size of a rat.

As for the birds, their reptilian cousins the Pterodactyls flew farther and better. There was just one thing about the birds that paralleled the physiology of the mammals. They, too, had evolved warm blood and its accompanying temperature control. Nevertheless, if one had been seen stripped of his feathers, he would still have seemed a slightly uncanny and unsightly lizard.

Neither the birds nor the mammals, however, were quite what they seemed. They were waiting for the Age of Flowers. They were waiting

15

for what flowers, and with them the true encased seed, would bring. Fish-eating, gigantic leather-winged reptiles, twenty-eight feet from wing tip to wing tip, hovered over the coasts that one day would be swarming with gulls.

Inland the monotonous green of the pine and spruce forests with their primitive wooden cone flowers stretched everywhere. No grass hindered the fall of the naked seeds to earth. Great sequoias towered to the skies. The world of that time has a certain appeal but it is a giant's world, a world moving slowly like the reptiles who stalked magnificently among the boles of its trees.

The trees themselves are ancient, slow-growing and immense, like the redwood groves that have survived to our day on the California coast. All is stiff, formal, upright and green, monotonously green. There is no grass as yet; there are no wide plains rolling in the sun, no tiny daisies dotting the meadows underfoot. There is little versatility about this scene; it is, in truth, a giant's world.

A few nights ago it was brought home vividly to me that the world has changed since that far epoch. I was awakened out of sleep by an unknown sound in my living room. Not a small sound—not a creaking timber or a mouse's scurry—but a sharp, rending explosion as though an unwary foot had been put down upon a wine glass. I had come instantly out of sleep and lay tense, unbreathing. I listened for another step. There was none.

Unable to stand the suspense any longer, I turned on the light and passed from room to room glancing uneasily behind chairs and into closets. Nothing seemed disturbed, and I stood puzzled in the corner of the living room floor. Then a small button-shaped object upon the rug caught my eye. It was hard and polished and glistening. Scattered over the length of the room were several more shining up at me like wary little eyes. A pine cone that had been lying in a dish had been blown the length of the coffee table. The dish itself could hardly have been the source of the explosion. Beside it I found two ribbon-like strips of velvety-green. I tried to place the two strips together to make a pod. They twisted resolutely away from each other and would no longer fit.

I relaxed in a chair, then, for I had reached a solution of the midnight disturbance. The twisted strips were wisteria pods that I had brought in a day or two previously and placed in the dish. They had chosen midnight to explode and distribute their multiplying fund of life down the length of the room. A plant, a fixed, rooted thing, immobilized in a single spot, had devised a way of propelling its offspring across open space. Immediately there passed before my eyes the million airy troopers of the milkweed pod and the clutching hooks of the sandburs. Seeds on the coyote's tail, seeds on the hunter's coat, thistledown mounting on the winds—all were somehow triumphing over life's limitations. Yet the ability to do this had not been with them at the beginning. It was the product of endless effort and experiment.

20

The seeds on my carpet were not going to lie stiffly where they had dropped like their antiquated cousins, the naked seeds on the pine-cone scales. They were travelers. Struck by the thought, I went out next day and collected several other varieties. I line them up now in a row on my desk—so many little capsules of life, winged, hooked or spiked. Every one is an angiosperm, a product of the true flowering plants. Contained in these little boxes is the secret of that far-off Cretaceous explosion of a hundred million years ago that changed the face of the planet. And somewhere in here, I think, as I poke seriously at one particularly resistant seedcase of a wild grass, was once man himself.

When the first simple flower bloomed on some raw upland late in the Dinosaur Age, it was wind pollinated, just like its early pine-cone relatives. It was a very inconspicuous flower because it had not yet evolved the idea of using the surer attraction of birds and insects to achieve the transportation of pollen. It sowed its own pollen and received the pollen of other flowers by the simple vagaries of the wind. Many plants in regions where insect life is scant still follow this principle today. Nevertheless, the true flower—and the seed that it produced—was a profound innovation in the world of life.

In a way, this event parallels, in the plant world, what happened among animals. Consider the relative chance for survival of the exteriorly deposited egg of a fish in contrast with the fertilized egg of a mammal, carefully retained for months in the mother's body until the young animal (or human being) is developed to a point where it may survive. The biological wastage is less—and so it is with the flowering plants. The primitive spore, a single cell fertilized at the beginning by a swimming sperm, did not promote rapid distribution, and the young plant, moreover, had to struggle up from nothing. No one had left it any food except what it could get by its own unaided efforts.

By contrast, the true flowering plants (angiosperm itself means "encased seed") grew a seed in the heart of a flower, a seed whose development was initiated by a fertilizing pollen grain independent of outside moisture. But the seed, unlike the developing spore, is already a fully equipped *embryonic plant* packed in a little enclosed box stuffed full of nutritious food. Moreover, by featherdown attachments, as in dandelion or milkweed seed, it can be wafted upward on gusts and ride the wind for miles; or with hooks it can cling to a bear's or a rabbit's hide; or like some of the berries, it can be covered with a juicy, attractive fruit to lure birds, pass undigested through their intestinal tracts and be voided miles away.

The ramifications of this biological invention were endless. Plants traveled as they had never traveled before. They got into strange environments heretofore never entered by the old spore plants or stiff pine-cone-seed plants. The well-fed, carefully cherished little embryos raised their heads everywhere. Many of the older plants with more primitive reproductive mechanisms began to fade away under this unequal contest. They contracted their range into secluded environments. Some, like the giant redwoods, lingered on as relics; many vanished entirely.

The world of the giants was a dying world. These fantastic little seeds skipping and hopping and flying about the woods and valleys brought with them an amazing adaptability. If our whole lives had not been spent in the midst of it, it would astound us. The old, stiff, sky-reaching wooden world had changed into something that glowed here and there with strange colors, put out queer, unheard-of fruits and little intricately carved seed cases, and, most important of all, produced concentrated foods in a way that the land had never seen before, or dreamed of back in the fish-eating, leaf-crunching days of the dinosaurs.

That food came from three sources, all produced by the reproductive system of the flowering plants. There were the tantalizing nectars and pollens intended to draw insects for pollenizing purposes, and which are responsible also for that wonderful jeweled creation, the hummingbird. There were the juicy and enticing fruits to attract larger animals, and in which tough-coated seeds were concealed, as in the tomato, for example. Then, as if this were not enough, there was the food in the actual seed itself, the food intended to nourish the embryo. All over the world, like hot corn in a popper, these incredible elaborations of the flowering plants kept exploding. In a movement that was almost instantaneous, geologically speaking, the angiosperms had taken over the world. Grass was beginning to cover the bare earth until, today, there are over six thousand species. All kinds of vines and bushes squirmed and writhed under new trees with flying seeds.

The explosion was having its effect on animal life also. Specialized groups of insects were arising to feed on the new sources of food and, incidentally and unknowingly, to pollinate the plant. The flowers bloomed and bloomed in ever larger and more spectacular varieties. Some were pale unearthly night flowers intended to lure moths in the evening twilight, some among the orchids even took the shape of female spiders in order to attract wandering males, some flamed redly in the light of noon or twinkled modestly in the meadow grasses. Intricate mechanisms splashed pollen on the breasts of hummingbirds, or stamped it on the bellies of black, grumbling bees droning assiduously from blossom to blossom. Honey ran, insects multiplied, and even the descendants of that toothed and ancient lizard-bird had become strangely altered. Equipped with prodding beaks instead of biting teeth they pecked the seeds and gobbled the insects that were really converted nectar.

Across the planet grasslands were now spreading. A slow continental upthrust which had been a part of the early Age of Flowers had cooled the world's climates. The stalking reptiles and the leather-winged black imps of the seashore cliffs had vanished. Only birds roamed the air now, hot-blooded and high-speed metabolic machines.

30

The mammals, too, had survived and were venturing into new domains, staring about perhaps a bit bewildered at their sudden eminence now that the thunder lizards were gone. Many of them, beginning as small browsers upon leaves in the forest, began to venture out upon this new sunlit world of the grass. Grass has a high silica content and demands a new type of very tough and resistant tooth enamel, but the seeds taken incidentally in the cropping of the grass are highly nutritious. A new world had opened out for the warm-blooded mammals. Great herbivores like the mammoths, horses and bisons appeared. Skulking about them had arisen savage flesh-feeding carnivores like the now extinct dire wolves and the saber-toothed tiger.

Flesh eaters though these creatures were, they were being sustained on nutritious grasses one step removed. Their fierce energy was being maintained on a high, effective level, through hot days and frosty nights, by the concentrated energy of the angiosperms. That energy, thirty per cent or more of the weight of the entire plant among some of the cereal grasses, was being accumulated and concentrated in the rich proteins and fats of the enormous game herds of the grasslands.

On the edge of the forest, a strange, old-fashioned animal still hesitated. His body was the body of a tree dweller, and though tough and knotty by human standards, he was, in terms of that world into which he gazed, a weakling. His teeth, though strong for chewing on the tough fruits of the forest, or for crunching an occasional unwary bird caught with his prehensile hands, were not the tearing sabers of the great cats. He had a passion for lifting himself up to see about, in his restless, roving curiosity. He would run a little stiffly and uncertainly, perhaps, on his hind legs, but only in those rare moments when he ventured out upon the ground. All this was the legacy of his climbing days; he had a hand with flexible fingers and no fine specialized hoofs upon which to gallop like the wind.

If he had any idea of competing in that new world, he had better forget it; teeth or hooves, he was much too late for either. He was a ne'er-do-well, and in-betweener. Nature had not done well by him. It was as if she had hesitated and never quite made up her mind. Perhaps as a consequence he had a malicious gleam in his eye, the gleam of an outcast who has been left nothing and knows he is going to have to take what he gets. One day a little band of these odd apes—for apes they were—shambled out upon the grass; the human story had begun.

Apes were to become men, in the inscrutable wisdom of nature, because flowers had produced seeds and fruits in such tremendous quantities that a new and totally different store of energy had become available in concentrated form. Impressive as the slow-moving, dimbrained dinosaurs had been, it is doubtful if their age had supported anything like the diversity of life that now rioted across the planet or flashed in and out among the trees. Down on the grass by a streamside,

35

one of those apes with inquisitive fingers turned over a stone and hefted it vaguely. The group clucked together in a throaty tongue and moved off through the tall grass foraging for seeds and insects. The one still held, sniffed, and hefted the stone he had found. He liked the feel of it in his fingers. The attack on the animal world was about to begin.

If one could run the story of that first human group like a speeded-up motion picture through a million years of time, one might see the stone in the hand change to the flint ax and the torch. All that swarming grassland world with its giant bison and trumpeting mammoths would go down in ruin to feed the insatiable and growing numbers of a carnivore who, like the great cats before him, was taking his energy indirectly from the grass. Later he found fire and it altered the tough meats and drained their energy even faster into a stomach ill adapted for the ferocious turn man's habits had taken.

His limbs grew longer, he strode more purposefully over the grass. The stolen energy that would take man across the continents would fail him at last. The great Ice Age herds were destined to vanish. When they did so, another hand like the hand that grasped the stone by the river long ago would pluck a handful of grass seed and hold it contemplatively.

In that moment, the golden towers of man, his swarming millions, his turning wheels, the vast learning of his packed libraries, would glimmer dimly there in the ancestor of wheat, a few seeds held in a muddy hand. Without the gift of flowers and the infinite diversity of their fruits, man and bird, if they had continued to exist at all, would be today unrecognizable. Archaeopteryx, the lizard-bird, might still be a nocturnal insectivore gnawing a roach in the dark. The weight of a petal has changed the face of the world and made it ours.

LINES OF INQUIRY
"How Flowers Changed the World"

Although this essay is explicitly concerned with explaining "how flowers changed the world," Eiseley doesn't actually get into this explanation in detail until the second half of his piece. What is the purpose of the material that he discusses in the first half of his piece? What topics does he discuss, what things does he describe, what stories does he tell in the first half, and exactly how does each bit of material pertain to the cause and effect process that he is trying to explain in this piece?

Given the title of this piece, it seems appropriate to consider exactly how the world was changed by the appearance of flowers. What specific changes, according to Eiseley, did flowers actually bring about in the world? How did flowers cause each of those changes? In particular, how did "the appearance of flowers [contain] also the equally mystifying emergence of man"? How did the appearance of flowers, in turn, lead to man's domination of the world, as Eiseley claims in the final sentence of his essay?

In what respects do you think it would be accurate to say that Eiseley's essay is essentially an anthropocentric piece of natural history? In other words, do you think it implies that man is the central being, final aim, or ultimate creature in the universe? In what respects do you think it would be inaccurate to define his views as anthropocentric? What do you consider to be the strengths and weaknesses of viewing the world anthropocentrically? For another point of view on this issue, look at Twain's essay, "Was the World Made for Man?"

THE BIRD AND THE MACHINE

I suppose their little bones have years ago been lost among the stones and winds of those high glacial pastures. I suppose their feathers blew eventually into the piles of tumbleweed beneath the straggling cattle fences and rotted there in the mountain snows, along with dead steers and all the other things that drift to an end in the corners of the wire. I do not quite know why I should be thinking of birds over the *New York Times* at breakfast, particularly the birds of my youth half a continent away. It is a funny thing what the brain will do with memories and how it will treasure them and finally bring them into odd juxtapositions with other things, as though it wanted to make a design, or get some meaning out of them, whether you want it or not, or even see it.

It used to seem marvelous to me, but I read now that there are machines that can do these things in a small way, machines that can crawl about like animals, and that it may not be long now until they do more things—maybe even make themselves—I saw that piece in the *Times* just now. And then they will, maybe—well, who knows—but you read about it more and more with no one making any protest, and already they can add better than we and reach up and hear things through the dark and finger the guns over the night sky.

This is the new world that I read about at breakfast. This is the world that confronts me in my biological books and journals, until there are times when I sit quietly in my chair and try to hear the little purr of the cogs in my head and the tubes flaring and dying as the messages go through them and the circuits snap shut or open. This is the great age, make no mistake about it; the robot has been born somewhat appropriately along with the atom bomb, and the brain they say now is just another type of more complicated feedback system. The engineers have its basic principles worked out; it's mechanical, you know; nothing to get superstitious about; and man can always improve on nature once he gets the idea. Well, he's got it all right and that's why, I guess, that I sit here in my chair, with the article crunched in my hand, remembering those two birds and that blue mountain sunlight. There is another magazine article on my desk that reads "Machines Are Getting Smarter Every Day." I don't deny it, but I'll still stick with the birds. It's life I believe in, not machines.

Maybe you don't believe there is any difference. A skeleton is all joints and pulleys, I'll admit. And when man was in his simpler stages of machine building in the eighteenth century, he quickly saw the resemblances. "What," wrote Hobbes, "is the heart but a spring, and the nerves but so many strings, and the joints but so many wheels, giving motion to the whole body?'' Tinkering about in their shops it was inevitable in the end that men would see the world as a huge machine "subdivided into an infinite number of lesser machines."

The idea took on with a vengeance. Little automatons toured the country—dolls controlled by clockwork. Clocks described as little worlds were taken on tours by their designers. They were made up of moving figures, shifting scenes, and other remarkable devices. The life of the cell was unknown. Man, whether he was conceived as possessing a soul or not, moved and jerked about like these tiny puppets. A human being thought of himself in terms of his own tools and implements. He had been fashioned like the puppets he produced and was only a more clever model made by a greater designer.

Then in the nineteenth century, the cell was discovered, and the single machine in its turn was found to be the product of millions of infinitesimal machines—the cells. Now, finally, the cell itself dissolved away into an abstract chemical machine, and that into some intangible, inexpressible flow of energy. The secret seems to lurk all about, the wheels get smaller and smaller, and they turn more rapidly, but when you try to seize it the life is gone—and so, by popular definition, some would say that life was never there in the first place. The wheels and the cogs are the secret and we can make them better in time—machines that will run faster and more accurately than real mice to real cheese.

I have no doubt it can be done, though a mouse harvesting seeds on an autumn thistle is to me a fine sight and more complicated, I think, in his multiform activity than a machine "mouse" running a maze. Also, I like to think of the possible shape of the future brooding in mice, just as it brooded once in a rather mousy insectivore who became a man. It leaves a nice fine indeterminate sense of wonder that even an electronic brain hasn't got, because you know perfectly well that if the electronic brain changes, it will be because of something man has done to it. But what man will do to himself he doesn't really know. A certain scale of time and a ghostly intangible thing called change are ticking in him. Powers and potentialities like the oak in the seed, or a red and awful ruin. Either way, it's impressive; and the mouse has it, too. Or those birds, I'll never forget those birds—yet before I measured their significance, I learned the lesson of time first of all. I was young then and left alone in a great desert—part of an expedition that had scattered its men over several hundred miles in order to carry on research more effectively. I learned there that time is a series of planes existing superficially in the same universe. The tempo is a human illusion, a subjective clock ticking in our own kind of protoplasm.

As the long months passed, I began to live on the slower planes and to observe more readily what passed for life there. I sauntered, I passed more and more slowly up and down the canyons in the dry baking heat of midsummer. I slumbered for long hours in the shade of huge brown boulders that had gathered in tilted companies out on the flats. I had forgotten the world of men and the world had forgotten me. Now and then I found a skull in the canyons, and these justified my remaining there. I took a serene cold interest in these discoveries. I had come, like many a naturalist before me, to view life with a wary and subdued attention. I had grown to take pleasure in the divested bone.

I sat once on a high ridge that fell away before me into a waste of sand dunes. I sat through hours of a long afternoon. Finally, as I glanced beside my boot an indistinct configuration caught my eye. It was a coiled rattlesnake, a big one. How long he had sat with me I do not know. I had not frightened him. We were both clocked in the sleep-walking tempo of the earlier world, baking in the same high air and sunshine. Perhaps he had been there when I came. He slept on as I left, his coils, so ill-discerned by me, dissolving once more among the stones and gravel from which I had barely made him out.

Another time I got on a higher ridge, among some tough little wind-warped pines half covered over with sand in a basinlike depression that caught everything carried by the air up to those heights. There were a few thin bones of birds, some cracked shells of indeterminable age, and the knotty fingers of pine roots bulged out of shape from their long and agonizing grasp upon the crevices of the rock. I lay under the pines in the sparse shade and went to sleep once more.

It grew cold finally, for autumn was in the air by then, and the few   10
things that lived thereabouts were sinking down into an even chillier scale of time. In the moments between sleeping and waking I saw the roots about me and slowly, slowly, a foot in what seemed many centuries, I moved my sleep-stiffened hands over the scaling bark and lifted my numbed face after the vanishing sun. I was a great awkward thing of knots and aching limbs, trapped up there in some long, patient endurance that involved the necessity of putting living fingers into rocks and by slow, aching expansion bursting those rocks asunder. I suppose, so thin and slow was the time of my pulse by then, that I might have stayed on to drift still deeper into the lower cadences of the frost, or the crystalline life that glistens pebbles, or shines in a snowflake, or dreams in the meteoric iron between the worlds.

It was a dim descent, but time was present in it. Somewhere far down in that scale the notion struck me that one might come the other way. Not many months thereafter I joined some colleagues heading higher into a remote windy tableland where huge bones were reputed to protrude like boulders from the turf. I had drowsed with reptiles and moved with the century-long pulse of trees; now, lethargically, I was climbing back up some invisible ladder of quickening hours. There had been talk of birds in connection with my duties. Birds are intense, fast-living creatures—reptiles, I suppose one might say, that have escaped out of the heavy sleep of time, transformed fairy creatures dancing over sunlit meadows. It is a youthful fancy, no doubt, but because of something that happened up there among the escarpments of that range, it remains with me a lifelong impression. I can never bear to see a bird imprisoned.

We came into that valley through the trailing mists of a spring night. It was a place that looked as though it might never have known the foot of man, but our scouts had been ahead of us and we knew all about the abandoned cabin of stone that lay far up on one hillside. It had been built in the land rush of the last century and then lost to the cattlemen again as the marginal soils failed to take to the plow.

There were spots like this all over that country. Lost graves marked by unlettered stones and old corroding rim-fire cartridge cases lying where somebody had made a stand among the boulders that rimmed the valley. They are all that remain of the range wars; the men are under the stones now. I could see our cavalcade winding in and out through the mist below us: torches, the reflection of the truck lights on our collecting tins, and the far-off bumping of a loose dinosaur thigh bone in the bottom of a trailer. I stood on a rock a moment looking down and thinking what it cost in money and equipment to capture the past.

We had, in addition, instructions to lay hands on the present. The word had come through to get them alive—birds, reptiles, anything. A zoo somewhere abroad needed restocking. It was one of those reciprocal matters in which science involves itself. Maybe our museum needed a stray ostrich egg and this was the payoff. Anyhow, my job was to help capture some birds and that was why I was there before the trucks.

The cabin had not been occupied for years. We intended to clean it out and live in it, but there were holes in the roof and the birds had come in and were roosting in the rafters. You could depend on it in a place like this where everything blew away, and even a bird needed some place out of the weather and away from coyotes. A cabin going back to nature in a wild place draws them till they come in, listening at the eaves, I imagine, pecking softly among the shingles till they find a hole, and then suddenly the place is theirs and man is forgotten.

Sometimes of late years I find myself thinking the most beautiful sight in the world might be the birds taking over New York after the last man has run away to the hills. I will never live to see it, of course, but I know just how it will sound because I've lived up high and I know the sort of watch birds keep on us. I've listened to sparrows tapping tentatively on the outside of air conditioners when they thought no one was listening, and I know how other birds test the vibrations that come up to them through the television aerials.

"Is he gone?" they ask, and the vibrations come up from below, "Not yet, not yet."

Well, to come back, I got the door open softly and I had the spot-light all ready to turn on and blind whatever birds there were so they couldn't see to get out through the roof. I had a short piece of ladder to put against the far wall where there was a shelf on which I expected to make the biggest haul. I had all the information I needed, just like any skilled assassin. I pushed the door open, the hinges squeaking only a little. A bird or two stirred—I could hear them—but nothing flew and there was a faint starlight through the holes in the roof.

I padded across the floor, got the ladder up and the light ready, and slithered up the ladder till my head and arms were over the shelf. Everything was dark as pitch except for the starlight at the little place back of the shelf near the eaves. With the light to blind them, they'd never make it. I had them. I reached my arm carefully over in order to be ready to seize whatever was there and I put the flash on the edge of the shelf where it would stand by itself when I turned it on. That way I'd be able to use both hands.

Everything worked perfectly except for one detail—I didn't know 20 what kind of birds were there. I never thought about it at all, and it wouldn't have mattered if I had. My orders were to get something interesting. I snapped on the flash and sure enough there was a great beating and feathers flying, but instead of my having them, they, or rather he, had me. He had my hand, that is, and for a small hawk not much bigger than my fist he was doing all right. I heard him give one short metallic cry when the light went on and my hand descended on the bird beside him; after that he was busy with his claws and his beak was sunk in my thumb. In the struggle I knocked the lamp over on the shelf, and his mate got her sight back and whisked neatly through the hole in the roof and off among the stars outside. It all happened in fifteen seconds and you might think I would have fallen down the lad-der, but no, I had a professional assassin's reputation to keep up, and the bird, of course, made the mistake of thinking the hand was the enemy and not the eyes behind it. He chewed my thumb up pretty effectively and lacerated my hand with his claws, but in the end I got him, having two hands to work with.

He was a sparrow hawk and a fine young male in the prime of life. I was sorry not to catch the pair of them, but as I dripped blood and folded his wings carefully, holding him by the back so that he couldn't strike again, I had to admit the two of them might have been more than I could have handled under the circumstances. The little fellow had saved his mate by diverting me, and that was that. He was born to it and made no outcry now, resting in my hand hopelessly but peering toward me in the shadows behind the lamp with a fierce, almost indifferent glance. He neither gave nor expected mercy and something out of the high air passed from him to me, stirring a faint embarrassment.

I quit looking into that eye and managed to get my huge carcass with its fist full of prey back down the ladder. I put the bird in a box too small to allow him to injure himself by struggle and walked out to welcome the arriving trucks. It had been a long day, and camp still to make in the darkness. In the morning that bird would be just another episode. He would go back with the bones in the truck to a small cage in a city where he would spend the rest of his life. And a good thing, too. I sucked my aching thumb and spat out some blood. An assassin has to get used to these things. I had a professional reputation to keep up.

In the morning, with the change that comes on suddenly in that high country, the mist that had hovered below us in the valley was gone. The sky was a deep blue, and one could see for miles over the high outcroppings of stone. I was up early and brought the box in which the little hawk was imprisoned out onto the grass where I was building a cage. A wind as cool as a mountain spring ran over the grass and stirred my hair. It was a fine day to be alive. I looked up and all around and at the hole in the cabin roof out of which the other little hawk had fled. There was no sign of her anywhere that I could see.

"Probably in the next county by now," I thought cynically, but before beginning work I decided I'd have a look at my last night's capture.

Secretively, I looked again all around the camp and up and down and opened the box. I got him right out in my hand with his wings folded properly and I was careful not to startle him. He lay limp in my grasp and I could feel his heart pound under the feathers but he only looked beyond me and up.

I saw him look that last look away beyond me into a sky so full of light that I could not follow his gaze. The little breeze flowed over me again, and nearby a mountain aspen shook all its tiny leaves. I suppose I must have had an idea then of what I was going to do, but I never let it come up into consciousness. I just reached over and laid the hawk on the grass.

He lay there a long minute without hope, unmoving, his eyes still fixed on that blue vault above him. It must have been that he was already so far away in heart that he never felt the release from my hand. He never even stood. He just lay with his breast against the grass.

In the next second after that long minute he was gone. Like a flicker of light, he had vanished with my eyes full on him but without actually seeing even a premonitory wing beat. He was gone straight into that towering emptiness of light and crystal that my eyes could scarcely bear to penetrate. For another long moment there was silence. I could not see him. The light was too intense. Then from far up somewhere a cry came ringing down.

I was young then and had seen little of the world, but when I heard that cry my heart turned over. It was not the cry of the hawk I had captured; for, by shifting my position against the sun, I was now seeing farther up. Straight out of the sun's eye, where she must have been soaring restlessly above us for untold hours, hurtled his mate. And from far up, ringing from peak to peak of the summits over us, came a cry of such unutterable and ecstatic joy that it sounds down across the years and tingles among the cups of my quiet breakfast table.

I saw them both now. He was rising fast to meet her. They met in 30 a great soaring gyre that turned to a whirling circle and a dance of wings. Once more, just once, their two voices, joined in a harsh wild medley of question and response, struck and echoed against the pinnacles of the valley. Then they were gone forever somewhere into those upper regions beyond the eyes of men.

I am older now, and sleep less, and have seen most of what there is to see and am not very much impressed any more, I suppose, by anything. "What Next in the Attributes of Machines?" my morning headline runs. "It Might Be the Power to Reproduce Themselves."

I lay the paper down and across my mind a phrase floats insinuatingly: "It does not seem that there is anything in the construction, constituents, or behavior of the human being which it is essentially impossible for science to duplicate and synthesize. On the other hand . . ."

All over the city the cogs in the hard, bright mechanisms have begun to turn. Figures move through computers, names are spelled out, a thoughtful machine selects the fingerprints of a wanted criminal from an array of thousands. In the laboratory an electronic mouse runs swiftly through a maze toward the cheese it can neither taste nor enjoy. On the second run it does better than a living mouse.

"On the other hand . . ." Ah, my mind takes up, on the other hand the machine does not bleed, ache, hang for hours in the empty sky in a torment of hope to learn the fate of another machine, nor does it cry out with joy nor dance in the air with the fierce passion of a bird. Far off, over a distance greater than space, that remote cry from the heart of heaven makes a faint buzzing among my breakfast dishes and passes on and away.

LINES OF INQUIRY
"The Bird and the Machine"

Although the bird is one of the title characters in this piece, Eiseley doesn't begin telling the story of the birds until the middle of his essay. Why do you suppose he withholds the story until that point? Why doesn't he tell it right off, rather than preceding it with the story of his time up in the canyons with the snake? How does the story of his time in the canyons reflect upon his story of the birds? How is your reaction to the story of the bird—and your understanding of the story—shaped by everything that precedes it? What about the machine? What story, if any, does he tell about that?

At the end of the first paragraph, Eiseley is moved by the strange process of his own thoughts to reflect on "how it is a funny thing what the brain will do with memories," how it will "bring them into odd juxtapositions with other things, as though it wanted to make a design, or get some meaning out of them." Trace the process of Eiseley's musings through the first eight paragraphs and try to account for the memories, the images, and the ideas that are mingled in each paragraph. What does this associative or meditative form have to do with the point of the piece, with the things that are uppermost in Eiseley's mind?

In another memory piece, "Once More to the Lake," White also is moved to reflect upon how the mind works, how "you remember one thing, and that suddenly reminds you of another thing." In what respects do Eiseley and White have similar ideas about the workings of the mind? In what respects different? In what respects do they depict their minds as working in similar ways? In what respects do they depict them as working differently?

THE LONG LONELINESS

There is nothing more alone in the universe than man. He is alone because he has the intellectual capacity to know that he is separated by a vast gulf of social memory and experiment from the lives of his animal associates. He has entered into the strange world of history, of social and intellectual change, while his brothers of the field and forest remain subject to the invisible laws of biological evolution. Animals are molded by natural forces they do not comprehend. To their minds there is no past and no future. There is only the everlasting present of a single generation—its trails in the forest, its hidden pathways of the air and in the sea.

Man, by contrast, is alone with the knowledge of his history until the day of his death. When we were children we wanted to talk to animals and struggled to understand why this was impossible. Slowly we gave up the attempt as we grew into the solitary world of human adulthood; the rabbit was left on the lawn, the dog was relegated to his kennel. Only in acts of inarticulate compassion, in rare and hidden moments of communion with nature, does man briefly escape his solitary destiny. Frequently in science fiction he dreams of worlds with creatures whose communicative power is the equivalent of his own.

It is with a feeling of startlement, therefore, and eager interest touching the lost child in every one of us, that the public has received the recent accounts of naval research upon the intelligence of one of our brother mammals—the sea-dwelling bottle-nosed porpoise or dolphin.

These small whales who left the land millions of years ago to return to the great mother element of life, the sea, are now being regarded by researchers as perhaps the most intelligent form of life on our planet next to man. Dr. John Lilly of the Communications Research Institute in the Virgin Islands reports that the brain of the porpoise is 40 per cent larger than man's and is just as complex in its functional units. Amazed by the rapidity with which captive porpoises solved problems that even monkeys found difficult, Dr. Lilly is quoted as expressing the view that "man's position at the top of the hierarchy [of intelligence] begins to be questioned."

Dr. Lilly found that his captives communicated in a series of underwater whistles and that, in addition, they showed an amazing "verbalizing" ability in copying certain sounds heard in the laboratory. The experimental animal obviously hoped to elicit by this means a reproduction of the pleasurable sensations he had been made to experience under laboratory conditions. It is reported that in spite of living in a medium different from the one that man inhabits, and therefore having

5

quite a different throat structure, one of the porpoises even uttered in a Donald-Duckish voice a short number series it had heard spoken by one of the laboratory investigators.

The import of these discoveries is tremendous and may not be adequately known for a long time. An animal from a little-explored medium, which places great barriers in the way of the psychologist, has been found to have not only a strong social organization but to show a degree of initiative in experimental communicative activity unmatched by man's closest relatives, the great apes. The porpoises reveal, moreover, a touching altruism and friendliness in their attempts to aid injured companions. Can it be, one inevitably wonders, that man is so locked in his own type of intelligence—an intelligence that is linked to a prehensile, grasping hand giving him power over his environment—that he is unable to comprehend the intellectual life of a highly endowed creature from another domain such as the sea?

Perhaps the water barrier has shut us away from a potentially communicative and jolly companion. Perhaps we have some things still to learn from the natural world around us before we turn to the far shores of space and whatever creatures may await us there. After all, the porpoise is a mammal. He shares with us an ancient way of birth and affectionate motherhood. His blood is warm, he breathes air as we do. We both bear in our bodies the remnants of a common skeleton torn asunder for divergent purposes far back in the dim dawn of mammalian life. The porpoise has been superficially streamlined like a fish.

His are not, however, the cold-blooded ways of the true fishes. Far higher on the tree of life than fishes, the dolphin's paddles are made-over paws, rather than fins. He is an ever-constant reminder of the versatility of life and its willingness to pass through strange dimensions of experience. There are environmental worlds on earth every bit as weird as what we may imagine to revolve by far-off suns. It is our superficial familiarity with this planet that inhibits our appreciation of the unknown until a porpoise, rearing from a tank to say Three-Two-Three, re-creates for us the utter wonder of childhood.

Unless we are specialists in the study of communication and its relation to intelligence, however, we are apt to oversimplify or define poorly what intelligence is, what communication and language are, and thus confuse and mystify both ourselves and others. The mysteries surrounding the behavior of the bottle-nosed porpoise, and even of man himself, are not things to be probed simply by the dissector's scalpel. They lie deeper. They involve the whole nature of the mind and its role in the universe.

We are forced to ask ourselves whether native intelligence in another form than man's might be as high as or even higher than his own, yet be marked by no such material monuments as man has placed upon the earth. At first glance we are alien to this idea, because man is

10

particularly a creature who has turned the tables on his environment so that he is now engrossed in shaping it, rather than being shaped by it. Man expresses himself upon his environment through the use of tools. We therefore tend to equate the use of tools in a one-to-one relationship with intelligence.

The question we must now ask ourselves, however, is whether this involves an unconsciously man-centered way of looking at intelligence. Let us try for a moment to enter the dolphin's kingdom and the dolphin's body, retaining, at the same time, our human intelligence. In this imaginative act, it may be possible to divest ourselves of certain human preconceptions about our kind of intelligence and at the same time to see more clearly why mind, even advanced mind, may have manifestations other than the tools and railroad tracks and laboratories that we regard as evidence of intellect. If we are particularly adept in escaping from our own bodies, we may even learn to discount a little the kind of world of rockets and death that our type of busy human curiosity, linked to a hand noted for its ability to open assorted Pandora's boxes, has succeeded in foisting upon the world as a symbol of universal intelligence.

We have now sacrificed, in our imagination, our hands for flippers and our familiar land environment for the ocean. We will go down into the deep waters as naked of possessions as when we entered life itself. We will take with us one thing alone that exists among porpoises as among men: an ingrained biological gregariousness—a sociality that in our new world will permit us to run in schools, just as early man ran in the packs that were his ancient anthropoid heritage. We will assume in the light of Dr. Lilly's researches that our native intelligence, as distinguished from our culturally transmitted habits, is very high. The waters have closed finally over us, our paws have been sacrificed for the necessary flippers with which to navigate.

The result is immediately evident and quite clear: No matter how well we communicate with our fellows through the water medium we will never build drowned empires in the coral; we will never inscribe on palace walls the victorious boasts of porpoise kings. We will know only water and the wastes of water beyond the power of man to describe. We will be secret visitors in hidden canyons beneath the mouths of torrential rivers. We will survey in innocent astonishment the flotsam that pours from the veins of continents—dead men, great serpents, giant trees—or perhaps the little toy boat of a child loosed far upstream will come floating past. Bottles with winking green lights will plunge by us into the all-embracing ooze. Meaningless appearances and disappearances will comprise our philosophies. We will hear the earth's heart ticking in its thin granitic shell. Volcanic fires will growl ominously in steam-filled crevices. Vapor, bird cries, and sea wrack will compose our memories. We will see death in many forms and, on occasion, the slow

majestic fall of battleships through the green light that comes from beyond our domain.

Over all that region of wondrous beauty we will exercise no more
control than the simplest mollusk. Even the octopus with flexible arms
will build little shelters that we cannot imitate. Without hands we will
have only the freedom to follow the untrammeled sea winds across
the planet.

Perhaps if those whistling sounds that porpoises make are truly   15
symbolic and capable of manipulation in our brains, we will wonder
about the world in which we find ourselves—but it will be a world not
susceptible to experiment. At best we may nuzzle in curiosity a passing
shipbottom and be harpooned for our pains. Our thoughts, in other
words, will be as limited as those of the first men who roved in little
bands in the times before fire and the writing that was to open to man
the great doorway of his past.

Man without writing cannot long retain his history in his head. His
intelligence permits him to grasp some kind of succession of generations; but without writing, the tale of the past rapidly degenerates into
fumbling myth and fable. Man's greatest epic, his four long battles with
the advancing ice of the great continental glaciers, has vanished from
human memory without a trace. Our illiterate fathers disappeared and
with them, in a few scant generations, died one of the great stories of
all time. This episode has nothing to do with the biological quality of
a brain as between then and now. It has to do instead with a device, an
invention made possible by the hand. That invention came too late in
time to record eyewitness accounts of the years of the Giant Frost.

Primitives of our own species, even today, are historically shallow
in their knowledge of the past. Only the poet who writes speaks his
message across the millennia to other hearts. Only in writing can the
cry from the great cross on Golgotha still be heard in the minds of men.
The thinker of perceptive insight, even if we allow him for the moment
to be a porpoise rather than a man, has only his individual glimpse of
the universe until such time as he can impose that insight upon unnum-
bered generations. In centuries of pondering, man has come upon but
one answer to this problem: speech translated into writing that passes
beyond human mortality.

Writing, and later printing, is the product of our adaptable many-
purposed hands. It is thus, through writing, with no increase in genetic,
inborn capacity since the last ice advance, that modern man carries in
his mind the intellectual triumphs of all his predecessors who were able
to inscribe their thoughts for posterity.

All animals which man has reason to believe are more than usually
intelligent—our relatives the great apes, the elephant, the raccoon, the
wolverine, among others—are problem solvers, and in at least a small
way manipulators of their environment. Save for the instinctive calls of

their species, however, they cannot communicate except by direct imitation. They cannot invent words for new situations nor get their fellows to use such words. No matter how high the individual intelligence, its private world remains a private possession locked forever within a single, perishable brain. It is this fact that finally balks our hunger to communicate even with the sensitive dog who shares our fireside.

Dr. Lilly insists, however, that the porpoises communicate in high-pitched, underwater whistles that seem to transmit their wishes and problems. The question then becomes one of ascertaining whether these sounds represent true language—in the sense of symbolic meanings, additive, learned elements—or whether they are simply the instinctive signals of a pack animal. To this there is as yet no clear answer, but the eagerness with which laboratory sounds and voices were copied by captive porpoises suggests a vocalizing ability extending perhaps to or beyond the threshold of speech.

Most of the intelligent land animals have prehensile, grasping organs for exploring their environment—hands in man and his anthropoid relatives, the sensitive inquiring trunk in the elephant. One of the surprising things about the porpoise is that his superior brain is unaccompanied by any type of manipulative organ. He has, however, a remarkable range-finding ability involving some sort of echo-sounding. Perhaps this acute sense—far more accurate than any man has been able to devise artificially—brings him greater knowledge of his watery surroundings than might at first seem possible. Human beings think of intelligence as geared to things. The hand and the tool are to us the unconscious symbols of our intellectual achievement. It is difficult for us to visualize another kind of lonely, almost disembodied intelligence floating in the wavering green fairyland of the sea—an intelligence possibly near or comparable to our own but without hands to build, to transmit knowledge by writing, or to alter by one hairsbreadth the planet's surface. Yet at the same time there are indications that this is a warm, friendly and eager intelligence quite capable of coming to the assistance of injured companions and striving to rescue them from drowning. Porpoises left the land when mammalian brains were still small and primitive. Without the stimulus provided by agile exploring fingers, these great sea mammals have yet taken a divergent road toward intelligence of a high order. Hidden in their sleek bodies is an impressively elaborated instrument, the reason for whose appearance is a complete enigma. It is as though both man and porpoise were each part of some great eye which yearned to look both outward on eternity and inward to the sea's heart—that fertile entity so like the mind in its swarming and grotesque life.

Perhaps man has something to learn after all from fellow creatures without the ability to drive harpoons through living flesh, or poison with strontium the planetary winds. One is reminded of those watery blue vaults in which, as in some idyllic eternity, Herman Melville once saw the sperm whales nurse their young. And as Melville wrote of the sperm whale, so we might now paraphrase his words in speaking of the porpoise. "Genius in the porpoise? Has the porpoise ever written a book, spoken a speech? No, his great genius is declared in his doing nothing particular to prove it. It is declared in his pyramidical silence." If man had sacrificed his hands for flukes, the moral might run, he would still be a philosopher, but there would have been taken from him the devastating power to wreak his thought upon the body of the world. Instead he would have lived and wandered, like the porpoise, homeless across currents and winds and oceans, intelligent, but forever the lonely and curious observer of unknown wreckage falling through the blue light of eternity. This role would now be a deserved penitence for man. Perhaps such a transformation would bring him once more into that mood of childhood innocence in which he talked successfully to all things living but had no power and no urge to harm. It is worth at least a wistful thought that someday the porpoise may talk to us and we to him. It would break, perhaps, the long loneliness that has made man a frequent terror and abomination even to himself.

LINES OF INQUIRY
"The Long Loneliness"

In paragraph 11, Eiseley decides to enter imaginatively into the point of view of the porpoise, and in paragraphs 12–15 he follows through on this decision. What did you discover from this imaginative excursion? What purpose(s) does this excursion serve in the later development of the essay, particularly in the final paragraph? Why do you suppose that Eiseley didn't continue the excursion beyond paragraph 15? In what respect(s), if any, does the excursion seem to be biased by "a man-centered way of looking" at things?

In paragraphs 16–19, Eiseley makes a special claim for writing as endowing human beings with unique powers. What special powers and achievements does Eiseley attribute to writing? In what respects does he regard these powers and achievements as also being the cause of man's "long loneliness"? Exactly what does Eiseley mean by the long loneliness? Why might it not be argued that every creature suffers from a long loneliness?

In this essay, as in his other pieces in this collection, the relationship of human beings to other creatures in the world concerns Eiseley. Based on a reading of these four pieces, what do you consider to be the most important elements in Eiseley's view of that relationship?

THE HIDDEN TEACHER

*Sometimes the best teacher teaches only once to a single child or to
a grownup past hope.*

—Anonymous

I

The putting of formidable
riddles did not arise with today's philosophers. In fact, there is a sense
in which the experimental method of science might be said merely to
have widened the area of man's homelessness. Over two thousand years
ago, a man named Job, crouching in the Judean desert, was moved to
challenge what he felt to be the injustice of his God. The voice in the
whirlwind, in turn, volleyed pitiless questions upon the supplicant—
questions that have, in truth, precisely the ring of modern science. For
the Lord asked of Job by whose wisdom the hawk soars, and who had
fathered the rain, or entered the storehouses of the snow.

A youth standing by, one Elihu, also played a role in this drama,
for he ventured diffidently to his protesting elder that it was not true
that God failed to manifest Himself. He may speak in one way or another, though men do not perceive it. In consequence of this remark
perhaps it would be well, whatever our individual beliefs, to consider
what may be called the hidden teacher, lest we become too much concerned with the formalities of only one aspect of the education by which
we learn.

We think we learn from teachers, and we sometimes do. But the
teachers are not always to be found in school or in great laboratories.
Sometimes what we learn depends upon our own powers of insight.
Moreover, our teachers may be hidden, even the greatest teacher. And
it was the young man Elihu who observed that if the old are not always
wise, neither can the teacher's way be ordered by the young whom he
would teach.

For example, I once received an unexpected lesson from a spider.

It happened far away on a rainy morning in the West. I had come   5
up a long gulch looking for fossils, and there, just at eye level, lurked
a huge yellow-and-black orb spider, whose web was moored to the tall
spears of buffalo grass at the edge of the arroyo. It was her universe,
and her senses did not extend beyond the lines and spokes of the great
wheel she inhabited. Her extended claws could feel every vibration
throughout that delicate structure. She knew the tug of wind, the fall
of a raindrop, the flutter of a trapped moth's wing. Down one spoke
of the web ran a stout ribbon of gossamer on which she could hurry
out to investigate her prey.

Curious, I took a pencil from my pocket and touched a strand of the web. Immediately there was a response. The web, plucked by its menacing occupant, began to vibrate until it was a blur. Anything that had brushed claw or wing against that amazing snare would be thoroughly entrapped. As the vibrations slowed, I could see the owner fingering her guidelines for signs of struggle. A pencil point was an intrusion into this universe for which no precedent existed. Spider was circumscribed by spider ideas; its universe was spider universe. All outside was irrational, extraneous, at best raw material for spider. As I proceeded on my way along the gully, like a vast impossible shadow, I realized that in the world of spider I did not exist.

Moreover, I considered, as I tramped along, that to the phagocytes, the white blood cells, clambering even now with some kind of elementary intelligence amid the thin pipes and tubing of my body—creatures without whose ministrations I could not exist—the conscious "I" of which I was aware had no significance to these amoeboid beings. I was, instead, a kind of chemical web that brought meaningful messages to them, a natural environment seemingly immortal if they could have thought about it, since generations of them had lived and perished, and would continue to so live and die, in that odd fabric which contained my intelligence—a misty light that was beginning to seem floating and tenuous even to me.

I began to see that, among the many universes in which the world of living creatures existed, some were large, some small, but that all, including man's, were in some way limited or finite. We were creatures of many different dimensions passing through each other's lives like ghosts through doors.

In the years since, my mind has many times returned to that far moment of my encounter with the orb spider. A message has arisen only now from the misty shreds of that webbed universe. What was it that had so troubled me about the incident? Was it that spidery indifference to the human triumph?

If so, that triumph was very real and could not be denied. I saw, had many times seen, both mentally and in the seams of exposed strata, the long backward stretch of time whose recovery is one of the great feats of modern science. I saw the drifting cells of the early seas from which all life, including our own, has arisen. The salt of those ancient seas is in our blood, its lime is in our bones. Every time we walk along a beach some ancient urge disturbs us so that we find ourselves shedding shoes and garments or scavenging among seaweed and whitened timbers like the homesick refugees of a long war.

And war it has been indeed—the long war of life against its inhospitable environment, a war that has lasted for perhaps three billion years. It began with strange chemicals seething under a sky lacking in oxygen; it was waged through long ages until the first green plants learned to

10

harness the light of the nearest star, our sun. The human brain, so frail, so perishable, so full of inexhaustible dreams and hungers, burns by the power of the leaf.

The hurrying blood cells charged with oxygen carry more of that element to the human brain than to any other part of the body. A few moments' loss of vital air and the phenomenon we know as consciousness goes down into the black night of inorganic things. The human body is a magical vessel, but its life is linked with an element it cannot produce. Only the green plant knows the secret of transforming the light that comes to us across the far reaches of space. There is no better illustration of the intricacy of man's relationship with other living things.

The student of fossil life would be forced to tell us that if we take the past into consideration the vast majority of earth's creatures—perhaps over 90 percent—have vanished. Forms that flourished for a far longer time than man has existed upon earth have become either extinct or so transformed that their descendants are scarcely recognizable. The specialized perish with the environment that created them, the tooth of the tiger fails at last, the lances of men strike down the last mammoth.

In three billion years of slow change and groping effort only one living creature has succeeded in escaping the trap of specialization that has led in time to so much death and wasted endeavor. It is man, but the word should be uttered softly, for his story is not yet done.

With the rise of the human brain, with the appearance of a creature   15 whose upright body enabled two limbs to be freed for the exploration and manipulation of his environment, there had at last emerged a creature with a specialization—the brain—that, paradoxically, offered escape from specialization. Many animals driven into the nooks and crannies of nature have achieved momentary survival only at the cost of later extinction.

Was it this that troubled me and brought my mind back to a tiny universe among the grass blades, a spider's universe concerned with spider thought?

Perhaps.

The mind that once visualized animals on a cave wall is now engaged in a vast ramification of itself through time and space. Man has broken through the boundaries that control all other life. I saw, at last, the reason for my recollection of that great spider on the arroyo's rim, fingering its universe against the sky.

The spider was a symbol of man in miniature. The wheel of the web brought the analogy home clearly. Man, too, lies at the heart of a web, a web extending through the starry reaches of sidereal space, as well as backward into the dark realm of prehistory. His great eye upon Mount Palomar looks into a distance of millions of light-years, his radio ear hears the whisper of even more remote galaxies, he peers through the electron microscope upon the minute particles of his own being. It is a web no creature of earth has ever spun before. Like the orb spider, man lies at the heart of it, listening. Knowledge has given him the memory of earth's history beyond the time of his emergence. Like the spider's claw, a part of him touches a world he will never enter in the flesh. Even now, one can see him reaching forward into time with new machines, computing, analyzing, until elements of the shadowy future will also compose part of the invisible web he fingers.

Yet still my spider lingers in memory against the sunset sky. Spider thoughts in a spider universe—sensitive to raindrop and moth flutter, nothing beyond, nothing allowed for the unexpected, the inserted pencil from the world outside.

Is man at heart any different from the spider, I wonder: man thoughts, as limited as spider thoughts, contemplating now the nearest star with the threat of bringing with him the fungus rot from earth, wars, violence, the burden of a population he refuses to control, cherishing again his dream of the Adamic Eden he had pursued and lost in the green forests of America. Now it beckons again like a mirage from beyond the moon. Let man spin his web, I thought further; it is his nature. But I considered also the work of the phagocytes swarming in the rivers of my body, the unresting cells in their mortal universe. What is it we are a part of that we do not see, as the spider was not gifted to discern my face, or my little probe into her world?

We are too content with our sensory extensions, with the fulfillment of that Ice Age mind that began its journey amidst the cold of vast tundras and that pauses only briefly before its leap into space. It is no longer enough to see as a man sees—even to the ends of the universe. It is not enough to hold nuclear energy in one's hand like a spear, as a man would hold it, or to see the lightning, or times past, or time to come, as a man would see it. If we continue to do this, the great brain—the human brain—will be only a new version of the old trap, and nature is full of traps for the beast that cannot learn.

It is not sufficient any longer to listen at the end of a wire to the rustlings of galaxies; it is not enough even to examine the great coil of DNA in which is coded the very alphabet of life. These are our extended perceptions. But beyond lies the great darkness of the ultimate Dreamer, who dreamed the light and the galaxies. Before act was, or substance existed, imagination grew in the dark. Man partakes of that ultimate wonder and creativeness. As we turn from the galaxies to the swarming cells of our own being, which toil for something, some entity beyond their grasp, let us remember man, the self-fabricator who came across an ice age to look into the mirrors and the magic of science. Surely he did not come to see himself or his wild visage only. He came because he is at heart a listener and a searcher for some transcendent realm beyond himself. This he has worshiped by many names, even in the dismal caves of his beginning. Man, the self-fabricator, is so by reason of gifts he had no part in devising—and so he searches as the single living cell in the beginning must have sought the ghostly creature it was to serve.

II

The young man Elihu, Job's counselor and critic, spoke simply of the "Teacher," and it is of this teacher I speak when I refer to gifts man had no part in devising. Perhaps—though it is purely a matter of emotional reactions to words—it is easier for us today to speak of this teacher as "nature," that omnipresent all which contained both the spider and my invisible intrusion into her carefully planned universe. But nature does not simply represent reality. In the shapes of life, it prepares the future; it offers alternatives. Nature teaches, though what it teaches is often hidden and obscure, just as the voice from the spinning dust cloud belittled Job's thought but gave back no answers to its own formidable interrogation.

A few months ago I encountered an amazing little creature on a windy corner of my local shopping center. It seemed, at first glance, some long-limbed, feathery spider teetering rapidly down the edge of a store front. Then it swung into the air and, as hesitantly as a spider on a thread, blew away into the parking lot. It returned in a moment on a gust of wind and ran toward me once more on its spindly legs with amazing rapidity.   25

With great difficulty I discovered the creature was actually a filamentous seed, seeking a hiding place and scurrying about with the uncanny surety of a conscious animal. In fact, it *did* escape me before I could secure it. Its flexible limbs were stiffer than milkweed down, and, propelled by the wind, it ran rapidly and evasively over the pavement. It was like a gnome scampering somewhere with a hidden packet—for all that I could tell, a totally new one: one of the jumbled alphabets of life.

A new one? So stable seem the years and all green leaves, a botanist might smile at my imaginings. Yet bear with me a moment. I would like to tell a tale, a genuine tale of childhood. Moreover, I was just old enough to know the average of my kind and to marvel at what I saw. And what I saw was straight from the hidden Teacher, whatever be his name.

It is told in the Orient of the Hindu god Krishna that his mother, wiping his mouth when he was a child, inadvertently peered in and beheld the universe, though the sight was mercifully and immediately veiled from her. In a sense, this is what happened to me. One day there arrived at our school a newcomer, who entered the grade above me. After some days this lad, whose look of sleepy-eyed arrogance is still before me as I write, was led into my mathematics classroom by the principal. Our class was informed severely that we should learn to work harder.

With this preliminary exhortation, great rows of figures were chalked upon the blackboard, such difficult mathematical problems as could be devised by adults. The class watched in helpless wonder. When the preparations had been completed, the young pupil sauntered forward and, with a glance of infinite boredom that swept from us to his fawning teachers, wrote the answers, as instantaneously as a modern computer, in their proper place upon the board. Then he strolled out with a carelessly exaggerated yawn.

Like some heavy-browed child at the wood's edge, clutching the last stone hand ax, I was witnessing the birth of a new type of humanity—one so beyond its teachers that it was being used for mean purposes while the intangible web of the universe in all its shimmering mathematical perfection glistened untaught in the mind of a chance little boy. The boy, by then grown self-centered and contemptuous, was being dragged from room to room to encourage us, the paleanthropes, to duplicate what, in reality, our teachers could not duplicate. He was too precious an object to be released upon the playground among us, and with reason. In a few months his parents took him away.

Long after, looking back from maturity, I realized that I had been exposed on that occasion, not to human teaching, but to the Teacher, toying with some sixteen billion nerve cells interlocked in ways past understanding. Or, if we do not like the anthropomorphism implied in the word teacher, then nature, the old voice from the whirlwind fumbling for the light. At all events, I had been the fortunate witness to life's unbounded creativity—a creativity seemingly still as unbalanced and chance-filled as in that far era when a black-scaled creature had broken from an egg and the age of the giant reptiles, the creatures of the prime, had tentatively begun.

Because form cannot be long sustained in the living, we collapse inward with age. We die. Our bodies, which were the product of a kind of hidden teaching by an alphabet we are only beginning dimly to discern, are dismissed into their elements. What is carried onward, assuming we have descendants, is the little capsule of instructions such as I encountered hastening by me in the shape of a running seed. We have learned the first biological lesson: that in each generation life passes through the eye of a needle. It exists for a time molecularly and in no recognizable semblance to its adult condition. It *instructs* its way again into man or reptile. As the ages pass, so do variants of the code. Occasionally, a species vanishes on a wind as unreturning as that which took the pterodactyls.

Or the code changes by subtle degrees through the statistical altering of individuals; until I, as the fading Neanderthals must once have done, have looked with still-living eyes upon the creature whose genotype was quite possibly to replace me. The genetic alphabets, like genuine languages, ramify and evolve along unreturning pathways.

If nature's instructions are carried through the eye of a needle, through the molecular darkness of a minute world below the field of human vision and of time's decay, the same, it might be said, is true of those monumental structures known as civilizations. They are transmitted from one generation to another in invisible puffs of air known as words—words that can also be symbolically incised on clay. As the delicate printing on the mud at the water's edge retraces a visit of autumn birds long since departed, so the little scrabbled tablets in perished cities carry the seeds of human thought across the deserts of millennia. In this instance the teacher is the social brain, but it, too, must be compressed into minute hieroglyphs, and the minds that wrought the miracle efface themselves amidst the jostling torrent of messages, which, like the genetic code, are shuffled and reshuffled as they hurry through eternity. Like a mutation, an idea may be recorded in the wrong time, to lie latent like a recessive gene and spring once more to life in an auspicious era.

Occasionally, in the moments when an archaeologist lifts the slab over a tomb that houses a great secret, a few men gain a unique glimpse through that dark portal out of which all men living have emerged, and through which messages again must pass. Here the Mexican archaeologist Ruz Lhuillier speaks of his first penetration of the great tomb hidden beneath dripping stalactites at the pyramid of Palenque: "Out of the dark shadows, rose a fairy-tale vision, a weird ethereal spectacle from another world. It was like a magician's cave carved out of ice, with walls glittering and sparkling like snow crystals." After shining his torch over hieroglyphs and sculptured figures, the explorer remarked wonderingly: "We were the first people for more than a thousand years to look at it."

Or again, one may read the tale of an unknown pharaoh who had secretly arranged that a beloved woman of his household should be buried in the tomb of the god-king—an act of compassion carrying a personal message across the millennia in defiance of all precedent.

Up to this point we have been talking of the single hidden teacher, the taunting voice out of that old Biblical whirlwind which symbolizes nature. We have seen incredible organic remembrance passed through the needle's eye of a microcosmic world hidden completely beneath the observational powers of creatures preoccupied and ensorcelled by dissolution and decay. We have seen the human mind unconsciously seize upon the principles of that very code to pass its own societal memory forward into time. The individual, the momentary living cell of the society, vanishes, but the institutional structures stand, or if they change, do so in an invisible flux not too dissimilar from that persisting in the stream of genetic continuity.

Upon this world, life is still young, not truly old as stars are measured. Therefore it comes about that we minimize the role of the synapsid reptiles, our remote forerunners, and correspondingly exalt our own intellectual achievements. We refuse to consider that in the old eye of the hurricane we may be, and doubtless are, in aggregate, a slightly more diffuse and dangerous dragon of the primal morning that still enfolds us.

Note that I say "in aggregate." For it is just here, among men, that the role of messages, and, therefore, the role of the individual teacher— or, I should say now, the hidden teachers—begin to be more plainly apparent and their instructions become more diverse. The dead pharaoh, though unintentionally, by a revealing act, had succeeded in conveying an impression of human tenderness that has outlasted the trappings of a vanished religion.

Like most modern educators I have listened to student demands to   40
grade their teachers. I have heard the words repeated until they have become a slogan, that no man over thirty can teach the young of this generation. How would one grade a dead pharaoh, millennia gone, I wonder, one who did not intend to teach, but who, to a few perceptive minds, succeeded by the simple nobility of an act.

Many years ago, a student who was destined to become an internationally known anthropologist sat in a course in linguistics and heard his instructor, a man of no inconsiderable wisdom, describe some linguistic peculiarities of Hebrew words. At the time, the young student, at the urging of his family, was contemplating a career in theology. As the teacher warmed to his subject, the student, in the back row, ventured excitedly, "I believe I can understand that, sir. It is very similar to what exists in Mohegan."

The linguist paused and adjusted his glasses. "Young man," he said, "Mohegan is a dead language. Nothing has been recorded of it since the eighteenth century. Don't bluff."

"But sir," the young student countered hopefully, "It can't be dead so long as an old woman I know still speaks it. She is Pequot-Mohegan. I learned a bit of vocabulary from her and could speak with her myself. She took care of me when I was a child."

"Young man," said the austere, old-fashioned scholar, "be at my house for dinner at six this evening. You and I are going to look into this matter."

A few months later, under careful guidance, the young student pub-   45
lished a paper upon Mohegan linguistics, the first of a long series of studies upon the forgotten languages and ethnology of the Indians of the northeastern forests. He had changed his vocation and turned to anthropology because of the attraction of a hidden teacher. But just who was the teacher? The young man himself, his instructor, or that solitary speaker of a dying tongue who had so yearned to hear her people's voice that she had softly babbled it to a child?

Later, this man was to become one of my professors. I absorbed much from him, though I hasten to make the reluctant confession that he was considerably beyond thirty. Most of what I learned was gathered over cups of coffee in a dingy campus restaurant. What we talked about were things some centuries older than either of us. Our common interest lay in snakes, scapulimancy, and other forgotten rites of benighted forest hunters.

I have always regarded this man as an extraordinary individual, in fact, a hidden teacher. But alas, it is all now so old-fashioned. We never protested the impracticality of his quaint subjects. We were all too ready to participate in them. He was an excellent canoeman, but he took me to places where I fully expected to drown before securing my degree. To this day, fragments of his unused wisdom remain stuffed in some back attic of my mind. Much of it I have never found the opportunity to employ, yet it has somehow colored my whole adult existence. I belong to that elderly professor in somewhat the same way that he, in turn, had become the wood child of a hidden forest mother.

There are, however, other teachers. For example, among the hunting peoples there were the animal counselors who appeared in prophetic dreams. Or, among the Greeks, the daemonic supernaturals who stood at the headboard while a man lay stark and listened—sometimes to dreadful things. "You are asleep," the messengers proclaimed over and over again, as though the man lay in a spell to hear his doom pronounced. "You, Achilles, you, son of Atreus. You are asleep, asleep," the hidden ones pronounced and vanished.

We of this modern time know other things of dreams, but we know also that they can be interior teachers and healers as well as the anticipators of disaster. It has been said that great art is the night thought of man. It may emerge without warning from the soundless depths of the unconscious, just as supernovas may blaze up suddenly in the farther reaches of void space. The critics, like astronomers, can afterward triangulate such worlds but not account for them.

A writer friend of mine with bitter memories of his youth, and   50
estranged from his family, who, in the interim, had died, gave me this account of the matter in his middle years. He had been working, with an unusual degree of reluctance, upon a novel that contained certain autobiographical episodes. One night he dreamed; it was a very vivid and stunning dream in its detailed reality.

He found himself hurrying over creaking snow through the blackness of a winter night. He was ascending a familiar path through a long-vanished orchard. The path led to his childhood home. The house, as he drew near, appeared dark and uninhabited, but, impelled by the power of the dream, he stepped upon the porch and tried to peer through a dark window into his own old room.

"Suddenly," he told me, "I was drawn by a strange mixture of repulsion and desire to press my face against the glass. I knew intuitively they were all there waiting for me within, if I could but see them. My mother and my father. Those I had loved and those I hated. But the window was black to my gaze. I hesitated a moment and struck a match. For an instant in that freezing silence I saw my father's face glimmer wan and remote behind the glass. My mother's face was there, with the hard, distorted lines that marked her later years.

"A surge of fury overcame my cowardice. I cupped the match before me and stepped closer, closer toward that dreadful confrontation. As the match guttered down, my face was pressed almost to the glass. In some quick transformation, such as only a dream can effect, I saw that it was my own face into which I stared, just as it was reflected in the black glass. My father's haunted face was but my own. The hard lines upon my mother's aging countenance were slowly reshaping themselves upon my living face. The light burned out. I awoke sweating from the terrible psychological tension of that nightmare. I was in a far port in a distant land. It was dawn. I could hear the waves breaking on the reef."

"And how do you interpret the dream?" I asked, concealing a sympathetic shudder and sinking deeper into my chair.

"It taught me something," he said slowly, and with equal slowness a kind of beautiful transfiguration passed over his features. All the tired lines I had known so well seemed faintly to be subsiding.

"Did you ever dream it again?" I asked out of a comparable experience of my own.

"No, never," he said, and hesitated. "You see, I had learned it was just I, but more, much more, I had learned that I was they. It makes a difference. And at the last, late—much too late—it was all right. I understood. My line was dying, but I understood. I hope they understood, too." His voice trailed into silence.

"It is a thing to learn," I said. "You were seeking something and it came." He nodded, wordless. "Out of a tomb," he added after a silent moment, "my kind of tomb—the mind."

On the dark street, walking homeward, I considered my friend's experience. Man, I concluded, may have come to the end of that wild being who had mastered the fire and the lightning. He can create the web but not hold it together, not save himself except by transcending his own image. For at last, before the ultimate mystery, it is himself he shapes. Perhaps it is for this that the listening web lies open: that by knowledge we may grow beyond our past, our follies, and ever closer to what the Dreamer in the dark intended before the dust arose and walked. In the pages of an old book it has been written that we are in the hands of a Teacher, nor does it yet appear what man shall be.

LINES OF INQUIRY
"The Hidden Teacher"

In paragraphs 4, 5, and 6, Eiseley tells about "an unexpected lesson" that he learned "from a spider," and he refers to or alludes to the spider throughout the remainder of the essay. Make a note of all the explicit and implicit references to the spider. How are these references connected to each other, constituting something like a web of related images and ideas in the essay? How are the spider images related, in turn, to the other images and stories that Eiseley tells about in the piece? Why do you suppose that he chooses to make the spider the predominant metaphor in the essay?

Taking into account all of the hidden teachers that Eiseley refers to in his essay, what characteristics exactly distinguish "the hidden teacher"? How is a hidden teacher different from the teachers "to be found in school or in great laboratories"? In what respects does the knowledge that comes from hidden teachers differ from the knowledge conveyed by school teachers? In what respects do these different kinds of knowledge also imply different beliefs and values? What are the hidden beliefs and values that Eiseley attributes to the hidden teachers?

To what extent do you consider this essay to be a critique of traditional education? To what extent do you consider it a critique of the scientific method? To what extent do you consider it a critique of materialistic values? In thinking about these questions, you might find it useful to compare and contrast Thoreau's "My House" and "Where I Lived, and What I Lived For."

ELLEN GOODMAN

1941 –

I never wanted to be a package-tour sort of columnist who covered thirteen countries in twenty-seven days. Nor do I want to write at arm's length about the Major Issues of Our Times. I think it's more important for all of us to be able to make links between our personal lives and public issues.

Linking the public and private realms has consistently been Ellen Goodman's special contribution to the editorial pages of newspapers across America. As one journalist has said, Goodman's "trademark is a disarming personal approach to weighty subjects." So, while she writes on topics "as diverse as quiche, summer vacations, and collecting coffee cups," she is best known for her incisive commentary on social turmoil, especially the shifting sex roles in contemporary society. From sober analysis of rape to humorous yet serious reflection on advertising's depiction of women, Goodman's perspective manages to blend a sharp feminist edge with a steady devotion to the values which have traditionally given meaning to women's lives—mothering, hometending, gardening, and a strong sense of community. As a result, her widely syndicated columns have managed to engage the interest of a very diverse readership.

A third-generation Bostonian, Goodman grew up in so nurturing and secure a family that as a child she "wanted everything to stay the same." Her mother was a patient woman who "would listen to your problems until you were sick of them." Her father was a politically active lawyer who "discouraged mushy thinking" and encouraged his daughters to express and defend their opinions. He also encouraged his daughters to take part in his two unsuccesful campaigns for Congress. So, by the time she was only ten, Goodman had "learned the voting patterns of wards and precincts the way other kids learned the batting averages of the Red Sox and the battles of World War II." So, too, she learned to be "very comfortable speaking up."

Her prep school graduation yearbook predicted she would be the first woman president, but instead of entering politics she married shortly after graduating from Radcliffe College in 1963, and went to work as a researcher for *Newsweek,* where, she says, "All of the researchers were women and all of the reporters were men. We didn't like it but that's the way it was." In 1965, she moved with her husband to Detroit and began writing for the Detroit *Free Press*. In 1967, after returning with her husband to Boston, she went to work for the Boston *Globe* as a columnist and feature writer for the women's section. But the political and social upheavals of the late sixties and early seventies worked their influence on Goodman, as they did on the lives and views of countless others, leading her to take a strong interest in the issues addressed by the feminist movement, as well as in the "great ambivalence between tradition and non-tradition" that was then an overwhelming cultural concern.

In 1971 Goodman's marriage ended in divorce. That same year, her columns broke the traditional newspaper divisions of the "male" editorial page and the "female" features section and moved to the *Globe's* editorial page. By 1976 her column was syndicated—it now appears in nearly four hundred newspapers throughout the country. In 1980 she received the Pulitzer Prize for distinguished commentary. She has published four collections of her columns: *Close to Home* (1979), *At Large* (1981), *Keeping in Touch* (1985), and *Making Sense* (1990).

Characteristically still "close to home" and "in touch" with her roots, Goodman lives in a Boston suburb, near her relatives and her birthplace, in a renovated townhouse and in what she calls a "renovated" family that includes her second husband, also a writer for the *Globe*, her daughter, and her two stepchildren.

Though Goodman's work appears on the editorial page, she has never been willing to give up writing about her day-to-day experience. So she has persistently and quite self-consciously sought to juxtapose the personal and the political, in the hopes of illuminating both:

> They used to tell me a columnist can't write about politics one day and housework the next. So I made it a point to do just that. It was a conscious decision. I wanted to add something to the newspaper profession. . . . My definition of the political is broader. It is a political issue if Americans feel anxious about their family life, feel anxious about the future of their children.

Goodman's point of view is that of a woman who has struggled with "the greatest social change of our time—the evolving roles of men and women." Her preoccupation with that evolution led her in 1974 to spend a year as a Nieman fellow at Harvard studying the dynamics of personal and social change in American society. The fruit of her study was *Turning Points* (1979), which she calls "a storybook of change." Based on interviews with men and women throughout the country, the book proved Goodman's seriousness as a social analyst and critic, and it also helped her to understand and accept her own ambivalence about change. "People want all the safety that comes from sameness and all the

absorb it. There's going to be much more career shifting, second careers, third careers."

So, it seems that just when students needed to be open to change, even serendipity, there they were, in their hair shirts, seeking the salves of a false security.

There was a certain bookkeeping attitude among students, and that was understandable. If you paid $20,000 for college, one male student had told her, then surely you should be guaranteed $5,000 more a year than someone who had not gone to college. He launched an anxiety attack against his college—because it wasn't a successful trade school. Relevancy wasn't a matter of social action. It was, he said, what looked good on a résumé. Scratch, scratch.

The woman knew that colleges were open to that kind of attack.   10
But she hoped that they would not become so practically impractical.

What, after all, do college students need to know if they are going to have three careers? What is the best preparation for five decades? My answer: Just what college was supposed to teach people from the beginning. How to think. About themselves and their lives and whatever work they plunge into, sidle into, or fall into.

The woman wanted to tell the senior something like that. But she couldn't reach her through the hair shirt.

The senior was totally convinced that her life was a problem to be solved. She believed she absolutely *had* to solve it by the day after Commencement. And, wherever she went, she wore this uncomfortable conviction like a second skin.

March 1978

LINES OF INQUIRY
"Anxiety Is the Class Uniform"

In Goodman's opening description of the senior, she portrays her as "wearing her anxiety like a hair shirt." What are the implications of this unusual figure of speech? What are the implications of Goodman's reference to her in paragraph 2 as "the senior in anxiety," who "had broken out in hives"? How does Goodman develop these descriptive expressions and images in the remainder of her piece? Exactly how does the portrayal of the senior that results from these images serve to make Goodman's point in this essay?

Goodman's title makes clear her concern for anxiety-ridden students. But exactly where does she place the blame for this state of affairs? On the students? Their teachers? Career planning? Professionally oriented education? What do you think is Goodman's primary point in this piece? To what extent do you think that student attitudes and collegiate situations have changed since Goodman wrote this piece in 1978? To what extent are her concerns still relevant?

Based on this piece, what do you think is Goodman's idea of the central purpose of education? How does her idea of education compare with Bacon's in "Of Studies"? Or with your own?

PROTECTION FROM THE PRYING CAMERA

Maybe it was the year-end picture roundup that finally did it. Maybe it was the double exposure to the same vivid photographs. Or perhaps it was the memory of three amateur photographers carefully standing in the cold last fall, calculating their f stops and exposures with light meters, trying to find the best angle, pointing their cameras at a drunk in a doorway. Or maybe it was simply my nine-year-old cousin playing Candid Camera at the family gathering.

But whatever the reason, it has finally hit me. We have become a nation of Kodachrome, Nikon, Instamatic addicts. But we haven't yet developed a clear idea of the ethics of picture-taking. We haven't yet determined the parameters of privacy in a world of flash cubes and telescopic lenses.

We "take" pictures. As psychologist Stanley Milgram puts it, "A photographer takes a picture, he does not create it or borrow it." But who has given us the right to "take" those pictures and under what circumstances?

Since the camera first became portable, we have easily and repeatedly aimed it at public people. It has always been open shooting season on them. With new technology, however, those intrusions have intensified. This year, someone with a camera committed the gross indecency of shooting an unaware Greta Garbo in the nude—and *People* printed it.

This year, again, Ron Galella "took" the image of Jacqueline Onassis and sold it as if it belonged to him. This year, we have pictures of a crumpled Wayne Hays, an indiscreet Nelson Rockefeller and two presidential candidates in every imaginable pose from the absurd to the embarrassing.

We have accepted the idea that public people are always free targets for the camera—without even a statute of limitations for Jackie or Garbo. We have also accepted the idea that a private person becomes public by being involved in a public event. The earthquake victims of Guatemala, the lynched leftists of Thailand, the terror-stricken of Ireland—their emotions and their bodies become frozen images.

The right of the public to know, to see and to be affected is considered more important than the right of the individual to mourn, or even die, in privacy.

What happens now, however, when cameras proliferate until they are as common as television sets? What happens when the image being "taken" is that of a butcher, a baker or a derelict, rather than a public figure? Do we all lose our right to privacy simply by stepping into view?

Should we be allowed to point cameras at each other? To regard each other as objects of art? Does the photographer or the photographed own the image?

Several years ago, *Time* photographer Steve Northup, who had   10
covered Vietnam, and Watergate, took a group of students around Cambridge shooting pictures. He quietly insisted that they ask every pizza-maker, truck driver and beautician for permission. His attitude toward private citizens was one of careful respect for the power of "exposure." In contrast to this, the average camera bug—like the average tourist—too often goes about snapping "quaint" people, along with "quaint" scenes: See the natives smile, see the natives carrying baskets of fruit, see the native children begging, see the drunk in the doorway. As Milgram wrote, "I find it hard to understand wherein the photographer has derived the right to keep for his own purposes the image of the peasant's face."

Where do we get the right to bring other people home in a canister? Where did we lose the right to control our image?

In a study that Milgram conducted last year, a full 65 percent of the people to whom his students talked in midtown Manhattan refused to have their pictures taken, refused to be photographed. I don't think they were camera shy, in the sense of being vain. Rather, they were reluctant to have their pictures "taken."

The Navahos long believed that the photographer took a piece of them away in his film. Like them, we are coming to understand the power of these frozen images. Photographs can help us to hold onto the truth of our past, to make our history and identity more real. Or they can rip something away from us as precious as the privacy which once clothed Greta Garbo.

January 1977

LINES OF INQUIRY
"Protection from the Prying Camera"

Notice how Goodman repeatedly plays upon the familiar expression, "picture-taking," as a means of provoking readers to sympathize with her position. What does she imply with her variations on this phrase? Notice how she plays upon other familiar expressions, such as "pointing cameras" and "shooting pictures." What are the implications of her variations on these expressions? What other verbal plays does Goodman use here in her attempt to make a persuasive case?

Given the title of this piece, it would seem that Goodman considers the camera to be an essentially intrusive and offensive device. What reasons does she have for being upset with picture-taking? What limits do you think she would like to impose on photographers? What kinds of rules do you think she would propose?

Probably, you've had your picture taken quite a few times, and you've probably also taken some pictures of others, so you're familiar with the pervasiveness of the camera in contemporary life. Have you ever felt a camera to be prying so much upon you or upon others that you wanted to do something about it? What benefits—what problems—do you think would arise from developing an "ethics of picture-taking"?

SINKING THE RELATIONSHIP

There was this kid in my grammar school, the kind of kid who only got valentines from those of us whose mothers made us send them to everyone. Even then, he would only get the ones that were 25 cards for 25 cents.

I mean, it was sad. But to tell you the truth, Willie was a real wonk.

Last week I ran into Willie the Wonk at the five and ten. It turns out that since we'd last met, Willie had gotten a Ph.D. and married, and then settled down and gotten divorced. Now, he was, and I quote, "relating to a woman in Providence." Together they were "really into exploring intimate relationships."

Now let me tell you, I covered my mouth lest anything untoward spill out. At that moment I regretted sending him even the crummy valentine that had come out on the perforated cardboard saying, "Gee, you're swell."

But, as they say, everything has its sunny side. Meeting Willie finally pushed me into making public my radical Valentine's Day proposal for 1977. Which is, ladies and gentlemen, boys and girls, sons and lovers, to renounce "relationships." In word, though not in deed. 5

I hereby propose striking out meaningful relationships (gag), intimate relationships (bleh), and working relationships (ugh).

Once upon a time, the only Relation Ship was a boat that carried the family over from the old country. Those were the days when only New Yorkers and battered wives got divorced. The rich may have had relationships, but they called them affairs. The only affairs Willie's forebears attended were the kind where they fought over who would take the centerpiece home.

Now, as I recall, somewhere along in the sixties, international relations became too grim and we all turned to our personal lives. Which we instantly turned equally grim. At that moment, the word "relationship" was born.

A relationship, unlike a love affair, is something which is carefully negotiated to be "self-actualizing" and "growth-oriented" and "nonbinding." It is written along the lines of the model approved by the National Mental Health Association. It is then signed by two consenting adults who are too embarrassed to tell their friends that they've fallen in love.

In truth, one never falls into a relationship. One is too mature, healthy, sensible and dreary for that. Rather, one enters a relationship as if it were a law firm. 10

"Relationship" is a cool, McLuhan-ish word. After all, one can re-late to almost anything—a food processor, a book, even Willie. The word has always sounded more mathematical than poetic. Try as they might, few poets could ever work with: "How do I relate to thee, let me count the ways," or "Come live with me and be my relationship."

It is even harder to write a relationship song: "Relationship is a many-splendored thing." "I relate to you a bushel and a peck."

It just won't sell. The term is too measured, calibrated, passionless. It is hard to send flowers to a relationship.

As for Working Relationships, well, that has always reminded me of a mom-and-pop store of the feelings. Meaningful Relationships make me think of the English professor who had us read *Hamlet* and count the water images. And Intimate Relationship sounds like something you'd only have with a bathing-suit saleslady.

It is time that we bid farewell and jump this particular ship. I hereby   15
take the pledge. Up with love, down with relationships. Even Willie the Wonk deserves better than that.

February 1977

LINES OF INQUIRY
"Sinking the Relationship"

Notice the following passages from the first two paragraphs of this piece: "There was this kid in my grammar school"; "I mean, it was sad"; "Willie was a real wonk". How could you describe the style of these passages? How would you characterize the tone of voice that Goodman projects in these passages? How typical are these passages of her style and tone in the rest of the piece? In her other pieces? What reason(s) do you suppose she might have in this piece for using such a style and tone?

In paragraphs 7–15, Goodman makes fun of the word "relationship." But why exactly do you think she is so strongly opposed to it? Do you think she opposes it completely, or do you think she is only opposed to it in certain contexts and situations? What advantages or disadvantages do you think would result from her proposal "to renounce 'relationships' "?

Can you think of any other words like relationship that might be equally as objectionable to Goodman? What objectionable qualities do these words have in common with "relationship"? What objectionable qualities do these words and "relationship" have in common with the words and expressions that Orwell objects to in "Politics and the English Language"?

IN LOVE FORNOW

They are in their twenties and in love. Not in love forever. In love fornow.

They haven't said this exactly. But as a certified FOF (friend of the family) I have heard it in their silences. Certain words don't come up when we talk. Words like *our future* or even *next year.*

They are sharing their plans with me. But these are not shared plans. She has applied to East Coast graduate schools, he has been interviewing for West Coast jobs. They tell me this casually, their limbs familiarly entwined on the sofa in the position they adopted a year ago to tell everyone they were in love.

As an FOF, I quietly take in this scene. Have my young friends mastered the ability to love in the now? I ask myself. Or are they missing the romantic glue of futurism? I wonder if this is what it's like to be young lovers today.

Sitting with them, I am reminded of my reading trip through this year's Valentine's Day cards. I flipped through dozens of messages. The poetic pledges of forever love were almost all marketed for old lovers. The mush quota was highest for the cards marked: To Grandma.

But the Valentines for young lovers were, by and large, careful, cool. Some risqué, some even raunchy, but not emotionally risky. The Valentines I read carried no promises that would last longer than flowers or chocolate. They were about love fornow.

The woman who had dubbed me the Friend of this Family stands beside me. At her son's age, she had been married for two years. She was the example she didn't want her two children to follow. Married at 22, divorced ten years later.

"We were too young." How many times had she said so to the two children of this marriage and divorce? Children who had watched her start a career at 32. Children who had watched their father start another family at 40. My friend had told her sons, "Wait a while. Get to know several people, including yourself."

This young man had listened. His whole college generation had listened to some variation on that parental or societal advice. They had learned to put reason over romance. This young couple were like the graduates in that Dow Chemical ad last year. They were able to say—"I am going to miss you next year"—and accept parting as the given at their stage of life.

"So what," I ask my friend when we retreat to privacy, "do you think of this reasonableness now? Is it not just what you wanted?"

"Yes," she says, but slowly, and goes on. "I think they are doing the right thing. There are too many changes ahead for them. They are too young to limit their options—jobs, schools, cities—for each other." Then she adds quietly, "But what about the option to have each other?"

We sit quietly with each other, thinking about the dramatic reversal of life patterns in two decades. The young people we know have a passion for finding the right work. And caution about finding the right relationship. Those in their twenties pursue careers wholeheartedly. And embrace love halfheartedly. The half that is missing may be the part that pulses with the idea of a future, the desire for forever.

My friend and I, FOFs for a dozen or more young people, figure that on average these began their first love affairs between 18 and 20. If our small statistical sample holds up, they are likely to be single until 28 or 30. The time lapse between intimacy and commitment, between first love and marriage, has expanded enormously from our twenties to theirs.

In the interim these young may become very good at conditional love, love "until," love fornow. But it seems to us that it is hard to love fully in a limited time zone. Love without a belief in a future is like a chocolate heart made of skim milk and Sweet 'n' Low.

The timing of our revisionist notion is probably lousy. This is the Love Carefully era. A balanced life is more prized than a sudden disorienting fall into love. On campuses, this Valentine's Day is celebrated by distributing condoms, not commitments.

Yet my friend and I, harbingers of realism, proponents of caution, survivors of one or more disasters, have, to our great surprise, discovered that we are more romantic than the young lovers in the next room. We wish them wholeheartedness. And the rich flavor of forever.

February 1988

LINES OF INQUIRY
"In Love Fornow"

In this essay about contemporary attitudes toward love and marriage, Goodman initially focuses her attention very dramatically on the situation of two young lovers, one of whom is the son of a divorced woman friend of hers. Why do you suppose that Goodman gradually seems to shift her attention from describing the young lovers "entwined on the sofa" to telling about herself and her friend who "sit quietly with each other"? How is this shift in focus related to the ideas about love and marriage that Goodman is concerned with in the piece?

In the title of her essay, Goodman combines two familiar words to produce a single new word, "fornow," which she subsequently uses to describe the love of the two young people in her story. Why do you suppose that she combines these two words rather than leaving them apart? Why doesn't she also combine some of the other words in her piece that refer to the timing of the young people's love, such as "our future" ("ourfuture") and "next year" ("nextyear")? Throughout the piece she also plays another word game, referring to herself as an "FOF (friend of the family)," yet doesn't choose to refer to the young lovers as YLs. How do you account for this apparent inconsistency in her piece? What ideas do you think Goodman is trying to convey or emphasize through these two word games?

"In Love Fornow" is not the only piece that Goodman has written about changing attitudes toward love and marriage, as you can see by looking at her previous piece in this collection, "Sinking the Relationship." What similarities, what differences, do you see in her perceptions of contemporary love and her thoughts on the subject? How do you account for the similarities, given the changing attitudes toward love that presumably have taken place in America during the ten years separating the publication of these two essays? What changes, if any, do you think have taken place in the five or six years since the publication of "In Love Fornow"?

STEPHEN JAY GOULD

1941 –

Evolution is one of the half-dozen shattering ideas that science has developed to overturn past hopes and assumptions, and to enlighten our current thoughts. Evolution is also more personal than the quantum, or the relative motion of earth and sun; it speaks directly to the questions of genealogy that so fascinate us—how and when did we arise, what are our biological relationships with other creatures? And evolution has built all those creatures in stunning variety—an endless source of delight (though not the reason for their existence!), not to mention of essays.

For the past fifteen years, Harvard paleontologist Stephen Jay Gould has been explaining and defending the "shattering idea" of Darwin's theory of evolution, as he puts it here in this passage from the preface to *The Flamingo's Smile*. With example after example, fact after fact, he tries to demonstrate how the inescapable logic of evolutionary theory "overturns past hopes and assumptions," challenging our most basic cultural prejudices. But evolution ought to "fascinate" and "delight" us as well, Gould thinks. It tells the story of who we are and where we came from. It helps us appreciate "the stunning variety" of life on earth. And properly understood, without fear or prejudice, it leads us to the realization that we, not nature, are finally responsible for our behavior and the values of our culture.

Though he writes about natural history, Gould grew up in New York and loves the life of the city. "I resonate when I walk across the Brooklyn Bridge and look at lower Manhattan," he said in an interview, and he is an avid baseball fan. As a child he was taken by his father, a court stenographer, to the American Museum of Natural History, where the sight of a Tyrannosaurus Rex convinced him that he wanted to become a paleontologist. "I was just so fascinated by it, because there wasn't any information about it. There were just these skeletons, these awesome skeletons." As an undergraduate at Antioch College, Gould integrated courses in geology, history, and philosophy, then did graduate work at Columbia University, writing a doctoral dissertation on the Bahamian land snail. Now a professor of geology at Harvard, he established himself in scientific circles when he collaborated in developing the controversial theory that evolution moves in abrupt fits and starts, rather than gradually and progressively over time.

In 1974 Gould was invited to write a column for *Natural History,* the monthly magazine of the American Museum, and though he at first regarded the essay form as "ephemeral," he soon established a reputation for the readable exposition of difficult ideas, becoming, like Loren Eiseley and Lewis Thomas, one of our most important bridges between science and the rest of the culture. His essays have been collected in *Ever Since Darwin* (1977); *The Panda's Thumb* (1980), winner of the National Book Award; *Hen's Teeth and Horses' Toes* (1983); *The Flamingo's Smile* (1985); and *Bully for Brontosaurus* (1991). In 1981, his book-length study of the scientific measurement of intelligence, *The Mismeasure of Man,* won the National Book Critics Award.

Evolutionary theory has from the beginning been Gould's dominant concern. As he puts it in a retrospective essay in *The Flamingo's Smile,* "I have a wonderful advantage among essayists because no other theme so beautifully encompasses both the particulars that fascinate and the generalities that instruct." Evolution, he argues over and over again, has no purpose. It just happens as "individuals struggle to increase the representation of their genes in future generations" and "that is all." So, he believes that harmony or order arises only as an "incidental result" of randomness. So, too, he argues that "Homo sapiens is not the foreordained product of a ladder that was reaching toward our exalted estate from the start. We are merely the surviving branch of a once luxuriant bush."

In other words, nature, according to Gould, is not exquisitely designed, nor is it proof of an exquisite designer. The bone structure of a horse, for example, is rickety and unsound, surviving only by accident, not at all the best way to design a running animal. The panda's thumb is not a perfect adaptation for the eating of bamboo but simply an enlarged wristbone resulting from a biological accident which the panda has clumsily adapted for its own purposes. Thus Gould finds it difficult to read nature as moral in any way. How can we derive a pleasing lesson from the spectacle of the offspring of cecidomyian gall midgets devouring their mothers in order to grow? The process is neither moral nor immoral but rather an adaptation that serves to the need of the animal to reproduce quickly.

But Gould's belief that "evolution is purposeless, nonprogressive, and materialistic" doesn't lead him to cynicism or despair. "Yes, the world has been different ever since Darwin," he says. "But no less exciting, instructing, or uplifting; for if we cannot find purpose in nature, we will have to define it for ourselves." Gould's real project is to get us to accept our responsibility for what we are rather than "fobbing it off" on nature; to help us recognize our arrogance in assuming that we are "the loftiest product of a preordained process" with the right to destroy the environment for our own purposes.

Throughout his work, Gould takes pleasure in exploring the facts of nature, turning each shell or fossil over and over in his mind like a delighted child, often with the intent of making a specific moral point. In many essays, in fact, he takes his argument into an attack on scientists and others who use the supposed design and purposefulness of nature—or their own biased interpretation of this design—as a way of defending unjust social policies. In *The Mismeasure of Man,* he exposes in intricate detail the work of scientists who have claimed to measure human intelligence objectively, revealing that they consistently, if inadvertently, distorted their data to support their prior prejudices about the inferiority of certain races. So, Gould shows us that "science is no inexorable march to truth," and that scientists are "ordinary human beings" who "unconsciously reflect in their theories the social and political constraints of their times."

Given his no-nonsense views of evolution and of scientific investigation, Gould is rarely inclined to be lyrical or mystical like Loren Eiseley and Lewis Thomas, the two other notable scientist-essayists with whom he is most often compared. Though his style is often witty and eloquent, marked by balanced and ringing phrases, he relies most of all on the strategies of detailed explanation, sustained analysis, and painstakingly logical argumentation. So, each of his essays is invariably grounded on a hard fact, a piece of evidence, a natural oddity, such as the structure of hen's teeth, the configuration of Siamese twins, the evolution of Mickey Mouse's features, or the disappearance of the .400 hitter. As Gould says, he "treats generality only as it emerges from little things that arrest us and open our eyes with an 'aha.' " To show us the emergence of the generality, to open our eyes, he takes us step by step through a logical exposition of the problem. Though he wants to be clear, even entertaining, he insists that he "will not simplify concepts." In his essays as in his specialized research, Gould's commitment is to "science and rationality in its proper sphere," because without science and rationality, "there can be no solution to the problems that engulf us."

A BIOLOGICAL HOMAGE TO MICKEY MOUSE

Age often turns fire to placidity. Lytton Strachey, in his incisive portrait of Florence Nightingale, writes of her declining years:

> Destiny, having waited very patiently, played a queer trick on Miss Nightingale. The benevolence and public spirit of that long life had only been equalled by its acerbity. Her virtue had dwelt in hardness. . . . And now the sarcastic years brought the proud woman her punishment. She was not to die as she had lived. The sting was to be taken out of her; she was to be made soft; she was to be reduced to compliance and complacency.

I was therefore not surprised—although the analogy may strike some people as sacrilegious—to discover that the creature who gave his name as a synonym for insipidity had a gutsier youth. Mickey Mouse turned a respectable fifty last year. To mark the occasion, many theaters replayed his debut performance in *Steamboat Willie* (1928). The original Mickey was a rambunctious, even slightly sadistic fellow. In a remarkable sequence, exploiting the exciting new development of sound, Mickey and Minnie pummel, squeeze, and twist the animals on board to produce a rousing chorus of "Turkey in the Straw." They honk a duck with a tight embrace, crank a goat's tail, tweak a pig's nipples, bang a cow's teeth as a stand-in xylophone, and play bagpipe on her udder.

Christopher Finch, in his semiofficial pictorial history of Disney's work, comments: "The Mickey Mouse who hit the movie houses in the late twenties was not quite the well-behaved character most of us are familiar with today. He was mischievous, to say the least, and even displayed a streak of cruelty." But Mickey soon cleaned up his act, leaving to gossip and speculation only his unresolved relationship with Minnie and the status of Morty and Ferdie. Finch continues: "Mickey . . . had become virtually a national symbol, and as such he was expected to behave properly at all times. If he occasionally stepped out of line, any number of letters would arrive at the Studio from citizens and organizations who felt that the nation's moral well-being was in their hands. . . . Eventually he would be pressured into the role of straight man."

As Mickey's personality softened, his appearance changed. Many Disney fans are aware of this transformation through time, but few (I suspect) have recognized the coordinating theme behind all the alterations—in fact, I am not sure that the Disney artists themselves explicitly

Mickey's evolution during 50 years (left to right). As Mickey became increasingly well behaved over the years, his appearance became more youthful. Measurements of three stages in his development revealed a larger relative head size, larger eyes, and an enlarged cranium—all traits of juvenility. © Walt Disney Productions

realized what they were doing, since the changes appeared in such a halting and piecemeal fashion. In short, the blander and inoffensive Mickey became progressively more juvenile in appearance. (Since Mickey's chronological age never altered—like most cartoon characters he stands impervious to the ravages of time—this change in appearance at a constant age is a true evolutionary transformation. Progressive juvenilization as an evolutionary phenomenon is called neoteny. More on this later.)

The characteristic changes of form during human growth have 5 inspired a substantial biological literature. Since the head-end of an embryo differentiates first and grows more rapidly in utero than the foot-end (an antero-posterior gradient, in technical language), a newborn child possesses a relatively large head attached to a medium-sized body with diminutive legs and feet. This gradient is reversed through growth as legs and feet overtake the front end. Heads continue to grow but so much more slowly than the rest of the body that relative head size decreases.

In addition, a suite of changes pervades the head itself during human growth. The brain grows very slowly after age three, and the bulbous cranium of a young child gives way to the more slanted, lower-browed configuration of adulthood. The eyes scarcely grow at all and relative eye size declines precipitously. But the jaw gets bigger and bigger. Children, compared with adults, have larger heads and eyes, smaller jaws, a more prominent, bulging cranium, and smaller, pudgier legs and feet. Adult heads are altogether more apish, I'm sorry to say.

Mickey, however, has traveled this ontogenetic pathway in reverse during his fifty years among us. He has assumed an ever more childlike appearance as the ratty character of *Steamboat Willie* became the cute and inoffensive host to a magic kingdom. By 1940, the former tweaker of pig's nipples gets a kick in the ass for insubordination (as the *Sorcerer's Apprentice* in *Fantasia*). By 1953, his last cartoon, he has gone fishing and cannot even subdue a squirting clam.

The Disney artists transformed Mickey in clever silence, often using suggestive devices that mimic nature's own changes by different routes. To give him the shorter and pudgier legs of youth, they lowered his pants line and covered his spindly legs with a baggy outfit. (His arms and legs also thickened substantially—and acquired joints for a floppier appearance.) His head grew relatively larger and its features more youthful. The length of Mickey's snout has not altered, but decreasing protrusion is more subtly suggested by a pronounced thickening. Mickey's eye has grown in two modes: first, by a major, discontinuous evolutionary shift as the entire eye of ancestral Mickey became the pupil of his descendants, and second, by gradual increase thereafter.

Mickey's improvement in cranial bulging followed an interesting path since his evolution has always been constrained by the unaltered convention of representing his head as a circle with appended ears and an oblong snout. The circle's form could not be altered to provide a bulging cranium directly. Instead, Mickey's ears moved back, increasing the distance between nose and ears, and giving him a rounded, rather than a sloping, forehead.

To give these observations the cachet of quantitative science, I applied my best pair of dial calipers to three stages of the official phylogeny—the thin-nosed, ears-forward figure of the early 1930s (stage 1), the latter-day Jack of Mickey and the Beanstalk (1947, stage 2), and the modern mouse (stage 3). I measured three signs of Mickey's creeping juvenility: increasing eye size (maximum height) as a percentage of head length (base of the nose to top of rear ear); increasing head length as a percentage of body length; and increasing cranial vault size measured by rearward displacement of the front ear (base of the nose to top of front ear as a percentage of base of the nose to top of rear ear).

All three percentages increased steadily—eye size from 27 to 42 percent of head length; head length from 42.7 to 48.1 percent of body length; and nose to front ear from 71.7 to a whopping 95.6 percent of

10

The "Evolution" of Mickey Mouse

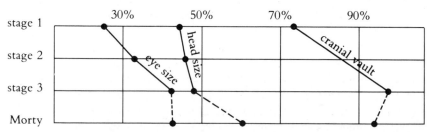

At an early stage in his evolution, Mickey had a smaller head, cranial vault, and eyes. He evolved toward the characteristics of his young nephew Morty (connected to Mickey by a dotted line).

nose to rear ear. For comparison, I measured Mickey's young "nephew" Morty Mouse. In each case, Mickey has clearly been evolving toward youthful stages of his stock, although he still has a way to go for head length.

You may, indeed, now ask what an at least marginally respectable scientist has been doing with a mouse like that. In part, fiddling around and having fun, of course. (I still prefer *Pinocchio* to *Citizen Kane.*) But I do have a serious point—two, in fact—to make. We must first ask why Disney chose to change his most famous character so gradually and persistently in the same direction? National symbols are not altered capriciously and market researchers (for the doll industry in particular) have spent a good deal of time and practical effort learning what features appeal to people as cute and friendly. Biologists also have spent a great deal of time studying a similar subject in a wide range of animals.

In one of his most famous articles, Konrad Lorenz argues that humans use the characteristic differences in form between babies and adults as important behavioral cues. He believes that features of juvenility trigger "innate releasing mechanisms" for affection and nurturing in adult humans. When we see a living creature with babyish features, we feel an automatic surge of disarming tenderness. The adaptive value of this response can scarcely be questioned, for we must nurture our babies. Lorenz, by the way, lists among his releasers the very features of babyhood that Disney affixed progressively to Mickey: "a relatively large head, predominance of the brain capsule, large and low-lying eyes, bulging cheek region, short and thick extremities, a springly elastic consistency, and clumsy movements." (I propose to leave aside for this article the contentious issue of whether or not our affectionate response to babyish features is truly innate and inherited directly from ancestral primates—as Lorenz argues—or whether it is simply learned from our immediate experience with babies and grafted upon an evolutionary predisposition for attaching ties of affection to certain learned signals. My argument works equally well in either case for I only claim that babyish features tend to elicit strong feelings of affection in adult humans, whether the biological basis be direct programming or the capacity to learn and fix upon signals. I also treat as collateral to my point the major thesis of Lorenz's article—that we respond not to the totality or *Gestalt,* but to a set of specific features acting as releasers. This argument is important to Lorenz because he wants to argue for evolutionary identity in modes of behavior between other vertebrates and humans, and we know that many birds, for example, often respond to abstract features rather than *Gestalten.* Lorenz' article, published in 1950, bears the title *Ganzheit und Teil in der tierischen und menschlichen Gemeinschaft*—"Entirety and part in animal and human society." Disney's piecemeal change of Mickey's appearance does make sense in this context—he operated in sequential fashion upon Lorenz's primary releasers.)

Lorenz emphasizes the power that juvenile features hold over us, and the abstract quality of their influence, by pointing out that we judge other animals by the same criteria—although the judgment may be utterly inappropriate in an evolutionary context. We are, in short, fooled by an evolved response to our own babies, and we transfer our reaction to the same set of features in other animals.

Many animals, for reasons having nothing to do with the inspira-   15
tion of affection in humans, possess some features also shared by human babies but not by human adults—large eyes and a bulging forehead with retreating chin, in particular. We are drawn to them, we cultivate them as pets, we stop and admire them in the wild—while we reject their small-eyed, long-snouted relatives who might make more affectionate companions or objects of admiration. Lorenz points out that the German names of many animals with features mimicking human babies end in the diminutive suffix *chen,* even though the animals are often larger than close relatives without such features—*Rotkehlchen* (robin), *Eichhörnchen* (squirrel), and *Kaninchen* (rabbit), for example.

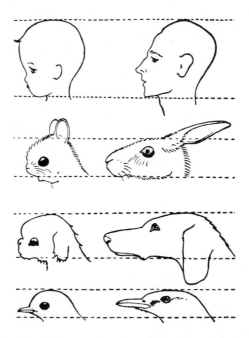

Humans feel affection for animals with juvenile features: large eyes, bulging craniums, retreating chins (left column). Small-eyed, long-snouted animals (right column) do not elicit the same response. From Studies in Animal and Human Behavior, *vol. II, by Konrad Lorenz, 1971. Methuen & Co. Ltd.*

In a fascinating section, Lorenz then enlarges upon our capacity for biologically inappropriate response to other animals, or even to inanimate objects that mimic human features. "The most amazing objects can acquire remarkable, highly specific emotional values by 'experiential attachment' of human properties. . . . Steeply rising, somewhat overhanging cliff faces or dark storm-clouds piling up have the same, immediate display value as a human being who is standing at full height and leaning slightly forwards"—that is, threatening.

We cannot help regarding a camel as aloof and unfriendly because it mimics, quite unwittingly and for other reasons, the "gesture of haughty rejection" common to so many human cultures. In this gesture, we raise our heads, placing our nose above our eyes. We then half-close our eyes and blow out through our nose—the "harumph" of the stereotyped upperclass Englishman or his well-trained servant. "All this," Lorenz argues quite cogently, "symbolizes resistance against all sensory modalities emanating from the disdained counterpart." But the poor camel cannot help carrying its nose above its elongate eyes, with mouth drawn down. As Lorenz reminds us, if you wish to know whether a camel will eat out of your hand or spit, look at its ears, not the rest of its face.

In his important book *Expression of the Emotions in Man and Animals,* published in 1872, Charles Darwin traced the evolutionary basis of many common gestures to originally adaptive actions in animals later internalized as symbols in humans. Thus, he argued for evolutionary continuity of emotion, not only of form. We snarl and raise our upper lip in fierce anger—to expose our nonexistent fighting canine tooth. Our gesture of disgust repeats the facial actions associated with the highly adaptive act of vomiting in necessary circumstances. Darwin concluded, much to the distress of many Victorian contemporaries: "With mankind some expressions, such as the bristling of the hair under the influence of extreme terror, or the uncovering of the teeth under that of furious rage, can hardly be understood, except on the belief that man once existed in a much lower and animal-like condition."

In any case, the abstract features of human childhood elicit powerful emotional responses in us, even when they occur in other animals. I submit that Mickey Mouse's evolutionary road down the course of his own growth in reverse reflects the unconscious discovery of this biological principle by Disney and his artists. In fact, the emotional status of most Disney characters rests on the same set of distinctions. To this extent, the magic kingdom trades on a biological illusion—our ability to abstract and our propensity to transfer inappropriately to other animals the fitting responses we make to changing form in the growth of our own bodies.

Donald Duck also adopts more juvenile features through time. His elongated beak recedes and his eyes enlarge; he converges on Huey, Louie, and Dewey as surely as Mickey approaches Morty. But Donald,   20

Dandified, disreputable Mortimer (here stealing Minnie's affections) has strikingly more adult features than Mickey. His head is smaller in proportion to body length; his nose is a full 80 percent of head length. © *Walt Disney Productions*

having inherited the mantle of Mickey's original misbehavior, remains more adult in form with his projecting beak and more sloping forehead.

Mouse villains or sharpies, contrasted with Mickey, are always more adult in appearance, although they often share Mickey's chronological age. In 1936, for example, Disney made a short entitled *Mickey's Rival*. Mortimer, a dandy in a yellow sports car, intrudes upon Mickey and Minnie's quiet country picnic. The thoroughly disreputable Mortimer has a head only 29 percent of body length, to Mickey's 45, and a snout 80 percent of head length, compared with Mickey's 49. (Nonetheless, and was it ever different, Minnie transfers her affection until an obliging bull from a neighboring field dispatches Mickey's rival.) Consider also the exaggerated adult features of other Disney characters—the swaggering bully Peg-leg Pete or the simple, if lovable, dolt Goofy.

As a second, serious biological comment on Mickey's odyssey in form, I note that his path to eternal youth repeats, in epitome, our own evolutionary story. For humans are neotenic. We have evolved by retaining to adulthood the originally juvenile features of our ancestors. Our australopithecine forebears, like Mickey in *Steamboat Willie,* had projecting jaws and low vaulted craniums.

Our embryonic skulls scarcely differ from those of chimpanzees. And we follow the same path of changing form through growth: relative decrease of the cranial vault since brains grow so much more slowly than bodies after birth, and continuous relative increase of the jaw. But

Cartoon villains are not the only Disney characters with exaggerated adult features. Goofy, like Mortimer, has a small head relative to body length and a prominent snout. © *Walt Disney Productions*

while chimps accentuate these changes, producing an adult strikingly different in form from a baby, we proceed much more slowly down the same path and never get nearly so far. Thus, as adults, we retain juvenile features. To be sure, we change enough to produce a notable difference between baby and adult, but our alteration is far smaller than that experienced by chimps and other primates.

A marked slowdown of developmental rates has triggered our neoteny. Primates are slow developers among mammals, but we have accentuated the trend to a degree matched by no other mammal. We have very long periods of gestation, markedly extended childhoods, and the longest life span of any mammal. The morphological features of eternal youth have served us well. Our enlarged brain is, at least in part, a result of extending rapid prenatal growth rates to later ages. (In all mammals, the brain grows rapidly in utero but often very little after birth. We have extended this fetal phase into postnatal life.)

But the changes in timing themselves have been just as important. 25
We are preeminently learning animals, and our extended childhood permits the transference of culture by education. Many animals display flexibility and play in childhood but follow rigidly programmed patterns as adults. Lorenz writes, in the same article cited above: "The

characteristic which is so vital for the human peculiarity of the true man—that of always remaining in a state of development—is quite certainly a gift which we owe to the neotenous nature of mankind."

In short, we, like Mickey, never grow up although we, alas, do grow old. Best wishes to you, Mickey, for your next half-century. May we stay as young as you, but grow a bit wiser.

LINES OF INQUIRY
"A Biological Homage to Mickey Mouse"

In paragraph 12, Gould says that in discussing Mickey Mouse he is "in part, fiddling around and having fun . . . but I do have a serious point—two, in fact—to make." What aspects of his organization, evidence, analysis, and style suggest that he is having fun; what aspects suggest that he is serious? What issues does he treat lightly; what issues does he treat seriously? In what respects are the playful and serious sides of this essay related?

As his title suggests, Gould's approach in this piece is to examine a cartoon character scientifically, to look at a fictitious animal as if it were a biological creature. What purpose(s) does he have for doing so? To what extent do you think Gould is concerned with the evolution of Mickey Mouse? To what extent do you think he is concerned with shedding light on the psychology of cartooning? To what extent do you think he is concerned with shedding light on the evolving pattern of human features? What other points is he concerned with in this piece?

Examine another cartoon character who has existed for a long time to see if this character has evolved (rather than aged) over time. Use Gould's analytic methods to take note of any significant changes in the character's facial or body features. Take note of any other significant changes that seem to have occurred in the character's physical behavior, gestures, style of dressing, and way of talking. How do you account for the change(s) or lack of change that you've noticed in this character?

WOMEN'S BRAINS

In the prelude to *Middle-march*, George Eliot lamented the unfulfilled lives of talented women:

> Some have felt that these blundering lives are due to the inconvenient indefiniteness with which the Supreme Power has fashioned the natures of women: if there were one level of feminine incompetence as strict as the ability to count three and no more, the social lot of women might be treated with scientific certitude.

Eliot goes on to discount the idea of innate limitation, but while she wrote in 1872, the leaders of European anthropometry were trying to measure "with scientific certitude" the inferiority of women. Anthropometry, or measurement of the human body, is not so fashionable a field these days, but it dominated the human sciences for much of the nineteenth century and remained popular until intelligence testing replaced skull measurement as a favored device for making invidious comparisons among races, classes, and sexes. Craniometry, or measurement of the skull, commanded the most attention and respect. Its unquestioned leader, Paul Broca (1824–80), professor of clinical surgery at the Faculty of Medicine in Paris, gathered a school of disciples and imitators around himself. Their work, so meticulous and apparently irrefutable, exerted great influence and won high esteem as a jewel of nineteenth-century science.

Broca's work seemed particularly invulnerable to refutation. Had he not measured with the most scrupulous care and accuracy? (Indeed, he had. I have the greatest respect for Broca's meticulous procedure. His numbers are sound. But science is an inferential exercise, not a catalog of facts. Numbers, by themselves, specify nothing. All depends upon what you do with them.) Broca depicted himself as an apostle of objectivity, a man who bowed before facts and cast aside superstition and sentimentality. He declared that "there is no faith, however respectable, no interest, however legitimate, which must not accommodate itself to the progress of human knowledge and bend before truth." Women, like it or not, had smaller brains than men and, therefore, could not equal them in intelligence. This fact, Broca argued, may reinforce a common prejudice in male society, but it is also a scientific truth. L. Manouvrier, a black sheep in Broca's fold, rejected the inferiority of women and wrote with feeling about the burden imposed upon them by Broca's numbers:

Women displayed their talents and their diplomas. They also invoked philosophical authorities. But they were opposed by *numbers* unknown to Condorcet or to John Stuart Mill. These numbers fell upon poor women like a sledge hammer, and they were accompanied by commentaries and sarcasms more ferocious than the most misogynist imprecations of certain church fathers. The theologians had asked if women had a soul. Several centuries later, some scientists were ready to refuse them a human intelligence.

Broca's argument rested upon two sets of data: the larger brains of men in modern societies, and a supposed increase in male superiority through time. His most extensive data came from autopsies performed personally in four Parisian hospitals. For 292 male brains, he calculated an average weight of 1,325 grams; 140 female brains averaged 1,144 grams for a difference of 181 grams, or 14 percent of the male weight. Broca understood, of course, that part of this difference could be attributed to the greater height of males. Yet he made no attempt to measure the effect of size alone and actually stated that it cannot account for the entire difference because we know, a priori, that women are not as intelligent as men (a premise that the data were supposed to test, not rest upon):

> We might ask if the small size of the female brain depends exclusively upon the small size of her body. Tiedemann has proposed this explanation. But we must not forget that women are, on the average, a little less intelligent than men, a difference which we should not exaggerate but which is, nonetheless, real. We are therefore permitted to suppose that the relatively small size of the female brain depends in part upon her physical inferiority and in part upon her intellectual inferiority.

In 1873, the year after Eliot published *Middlemarch,* Broca measured   5
the cranial capacities of prehistoric skulls from L'Homme Mort cave. Here he found a difference of only 99.5 cubic centimeters between males and females, while modern populations range from 129.5 to 220.7. Topinard, Broca's chief disciple, explained the increasing discrepancy through time as a result of differing evolutionary pressures upon dominant men and passive women:

> The man who fights for two or more in the struggle for existence, who has all the responsibility and the cares of tomorrow, who is constantly active in combating the environment and human rivals, needs more brain than the woman whom he must protect and nourish, the sedentary woman, lacking any interior occupations, whose role is to raise children, love, and be passive.

In 1879, Gustave Le Bon, chief misogynist of Broca's school, used these data to publish what must be the most vicious attack upon women in modern scientific literature (no one can top Aristotle). I do not claim his views were representative of Broca's school, but they were published in France's most respected anthropological journal. Le Bon concluded:

> In the most intelligent races, as among the Parisians, there are a large number of women whose brains are closer in size to those of gorillas than to the most developed male brains. This inferiority is so obvious that no one can contest it for a moment; only its degree is worth discussion. All psychologists who have studied the intelligence of women, as well as poets and novelists, recognize today that they represent the most inferior forms of human evolution and that they are closer to children and savages than to an adult, civilized man. They excel in fickleness, inconstancy, absence of thought and logic, and incapacity to reason. Without doubt there exist some distinguished women, very superior to the average man, but they are as exceptional as the birth of any monstrosity, as, for example, of a gorilla with two heads; consequently, we may neglect them entirely.

Nor did Le Bon shrink from the social implications of his views. He was horrified by the proposal of some American reformers to grant women higher education on the same basis as men:

> A desire to give them the same education, and, as a consequence, to propose the same goals for them, is a dangerous chimera. . . . The day when, misunderstanding the inferior occupations which nature has given her, women leave the home and take part in our battles; on this day a social revolution will begin, and everything that maintains the sacred ties of the family will disappear.

Sound familiar?[1]

I have reexamined Broca's data, the basis for all this derivative pronouncement, and I find his numbers sound but his interpretation ill-founded, to say the least. The data supporting his claim for increased difference through time can be easily dismissed. Broca based his contention on the samples from L'Homme Mort alone—only seven male and six female skulls in all. Never have so little data yielded such far ranging conclusions.

In 1888, Topinard published Broca's more extensive data on the Parisian hospitals. Since Broca recorded height and age as well as brain size, we may use modern statistics to remove their effect. Brain weight decreases with age, and Broca's women were, on average, considerably older than his men. Brain weight increases with height, and his average

---

[1] When I wrote this essay, I assumed that Le Bon was a marginal, if colorful, figure. I have since learned that he was a leading scientist, one of the founders of social psychology, and best known for a seminal study on crowd behavior, still cited today (*La psychologie des foules*, 1895), and for his work on unconscious motivation.

man was almost half a foot taller than his average woman. I used multiple regression, a technique that allowed me to assess simultaneously the influence of height and age upon brain size. In an analysis of the data for women, I found that, at average male height and age, a woman's brain would weigh 1,212 grams. Correction for height and age reduces Broca's measured difference of 181 grams by more than a third, to 113 grams.

I don't know what to make of this remaining difference because I   10
cannot assess other factors known to influence brain size in a major way. Cause of death has an important effect: degenerative disease often entails a substantial diminution of brain size. (This effect is separate from the decrease attributed to age alone.) Eugene Schreider, also working with Broca's data, found that men killed in accidents had brains weighing, on average, 60 grams more than men dying of infectious diseases. The best modern data I can find (from American hospitals) records a full 100-gram difference between death by degenerative arteriosclerosis and by violence or accident. Since so many of Broca's subjects were elderly women, we may assume that lengthy degenerative disease was more common among them than among the men.

More importantly, modern students of brain size still have not agreed on a proper measure for eliminating the powerful effect of body size. Height is partly adequate, but men and women of the same height do not share the same body build. Weight is even worse than height, because most of its variation reflects nutrition rather than intrinsic size— fat versus skinny exerts little influence upon the brain. Manouvrier took up this subject in the 1880s and argued that muscular mass and force should be used. He tried to measure this elusive property in various ways and found a marked difference in favor of men, even in men and women of the same height. When he corrected for what he called "sexual mass," women actually came out slightly ahead in brain size.

Thus, the corrected 113-gram difference is surely too large; the true figure is probably close to zero and may as well favor women as men. And 113 grams, by the way, is exactly the average difference between a 5 foot 4 inch and a 6 foot 4 inch male in Broca's data. We would not (especially us short folks) want to ascribe greater intelligence to tall men. In short, who knows what to do with Broca's data? They certainly don't permit any confident claim that men have bigger brains than women.

To appreciate the social role of Broca and his school, we must recognize that his statements about the brains of women do not reflect an isolated prejudice toward a single disadvantaged group. They must be weighed in the context of a general theory that supported contemporary social distinctions as biologically ordained. Women, blacks, and poor people suffered the same disparagement, but women bore the brunt of Broca's argument because he had easier access to data on women's brains. Women were singularly denigrated but they also stood as surrogates for other disenfranchised groups. As one of Broca's disciples wrote in 1881: "Men of the black races have a brain scarcely heavier than that of white woman." This juxtaposition extended into many other realms of anthropological argument, particularly to claims that, anatomically and emotionally, both women and blacks were like white children—and that white children, by the theory of recapitulation, represented an ancestral (primitive) adult stage of human evolution. I do not regard as empty rhetoric the claim that women's battles are for all of us.

Maria Montessori did not confine her activities to educational reform for young children. She lectured on anthropology for several years at the University of Rome, and wrote an influential book entitled *Pedagogical Anthropology* (English edition, 1913). Montessori was no egalitarian. She supported most of Broca's work and the theory of innate criminality proposed by her compatriot Cesare Lombroso. She measured the circumference of children's heads in her schools and inferred that the best prospects had bigger brains. But she had no use for Broca's conclusions about women. She discussed Manouvrier's work at length and made much of his tentative claim that women, after proper correction of the data, had slightly larger brains than men. Women, she concluded, were intellectually superior, but men had prevailed heretofore by dint of physical force. Since technology has abolished force as an instrument of power, the era of women may soon be upon us: "In such an epoch there will really be superior human beings, there will really be men strong in morality and in sentiment. Perhaps in this way the reign of women is approaching, when the enigma of her anthropological superiority will be deciphered. Woman was always the custodian of human sentiment, morality and honor."

This represents one possible antidote to "scientific" claims for the constitutional inferiority of certain groups. One may affirm the validity of biological distinctions but argue that the data have been misinterpreted by prejudiced men with a stake in the outcome, and that disadvantaged groups are truly superior. In recent years, Elaine Morgan has followed this strategy in her *Descent of Woman,* a speculative reconstruction of human prehistory from the woman's point of view—and as farcical as more famous tall tales by and for men.

I prefer another strategy. Montessori and Morgan followed Broca's philosophy to reach a more congenial conclusion. I would rather label the whole enterprise of setting a biological value upon groups for what it is: irrelevant and highly injurious. George Eliot well appreciated the special tragedy that biological labeling imposed upon members of disadvantaged groups. She expressed it for people like herself—women of extraordinary talent. I would apply it more widely—not only to those whose dreams are flouted but also to those who never realize that they may dream—but I cannot match her prose. In conclusion, then, the rest of Eliot's prelude to *Middlemarch:*

> The limits of variation are really much wider than anyone would imagine from the sameness of women's coiffure and the favorite love stories in prose and verse. Here and there a cygnet is reared uneasily among the ducklings in the brown pond, and never finds the living stream in fellowship with its own oary-footed kind. Here and there is born a Saint Theresa, foundress of nothing, whose loving heartbeats and sobs after an unattained goodness tremble off and are dispersed among hindrances instead of centering in some long-recognizable deed.

LINES OF INQUIRY
"Women's Brains"

In paragraph 3, Gould asserts that "science is an inferential exercise, not a catalog of facts. Numbers, by themselves, specify nothing. All depends upon what you do with them." What does Gould do with numbers? Exactly how does it differ from what Broca and his followers did with numbers? Specifically, what distinguishes Gould's and Broca's methods of calculating and interpreting the facts about women's brains?

It might also be said that quotations, by themselves, specify nothing. All depends upon what you do with them. What does Gould do with quotations in this essay? Why does he begin and end his piece with passages by George Eliot? Why does he quote so extensively from Broca and his followers, particularly from Le Bon? Why does he quote from Montessori? What purpose do all of these quotations serve in connection with the points that Gould is trying to make about women's brains and "biological labeling"?

Gould is not the only essayist in this collection to write about the denigration of women, as you can see by reading Walker's "In Search of our Mothers' Gardens" and Woolf's "Women and Fiction." What common themes do you see in these essays? What distinctive ideas and approaches do you see in each?

THE STREAK
OF STREAKS

My father was a court stenographer. At his less than princely salary, we watched Yankee games from the bleachers or high in the third deck. But one of the judges had season tickets, so we occasionally sat in the lower boxes when hizzoner couldn't attend. One afternoon, while DiMaggio was going 0 for 4 against, of all people, the lowly St. Louis Browns, the great man fouled one in our direction. "Catch it, Dad," I screamed. "You never get them," he replied, but stuck up his hand like the Statue of Liberty—and the ball fell right in. I mailed it to DiMaggio, and, bless him, he actually sent the ball back, signed and in a box marked "insured." Insured, that is, to make me the envy of the neighborhood, and DiMaggio the model and hero of my life.

I met DiMaggio a few years ago on a small playing field at the Presidio of San Francisco. My son, wearing DiMaggio's old number 5 on his Little League jersey, accompanied me, exactly one generation after my father caught that ball. DiMaggio gave him a pointer or two on batting and then signed a baseball for him. One generation passeth away, and another generation cometh: But the earth abideth forever.

My son, uncoached by Dad, and given the chance that comes but once in a lifetime, asked DiMaggio as his only query about life and career: "Suppose you had walked every time up during one game of your 56-game hitting streak? Would the streak have been over?" DiMaggio replied that, under 1941 rules, the streak would have ended, but that this unfair statute has since been revised, and such a game would not count today.

My son's choice for a single question tells us something vital about the nature of legend. A man may labor for a professional lifetime, especially in sport or in battle, but posterity needs a single transcendant event to fix him in permanent memory. Every hero must be a Wellington on the right side of his personal Waterloo; generality of excellence is too diffuse. The unambiguous factuality of a single achievement is adamantine. Detractors can argue forever about the general tenor of your life and works, but they can never erase a great event.

In 1941, as I gestated in my mother's womb, Joe DiMaggio got   5 at least one hit in each of 56 successive games. Most records are only incrementally superior to runners-up; Roger Maris hit 61 homers in 1961, but Babe Ruth hit 60 in 1927 and 59 in 1921, while Hank Greenberg (1938) and Jimmy Foxx (1932) both hit 58. But DiMaggio's

56-game hitting streak is ridiculously, almost unreachably far from all challengers (Wee Willie Keeler and Pete Rose, both with 44, come second). Among sabermetricians (a happy neologism based on an acronym for members of the Society for American Baseball Research, and referring to the statistical mavens of the sport)—a contentious lot not known for agreement about anything—we find virtual consensus that DiMaggio's 56-game hitting streak is the greatest accomplishment in the history of baseball, if not all modern sport.

The reasons for this respect are not far to seek. Single moments of unexpected supremacy—Johnny Vander Meer's back-to-back no-hitters in 1938, Don Larsen's perfect game in the 1956 World Series—can occur at any time to almost anybody, and have an irreducibly capricious character. Achievements of a full season—such as Maris's 61 homers in 1961 and Ted Williams's batting average of .406, also posted in 1941 and not equaled since—have a certain overall majesty, but they don't demand unfailing consistency every single day; you can slump for a while, so long as your average holds. But a streak must be absolutely exceptionless; you are not allowed a single day of subpar play, or even bad luck. You bat only four or five times in an average game. Sometimes two or three of these efforts yield walks, and you get only one or two shots at a hit. Moreover, as tension mounts and notice increases, your life becomes unbearable. Reporters dog your every step; fans are even more intrusive than usual (one stole DiMaggio's favorite bat right in the middle of his streak). You cannot make a single mistake.

Thus Joe DiMaggio's 56-game hitting streak is both the greatest factual achievement in the history of baseball and a principal icon of American mythology. What shall we do with such a central item of our cultural history?

Statistics and mythology may strike us as the most unlikely of bedfellows. How can we quantify Caruso or measure *Middlemarch?* But if God could mete out heaven with the span (Isaiah 40:12), perhaps we can say something useful about hitting streaks. The statistics of "runs," defined as continuous series of good or bad results (including baseball's streaks and slumps), is a well-developed branch of the profession, and can yield clear—but wildly counterintuitive—results. (The fact that we find these conclusions so surprising is the key to appreciating DiMaggio's achievement, the point of this article, and the gateway to an important insight about the human mind.)

Start with a phenomenon that nearly everyone both accepts and considers well understood—"hot hands" in basketball. Now and then, someone just gets hot, and can't be stopped. Basket after basket falls in—or out as with "cold hands," when a man can't buy a bucket for love or money (choose your cliché). The reason for this phenomenon is clear enough: It lies embodied in the maxim, "When you're hot, you're hot; and when you're not, you're not." You get that touch, build confidence; all nervousness fades, you find your rhythm; swish, swish, swish. Or you miss a few, get rattled, endure the booing, experience despair; hands start shaking and you realize that you shoulda stood in bed.

Everybody knows about hot hands. The only problem is that no   10 such phenomenon exists. Stanford psychologist Amos Tversky studied every basket made by the Philadelphia 76ers for more than a season. He found, first of all, that the probability of making a second basket did not rise following a successful shot. Moreover, the number of "runs," or baskets in succession, was no greater than what a standard random, or coin-tossing, model would predict. (If the chance of making each basket is 0.5, for example, a reasonable value for good shooters, five hits in a row will occur, on average, once in 32 sequences—just as you can expect to toss five successive heads about once in 32 times, or 0.5^5.)

Of course Larry Bird, the great forward of the Boston Celtics, will have more sequences of five than Joe Airball—but not because he has greater will or gets in that magic rhythm more often. Larry has longer runs because his average success rate is so much higher, and random models predict more frequent and longer sequences. If Larry shoots field goals at 0.6 probability of success, he will get five in a row about once every 13 sequences (0.6^5). If Joe, by contrast, shoots only 0.3, he will get his five straight only about once in 412 times. In other words, we need no special explanation for the apparent pattern of long runs. There is no ineffable "causality of circumstance" (to coin a phrase), no definite reason born of the particulars that make for heroic myths— courage in the clinch, strength in adversity, etc. You only have to know a person's ordinary play in order to predict his sequences. (I rather suspect that we are convinced of the contrary not only because we need myths so badly, but also because we remember the successes and simply allow the failures to fade from memory. More on this later.) But how does this revisionist pessimism work for baseball?

My colleague Ed Purcell, Nobel laureate in physics but, for purposes of this subject, just another baseball fan, has done a comprehensive study of all baseball streak and slump records. His firm conclusion is easily and swiftly summarized. Nothing ever happened in baseball above and beyond the frequency predicted by coin-tossing models. The longest runs of wins or losses are as long as they should be, and occur about as often as they ought to. Even the hapless Orioles, at 0 and 21 to start the 1988 season, only fell victim to the laws of probability (and not to the vengeful God of racism, out to punish major league baseball's only black manager).*

But "treasure your exceptions," as the old motto goes. Purcell's rule has but one major exception, one sequence so many standard deviations

---

* When I wrote this essay, Frank Robinson, the Baltimore skipper, was the only black man at the helm of a major league team. For more on the stats of Baltimore's slump, see my article "Winning and Losing: It's All in the Game," *Rotunda,* Spring 1989.

above the expected distribution that it should never have occurred at all: Joe DiMaggio's 56-game hitting streak in 1941. The intuition of baseball aficionados has been vindicated. Purcell calculated that to make it likely (probability greater than 50 percent) that a run of even 50 games will occur once in the history of baseball up to now (and 56 is a lot more than 50 in this kind of league), baseball's rosters would have to include either four lifetime .400 batters or 52 lifetime .350 batters over careers of 1,000 games. In actuality, only three men have lifetime batting averages in excess of .350, and no one is anywhere near .400 (Ty Cobb at .367, Rogers Hornsby at .358, and Shoeless Joe Jackson at .356). DiMaggio's streak is the most extraordinary thing that ever happened in American sports. He sits on the shoulders of two bearers—mythology and science. For Joe DiMaggio accomplished what no other ballplayer has done. He beat the hardest taskmaster of all, a woman who makes Nolan Ryan's fastball look like a cantaloupe in slow motion—Lady Luck.

A larger issue lies behind basic documentation and simple appreciation. For we don't understand the truly special character of DiMaggio's record because we are so poorly equipped, whether by habits of culture or by our modes of cognition, to grasp the workings of random processes and patterning in nature.

Omar Khayyám, the old Persian tentmaker, understood the quandary of our lives (*Rubaiyat of Omar Khayyám,* Edward Fitzgerald, trans.):   15

> Into this Universe, and Why not knowing,
> Nor Whence, like Water willy-nilly flowing;
> And out of it, as Wind along the Waste,
> I know not Whither, willy-nilly blowing.

But we cannot bear it. We must have comforting answers. We see pattern, for pattern surely exists, even in a purely random world. (Only a highly nonrandom universe could possibly cancel out the clumping that we perceive as pattern. We think we see constellations because stars are dispersed at random in the heavens, and therefore clump in our sight.) Our error lies not in the perception of pattern but in automatically imbuing pattern with meaning, especially with meaning that can bring us comfort, or dispel confusion. Again, Omar took the more honest approach:

> Ah, love! could you and I with Fate conspire
> To grasp this sorry Scheme of Things entire,
> Would not we shatter it to bits—and then
> Re-mould it nearer to the Heart's Desire!

We, instead, have tried to impose that "heart's desire" upon the actual earth and its largely random patterns (Alexander Pope, *Essay on Man,* end of Epistle 1):

> All Nature is but Art, unknown to thee;
> All Chance, Direction, which thou canst not see;
> All Discord, Harmony not understood:
> All partial Evil, universal Good.

Sorry to wax so poetic and tendentious about something that leads back to DiMaggio's hitting streak, but this broader setting forms the source of our misinterpretation. We believe in "hot hands" because we must impart meaning to a pattern—and we like meanings that tell stories about heroism, valor, and excellence. We believe that long streaks and slumps must have direct causes internal to the sequence itself, and we have no feel for the frequency and length of sequences in random data. Thus, while we understand that DiMaggio's hitting streak was the longest ever, we don't appreciate its truly special character because we view all the others as equally patterned by cause, only a little shorter. We distinguish DiMaggio's feat merely by quantity along a continuum of courage; we should, instead, view his 56-game hitting streak as a unique assault upon the otherwise unblemished record of Dame Probability.

Amos Tversky, who studied "hot hands," has performed, with Daniel Kahneman, a series of elegant psychological experiments. These long-term studies have provided our finest insight into "natural reasoning" and its curious departure from logical truth. To cite an example, they construct a fictional description of a young woman: "Linda is 31 years old, single, outspoken, and very bright. She majored in philosophy. As a student, she was deeply concerned with issues of discrimination and social justice, and also participated in anti-nuclear demonstrations." Subjects are then given a list of hypothetical statements about Linda: They must rank these in order of presumed likelihood, most to least probable. Tversky and Kahneman list eight statements, but five are a blind, and only three make up the true experiment:

> Linda is active in the feminist movement;
> Linda is a bank teller;
> Linda is a bank teller and is active in the feminist movement.

Now it simply must be true that the third statement is least likely, since any conjunction has to be less probable than either of its parts considered separately. Everybody can understand this when the principle is explained explicitly and patiently. But all groups of subjects, sophisticated students who have pondered logic and probability as well as folks off the street corner, rank the last statement as more probable than the second. (I am particularly fond of this example because I know that the third statement is least probable, yet a little homunculus in my head continues to jump up and down, shouting at me—"but she can't just be a bank teller; read the description.")

20

Why do we so consistently make this simple logical error? Tversky and Kahneman argue, correctly I think, that our minds are not built (for whatever reason) to work by the rules of probability, though these rules clearly govern our universe. We do something else that usually serves us well, but fails in crucial instances: We "match to type." We abstract what we consider the "essence" of an entity, and then arrange our judgments by their degree of similarity to this assumed type. Since we are given a "type" for Linda that implies feminism, but definitely not a bank job, we rank any statement matching the type as more probable than another that only contains material contrary to the type. This propensity may help us to understand an entire range of human preferences, from Plato's theory of form to modern stereotyping of race or gender.

We might also understand the world better, and free ourselves of unseemly prejudice, if we properly grasped the workings of probability and its inexorable hold, through laws of logic, upon much of nature's pattern. "Matching to type" is one common error; failure to understand random patterning in streaks and slumps is another—hence Tversky's study of both the fictional Linda and the 76ers' baskets. Our failure to appreciate the uniqueness of DiMaggio's streak derives from the same unnatural and uncomfortable relationship that we maintain with probability. (If we knew Lady Luck better, Las Vegas might still be a roadstop in the desert.)

My favorite illustration of this basic misunderstanding, as applied to DiMaggio's hitting streak, appeared in a recent article by baseball writer John Holway, "A Little Help from His Friends," and subtitled "Hits or Hype in '41" (*Sports Heritage,* 1987). Holway points out that five of DiMaggio's successes were narrow escapes and lucky breaks. He received two benefits-of-the-doubt from official scorers on plays that might have been judged as errors. In each of two games, his only hit was a cheapie. In game 16, a ball dropped untouched in the outfield and had to be called a hit, even though the ball had been misjudged and could have been caught; in game 54, DiMaggio dribbled one down the third-base line, easily beating the throw because the third baseman, expecting the usual, was playing far back. The fifth incident is an oft-told tale, perhaps the most interesting story of the streak. In game 38, DiMaggio was 0 for 3 going into the last inning. Scheduled to bat fourth, he might have been denied a chance to hit at all. Johnny Sturm popped up to begin the inning, but Red Rolfe then walked. Slugger Tommy Henrich, up next, was suddenly swept with a premonitory fear: Suppose I ground into a double play and end the inning? An elegant solution immediately occurred to him: Why not bunt (an odd strategy for a power hitter). Henrich laid down a beauty; DiMaggio, up next, promptly drilled a double to left.

I enjoyed Holway's account, but his premise is entirely, almost preciously, wrong. First of all, none of the five incidents represents an egregious miscall. The two hits were less than elegant, but undoubtedly legitimate; the two boosts from official scorers were close calls on judgment plays, not gifts. As for Henrich, I can only repeat manager Joe McCarthy's comment when Tommy asked him for permission to bunt: "Yeah, that's a good idea." Not a terrible strategy either—to put a man into scoring position for an insurance run when you're up 3–1.

But these details do not touch the main point: Holway's premise is false because he accepts the conventional mythology about long sequences. He believes that streaks are unbroken runs of causal courage— so that any prolongation by hook-or-crook becomes an outrage against the deep meaning of the phenomenon. But extended sequences are not pure exercises in valor. Long streaks always are, and must be, a matter of extraordinary luck imposed upon great skill. Please don't make the vulgar mistake of thinking that Purcell or Tversky or I or anyone else would attribute a long streak to "just luck"—as though everyone's chances are exactly the same, and streaks represent nothing more than the lucky atom that kept moving in one direction. Long hitting streaks happen to the greatest players—Sisler, Keeler, DiMaggio, Rose— because their general chance of getting a hit is so much higher than average. Just as Joe Airball cannot match Larry Bird for runs of baskets, Joe's cousin Bill Ofer, with a lifetime batting average of .184, will never have a streak to match DiMaggio's with a lifetime average of .325. The statistics show something else, and something fascinating: There is no "causality of circumstance," no "extra" that the great can draw from the soul of their valor to extend a streak beyond the ordinary expectation of cointossing models for a series of unconnected events, each occurring with a characteristic probability for that particular player. Good players have higher characteristic probabilities, hence longer streaks.

Of course DiMaggio had a little luck during his streak. That's what streaks are all about. No long sequence has ever been entirely sustained in any other way (the Orioles almost won several of those 21 games). DiMaggio's remarkable achievement—its uniqueness, in the unvarnished literal sense of that word—lies in whatever he did to extend his success well beyond the reasonable expectations of random models that have governed every other streak or slump in the history of baseball.

Probability does pervade the universe—and in this sense, the old chestnut about baseball imitating life really has validity. The statistics of streaks and slumps, properly understood, do teach an important lesson about epistemology, and life in general. The history of a species, or any natural phenomenon that requires unbroken continuity in a world of trouble, works like a batting streak. All are games of a gambler

25

playing with a limited stake against a house with infinite resources. The gambler must eventually go bust. His aim can only be to stick around as long as possible, to have some fun while he's at it, and, if he happens to be a moral agent as well, to worry about staying the course with honor. The best of us will try to live by a few simple rules: Do justly, love mercy, walk humbly with thy God, and never draw to an inside straight.

DiMaggio's hitting streak is the finest of legitimate legends because it embodies the essence of the battle that truly defines our lives. DiMaggio activated the greatest and most unattainable dream of all humanity, the hope and chimera of all sages and shamans: He cheated death, at least for a while.

LINES OF INQUIRY
"The Streak of Streaks"

Like a skilled journalist, Gould begins this essay with a "hook," a grabby little story or bit of information that not only arouses a reader's interest but also relates to the topic and significance of the piece as a whole. In what ways does Gould's opening story about his father and himself relate to the topic and implications of his piece? In what ways does Gould's next little story, another "hook," relate to the preceding one as well as to the piece as a whole? How, in turn, does Gould manage to develop this essay, so that he is able to move from such apparently trivial accounts of personal experience to such a momentous set of claims as he makes in his final paragraph?

The title of an essay may or may not be an indication of its central concern. To what extent do you think this essay is primarily concerned with statistically accounting for DiMaggio's "streak of streaks"? To what extent do you think it is concerned instead with exposing the logical errors that people typically commit in attempting to account for random processes? To what extent do you think it is concerned instead with reflecting upon the profound relationship between baseball "and life in general"? To what extent do you think it is concerned instead with reflecting upon the randomness of existence itself?

Gould is not the only essayist in this collection to be concerned with streaks, as you can see by looking at Edward Hoagland's "A Run of Bad Luck." In what respects do Gould and Hoagland seem to agree in their approach to streaks and runs? To disagree? Whose approach makes more sense in terms of your own experience with streaks and runs?

THE MEDIAN ISN'T
THE MESSAGE

My life has recently inter-
sected, in a most personal way, two of Mark Twain's famous quips. One
I shall defer to the end of this essay. The other (sometimes attributed to
Disraeli) identifies three species of mendacity, each worse than the one
before—lies, damned lies, and statistics.

Consider the standard example of stretching truth with numbers—
a case quite relevant to my story. Statistics recognizes different measures of an "average," or central tendency. The *mean* represents our usual
concept of an overall average—add up the items and divide them by the
number of sharers (100 candy bars collected for five kids next Hal-
loween will yield 20 for each in a fair world). The *median,* a different
measure of central tendency, is the halfway point. If I line up five kids
by height, the median child is shorter than two and taller than the other
two (who might have trouble getting their mean share of the candy). A
politician in power might say with pride, "The mean income of our
citizens is $15,000 per year." The leader of the opposition might retort,
"But half our citizens make less than $10,000 per year." Both are right,
but neither cites a statistic with impassive objectivity. The first invokes
a mean, the second a median. (Means are higher than medians in such
cases because one millionaire may outweigh hundreds of poor people in
setting a mean, but can balance only one mendicant in calculating a
median.)

The larger issue that creates a common distrust or contempt for
statistics is more troubling. Many people make an unfortunate and
invalid separation between heart and mind, or feeling and intellect. In
some contemporary traditions, abetted by attitudes stereotypically
centered upon Southern California, feelings are exalted as more "real"
and the only proper basis for action, while intellect gets short shrift as
a hang-up of outmoded elitism. Statistics, in this absurd dichotomy,
often becomes the symbol of the enemy. As Hilaire Belloc wrote,
"Statistics are the triumph of the quantitative method, and the quantitative method is the victory of sterility and death."

This is a personal story of statistics, properly interpreted, as profoundly nurturant and life-giving. It declares holy war on the down-
grading of intellect by telling a small story to illustrate the utility of
dry, academic knowledge about science. Heart and head are focal points
of one body, one personality.

In July 1982, I learned that I was suffering from abdominal mesothelioma, a rare and serious cancer usually associated with

5

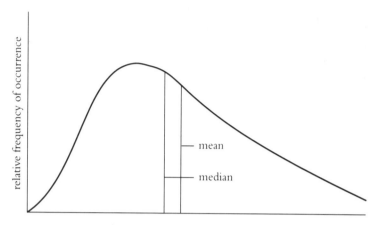

A right-skewed distribution showing that means must be higher than medians, and that the right side of the distribution extends out into a long tail. BEN GAMIT.

exposure to asbestos. When I revived after surgery, I asked my first question of my doctor and chemotherapist: "What is the best technical literature about mesothelioma?" She replied, with a touch of diplomacy (the only departure she has ever made from direct frankness), that the medical literature contained nothing really worth reading.

Of course, trying to keep an intellectual away from literature works about as well as recommending chastity to *Homo sapiens,* the sexiest primate of all. As soon as I could walk, I made a beeline for Harvard's Countway medical library and punched mesothelioma into the computer's bibliographic search program. An hour later, surrounded by the latest literature on abdominal mesothelioma, I realized with a gulp why my doctor had offered that humane advice. The literature couldn't have been more brutally clear: Mesothelioma is incurable, with a median mortality of only eight months after discovery. I sat stunned for about fifteen minutes, then smiled and said to myself: So that's why they didn't give me anything to read. Then my mind started to work again, thank goodness.

If a little learning could ever be a dangerous thing, I had encountered a classic example. Attitude clearly matters in fighting cancer. We don't know why (from my old-style materialistic perspective, I suspect that mental states feed back upon the immune system). But match people with the same cancer for age, class, health, and socioeconomic status, and, in general, those with positive attitudes, with a strong will and purpose for living, with commitment to struggle, and with an active response to aiding their own treatment and not just a passive acceptance of anything doctors say tend to live longer. A few months later I asked Sir Peter Medawar, my personal scientific guru and a Nobelist in immunology, what the best prescription for success against cancer might be. "A sanguine personality," he replied. Fortunately (since one can't reconstruct oneself at short notice and for a definite purpose), I am, if anything, even-tempered and confident in just this manner.

Hence the dilemma for humane doctors: Since attitude matters so critically, should such a somber conclusion be advertised, especially since few people have sufficient understanding of statistics to evaluate what the statements really mean? From years of experience with the small-scale evolution of Bahamian land snails treated quantitatively, I have developed this technical knowledge—and I am convinced that it played a major role in saving my life. Knowledge is indeed power, as Francis Bacon proclaimed.

The problem may be briefly stated: What does "median mortality of eight months" signify in our vernacular? I suspect that most people, without training in statistics, would read such a statement as "I will probably be dead in eight months"—the very conclusion that must be avoided, both because this formulation is false, and because attitude matters so much.

I was not, of course, overjoyed, but I didn't read the statement in   10 this vernacular way either. My technical training enjoined a different perspective on "eight months median mortality." The point may seem subtle, but the consequences can be profound. Moreover, this perspective embodies the distinctive way of thinking in my own field of evolutionary biology and natural history.

We still carry the historical baggage of a Platonic heritage that seeks sharp essences and definite boundaries. (Thus we hope to find an unambiguous "beginning of life" or "definition of death," although nature often comes to us as irreducible continua.) This Platonic heritage, with its emphasis on clear distinctions and separated immutable entities, leads us to view statistical measures of central tendency wrongly, indeed opposite to the appropriate interpretation in our actual world of variation, shadings, and continua. In short, we view means and medians as hard "realities," and the variation that permits their calculation as a set of transient and imperfect measurements of this hidden essence. If the median is the reality and variation around the median just a device for calculation, then "I will probably be dead in eight months" may pass as a reasonable interpretation.

But all evolutionary biologists know that variation itself is nature's only irreducible essence. Variation is the hard reality, not a set of imperfect measures for a central tendency. Means and medians are the abstractions. Therefore, I looked at the mesothelioma statistics quite differently—and not only because I am an optimist who tends to see the doughnut instead of the hole, but primarily because I know that variation itself is the reality. I had to place myself amidst the variation.

When I learned about the eight-month median, my first intellectual reaction was: Fine, half the people will live longer; now what are my chances of being in that half. I read for a furious and nervous hour and concluded, with relief: damned good. I possessed every one of the characteristics conferring a probability of longer life: I was young; my disease had been recognized in a relatively early stage; I would receive the nation's best medical treatment; I had the world to live for; I knew how to read the data properly and not despair.

Another technical point then added even more solace. I immediately recognized that the distribution of variation about the eight-month median would almost surely be what statisticians call "right skewed." (In a symmetrical distribution, the profile of variation to the left of the central tendency is a mirror image of variation to the right. Skewed distributions are asymmetrical, with variation stretching out more in one direction than the other—left skewed if extended to the left, right skewed if stretched out to the right.) The distribution of variation had to be right skewed, I reasoned. After all, the left of the distribution contains an irrevocable lower boundary of zero (since mesothelioma can only be identified at death or before). Thus, little space exists for the distribution's lower (or left) half—it must be scrunched up between zero and eight months. But the upper (or right) half can extend out for years and years, even if nobody ultimately survives. The distribution must be right skewed, and I needed to know how long the extended tail ran—for I had already concluded that my favorable profile made me a good candidate for the right half of the curve.

The distribution was, indeed, strongly right skewed, with a long tail (however small) that extended for several years above the eight-month median. I saw no reason why I shouldn't be in that small tail, and I breathed a very long sigh of relief. My technical knowledge had helped. I had read the graph correctly. I had asked the right question and found the answers. I had obtained, in all probability, that most precious of all possible gifts in the circumstances—substantial time. I didn't have to stop and immediately follow Isaiah's injunction to Hezekiah—set thine house in order: for thou shalt die, and not live. I would have time to think, to plan, and to fight.

One final point about statistical distributions. They apply only to a prescribed set of circumstances—in this case to survival with mesothelioma under conventional modes of treatment. If circumstances change, the distribution may alter. I was placed on an experimental protocol of treatment and, if fortune holds, will be in the first cohort of a new distribution with high median and a right tail extending to death by natural causes at advanced old age.*

It has become, in my view, a bit too trendy to regard the acceptance of death as something tantamount to intrinsic dignity. Of course I agree with the preacher of Ecclesiastes that there is a time to love and a time to die—and when my skein runs out I hope to face the end calmly and in

15

---

* So far so good.

my own way. For most situations, however, I prefer the more martial view that death is the ultimate enemy—and I find nothing reproachable in those who rage mightily against the dying of the light.

The swords of battle are numerous, and none more effective than humor. My death was announced at a meeting of my colleagues in Scotland, and I almost experienced the delicious pleasure of reading my obituary penned by one of my best friends (the so-and-so got suspicious and checked; he too is a statistician, and didn't expect to find me so far out on the left tail). Still, the incident provided my first good laugh after the diagnosis. Just think, I almost got to repeat Mark Twain's most famous line of all: The reports of my death are greatly exaggerated.*

LINES OF INQUIRY
"The Median Isn't the Message"

In the third paragraph of this brief essay, Gould declares that "this is a personal story of statistics, properly interpreted, as profoundly nurturant and life-giving." How does Gould tell his story so as to arouse interest and build suspense? How does he develop his story, so as to show what he means by the proper interpretation of statistics, without losing the continuity of his narrative? How does he develop his story, so as to make his point about the "utility of dry, academic knowledge about science"?

At several points in his essay, Gould makes clear that "in fighting cancer," he believes in the value not only of "dry, academic knowledge" but also of an "even-tempered, confident," possibly even somewhat playful and cocky attitude toward experience. Beyond his outright claim of possessing such an attitude, what implicit evidence do you see in this essay—in Gould's prose style, his narrative technique, his literary allusions, and technical explanations—to suggest that he possesses such an attitude? What evidence do you see in Gould's other essays to suggest that he possesses such an attitude?

In this essay, as in his other pieces in this collection, Gould seeks to demonstrate the crucial importance of knowing how to interpret numbers "properly." What similarities, what differences, do you notice in the way that he announces, develops, illustrates, and proves this point in each of his essays. How do you account for the differences?

---

* Since writing this, my death has actually been reported in two European magazines, five years apart. *Fama volat* (and lasts a long time). I squawked very loudly both times and demanded a retraction; guess I just don't have Mr. Clemens's *savoir faire*.

EDWARD HOAGLAND

1937 –

*Pain, love, boredom, and glee, and anticipation or anxiety—these
are the pilings we build our lives from. In love we beget more love
and in pain we beget more pain. Since we must like it or lump it,
we like it. And why not, indeed?*

Edward Hoagland builds
his essays from the "pilings" of both pain and love, boredom and glee,
as he puts it in this excerpt from his essay exploring "The Threshold
and the Jolt of Pain"—formed out of both the darkness and the light of
his own nature. Whether he writes about the city or the country, the
behavior of people or of animals, Hoagland is fascinated with the actual
experience of living in the world, in all its complexity. He is ecstatic
and admittedly "kinky" by turns, sometimes celebrating the beauties of
the natural landscape, sometimes delving into his own sadistic impulses. Whatever he uncovers in his own sensibility, whatever he observes in the behavior of others moves him in the end to "like it" rather
than "lump it." For him even pain can be "converted to serve as a
purpose," since it jolts us for a moment into a new vitality.

Hoagland grew up in a rural suburb of New York, where he experienced the joys of both the country and the city, both of which are
centers of interest in his writing. "The out-of-doors was everything to
me. I spent the summer mornings . . . vaulting the brooks, climbing
the pines, creeping along the rabbit paths." Yet he also grew up a "city
rat," walking the streets of New York "delightedly," an expert in the
"innumerable street nooks and faces which epitomized New York." All
his life, to paraphrase the title of one of his more famous essays, "home
has been two places." A more problematic relationship in Hoagland's
background is the tension between his upper-middle-class upbringing
and his desire for a wider range of experiences. The son of affluent
parents, Hoagland went to Deerfield Academy and then "sumptuous"
Harvard, rubbing elbows with Kennedys, Rockefellers, and Du Ponts.
But partly as a "clumsy penance" for his life of privilege, partly out of
a hunger for new sensations, Hoagland has also spent much of his time

living with winos on Skid Row, sleeping in flophouses, tramping across the country, fighting forest fires, or working in a circus. "To live is to see," he says in one of his later travel essays, "and traveling sometimes speeds up the process."

As a young man Hoagland felt himself to be an "oddball," a "little askew," and worried about a streak of cruelty and even masochism he discovered in himself: "I was a bunch of nerves." What most set him apart was a severe stammer—something he still struggles with today— an inability to talk under pressure that earlier in his life made social situations unbearable, driving Hoagland deeper into himself. The effects of this stammer are evident in his writing, particularly in his fascination with animals and his detachment as an observer. "Words are spoken at considerable cost to me," he says, "so a great value is placed on each one. That has had some effect on me as a writer. As a child, since I couldn't talk to people, I became close to animals. I became an observer, and in all my books, even the novels, witnessing things is what counts." In fact, Hoagland has even suggested that "being in these vocal handcuffs has made me a desperate, devoted writer" in the first place, the written word allowing him to express what he could not say out loud.

His first novel, *Cat Man* (1956), a depiction of life in a traveling circus, was published soon after his graduation from Harvard, and he has since produced two other novels, *The Circle Home* (1960) and *The Peacock's Tail* (1965). But in the late 1960s, after writing the first of his many essays and reviews, Hoagland began to realize that "what I wanted to do most was to tell my own story" and "that the easiest way to do so was by writing directly to the reader without filtering myself through the artifices of fiction." At first these nonfiction pieces had seemed like quick and easy work, a nice break from the "main-force adventure" of writing novels. "But then I realized that since the essays themselves were breaking ground for me, perhaps they were just as directly to the point." They were a "relief," a more generous, open-ended way of expressing the feelings "bottled up" inside of him. But more than that, as he refined and perfected his technique, Hoagland saw that the essay is an art form in itself, capable of embodying experience and ideas not expressible in other ways, as he has explained in his essay on the essay, "What I Think, What I Am." Over the last twenty years, devoting himself exclusively to the essay, he has produced four essay collections— *The Courage of Turtles* (1971), *Walking the Dead Diamond River* (1973), *Red Wolves and Black Bears* (1976), and *The Tugman's Passage* (1982)— and two travel books—*Notes from the Century Before: A Journal of British Columbia* (1969) and *African Calliope: a Journey to the Sudan* (1979).

Hoagland divides his time now between a Greenwich Village apartment and an isolated cabin in Vermont, writing essays on a wide variety of subjects, from boxing and taxidermy to marriage and success. Like E. B. White, though with an entirely different tone and outlook, he alternates between writing about life in the country, where "the peepers sing in a ringing, monotonous, fitfully exhilarating call" and "the wood frogs congregate in the woodside pools," and life in the city, where commuters dodge muggers and choke on the smoggy air. "The problem everywhere nowadays turns on how we shall decide to live." Hoagland keeps a foot in both the country and the city, balancing the values of each without retreating from the challenges of contemporary life. Another of his central preoccupations is the idea of skill and performance, in tugboat captains, animal trainers, athletes, rodeo performers, and other writers. As he says of boxing, "I go to admire a trial of skills." He also remains fascinated with animals, especially turtles and bears, but also with any animal that is hunted or tamed. What compels him is the physicality and power of animals as they resist human attempts to subdue them, and also their strangeness, their otherness.

Hoagland is also compelled by his own strange, dark impulses, and he is arrestingly frank and precise in describing such feelings. "There is a monster in me that I keep at bay," he says, "a secret hunchback residing inside of me." In writing of an early lover, for example, he admits that "I was not an ogre to her, but I did by stages develop the habit of beating her briefly with my belt or hairbrush before we made love, a practice which I have foregone ever since." In other essays he describes with a kind of steady, almost scientific relish his secret satisfaction in seeing people and animals trapped or hurt, his own enjoyment at being restrained or abused, even his desire to beat his infant daughter.

Hoagland explores such feelings not for the sake of sensationalism but rather out of a belief in the importance of honesty, and more than that, for the purpose in the end of making a moral point. "What is kinky in me worries me less than the dead spots," he says. "Kinkiness, like a reversible coat, can be turned inside out." So, Hoagland values most the ability to be aware, fully human, not deadened by the routines and pressures of daily life. Admitting to kinkiness can be one step to recognizing the other side of human nature, the human capacity for joy, which is equally Hoagland's subject. "I'm an optimist in the same way that I'm right-handed, and will always be. It's simpler to be an optimist and it's a sensible defense against the uncertainties and abysses which otherwise confront us prematurely."

Thus when he isn't divulging some intimacy of his inner life, Hoagland describes as accurately as he can the splendor of the circus, the thrill of the city, the serenity of the morning forest, or the courage of turtles. Given the extraordinary range of his interests and the vigor of his impulses, Hoagland's essays are often rambling, full of tangents and false cues, intricate digressions, fractures. Yet the vividness of his metaphors, the strength of his verbs, and the drive of his sentences also enable him to achieve "a combination of personality and originality and energetic loose ends" that for him characterizes the essay.

THE COURAGE
OF TURTLES

Turtles are a kind of bird with the governor turned low. With the same attitude of removal, they cock a glance at what is going on, as if they need only to fly away. Until recently they were also a case of virtue rewarded, at least in the town where I grew up, because, being humble creatures, there were plenty of them. Even when we still had a few bobcats in the woods the local snapping turtles, growing up to forty pounds, were the largest carnivores. You would see them through the amber water, as big as greeny wash basins at the bottom of the pond, until they faded into the inscrutable mud as if they hadn't existed at all.

When I was ten I went to Dr. Green's Pond, a two-acre pond across the road. When I was twelve I walked a mile or so to Taggart's Pond, which was lusher, had big water snakes and a waterfall; and shortly after that I was bicycling way up to the adventuresome vastness of Mud Pond, a lake-sized body of water in the reservoir system of a Connecticut city, possessed of cat-backed little islands and empty shacks and a forest of pines and hardwoods along the shore. Otters, foxes and mink left their prints on the bank; there were pike and perch. As I got older, the estates and forgotten back lots in town were parceled out and sold for nice prices, yet, though the woods had shrunk, it seemed that fewer people walked in the woods. The new residents didn't know how to find them. Eventually, exploring, they did find them, and it required some ingenuity and doubling around on my part to go for eight miles without meeting someone. I was grown by now, I lived in New York, and that's what I wanted on the occasional weekends when I came out.

Since Mud Pond contained drinking water I had felt confident nothing untoward would happen there. For a long while the developers stayed away, until the drought of the mid-1960s. This event, squeezing the edges in, convinced the local water company that the pond really wasn't a necessity as a catch basin, however; so they bulldozed a hole in the earthen dam, bulldozed the banks to fill in the bottom, and landscaped the flow of water that remained to wind like an English brook and provide a domestic view for the houses which were planned. Most of the painted turtles of Mud Pond, who had been inaccessible as they sunned on their rocks, wound up in boxes in boys' closets within a matter of days. Their footsteps in the dry leaves gave them away as they wandered forlornly. The snappers and the little musk turtles, neither of whom leave the water except once a year to lay their eggs, dug into the drying mud for another siege of hot weather, which they were accustomed to doing whenever the pond got low. But this time it was low for good; the mud baked over them and slowly entombed them. As for the ducks, I couldn't stroll in the woods and not feel guilty, because they were crouched beside every stagnant pothole, or were slinking between the bushes with their heads tucked into their shoulders so that I wouldn't see them. If they decided I had, they beat their way up through the screen of trees, striking their wings dangerously, and wheeled about with that headlong, magnificent velocity to locate another poor puddle.

I used to catch possums and black snakes as well as turtles, and I kept dogs and goats. Some summers I worked in a menagerie with the big personalities of the animal kingdom, like elephants and rhinoceroses. I was twenty before these enthusiasms began to wane, and it was then that I picked turtles as the particular animal I wanted to keep in touch with. I was allergic to fur, for one thing, and turtles need minimal care and not much in the way of quarters. They're personable beasts. They see the same colors we do and they seem to see just as well, as one discovers in trying to sneak up on them. In the laboratory they unravel the twists of a maze with the hot-blooded rapidity of a mammal. Though they can't run as fast as a rat, they improve on their errors just as quickly, pausing at each crossroads to look left and right. And they rock rhythmically in place, as we often do, although they are hatched from eggs, not the womb. (A common explanation psychologists give for our pleasure in rocking quietly is that it recapitulates our mother's heartbeat *in utero.*)

Snakes, by contrast, are dryly silent and priapic. They are smooth   5 movers, legalistic, unblinking, and they afford the humor which the humorless do. But they make challenging captives; sometimes they don't eat for months on a point of order—if the light isn't right, for instance. Alligators are sticklers too. They're like war-horses, or German shepherds, and with their bar-shaped, vertical pupils adding emphasis, they have the *idée fixe* of eating, eating, even when they choose to refuse all food and stubbornly die. They delight in tossing a salamander up towards the sky and grabbing him in their long mouths as he comes down. They're so eager that they get the jitters, and they're too much of a proposition for a casual aquarium like mine. Frogs are depressingly defenseless: that moist, extensive back, with the bones almost sticking through. Hold a frog and you're holding its skeleton. Frogs' tasty legs are the staff of life to many animals—herons, raccoons, ribbon snakes—though they themselves are hard to feed. It's not an enviable role to be the staff of life, and after frogs you descend down the evolutionary ladder a big step to fish.

Turtles cough, burp, whistle, grunt and hiss, and produce social judgments. They put their heads together amicably enough, but then one drives the other back with the suddenness of two dogs who have been conversing in tones too low for an onlooker to hear. They pee in fear when they're first caught, but exercise both pluck and optimism in trying to escape, walking for hundreds of yards within the confines of their pen, carrying the weight of that cumbersome box on legs which are cruelly positioned for walking. They don't feel that the contest is unfair; they keep plugging, rolling like sailorly souls—a bobbing, infirm gait, a brave, sea-legged momentum—stopping occasionally to study the lay of the land. For me, anyway, they manage to contain the rest of the animal world. They can stretch out their necks like a giraffe, or loom underwater like an apocryphal hippo. They browse on lettuce thrown on the water like a cow moose which is partly submerged. They have a penguin's alertness, combined with a build like a Brontosaurus when they rise up on tiptoe. Then they hunch and ponderously lunge like a grizzly going forward.

Baby turtles in a turtle bowl are a puzzle in geometrics. They're as decorative as pansy petals, but they are also self-directed building blocks, propping themselves on one another in different arrangements, before upending the tower. The timid individuals turn fearless, or vice versa. If one gets a bit arrogant he will push the others off the rock and afterwards climb down into the water and cling to the back of one of those he has bullied, tickling him with his hind feet until he bucks like a bronco. On the other hand, when this same milder-mannered fellow isn't exerting himself, he will stare right into the face of the sun for hours. What could be more lionlike? And he's at home in or out of the water and does lots of metaphysical tilting. He sinks and rises, with an infinity of levels to choose from; or, elongating himself, he climbs out on the land again to perambulate, sits boxed in his box, and finally slides back in the water, submerging into dreams.

I have five of these babies in a kidney-shaped bowl. The hatchling, who is a painted turtle, is not as large as the top joint of my thumb. He eats chicken gladly. Other foods he will attempt to eat but not with sufficient perseverance to succeed because he's so little. The yellow-bellied terrapin is probably a yearling, and he eats salad voraciously, but no meat, fish or fowl. The Cumberland terrapin won't touch salad or chicken but eats fish and all of the meats except for bacon. The little snapper, with a black crenelated shell, feasts on any kind of meat, but rejects greens and fish. The fifth of the turtles is African. I acquired him only recently and don't know him well. A mottled brown, he unnerves the green turtles, dragging their food off to his lairs. He doesn't seem to want to be green—he bites the algae off his shell, hanging meanwhile at daring, steep, head-first angles.

The snapper was a Ferdinand until I provided him with deeper water. Now he snaps at my pencil with his downturned and fearsome mouth, his swollen face like a napalm victim's. The Cumberland has an elliptical red mark on the side of his green-and-yellow head. He is

benign by nature and ought to be as elegant as his scientific name
(Pseudemys scripta elegans), except he has contracted a disease of the air
bladder which has permanently inflated it; he floats high in the water at
an undignified slant and can't go under. There may have been internal
bleeding, too, because his carapace is stained along its ridge. Unfortunately, like flowers, baby turtles often die. Their mouths fill up with a
white fungus and their lungs with pneumonia. Their organs clog up
from the rust in the water, or diet troubles, and, like a dying man's, their
eyes and heads become too prominent. Toward the end, the edge of the
shell becomes flabby as felt and folds around them like a shroud.

While they live they're like puppies. Although they're vivacious,   10
they would be a bore to be with all the time, so I also have an adult wood
turtle about six inches long. Her shell is the equal of any seashell for
sculpturing, even a Cellini shell; it's like an old, dusty, richly engraved
medallion dug out of a hillside. Her legs are salmon-orange bordered
with black and protected by canted, heroic scales. Her plastron—the
bottom shell—is splotched like a margay cat's coat, with black ocelli on
a yellow background. It is convex to make room for the female organs
inside, whereas a male's would be concave to help him fit tightly on top
of her. Altogether, she exhibits every camouflage color on her limbs and
shells. She has a turtleneck neck, a tail like an elephant's, wise old
pachydermous hind legs and the face of a turkey—except that when I
carry her she gazes at the passing ground with a hawk's eyes and mouth.
Her feet fit to the fingers of my hand, one to each one, and she rides
looking down. She can walk on the floor in perfect silence, but usually
she lets her shell knock portentously, like a footstep, so that she resembles some grand, concise, slow-moving id. But if an earthworm is
presented, she jerks swiftly ahead, poises above it and strikes like a
mongoose, consuming it with wild vigor. Yet she will climb on my lap
to eat bread or boiled eggs.

If put into a creek, she swims like a cutter, nosing forward to inter-
cept a strange turtle and smell him. She drifts with the current to go
downstream, maneuvering behind a rock when she wants to take stock,
or sinking to the nether levels, while bubbles float up. Getting out,
choosing her path, she will proceed a distance and dig into a pile of
humus, thrusting herself to the coolest layer at the bottom. The hole
closes over her until it's as small as a mouse's hole. She's not as aquatic as
a musk turtle, not quite as terrestrial as the box turtles in the same
woods, but because of her versatility she's marvelous, she's everywhere.
And though she breathes the way we breathe, with scarcely perceptible
movements of her chest, sometimes instead she pumps her throat rumi-
natively, like a pipe smoker sucking and puffing. She waits and blinks,
pumping her throat, turning her head, then sets off like a loping tiger in
slow motion, hurdling the jungly lumber, the pea vine and twigs. She
estimates angles so well that when she rides over the rocks, sliding down

a drop-off with her rugged front legs extended, she has the grace of a rodeo mare.

But she's well off to be with me rather than at Mud Pond. The other turtles have fled—those that aren't baked into the bottom. Creeping up the brooks to sad, constricted marshes, burdened as they are with that box on their backs, they're walking into a setup where all their enemies move thirty times faster than they. It's like the nightmare most of us have whimpered through, where we are weighted down disastrously while trying to flee; fleeing our home ground, we try to run.

I've seen turtles in still worse straits. On Broadway, in New York, there is a penny arcade which used to sell baby terrapins that were scrawled with bon mots in enamel paint, such as KISS ME BABY. The manager turned out to be a wholesaler as well, and once I asked him whether he had any larger turtles to sell. He took me upstairs to a loft room devoted to the turtle business. There were desks for the paper work and a series of racks that held shallow tin bins atop one another, each with several hundred babies crawling around in it. He was a smudgy-complexioned, serious fellow and he did have a few adult terrapins, but I was going to school and wasn't actually planning to buy; I'd only wanted to see them. They were aquatic turtles, but here they went without water, presumably for weeks, lurching about in those dry bins like handicapped citizens, living on gumption. An easel where the artist worked stood in the middle of the floor. She had a palette and a clip attachment for fastening the babies in place. She wore a smock and a beret, and was homely, short and eccentric-looking, with funny black hair, like some of the ladies who show their paintings in Washington Square in May. She had a cold, she was smoking, and her hand wasn't very steady, although she worked quickly enough. The smile that she produced for me would have looked giddy if she had been happier, or drunk. Of course the turtles' doom was sealed when she painted them, because their bodies inside would continue to grow but their shells would not. Gradually, invisibly, they would be crushed. Around us their bellies—two thousand belly shells—rubbed on the bins with a mournful, momentous hiss.

Somehow there were so many of them I didn't rescue one. Years later, however, I was walking on First Avenue when I noticed a basket of living turtles in front of a fish store. They were as dry as a heap of old bones in the sun; nevertheless, they were creeping over one another gimpily, doing their best to escape. I looked and was touched to discover that they appeared to be wood turtles, my favorites, so I bought one. In my apartment I looked closer and realized that in fact this was a diamond-back terrapin, which was bad news. Diamond-backs are tide-water turtles from brackish estuaries, and I had no sea water to keep him in. He spent his days thumping interminably against the baseboards, pushing for an opening through the wall. He drank thirstily but would not eat and had none of the hearty, accepting qualities of wood turtles. He was morose, paler in color, sleeker and more Oriental in the carved ridges and rings that formed his shell. Though I felt sorry for him, finally I found his unrelenting presence exasperating. I carried him, struggling in a paper bag, across town to the Morton Street Pier on the Hudson. It was August but gray and windy. He was very surprised when I tossed him in; for the first time in our association, I think, he was afraid. He looked afraid as he bobbed about on top of the water, looking up at me from ten feet below. Though we were both accustomed to his resistance and rigidity, seeing him still pitiful, I recognized that I must have done the wrong thing. At least the river was salty, but it was also bottomless; the waves were too rough for him, and the tide was coming in, bumping him against the pilings underneath the pier. Too late, I realized that he wouldn't be able to swim to a peaceful inlet in New Jersey, even if he could figure out which way to swim. But since, short of diving in after him, there was nothing I could do, I walked away.

[1968]

LINES OF INQUIRY
"The Courage of Turtles"

Though Hoagland tells about his childhood and adolescent experience with turtles in chronological order, he tells about his different adult experiences with them in reverse chronological order. What are the effects of this reversed chronology? For example, what impression do you get of turtles—and of Hoagland—from his concluding story about the diamond-back terrapin? How do these concluding impressions compare with Hoagland's previous depiction of turtles—and of himself? Imagine how your impression of turtles—and of Hoagland—might be altered if the piece were chronologically organized from beginning to end and concluded, therefore, with the story about Hoagland and his pet wood turtle.

After the first paragraph of this essay, Hoagland doesn't focus on turtles again until the sixth paragraph. How do you account for this apparent digression from the theme of his essay? And once he does turn his attention entirely to turtles, little that he has to say about them seems to pertain to their "courage." How do you account for this apparent digression from the theme of his essay? Assuming that the piece is not about "the courage of turtles," what do you think is its major theme?

The situation of animals and their relationship to human beings is also explored in Dillard's "The Deer at Providencia," Eiseley's "The Bird and the Machine," and Walker's "Am I Blue?" Read or reread one of these pieces and consider what ideas and concerns Hoagland shares with that essayist, as well as what issues are of interest to him alone.

A RUN OF BAD LUCK

Bad ions in the air, bad stars, or bad luck: call it what you will—a run of bad luck, in fact. I was driving down the Thruway in Vermont to consult a doctor in New York, and hit a deer. Didn't see the deer till the impact, sharing its surprise. Deer, unlike domestic animals, are afraid of cars and leap as you pass, either into you or away. It lay in the deep grass, heaving like a creature stranded on the beach.

Sure enough, as befitted the omen, in New York City the doctor's news was bad. Then within a day or two, Pier 50, a huge ramshackle structure across the street from where I live, caught fire and burned hectically for seven hours, although surrounded by fireboats, as only an abandoned pier can. The neighborhood was layered in smoke for a couple of days—for me, acrid testimony to what the doctor had said. There were also a few of the usual New York hang-up phone calls, and then, as if to push me into a sump of depression, somebody—a vandal aroused by the fire, or someone who thought I had parked in his parking space—poured sugar into the gas tank of my car, not enough to destroy the engine but enough so that I returned to Vermont in relief.

In the meantime, my mother, in another city, had gone into the hospital for surgery, and one evening that week my daughter and I were out walking along a wooded road (I was carrying her on my shoulders), when a car passing another car bore down on us at high speed, its roar not easy to distinguish from that of the slower one; I barely heard it in time. This, in the context of the other incidents, particularly shook me because it seemed to bear a hint of malevolence; I felt very small. Then, within days, my next-door neighbor there, an old man as close as a relative to us, died of a stroke. Another good friend and country mentor went into the hospital after a heart attack. News came from New York as well that a friend in the city had killed herself. I marshaled a motley assortment of tranquilizers and sleeping pills left over from the past—divorce, career crisis, other bad occasions. I had that feeling of luck running out, that I must be *very careful,* although, on the contrary, I was becoming deadened, not alert. At such a time, the opposite of invulnerable, one must take care to move in a gingerly fashion and not get so rattled that an accident happens. I had considered myself a sort of a Sunday's child much of my life, but suddenly intimations of death and calamity were all about.

I remembered talking to a woman who had survived a snowslide by swimming along on the surface while whooshing downhill for a hundred yards—as people caught in an undertow or even in quicksand save themselves by flattening out and floating if they can. Just so, I should ride the current until it turned. The best advice I have heard on bearing pain is to fix one's mind upon the idea that the pain is in one place—the other side of the room—and that you are in another; then, where you are, play cards or whatever. Cooking, fooling with my daughter, I realized more distinctly than at any time in years that although in fact my life was not at stake right now, I believed in some form of reincarnation or immortality—this a conviction, not a wish. I pray in airplanes during takeoff, but it is with a sense of praying *pro forma,* as if the location of my belief weren't really there, but were more generalized, in a bigger God. There are ideas central to society which we seldom question in order that society will hold together—as, for instance, the notion basic to medical care that everybody has a contribution to make, or "a right to life." But there are other conceptions, such as the idea of God, which we disparage and scarcely consider, until later, smiling sheepishly in our mind's eye as if we had disputed the fact that the moon moves in the sky, we admit to having been wrong, and to having known all along that we were wrong.

Once, highborn ladies would flee to a convent if some unnerving   5
sequence of events overtook them, not necessarily taking orders, but resting, collecting their wits. And when they strolled in the cloister around a bubbling fountain, the walkway itself possessed a soothing, perpetual quality, with each right-angle turn leading straight to another. Walking for many hours, they looked at the lindenwood saints, the robust faces—at the Virgin's implacable verve, or else at a dolor portrayed with an equally saving exaggeration. Coincidentally, I went to New York's own Cloisters, and because the reality of each bad event had been dulled by the others, it was for me one of those queer times when people recognize how much they can adjust to—how quickly, for example, they could settle into the routine of life in a prison camp.

Of course I had my daughter to entertain, and in the country I walked in the woods, watching the aspens quake (said by legend to occur because Christ's cross was of aspen). I have an old army siren, hand-cranked, that I climbed with up on the mountain at twilight, to persuade a family of coyotes nearby to answer. I was relieved that the random incidents seemed to have ended. I thought of two friends in the city who had recently suffered crises—heart attacks at forty. One fellow, as the pain surged through him, found himself muttering stubbornly, "No groveling, Death!" When he was out of danger he wrote seventy-some letters to friends from his hospital bed, each with a numbered series of thoughts directed to the recipient. The other man is that rare case where one can put one's finger exactly on the characteristics of which one is so fond. He married the same woman twice. Although it didn't work out either time, she was well worth marrying twice, and to my way of thinking this showed that he was at once a man of fervent, rash, abiding love, and yet a man of flexibility, ready to admit an error and to act to correct it.

Both my mother and country mentor were now on the mend, and my own doctor reported good news. Prospects began looking up. What I'd gained from the period, besides a flood of relief, was the memory of how certain I'd been that the intricacy and brilliance of life cannot simply fold up with one's death—that, as in the metaphor of a fountain, or the great paradigm of rain and the ocean, it sinks down but comes up, blooms up and sinks down again.

LINES OF INQUIRY
"A Run of Bad Luck"

In the preface to his first collection of essays, Hoagland says that writing essays is "the next thing to writing letters." What aspects of style, detailing, and organization make "A Run of Bad Luck" seem like a letter? How would you respond to it, if you actually received this as a letter? On the other hand, how does this piece differ from a letter? What aspects of style, organization, and content make this an essay?

Though Hoagland devotes much of this essay to describing "a run of bad luck," he ends by saying that what he gained from the experience "was the memory of how certain I'd been that the intricacy and brilliance of life cannot simply fold up with one's death." How does he manage to arrive at this affirmative conclusion? How exactly does he get from the terrible things in the beginning to the optimism at the end? What does his belief in "some form of reincarnation or immortality" have to do with this movement from dread to joy? How does this conviction also relate to the dread and fear he felt during his run of bad luck?

Think about a run of bad luck that you—or someone close to you—have lived through. How did it begin? What happened over the course of it? How did it end? Did you feel any of the dread that Hoagland describes, or the superstition? What did you think about it all when the run of bad luck was over?

SPRING

Foxes jubilantly mouse in the fields or dig up moles; raccoons munch grubs. Wild turkeys venture out of the woods with beagly gobbles. May's perfervid grass, stippled with white clover flowers, is a definitive green, and the ground underfoot has regained its resilience. Infant raspberry-red cones hang on some spruces' boughs. Small ferns that went tatty and brown in the snow are springing up fresh. The mountains are color-coded in temperature zones; and deer, fattening in the fields, only frisk away when a dog rushes after them, instead of fearfully panting.

Blue herons sit on their nests, and there are other surprises a walk may bring—a migrating osprey, even a gyrfalcon. As the first flocks of barnstorming swallows arrive, the snowshoe hares are losing the last of their white camouflage, assuming dun colors. Red squirrels chitter like ringing phones, flourishing their tails imperiously, like a bandmaster's hands. A rainy warm evening brings out the toads, traveling toward their breeding pools, though snakes lie in wait for them.

A friend who used to whistle walking to school now whistles to his caged cockatiel through the winter. But in the spring he and this crested bird almost ignore one another, keeping an ear peeled out-of-doors for wrens, ovenbirds, catbirds. The trout fishing gets good as the wild cherries bloom; and when oak leaves and maple seed-keys reach a certain early stage of development, he can find morel mushrooms. Winter's astringence seems to leap from the soil in rhubarb pies, but sweet peas will soon follow. Taking a sauna is no longer punishing when he plunges out of the hotbox into the pool. The steely sky turns dove gray, and in the moonlight (back in February, often so brutal), tree shadows finger the meadow. The breeze smells like honey, the moon has grown tender.

LINES OF INQUIRY
"Spring"

In this very brief essay, Hoagland relies entirely on specific images to convey his impression of Spring. What kinds of images seem to dominate the essay as a whole? What kinds of images seem to prevail in each paragraph? Try some different ways of arranging the three paragraphs. Or try some different ways of arranging the individual images themselves. How does each of your rearrangements affect the pacing, the development, and the overall experience of the essay?

What impression of Spring is conveyed by the first paragraph? By the second paragraph? By the third? By the essay as a whole? How does Hoagland's impression of Spring compare with your own? What images come to your mind when you think of Spring?

For another essay about Spring, see Orwell's "Some Thoughts on the Common Toad." What similarities, what differences, do you notice in the images they record and the impressions they convey of Spring? What similarities, what differences, do you notice in their overall approach to writing about Spring? How do you account for the differences?

WHAT I THINK, WHAT I AM

Our loneliness makes us avid column readers these days. The personalities in the San Francisco *Chronicle,* Chicago *Daily News,* New York *Post* constitute our neighbors now, some of them local characters but also the opinionated national stars. And movie reviewers thrive on our yearning for somebody emotional who is willing to pay attention to us and return week after week, year after year, through all the to-and-fro of other friends, to flatter us by pouring out his/her heart. They are essayists of a type, as Elizabeth Hardwick is, James Baldwin was.

We sometimes hear that essays are an old-fashioned form, that so-and-so is the "last essayist," but the facts of the marketplace argue quite otherwise. Essays of nearly any kind are so much easier than short stories for a writer to sell, so many more see print, it's strange that though two fine anthologies remain that publish the year's best stories, no comparable collection exists for essays. Such changes in the reading public's taste aren't always to the good, needless to say. The art of telling stories predated even cave painting, surely; and if we ever find ourselves living in caves again, it (with painting and drumming) will be the only art left, after movies, novels, photography, essays, biography, and all the rest have gone down the drain—the art to build from.

One has the sense with the short story as a form that while everything may have been done, nothing has been overdone; it has a permanence. Essays, if a comparison is to be made, although they go back four hundred years to Montaigne, seem a mercurial, newfangled, sometimes hokey affair that has lent itself to many of the excesses of the age, from spurious autobiography to spurious hallucination, as well as to the shabby careerism of traditional journalism. It's a greased pig. Essays are associated with the way young writers fashion a name—on plain, crowded newsprint in hybrid vehicles like the *Village Voice, Rolling Stone,* the *New York Review of Books,* instead of the thick paper stock and thin readership of *Partisan Review.*

Essays, however, hang somewhere on a line between two sturdy poles: this is what I think, and this is what I am. Autobiographies which aren't novels are generally extended essays, indeed. A personal essay is like the human voice talking, its order the mind's natural flow, instead of a systematized outline of ideas. Though more wayward or informal than an article or treatise, somewhere it contains a point which is its real center, even if the point couldn't be uttered in fewer words than the essayist has used. Essays don't usually boil down to a summary, as articles do, and the style of the writer has a "nap" to it, a combination of personality and originality and energetic loose ends that stand up like the nap on a piece of wool and can't be brushed flat. Essays belong to the animal kingdom, with a surface that generates sparks, like a coat of fur, compared with the flat, conventional cotton of the magazine article writer, who works in the vegetable kingdom, instead. But essays, on the other hand, may have fewer "levels" than fiction, because we are not supposed to argue much about their meaning. In the old distinction between teaching and storytelling, the essayist, however cleverly he camouflages his intentions, is a bit of a teacher or reformer, and an essay is intended to convey the same point to each of us.

This emphasis upon mind speaking to mind is what makes essays   5 less universal in their appeal than stories. They are addressed to an educated, perhaps a middle-class, reader, with certain presuppositions, a frame of reference, even a commitment to civility that is shared—not the grand and golden empathy inherent in every man or woman that a storyteller has a chance to tap.

Nevertheless, the artful "I" of an essay can be as chameleon as any narrator in fiction; and essays do tell a story quite as often as a short story stakes a claim to a particular viewpoint. Mark Twain's piece called "Corn-pone Opinions," for example, which is about public opinion, begins with a vignette as vivid as any in *Huckleberry Finn.* Twain says that when he was a boy of fifteen, he used to hang out a back window and listen to the sermons preached by a neighbor's slave standing on top of a woodpile: "He imitated the pulpit style of the several clergymen of the village, and did it well and with fine passion and energy. To me he was a wonder. I believed he was the greatest orator in the United States and would some day be heard from. But it did not happen; in the distribution of rewards he was overlooked. . . . He interrupted his preaching now and then to saw a stick of wood, but the sawing was a pretense—he did it with his mouth, exactly imitating the sound the bucksaw makes in shrieking its way through the wood. But it served its purpose, it kept his master from coming out to see how the work was getting along."

A novel would go on and tell us what happened next in the life of the slave—and we miss that. But the extraordinary flexibility of essays is what has enabled them to ride out rough weather and hybridize into forms that suit the times. And just as one of the first things a fiction writer learns is that he needn't actually be writing fiction to write a short story—that he can tell his own history or anybody else's as exactly as he remembers it and it will be "fiction" if it remains primarily a story—an essayist soon discovers that he doesn't have to tell the whole truth and nothing but the truth; he can shape or shave his memories, as long as the purpose is served of elucidating a truthful point. A personal essay frequently is not autobiographical at all, but what it does keep in common with autobiography is that, through its tone and tumbling progression, it conveys the quality of the author's mind. Nothing gets in the way. Because essays are directly concerned with the mind and the mind's idiosyncrasy, the very freedom the mind possesses is bestowed on this branch of literature that does honor to it, and the fascination of the mind is the fascination of the essay.

1976

LINES OF INQUIRY
"What I Think, What I Am"

Given Hoagland's attempt to define the essay in this piece, how well does he conform to his own definition? Does this essay about the the essay fit Hoagland's definition of the essay? Does it seem to be organized according to "the mind's natural flow," or is it "systematized" instead like an "outline of ideas"? Does it have "a combination of personality and originality and energetic loose ends that stand up like the nap on a piece of wool" or is it instead more nearly like "the flat conventional cotton of the magazine writer"?

Throughout this piece, Hoagland examines the essay in relation to the short story and the article. According to Hoagland, what qualities does the essay have in common with each of these kinds of writing? In what important respects does it differ from both fiction and the article? Why do you suppose that he puts so much emphasis on the character of the "I" in relating the essay to the article and the story? How is the "I" of the essay similar to and different from that of the story?

For another American essayist's view of the essay, look at E. B. White's "The Essayist and the Essay." In what respects do they seem to agree, in what respects do they seem to disagree, about the nature of the essay? About the purpose of the essay? About the form of the essay? About the role of the essayist? About the place of personality in the essay? Whose ideas seem most applicable to the essays you've recently been reading and writing?

MARTIN LUTHER KING, JR.

1 9 2 9 — 6 8

In a world facing the revolt of ragged and hungry masses of God's children; in a world torn between the tensions of East and West, white and colored, individualists and collectivists; in a world whose cultural and spiritual power lags so far behind her technological capabilities that we live each day on the verge of nuclear co-annihilation; in this world, nonviolence is no longer an option for intellectual analysis, it is an imperative for action.

Martin Luther King's impassioned call for action in the form of nonviolent resistance to racial injustice was heard throughout America from the mid-fifties to his death in 1968. And it was heeded. Under his leadership, civil rights protesters marched, boycotted, staged sit-ins, faced police dogs and fire hoses, and won strategic victories in the struggle to achieve equal opportunity for black Americans. King always couched his urgent pleas for change in the framework of moral argument, and he stressed the interdependence of citizens throughout the world as well as the nation to explain the need for "helping to make this nation and this world a better place to live in—for *all* men, black and white alike."

King was born and raised in Atlanta, Georgia, where his father had raised himself out of poverty to become pastor of Ebenezer Baptist Church and one of the most respected leaders of Atlanta's middle-class black community. His mother was a gentle and genteel woman, the daughter of an influential Atlanta preacher who had been born a slave and had founded Ebenezer Baptist Church. So, King grew up in a comfortable and deeply religious home in which the church's presence always was felt. A precocious child who from an early age exhibited a love of books and language, according to one biographer he possessed "a remarkable vocabulary that dazzled teachers and peers alike" and "sailed through school, skipping grades as he went." King later said that his "greatest talent, strongest tradition, and most constant interest was the eloquent statement of ideas." He gave evidence of his eloquence and his budding social concerns in high school by winning an oratorical contest with a speech on "The Negro and the Constitution."

King entered Morehouse College in Atlanta in 1944, when he was only fifteen, and graduated four years later with a degree in sociology. At Morehouse he came under the influence of black intellectuals who introduced him to a world of new ideas that freed him, as he later said, of "the shackles of fundamentalism," showing him that the insights of sociology and religion were not at odds, but instead could cooperate to shape a commitment to social and spiritual activism for the improvement of his race. Inspired by this vision, he decided to enter the ministry, was ordained at seventeen, and became assistant pastor to his father at Ebenezer Baptist Church.

After graduating from Morehouse, King entered Crozer Seminary in Pennsylvania to study for a B.A. in divinity. Though he was a model student, earning As in all his courses, the conventional Crozer curriculum did not satisfy his quest for a definition of what the church's role might be as a force for social protest. So, he began to read widely in history and political philosophy, and thus encountered the thinking of Mahatma Ghandi, the Indian leader who had used nonviolent resistance and "soul force" to free his country from British colonialism. King was profoundly influenced by Ghandi as well as by Thoreau's "Civil Disobedience," and from their ideas and examples he began to synthesize the commitment to "militant nonviolent resistance" that would become his major contribution to the civil rights movement.

From Crozer he went to Boston University to earn a Ph.D. in philosophical theology. In Boston he met Coretta Scott, a fellow Southerner who was studying music at the Boston Conservatory, and they were married in 1953. As a doctoral student King continued to excel, and his passionate love for the intellectual life led him to decide on a career as a teacher and writer in the academic world. But he felt that he first needed to serve for a few years as an active minister. So in May 1954 he accepted the pastorate of the Dexter Avenue Baptist Church in Montgomery, Alabama, the "cradle of the Confederacy." It was a historic juncture, for within months of King's arrival in Montgomery, Rosa Parks was arrested for refusing to give up her seat on a city bus to a white man, and King found himself spearheading what proved to be a successful boycott of the city bus system to protest racist seating policies. Thus he was suddenly thrust into the forefront as a national leader in the civil rights movement.

In 1960, in order to devote more of his time to the movement, he resigned his pastorate in Montgomery and moved his family back to Atlanta, where he once again served as associate pastor at his father's church. Leading a social reform movement allowed King to exercise his extraordinary intelligence, his moral and personal force, and his charismatic powers of oratory. Yet in other ways King was an unlikely public figure, attracted as he was to the retiring life of the scholar and author. Indeed, he once called himself an "ambivert," a "cross between an extrovert and an introvert." Throughout his life, in fact, he somehow managed to balance his public commitments to preaching and social reforming with his personal interests in reading and writing about religion, philosophy, and social issues. Thus before his early death, he managed to produce two collections of his sermons, rewritten for publication, *The Strength to Love* (1963) and *The Trumpet of Conscience* (1967), as well as three other books, *Stride Toward Freedom* (1958), *Why We Can't Wait* (1964), and *Where Do We Go From Here: Chaos or Community?* (1967), and a host of articles and essays that bear witness to the depth and breadth of King's social concerns. Indeed, they clearly reveal how his social concerns expanded from a desire for racial equality to a concern for the plight of the poor and disadvantaged of every color and beyond that to a concern for harmony and community throughout the world.

King is probably most well remembered, of course, for "I Have a Dream," his stirring speech which climaxed the massive civil rights march on Washington in March 1963. For in that speech, he gave powerful voice to the idea of America as being "essentially a dream, a dream as yet unfulfilled." His criticism, though, was inspired by a powerful faith in America's future, a profound optimism that the dream could and would become reality. So, when he received the Nobel Peace Prize in 1964, he declared that "I accept this award today with an abiding faith in America and an audacious faith in the future of mankind." By the late sixties, however, a new generation of black leaders was restless and impatient with King's moderate pacifist approach to social change. They called for "Black Power," for active resistance, and thus opposed King for being a "militant conservative." Though wearied by attacks from both white defenders of the status quo and black power advocates, King doggedly stood by his commitment to peaceful nonviolent resistance, insisting with even greater determination that violence would lead only to greater violence, that the only appropriate weapon is "fabricated of love."

The violence which had been repeatedly directed at King since the earliest days of his protest activities reached its peak when he was assassinated in April 1968, in Memphis, where he had gone to march in support of a strike by the city's sanitation workers. In 1977, he was posthumously awarded the Presidential Medal of Freedom for having "made our nation stronger because he made it better." In 1983, his birthday, January 15, was declared a national holiday, in honor of his tireless commitment to justice and peace. But perhaps the greatest tributes to King have come from the generation of younger blacks and other minorities who have been inspired by his example to act on their civil rights. As Alice Walker has written, "at the moment I saw his resistance I knew I would never be able to live in this country without resisting everything that sought to disinherit me."

AN EXPERIMENT IN LOVE: NONVIOLENT RESISTANCE

From the beginning a basic philosophy guided the movement. This guiding principle has since been referred to variously as nonviolent resistance, noncooperation, and passive resistance. But in the first days of the protest none of these expressions was mentioned; the phrase most often heard was "Christian love." It was the Sermon on the Mount, rather than a doctrine of passive resistance, that initially inspired the Negroes of Montgomery to dignified social action. It was Jesus of Nazareth that stirred the Negroes to protest with the creative weapon of love.

As the days unfolded, however, the inspiration of Mahatma Gandhi began to exert its influence. I had come to see early that the Christian doctrine of love operating through the Gandhian method of nonviolence was one of the most potent weapons available to the Negro in his struggle for freedom. About a week after the protest started, a white woman who understood and sympathized with the Negroes' efforts wrote a letter to the editor of the *Montgomery Advertiser* comparing the bus protest with the Gandhian movement in India. Miss Juliette Morgan, sensitive and frail, did not long survive the rejection and condemnation of the white community, but long after she died in the summer of 1957 the name of Mahatma Gandhi was well known in Montgomery. People who had never heard of the little brown saint of India were now saying his name with an air of familiarity. Nonviolent resistance had emerged as the technique of the movement, while love stood as the regulating ideal. In other words, Christ furnished the spirit and motivation, while Gandhi furnished the method.

One of the glories of the Montgomery movement was that Baptists, Methodists, Lutherans, Presbyterians, Episcopalians, and others all came together with a willingness to transcend denominational lines. Although no Catholic priests were actively involved in the protest, many of their parishioners took part. All joined hands in the bond of Christian love. Thus the mass meetings accomplished on Monday and Thursday nights what the Christian Church had failed to accomplish on Sunday mornings.

In my weekly remarks as president of the resistance committee, I stressed that the use of violence in our struggle would be both impractical and immoral. To meet hate with retaliatory hate would do nothing but intensify the existence of evil in the universe. Hate begets hate; violence begets violence; toughness begets a greater toughness. We must meet the forces of hate with the power of love; we must meet physical force with soul force. Our aim must never be to defeat or humiliate the white man, but to win his friendship and understanding.

In a real sense, Montgomery's Negroes showed themselves willing   5
to grapple with a new approach to the crisis in race relations. It is probably true that most of them did not believe in nonviolence as a philosophy of life, but because of their confidence in their leaders and because nonviolence was presented to them as a simple expression of Christianity in action, they were willing to use it as a technique. Admittedly, nonviolence in the truest sense is not a strategy that one uses simply because it is expedient at the moment; nonviolence is ultimately a way of life that men live by because of the sheer morality of its claim. But even granting this, the willingness to use nonviolence as a technique is a step forward. For he who goes this far is more likely to adopt nonviolence later as a way of life.

It must be emphasized that nonviolent resistance is not a method for cowards; it does resist. If one uses this method because he is afraid or merely because he lacks the instruments of violence, he is not truly nonviolent. This is why Gandhi often said that if cowardice is the only alternative to violence, it is better to fight. He made this statement conscious of the fact that there is always another alternative: no individual or group need submit to any wrong, nor need they use violence to right that wrong; there is the way of nonviolent resistance. This is ultimately the way of the strong man. It is not a method of stagnant passivity. The phrase "passive resistance" often gives the false impression that this is a sort of "do-nothing method" in which the resister quietly and passively accepts evil. But nothing is further from the truth. For while the nonviolent resister is passive in the sense that he is not physically aggressive toward his opponent, his mind and emotions are always active, constantly seeking to persuade his opponent that he is wrong. The method is passive physically but strongly active spiritually. It is not passive non-resistance to evil, it is active nonviolent resistance to evil.

A second basic fact that characterizes nonviolence is that it does not seek to defeat or humiliate the opponent, but to win his friendship and understanding. The nonviolent resister must often express his protest through noncooperation or boycotts, but he realizes that these are not ends in themselves; they are merely means to awaken a sense of moral shame in the opponent. The end is redemption and reconciliation. The aftermath of nonviolence is the creation of the beloved community, while the aftermath of violence is tragic bitterness.

A third characteristic of this method is that the attack is directed against forces of evil rather than against persons who happen to be doing the evil. It is evil that the nonviolent resister seeks to defeat, not the persons victimized by evil. If he is opposing racial injustice, the nonviolent resister has the vision to see that the basic tension is not between races. As I like to say to the people in Montgomery: "The tension in this city is not between white people and Negro people. The tension is, at bottom, between justice and injustice, between the forces of light and the forces of darkness. And if there is a victory, it will be a victory not merely for fifty thousand Negroes, but a victory for justice and the forces of light. We are out to defeat injustice and not white persons who may be unjust."

A fourth point that characterizes nonviolent resistance is a willingness to accept suffering without retaliation, to accept blows from the opponent without striking back. "Rivers of blood may have to flow before we gain our freedom, but it must be our blood," Gandhi said to his countrymen. The nonviolent resister is willing to accept violence if necessary, but never to inflict it. He does not seek to dodge jail. If going to jail is necessary, he enters it "as a bridegroom enters the bride's chamber."

One may well ask: "What is the nonviolent resister's justification   10 for this ordeal to which he invites men, for this mass political application of the ancient doctrine of turning the other cheek?" The answer is found in the realization that unearned suffering is redemptive. Suffering, the nonviolent resister realizes, has tremendous educational and transforming possibilities. "Things of fundamental importance to people are not secured by reason alone, but have to be purchased with their suffering," said Gandhi. He continues: "Suffering is infinitely more powerful than the law of the jungle for converting the opponent and opening his ears which are otherwise shut to the voice of reason."

A fifth point concerning nonviolent resistance is that it avoids not only external physical violence but also internal violence of spirit. The nonviolent resister not only refuses to shoot his opponent but he also refuses to hate him. At the center of nonviolence stands the principle of love. The nonviolent resister would contend that in the struggle for human dignity, the oppressed people of the world must not succumb to the temptation of becoming bitter or indulging in hate campaigns. To retaliate in kind would do nothing but intensify the existence of hate in the universe. Along the way of life, someone must have sense enough and morality enough to cut off the chain of hate. This can only be done by projecting the ethic of love to the center of our lives.

In speaking of love at this point, we are not referring to some sentimental or affectionate emotion. It would be nonsense to urge men to love their oppressors in an affectionate sense. Love in this connection means understanding, redemptive good will. When we speak of loving those who oppose us, we refer to neither *eros* nor *philia;* we speak of a love which is expressed in the Greek word *agape. Agape* means understanding, redeeming good will for all men. It is an overflowing love which is purely spontaneous, unmotivated, groundless, and creative. It is not set in motion by any quality or function of its object. It is the love of God operating in the human heart.

Agape is disinterested love. It is a love in which the individual seeks not his own good, but the good of his neighbor (1 Cor. 10:24). *Agape* does not begin by discriminating between worthy and unworthy people, or any qualities people possess. It begins by loving others *for their sakes*. It is an entirely "neighbor-regarding concern for others," which discovers the neighbor in every man it meets. Therefore, *agape* makes no distinction between friends and enemy; it is directed toward both. If one loves an individual merely on account of his friendliness, he loves him for the sake of the benefits to be gained from the friendship, rather than for the friend's own sake. Consequently, the best way to assure oneself that love is disinterested is to have love for the enemy-neighbor from whom you can expect no good in return, but only hostility and persecution.

Another basic point about *agape* is that it springs from the *need* of the other person—his need for belonging to the best in the human family. The Samaritan who helped the Jew on the Jericho Road was "good!" because he responded to the human need that he was presented with. God's love is eternal and fails not because man needs his love. Saint Paul assures us that the loving act of redemption was done "while we were yet sinners"—that is, at the point of our greatest need for love. Since the white man's personality is greatly distorted by segregation, and his soul is greatly scarred, he needs the love of the Negro. The Negro must love the white man, because the white man needs his love to remove his tensions, insecurities, and fears.

Agape is not a weak, passive love. It is love in action. *Agape* is love   15
seeking to preserve and create community. It is insistence on community even when one seeks to break it. *Agape* is a willingness to go to any length to restore community. It doesn't stop at the first mile, but it goes the second mile to restore community. It is a willingness to forgive, not seven times, but seventy times seven to restore community. The cross is the eternal expression of the length to which God will go in order to restore broken community. The resurrection is a symbol of God's triumph over all the forces that seek to block community. The Holy Spirit is the continuing community creating reality that moves through history. He who works against community is working against the whole of creation. Therefore, if I respond to hate with a reciprocal hate I do nothing but intensify the cleavage in broken community. I can only close the gap in broken community by meeting hate with love. If I meet hate with hate, I become depersonalized, because creation is so designed that my personality can only be fulfilled in the context of community. Booker T. Washington was right: "Let no man pull you so low as to make you hate him." When he pulls you that low he brings you to the point of defying creation, and thereby becoming depersonalized.

In the final analysis, *agape* means a recognition of the fact that all life is interrelated. All humanity is involved in a single process, and all men are brothers. To the degree that I harm my brother, no matter what he is doing to me, to that extent I am harming myself. For example, white men often refuse federal aid to education in order to avoid giving the Negro his rights; but because all men are brothers they cannot deny Negro children without harming their own. They end, all efforts to the contrary, by hurting themselves. Why is this? Because men are brothers. If you harm me, you harm yourself.

A sixth basic fact about nonviolent resistance is that it is based on the conviction that the universe is on the side of justice. Consequently, the believer in nonviolence has deep faith in the future. This faith is another reason why the nonviolent resister can accept suffering without retaliation. For he knows that in his struggle for justice he has cosmic companionship. It is true that there are devout believers in nonviolence who find it difficult to believe in a personal God. But even these persons believe in the existence of some creative force that works for universal wholeness. Whether we call it an unconscious process, an impersonal Brahman, or a Personal Being of matchless power and infinite love, there is a creative force in this universe that works to bring the disconnected aspects of reality into a harmonious whole.

LINES OF INQUIRY
"An Experiment in Love: Nonviolent Resistance"

In this piece, King is evidently concerned with both defining and justifying the practice of nonviolent resistance. Given this dual purpose, how do you account for the selection and organization of material that he discusses here? For example, why does he begin by telling how nonviolent resistance "emerged as the technique of the movement"? Why does he then take up his six points about nonviolent resistance in exactly the order that he follows? What would be the effect of rearranging, or even reversing, the order of the points? Why does he place his discussion of *agape* between his fifth and sixth points? Why doesn't he discuss this concept much earlier or later in the piece?

In his opening paragraph, King notes that the "guiding principle" of the civil rights movement has "been referred to variously as nonviolent resistance, noncooperation, and passive resistance," but subsequently he only refers to it as "nonviolent resistance"? Why does he evidently prefer to call it nonviolent resistance? Why does he not use the three terms interchangeably? Why does he define the concept of nonviolent resistance by reference not only to the Christian idea of love but also to the Greek idea of love known as *agape?*

In what respects does King's idea of nonviolent resistance change, in what respects does it remain the same, in his other civil rights pieces that appear in this collection? In what respects is King's idea of nonviolent resistance comparable to the idea of resistance that Bettelheim defends in "The Ignored Lesson of Anne Frank"? In what respects do their ideas differ?

LETTER FROM BIRMINGHAM JAIL

April 16, 1963

My Dear Fellow Clergymen:

While confined here in the Birmingham city jail, I came across your recent statement calling my present activities "unwise and untimely." Seldom do I pause to answer criticism of my work and ideas. If I sought to answer all the criticisms that cross my desk, my secretaries would have little time for anything other than such correspondence in the course of the day, and I would have no time for constructive work. But since I feel that you are men of genuine good will and that your criticisms are sincerely set forth, I want to try to answer your statement in what I hope will be patient and reasonable terms.

I think I should indicate why I am here in Birmingham, since you have been influenced by the view which argues against "outsiders coming in." I have the honor of serving as president of the Southern Christian Leadership Conference, an organization operating in every southern state, with headquarters in Atlanta, Georgia. We have some eighty-five affiliated organizations across the South, and one of them is the Alabama Christian Movement for Human Rights. Frequently we share staff, educational and financial resources with our affiliates. Several months ago the affiliate here in Birmingham asked us to be on call to engage in a nonviolent direct-action program if such were deemed necessary. We readily consented, and when the hour came we lived up to our promise. So I, along with several members of my staff, am here because I was invited here. I am here because I have organizational ties here.

But more basically, I am in Birmingham because injustice is here. Just as the prophets of the eighth century B.C. left their villages and

---

AUTHOR'S NOTE: This response to a published statement by eight fellow clergymen from Alabama (Bishop C. C. J. Carpenter, Bishop Joseph A. Durick, Rabbi Hilton L. Grafman, Bishop Paul Hardin, Bishop Holan B. Harmon, the Reverend George M. Murray, the Reverend Edward V. Ramage and the Reverend Earl Stallings) was composed under somewhat constricting circumstances. Begun on the margins of the newspaper in which the statement appeared while I was in jail, the letter was continued on scraps of writing paper supplied by a friendly Negro trusty, and concluded on a pad my attorneys were eventually permitted to leave me. Although the text remains in substance unaltered, I have indulged in the author's prerogative of polishing it for publication.

carried their "thus saith the Lord" far beyond the boundaries of their home towns, and just as the Apostle Paul left his village of Tarsus and carried the gospel of Jesus Christ to the far corners of the Greco-Roman world, so am I compelled to carry the gospel of freedom beyond my own home town. Like Paul, I must constantly respond to the Macedonian call for aid.

Moreover, I am cognizant of the interrelatedness of all communities and states. I cannot sit idly by in Atlanta and not be concerned about what happens in Birmingham. Injustice anywhere is a threat to justice everywhere. We are caught in an inescapable network of mutuality, tied in a single garment of destiny. Whatever affects one directly, affects all indirectly. Never again can we afford to live with the narrow, provincial "outside agitator" idea. Anyone who lives inside the United States can never be considered an outsider anywhere within its bounds.

You deplore the demonstrations taking place in Birmingham. But   5 your statement, I am sorry to say, fails to express a similar concern for the conditions that brought about the demonstrations. I am sure that none of you would want to rest content with the superficial kind of social analysis that deals merely with effects and does not grapple with underlying causes. It is unfortunate that demonstrations are taking place in Birmingham, but it is even more unfortunate that the city's white power structure left the Negro community with no alternative.

In any nonviolent campaign there are four basic steps: collection of the facts to determine whether injustices exist; negotiation; self-purification; and direct action. We have gone through all these steps in Birmingham. There can be no gainsaying the fact that racial injustice engulfs this community. Birmingham is probably the most thoroughly segregated city in the United States. Its ugly record of brutality is widely known. Negroes have experienced grossly unjust treatment in the courts. There have been more unsolved bombings of Negro homes and churches in Birmingham than in any other city in the nation. These are the hard brutal facts of the case. On the basis of these conditions, Negro leaders sought to negotiate with the city fathers. But the latter consistently refused to engage in good-faith negotiation.

Then, last September, came the opportunity to talk with leaders of Birmingham's economic community. In the course of the negotiations, certain promises were made by the merchants—for example, to remove the stores' humiliating racial signs. On the basis of these promises, the Reverend Fred Shuttlesworth and the leaders of the Alabama Christian Movement for Human Rights agreed to a moratorium on all demonstrations. As the weeks and months went by, we realized that we were the victims of a broken promise. A few signs, briefly removed, returned; the others remained.

As in so many past experiences, our hopes had been blasted, and the shadow of deep disappointment settled upon us. We had no alternative except to prepare for direct action, whereby we would present our very bodies as a means of laying our case before the conscience of the local and the national community. Mindful of the difficulties involved, we decided to undertake a process of self-purification. We began a series of workshops on nonviolence, and we repeatedly asked ourselves: "Are you able to accept blows without retaliating?" "Are you able to endure the ordeal of jail?" We decided to schedule our direct-action program for the Easter season, realizing that except for Christmas, this is the main shopping period of the year. Knowing that a strong economic-withdrawal program would be the by-product of direct action, we felt that this would be the best time to bring pressure to bear on the merchants for the needed change.

Then it occurred to us that Birmingham's mayoralty election was coming up in March, and we speedily decided to postpone action until after election day. When we discovered that the Commissioner of Public Safety, Eugene "Bull" Connor, had piled up enough votes to be in the run-off, we decided again to postpone action until the day after the run-off so that the demonstrations could not be used to cloud the issues. Like many others, we waited to see Mr. Connor defeated, and to this end we endured postponement after postponement. Having aided in this community need, we felt that our direct-action program could be delayed no longer.

You may well ask: "Why direct action? Why sit-ins, marches and   10
so forth? Isn't negotiation a better path?" You are quite right in calling for negotiation. Indeed, this is the very purpose of direct action. Nonviolent direct action seeks to create such a crisis and foster such a tension that a community which has constantly refused to negotiate is forced to confront the issue. It seeks so to dramatize the issue that it can no longer be ignored. My citing the creation of tension as part of the work of the nonviolent-resister may sound rather shocking. But I must confess that I am not afraid of the word "tension." I have earnestly opposed violent tension, but there is a type of constructive nonviolent tension which is necesssary for growth. Just as Socrates felt that it was necessary to create a tension in the mind so that individuals could rise from the bondage of myths and half-truths to the unfettered realm of creative analysis and objective appraisal, so must we see the need for nonviolent gadflies to create the kind of tension in society that will help men rise from the dark depths of prejudice and racism to the majestic heights of understanding and brotherhood.

The purpose of our direct-action program is to create a situation so crisis-packed that it will inevitably open the door to negotiation. I therefore concur with you in your call for negotiation. Too long has our beloved Southland been bogged down in a tragic effort to live in monologue rather than dialogue.

One of the basic points in your statement is that the action that I and my associates have taken in Birmingham is untimely. Some have asked: "Why didn't you give the new city administration time to act?"

The only answer that I can give to this query is that the new Birmingham administration must be prodded about as much as the outgoing one, before it will act. We are sadly mistaken if we feel that the election of Albert Boutwell as mayor will bring the millennium to Birmingham. While Mr. Boutwell is a much more gentle person than Mr. Connor, they are both segregationists, dedicated to maintenance of the status quo. I have hope that Mr. Boutwell will be reasonable enough to see the futility of massive resistance to desegregation. But he will not see this without pressure from devotees of civil rights. My friends, I must say to you that we have not made a single gain in civil rights without determined legal and nonviolent pressure. Lamentably, it is an historical fact that privileged groups seldom give up their privileges voluntarily. Individuals may see the moral light and voluntarily give up their unjust posture; but, as Reinhold Niebuhr has reminded us, groups tend to be more immoral than individuals.

We know through painful experience that freedom is never voluntarily given by the oppressor; it must be demanded by the oppressed. Frankly, I have yet to engage in a direct-action campaign that was "well timed" in the view of those who have not suffered unduly from the disease of segregation. For years now I have heard the word "Wait!" It rings in the ear of every Negro with piercing familiarity. This "Wait" has almost always meant "Never." We must come to see, with one of our distinguished jurists, that "justice too long delayed is justice denied."

We have waited for more than 340 years for our constitutional and Godgiven rights. The nations of Asia and Africa are moving with jet-like speed toward gaining political independence, but we still creep at horse-and-buggy pace toward gaining a cup of coffee at a lunch counter. Perhaps it is easy for those who have never felt the stinging darts of segregation to say, "Wait." But when you have seen vicious mobs lynch your mothers and fathers at will and drown your sisters and brothers at whim; when you have seen hate-filled policemen curse, kick and even kill your black brothers and sisters; when you see the vast majority of your twenty million Negro brothers smothering in an airtight cage of poverty in the midst of an affluent society; when you suddenly find your tongue twisted and your speech stammering as you seek to explain to your six-year-old daughter why she can't go to the public amusement park that has just been advertised on television, and see tears welling up in her eyes when she is told that Funtown is closed to colored children, and see ominous clouds of inferiority beginning to form in her little mental sky, and see her beginning to distort her personality by developing an unconscious bitterness toward white people; when you have to concoct an answer for a five-year-old son who is asking: "Daddy, why do white people treat colored people so mean?"; when you take a cross-country drive and find it necessary to sleep night after night in the uncomfortable corners of your automobile because no

motel will accept you; when you are humiliated day in and day out by
nagging signs reading "white" and "colored"; when your first name
becomes "nigger," your middle name becomes "boy" (however old
you are) and your last name becomes "John," and your wife and mother
are never given the respected title "Mrs."; when you are harried by day
and haunted by night by the fact that you are a Negro, living constantly
at tiptoe stance, never quite knowing what to expect next, and are plagued
with inner fears and outer resentments; when you are forever fighting
a degenerating sense of "nobodiness"—then you will understand why
we find it difficult to wait. There comes a time when the cup of endurance runs over, and men are no longer willing to be plunged into the
abyss of despair. I hope, sirs, you can understand our legitimate and
unavoidable impatience.

You express a great deal of anxiety over our willingness to break   15
laws. This is certainly a legitimate concern. Since we so diligently urge
people to obey the Supreme Court's decision of 1954 outlawing segregation in the public schools, at first glance it may seem rather paradoxical for us consciously to break laws. One may well ask: "How can you
advocate breaking some laws and obeying others?" The answer lies in
the fact that there are two types of laws: just and unjust. I would be the
first to advocate obeying just laws. One has not only a legal but a moral
responsibility to obey just laws. Conversely, one has a moral responsibility to disobey unjust laws. I would agree with St. Augustine that "an
unjust law is no law at all."

Now, what is the difference between the two? How does one determine whether a law is just or unjust? A just law is a man-made code
that squares with the moral law or the law of God. An unjust law is a
code that is out of harmony with the moral law. To put it in the terms
of St. Thomas Aquinas: An unjust law is a human law that is not rooted
in eternal law and natural law. Any law that uplifts human personality
is just. Any law that degrades human personality is unjust. All segregation statutes are unjust because segregation distorts the soul and dam-
ages the personality. It gives the segregator a false sense of superiority
and the segregated a false sense of inferiority. Segregation, to use the
terminology of the Jewish philosopher Martin Buber, substitutes an "I-
it" relationship for an "I-thou" relationship and ends up relegating persons to the status of things. Hence segregation is not only politically,
economically and sociologically unsound, it is morally wrong and sin-
ful. Paul Tillich has said that sin is separation. Is not segregation an
existential expression of man's tragic separation, his awful estrangement, his terrible sinfulness? Thus it is that I can urge men to obey the
1954 decision of the Supreme Court, for it is morally right; and I can
urge them to disobey segregation ordinances, for they are morally wrong.

Let us consider a more concrete example of just and unjust laws.
An unjust law is a code that a numerical or power majority group compels a minority group to obey but does not make binding on itself. This

is *difference* made legal. By the same token, a just law is a code that a majority compels a minority to follow and that it is willing to follow itself. This is *sameness* made legal.

Let me give another explanation. A law is unjust if it is inflicted on a minority that, as a result of being denied the right to vote, had no part in enacting or devising the law. Who can say that the legislature of Alabama which set up that state's segregation laws was democratically elected? Throughout Alabama all sorts of devious methods are used to prevent Negroes from becoming registered voters, and there are some counties in which even though Negroes constitute a majority of the population, not a single Negro is registered. Can any law enacted under such circumstances be considered democratically structured?

Sometimes a law is just on its face and unjust in its application. For instance, I have been arrested on a charge of parading without a permit. Now, there is nothing wrong in having an ordinance which requires a permit for a parade. But such an ordinance becomes unjust when it is used to maintain segregation and to deny citizens the First-Amendment privilege of peaceful assembly and protest.

I hope you are able to see the distinction I am trying to point out.   20
In no sense do I advocate evading or defying the law, as would the rabid segregationist. That would lead to anarchy. One who breaks an unjust law must do so openly, lovingly, and with a willingness to accept the penalty. I submit that an individual who breaks a law that conscience tells him is unjust, and who willingly accepts the penalty of imprisonment in order to arouse the conscience of the community over its injustice, is in reality expressing the highest respect for law.

Of course, there is nothing new about this kind of civil disobedience. It was evidenced sublimely in the refusal of Shadrach, Meshach and Abednego to obey the laws of Nebuchadnezzar, on the ground that a higher moral law was at stake. It was practiced superbly by the early Christians, who were willing to face hungry lions and the excruciating pain of chopping blocks rather than submit to certain unjust laws of the Roman Empire. To a degree, academic freedom is a reality today because Socrates practiced civil disobedience. In our own nation, the Boston Tea Party represented a massive act of civil disobedience.

We should never forget that everything Adolf Hitler did in Germany was "legal" and everything the Hungarian freedom fighters did in Hungary was "illegal." It was "illegal" to aid and comfort a Jew in Hitler's Germany. Even so, I am sure that, had I lived in Germany at the time, I would have aided and comforted my Jewish brothers. If today I lived in a Communist country where certain principles dear to the Christian faith are suppressed, I would openly advocate disobeying that country's anti-religious laws.

I must make two honest confessions to you, my Christian and Jewish brothers. First, I must confess that over the past few years I have been gravely disappointed with the white moderate. I have almost reached the regrettable conclusion that the Negro's great stumbling block in his stride toward freedom is not the White Citizen's Counciler or the Ku Klux Klanner, but the white moderate, who is more devoted to "order" than to justice; who prefers a negative peace which is the absence of tension to a positive peace which is the presence of justice; who constantly says: "I agree with you in the goal you seek, but I cannot agree with your methods of direct action"; who paternalistically believes he can set the timetable for another man's freedom; who lives by a mythical concept of time and who constantly advises the Negro to wait for a "more convenient season." Shallow understanding from people of good will is more frustrating than absolute misunderstanding from people of ill will. Lukewarm acceptance is much more bewildering than outright rejection.

I had hoped that the white moderate would understand that law and order exist for the purpose of establishing justice and that when they fail in this purpose they become the dangerously structured dams that block the flow of social progress. I had hoped that the white moderate would understand that the present tension in the South is a necessary phase of the transition from an obnoxious negative peace, in which the Negro passively accepted his unjust plight, to a substantive and positive peace, in which all men will respect the dignity and worth of human personality. Actually, we who engage in nonviolent direct action are not the creators of tension. We merely bring to the surface the hidden tension that is already alive. We bring it out in the open, where it can be seen and dealt with. Like a boil that can never be cured so long as it is covered up but must be opened with all its ugliness to the natural medicines of air and light, injustice must be exposed, with all the tension its exposure creates, to the light of human conscience and the air of national opinion before it can be cured.

In your statement you assert that our actions, even though peaceful, must be condemned because they precipitate violence. But is this a logical assertion? Isn't this like condemning a robbed man because his possession of money precipitated the evil act of robbery? Isn't this like condemning Socrates because his unswerving commitment to truth and his philosophical inquiries precipitated the act by the misguided populace in which they made him drink hemlock? Isn't this like condemning Jesus because his unique God-consciousness and never-ceasing devotion to God's will precipitated the evil act of crucifixion? We must come to see that, as the federal courts have consistently affirmed, it is wrong to urge an individual to cease his efforts to gain his basic constitutional rights because the quest may precipitate violence. Society must protect the robbed and punish the robber.

I had also hoped that the white moderate would reject the myth concerning time in relation to the struggle for freedom. I have just

25

received a letter from a white brother in Texas. He writes: "All Christians know that the colored people will receive equal rights eventually, but it is possible that you are in too great a religious hurry. It has taken Christianity almost two thousand years to accomplish what it has. The teachings of Christ take time to come to earth." Such an attitude stems from a tragic misconception of time, from the strangely irrational notion that there is something in the very flow of time that will inevitably cure all ills. Actually, time itself is neutral; it can be used either destructively or constructively. More and more I feel that the people of ill will have used time much more effectively than have the people of good will. We will have to repent in this generation not merely for the hateful words and actions of the bad people but for the appalling silence of the good people. Human progress never rolls in on wheels of inevitability; it comes through the tireless efforts of men willing to be coworkers with God, and without this hard work, time itself becomes an ally of the forces of social stagnation. We must use time creatively, in the knowledge that the time is always ripe to do right. Now is the time to make real the promise of democracy and transform our pending national elegy into a creative psalm of brotherhood. Now is the time to lift our national policy from the quicksand of racial injustice to the solid rock of human dignity.

You speak of our activity in Birmingham as extreme. At first I was rather disappointed that fellow clergymen would see my nonviolent efforts as those of an extremist. I began thinking about the fact that I stand in the middle of two opposing forces in the Negro community. One is a force of complacency, made up in part of Negroes who, as a result of long years of oppression, are so drained of self-respect and a sense of "somebodiness" that they have adjusted to segregation; and in part of a few middle-class Negroes who, because of a degree of academic and economic security and because in some ways they profit by segregation, have become insensitive to the problems of the masses. The other force is one of bitterness and hatred, and it comes perilously close to advocating violence. It is expressed in the various black nationalist groups that are springing up across the nation, the largest and best-known being Elijah Muhammad's Muslim movement. Nourished by the Negro's frustration over the continued existence of racial discrimination, this movement is made up of people who have lost faith in America, who have absolutely repudiated Christianity, and who have concluded that the white man is an incorrigible "devil."

I have tried to stand between these two forces, saying that we need emulate neither the "do-nothingism" of the complacent nor the hatred and despair of the black nationalist. For there is the more excellent way of love and nonviolent protest. I am grateful to God that, through the influence of the Negro church, the way of nonviolence became an integral part of our struggle.

If this philosophy had not emerged, by now many streets of the South would, I am convinced, be flowing with blood. And I am further convinced that if our white brothers dismiss as "rabble-rousers" and "outside agitators" those of us who employ nonviolent direct action, and if they refuse to support our non-violent efforts, millions of Negroes will, out of frustration and despair, seek solace and security in black-nationalist ideologies—a development that would inevitably lead to a frightening racial nightmare.

Oppressed people cannot remain oppressed forever. The yearning for freedom eventually manifests itself, and that is what has happened to the American Negro. Something within has reminded him of his birthright of freedom, and something without has reminded him that it can be gained. Consciously or unconsciously, he has been caught up by the *Zeitgeist,* and with his black brothers of Africa and his brown and yellow brothers of Asia, South America and the Caribbean, the United States Negro is moving with a sense of great urgency toward the promised land of racial justice. If one recognizes this vital urge that has engulfed the Negro community, one should readily understand why public demonstrations are taking place. The Negro has many pent-up resentments and latent frustrations, and he must release them. So let him march; let him make prayer pilgrimages to the city hall; let him go on freedom rides—and try to understand why he must do so. If his repressed emotions are not released in nonviolent ways, they will seek expression through violence; this is not a threat but a fact of history. So I have not said to my people: "Get rid of your discontent." Rather, I have tried to say that this normal and healthy discontent can be channeled into the creative outlet of nonviolent direct action. And now this approach is being termed extremist.

But though I was initially disappointed at being categorized as an extremist, as I continued to think about the matter I gradually gained a measure of satisfaction from the label. Was not Jesus an extremist for love: "Love your enemies, bless them that curse you, do good to them that hate you, and pray for them which despitefully use you, and persecute you." Was not Amos an extremist for justice: "Let justice roll down like waters and righteousness like an ever-flowing stream." Was not Paul an extremist for the Christian gospel: "I bear in my body the marks of the Lord Jesus." Was not Martin Luther an extremist: "Here I stand; I cannot do otherwise, so help me God." And John Bunyan: "I will stay in jail to the end of my days before I make a butchery of my conscience." And Abraham Lincoln: "This nation cannot survive half slave and half free." And Thomas Jefferson: "We hold these truths to be self-evident, that all men are created equal. . . ." So the question is not whether we will be extremists, but what kind of extremists we will be. Will we be extremists for hate or for love? Will we be extremists for the preservation of injustice or for the extension of justice? In that dramatic scene on Calvary's hill three men were crucified. We must never forget that all three were crucified for the same crime—the crime of extremism. Two were extremists for immorality, and thus fell below their environment. The other, Jesus Christ, was an extremist for love, truth and goodness, and thereby rose above his environment. Perhaps the South, the nation and the world are in dire need of creative extremists.

I had hoped that the white moderate would see this need. Perhaps I was too optimistic; perhaps I expected too much. I suppose I should have realized that few members of the oppressor race can understand the deep groans and passionate yearnings of the oppressed race, and still fewer have the vision to see that injustice must be rooted out by strong, persistent and determined action. I am thankful, however, that some of our white brothers in the South have grasped the meaning of this social revolution and committed themselves to it. They are still all too few in quantity, but they are big in quality. Some—such as Ralph McGill, Lillian Smith, Harry Golden, James McBride Dabbs, Ann Braden and Sarah Patton Boyle—have written about our struggle in eloquent and prophetic terms. Others have marched with us down nameless streets of the South. They have languished in filthy, roach-infested jails, suffering the abuse and brutality of policemen who view them as "dirty nigger-lovers." Unlike so many of their moderate brothers and sisters, they have recognized the urgency of the moment and sensed the need for powerful "action" antidotes to combat the disease of segregation.

Let me take note of my other major disappointment. I have been so greatly disappointed with the white church and its leadership. Of course, there are some notable exceptions. I am not unmindful of the fact that each of you has taken some significant stands on this issue. I commend you, Reverend Stallings, for your Christian stand on this past Sunday, in welcoming Negroes to your worship service on a nonsegregated basis. I commend the Catholic leaders of this state for integrating Spring Hill College several years ago.

But despite these notable exceptions, I must honestly reiterate that I have been disappointed with the church. I do not say this as one of those negative critics who can always find something wrong with the church. I say this as a minister of the gospel, who loves the church; who was nurtured in its bosom; who has been sustained by its spiritual blessings and who will remain true to it as long as the cord of life shall lengthen.

When I was suddenly catapulted into the leadership of the bus protest in Montgomery, Alabama, a few years ago, I felt we would be supported by the white church. I felt that the white ministers, priests and rabbis of the South would be among our strongest allies. Instead, some have been outright opponents, refusing to understand the freedom movement and misrepresenting its leaders; all too many others

have been more cautious than courageous and have remained silent behind the anesthetizing security of stained-glass windows.

In spite of my shattered dreams, I came to Birmingham with the
hope that the white religious leadership of this community would see
the justice of our cause and, with deep moral concern, would serve as
the channel through which our just grievances could reach the power
structure. I had hoped that each of you would understand. But again I
have been disappointed.

I have heard numerous southern religious leaders admonish their
worshipers to comply with a desegregation decision because it is the
law, but I have longed to hear white ministers declare: "Follow this
decree because integration is morally right and because the Negro is
your brother." In the midst of blatant injustices inflicted upon the Negro, I have watched white churchmen stand on the sideline and mouth
pious irrelevancies and sanctimonious trivialities. In the midst of a mighty
struggle to rid our nation of racial and economic injustice, I have heard
many ministers say: "Those are social issues, with which the gospel has
no real concern." And I have watched many churches commit themselves to a completely other-worldly religion which makes a strange,
un-Biblical distinction between body and soul, between the sacred and
the secular.

I have traveled the length and breadth of Alabama, Mississippi and
all the other southern states. On sweltering summer days and crisp autumn mornings I have looked at the South's beautiful churches with
their lofty spires pointing heavenward. I have beheld the impressive
outlines of her massive religious-education buildings. Over and over I
have found myself asking: "What kind of people worship here? Who is
their God? Where were their voices when the lips of Governor Barnett
dripped with words of interposition and nullification? Where were they
when Governor Wallace gave a clarion call for defiance and hatred?
Where were their voices of support when bruised and weary Negro
men and women decided to rise from the dark dungeons of complacency to the bright hills of creative protest?"

Yes, these questions are still in my mind. In deep disappointment I
have wept over the laxity of the church. But be assured that my tears
have been tears of love. There can be no deep disappointment where
there is not deep love. Yes, I love the church. How could I do otherwise? I am in the rather unique position of being the son, the grandson
and the great-grandson of preachers. Yes, I see the church as the body
of Christ. But, oh! How we have blemished and scarred that body
through social neglect and through fear of being nonconformists.

There was a time when the church was very powerful—in the time   40
when the early Christians rejoiced at being deemed worthy to suffer for
what they believed. In those days the church was not merely a ther-
mometer that recorded the ideas and principles of popular opinion; it

was a thermostat that transformed the mores of society. Whenever the early Christians entered a town, the people in power became disturbed and immediately sought to convict the Christians for being "disturbers of the peace" and "outside agitators." But the Christians pressed on, in the conviction that they were "a colony of heaven," called to obey God rather than man. Small in number, they were big in commitment. They were too God-intoxicated to be "astronomically intimidated." By their effort and example they brought an end to such ancient evils as infanticide and gladiatorial contests.

Things are different now. So often the contemporary church is a weak, ineffectual voice with an uncertain sound. So often it is an arch-defender of the status quo. Far from being disturbed by the presence of the church, the power structure of the average community is consoled by the church's silent—and often even vocal—sanction of things as they are.

But the judgment of God is upon the church as never before. If today's church does not recapture the sacrificial spirit of the early church, it will lose its authenticity, forfeit the loyalty of millions, and be dismissed as an irrelevant social club with no meaning for the twentieth century. Every day I meet young people whose disappointment with the church has turned into outright disgust.

Perhaps I have once again been too optimistic. Is organized religion too inextricably bound to the status quo to save our nation and the world? Perhaps I must turn my faith to the inner spiritual church, the church within the church, as the true *ekklesia* and the hope of the world. But again I am thankful to God that some noble souls from the ranks of organized religion have broken loose from the paralyzing chains of conformity and joined us as active partners in the struggle for freedom. They have left their secure congregations and walked the streets of Albany, Georgia, with us. They have gone down the highways of the South on tortuous rides for freedom. Yes, they have gone to jail with us. Some have been dismissed from their churches, have lost the support of their bishops and fellow ministers. But they have acted in the faith that right defeated is stronger than evil triumphant. Their witness has been the spiritual salt that has preserved the true meaning of the gospel in these troubled times. They have carved a tunnel of hope through the dark mountain of disappointment.

I hope the church as a whole will meet the challenge of this decisive hour. But even if the church does not come to the aid of justice, I have no despair about the future. I have no fear about the outcome of our struggle in Birmingham, even if our motives are at present misunderstood. We will reach the goal of freedom in Birmingham and all over the nation, because the goal of America is freedom. Abused and scorned though we may be, our destiny is tied up with America's destiny. Before the pilgrims landed at Plymouth, we were here. Before the pen of

Jefferson etched the majestic words of the Declaration of Independence across the pages of history, we were here. For more than two centuries our forebears labored in this country without wages; they made cotton king; they built the homes of their masters while suffering gross injustice and shameful humiliation—and yet out of a bottomless vitality they continued to thrive and develop. If the inexpressible cruelties of slavery could not stop us, the opposition we now face will surely fail. We will win our freedom because the sacred heritage of our nation and the eternal will of God are embodied in our echoing demands.

Before closing I feel impelled to mention one other point in your 45 statement that has troubled me profoundly. You warmly commended the Birmingham police force for keeping "order" and "preventing violence." I doubt that you would have so warmly commended the police force if you had seen its dogs sinking their teeth into unarmed, nonviolent Negroes. I doubt that you would so quickly commend the policemen if you were to observe their ugly and inhumane treatment of Negroes here in the city jail; if you were to watch them push and curse old Negro women and young Negro girls; if you were to see them slap and kick old Negro men and young boys; if you were to observe them as they did on two occasions, refuse to give us food because we wanted to sing our grace together. I cannot join you in your praise of the Birmingham police department.

It is true that the police have exercised a degree of discipline in handling the demonstrators. In this sense they have conducted themselves rather "nonviolently" in public. But for what purpose? To preserve the evil system of segregation. Over the past few years I have consistently preached that nonviolence demands that the means we use must be as pure as the ends we seek. I have tried to make clear that it is wrong to use immoral means to attain moral ends. But now I must affirm that it is just as wrong, or perhaps even more so, to use moral means to preserve immoral ends. Perhaps Mr. Connor and his policemen have been rather nonviolent in public, as was Chief Pritchett in Albany, Georgia, but they have used the moral means of nonviolence to maintain the immoral end of racial injustice. As T. S. Eliot has said: "The last temptation is the greatest treason: To do the right deed for the wrong reason."

I wish you had commended the Negro sit-inners and demonstrators of Birmingham for their sublime courage, their willingness to suffer and their amazing discipline in the midst of great provocation. One day the South will recognize its real heroes. They will be the James Merediths, with the noble sense of purpose that enables them to face jeering and hostile mobs, and with the agonizing loneliness that characterizes the life of the pioneer. They will be old, oppressed, battered Negro women, symbolized in a seventy-two-year-old woman in Montgomery, Alabama, who rose up with a sense of dignity and with her people decided not to ride segregated buses, and who responded with ungrammatical profundity to one who inquired about her weariness: "My feet is tired, but my soul is at rest." They will be the young high school and college students, the young ministers of the gospel and a host of their elders, courageously and nonviolently sitting in at lunch counters and willingly going to jail for conscience's sake. One day the South will know that when these disinherited children of God sat down at lunch counters, they were in reality standing up for what is best in the American dream and for the most sacred values in our Judaeo-Christian heritage, thereby bringing our nation back to those great wells of democracy which were dug by the founding fathers in their formulation of the Constitution and the Declaration of Independence.

Never before have I written so long a letter. I'm afraid it is much too long to take your precious time. I can assure you that it would have been much shorter if I had been writing from a comfortable desk, but what else can one do when he is alone in a narrow jail cell, other than write long letters, think long thoughts and pray long prayers?

If I have said anything in this letter that overstates the truth and indicates an unreasonable impatience, I beg you to forgive me. If I have said anything that understates the truth and indicates my having a patience that allows me to settle for anything less than brotherhood, I beg God to forgive me.

I hope this letter finds you strong in the faith. I also hope that circumstances will soon make it possible for me to meet each of you, not as an integrationist or a civil-rights leader but as a fellow clergyman and a Christian brother. Let us all hope that the dark clouds of racial prejudice will soon pass away and the deep fog of misunderstanding will be lifted from our fear-drenched communities, and in some not too distant tomorrow the radiant stars of love and brotherhood will shine over our great nation with all their scintillating beauty.

50

Yours for the cause of Peace and Brotherhood,
Martin Luther King, Jr.

LINES OF INQUIRY
"Letter from Birmingham Jail"

As King indicates in his Author's Note on the first page, this letter was written in "response to a published statement by eight fellow clergymen from Alabama" who had objected to the civil rights protest that King was then leading in Birmingham, Alabama. Identify the various kinds of arguments, evidence, appeals, and assumptions that he uses to answer each of their objections. In what respects do you suppose his varied supporting material was meant to appeal to the eight clergyman? In what respects does it seem to be intended for the worldwide audience that was then closely following King's activities? In what respect does it seem to be occasioned by the substance of each controversial issue?

How do you account for the order in which King takes up the clergymen's objections? Why does he begin by answering their arguments against "outsiders coming in," then move on to their arguments against public demonstrations, then to their arguments against the timing of the protests, then to their arguments against the legality of the protests, then to their arguments against the extremity of the protests? Why does he then devote most of the remainder of his letter to an extended attack on "the white church and its leadership"? What do you consider to be the major source—the essence—of his "disappointment" with the white church?

In "Civil Disobedience," Thoreau offers a lengthy defense of the protest he made against the racial prejudice of his own time. What common issues do King and Thoreau address in their self-defense? What similar arguments do they offer in their defense? In what respects are their arguments most notably different, and how do you account for the differences?

I HAVE A DREAM

I am happy to join with you today in what will go down in history as the greatest demonstration for freedom in the history of our nation.

Five score years ago, a great American, in whose symbolic shadow we stand today, signed the Emancipation Proclamation. This momentous decree came as a great beacon light of hope to millions of Negro slaves who had been seared in the flames of withering injustice. It came as a joyous daybreak to end the long night of their captivity.

But one hundred years later, the Negro still is not free; one hundred years later, the life of the Negro is still sadly crippled by the manacles of segregation and the chains of discrimination; one hundred years later, the Negro lives on a lonely island of poverty in the midst of a vast ocean of material prosperity; one hundred years later, the Negro is still languished in the corners of American society and finds himself in exile in his own land.

So we've come here today to dramatize a shameful condition. In a sense we've come to our nation's capital to cash a check. When the architects of our republic wrote the magnificent words of the Constitution and the Declaration of Independence, they were signing a promissory note to which every American was to fall heir. This note was the promise that all men, yes, black men as well as white men, would be guaranteed the unalienable rights of life, liberty, and the pursuit of happiness.

It is obvious today that America has defaulted on this promissory note in so far as her citizens of color are concerned. Instead of honoring this sacred obligation, America has given the Negro people a bad check, a check which has come back marked "insufficient funds." But we refuse to believe that the bank of justice is bankrupt. We refuse to believe that there are insufficient funds in the great vaults of opportunity of this nation. And so we've come to cash this check, a check that will give us upon demand the riches of freedom and the security of justice.

We have also come to this hallowed spot to remind America of the fierce urgency of now. This is no time to engage in the luxury of cooling off or to take the tranquilizing drug of gradualism. Now is the time to make real the promises of democracy; now is the time to rise from the dark and desolate valley of segregation to the sunlit path of racial justice; now is the time to lift our nation from the quicksands of racial injustice to the solid rock of brotherhood; now is the time to make justice a reality for all of God's children. It would be fatal for the nation to overlook the urgency of the moment. This sweltering summer of the Negro's legitimate discontent will not pass until there is an invigorating autumn of freedom and equality.

Nineteen sixty-three is not an end, but a beginning. And those who hope that the Negro needed to blow off steam and will now be content, will have a rude awakening if the nation returns to business as usual. There will be neither rest nor tranquility in America until the Negro is granted his citizenship rights. The whirlwinds of revolt will continue to shake the foundations of our nation until the bright day of justice emerges.

But there is something that I must say to my people, who stand on the worn threshold which leads into the palace of justice. In the process of gaining our rightful place, we must not be guilty of wrongful deeds. Let us not seek to satisfy our thirst for freedom by drinking from the cup of bitterness and hatred. We must forever conduct our struggle on the high plain of dignity and discipline. We must not allow our creative protests to degenerate into physical violence. Again and again we must rise to the majestic heights of meeting physical force with soul force. The marvelous new militancy, which has engulfed the Negro community, must not lead us to a distrust of all white people. For many of our white brothers, as evidenced by their presence here today, have come to realize that their destiny is tied up with our destiny. And they have come to realize that their freedom is inextricably bound to our freedom. We cannot walk alone. And as we walk, we must make the pledge that we shall always march ahead. We cannot turn back.

There are those who are asking the devotees of Civil Rights, "When will you be satisfied?" We can never be satisfied as long as the Negro is the victim of the unspeakable horrors of police brutality; we can never be satisfied as long as our bodies, heavy with the fatigue of travel, cannot gain lodging in the motels of the highways and the hotels of the cities; we cannot be satisfied as long as the Negro's basic mobility is from a smaller ghetto to a larger one; we can never be satisfied as long as our children are stripped of their selfhood and robbed of their dignity by signs stating "For Whites Only"; we cannot be satisfied as long as the Negro in Mississippi cannot vote and a Negro in New York believes he has nothing for which to vote. No! No, we are not satisfied, and we will not be satisfied until "justice rolls down like waters and righteousness like a mighty stream."

I am not unmindful that some of you have come here out of great 10 trials and tribulations. Some of you have come fresh from narrow jail cells. Some of you have come from areas where your quest for freedom left you battered by the storms of persecution and staggered by the winds of police brutality. You have been the veterans of creative suffering. Continue to work with the faith that unearned suffering is redemptive. Go back to Mississippi. Go back to Alabama. Go back to South Carolina. Go back to Georgia. Go back to Louisiana. Go back to the slums and ghettos of our Northern cities, knowing that somehow this situation can and will be changed. Let us not wallow in the valley of despair.

I say to you today, my friends, so even though we face the difficulties of today and tomorrow, I still have a dream. It is a dream deeply rooted in the American dream. I have a dream that one day this nation will rise up and live out the true meaning of its creed, "We hold these truths to be self-evident, that all men are created equal." I have a dream that one day on the red hills of Georgia, sons of former slaves and the sons of former slave owners will be able to sit down together at the table of brotherhood. I have a dream that one day even the state of Mississippi, a state sweltering with the heat of injustice, sweltering with the heat of oppression, will be transformed into an oasis of freedom and justice. I have a dream that my four little children will one day live in a nation where they will not be judged by the color of their skin, but by the content of their character.

I HAVE A DREAM TODAY!

I have a dream that one day down in Alabama—with its vicious racists, with its Governor having his lips dripping with the words of interposition and nullification—one day right there in Alabama, little black boys and black girls will be able to join hands with little white boys and white girls as sisters and brothers.

I HAVE A DREAM TODAY!

I have a dream that one day every valley shall be exalted, and every   15
hill and mountain shall be made low. The rough places will be plain and the crooked places will be made straight, "and the glory of the Lord shall be revealed, and all flesh shall see it together."

This is our hope. This is the faith that I go back to the South with. With this faith we will be able to hew out of the mountain of despair a stone of hope. With this faith we will be able to transform the jangling discords of our nation into a beautiful symphony of brotherhood. With this faith we will be able to work together, to pray together, to struggle together, to go to jail together, to stand up for freedom together, knowing that we will be free one day. And this will be the day. This will be the day when all of God's children will be able to sing with new meaning, "My country 'tis of thee, sweet land of liberty, of thee I sing. Land where my father died, land of the pilgrim's pride, from every mountainside, let freedom ring." And if America is to be a great nation, this must become true.

So let freedom ring from the prodigious hilltops of New Hampshire; let freedom ring from the mighty mountains of New York; let freedom ring from the heightening Alleghenies of Pennsylvania; let freedom ring from the snow-capped Rockies of Colorado; let freedom ring from the curvaceous slopes of California. But not only that. Let freedom ring from Stone Mountain of Georgia; let freedom ring from

Lookout Mountain of Tennessee; let freedom ring from every hill and mole hill of Mississippi. "From every mountainside, let freedom ring."

And when this happens, and when we allow freedom to ring, when we let it ring from every village and every hamlet, from every state and every city, we will be able to speed up that day when all of God's children, black men and white men, Jews and Gentiles, Protestants and Catholics, will be able to join hands and sing in the words of the old Negro spiritual: "Free at last. Free at last. Thank God Almighty, we are free at last."

LINES OF INQUIRY
"I Have a Dream"

King relies heavily in this piece on a stylistic device known as *anaphora,* which involves the repetition of a word or group of words at the beginning of two or more successive clauses or sentences. Make a note of all the words that he chooses to repeat in this way. What do you suppose accounts for each such instance of anaphora? What do you suppose accounts for the relative length of each case of anaphora? Be sure to read the piece aloud to get an understanding of how it would have sounded to a listening audience and how the sound of it would have been determined by King's use of anaphora.

King also relies heavily on analogies, metaphors, and other figures of speech, as when he compares the Constitution and Declaration of Independence to "a promissory note to which every American was to fall heir." Make a note of all the figures of speech that you can find in this piece. Why does King rely so heavily on these figures? Why does he develop some of these figures at length, such as the "promissory note" and the "bad check" metaphors, whereas others, such as "to rise from the dark and desolate valley of segregation to the sunlit path of racial justice," are mentioned only once?

What is the essence of King's dream as he defines it in this piece? Judging from King's "Black Power" essay (1967), how far did he think he had come at that point in achieving his dream? Judging from Walker's "The Civil Rights Movement" (1967), how far did she think he had come at that point in achieving his dream? Judging from the current state of affairs in the United States, how close is the nation to achieving King's dream?

Black Power

The Black Power movement of today, like the Garvey "Back to Africa" movement of the 1920s, represents a dashing of hope, a conviction of the inability of the Negro to win and a belief in the infinitude of the ghetto. While there is much grounding in past experience for all these feelings, a revolution cannot succumb to any of them. Today's despair is a poor chisel to carve out tomorrow's justice.

Black Power is an implicit and often explicit belief in black separatism. Notice that I do not call it black racism. It is inaccurate to refer to Black Power as racism in reverse, as some have recently done. Racism is a doctrine of the congenital inferiority and worthlessness of a people. While a few angry proponents of Black Power have, in moments of bitterness, made wild statements that come close to this kind of racism, the major proponents of Black Power have never contended that the white man is innately worthless.

Yet behind Black Power's legitimate and necessary concern for group unity and black identity lies the belief that there can be a separate black road to power and fulfillment. Few ideas are more unrealistic. There is no salvation for the Negro through isolation.

One of the chief affirmations of Black Power is the call for the mobilization of political strength for black people. But we do not have to look far to see that effective political power for Negroes cannot come through separatism. Granted that there are cities and counties in the country where the Negro is in a majority, there are so few that concentration on them alone would still leave the vast majority of Negroes outside the mainstream of American political life.

Out of the eight-odd counties in Alabama, the state where SNCC 80 sought to develop an all-black party, only nine have a majority of Negroes. Even if blacks could control each of these counties, they would have little influence in overall state politics and could do little to improve conditions in the major Negro population centers of Birmingham, Mobile and Montgomery. There are still relatively few congressional districts in the South that have such large black majorities that Negro candidates could be elected without the aid of whites. Is it a sounder program to concentrate on the election of two or three Negro congressmen from predominantly Negro districts or to concentrate on the election of fifteen or twenty Negro congressmen from southern districts where a coalition of Negro and white moderate voters is possible?

Moreover, any program that elects all black candidates simply because they are black and rejects all white candidates simply because they are white is politically unsound and morally unjustifiable. It is true that in many areas of the South Negroes still must elect Negroes in order to be effectively represented. SNCC staff members are eminently correct when they point out that in Lowndes County, Alabama, there are no white liberals or moderates and no possibility for cooperation between the races at the present time. But the Lowndes County experience cannot be made a measuring rod for the whole of America. The basic thing in determining the best candidate is not his color but his integrity.

Black Power alone is no more insurance against social injustice than white power. Negro politicians can be as opportunistic as their white counterparts if there is not an informed and determined constituency demanding social reform. What is most needed is a coalition of Negroes and liberal whites that will work to make both major parties truly responsive to the needs of the poor. Black Power does not envision or desire such a program.

Just as the Negro cannot achieve political power in isolation, neither can he gain economic power through separatism. While there must be a continued emphasis on the need for blacks to pool their economic resources and withdraw consumer support from discriminating firms, we must not be oblivious to the fact that the larger economic problems confronting the Negro community will only be solved by federal programs involving billions of dollars. One unfortunate thing about Black Power is that it gives priority to race precisely at a time when the impact of automation and other forces have made the economic question fundamental for blacks and whites alike. In this context a slogan "Power for Poor People" would be much more appropriate than the slogan "Black Power."

However much we pool our resources and "buy black," this cannot create the multiplicity of new jobs and provide the number of low-cost houses that will lift the Negro out of the economic depression caused by centuries of deprivation. Neither can our resources supply quality integrated education. All of this requires billions of dollars which only an alliance of liberal-labor-civil-rights forces can stimulate. In short, the Negroes' problem cannot be solved unless the whole of American society takes a new turn toward greater economic justice.

In a multiracial society no group can make it alone. It is a myth   85
to believe that the Irish, the Italians and the Jews—the ethnic groups that Black Power advocates cite as justification for their views—rose to power through separatism. It is true that they stuck together. But their group unity was always enlarged by joining in alliances with other groups such as political machines and trade unions. To succeed in a

pluralistic society, and an often hostile one at that, the Negro obviously needs organized strength, but that strength will only be effective when it is consolidated through constructive alliances with the majority group.

Those proponents of Black Power who have urged Negroes to shun alliances with whites argue that whites as a group cannot have a genuine concern for Negro progress. Therefore, they claim, the white man's main interest in collaborative effort is to diminish Negro militancy and deflect it from constructive goals.

Undeniably there are white elements that cannot be trusted, and no militant movement can afford to relax its vigilance against halfhearted associates or conscious betrayers. Every alliance must be considered on its own merits. Negroes may embrace some and walk out on others where their interests are imperiled. Occasional betrayals, however, do not justify the rejection of the principle of Negro-white alliance.

The oppression of Negroes by whites has left an understandable residue of suspicion. Some of this suspicion is a healthy and appropriate safeguard. An excess of skepticism, however, becomes a fetter. It denies that there can be reliable white allies, even though some whites have died heroically at the side of Negroes in our struggle and others have risked economic and political peril to support our cause.

The history of the movement reveals that Negro-white alliances have played a powerfully constructive role, especially in recent years. While Negro initiative, courage and imagination precipitated the Birmingham and Selma confrontations and revealed the harrowing injustice of segregated life, the organized strength of Negroes alone would have been insufficient to move Congress and the administration without the weight of the aroused conscience of white America. In the period ahead Negroes will continue to need this support. Ten percent of the population cannot by tensions alone induce ninety percent to change a way of life.

Within the white majority there exists a substantial group who cherish democratic principles above privilege and who have demonstrated a will to fight side by side with the Negro against injustice. Another and more substantial group is composed of those having common needs with the Negro and who will benefit equally with him in the achievement of social progress. There are, in fact, more poor white Americans than there are Negro. Their need for a war on poverty is no less desperate than the Negro's. In the South they have been deluded by race prejudice and largely remained aloof from common action. Ironically, with this posture they were fighting not only the Negro but themselves. Yet there are already signs of change. Without formal alliances, Negroes and whites have supported the same candidates in many *de facto* electoral coalitions in the South because each sufficiently served his own needs.

The ability of Negroes to enter alliances is a mark of our growing   90
strength, not of our weakness. In entering an alliance, the Negro is not
relying on white leadership or ideology; he is taking his place as an
equal partner in a common endeavor. His organized strength and his
new independence pave the way for alliances. Far from losing independence in an alliance, he is using it for constructive and multiplied gains.

Negroes must shun the very narrow-mindedness that in others has
so long been the source of our own afflictions. We have reached the
stage of organized strength and independence to work securely in
alliances. History has demonstrated with major victories the effectiveness, wisdom and moral soundness of Negro-white alliance. The cooperation of Negro and white based on the solid ground of honest
conscience and proper self-interest can continue to grow in scope and
influence. It can attain the strength to alter basic institutions by democratic means. Negro isolation can never approach this goal.

In the final analysis the weakness of Black Power is its failure to see
that the black man needs the white man and the white man needs the
black man. However much we may try to romanticize the slogan, there
is no separate black path to power and fulfillment that does not intersect white paths, and there is no separate white path to power and
fulfillment, short of social disaster, that does not share that power with
black aspirations for freedom and human dignity. We are bound together in a single garment of destiny. The language, the cultural patterns, the music, the material prosperity and even the food of America
are an amalgam of black and white.

James Baldwin once related how he returned home from school and
his mother asked him whether his teacher was colored or white. After a
pause he answered: "She is a little bit colored and a little bit white."[4]
This is the dilemma of being a Negro in America. In physical as well as
cultural terms every Negro is a little bit colored and a little bit white. In
our search for identity we must recognize this dilemma.

Every man must ultimately confront the question "Who am I?" and
seek to answer it honestly. One of the first principles of personal adjustment is the principle of self-acceptance. The Negro's greatest dilemma
is that in order to be healthy he must accept his ambivalence. The
Negro is the child of two cultures—Africa and America. The problem is
that in the search for wholeness all too many Negroes seek to embrace
only one side of their natures. Some, seeking to reject their heritage, are
ashamed of their color, ashamed of black art and music, and determine
what is beautiful and good by the standards of white society. They end
up frustrated and without cultural roots. Others seek to reject everything American and to identify totally with Africa, even to the point of
wearing African clothes. But this approach leads also to frustration

---

[4] In *The Negro Protest,* Kenneth B. Clark (ed.), Beacon, 1963.

because the American Negro is not an African. The old Hegelian synthesis still offers the best answer to many of life's dilemmas. The American Negro is neither totally African nor totally Western. He is Afro-American, a true hybrid, a combination of two cultures.

Who are we? We are the descendants of slaves. We are the off- 95
spring of noble men and women who were kidnapped from their native land and chained in ships like beasts. We are the heirs of a great and exploited continent known as Africa. We are the heirs of a past of rope, fire and murder. I for one am not ashamed of this past. My shame is for those who became so inhuman that they could inflict this torture upon us.

But we are also Americans. Abused and scorned though we may be, our destiny is tied up with the destiny of America. In spite of the psychological appeals of identification with Africa, the Negro must face the fact that America is now his home, a home that he helped to build through "blood, sweat and tears." Since we are Americans the solution to our problem will not come through seeking to build a separate black nation within a nation, but by finding that creative minority of the concerned from the ofttimes apathetic majority, and together moving toward that colorless power that we all need for security and justice.

In the first century B.C., Cicero said: "Freedom is participation in power." Negroes should never want all power because they would deprive others of their freedom. By the same token, Negroes can never be content without participation in power. America must be a nation in which its multiracial people are partners in power. This is the essence of democracy toward which all Negro struggles have been directed since the distant past when he was transplanted here in chains.

Probably the most destructive feature of Black Power is its unconscious and often conscious call for retaliatory violence. Many well-meaning persons within the movement rationalize that Black Power does not really mean black violence, that those who shout the slogan don't really mean it that way, that the violent connotations are solely the distortions of a vicious press. That the press has fueled the fire is true. But as one who has worked and talked intimately with devotees of Black Power, I must admit that the slogan is mainly used by persons who have lost faith in the method and philosophy of nonviolence. I must make it clear that no guilt by association is intended. Both Floyd McKissick and Stokely Carmichael have declared themselves opponents of aggressive violence. This clarification is welcome and useful, despite the persistence of some of their followers in examining the uses of violence.

Over cups of coffee in my home in Atlanta and my apartment in Chicago, I have often talked late at night and over into the small hours of the morning with the proponents of Black Power who argued passionately about the validity of violence and riots. They don't quote Gandhi or Tolstoy. Their bible is Frantz Fanon's *The Wretched of the*

Earth.[5] This black psychiatrist from Martinique, who went to Algeria to work with the National Liberation Front in its fight against the French, argues in his book—a well-written book, incidentally, with many penetrating insights—that violence is a psychologically healthy and tactically sound method for the oppressed. And so, realizing that they are a part of that vast company of the "wretched of the earth," these young American Negroes, who are predominantly involved in the Black Power movement, often quote Fanon's belief that violence is the only thing that will bring about liberation. As they say, "Sing us no songs of nonviolence, sing us no songs of progress, for nonviolence and progress belong to middle-class Negroes and whites and we are not interested in you."

As we have seen, the first public expression of disenchantment   100
with nonviolence arose around the question of "self-defense." In a sense this is a false issue, for the right to defend one's home and one's person when attacked has been guaranteed through the ages by common law. In a nonviolent demonstration, however, self-defense must be approached from another perspective.

The cause of a demonstration is the existence of some form of exploitation or oppression that has made it necessary for men of courage and good will to protest the evil. For example, a demonstration against *de facto* school segregation is based on the awareness that a child's mind is crippled by inadequate educational opportunities. The demonstrator agrees that it is better to suffer publicly for a short time to end the crippling evil of school segregation than to have generation after generation of children suffer in ignorance. In such a demonstration the point is made that the schools are inadequate. This is the evil one seeks to dramatize; anything else distracts from that point and interferes with the confrontation of the primary evil. Of course no one wants to suffer and be hurt. But it is more important to get at the cause than to be safe. It is better to shed a little blood from a blow on the head or a rock thrown by an angry mob than to have children by the thousands finishing high school who can only read at a sixth-grade level.

Furthermore, it is dangerous to organize a movement around self-defense. The line of demarcation between defensive violence and aggressive violence is very thin. The minute a program of violence is enunciated, even for self-defense, the atmosphere is filled with talk of violence, and the words falling on unsophisticated ears may be interpreted as an invitation to aggression.

One of the main questions that the Negro must confront in his pursuit of freedom is that of effectiveness. What is the most effective way to achieve the desired goal? If a method is not effective, no matter how much steam it releases, it is an expression of weakness, not of

---

[5] Evergreen, 1966.

strength. Now the plain, inexorable fact is that any attempt of the American Negro to overthrow his oppressor with violence will not work. We do not need President Johnson to tell us this by reminding Negro rioters that they are outnumbered ten to one. The courageous efforts of our own insurrectionist brothers, such as Denmark Vesey and Nat Turner, should be eternal reminders to us that violent rebellion is doomed from the start. In violent warfare one must be prepared to face the fact that there will be casualties by the thousands. Anyone leading a violent rebellion must be willing to make an honest assessment regarding the possible casualties to a minority population confronting a well-armed, wealthy majority with a fanatical right wing that would delight in exterminating thousands of black men, women and children.

Arguments that the American Negro is a part of a world which is two-thirds colored and that there will come a day when the oppressed people of color will violently rise together to throw off the yoke of white oppression are beyond the realm of serious discussion. There is no colored nation, including China, that now shows even the potential of leading a violent revolution of color in any international proportions. Ghana, Zambia, Tanganyika and Nigeria are so busy fighting their own battles against poverty, illiteracy and the subversive influence of neo-colonialism that they offer little hope to Angola, Southern Rhodesia and South Africa, much less to the American Negro. The hard cold facts today indicate that the hope of the people of color in the world may well rest on the American Negro and his ability to reform the structure of racist imperialism from within and thereby turn the technology and wealth of the West to the task of liberating the world from want.

The futility of violence in the struggle for racial justice has been tragically etched in all the recent Negro riots. There is something painfully sad about a riot. One sees screaming youngsters and angry adults fighting hopelessly and aimlessly against impossible odds. Deep down within them you perceive a desire for self-destruction, a suicidal longing. Occasionally Negroes contend that the 1965 Watts riot and other riots in various cities represented effective civil rights action. But those who express this view always end up with stumbling words when asked what concrete gains have been won as a result. At best the riots have produced a little additional antipoverty money, allotted by frightened government officials, and a few water sprinklers to cool the children of the ghettos. It is something like improving the food in a prison while the people remain securely incarcerated behind bars. Nowhere have the riots won any concrete improvement such as have the organized protest demonstrations.

It is not overlooking the limitations of nonviolence and the distance we have yet to go to point out the remarkable record of achievements that have already come through nonviolent action. The 1960 sit-ins desegregated lunch counters in more than 150 cities within a year. The 1961 freedom rides put an end to segregation in interstate travel. The 1956 bus boycott in Montgomery, Alabama, ended segregation on the buses not only of that city but in practically every city of the South. The 1963 Birmingham movement and the climactic March on Washington won passage of the most powerful civil rights law in a century. The 1965 Selma movement brought enactment of the Voting Rights Law. Our nonviolent marches in Chicago last summer brought about a housing agreement which, if implemented, will be the strongest step toward open housing taken in any city in the nation. Most significant is the fact that this progress occurred with minimum human sacrifice and loss of life. Fewer people have been killed in ten years of nonviolent demonstrations across the South than were killed in one night of rioting in Watts.

When one tries to pin down advocates of violence as to what acts would be effective, the answers are blatantly illogical. Sometimes they talk of overthrowing racist state and local governments. They fail to see that no internal revolution has ever succeeded in overthrowing a government by violence unless the government has already lost the allegiance and effective control of its armed forces. Anyone in his right mind knows that this will not happen in the United States. In a violent racial situation, the power structure has the local police, the state troopers, the national guard and finally the army to call on, all of which are predominantly white.

Furthermore, few if any violent revolutions have been successful unless the violent minority had the sympathy and support of the non-resisting majority. Castro may have had only a few Cubans actually fighting with him, but he would never have overthrown the Batista regime unless he had had the sympathy of the vast majority of the Cuban people. It is perfectly clear that a violent revolution on the part of American blacks would find no sympathy and support from the white population and very little from the majority of the Negroes themselves.

This is no time for romantic illusions and empty philosophical debates about freedom. This is a time for action. What is needed is a strategy for change, a tactical program that will bring the Negro into the mainstream of American life as quickly as possible. So far, this has only been offered by the nonviolent movement. Without recognizing this we will end up with solutions that don't solve, answers that don't answer and explanations that don't explain.

Beyond the pragmatic invalidity of violence is its inability to appeal to conscience. Some Black Power advocates consider an appeal to conscience irrelevant. A Black Power exponent said to me not long ago: "To hell with conscience and morality. We want power." But power and morality must go together, implementing, fulfilling and ennobling each other. In the quest for power I cannot bypass the concern for morality. I refuse to be driven to a Machiavellian cynicism with respect to power. Power at its best is the right use of strength. The words of Alfred the Great are still true: "Power is never good unless he who has it is good."

Nonviolence is power, but it is the right and good use of power.   110
Constructively it can save the white man as well the Negro. Racial segregation is buttressed by such irrational fears as loss of preferred economic privilege, altered social status, intermarriage and adjustment to new situations. Through sleepless nights and haggard days numerous white people struggle pitifully to combat these fears. By following the path of escape, some seek to ignore the questions of race relations and to close their minds to the issues involved. Others, placing their faith in legal maneuvers, counsel massive resistance. Still others hope to drown their fears by engaging in acts of meanness and violence toward their Negro brethren. But how futile are all these remedies! Instead of eliminating fear, they instill deeper and more pathological fears. The white man, through his own efforts, through education and goodwill, through searching his conscience and through confronting the fact of integration, must do a great deal to free himself of these paralyzing fears. But to master fear he must also depend on the spirit the Negro generates toward him. Only through our adherence to nonviolence—which also means love in its strong and commanding sense—will the fear in the white community be mitigated.

A guilt-ridden white minority fears that if the Negro attains power, he will without restraint or pity act to revenge the accumulated injustices and brutality of the years. The Negro must show that the white man has nothing to fear, for the Negro is willing to forgive. A mass movement exercising nonviolence and demonstrating power under discipline should convince the white community that as such a movement attained strength, its power would be used creatively and not for revenge.

In a moving letter to his nephew on the one hundredth anniversary of emancipation, James Baldwin wrote concerning white people:

> The really terrible thing, old buddy, is that *you* must accept *them*. And I mean that very seriously. You must accept them and accept them with love. For these innocent people have no other hope. They are, in effect, still trapped in a history which they do not understand; and until they understand it, they cannot be released from it. They have had to believe for many years, and for innumerable reasons, that black men are inferior to white men. Many of them, indeed, know better, but, as you will discover, people find it very difficult to act on what they know. To act is to be committed, and to be committed is to be in danger. In this case, the danger, in the minds of most white Americans, is the loss of their identity. . . . But these men are your brothers—your lost, younger brothers. And if the word *integration* means anything, this is what it means: that we, with love, shall force our

brothers to see themselves as they are, to cease fleeing from reality and begin to change it. . . .[6]

The problem with hatred and violence is that they intensify the fears of the white majority, and leave them less ashamed of their prejudices toward Negroes. In the guilt and confusion confronting our society, violence only adds to the chaos. It deepens the brutality of the oppressor and increases the bitterness of the oppressed. Violence is the antithesis of creativity and wholeness. It destroys community and makes brotherhood impossible.

My friend John Killens recently wrote in the *Negro Digest:* "Integration comes after liberation. A slave cannot integrate with his master. In the whole history of revolts and revolutions, integration has never been the main slogan of the revolution. The oppressed fights to free himself from his oppressor, not to integrate with him. Integration is the step after freedom when the freedman makes up his mind as to whether he wishes to integrate with his former master."[7]

At first glance this sounds very good. But after reflection one has to face some inescapable facts about the Negro and American life. This is a multiracial nation where all groups are dependent on each other, whether they want to recognize it or not. In this vast interdependent nation no racial group can retreat to an island entire of itself. The phenomena of integration and liberation cannot be as neatly divided as Killens would have it.

There is no theoretical or sociological divorce between liberation and integration. In our kind of society liberation cannot come without integration and integration cannot come without liberation. I speak here of integration in both the ethical and the political senses. On the one hand, integration is true intergroup, interpersonal living. On the other hand, it is the mutual sharing of power. I cannot see how the Negro will be totally liberated from the crushing weight of poor education, squalid housing and economic strangulation until he is integrated, with power, into every level of American life.

Mr. Killens's assertion might have some validity in a struggle for independence against a foreign invader. But the Negro's struggle in America is quite different from and more difficult than the struggle for independence. The American Negro will be living tomorrow with the very people against whom he is struggling today. The American Negro is not in a Congo where the Belgians will go back to Belgium after the battle is over, or in an India where the British will go back to England after independence is won. In the struggle for national independence one can talk about liberation now and integration later, but in the

115

---

[6] *The Fire Next Time,* Dial, 1963, pp. 22–23.
[7] November 1966.

struggle for racial justice in a multiracial society where the oppressor and the oppressed are both "at home," liberation must come through integration.

Are we seeking power for power's sake? Or are we seeking to make the world and our nation better places to live? If we seek the latter, violence can never provide the answer. The ultimate weakness of violence is that it is a descending spiral, begetting the very thing it seeks to destroy. Instead of diminishing evil, it multiplies it. Through violence you may murder the liar, but you cannot murder the lie, nor establish the truth. Through violence you may murder the hater, but you do not murder hate. In fact, violence merely increases hate. So it goes. Returning violence for violence multiplies violence, adding deeper darkness to a night already devoid of stars. Darkness cannot drive out darkness: only light can do that. Hate cannot drive out hate: only love can do that.

The beauty of nonviolence is that in its own way and in its own time it seeks to break the chain reaction of evil. With a majestic sense of spiritual power, it seeks to elevate truth, beauty and goodness to the throne. Therefore I will continue to follow this method because I think it is the most practically sound and morally excellent way for the Negro to achieve freedom.

LINES OF INQUIRY
"Black Power"

King's complex argument against the black power movement is further complicated by his attempt to offer black people a drastically different approach to their political, economic, and social problems without alienating the proponents of the black power movement. What issues does King raise, what techniques does he use, to attack black power without offending its proponents? What issues does he raise, what techniques does he use, to defend his idea of a Negro-white alliance without alienating the proponents of black power?

Among King's objections to the movement is his claim that "probably the most destructive feature of black power is its unconscious and often conscious call for retaliatory violence." What do you think he means by an unconscious call? And how do you suppose the call could be both unconscious and conscious? Why does King devote more attention to discussing this objection than to any of the others that he raises?

Based on your personal experience, firsthand observation, and reading, what do you think has come of the black power movement in America? In what ways does it seem to have affected black culture in America? In what ways does it seem to have affected white culture in America? In what ways does it seem to have affected racial relations in America?

NANCY MAIRS

1943 –

I've been drilled in the rules of polite discourse. I know that talking openly about certain matters — "telling the truth about my own experiences as a body," as Virginia Woolf put it — isn't "nice," especially for a woman. Time and again I've felt myself shrink from the task, and probably I've yielded in ways I don't even recognize. I believe, however, that the proscriptions traditionally placed on a woman's speech foster feelings of shame that lead her to trivialize her own experiences and prevent her from discovering the depth and complexities of her life. In defiance of the conventions of poetic silence, I've spoken as plainly and truthfully as the squirms and wriggles of the human psyche will permit.

Here Nancy Mairs stakes the claim that she mines persistently in her writing—breaking the "rules" about what can and cannot be revealed about one's life in writing for a public audience. Despite the traditional injunctions to women to be silent and modest about their bodily and psychic lives, Mairs does not blink at revealing anything about her existence, no matter how deeply personal or private it might be. Indeed, Mairs, who has struggled for years with both chronic depression and multiple sclerosis, has experienced her psyche and body not only as terrains to be explored in her writing, but also as battlegrounds for conflicting ideologies and for survival itself. Though her writing is fueled by a feminist passion, her vision is essentially inclusive and communal:

> I think that my "story," though intensely personal, is not at all private. Beneath its idiosyncrasies lie vast strata of commonality, communality. I don't see how anyone engaged in self-representation can fail to recognize in the autobiographical self, constructed as it is in language, all the others whom the writing self shelters.

Mairs was born in California, a birthplace that was, as she put it, an "accident of war," for both of her parents were native New Englanders, but her father, a graduate of the U.S. Naval Academy, was then based on the West coast. After her father's accidental death in Guam in 1947, her mother moved back to New England, taking Mairs and her younger sister to live near their grandparents. Growing up in New Hampshire and Massachusetts, and summering in Maine, she absorbed the Puritan values and habits against which she would later rebel:

> I am the "difficult" child. This is not at all the same as being a "bad" child, though I am occasionally bad as well. Rather, the difficult child is the one who deviates from the family's (and possibly, though not necessarily, society's) most cherished values, which in my case tend toward the Yankee

conventions of thrift, diligence, restraint, direction, modesty, a cheerful though undemonstrative disposition, and, as soon as we're old enough, a vote for the Republican ticket.

If reticence, controlled emotion, and dedication to the predictable constituted Mairs's regional and familial heritage, her behavior as represented in her written life is the exact opposite of those strictures. For in her writing Mairs is flagrantly public, revelatory, effusive, loquacious, and iconoclastic. And in her life itself, Mairs has not only abandoned New England Congregationalism for the lavish symbology of Roman Catholicism, but she has also abandoned New England for the landscape of the Southwest, where she has lived for the past twenty years.

Before moving to the Southwest, Mairs attended Wheaton College in Massachusetts, where she took a B.A. in English in 1964. During her final year at Wheaton, Mairs married the man to whom she is married still, a teacher and social activist. The couple lived in Boston during the early years of their marriage, and it was during this period that Mairs' chronic depression first became seriously evident. Shortly after the birth of her first child, a daughter, Mairs's emotional distress became acute. Suffering from postpartum depression, severe agoraphobia, dismay over her inability to write, and a feeling of being suffocated by domesticity, she spent six months in a state mental hospital where she received shock treatments and made her first suicide attempt. Marriage and motherhood, she wrote later, had "strangled me, choked me on my own ashes." She was released from the hospital, although, as she has written, she did not soon "get well"; rather, she got "functional." Indeed, she partly blames the doctors who treated her during the early stages of her illness for how long it took her to understand that she was not "crazy," but was instead suffering from a common chronic illness treatable with medication. Though her illness is treatable, the fact remains that for many years she has been haunted by bouts of depression and suicidal impulses—episodes she calls "the sudden quiet descent into the will of death."

After her release from the hospital, Mairs feared that her life had "fallen way behind schedule"; it was time for a second child, and her son was born not long after. Following his birth she returned to work, holding various editorial and technical writing jobs in the Boston area for several years. Then, still compelled to pursue the serious writing she had always believed would be her real work, she decided to "risk a new exploration of old dreams" and attended a poetry workshop taught by her aunt, the poet Jean Pedrick. It proved to be a turning point, for a year later Mairs and her family moved to Tucson so that she could enter a creative writing program at the University of Arizona, where she earned an M.F.A. in Poetry and then a Ph.D. in English.

Since moving to Tucson, where she continues to live, Mairs has published a collection of poems, *All the Rooms in the Yellow House,* which won the Western States Book Awards first prize in poetry in 1984; a collection of personal essays, which had been her doctoral dissertation, *Plaintext: Deciphering a Woman's Life* (1986); a memoir, *Remembering the Bone House: An Erotics of Space and Place* (1989); and a second collection of essays, *Carnal Acts* (1990). Both the titles and contents of her three prose books reveal how significantly she has been influenced in her thinking and writing by the French feminist philosophers Hélène Cixous and Julia Kristeva, who insist on the interconnections of text and body, on the urgency for women to "write their bodies" so that women's experience can be seen and known in the heretofore masculinist realm of signification from which women have been largely absent.

Though the French feminists provided Mairs with a philosophic rationale for her confessional mode of writing, her deepest artistic connections are with the work of the confessional poets Anne Sexton and Sylvia Plath. Like Sexton and Plath, both of whom were also haunted by depression and both of whom committed suicide, Mairs has refused to deny or cover up the specificities of her life as a woman. Indeed, like them, Mairs has incessantly used the most intimate details of her psychic and sexual life as the essential material of her art. Unlike them, however, she has never romanticized the connection between art and madness:

> I don't think the artist creates because she is mad. I think she wrings out what she can despite the misery and terror, despite the long blank afternoons she spends huddled in one corner of her livingroom couch, the voices resonating around the curve of her skull . . . . And I think she might wring out more if she didn't feed her time and energy into these states.

As if her psychic problems were not enough of an affliction, Mairs has also been progressively hobbled by the ravages of multiple sclerosis, the symptoms of which first appeared soon after she moved to Tucson. She has written poignantly about being crippled by MS and about the strategies she has developed to cope with it, but she has also written of the ways that "being a cripple" has intensified and even enhanced her vision:

> I think there's an authentic alternative to either denial or masochism in response to a difficult life. You can use your hardships to augment your understanding of and appreciation for yourself and the world you dwell in. Because a difficult life is more complex than an easy one, it offers opportunities for developing a greater range of response to experience: a true generosity of spirit.

The "greater range of response to experience" she acquired from her affliction with MS has also had something to do with her shift from poetry to essays. Writing poems was something Mairs could do, she has said, only when she was in a state of being obsessively and tragically "in love"; as her recovery from crippling depression progressed, she became less susceptible to such episodes. On the other hand, as she became progressively more enfeebled by MS, she evidently acquired an increasing preoccupation with the homely but exquisitely pointed details of her physical and neural situation. So, it might be said that MS led Mairs to fulfill the part-playful, part-serious prediction she once made when she was still writing poetry—that her aging and changing desires would one day lead her to "take up writing essays."

Ultimately, though, Mairs's view of what it means to record personal experience in language is by no means naive, for she emphatically distinguishes between "life (what one does day after day) and 'a life' (the report one makes on the outcome of what one does day after day)." Thus her essays, as she makes clear, involve a quite complex and by no means literal relationship to her self and her life:

> Every piece of writing, whether 'fictional' or 'factual,' entails the creation of a persona, of course: a mask. I am not the woman whose voice animates my essays . . . . But I am more the woman of my essays than I am the woman of my fiction, because she and I share the same past. And so, understanding with greater clarity as I kept writing that I wanted to make sense of my own experience as it illuminates human experience more generally, I turned to writing nonfiction. Rather than remove myself from my life . . . . I've tried to scribble myself deeper and deeper into it.

ON TOUCHING BY ACCIDENT

Those of us who would be suicides come at odd bits of knowledge about the failings of the human heart. Not necessarily literal heart failure, of course: A good many of us stop short of that point, for one reason or another. Virginia Woolf, for instance, who swallowed a lethal dose of veronal in 1913, did not take her final walk, into the River Ouse with her pockets full of stones, until 1941. We may survive. We often do. The failings I'm talking about have to do not with death, which is another matter altogether ("the one experience," Woolf noted, "I shall never describe"), but with life—with lives. The last time I tried to kill myself, a number of things happened to me, most of them predictable and some of them not very pleasant. But one of them was odd enough that still, months later, I return to the thought of it, amused and puzzled and more than a little anxious about its significance.

I am a depressive. Researchers know surprisingly little about my condition, which is called "unipolar" depression to distinguish it from "bipolar" or manic depression. It may be caused by a chemical imbalance in the brain. It occurs cyclically, and each person has his own cycle—or, more likely, her own cycle, since far more women suffer from depression than men. No one knows why, though some very good reasons have been proposed. (A thorough review of depression in women is Maggie Scarf's *Unfinished Business: Pressure Points in the Lives of Women* [New York: Ballantine Books, 1980].) Depression is characterized by disturbances in normal physiological functions like eating and sleeping and by suicidal thoughts or acts arising from a sense of personal worthlessness and despair. As a rule, a depressive does not attempt suicide until she begins to feel better, probably because, in the depths of depression, she has felt too powerless even to kill herself. Several doctors have told me, with a good deal of satisfaction, that I am a textbook case. I do not like being a textbook case. I feel dull. Nonetheless, every so often I fall off the edge of the world into a void even blacker than the one that kept medieval sailors in charted waters; and as soon as I begin to emerge, I grab for the bottle of pills.

Just so the last time. Gradually my consciousness filled with the image of a thin sharp blade drawing again and again across the blue veins in my wrist. This image is symbolic only—except for one youthful attempt, I have never tried to slash my wrists and would not now choose to do so—and I am never entirely free from it. But when it becomes so repetitive that it screens out the faces and voices of people around me, even my own face in the mirror, then I know I am in mortal danger. (Wonderful how such clichés take on their original purity and force in a literal context.) I kept checking myself for signs of survival: I polished my fingernails and had a permanent; I bought a director's chair in which to sit in the sun and a soft plum-colored velveteen blazer; I sent a short story to *The New Yorker.* People who do such things, I reasoned, do not commit suicide. Finally, however, exhausted by the moment-to-moment decisions to stay alive, I decided on a Tuesday that I would kill myself on Friday night.

From then on, I was frantically busy. I had to sort through the tottering piles on my desks at home and in my office. I had to catch up on the teaching duties I had neglected and plan activities for the rest of the semester, so that whoever took over could do so with the least possible disruption of my students' learning. I had to write a long letter to George, listing the names and numbers of people to notify, reminding him that my body was to be donated for research into multiple sclerosis, detailing the distribution of my personal effects. During that time I also did a couple of interviews for a television program about the disabled that I was hosting. I had a drink with a friend. I invited my daughter to spend a night with me in the apartment to which I'd moved a few weeks before and bought her a pink striped shirt and a pair of purple jeans at the same time I bought my blazer.

By Friday night I was tired. I thought about staying home from   5
the Hallowe'en party I'd said I'd go to, but finally I put on my new blazer and went (and all evening harlequins and witches and men with gigantic bosoms and miniskirts asked me, "Where's your costume?" and I said, carefully, each time, "You're looking at it"). I had a pretty good time. To be sure, the man with whom I was in love, who had recently thrown me over (another pure and forceful cliché), was there, annihilating me; but then, a well-known novelist flirted with me, so I must have had some substance. I was kissed by a pirate and possibly also by a devil. I didn't drink much. I left early.

When I got home, the back yard of my little apartment building, where I parked my car, was dark; but there was a moon, and I'd left my porch light on, so I could find my door. As I stuck the key into the lock, a figure danced out of the darkness—a clown, I think, in a pink ruffled suit—and pleaded, "Oh, can I use your bathroom? I'm at this party over there"—vague gesture—"and the line to the bathroom is *miles* long and I've been drinking all this *beer* and I'm about to *burst* and . . . ." "Sure," I said, swinging the door in. "It's in there." While she peed torrentially, I turned on the radio, opened a beer, and put down fresh food for Bête Noire, who was twisting around my ankles like a dervish. The clown flushed and came out, yanking at her ruffles. "This is so *hard* to get in and out of," she moaned. "Oh, thank you. You saved my *life.* I just couldn't have waited any longer." She was pink and plump. I didn't think she was old enough for the beer. "Oh, *there* you are," she called to a shadow that loomed on the doorstep, and off she bounded, recounting my heroic rescue of her in her moment of greatest need.

I closed the door behind her. I went into the bathroom and started taking Elavil while I washed my face and undressed. I went back into the tidy white bedroom/living room/kitchen/study and sat down at my desk. Still taking the Elavil, three by three, I finished my letter to George and tried to write in my journal, but my vision was too badly blurred. I dropped the bottle of Elavil and couldn't see to pick up the small yellow tablets. That clumsiness probably saved my life. That, and Bête Noire. I had at first thought I would turn on my stove and heater, which had no pilot lights, and thus hasten the work of the drug. But Bête was so tiny that I knew that the gas would kill her long before me, and I couldn't bear the thought of her black body still and lifeless. By this time I had no sense of myself or anyone else as a living creature; and when, later, a psychiatrist asked if I hadn't tried to call for help after taking all those pills, I had to say that I didn't know there was anyone to call; yet I couldn't kill the kitten.

George found me eighteen hours later and took me to the emergency room, where, after a few hours on a heart monitor and the obligatory psychiatric interview, I was pronounced a survivor and sent home. I had at some point roused having to go to the bathroom and, unable to get even to my hands and knees, had dragged myself around my apartment, battering my body and smearing the floor with blood and urine; but I heal quickly. Before long the bruises faded and the scabs fell off. I was still shaky but no longer suicidal. I had let a lot of my responsibilities slide, so I threw myself into activity and forgot the whole mess as much and as quickly as possible.

Then one day, six weeks or so later, when I was having lunch with a friend and we were swapping stories of failed love and suicide, I saw suddenly the round pink ruffled form of the little clown dancing through my door and into my bathroom. I had wholly forgotten her and the young man waiting for her in the shadows under my cedar trees. I was startled by the memory—so quick, so complete—startled and amused, and I began to describe it to my friend. Just then, though, the man who had thrown me over, with whom I was still in love, asked if he might join us, and naturally we had to speak of other things. I never finished my story about the clown.

I have thought of her often since then, however. She entered my life so lightly, this child, needing only a place to empty her bladder so that she wouldn't disgrace herself, at just the moment when I was planning to leave, though she couldn't have known that. And I wonder whether I have done just the same thing myself, wandering through some other's desolation in my costume—tight jeans, soft shirt, dusky velveteen blazer, cane—needing some quick favor on my way. How many times? And when?

10

LINES OF INQUIRY
"On Touching by Accident"

Though Mairs devotes most of this brief essay to a discussion of suicide and to telling about one of her own suicidal attempts, the title of her piece and its opening and closing paragraphs suggest that she is more concerned about her brief encounter with the "little clown" who suddenly appeared at the moment she was on the verge of attempting suicide. How were you affected by the incident with the "little clown" and by what she said to Mairs? How was Mairs initially affected by the incident? How was she subsequently affected by the incident? How do you account for the difference between Mairs's initial and subsequent reactions to the little clown?

Mairs claims in the opening sentence of her essay that "would-be suicides come at odd bits of knowledge about the failings of the human heart." What failings do you think she is referring to in the story that follows? In what sense(s) does she seem to have come to a recognition of those failings by virtue of her status as a "would-be suicide"? What additional insights, if any, did this essay give you into "the failings of the human heart"?

If you take a few moments to think about your own past experience, you'll probably discover that you too have had the experience of "touching" or of being touched "by accident." What were you doing when the "touching" took place? What did you think about the "accident" when it was happening? What do you think about it now?

ON BEING A CRIPPLE

To escape is nothing. Not to escape is nothing.
                    Louise Bogan

The other day I was think-
ing of writing an essay on being a cripple. I was thinking hard in one of
the stalls of the women's room in my office building, as I was shoving
my shirt into my jeans and tugging up my zipper. Preoccupied, I
flushed, picked up my book bag, took my cane down from the hook, and
unlatched the door. So many movements unbalanced me, and as I pulled
the door open I fell over backward, landing fully clothed on the toilet
seat with my legs splayed in front of me: the old beetle-on-its-back
routine. Saturday afternoon, the building deserted, I was free to laugh
aloud as I wriggled back to my feet, my voice bouncing off the yellow-
ish tiles from all directions. Had anyone been there with me, I'd have
been still and faint and hot with chagrin. I decided that it was high time
to write the essay.

First, the matter of semantics. I am a cripple. I choose this word to
name me. I choose from among several possibilities, the most common
of which are "handicapped" and "disabled." I made the choice a number
of years ago, without thinking, unaware of my motives for doing so.
Even now, I'm not sure what those motives are, but I recognize that they
are complex and not entirely flattering. People—crippled or not—
wince at the word "cripple," as they do not at "handicapped" or "disabled." Perhaps I want them to wince. I want them to see me as a tough
customer, one to whom the fates/gods/viruses have not been kind, but
who can face the brutal truth of her existence squarely. As a cripple, I
swagger.

But, to be fair to myself, a certain amount of honesty underlies my
choice. "Cripple" seems to me a clean word, straightforward and precise. It has an honorable history, having made its first appearance in the
Lindisfarne Gospel in the tenth century. As a lover of words, I like
the accuracy with which it describes my condition: I have lost the full
use of my limbs. "Disabled," by contrast, suggests any incapacity, physical or mental. And I certainly don't like "handicapped," which implies
that I have deliberately been put at a disadvantage, by whom I can't
imagine (my God is not a Handicapper General), in order to equalize
chances in the great race of life. These words seem to me to be moving away from my condition, to be widening the gap between word
and reality. Most remote is the recently coined euphemism "differently abled," which partakes of the same semantic hopefulness that

transformed countries from "undeveloped" to "underdeveloped," then to "less developed," and finally to "developing" nations. People have continued to starve in those countries during the shift. Some realities do not obey the dictates of language.

Mine is one of them. Whatever you call me, I remain crippled. But I don't care what you call me, so long as it isn't "differently abled," which strikes me as pure verbal garbage designed, by its ability to describe anyone, to describe no one. I subscribe to George Orwell's thesis that "the slovenliness of our language makes it easier for us to have foolish thoughts." And I refuse to participate in the degeneration of the language to the extent that I deny that I have lost anything in the course of this calamitous disease; I refuse to pretend that the only differences between you and me are the various ordinary ones that distinguish any one person from another. But call me "disabled" or "handicapped" if you like. I have long since grown accustomed to them; and if they are vague, at least they hint at the truth. Moreover, I use them myself. Society is no readier to accept crippledness than to accept death, war, sex, sweat, or wrinkles. I would never refer to another person as a cripple. It is the word I use to name only myself.

I haven't always been crippled, a fact for which I am soundly   5 grateful. To be whole of limb is, I know from experience, infinitely more pleasant and useful than to be crippled; and if that knowledge leaves me open to bitterness at my loss, the physical soundness I once enjoyed (though I did not enjoy it half enough) is well worth the occasional stab of regret. Though never any good at sports, I was a normally active child and young adult. I climbed trees, played hopscotch, jumped rope, skated, swam, rode my bicycle, sailed. I despised team sports, spending some of the wretchedest afternoons of my life, sweaty and humiliated, behind a field-hockey stick and under a basketball hoop. I tramped alone for miles along the bridle paths that webbed the woods behind the house I grew up in. I swayed through countless dim hours in the arms of one man or another under the scattered shot of light from mirrored balls, and gyrated through countless more as Tab Hunter and Johnny Mathis gave way to the Rolling Stones, Creedence Clearwater Revival, Cream. I walked down the aisle. I pushed baby carriages, changed tires in the rain, marched for peace.

When I was twenty-eight I started to trip and drop things. What at first seemed my natural clumsiness soon became too pronounced to shrug off. I consulted a neurologist, who told me that I had a brain tumor. A battery of tests, increasingly disagreeable, revealed no tumor. About a year and a half later I developed a blurred spot in one eye. I had, at last, the episodes "disseminated in space and time" requisite for a diagnosis: multiple sclerosis. I have never been sorry for the doctor's initial misdiagnosis, however. For almost a week, until the negative results of the tests were in, I thought that I was going to die right away.

Every day for the past nearly ten years, then, has been a kind of gift. I accept all gifts.

Multiple sclerosis is a chronic degenerative disease of the central nervous system, in which the myelin that sheathes the nerves is somehow eaten away and scar tissue forms in its place, interrupting the nerves' signals. During its course, which is unpredictable and uncontrollable, one may lose vision, hearing, speech, the ability to walk, control of bladder and/or bowels, strength in any or all extremities, sensitivity to touch, vibration, and/or pain, potency, coordination of movements— the list of possibilities is lengthy and, yes, horrifying. One may also lose one's sense of humor. That's the easiest to lose and the hardest to survive without.

In the past ten years, I have sustained some of these losses. Characteristic of MS are sudden attacks, called exacerbations, followed by remissions, and these I have not had. Instead, my disease has been slowly progressive. My left leg is now so weak that I walk with the aid of a brace and a cane; and for distances I use an Amigo, a variation on the electric wheelchair that looks rather like an electrified kiddie car. I no longer have much use of my left hand. Now my right side is weakening as well. I still have the blurred spot in my right eye. Overall, though, I've been lucky so far. My world has, of necessity, been circumscribed by my losses, but the terrain left me has been ample enough for me to continue many of the activities that absorb me: writing, teaching, raising children and cats and plants and snakes, reading, speaking publicly about MS and depression, even playing bridge with people patient and honorable enough to let me scatter cards every which way without sneaking a peek.

Lest I begin to sound like Pollyanna, however, let me say that I don't like having MS. I hate it. My life holds realities—harsh ones, some of them—that no right-minded human being ought to accept without grumbling. One of them is fatigue. I know of no one with MS who does not complain of bone-weariness; in a disease that presents an astonishing variety of symptoms, fatigue seems to be a common factor. I wake up in the morning feeling the way most people do at the end of a bad day, and I take it from there. As a result, I spend a lot of time *in extremis* and, impatient with limitation, I tend to ignore my fatigue until my body breaks down in some way and forces rest. Then I miss picnics, dinner parties, poetry readings, the brief visits of old friends from out of town. The offspring of a puritanical tradition of exceptional venerability, I cannot view these lapses without shame. My life often seems a series of small failures to do as I ought.

I lead, on the whole, an ordinary life, probably rather like the one I would have led had I not had MS. I am lucky that my predilections were already solitary, sedentary, and bookish—unlike the world-famous French cellist I have read about, or the young woman I talked with one long afternoon who wanted only to be a jockey. I had just begun graduate school when I found out something was wrong with me, and I have remained, interminably, a graduate student. Perhaps I would not have if I'd thought I had the stamina to return to a full-time job as a technical editor; but I've enjoyed my studies.

In addition to studying, I teach writing courses. I also teach medical students how to give neurological examinations. I pick up freelance editing jobs here and there. I have raised a foster son and sent him into the world, where he has made me two grandbabies, and I am still escorting my daughter and son through adolescence. I go to Mass every Saturday. I am a superb, if messy, cook. I am also an enthusiastic laundress, capable of sorting a hamper full of clothes into five subtly differentiated piles, but a terrible housekeeper. I can do italic writing and, in an emergency, bathe an oil-soaked cat. I play a fiendish game of Scrabble. When I have the time and the money, I like to sit on my front steps with my husband, drinking Amaretto and smoking a cigar, as we imagine our counterparts in Leningrad and make sure that the sun gets down once more behind the sharp childish scrawl of the Tucson Mountains.

This lively plenty has its bleak complement, of course, in all the things I can no longer do. I will never run again, except in dreams, and one day I may have to write that I will never walk again. I like to go camping, but I can't follow George and the children along the trails that wander out of a campsite through the desert or into the mountains. In fact, even on the level I've learned never to check the weather or try to hold a coherent conversation: I need all my attention for my wayward feet. Of late, I have begun to catch myself wondering how people can propel themselves without canes. With only one usable hand, I have to select my clothing with care not so much for style as for ease of ingress and egress, and even so, dressing can be laborious. I can no longer do fine stitchery, pick up babies, play the piano, braid my hair. I am immobilized by acute attacks of depression, which may or may not be physiologically related to MS but are certainly its logical concomitant.

These two elements, the plenty and the privation, are never pure, nor are the delight and wretchedness that accompany them. Almost every pickle that I get into as a result of my weakness and clumsiness—and I get into plenty—is funny as well as maddening and sometimes painful. I recall one May afternoon when a friend and I were going out for a drink after finishing up at school. As we were climbing into opposite sides of my car, chatting, I tripped and fell, flat and hard, onto the asphalt parking lot, my abrupt departure interrupting him in midsentence. "Where'd you go?" he called as he came around the back of the car to find me hauling myself up by the door frame. "Are you all right?" Yes, I told him, I was fine, just a bit rattly, and we drove off to find a shady patio and some beer. When I got home an hour or so later, my daughter greeted me with "What have you done to yourself?" I looked down. One elbow of my white turtleneck with the green froggies, one knee of my white trousers, one white kneesock were bloodsoaked. We peeled off the clothes and inspected the damage, which was nasty enough but not alarming. That part wasn't funny: The abrasions took a long time to heal, and one got a little infected. Even so, when I think of my friend talking earnestly, suddenly, to the hot thin air while I dropped from his view as though through a trap door, I find the image as silly as something from a Marx Brothers movie.

I may find it easier than other cripples to amuse myself because I live propped by the acceptance and the assistance and, sometimes, the amusement of those around me. Grocery clerks tear my checks out of my checkbook for me, and sales clerks find chairs to put into dressing rooms when I want to try on clothes. The people I work with make sure I teach at times when I am least likely to be fatigued, in places I can get to, with the materials I need. My students, with one anonymous exception (in an end-of-the-semester evaluation), have been unperturbed by my disability. Some even like it. One was immensely cheered by the information that I paint my own fingernails; she decided, she told me, that if I could go to such trouble over fine details, she could keep on writing essays. I suppose I became some sort of bright-fingered muse. She wrote good essays, too.

The most important struts in the framework of my existence, 15 of course, are my husband and children. Dismayingly few marriages survive the MS test, and why should they? Most twenty-two- and nineteen-year-olds, like George and me, can vow in clear conscience, after a childhood of chicken pox and summer colds, to keep one another in sickness and in health so long as they both shall live. Not many are equipped for catastrophe: the dismay, the depression, the extra work, the boredom that a degenerative disease can insinuate into a relationship. And our society, with its emphasis on fun and its association of fun with physical performance, offers little encouragement for a whole spouse to stay with a crippled partner. Children experience similar stresses when faced with a crippled parent, and they are more helpless, since parents and children can't usually get divorced. They hate, of course, to be different from their peers, and the child whose mother is tacking down the aisle of a school auditorium packed with proud parents like a Cape Cod dinghy in a stiff breeze jolly well stands out in a crowd. Deprived of legal divorce, the child can at least deny the mother's disability, even her existence, forgetting to tell her about recitals and PTA meetings, refusing to accompany her to stores or church or the movies, never inviting friends to the house. Many do.

But I've been limping along for ten years now, and so far George and the children are still at my left elbow, holding tight. Anne and Matthew vacuum floors and dust furniture and haul trash and rake up dog droppings and button my cuffs and bake lasagna and Toll House cookies with just enough grumbling so I know that they don't have brain fever. And far from hiding me, they're forever dragging me by racks of fancy clothes or through teeming school corridors, or welcoming gaggles of friends while I'm wandering through the house in Anne's filmy pink babydoll pajamas. George generally calls before he brings someone home, but he does just as many dumb thankless chores as the children. And they all yell at me, laugh at some of my jokes, write me funny letters when we're apart—in short, treat me as an ordinary human being for whom they have some use. I think they like me. Unless they're faking. . . .

Faking. There's the rub. Tugging at the fringes of my consciousness always is the terror that people are kind to me only because I'm a cripple. My mother almost shattered me once, with that instinct mothers have—blind, I think, in this case, but unerring nonetheless—for striking blows along the fault-lines of their children's hearts, by telling me, in an attack on my selfishness, "We all have to make allowances for you, of course, because of the way you are." From the distance of a couple of years, I have to admit that I haven't any idea just what she meant, and I'm not sure that she knew either. She was awfully angry. But at the time, as the words thudded home, I felt my worst fear, suddenly realized. I could bear being called selfish: I am. But I couldn't bear the corroboration that those around me were doing in fact what I'd always suspected them of doing, professing fondness while silently putting up with me because of the way I am. A cripple. I've been a little cracked ever since.

Along with this fear that people are secretly accepting shoddy goods comes a relentless pressure to please—to prove myself worth the burdens I impose, I guess, or to build a substantial account of goodwill against which I may write drafts in times of need. Part of the pressure arises from social expectations. In our society, anyone who deviates from the norm had better find some way to compensate. Like fat people, who are expected to be jolly, cripples must bear their lot meekly and cheerfully. A grumpy cripple isn't playing by the rules. And much of the pressure is self-generated. Early on I vowed that, if I had to have MS, by God I was going to do it well. This is a class act, ladies and gentlemen. No tears, no recriminations, no faint-heartedness.

One way and another, then, I wind up feeling like Tiny Tim, peering over the edge of the table at the Christmas goose, waving my crutch, piping down God's blessing on us all. Only sometimes I don't want to play Tiny Tim. I'd rather be Caliban, a most scurvy monster. Fortunately, at home no one much cares whether I'm a good cripple or a bad cripple as long as I make vichyssoise with fair regularity. One evening several years ago, Anne was reading at the dining-room table while I cooked dinner. As I opened a can of tomatoes, the can slipped in my left hand and juice spattered me and the counter with bloody spots. Fatigued and infuriated, I bellowed, "I'm so sick of being crippled!" Anne glanced at me over the top of her book. "There now," she said, "do you feel better?" "Yes," I said, "yes, I do." She went back to her reading. I felt better. That's about all the attention my scurviness ever gets.

Because I hate being crippled, I sometimes hate myself for being a   20
cripple. Over the years I have come to expect—even accept—attacks of violent self-loathing. Luckily, in general our society no longer connects deformity and disease directly with evil (though a charismatic once told me that I have MS because a devil is in me) and so I'm allowed to move largely at will, even among small children. But I'm not sure that this revision of attitude has been particularly helpful. Physical imperfection, even freed of moral disapprobation, still defies and violates the ideal, especially for women, whose confinement in their bodies as objects of desire is far from over. Each age, of course, has its ideal, and I doubt that ours is any better or worse than any other. Today's ideal wom n, who lives on the glossy pages of dozens of magazines, seems to be betw en the ages of eighteen and twenty-five; her hair has body, her teeth fla white, her breath smells minty, her underarms are dry; she has a career ut is still a fabulous cook, especially of meals that take less than twenty minutes to prepare; she does not ordinarily appear to have a husband or children; she is trim and deeply tanned; she jogs, swims, plays tennis, rides a bicycle, sails, but does not bowl; she travels widely, even to out-of-the-way places like Finland and Samoa, always in the company of the ideal man, who possesses a nearly identical set of characteristics. There are a few exceptions. Though usually white and often blonde, she may be black, Hispanic, Asian, or Native American, so long as she is unusually sleek. She may be old, provided she is selling a laxative or is Lauren Bacall. If she is selling a detergent, she may be married and have a flock of strikingly messy children. But she is never a cripple.

Like many women I know, I have always had an uneasy relationship with my body. I was not a popular child, largely, I think now, because I was peculiar: intelligent, intense, moody, shy, given to unexpected actions and inexplicable notions and emotions. But as I entered adolescence, I believed myself unpopular because I was homely: my breasts too flat, my mouth too wide, my hips too narrow, my clothing never quite right in fit or style. I was not, in fact, particularly ugly, old photographs inform me, though I was well off the ideal; but I carried this sense of self-alienation with me into adulthood, where it regenerated in response to the depredations of MS. Even with my brace I walk with a limp so pronounced that, seeing myself on the videotape of a television program on the disabled, I couldn't believe that anything but an inchworm could make progress humping along like that. My shoulders droop and my pelvis thrusts forward as I try to balance myself upright, throwing my frame into a bony S. As a result of contractures, one shoulder is higher than the other and I carry one arm bent in front of me, the fingers curled into a claw. My left arm and leg have wasted into pipe-stems, and I try always to keep them covered. When I think about how my body must look to others, especially to men, to whom I have been trained to display myself, I feel ludicrous, even loathsome.

At my age, however, I don't spend much time thinking about my appearance. The burning egocentricity of adolescence, which assures one that all the world is looking all the time, has passed, thank God, and I'm generally too caught up in what I'm doing to step back, as I used to, and watch myself as though upon a stage. I'm also too old to believe in the accuracy of self-image. I know that I'm not a hideous crone, that in fact, when I'm rested, well dressed, and well made up, I look fine. The self-loathing I feel is neither physically nor intellectually substantial. What I hate is not me but a disease.

I am not a disease.

And a disease is not—at least not singlehandedly—going to determine who I am, though at first it seemed to be going to. Adjusting to a chronic incurable illness, I have moved through a process similar to that outlined by Elizabeth Kübler-Ross in *On Death and Dying.* The major difference—and it is far more significant than most people recognize—is that I can't be sure of the outcome, as the terminally ill cancer patient can. Research studies indicate that, with proper medical care, I may achieve a "normal" life span. And in our society, with its vision of death as the ultimate evil, worse even than decrepitude, the response to such news is, "Oh well, at least you're not going to *die.*" Are there worse things than dying? I think that there may be.

I think of two women I know, both with MS, both enough older   25 than I to have served me as models. One took to her bed several years ago and has been there ever since. Although she can sit in a high-backed wheel-chair, because she is incontinent she refuses to go out at all, even though incontinence pants, which are readily available at any pharmacy, could protect her from embarrassment. Instead, she stays at home and insists that her husband, a small quiet man, a retired civil servant, stay there with her except for a quick weekly foray to the supermarket. The other woman, whose illness was diagnosed when she was eighteen, a nursing student engaged to a young doctor, finished her training, married her doctor, accompanied him to Germany when he was in the service, bore three sons and a daughter, now grown and gone. When she can, she travels with her husband; she plays bridge, embroiders, swims regularly; she works, like me, as a symptomatic-patient instructor of medical students in neurology. Guess which woman I hope to be.

At the beginning, I thought about having MS almost incessantly. And because of the unpredictable course of the disease, my thoughts were always terrified. Each night I'd get into bed wondering whether I'd get out again the next morning, whether I'd be able to see, to speak, to hold a pen between my fingers. Knowing that the day might come when I'd be physically incapable of killing myself, I thought perhaps

I ought to do so right away, while I still had the strength. Gradually I came to understand that the Nancy who might one day lie inert under a bedsheet, arms and legs paralyzed, unable to feed or bathe herself, unable to reach out for a gun, a bottle of pills, was not the Nancy I was at present, and that I could not presume to make decisions for that future Nancy, who might well not want in the least to die. Now the only provision I've made for the future Nancy is that when the time comes— and it is likely to come in the form of pneumonia, friend to the weak and the old—I am not to be treated with machines and medications. If she is unable to communicate by then, I hope she will be satisfied with these terms.

Thinking all the time about having MS grew tiresome and intrusive, especially in the large and tragic mode in which I was accustomed to considering my plight. Months and even years went by without catastrophe (at least without one related to MS), and really I was awfully busy, what with George and children and snakes and students and poems, and I hadn't the time, let alone the inclination, to devote myself to being a disease. Too, the richer my life became, the funnier it seemed, as though there were some connection between largesse and laughter, and so my tragic stance began to waver until, even with the aid of a brace and a cane, I couldn't hold it for very long at a time.

After several years I was satisfied with my adjustment. I had suffered my grief and fury and terror, I thought, but now I was at ease with my lot. Then one summer day I set out with George and the children across the desert for a vacation in California. Part way to Yuma I became aware that my right leg felt funny. "I think I've had an exacerbation," I told George. "What shall we do?" he asked. "I think we'd better get the hell to California," I said, "because I don't know whether I'll ever make it again." So we went on to San Diego and then to Orange, up the Pacific Coast Highway to Santa Cruz, across to Yosemite, down to Sequoia and Joshua Tree, and so back over the desert to home. It was a fine two-week trip, filled with friends and fair weather, and I wouldn't have missed it for the world, though I did in fact make it back to California two years later. Nor would there have been any point in missing it, since in MS, once the symptoms have appeared, the neurological damage has been done, and there's no way to predict or prevent that damage.

The incident spoiled my self-satisfaction, however. It renewed my grief and fury and terror, and I learned that one never finishes adjusting to MS. I don't know now why I thought one would. One does not, after all, finish adjusting to life, and MS is simply a fact of my life—not my favorite fact, of course—but as ordinary as my nose and my tropical fish and my yellow Mazda station wagon. It may at any time get worse, but no amount of worry or anticipation can prepare me for a new loss. My life is a lesson in losses. I learn one at a time.

And I had best be patient in the learning, since I'll have to do it   30
like it or not. As any rock fan knows, you can't always get what you
want. Particularly when you have MS. You can't, for example, get
cured. In recent years researchers and the organizations that fund research have started to pay MS some attention even though it isn't fatal;
perhaps they have begun to see that life is something other than a
quantitative phenomenon, that one may be very much alive for a very
long time in a life that isn't worth living. The researchers have made
some progress toward understanding the mechanism of the disease: It
may well be an autoimmune reaction triggered by a slow-acting virus.
But they are nowhere near its prevention, control, or cure. And most of
us want to be cured. Some, unable to accept incurability, grasp at one
treatment after another, no matter how bizarre: megavitamin therapy,
gluten-free diet, injections of cobra venom, hypothermal suits,
lymphocytopharesis, hyperbaric chambers. Many treatments are probably harmless enough, but none are curative.

The absence of a cure often makes MS patients bitter toward their
doctors. Doctors are, after all, the priests of modern society, the new
shamans, whose business is to heal, and many an MS patient roves from
one to another, searching for the "good" doctor who will make him
well. Doctors too think of themselves as healers, and for this reason
many have trouble dealing with MS patients, whose disease in its in-
transigence defeats their aims and mocks their skills. Too few doctors,
it is true, treat their patients as whole human beings, but the reverse is
also true. I have always tried to be gentle with my doctors, who often
have more at stake in terms of ego than I do. I may be frustrated,
maddened, depressed by the incurability of my disease, but I am not
diminished by it, and they are. When I push myself up from my seat
in the waiting room and stumble toward them, I incarnate the limitation of their powers. The least I can do is refuse to press on their
tenderest spots.

This gentleness is part of the reason that I'm not sorry to be a
cripple. I didn't have it before. Perhaps I'd have developed it anyway—
how could I know such a thing?—and I wish I had more of it, but I'm
glad of what I have. It has opened and enriched my life enormously, this
sense that my frailty and need must be mirrored in others, that in
searching for and shaping a stable core in a life wrenched by change and
loss, change and loss, I must recognize the same process, under individual conditions, in the lives around me. I do not deprecate such knowledge, however I've come by it.

All the same, if a cure were found, would I take it? In a minute. I may
be a cripple, but I'm only occasionally a loony and never a saint. Anyway,
in my brand of theology God doesn't give bonus points for a limp. I'd take
a cure; I just don't need one. A friend who also has MS startled me once by
asking, "Do you ever say to yourself, 'Why me, Lord?'" "No, Michael, I

don't," I told him, "because whenever I try, the only response I can think of is 'Why not?'" If I could make a cosmic deal, who would I put in my place? What in my life would I give up in exchange for sound limbs and a thrilling rush of energy? No one. Nothing. I might as well do the job myself. Now that I'm getting the hang of it.

LINES OF INQUIRY
"On Being a Cripple"

This essay provides a richly detailed account of Mairs's experience with MS, but it does not tell the story of her experience in chronological order. Identify all of the paragraphs and passages that deal with the earlier phases of her experience. Identify those that deal with the later phases of her experience. What difference(s) do you notice between her earlier and later reactions and attitudes toward MS? How do you account for the differences? Why do you suppose that she doesn't tell about her experience in chronological order?

In paragraphs 2, 3, and 4, Mairs makes a deliberate point of referring to herself as a "cripple" rather than as a "disabled" or "handicapped" or "differently abled" person. Why does she prefer to call herself "a cripple"? In what ways do you think her preference for this term is related to the way she depicts her condition in the rest of the essay? What insights did you gain into the nature of a crippled person's existence from Mairs's account of her experience with MS?

How does Mairs's depiction of "being a cripple" compare with your own prior conception, or observation, or experience of being crippled? In what respects are your perceptions most similar to hers? In what respects do they differ? In what ways, if any, have you revised your perceptions on the basis of reading her essay? In what ways have your thoughts about the subject remained the same?

ON NOT LIKING SEX

"The other day, sitting in a tweed chair with my knees crossed, drinking a cup of coffee and smoking a cigarette, I looked straight at my therapist and said, 'I don't like sex.' I have known this man for years now. I have told him that I don't like my husband, my children, my parents, my students, my life. I may even have said at some time, 'I don't like sex very much.' But the difference between not liking sex very much and not liking sex is vast, vaster even than the Catholic Church's gulf between salvation and damnation, because there's no limbo, no purgatory. An irony here: For in another age (perhaps in this age within the bosom of the Holy Mother Church) I would be the woman whose price is above rubies, pure and virtuous, purity and virtue having always attached themselves, at least for women, to the matter of sex. As it is, I am, in my metaphor, one of the damned. My therapist has a homelier metaphor. I have, he says, what our society considers 'the worst wart.' In 1981 in the United States of America one cannot fail to like sex. It's not normal. It's not nice."

This paragraph opened a brief essay I wrote a couple of years ago entitled "On Not Liking Sex." The essay, which I have preserved here in quotation marks, was a brittle, glittery piece, a kind of spun confection of the verbal play I'd like to engage in at cocktail parties but can muster only at a solitary desk with a legal-size yellow pad in front of me. It was, in fact, as you can see if you read it straight through, cocktail party chatter. And yet it was true, insofar as any truth can be translated into words. That is, it said some things, and suggested others, about me and the times I live in which were accurate enough as far as they went.

But they certainly didn't go very far. Hardly to the end of the block. Certainly not across the street. This essay is an almost perfect example of a phenomenon I've only recently become aware of, though clearly at a deeper level I've understood its workings for a very long time, a kind of pretense at serious writing which I use to keep busy and out of trouble: the kind of trouble you get when you run smack into an idea so significant and powerful that the impact jars you to the bone. It's a way of staying out of the traffic. It is not babble, and it is not easy. On the contrary, it requires painstakingly chosen diction, deliberately controlled syntax, and seamless organization. A rough spot is a trouble spot, a split, a crack, out of which something dreadful (probably black, probably with a grin) may leap and squash you flat.

If this essay was an exercise in making careful statements that would ensure that I never said what I really had to say, then what did I have to say? I don't know. If I'd known then, I couldn't have written such a piece in the first place. And the only progress I've made since then is to have gained a little courage in the face of things that leap out of cracks in the pavement. If I look at the essay again closely, if I listen for the resonances among the words with the not-yet-words, perhaps I can discover some portion of the significance—for the woman just turned forty in the 1980s in the United States of America—of not liking sex.

The title and the first paragraph, by using words as though, like algebraic notation, they had fixed meanings in the context of a given problem, claim to have signified an attitude they have in fact obscured. Even if *on* and *not* may be allowed a certain fixity as they function here, *liking* and *sex* may not. *Sex,* in its most general sense, is simply the way one is: male or female just as black or brown, blue- or hazel-eyed, long- or stubby-fingered, able or not to curl one's tongue into a tube. The genes take care of it. One may dislike one's sex, apparently, just as my daughter dislikes her nose, which is round and tends toward rosy under the sun; some people, thanks to the technological genius of modern medicine, even change theirs. But I like my sex. I suffer from penis envy, of course, to the extent that freedom and privilege have attached themselves to this fleshy sign; I've never wished for the actual appendage, however, except on long car trips through sparsely populated areas. In fact, looked at this way, *not liking sex* doesn't make sense to me at all, any more than do *having sex, wanting sex, demanding sex, refusing sex.* Such phrases clarify the specialized use of the word as shorthand for sexual activity, particularly sexual intercourse.

So I don't like sexual activity. But *like* can mean both to take pleasure in, enjoy, and to wish to have, want; and wanting something seems to me quite a different matter from enjoying it. The former is volitional, a reaching out for experience, whereas the latter is a response to an experience (whether sought for or not) already in progress. In these terms I can and often do enjoy sex. But I do not necessarily want to engage in sexual activity even though I may enjoy doing so.

> "The human psyche being the squirmy creature that it is, I have trouble pinning down my objections to sex. I do not seem to object to the act itself which, if I can bring myself to commit it, I like very well. I object to the idea. My objections are undoubtedly, in part, Puritanical. Not for nothing did John Howland, Stephen Hopkins, Thomas Rogers, and Elder William Brewster bring on the Mayflower the seed that would one day bloom in me. If it feels good, it's bad. Sex feels good. My objections may also be aesthetic: It's a sweaty, slimy business. Certainly they are mythic, Eros and Thanatos colliding in the orgasm to explode the frail self back into the atoms of the universe. Love is Death."

The human psyche squirms indeed, especially when it is striving to distance itself from its desires by creating platonic distinctions between things in themselves and the ideas of things. I don't object to the idea of sex. In fact, I don't feel any particular response one way or the other to the idea of sex. Sex for me as for most, I should think, is not ideational but sensual, and it is this distinction that gives me trouble, a distinction that resembles that between wanting and enjoying. I don't object to the *idea* of sex: I object to the *sense* of sex. An act is a sign. Directly apprehended, it has always at least one meaning and usually a multiplicity of meanings. These I must sort out—their implications, their resonances—in order to understand how I, with a singularly human perversity, can not want what I enjoy.

Puritanism, aesthetics, and myth all play a part in this response, no doubt, though the reference to the Mayflower is misleading (the Pilgrims were not Puritans, though many of their descendants were), and as far as I know, the Puritans did not prohibit the sex act—no matter what it felt like—so long as it was confined to the marriage bed. The kind of puritanism that has dogged me is more diffuse than that of my foremothers, perhaps the inevitable legacy of their hard-scrabble existence in tiny communities clinging to the flinty, bitter-wintered New England coast, no longer a religion but still a code of conduct, closemouthed, grudging of joy, quick to judge and reject. We conducted ourselves at all levels with restraint. Our disapproval of Catholics was not particularly theological; rather, we thought them primitive, childishly taken with display, with their candles and crosses and croziers, play-acting at religion. We painted our houses white with black or green shutters, grey with blue shutters, sometimes soft yellow or dark brown, and we shuddered at the pink and turquoise and lime green on the little capes and ranches that belonged, we assumed, to the Italians. When we met, we greeted one another with a nod, perhaps a small smile, a few words, a firm handshake, even a kiss on the cheek, depending on the degree of our intimacy, but we did not fall into each other's arms with loud smackings, everybody jabbering at once. As a child I was given to fits of weeping and outbursts of delight which to this day my mother refers to with a sigh as "Nancy's dramatics"; I do not, of course, have them now.

Here is the real aesthetics of the matter: the refinement of decoration and gesture to a state so etiolated that voices pierce, perfumes smother, colors clash and scream and shout. I still dislike wearing red and certain shades of pink and orange. The entire sensory world impinges—presses, pinches, pummels—unless one keeps a distance. Touch comes, eventually, to burn. Sex isn't bad so much because it feels good as because it's poor form—the kind of rowdy, riotous behavior one squelches in children as they become young ladies (honest to God, I was never permitted to refer to female human beings as women but only as ladies) and gentlemen. Sex is indecorous.

As for the sweat and slime, the basis for this objection strikes me as more medical than aesthetic. After all, one can get a good deal grubbier on a hike up a small mountain, which is just good clean fun. But the body itself is not clean. It is, according to pathologists like my ancestor Rudolf Virchow, a veritable pesthouse. I grew up knowing that my breath was pestilent ("cover your mouth when you sneeze"), that my mouth was pestilent ("don't kiss me—you've got a cold"). And then along came men, themselves crawling with germs, who breathed on me, who wanted to put their mouths on mine and make me sick. Rudolf may have done wonders for German public health, but he sure put a kink in my private sex life. Oddly enough, this phobia of germs did not include my genitalia, perhaps because they lay untouched and unpondered until long after it had been formed. Nowadays, with the threat of venereal disease widely publicized, I don't suppose one can be so insouciant. The germs lurk at every orifice, and sex is simply contrary to good sanitary practices.

Poor sanitary practices may give you a cold or a stomach flu or herpes, but they are not, in Tucson in 1983, likely to do you in. The equation of sex with death is of another order altogether, though not the less dreadful for not being literal. As late as the Renaissance *to die* was used as we use *to come* to signify orgasm; and although we have abandoned the explicit connection, we have not lost the construct that underlies it. Orgasm shares, briefly, the characteristics we imagine death to have, the annihilation (or at least the transmogrification) of consciousness, the extinction of the *I* that forms and controls being. The loss of my hard-won identity, even for an instant, risks forfeiture of self: not perhaps the death that ends in the coffin but certainly the death that ends in the cell: I am afraid of going away and never coming back.

> "But most strongly, my objections are what I reluctantly term 'political.' My reluctance stems from the sense that 'political' in this context implies the kind of radical lesbianism that suggests that medical technology is sufficiently advanced to permit the elimination of the male entirely. I learned, in one of the most poignant affairs of my life, that I am not lesbian. Nor am I even a good feminist, since I seldom think abstractly and tend to run principles together like the paints on a sloppy artist's palette, the results being colorful but hardly coherent. No, when I say 'political,' I mean something purely personal governing the nature of the relationship between me and a given man. In this sense, sex is a political act. In it, I lose power, through submission or, in one instance, through force. In either case, my integrity is violated; I become possessed."

Here's the heart of the matter—politics—and I've dashed it off and done it up with ribbons of lesbianism and feminism so that the plain package hardly shows. True, I'm not lesbian, but thanks to the fundamental heterosexual bias of our culture no one would be likely to assume that I was. And I am, in fact, a perfectly good if unsystematic feminist. Who in my audience, I wonder, was I worried about when I made that self-deprecatory moue, as if to say, "Don't expect too much of me; I'm just a nonradical heterosexual little woman, a bit daffy perhaps, but harmless"? And what the hell (now that I've got the ribbons off) is in the box that made me wrap it up so tight?

Politics. Power. Submission. Force. Violation. Possession. Sex is not merely a political act; it is an act of war. And no act is ever "purely personal." It is a nexus that accretes out of earlier and other acts older than memory, older than dreams: the exchange of women, along with goods, gestures, and words, in the creation of allies; the ascription to women of all that lurks terrible in the darkened brain; the protection and penetration of the maidenhead in rituals for ensuring paternity and perpetuating lineage; the conscription of women's sons for the destruction of human beings, of women's daughters for their reproduction; enforcement of silence; theft of subjectivity; immurement; death. If I think that what I do, in or out of bed, originates in me, I am a much madder woman than I believe myself to be. I am no original but simply a locus of language in a space and time that permits one—in politics as in sex—to fuck or get fucked. Aggression is the germ in all the words.

From such an angle, sex is always rape, and indeed I tangle the two words at the level just below articulation. Perhaps I do so because my first sexual intercourse was a rape. At least it occurred in the safety of my own bed by someone I knew intimately, so that although I was furious, I was never in fear for my life. We were both nineteen, had been high-school sweethearts grown apart, and he had come to spend a weekend at the Farm, where I was working as a mother's helper for the summer. We spent the evening deep in conversation, I remember, and after I went to bed, he came into my room, jumped on top of me, deflowered me, and went away again. I don't believe we ever exchanged a word or an embrace. I felt some pain, and in the morning I found blood on my thighs and on the sheets, which I had secretly to wash, so I know that all of this really happened, but I never permitted myself the least feeling about it, not as much as I might have given a nightmare. I *knew* that I was furious, but I *felt* nothing. I don't know what response he expected, but he got none at all. He left the next day, without my ever having spoken to him, and we never met again.

Nor do I know what effect he intended his act to have. I'm sure that he was marking me, for we grew up at the tail end of the time when virginity had real significance, and in defloration he claimed me in only a slightly more subtle manner than incising his initials into some hidden area of my flesh. He knew that I was in love with another man, that I planned to be married within a year, and for a long time I believed that he was trying, through some sort of magical thinking, to force me to marry him instead. We really did believe that a woman belonged to the man who first "had" her. But now I think that he wasn't marking me for himself so much as spoiling me for George. Whatever its true interpretation, his act makes clear my absence from the transaction. The business was between him and George, the item of exchange one tarnished coin.

To sense myself such a cipher robs me of power. In sex, as in many other instances, I feel powerless. Part of this feeling arises from the fact that, as new symptoms of multiple sclerosis appear and worsen, my power literally drains away. But to what extent is multiple sclerosis merely the physical inscription of my way of being in the world? In sex, as in the rest of my life, I am acted upon. I am the object, not the agent. I live in the passive voice. The phallus penetrates me; I do not surround, engulf, incorporate the phallus. No wonder Caleb raped me. Rape was his only grammatical option.

15

Thus, I see that in a queer and cruel way I raped him by forcing him to rape me. I always made myself the object of his desire. How many times, I remember now, we came to the brink of intercourse, and always at the last I turned him away, pretending that I couldn't overcome my moral scruples. What I really couldn't overcome was a barrier so ludicrous that I don't expect you to believe it: my underpants. I couldn't figure out how to get rid of them. The women in films and romantic novels, where I'd gotten my impressions of the mechanics of intercourse, didn't struggle with underpants. Did I think they just melted away? After all, I took my underpants off every day as matter-of-factly as I kicked them under the bed to drive my mother wild with despair over my inability to keep some man a decent house. Why then could I not just take them off an extra time? The gesture seemed too overt, too clumsy and pedestrian for the occasion. I couldn't bear to look a fool. So I lay in bondage to the concept of woman as image, not agent, kept a virgin till I was nineteen by Carter Lollipop Pants, red ones and navy ones, their combed cotton grim as iron through my crotch. But for Caleb, who knew nothing of my quandary, I was withholding a treasure that must have seemed of great worth, since I guarded it so jealously. I think I can understand his fury when I threatened to give it to someone else.

Ah, but I'm so old now. I can't blame myself for having been a fool, or him for having believed me a pearl of great price instead of a human being, for whatever she was worth. We were both too young to give tongue to the grammar of our intercourse. All I can do now is use the leverage of my understanding to pry open the box I have stripped and look at the contents squarely. In sex, that political act, I lose power because I have still not learned what it might be and how to claim it.

"For this reason, I have preferred casual lovers to a permanent, long-term partner. They have fewer expectations, thus minimizing possession and obligation. Less is at stake. With them, I can concentrate on the act itself without worrying about its implications. They will be gone long before they learn enough about me to threaten my privacy or come to consider sexual access a right or even a privilege. But even lovers, the romantic ones at least, are risky. They can be more interested in being in love than in bed. My latest lover pitched me out on the grounds that he wasn't in love with me (don't ask me why he took me in—life is complicated enough as it is); and with the irony that won't work in fiction but does splendidly in life, I had fallen in love with him, only the second time that I have done so and the only time that doing so was a mistake. The experience was so nearly disastrous that I learned precipitously the lesson that had long been floating just outside the periphery of my vision: Celibacy is power."

An agoraphobe, a depressive, I have long since learned that avoidance is the most comfortable way to cope with situations that make me uneasy, and God knows sex makes me uneasy. In the playfulness of the opening of a sexual relationship, the issue of power is eclipsed by curiosity, exhilaration, voluptuousness. I find my delight in the process chronicled in my journal: "I sit beside Richard. It is terribly hot—I can feel the steam from both our bodies. We play the touching game—arms touch, knees brush, shoulders press together—at first by 'accident,' testing for response, then deliberately. I love this game, as often as I've played it and as silly as it is; it has a kind of rhythm and elegance when played properly, with good humor, without haste. Richard is very good at it. When, at one point, we have looked at one another for a long moment, he smiles a little and I say, 'What?' He starts to say something, then breaks off: 'You know.' I laugh and say, 'I've been wondering what would happen if I leaned over and kissed you.' It is a dumb idea—I don't know most of the people there very well, but Richard does, and they all know that I'm married. 'I think we'd better wait to do that on our own,' he replies. 'Soon.' 'Yes,' I say, 'yes, soon.' If I hadn't driven my own car, it could have been right then. Wasn't. The kiss is yet to come."

But in truth I do not like sex, even in brief affairs. In the rush of excitement I think I do, but afterwards I am always embarrassed by it. If I could stay balanced in the delicious vertigo of flirtation, I might not feel ashamed, but I can't. I always want to tumble dizzily into bed. And after I've been there, even once, my privacy has been not merely threatened but ruptured. My privacy I carry around me as a bubble of space. Quite literally. I hate to be touched. I hate to be known. If the bubble is pricked, I may disintegrate, leaking out vaporously and vanishing on the wind. The man who has even once seen me up close, naked and transported, knows more about me than I can bear for him to know. For this reason, I have not, in fact, preferred casual lovers to a permanent, long-term partner; if I had, I wouldn't still be married after twenty years. I have taken a casual lover every now and then in the hope that I can reduce sex to pure, unfreighted fun; but the baggage always catches up with me.

One of the cases, of course, carries love. Lovers and husbands alike 20 are risky to a woman who cannot bear to be loved any more than to be touched. I can feel love creep around me, pat me with soft fingers, and I stiffen and struggle for breath. By contrast, I quite readily fall in love and have loved, in some way, all but one of the men I've slept with. So what all the bobbing and weaving about my "latest lover" might mean I'm not sure. I hadn't, at the time I wrote the essay, got over him, and my immediate judgment now is that one oughtn't to try to write the truth while in the kind of turmoil that at that time was threatening my sanity and therefore my life. But on second thought I see that here are simply two truths. I wrote the truth when I said that I'd fallen in love with only two lovers in my life, though I can't think now who I had in mind; I write the truth when I say that I've fallen in love with all but one. Quod scripsi, scripsi. Anyway, I must have learned some lesson from the bitterness the last one brought me, for I have not taken another.

All the same, celibacy is not power. Celibacy is celibacy: the withholding of oneself from sexual union. When it is actively chosen as a means of redirecting one's attention, as it is by some religious, it may both reflect and confer personal power. But when it is clutched at as a means of disengaging oneself from the tentacles of human conflict, it is simply one more technique for avoiding distress. As I stay at home to avoid agoraphobic attacks, I stay out of bed to avoid claustrophobic ones. I am celibate not for the love of God but for the fear of love.

> "Avoiding sex altogether is not difficult. You must simply rent a tiny apartment, large enough only for yourself and possibly a very small black cat, and let no one into it. If you want friends, meet them at their houses, if they'll have you, at bars and restaurants, at art galleries, poetry readings, concerts. But don't take them home with you. Keep your space inviolate. During attacks of loneliness and desire, smoke cigarettes. Drink Amaretto. Throw the I Ching. Write essays. Letting someone into your space is tantamount to letting him between your legs, and more dangerous, since you risk his touching the inner workings of your life, not merely your body. Ask him if he wouldn't rather drive into the country for a picnic."

This advice is sound. I have tested all of it. Then I swallowed a handful of Elavil one Hallowe'en and almost succeeded in avoiding sex altogether.

> "All this I have learned. What I haven't learned is what to do with the grief and guilt that not liking sex inevitably arouses. The grief is so protean and private that I will not attempt to articulate it. But the guilt is a decidedly public matter, since it could not exist—not in its present form anyway—in the absence of post-Freudian social pressure to regard sex as the primary source not of joy (I doubt that contemporary society knows much about joy) but of satisfaction. If I don't like sex, I am abnormal, repressed, pathetic, sick—the labels vary but the significance is consistent—I do not belong in the ranks of healthy human beings, health requiring as one of its terms sexual activity and fulfillment."

By separating out grief from the complex of responses I feel to not wanting sex, and by tying it off as a "private" matter, I hoped perhaps that, like a vestigial finger or toe, it would drop away. But the dissociation is not authentic, because in fact all my responses are private insofar as the construct they form is my peculiar *I,* and all are public insofar as that *I* is a linguistic product spoken by a patriarchal culture that insists that my God-created function is to rejoice, through my person, the heart of a man. Moreover, failure to do so results not in guilt, as I have stated it, but in shame, which is a truly protean (and, say some feminists, distinctively feminine) emotion, pervasive and inexpiable. About guilt one can do something: Like a wound in the flesh, with proper cleansing it will heal, the scar, however twisted and lumpy, proof against infection. Shame, like the vaginal wound always open to invasion, is an inoperable state. My tongue has given me these distinctions. With it I must acknowledge my shame.

Shamelessness, like shame, is not a masculine condition. That is, there is no *shameless man* as there is a *shameless woman* or, as my grandmother used to say, a *shameless hussy.* A man without shame is in general assumed simply to have done nothing he need feel guilty about. A woman without shame is a strumpet, a trollop, a whore, a witch. The connotations have been, immemorially, sexual. Here is the thirteenth-century author of the *Ancrene Riwle,* a priest instructing three anchoresses in the correct manner of confession: "A woman will say, 'I have been foolish' or 'I had a lover,' whereas she should confess, 'I am a stud mare, a stinking whore.'" And somewhat later, in the *Malleus Maleficarum,* a warning to Inquisitors: "All witchcraft comes from carnal Lust which is in Women insatiable." My sexuality has been the single most powerful disruptive force mankind has ever perceived, and its repression has been the work of centuries.

Now, suddenly, the message has changed. Now, after ages of covering my face and my genitals—St. Paul's veil over my hair, my breasts bound, my waist girded in whalebone, my face masked with kohl and rouge, my length swathed in white cambric pierced by a lace-edged buttonhole through which to guide the erect penis to my hidden treasure—I am supposed to strip to the skin and spread my legs and strive for multiple orgasm.   25

Knowing what The Fathers have given me to know of the dangers of female sexuality, how could I dare?

> "If I got this message from one person at a time, I might be able to deal with it with rationality, distance, even amusement. But I get it impersonally, from all sides, in a barrage so relentless that the wonder is that I survive my guilt, let alone cope with it. I get the message from the bookshelves, where I find not only *The Joy of Sex* but also *More Joy of Sex,* written by a man whose very name promises physical contentment. (I have read some of these books.

They contain many instructions on how to do it well. I know how to do it well. I just don't know whether I want to do it at all.) The message comes with my jeans, which I may buy no longer merely for durability and comfort but for the ache they will create in some man's crotch. It foams in my toothpaste, my bath soap, even my dish detergent. It follows me through the aisles of the supermarket and the drugstore. It ridicules my breastless body, my greying hair."

Or has the message really changed? The body swaddled has become the body naked but it is, all the same, the female body, artifice of desire, still inscribed after stripping with the marks of straps cut into the shoulders, underwires into the breasts, zipper into the belly, squeezed and shaved and deodorized until it is shapely and sanitary enough to arouse no dread of its subjective possibilities. The mechanics of its eroticism have been altered so that, instead of receiving male desire as a patient vessel, it is supposed to validate male performance by resonating when it is played upon. Nonetheless, it remains a thing, alien, "other," as Simone de Beauvoir has pointed out, to the man who dreams of it—and also to the woman who wears it, sculpturing it to the specifications of the male-dominated advertising, publishing, fashion, and cosmetic industries.

An object does not know its own value. Even a sentient being, made into an object, will feel uncertain of her worth except as it is measured by the standards of the agora, the market place, which will reflect whatever male fantasies about women are current. Thanks to astonishing technological advances in the broadcasting of these standards, almost everyone in the world knows what they are and can weigh his object or her self against them, no matter how bizarre the means for their attainment may be. Somewhere I read that it takes the concerted pushing and pulling of three people to get a high-fashion model zipped into her jeans and propped into position for photographing. We all see the photographs, though not the three laborers behind them, and believe that the ideal woman looks like that. Thus a standard has been fixed, and most of us, lacking the appropriate sturdy personnel, won't meet it.

Through such manipulation I have learned to despise my body. I have, perhaps, more reason than most for doing so, since my body is not merely aging but also crippled. On the fair market, its value is slipping daily as the musculature twists and atrophies, the digestive system grinds spasmodically, the vision blurs, the gait lurches and stumbles. But long before I knew I had multiple sclerosis, I hadn't much use for it. Nor have I had much use for the man who desires it. He lacks taste, it seems to me: the kind of man who prefers Formica to teak, Melmac to Limoges, canned clam chowder to bouillabaisse. Who wants to have sex with a man who can't do better than you?

"Were I living in the Middle Ages, my difficulty could be quickly solved. I would become an anchoress, calling from my cell, 'And all shall be well, and all manner of thing shall be well.' God would love me. My fellow creatures would venerate me. But the wheel has turned and tipped me into a time when God has been dead for a century and my fellow creatures are likely to find me more pitiable than venerable. I shall no doubt be lonelier than any anchoress.

Nonetheless, my bed will stay narrow."

I love closure. Especially in any kind of writing. I like to tie off   30
the tale with some statement that sounds as though nothing further can be said. Never mind the Princess's hysterical weeping on the morning after her wedding night, her later infidelities, the first son's cleft palate, the Prince's untimely death during an ill-advised raid on a neighboring kingdom, the old King's driveling madness: They lived happily ever after, or, if the tale is a modern one like mine, unhappily ever after. But their development ceased. I love closure enough to pretend that quick resolution lies along the length of a cell (in which I might prostrate myself praying not "All shall be well" but "I am a stud mare, a stinking whore"), enough to believe that virtue lies easy in a narrow bed. True, at the time I wrote the essay I was sleeping alone in a narrow bed, but it's widened again now to queen size, with George in one half, or sometimes two thirds, and often Vanessa Bell and Lionel Tigress too.

My sexuality is too complicated a text to be truncated neatly at any point. What has woven it together until now, I see, to prevent it from being a mere tangle of random terror and revulsion, has been my coherent inverse equation of autonomy with physical violation. Such a connection is predicated upon the denial of my own subjectivity in sexual experience. Afraid of being reduced by another to an object, I have persisted in seeing myself as such. Why did I lie, limp as a doll, while Caleb butted at me? Why didn't I writhe, scratch, bite? Why didn't I at least give him a thorough tongue-lashing the next morning before he left my life forever? Over and over I have demanded that I be raped and have then despised both the rapist and myself.

I understand now some of the teachings that helped me compose such a tale of invasion, illness, self-immolation. And I will not close it off with an *ever after,* happy or unhappy. Tomorrow the Princess gets out of bed again: She washes her hair, drinks her coffee, scribbles some pages, tells a joke to her son, bakes a spinach quiche. And the day after. And the day after that. All the while she is telling herself a story. In it, she is aging now, and she drags one foot behind her when she walks. These are changes she can scrutinize in her mirror. They tell her that the true texts are the ones that do not end but revolve and reflect and spin out new constellations of meaning day after day, page after page, joke after joke, quiche after quiche. She has been learning much about vision and revision. She has been learning much about forgiveness.

In this story, she is the writer of essays. She has a black typewriter and several reams of paper. One day, she thinks, she could find herself writing an essay called "On Liking Sex." There's that to consider.

LINES OF INQUIRY
"On Not Liking Sex"

This essay actually contains two essays "On Not Liking Sex"—the earlier one a provocation of the other, the later one, in turn, a running commentary upon its earlier counterpart. In what respects do you think Mairs is primarily trying to offer a more detailed discussion so as to account for her earlier thinking? In what respects do you think she is instead trying to correct what she considers to be carelessly worded or potentially misleading statements in the earlier essay? In what respects do you think she has actually changed her mind about sex between the earlier and later essay? In what respects might it be said that the final paragraph of her later essay calls into question everything she has just finished saying about sex and therefore calls upon her to write yet another essay on the subject?

In paragraph 9 of her essay, Mairs asserts that "politics" is "the heart of the matter." In what sense(s) is politics at the heart of her reasons for not liking sex? In what sense(s), on the other hand, does she seem to suggest that her reasons for not liking sex are profoundly personal? In what sense(s) does she seem to imply that the political and the personal are so deeply intertwined that they cannot be disentangled?

Mairs touches on sex and her own sexuality in two other essays in this collection—"On Being a Cripple" and "Carnal Acts." In what respects, if any, do these essays convey similar attitudes toward sex? In what respects do they convey different attitudes toward it? How do you account for the differences?

CARNAL ACTS

Inviting me to speak at her small liberal-arts college during Women's Week, a young woman set me a task: "We would be pleased," she wrote, "if you could talk on how you cope with your MS disability, and also how you discovered your voice as a writer." Oh, Lord, I thought in dismay, how am I going to pull this one off? How can I yoke two such disparate subjects into a coherent presentation, without doing violence to one, or the other, or both, or myself? This is going to take some fancy footwork, and my feet scarcely carry out the basic steps, let alone anything elaborate.

To make matters worse, the assumption underlying each of her questions struck me as suspect. To ask *how* I cope with multiple sclerosis suggests that I *do* cope. Now, "to cope," *Webster's Third* tells me, is "to face or encounter and to find necessary expedients to overcome problems and difficulties." In these terms, I have to confess, I don't feel like much of a coper. I'm likely to deal with my problems and difficulties by squawking and flapping around like that hysterical chicken who was convinced the sky was falling. Never mind that in my case the sky really *is* falling. In response to a clonk on the head, regardless of its origin, one might comport oneself with a grace and courtesy I generally lack.

As for "finding" my voice, the implication is that it was at one time lost or missing. But I don't think it ever was. Ask my mother, who will tell you a little wearily that I was speaking full sentences by the time I was a year old and could never be silenced again. As for its being a writer's voice, it seems to have become one early on. Ask Mother again. At the age of eight I rewrote the Trojan War, she will say, and what Nestor was about to do to Helen at the end doesn't bear discussion in polite company.

Faced with these uncertainties, I took my own teacherly advice, something, I must confess, I don't always do. "If an idea is giving you trouble," I tell my writing students, "put it on the back burner and let it simmer while you do something else. Go to the movies. Reread a stack of old love letters. Sit in your history class and take detailed notes on the Teapot Dome scandal. If you've got your idea in mind, it will go on cooking at some level no matter what else you're doing." "I've had an idea for my documented essay on the back burner," one of my students once scribbled in her journal, "and I think it's just boiled over!"

I can't claim to have reached such a flash point. But in the weeks I've had the themes "disability" and "voice" sitting around in my head, they seem to have converged on their own, without my having to wrench them together and bind them with hoops of tough rhetoric.

They *are* related, indeed interdependent, with an intimacy that has for some reason remained, until now, submerged below the surface of my attention. Forced to juxtapose them, I yank them out of the depths, a little startled to discover how they were intertwined down there out of sight. This kind of discovery can unnerve you at first. You feel like a giant hand that, pulling two swimmers out of the water, two separate heads bobbling on the iridescent swells, finds the two bodies below, legs coiled around each other, in an ecstasy of copulation. You don't quite know where to turn your eyes.

Perhaps the place to start illuminating this erotic connection between who I am and how I speak lies in history. I have known that I have multiple sclerosis for about seventeen years now, though the disease probably started long before. The hypothesis is that the disease process, in which the protective covering of the nerves in the brain and spinal cord is eaten away and replaced by scar tissue, "hard patches," is caused by an autoimmune reaction to a slow-acting virus. Research suggests that I was infected by this virus, which no one has ever seen and which therefore, technically, doesn't even "exist," between the ages of four and fifteen. In effect, living with this mysterious mechanism feels like having your present self, and the past selves it embodies, haunted by a capricious and meanspirited ghost, unseen except for its footprints, which trips you even when you're watching where you're going, knocks glassware out of your hand, squeezes the urine out of your bladder before you reach the bathroom, and weights your whole body with a weariness no amount of rest can relieve. An alien invader must be at work. But of course it's not. It's your own body. That is, it's you.

This, for me, has been the most difficult aspect of adjusting to a chronic incurable degenerative disease: the fact that it has rammed my "self" straight back into the body I had been trained to believe it could, through highminded acts and aspirations, rise above. The Western tradition of distinguishing the body from the mind and/or the soul is so ancient as to have become part of our collective unconscious, if one is inclined to believe in such a noumenon, or at least to have become an unquestioned element in the social instruction we impose upon infants from birth, in much the same way we inculcate, without reflection, the gender distinctions "female" and "male." I *have* a body, you are likely to say if you talk about embodiment at all; you don't say, I *am* a body. A body is a separate entity possessable by the "I"; the "I" and the body aren't, as the copula would make them, grammatically indistinguishable.

To widen the rift between the self and the body, we treat our bodies as subordinates, inferior in moral status. Open association with them shames us. In fact, we treat our bodies with very much the same distance and ambivalence women have traditionally received from men in our culture. Sometimes this treatment is benevolent, even respectful, but all too often it is tainted by outright sadism. I think of the body-building regimens that have become popular in the last decade or so, with the complicated vacillations they reflect between self-worship and self-degradation: joggers and aerobic dancers and weightlifters all beating their bodies into shape. "No pain, no gain," the saying goes. "Feel the burn." Bodies get treated like wayward women who have to be shown who's boss, even if it means slapping them around a little. I'm not for a moment opposing rugged exercise here. I'm simply questioning the spirit in which it is often undertaken.

Since, as Hélène Cixous points out in her essay on women and writing, "Sorties,"* thought has always worked "through dual, hierarchical oppositions" (p. 64), the mind/body split cannot possibly be innocent. The utterance of an "I" immediately calls into being its opposite, the "not-I," Western discourse being unequipped to conceive "that which is neither 'I' nor 'not-I,'" "that which is both 'I' and 'not-I,'" or some other permutation which language doesn't permit me to speak. The "not-I" is, by definition, other. And we've never been too fond of the other. We prefer the same. We tend to ascribe to the other those qualities we prefer not to associate with our selves: it is the hidden, the dark, the secret, the shameful. Thus, when the "I" takes possession of the body, it makes the body into an other, direct object of a transitive verb, with all the other's repudiated and potentially dangerous qualities.

At the least, then, the body had best be viewed with suspicion.   10
And a woman's body is particularly suspect, since so much of it is in fact hidden, dark, secret, carried about on the inside where, even with the aid of a speculum, one can never perceive all of it in the plain light of day, a graspable whole. I, for one, have never understood why anyone would want to carry all that delicate stuff around on the outside. It would make you awfully anxious, I should think, put you constantly on the defensive, create a kind of siege mentality that viewed all other beings, even your own kind, as threats to be warded off with spears and guns and atomic missiles. And you'd never get to experience that inward dreaming that comes when your flesh surrounds all your treasures, holding them close, like a sturdy shuttered house. Be my personal skepticism as it may, however, as a cultural woman I bear just as much shame as any woman for my dark, enfolded secrets. Let the word for my external genitals tell the tale: my pudendum, from the Latin infinitive meaning "to be ashamed."

It's bad enough to carry your genitals like a sealed envelope bearing the cipher that, once unlocked, might loose the chaotic flood of female pleasure—*jouissance,* the French call it—upon the world-of-the-same. But I have an additional reason to feel shame for my body, less explicitly

---

* In *The Newly Born Woman,* translated by Betsy Wing (Minneapolis: University of Minnesota Press, 1986).

connected with its sexuality: it is a crippled body. Thus it is doubly other, not merely by the homo-sexual standards of patriarchal culture but by the standards of physical desirability erected for every body in our world. Men, who are by definition exonerated from shame in sexual terms (this doesn't mean that an individual man might not experience sexual shame, of course; remember that I'm talking in general about discourse, not folks), may—more likely must—experience bodily shame if they are crippled. I won't presume to speak about the details of their experience, however. I don't know enough. I'll just go on telling what it's like to be a crippled woman, trusting that, since we're fellow creatures who've been living together for some thousands of years now, much of my experience will resonate with theirs.

I was never a beautiful woman, and for that reason I've spent most of my life (together with probably at least 95 percent of the female population of the United States) suffering from the shame of falling short of an unattainable standard. The ideal woman of my generation was . . . perky, I think you'd say, rather than gorgeous. Blond hair pulled into a bouncing ponytail. Wide blue eyes, a turned-up nose with maybe a scattering of golden freckles across it, a small mouth with full lips over straight white teeth. Her breasts were large but well harnessed high on her chest; her tiny waist flared to hips just wide enough to give the crinolines under her circle skirt a starting outward push. In terms of personality, she was outgoing, even bubbly, not pensive or mysterious. Her milieu was the front fender of a white Corvette convertible, surrounded by teasing crewcuts, dressed in black flats, a sissy blouse, and the letter sweater of the Corvette owner. Needless to say, she never missed a prom.

Ten years or so later, when I first noticed the symptoms that would be diagnosed as MS, I was probably looking my best. Not beautiful still, but the ideal had shifted enough so that my flat chest and narrow hips gave me an elegantly attenuated shape, set off by a thick mass of long, straight, shining hair. I had terrific legs, long and shapely, revealed nearly to the pudendum by the fashionable miniskirts and hot pants I adopted with more enthusiasm than delicacy of taste. Not surprisingly, I suppose, during this time I involved myself in several pretty torrid love affairs.

The beginning of MS wasn't too bad. The first symptom, besides the pernicious fatigue that had begun to devour me, was "foot drop," the inability to raise my left foot at the ankle. As a consequence, I'd started to limp, but I could still wear high heels, and a bit of a limp might seem more intriguing than repulsive. After a few months, when the doctor suggested a cane, a crippled friend gave me quite an elegant wood-and-silver one, which I carried with a fair amount of panache. The real blow to my self-image came when I had to get a brace. As braces go, it's not bad: lightweight plastic molded to my foot and leg, fitting down into an ordinary shoe and secured around my calf by a Velcro strap. It reduces my limp and, more important, the danger of tripping and falling. But it meant the end of high heels. And it's ugly. Not as ugly as I think it is, I gather, but still pretty ugly. It signified for me, and perhaps still does, the permanence and irreversibility of my condition. The brace makes my MS concrete and forces me to wear it on the outside. As soon as I strapped the brace on, I climbed into trousers and stayed there (though not in the same trousers, of course). The idea of going around with my bare brace hanging out seemed almost as indecent as exposing my breasts. Not until 1984, soon after I won the Western States Book Award for poetry, did I put on a skirt short enough to reveal my plasticized leg. The connection between winning a writing award and baring my brace is not merely fortuitous; being affirmed as a writer really did embolden me. Since then, I've grown so accustomed to wearing skirts that I don't think about my brace any more than I think about my cane. I've incorporated them, I suppose: made them, in their necessity, insensate but fundamental parts of my body.

Meanwhile, I had to adjust to the most outward and visible sign   15
of all, a three-wheeled electric scooter called an Amigo. This lessens my fatigue and increases my range terrifically, but it also shouts out to the world, "Here is a woman who can't stand on her own two feet." At the same time, paradoxically, it renders me invisible, reducing me to the height of a seven-year-old, with a child's attendant low status. "Would she like smoking or nonsmoking?" the gate agent assigning me a seat asks the friend traveling with me. In crowds I see nothing but buttocks. I can tell you the name of every type of designer jeans ever sold. The wearers, eyes front, trip over me and fall across my handlebars into my lap. "Hey!" I want to shout to the lofty world. "Down here! There's a person down here!" But I'm not, by their standards, quite a person anymore.

My self-esteem diminishes further as age and illness strip from me the features that made me, for a brief while anyway, a good-looking, even sexy, young woman. No more long, bounding strides: I shuffle along with the timid gait I remember observing, with pity and impatience, in the little old ladies at Boston's Symphony Hall on Friday afternoons. No more lithe, girlish figure: my belly sags from the loss of muscle tone, which also creates all kinds of intestinal disruptions, hopelessly humiliating in a society in which excretory functions remain strictly unspeakable. No more sex, either, if society had its way. The sexuality of the disabled so repulses most people that you can hardly get a doctor, let alone a member of the general population, to consider the issues it raises. Cripples simply aren't supposed to Want It, much less Do It. Fortunately, I've got a husband with a strong libido and a weak sense of social propriety, or else I'd find myself perforce practicing a vow of chastity I never cared to take.

Afflicted by the general shame of having a body at all, and the specific shame of having one weakened and misshapen by disease, I ought not to be able to hold my head up in public. And yet I've gotten into the habit of holding my head up in public, sometimes under excruciating circumstances. Recently, for instance, I had to give a reading at the University of Arizona. Having smashed three of my front teeth in a fall onto the concrete floor of my screened porch, I was in the process of getting them crowned, and the temporary crowns flew out during dinner right before the reading. What to do? I wanted, of course, to rush home and hide till the dental office opened the next morning. But I couldn't very well break my word at this last moment. So, looking like Hansel and Gretel's witch, and lisping worse than the Wife of Bath, I got up on stage and read. Somehow, over the years, I've learned how to set shame aside and do what I have to do.

Here, I think, is where my "voice" comes in. Because, in spite of my demurral at the beginning, I do in fact cope with my disability at least some of the time. And I do so, I think, by speaking about it, and about the whole experience of being a body, specifically a female body, out loud, in a clear, level tone that drowns out the frantic whispers of my mother, my grandmothers, all the other trainers of wayward childish tongues: "Sssh! Sssh! Nice girls don't talk like that. Don't mention sweat. Don't mention menstrual blood. Don't ask what your grandfather does on his business trips. Don't laugh so loud. You sound like a loon. Keep your voice down. Don't tell. Don't tell. Don't tell." Speaking out loud is an antidote to shame. I want to distinguish clearly here between "shame," as I'm using the word, and "guilt" and "embarrassment," which, though equally painful, are not similarly poisonous. Guilt arises from performing a forbidden act or failing to perform a required one. In either case, the guilty person can, through reparation, erase the offense and start fresh. Embarrassment, less opprobrious though not necessarily less distressing, is generally caused by acting in a socially stupid or awkward way. When I trip and sprawl in public, when I wet myself, when my front teeth fly out, I feel horribly embarrassed, but, like the pain of childbirth, the sensation blurs and dissolves in time. If it didn't, every child would be an only child, and no one would set foot in public after the onset of puberty, when embarrassment erupts like a geyser and bathes one's whole life in its bitter stream. Shame may attach itself to guilt or embarrassment, complicating their resolution, but it is not the same emotion. I feel guilt or embarrassment for something I've done; shame, for who I am. I may stop doing bad or stupid things, but I can't stop being. How then can I help but be ashamed? Of the three conditions, this is the one that cracks and stifles my voice.

I can subvert its power, I've found, by acknowledging who I am, shame and all, and, in doing so, raising what was hidden, dark, secret about my life into the plain light of shared human experience. What we aren't permitted to utter holds us, each isolated from every other, in a kind of solipsistic thrall. Without any way to check our reality against anyone else's, we assume that our fears and shortcomings are ours alone. One of the strangest consequences of publishing a collection of personal essays called *Plaintext* has been the steady trickle of letters and telephone calls saying essentially, in a tone of unmistakable relief, "Oh, me too! Me too!" It's as though the part I thought was solo has turned out to be a chorus. But none of us was singing loud enough for the others to hear.

Singing loud enough demands a particular kind of voice, I think.   20 And I was wrong to suggest, at the beginning, that I've always had my voice. I have indeed always had *a* voice, but it wasn't *this* voice, the one with which I could call up and transform my hidden self from a naughty girl into a woman talking directly to others like herself. Recently, in the process of writing a new book, a memoir entitled *Remembering the Bone House,* I've had occasion to read some of my early writing, from college, high school, even junior high. It's not an experience I recommend to anyone susceptible to shame. Not that the writing was all that bad. I was surprised at how competent a lot of it was. Here was a writer who already knew precisely how the language worked. But the voice . . . oh, the voice was all wrong: maudlin, rhapsodic, breaking here and there into little shrieks, almost, you might say, hysterical. It was a voice that had shucked off its own body, its own homely life of Cheerios for breakfast and seventy pages of Chaucer to read before the exam on Tuesday and a planter's wart growing painfully on the ball of its foot, and reeled now wraithlike through the air, seeking incarnation only as the heroine who enacts her doomed love for the tall, dark, mysterious stranger. If it didn't get that part, it wouldn't play at all.

Among all these overheated and vaporous imaginings, I must have retained some shred of sense, because I stopped writing prose entirely, except for scholarly papers, for nearly twenty years. I even forgot, not exactly that I had written prose, but at least what kind of prose it was. So when I needed to take up the process again, I could start almost fresh, using the vocal range I'd gotten used to in years of asking the waiter in the Greek restaurant for an extra anchovy on my salad, congratulating the puppy on making a puddle outside rather than inside the patio door, pondering with my daughter the vagaries of female orgasm, saying goodbye to my husband, and hello, and goodbye, and hello. This new voice—thoughtful, affectionate, often amused—was essential because what I needed to write about when I returned to prose was an attempt I'd made not long before to kill myself, and suicide simply refuses to be spoken of authentically in high-flown romantic language. It's too ugly. Too shameful. Too strictly a bodily event. And, yes, too funny as well, though people are sometimes shocked to find humor shoved up against suicide. They don't like the incongruity. But let's face it, life (real life, I mean, not the edited-for-television version) is a cacophonous affair from start to finish. I might have wanted to portray my suicidal self as a languishing maiden, too exquisitely sensitive to sustain life's wounding pressures on her soul. (I didn't want to, as a matter of fact, but I might have.) The truth remained, regardless of my desires, that when my husband lugged me into the emergency room, my hair matted, my face swollen and gray, my nightgown streaked with blood and urine, I was no frail and tender spirit. I was a body, and one in a hell of a mess.

I "should" have kept quiet about that experience. I know the rules of polite discourse. I should have kept my shame, and the nearly lethal sense of isolation and alienation it brought, to myself. And I might have, except for something the psychiatrist in the emergency room had told my husband. "You might as well take her home," he said. "If she wants to kill herself, she'll do it no matter how many precautions we take. They always do." *They* always do. I was one of "them," whoever they were. I was, in this context anyway, not singular, not aberrant, but typical. I think it was this sense of commonality with others I didn't even know, a sense of being returned somehow, in spite of my appalling act, to the human family, that urged me to write that first essay, not merely speaking out but calling out, perhaps. "Here's the way I am," it said. "How about you?" And the answer came, as I've said: "Me too! Me too!"

This has been the kind of work I've continued to do: to scrutinize the details of my own experience and to report what I see, and what I think about what I see, as lucidly and accurately as possible. But because feminine experience has been immemorially devalued and repressed, I continue to find this task terrifying. "Every woman has known the torture of beginning to speak aloud," Cixous writes, "heart beating as if to break, occasionally falling into loss of language, ground and language slipping out from under her, because for woman speaking—even just opening her mouth—in public is something rash, a transgression" (p. 92).

The voice I summon up wants to crack, to whisper, to trail back into silence. "I'm sorry to have nothing more than this to say," it wants to apologize. "I shouldn't be taking up your time. I've never fought in a war, or even in a schoolyard free-for-all. I've never tried to see who could piss farthest up the barn wall. I've never even been to a whorehouse. All the important formative experiences have passed me by. I was raped once. I've borne two children. Milk trickling out of my breasts, blood trickling from between my legs. You don't want to hear about it. Sometimes I'm too scared to leave my house. Not scared *of* anything, just scared: mouth dry, bowels writhing. When the fear got really bad, they locked me up for six months, but that was years ago. I'm getting old now. Misshapen, too. I don't blame you if you can't get it up. No one could possibly desire a body like this. It's not your fault. It's mine. Forgive me. I didn't mean to start crying. I'm sorry . . . sorry . . . sorry. . . ."

An easy solace to the anxiety of speaking aloud: this slow subsi-   25
dence beneath the waves of shame, back into what Cixous calls "this body that has been worse than confiscated, a body replaced with a disturbing stranger, sick or dead, who so often is a bad influence, the cause and place of inhibitions. By censuring the body," she goes on, "breath and speech are censored at the same time" (p. 97). But I am not going back, not going under one more time. To do so would demonstrate a failure of nerve far worse than the depredations of MS have caused. Paradoxically, losing one sort of nerve has given me another. No one is going to take my breath away. No one is going to leave me speechless. To be silent is to comply with the standard of feminine grace. But my crippled body already violates all notions of feminine grace. What more have I got to lose? I've gone beyond shame. I'm shameless, you might say. You know, as in "shameless hussy"? A woman with her bare brace and her tongue hanging out.

I've "found" my voice, then, just where it ought to have been, in the body-warmed breath escaping my lungs and throat. Forced by the exigencies of physical disease to embrace my self in the flesh, I couldn't write bodiless prose. The voice is the creature of the body that produces it. I speak as a crippled woman. At the same time, in the utterance I redeem both "cripple" and "woman" from the shameful silences by which I have often felt surrounded, contained, set apart; I give myself permission to live openly among others, to reach out for them, stroke them with fingers and sighs. No body, no voice; no voice, no body. That's what I know in my bones.

LINES OF INQUIRY
"Carnal Acts"

Though the title of this piece is quite striking and suggestive, Mairs never uses it, or alludes to it, or even explains what she means by it in the essay itself. How do you feel about the fact that the title never turns up in the essay itself? When you first encountered the title, what did you think it meant? What do you think the title means now that you've had an opportunity to read the essay and think about its implications? Check the dictionary to find out the primary meanings of "carnal." In what sense(s) do you think this essay is about "acts" that might be thought of as "carnal"?

As Mairs asserts in paragraph 5, she considers her disability from MS and her voice as a writer to be not only "related," but "interdependent," indeed "intertwined." In what respect(s) does she see her disability and her voice as being related? Why does she speak of them as being not just related, but "interdependent" and "intertwined"? Why do you suppose that at the opening of paragraph 6 she defines the relationship as "this erotic connection between who I am and how I speak"? In what sense(s) might this connection be thought of as "erotic"?

In the middle of paragraph 20, Mairs characterizes the voice of her "early writing, from college, high school, even junior high" as being "maudlin, rhapsodic, breaking here and there into little shrieks, almost, you might say, hysterical." How would you characterize the voice you hear in this essay? Look at some of your own recent writing and consider how you would characterize your own written voice. What aspects of your style do you consider to be most influential in creating the voice that you hear in your writing? In what way(s), if any, do you think that your written voice might be related, interdependent, possibly even intertwined with the condition of your body?

MARGARET MEAD

1901 – 78

I have spent most of my life studying the lives of other peoples, faraway peoples, so that Americans might better understand themselves.

In this passage from her autobiography, *Blackberry Winter* (1972), Margaret Mead does not really do justice to the far-reaching scope of her efforts and influence. True enough, she did devote herself to "studying the lives of other peoples," particularly primitive peoples of the South Pacific, and she did use her studies of these other cultures to help Americans "better understand themselves" and their changing cultural situation. But her progressive and reformist instincts were not limited only to American self-understanding. Indeed, as a cultural anthropologist, she addressed virtually all the circumstances that impinge on the condition of human beings throughout the world—the family, the community, the environment, education, nutrition, religion, sex, race, technology, and war. She worked her good influence not only as a worldwide researcher and teacher, but also as a member of national and international commissions, as an officer of national and international organizations, and as an author and editor of forty-five books and several hundred articles. So it is hardly surprising that in 1969, *Time* magazine named her "Mother of the World."

Born in Philadelphia, she was the oldest of five children of an exceptionally well-educated family. Her father, a professor of economics who had "an enormous respect for facts," gave her a vivid "sense of the way theory and practice must be related." Her mother, who earned a doctorate for her research on Italian immigrant families, gave her an intense "concern for other people and the state of the world." But her paternal grandmother, a former schoolteacher and principal, who lived with the family, was "the most decisive influence" in her life. During most of her childhood years, Mead did not attend school, but was educated at home by her grandmother, who taught her early on "to observe the world around [her] and to note what [she] saw." From her resourceful and strong-willed grandmother, she ultimately gained a special respect not only for the capacities of women, but also for the importance of grandparents in the life of the family, especially in the development of children and adolescents.

After graduating from high school in 1918, she spent an unhappy freshman year at DePauw University, "confronted by the snobbery and cruelty of the sorority system at its worst." So, she transferred to Barnard, the women's college of Columbia University, and found there an intellectually stimulating group of friends. She found also that though not quite talented enough to succeed as a creative writer, she could "make a true contribution" in one of the social sciences. Her eventual choice of anthropology was sparked by an elective course in her senior year with Franz Boas, one of the leading figures in the early development of the field, and by a friendship that she developed with Ruth Benedict, the gifted disciple and teaching assistant of Boas. From Boas and Benedict, she discovered the unique value of studying primitive cultures not only in and of themselves, but also in relation to other cultures, and in connection with a variety of questions concerning the influence of culture on human development.

As a graduate student at Columbia, she developed so strong an interest in Polynesian culture that she convinced Boas to support her in doing fieldwork there, despite his fear of the risks she would run living and working in a primitive tropical village—"in a world that had not been constructed for a woman to work in." So in the late summer of 1925, after a brief vacation with her husband of two years' standing, she went off on her own to a tiny village in Samoa, to examine the influence of that primitive culture on the development of its young people, especially adolescent girls. The results of her nine-month study, which she wrote up in her first published book, *Coming of Age in Samoa* (1928), earned her a doctorate in 1929. It also brought her immediate nationwide attention for her vividly clear description of the culture and for her striking insights into the problems of American adolescents, whose situation she illuminated by detailing "the ways in which Samoan education, in its broadest sense, differs from our own."

Knowing as she did that "the last primitive peoples . . . would soon become changed beyond recovery," Mead devoted much of the next ten years to fieldwork in other primitive South Pacific cultures. During that time, she was twice divorced and twice remarried, both times to anthropologists whom she had met in the South Pacific. In the course of her pre-World War II research, she broadened the perspective of anthropology by taking into account the knowledge to be gained from other social sciences. She also developed important new methods for observing, recording, and analyzing specific aspects of primitive culture, which she described in several books, most notably *Growing Up in New Guinea* (1930) and *Sex and Temperament in Three Primitive*

Societies (1935). In these and other studies, she persistently used her insights into primitive culture to raise bold questions about aspects of modern American culture, particularly about the traditional roles of men and women, which she explored at greater length in *Male and Female: A Study of the Sexes in a Changing World* (1949).

During World War II, when firsthand cultural observation was virtually impossible, Mead, in collaboration with other social scientists, spearheaded the development of a new methodology for "the study of culture at a distance." Using this method to define the underlying character of various national groups, she and her colleagues provided strategically useful wartime and postwar information about the culture and behavior of Germany, Japan, and Russia. After the war, she returned to Manus, the New Guinea village that she had first studied in 1928, and in *New Lives for Old* (1956) she recorded the dramatic cultural changes that had taken place there during the wartime presence of Americans. During the sixties, she became increasingly concerned with the worldwide cultural changes that she perceived to be taking place as a result of young people having "grown up in a world their elders never knew," and she systematically examined those changes in *Culture and Commitment: A Study of the Generation Gap* (1970).

During most of her professional life, she not only served as a curator at the American Museum of Natural History in New York City, but she also taught at Columbia University as well as at more than forty other schools throughout the country. On top of everything else, she kept up a monthly column in *Redbook* magazine during the last seventeen years of her life. In her columns, as in her other writing, she spoke out on a broad range of issues, in a vividly clear, detailed, and humane style. Given her persistent desire to help others "better understand themselves," she knew that "what one says must be intelligible and bearable for those about whom one writes and, at the same time, for the members of one's own culture and for the people of all the other cultures in the world who may read what one has written."

A DAY IN SAMOA

The life of the day begins at dawn, or if the moon has shown until daylight, the shouts of the young men may be heard before dawn from the hillside. Uneasy in the night, populous with ghosts, they shout lustily to one another as they hasten with their work. As the dawn begins to fall among the soft brown roofs and the slender palm trees stand out against a colourless, gleaming sea, lovers slip home from trysts beneath the palm trees or in the shadow of beached canoes, that the light may find each sleeper in his appointed place. Cocks crow, negligently, and a shrill-voiced bird cries from the breadfruit trees. The insistent roar of the reef seems muted to an undertone for the sounds of a waking village. Babies cry, a few short wails before sleepy mothers give them the breast. Restless little children roll out of their sheets and wander drowsily down to the beach to freshen their faces in the sea. Boys, bent upon an early fishing, start collecting their tackle and go to rouse their more laggard companions. Fires are lit, here and there, the white smoke hardly visible against the paleness of the dawn. The whole village, sheeted and frowsy, stirs, rubs its eyes, and stumbles towards the beach. "Talofa!" "Talofa!" "Will the journey start to-day?" "Is it bonito fishing your lordship is going?" Girls stop to giggle over some young ne'er-do-well who escaped during the night from an angry father's pursuit and to venture a shrewd guess that the daughter knew more about his presence than she told. The boy who is taunted by another, who has succeeded him in his sweetheart's favour, grapples with his rival, his foot slipping in the wet sand. From the other end of the village comes a long drawn-out, piercing wail. A messenger has just brought word of the death of some relative in another village. Half-clad, unhurried women, with babies at their breasts, or astride their hips, pause in their tale of Losa's outraged departure from her father's house to the greater kindness in the home of her uncle, to wonder who is dead. Poor relatives whisper their requests to rich relatives, men make plans to set a fish trap together, a woman begs a bit of yellow dye from a kinswoman, and through the village sounds the rhythmic tattoo which calls the young men together. They gather from all parts of the village, digging sticks in hand, ready to start inland to the plantation. The older men set off upon their more lonely occupations, and each household, reassembled under its peaked roof, settles down to the routine of the morning. Little children, too hungry to wait for the late breakfast, beg lumps of cold taro which they munch greedily. Women carry piles of washing to the sea or to the spring at the far end of the village, or set off inland after weaving materials. The older girls go fishing on the reef, or perhaps set themselves to weaving a new set of Venetian blinds.

In the houses, where the pebbly floors have been swept bare with a stiff long-handled broom, the women great with child and the nursing mothers sit and gossip with one another. Old men sit apart, unceasingly twisting palm husk on their bare thighs and muttering old tales under their breath. The carpenters begin work on the new house, while the owner bustles about trying to keep them in a good humour. Families who will cook today are hard at work; the taro, yams and bananas have already been brought from inland; the children are scuttling back and forth, fetching sea water, or leaves to stuff the pig. As the sun rises higher in the sky, the shadows deepen under the thatched roofs, the sand is burning to the touch, the hibiscus flowers wilt on the hedges, and little children bid the smaller ones, "Come out of the sun." Those whose excursions have been short return to the village, the women with strings of crimson jelly fish, or baskets of shell fish, the men with cocoanuts, carried in baskets slung on a shoulder pole. The women and children eat their breakfasts, just hot from the oven, if this is cook day, and the young men work swiftly in the mid-day heat, preparing the noon feast for their elders.

It is high noon. The sand burns the feet of the little children, who leave their palm leaf balls and their pin-wheels of frangipani blossoms to wither in the sun, as they creep into the shade of the houses. The women who must go abroad carry great banana leaves as sun-shades or wind wet cloths about their heads. Lowering a few blinds against the slanting sun, all who are left in the village wrap their heads in sheets and go to sleep. Only a few adventurous children may slip away for a swim in the shadow of a high rock, some industrious woman continues with her weaving, or a close little group of women bend anxiously over a woman in labour. The village is dazzling and dead; any sound seems oddly loud and out of place. Words have to cut through the solid heat slowly. And then the sun gradually sinks over the sea.

A second time, the sleeping people stir, roused perhaps by the cry of "a boat," resounding through the village. The fishermen beach their canoes, weary and spent from the heat, in spite of the slaked lime on their heads, with which they have sought to cool their brains and redden their hair. The brightly coloured fishes are spread out on the floor, or piled in front of the houses until the women pour water over them to free them from taboo. Regretfully, the young fishermen separate out the "Taboo fish," which must be sent to the chief, or proudly they pack the little palm leaf baskets with offerings of fish to take to their sweethearts. Men come home from the bush, grimy and heavy laden, shouting as they come, greeted in a sonorous rising cadence by those who have remained at home. They gather in the guest house for their evening kava drinking. The soft clapping of hands, the high-pitched intoning of the talking chief who serves the kava echoes through the village. Girls gather flowers to weave into necklaces; children, lusty from their naps and bound to no particular task, play circular games in the half shade of the late afternoon. Finally the sun sets, in a flame which stretches from the mountain behind to the horizon on the sea, the last bather comes up from the beach, children straggle home, dark little figures etched against the sky; lights shine in the houses, and each household gathers for its evening meal. The suitor humbly presents his offering, the children have been summoned from their noisy play, perhaps there is an honoured guest who must be served first, after the soft, barbaric singing of Christian hymns and the brief and graceful evening prayer. In front of a house at the end of the village, a father cries out the birth of a son. In some family circles a face is missing, in others little runaways have found a haven! Again quiet settles upon the village, as first the head of the household, then the women and children, and last of all the patient boys, eat their supper.

After supper the old people and the little children are bundled off 5 to bed. If the young people have guests the front of the house is yielded to them. For day is the time for the councils of old men and the labours of youth, and night is the time for lighter things. Two kinsmen, or a chief and his councillor, sit and gossip over the day's events or make plans for the morrow. Outside a crier goes through the village announcing that the communal breadfruit pit will be opened in the morning, or that the village will make a great fish trap. If it is moonlight, groups of young men, women by twos and threes, wander through the village, and crowds of children hunt for land crabs or chase each other among the breadfruit trees. Half the village may go fishing by torchlight and the curving reef will gleam with wavering lights and echo with shouts of triumph or disappointment, teasing words or smothered cries of outraged modesty. Or a group of youths may dance for the pleasure of some visiting maiden. Many of those who have retired to sleep, drawn by the merry music, will wrap their sheets about them and set out to find the dancing. A white-clad, ghostly throng will gather in a circle about the gaily lit house, a circle from which every now and then a few will detach themselves and wander away among the trees. Sometimes sleep will not descend upon the village until long past midnight; then at last there is only the mellow thunder of the reef and the whisper of lovers, as the village rests until dawn.

LINES OF INQUIRY
"A Day in Samoa"

In keeping with her title, Mead describes the events that take place during a typical day in Samoa. What kinds of details does Mead emphasize in her description to help you *feel* what it might be like to live through a day in Samoa? How does she try to keep her description from turning into a mechanical summary of information? How does she describe a typical day so that it seems lively and interesting from beginning to end? How, in turn, does she organize her material overall, and in each of her five paragraphs, so as to provide an orderly description of the day?

As a cultural anthropologist, Mead tells about "a day in Samoa," because she aims to reveal the typical incidents and patterns of life in this tropical island culture. What incidents and patterns of life seem to stand out as being most distinctive and important in Samoan culture? What incidents and patterns of life did you find most surprising and unusual? In what respects does a day in Samoa seem most different from a day in your own culture? In what respects, if any, does a day there seem like a day in your own culture?

Imagine that a cultural anthropologist were to observe a typical day on your campus, or in your hometown. What incidents and patterns of life do you think such an observer would consider to be most distinctive and important in providing an accurate description of a typical day in your culture? What incidents or patterns of life do you suppose would strike an anthropologist as most surprising and unusual?

SCENES FROM MANUS LIFE

I

*T*o the Manus native the world is a greater platter, curving upwards on all sides, from his flat lagoon village where the pile houses stand like long-legged birds, placid and unstirred by the changing tides. One long edge of the platter is the mainland, rising from its fringe of mangrove swamps in fold after fold of steep, red clay. The mainland is approached across a half mile of lagoon, where the canoe leaves a path in the thicket of scum-coated sea growth, and is entered by slowly climbing the narrow tortuous beds of the small rivers which wind stagnant courses through the dark forbidding swamps. On the mainland live the Usiai, the men of the bush, whom the Manus people meet daily at set hours near the river mouths. Here the Manus fishermen, the landless rulers of the lagoons and reefs, bargain with the Usiai for taro, sago, yams, wood for housebuilding, betel nut for refreshments, logs for the hulls of their great outrigger canoes,—buying with their fish all the other necessities of life from the timid, spindly-legged bush people. Here also the people of Peri come to work the few sago patches which they long ago traded or stole from the Usiai; here the children come for a fresh water swim, and the women to gather firewood and draw water. The swamps are infested with sulky Usiai, hostile demons and fresh water monsters. Because of them the Manus dislike both the rivers and the land and take pains never to look into the still waters lest part of their soul stuff remain there.

At the other edge of the platter is the reef, beyond which lies the open sea and the islands of their own archipelago, where they sail to trade for cocoanuts, oil, carved wooden bowls and carved bedsteads. Beyond, still higher up the sea wall, lies Rabaul, the capital of the white man's government of the Territory of New Guinea, and far up on the rim of the world lies Sydney, the farthest point of their knowledge. Stretching away to right and left along the base of the platter lie other villages of the Manus people, standing in serried ranks in brown lagoons, and far away at each end of the platter lies the gentle slope of the high sea wall which canoes must climb if they would sail upon it.

Around the stout house piles, the tides run, now baring the floor of the lagoon until part of the village is left high and dry in the mud, now swelling with a soft insistence nearly to the floor slats of the houses. Here and there, around the village borders, are small abrupt islands, without level land, and unfit for cultivation. Here the women spread out leaves to dry for weaving, the children scramble precariously from rock to rock. Bleaching on the farther islands lie the white bones of the dead.

This small world of water dwellings, where men who are of one kin build their houses side by side, and scatter sago on the edge of the little island which they have inherited from their fathers, shelters not only the living but also the spirits of the dead. These live protected from the inclemency of wind and rain beneath the house thatch. Disowned by their descendants, they flutter restlessly about the borders of the small islets of coral rubble which stand in the centre of the village and do duty as village greens, places of meeting and festivity.

Within the village bounds, the children play. At low tide they 5 range in straggling groups about the shallows, spearing minnows or pelting each other with seaweed. When the water rises the smaller ones are driven up upon the little islets or into the houses, but the taller still wade about sailing toy boats, until the rising tide drives them into their small canoes to race gaily upon the surface of the water. Within the village the sharks of the open sea do not venture, nor are the children in danger from the crocodiles of the mainland. The paint with which their fathers decorate their faces for a voyage into the open seas as a protection against malicious spirits is not needed here. Naked, except for belts or armlets of beads or necklaces of dogs' teeth, they play all day at fishing, swimming, boating, mastering the arts upon which their landless fathers have built their secure position as the dominant people of the archipelago. Up the sides of the universe lie dangers, but here in the watery bottom, the children play, safe beneath the eyes of their spirit ancestors.

II

*I*n the centre of a long house are gathered a group of women. Two of them are cooking sago and cocoanut in shallow broken pieces of earthenware pottery, another is making beadwork. One old woman, a widow by her rope belt and black rubber-like breast bands, is shredding leaves and plaiting them into new grass skirts to add to those which hang in a long row from above her head. The thatched roof is black from the thick wood smoke, rising incessantly from the fires which are never allowed to go out. On swinging shelves over the fires, fish are smoking. A month-old baby lies on a leaf mat, several other small children play about, now nursing at their mothers' breasts, now crawling away, now returning to cry for more milk. It is dark and hot in the house. The only breath of air comes up through the slats in the floor and from trap door entrances at the far ends of the house. The women have laid aside their long drab cotton cloaks, which they must always wear in public to hide their faces from their male relatives-in-law. Beads of sweat glisten on their shiny shaven heads, sign of the wedded estate. Their grass skirts, which are only two tails worn one before and one behind, leaving the thighs bare, are wilted and work-bedraggled.

One woman starts to gather up her beads: "Come, Alupwa," she says to her three-year-old daughter.

"I don't want to." The fat little girl wriggles and pouts.

"Yes, come, I must go home now. I have stayed here long enough making bead-work. Come."

"I don't want to."   10

"Yes, come, father will be home from market and hungry after fishing all night."

"I won't." Alupwa purses her lips into ugly defiance.

"But come daughter of mine, we must go home now."

"I won't."

"If thou dost not come now, I must return for thee and what if in the   15
meantime, my sister-in-law, the wife of my husband's brother, should take the canoe? Thou wouldst cry and who would fetch thee home?"

"Father!" retorted the child impudently.

"Father will scold me if thou art not home. He likes it not when thou stayest for a long while with my kinsfolk," replies the mother, glancing up at the skull bowl, where the grandfather's skull hangs from the ceiling.

"Never mind!" The child jerks away from her mother's attempt to detain her and turning, slaps her mother roundly in the face. Every one laughs merrily.

Her mother's sister adds: "Alupwa, thou shouldst go home now with thy mother," whereupon the child slaps her also. The mother gives up the argument and begins working on her beads again, while Alupwa prances to the front of the house and returns with a small green fruit from which the older children make tops. This she begins to eat with a sly glance at her mother.

"Don't eat that, Alupwa, it is bad." Alupwa defiantly sets her   20
teeth into the rind. "Don't eat it. Dost not hear me?" Her mother takes hold of the child's hand and tries to wrest it away from her. Alupwa immediately begins to shriek furiously. The mother lets go of her hand with a hopeless shrug and the child puts the fruit to her lips again. But one of the older women intervenes.

"It is bad that she should eat that thing. It will make her sick."

"Well, then do thou take it from her. If I do she will hate me." The older woman grasps the wrist of the screaming child and wrenches the fruit from her.

"Daughter of Kea!" At the sound of her husband's voice, the mother springs to her feet, gathering up her cloak. The other women hastily seize their cloaks against their brother-in-law's possible entrance into the house. But Alupwa, tears forgotten, scampers out to the trap door, climbs down the ladder to the veranda, out along the outrigger poles to the canoe platform, and along the sharp gunwale to nestle happily against her father's leg. His hand plays affectionately with her hair as he scowls up at his wife who is sullenly descending the ladder.

III

*I*t is night in Peri. From the windowless houses with their barred entrances, no house fires shine out into the village. Now and then a shower of incandescent ashes falls into the sea, betraying that folk are still awake within the silent houses. Under a house, at the other end of the village, a dark figure is visible against the light cast by a fan-shaped torch of palm leaves. It is a man who is searing the hull of his water-worn canoe with fire. Out in the shallows near the pounding reef, can be seen the scattered bamboo torches of fishermen. A canoe passes down the central waterway, and stops, without a sound, under the verandah of a house. The occupant of the canoe stands, upright, leaning on his long punt, listening. From the interior of the house comes the sound of low sibilant, indrawn whistlings. The owner of the house is holding a séance and through the whistles of the spirit, who is in possession of the mouth of the medium, he communicates with the spirits of the dead. The whistling ceases, and a woman's voice exclaims: "Ah, Pokus is here and thou mayst question him."

The listener recognizes the name of Pokus, although the voice of   25 his mortal mother, the medium, is strained and disguised. His lips form the words: "Wife of Pokanas is conducting the séance."

The owner of the house speaks, quickly, in a voice of command: "Thou, Pokus, tell me. Why is my child sick? All day he is sick. Is it because I sold those pots which I should have kept for my daughter's dowry? Speak, thou, tell me."

Again the whistling. Then the woman's voice drowsily. "He says he does not know."

"Then let him go and ask Selanbelot, my father's brother, whose skull I have given room under my roof. Let him ask him why my child is sick."

Again whistling. Then the woman's voice, softly: "He says he will go and ask him."

From the next house comes the sharp angry wail of a child. The   30 floor creaks above the listener's head and the medium says in her ordinary voice, "Thou, Pokanas. Wake up. The child is crying. Dost thou sleep? Listen, the child is crying, go quickly."

A heavy man climbs down the ladder and perceiving the man in the canoe: "Who is it? Thou, Saot?"

"Take me quickly in thy canoe. The child has wakened and is frightened." As the young man punts the father across to his child, the whistling begins again.

IV

*A*gainst the piles at the back of his veranda a man lounges wearily. After a whole night's fishing and the morning at the market he is very sleepy. His hair is combed stiffly back from his head in a pompadour. Around his throat is a string of dogs' teeth. From his distended ear lobes dangle little notched rings of coconut shell, and through the pierced septum of his nose is passed a long slender crescent of pearl shell. His G-string of trade cloth is held fast by a woven belt, patterned in yellow and brown. On his upper arms are wide woven armlets coated with black, rubber-like gum; in these are stuck the pieces of the rib bones of his dead father. On the rough floor boards lies a small grass bag, from which projects a polished gourd on which intricate designs have been burned. In the mouth of the gourd is thrust a wooden spatula, the end carved to represent a crocodile eating a man. The carved head extends in staring unconcern from the crocodile's ornate jaws. The lounger stirs and draws from the bag the lime gourd, a cluster of bright green betel nuts and a bunch of pepper leaves. He puts a betel nut in his mouth, leisurely rolls a pepper leaf into a long funnel, bites off the end, and dipping the spatula into the powdered lime, adds a bit of lime to the mixture which he is already chewing vigorously.

The platform shakes as a canoe collides with one of the piles. The man begins hastily gathering up the pepper leaves and betel nut to hide them from a possible visitor. But he is not quick enough. A small head appears above the edge of the verandah and his six-year-old son, Popoli, climbs up dripping. The child's hair is long and strands of it are caked together with red mud; before they can be cut off, his father must give a large feast. The child has spied the treasure and hanging onto the edge of the verandah he whines out in the tone which all Manus natives use when begging betel nut: "A little betel?" The father throws him a nut. He tears the skin off with his teeth and bites it greedily.

"Another," the child's voice rises to a higher pitch. The father 35 throws him a second nut, which the child grasps firmly in his wet little fist, without acknowledgment. "Some pepper leaf?"

The father frowns. "I have very little, Popoli."

"Some pepper leaf." The father tears off a piece of a leaf and throws it to him.

The child scowls at the small piece. "This is too little. More! More! More!" His voice rises to a howl of rage.

"I have but a little, Popoli. I go not to market until the morrow. I go this afternoon to Patusi and I want some for my voyaging." The father resolutely begins to stuff the leaves farther into the bag, and as he does so, his knife slips out of the bag and falls through a crack into the sea.

"Wilt get it, Popoli?"

But the child only glares furiously. "No. I won't, thou, thou 40 stingy one, thou hidest thy pepper leaf from me." And the child dives off the verandah and swims away, leaving his father to climb down and rescue the knife himself.

V

On a shaded verandah a group of children are playing cat's cradle.

"Molung is going to die," remarks one little girl, looking up from her half-completed string figure.

"Who says so?" demands a small boy, leaning over to light his cigarette at a glowing bit of wood which lies on the floor.

"My mother. Molung has a snake in her belly."

The other children pay no attention to this announcement, but one four-year-old adds after a moment's reflection, "She had a baby in her belly." 45

"Yes, but the baby came out. It lives in the back of our house. My grandmother looks out for it." "If Molung dies, you can keep the baby," says the small boy. "Listen!"

From the house across the water a high piercing wail of many voices sounds, all crying in chorus, "My mother, my mother, my mother, oh, what can be the matter?"

"Is she dead yet?" asks the small boy, wriggling to the edge of the verandah. Nobody answers him. "Look." From the rear of the house of illness, a large canoe slides away, laden high with cooking pots. An old woman, gaunt of face, and with head uncovered in her haste, punts the canoe along the waterway.

"That's Ndrantche, the mother of Molung," remarks the first little girl.

"Look, there goes Ndrantche with a canoe full of pots," shout the children. 50

Two women come to the door of the house and look out. "Oho," says one. "She's getting the pots away so that when all the mourners come, the pots won't be broken."

"When will Molung die?" asks little Itong, and "Come for a swim," she adds, diving off the verandah without waiting for an answer.

LINES OF INQUIRY
"Scenes from Manus Life"

Mead's essay consists of five numbered segments, beginning with an introductory segment about the Manus people's lagoon village, followed by four segments each of which focuses on a separate place in the village. How do you account for her organization of segments II through V? For example, what is the effect of her beginning with the scene about Alupwa and her mother, then moving to the scene about the seance, then depicting the scene about Popoli and his father, then concluding with the scene of the children at play on a verandah? Try some different ways of arranging these four segments. How does each of your rearrangements affect the pacing, the buildup, the climax, and the overall significance of the piece?

After the introductory segment, each of the next four segments offers a vividly detailed picture, somewhat like a snapshot or vignette, of a particular scene or happening in and around the lagoon. What kinds of details, images, and scenes does Mead emphasize in this sequence of snapshots? What impression of Manus life do you get from each of these scenes individually? What impression do you get from them collectively? What more would you like to know about Manus life that Mead does not convey in this piece?

In her preceding essay, "A Day in Samoa," Mead depicts life in another tropical village culture. What similarities—and differences—do you note between the culture and the way of life in each of these villages? What similarities—and differences—do you notice in the structure, style, and detailing of each piece? What do you consider to be the benefits and limitations of the different methods that Mead uses to depict life in each of the villages?

ADOLESCENTS

At adolescence children begin to move toward an unknown future. The translucent walls of childhood no longer close them in, for suddenly they discover the wide gateways and the gates ready to swing open at a touch of the hand. The way is open for them to move away from the family, away from the familiar gardens and ponds and woods where they came to know the natural world, away from the fireside stories told them by their grandmothers, away from the brothers and sisters who will always be older and younger than they, and away from the playmates who shared their earliest games.

Up to adolescence the child lived in a circumscribed world. However individual and gifted, lively and intelligent he seemed to his parents, he was still a child for whom others had to plan, who had to be admonished, hedged about with protective rules, and kept within bounds. But with adolescence the old rules lose their meaning, and children begin to look beyond the old boundaries with new farseeing eyes. The adolescent boy gives up the dream of competition with his father in which he sometimes triumphed and sometimes despaired of ever accomplishing as much as his father had. Instead, he now looks forward to what he actually may become. The adolescent girl who once held her doll as her mother held her baby now looks forward in earnest, picturing the woman she will become and the living child she may rock in her arms. At adolescence, children stand at the gates, vividly seeing—and yet not seeing—the pathways of their own lives. For better or worse, each family has accomplished the task of caring for its sons and daughters, and they have learned, well or badly, the essential lessons their parents could teach them.

For the adolescent the paths leading out from the swinging gates are both entrancing and frightening. Even for the youth who has been an intrepid child traveler, the first journeys away from home may seem too difficult to accomplish. Girls who ranged the streams and mountains beside their brothers become shy and timid, their hands hot and cold, their smiles precarious. One day they want to dress as children, the next as women of the world. Each adolescent in his own way hesitates at the threshold. One sallies out and then, frightened by his own temerity, hurries back; but safely inside he looks out longingly, ready to be off again. Another hangs back, willing and unwilling, until at some sign known only to himself he moves ahead boldly, once and for all.

Everywhere in the world people mark the moment when a girl passes from childhood to physical maturity and the time when the boy's voice cracks and deepens and his beard, slight as it may be for some racial stocks, begins to grow. For the elders these changes signal the end of one kind of responsibility and the beginning of another more onerous one. Little children must be ceaselessly guarded and cared for, but adolescents, who still are in need of protection, are creatures whom it is almost impossible to protect. Their safety now depends on their earlier learning in childhood and on the way the other adolescents around them are growing toward adulthood.

In a society in which boys go out on dangerous raids, a mother   5 may make magic to protect her adolescent son's life, but any attempt to keep him at home when others go out will also endanger him. Where adolescent girls have a special house to which boys come with flutes to court them, a father may tremble for his daughter's safety and fear that the wooing may go wrong, but by interfering he will only create new difficulties. In every society adolescents take over the world's ways and parents must yield their assent.

Sometimes parents are permitted to lock up their daughters, and girls can only whisper to their lovers through barred windows. Sometimes boys are shut up in schools where older boys teach and harry them and men wearing the masks of frightening authority give them a last set of admonitions about manliness. Sometimes, at the beginning of adolescence, boys are sent as war scouts on dangerous missions and on long night errands through the enemy-infested bush. And sometimes each boy must go out alone and wait, fasting and vigilant, in the hope of winning the protection of a guardian spirit. Whatever the customary ways are for children to emerge into youth, these indicate the kinds of paths adolescents must take. Individual families can neither shield their children nor safely direct them along different paths. Individual parents who set themselves against custom become involved in a much greater struggle than those who watch with bated breath as their children set out on their first adventures.

The world over, adolescence is the period of greatest differentiation between boys and girls, not only in the anxieties felt by their parents but also in the dreams that animate them. Yet the boy and the girl, each in a different way, are equally preoccupied by the task of becoming, physically, a man and a woman—no longer someone's child, but potentially the parent of a child. Within their own bodies changes are taking place that they cannot ignore, and in the world outside they are confronted by alterations in treatment that match their visible growth and approaching maturity.

In some societies adolescents are left to realize change at their own pace. No one records their age. No one complains about the slow pace of this boy or the fast pace of that girl in growing up. Children are safe in their childhood as long as they are unready; and each chooses when to begin courtship and the first tentative search for a mate. One by one, the boys drift away from the boys' gang, take on the stance of young

men, and move toward the girls who also, one by one, grow into readiness to receive them. No one will hurry them.

But in most societies adults express old fears and new fears, old
hopes and new hopes as they urge on and hold back adolescent boys
and girls, guard them and leave them to fend for themselves. All the
girls may be betrothed early in childhood and sent to their prospective
husbands' homes before they reach puberty. In this the girls have no
choice. They must accept their new families as unquestioningly as they
accepted the families into which they were born. And the boys, given
their wives, have as little choice and yet are expected to be grateful to
those who have made this provision for their future.

At the other extreme are the adolescents who are trapped in the   10
neglect and poverty of great cities. Growing up in families whose kin-
ship ties are disrupted and whose links to a more stable past are broken,
they can expect no help from parents who do not understand their new
urban life. Unschooled, unprotected, and unguided, each adolescent is
left to follow the initiative of other adolescents. In a society that makes
no coherent plan for them and coming from families who do not know
what plans to make, they turn to radio and television, mass magazines
and comic strips in search of guidance. Children of the mass media,
they learn from headlines how other adolescents, equally at sea, dress
and talk, think and act. In a simpler society, adolescents share the channeled dreams of all young people, and their parents, whose adolescence
differed hardly at all from their own, can set up guideposts that will
lead a new generation safely into adulthood. In contrast, modern adolescents are exposed to the fads and extreme actions of hundreds of
thousands of young people who drift on a chartless course between a
narrower, traditional world and a world whose dimensions are still un-
clear. All they have to follow are the published statistics of how many
of them are now—this year, this month, this week—turning in questing
masses first in one direction and then in another. For these adolescents,
as in no other generation, the end of the journey in adulthood is unknown.

An unbridgeable gulf seems to separate the life of the five boys who
are growing up in a shepherd hamlet, each of whom will choose a wife
from among the six girls in that hamlet or the twenty girls living in
nearby villages, from the life of young people who crowd, ten thousand strong, to welcome a television star at an airport. Yet the tasks
confronting the shepherd boy are no different from those facing the
teen-age city boy who moves so lightly to the rhythm set last week by
a new hit record. For now, at adolescence, both boys must give up the
dependence of childhood and move toward the autonomy and interdependence of adulthood.

Wherever a boy grows up, he must learn to leave home without
fear, leaving behind him the old battles of childhood, and learn to return home from school or work or an assignment in a far city or over-

seas ready to treat his parents differently. Where he is permitted choice, he must be prepared to make a choice. Where no choice is open to him, the decision to go another way means that he must be prepared to blaze a new and lonely path. If he succeeds, he may open that path to others. If he fails, others coming after him may have a harder time.

For the young boy who rebels against the choices that have been made for him—refuses the wife who has been chosen in his name, deserts the craft to which he has been apprenticed, leaves the school or college to which he has been sent—the battle is a lonely one. At the moment of rebellion the battle is joined not with his whole society—for if it is, he becomes a criminal—but with his own parents whose demands he cannot meet. Such a battle generates an almost unbearable tension, as his old childish love and dependence must be opposed both to a desire for independence which his parents approve and to a course which they disapprove. In some societies, it is not only the rebel who suffers, but also the boy struggling to meet the demands made on him—to show bravery in battle, seek a vision on a mountainside, endure a period of poverty and self-discipline in a monastery, work as an ill-fed and much-abused apprentice, last out the hard grind before he can enter a profession, practice every day the difficult skills that will make him an athlete, a mountain guide, or a pilot. If he fails, or even thinks he has failed, he has been taught to feel he will betray his parents, and he may be tempted to revenge himself on them by killing the child they failed to rear in their image of what their child should be. In still other societies grandfathers stand behind the springing young boys, guarding their inexperience. But elsewhere there are no such safeguards. Fathers relinquish their authority early, and boys of thirteen or fourteen, long before they can break away in rebellion, are pushed into manhood and have the cares and responsibilities of manhood thrust on their shoulders.

The problems girls face, the world over, are not those that confront their brothers, but very different ones. For the adolescent girl may still feel like a child or she may still long to roam the hills with her brothers as she did when she was a child, but now, unlike a child, she can conceive. And long before she has the discretion or the judgment to choose among suitors or to weigh the temptation of the moment against her hopes for the future, her body, outstripping her imagination, or her imagination, outstripping her physical readiness, may involve her in an irrevocable act. The boy who breaks his bow string, turns tail in battle, hesitates before an order, or fails in school can still retrieve his losses by stringing the bow better, returning to school, learning to obey and to command. But for the girl herself and for society, the change is irreversible. It does not matter whether the child she has conceived is lost immediately after conception, whether it is born in wedlock or out of wedlock, whether it lives or dies. The event cannot be set aside. One more child, if it lives, will have started life in one way and not in another, and the girl herself can go on, but she cannot begin afresh.

Because parenthood for the girl and parenthood for the boy are fundamentally different, it has taken a very long time to develop contexts in which girls can be allowed to become persons before they become mothers. And because, in the end, the education of boys depends partly on the mothers who rear them, and the sisters with whom they play and compete or whom they cherish and protect, it also took a long time before boys were permitted to become full persons. Throughout human history, most peoples have been intent, most of the time, on turning most young boys and girls into parents whose primary task it has been to rear children who, in their turn, would become parents also. With rare exceptions, girls have always been reared to become parents, and persons only incidentally, and boys, too, have been reared to become parents, and persons only if they have belonged to some specially privileged elite.

But very slowly the burden has been lifting. Each small savage society had to lay on every able member the responsibility of reproduction first and then for continual, unremitting daily concern for food and for protection against cold and danger. The burden was lifted first from the sons of those of high rank and, occasionally, the youth of high promise, and later from a few daughters who shared, almost accidentally, in their brothers' privileges. Gradually it has been lifted also from larger and larger numbers of young people in those countries that have conquered the relentless problems of hunger and cold. In the past, most boys, as soon as they left childhood, had no choice but to hunt, herd sheep, fish, toil in the fields, or work at a craft, or, in more recent times, work as unskilled laborers who never earned more than was enough to buy tomorrow's food and pay next week's rent. But in modern societies, it has been possible to keep an ever larger number of adolescents in school and to give them an opportunity to think further than their fathers thought, explore the life of other periods and other cultures, and to become both civilized men, inheritors of the past, and modern men, ready to make a different future. And as our capacity to free more adolescents has increased, our willingness also has grown to permit them to become what they have the potentiality to be as persons.

This change has coincided with a tremendous increase in the world's population. In the past, men struggled desperately to preserve the small tribes or nations to which they owed their sense of identity. Today we are engaged in a common enterprise in the attempt to preserve mankind, as all men are endangered by the weapons of destruction they have now—and will always have—the knowledge to build. In the past people counted the children who were born, wept for the many who died, and wondered whether the living were enough to do the work, guard the group from danger, and reproduce the group in the next generation. Now we know we must stem the uncontrolled growth of the earth's population. When almost all children live, fewer children need be born. When almost no mothers die, fewer women need bear children. When as many children grow up in small families as once survived only in very large families, so many of whose children died, men and women need not marry so early or devote so large a part of their lives to parenthood. Now, when our task is to balance the world's population at a level at which every child who is born anywhere, in the most remote valley and on the highest plateau, will have an opportunity to become a person, we do not need to organize the world in such a way that the relentless, unremitting needs of parenthood and poverty weigh down adolescents as soon as they leave childhood behind, making them old before their time. Our new command of nature, which makes it possible for the first time in human history to organize a world without war, save the children who are born, and feed and clothe every child, also allows us to offer to all adolescents, not only the chosen and privileged few, a chance to grow further.

Man's history has been one of longer and longer periods of growth. In the very distant past, before men as we know them had evolved, the period of growth must have been even shorter and boys must have been ready for the tasks of procreation and parenthood very young. Later, when members of our own species were living under extremely primitive conditions, boys had learned all they needed to know in order to survive by the time they were six or seven years of age, but they matured more slowly. At adolescence they were ready to assume the responsibilities of manhood, and so it has remained for primitive men, for peasants, and for the poor in industrial cities. The demands made on them permitted them to grow no more. Even when the years of education lengthened a little in the more fortunate modern countries, the idea survived that growth stopped somewhere in mid-adolescence. There was, as there still is, a general expectation that most young people would give up learning and growing when they left school. Set in a mold, they were ready to work day in and day out, because otherwise they and their children would not eat. They stepped from childhood to adolescence and from early adolescence immediately into maturity, and then aged early.

But in the last ten thousand years—and possibly for a longer time—some societies began to benefit from the accumulated knowledge that made it possible for men to plan ahead—to raise more food than they immediately needed, to store food, and to feed a larger number of people—so that some men were freed to study, to think, and to build a larger tradition. In time, in some societies, men watched the stars and measured the phases of the sun and the moon, designed great buildings, carved, painted, created systems of notation, built cities and organized nations, and dreamed of including all men, not merely the members of their own tribe, their own city, or their own race, within one system of values, cherishing common goals.

With leisure and the freedom given to some young men to pursue   20
the new arts and sciences of civilization, a new human capacity was discovered: the idealism of adolescence. Among a primitive people, as each new generation lives much the same life the parent generation also lived, adolescents do not reveal their capacity to dream soaring dreams, make mighty plans, leap in thought to new formulations of the relations of mind and matter, and visualize the place of man on earth, in the solar system, in the galaxy, in an expanding universe. Until men lived in the kinds of societies in which leisure was a possibility, and a few adolescents had time to grow further away from childhood, youth was untouched by idealism. Indeed, in many societies, young people were more cowed, more submissive, and less rebellious than their aging and less responsible elders.

With the development of civilization, as knowledge accumulated and systems of writing made it possible to preserve and communicate to others, as yet unborn, what was known, new processes of development were also revealed in adolescents. Moving away from childhood, boys and young men were no longer exposed only to the drudgery and the small excitements of the daily round. Some of them, at least, heard and saw and read about the things earlier great men had dreamed of and sung of, written about, and built. The spacious vision of the exceptional man did not die with him, but became the property of young men who came after him. In each generation there were young men, and occasionally young women, who could match the unsatisfactory present against the prophecies of a better future or the dream of a golden past, and these young people, in their turn, were led to prophesy, strike out in bold adventure, break the bonds of tradition, discover new fields, and plunge forward into some new understanding of the universe and man.

In any growing civilization, some young men have been allowed to live out and prolong their adolescence, free from the pressure to marry and from the necessity of working for their bread. This leisure not only has given them time to grow, but also time for friendship before parenthood. It is essentially in the continuation of companionship outside the family, in relationships other than those concerned with courtship, marriage, and parenthood, that adolescents can seek and find the strength and the vision to carry one step farther the civilization into which they were born and of which they are the heirs. The urgent desire, everywhere in the world, to give children more schooling and more time to learn has at its base a very profound need. The rationale of educational plans in the contemporary world is the necessity of having a more literate population, able to do the work of a more literate and complicated society. But the underlying need goes far beyond this. Giving children time to prolong their growing is intrinsic to the very creation of that literate and complicated society. Without vision the people perish, and the power of seeing visions must be fostered in adolescents if we are to have the visionaries the world needs.

For many centuries civilizations have struggled with the problem of how to give men—and sometimes women—the freedom in which inspiration, knowledge, and art can flower. One solution has been to create a dichotomy in which the life of sex and parenthood has been set apart from a life of celibacy, asceticism, and thought or prayer. In a society that accepted this solution, the parent was never so specialized or developed a person as were those who carried on the spiritual, intellectual, and artistic work of the world. Moreover, every child was presented with two conflicting life paths, as he had to choose between the pursuit of knowledge, on the one hand, and the life of the family, on the other. Only in the next generation, if he chose to have children, might a son realize his other dreams and, turning away from parenthood, devote himself entirely to religion, the arts, scholarship, or science. In other societies, all boys have lived for a period apart from the secular world, as a way of giving them access to traditional knowledge and insight into the spiritual resources of a great religion, as one aspect of their on-going lives. In still other societies, childhood and old age were equated in the sense that the intensive learning of childhood, practiced throughout life, came to flower only when men retired from everyday responsibilities and could devote themselves wholly to thought, poetry, painting, and music. But all these have been essentially conservative solutions, the solutions worked out by societies among whom only a few were the chosen carriers of a great tradition, and only a few had the freedom to become creative individuals.

In most modern societies this selection and segregation of the few from the many is breaking down. Those who dedicate themselves wholly to important work now live in the world. Even though they may not marry, they do not live a life apart. However, where once the population was divided into the many who bore and reared children and the few who had time all their lives to think and to grow, there is now developing in many parts of the modern world a new dichotomy based on sex. For increasingly, adolescent boys are being educated, while girls, like the vast majority of men and women in medieval Europe who chose parenthood, are asked to set aside their dreams of what they might become in favor of immediate marriage and parenthood.

In creating this new dichotomy we resemble the primitive peoples   25
who did not understand paternity. For we do not take into account fatherhood or realize that in establishing a kind of society in which girls must become mothers as adolescents, before they have had time to become individuals, we also are forcing boys to become fathers before

they have become individuals. In our civilization we are the beneficiaries of poor societies in which only a few had leisure, but we are not yet
fully conscious of the power our new affluence gives us to make all
men the beneficiaries of that past and to open the way for every adolescent to grow slowly through a long youth into mature individuality.

All around the world, youth is stirring. Often that stirring is the
blind movement of disorganized mobs. There is a restlessness that is
widely expressed in demands for privilege, for power, for change, for
marriage as a right rather than as a responsibility, and for parenthood
as a pleasure rather than as a vocation. That blind movement and those
demands express the deep contradictions characteristic of our time—a
time of transition.

Perhaps even more important than the revolution in the lives of
peoples who for centuries have been subjected to tyranny and alien authority is the surging revolution of young people who are seeking a
new place in a new kind of world. The more rapidly the world changes,
the greater is the contrast between older people, who have had to learn
so many new things during their lifetime, and younger people, who
take the same things for granted. Young people who all their lives have
been familiar with cars and how they are driven, who know how a jet
plane is operated and how a computer is built, have an appearance of
startling precocity as they move among adults for whom this knowledge and these skills are still new and strange. How can parents feel
that their adolescent children are, in fact, adolescents, when these children know so much that they, the parents, learned only yesterday and
with great difficulty? The authority in adult voices flickers, hesitates,
grows shrill, and young people, sensing adult uncertainty and weakness, press harder against the barriers that hold them back from full
participation in life. From their viewpoint they are asking for full citizenship and the right to be men and women at once, because they are
already more skilled and knowledgeable than their parents. But the fulfillment of their demands would have the effect of putting the clock
back, rather than moving it forward, and of reinstating a kind of world
in which all young people were set to work at sober, confining tasks as
soon as they were able to undertake them. At the threshold of a new
age, it is as if a generation was turning in blind flight from its
vast possibilities.

For all over the world a new age is struggling to be born, an age in
which all children can grow up in families and all adolescents can have
time to become individuals who are able to meet the demands of a fully
adult life. In this new age, in which adolescents need not be forced to
become mothers and fathers and grow old before their time, we can set
a new value on adolescence of the mind and the spirit. In a society in
which no one will be forced into premature adulthood, many people
will remain adolescents all their lives, following a vision that is not yet

clear, puzzling over a theory that is not yet fully formulated, attempting to create in sound or in color, in meditation or in prayer, in the laboratory or in the library, in the halls of government or in the councils of the nations something as yet unknown.

For long ages the prospect opening out from childhood closed in almost at once. Only a few were free long enough to glimpse a wider horizon, a visionary gleam. With the knowledge gained through their labor and their imagination, still more could be set free. When childhood stretched only a few years ahead, early man was set free to learn a little; when adolescence was prolonged, the men of earlier civilizations were able to leap ahead. In the future we may hope to meet the magnificent responsibilities of our knowledge through the visions of boys and girls who will remain all their lives, not only as adolescents but as adults, open to the widest prospects, "moving about in worlds not realized."

LINES OF INQUIRY
"Adolescents"

Mead opens this essay with a very specific image that depicts adolescents suddenly discovering "the wide gateways and the gates ready to swing open at a touch of the hand." What does this opening image imply about Mead's idea of adolescence? How does she develop this image in the remainder of the opening paragraph and in the next two paragraphs? What additional implications does the image carry as Mead elaborates on it over the course of these paragraphs? In what ways does the image relate to Mead's subsequent discussion of adolescence? How does it relate to her concluding discussion of the topic?

Notice that Mead titles her essay "Adolescents" rather than "Adolescence." What do you make of this title? What do you infer about her idea of adolescence from the fact that her examples of adolescent experience reflect so many different cultures and periods of history? Near the end of her essay, Mead hopefully envisions "a new age," in which "many people will remain adolescents all their lives." What does this vision imply about Mead's idea of adolescence?

How does Mead's idea of adolescence compare with the behavior of the adolescents whom Wolfe portrays in "The Pump House Gang"? How does her idea of adolescence compare with your own experience of it? What do you think is the essence of adolescence? What distinguishes adolescents from children and adults?

WARFARE: AN INVENTION—
NOT A BIOLOGICAL NECESSITY

Is war a biological neces-
sity, a sociological inevitability or just a bad invention? Those who argue for the first view endow man with such pugnacious instincts that
some outlet in aggressive behavior is necessary if man is to reach full
human stature. It was this point of view which lay back of William
James's famous essay, "The Moral Equivalent of War," in which he
tried to retain the warlike virtues and channel them in new directions.
A similar point of view has lain back of the Soviet Union's attempt to
make competition between groups rather than between individuals. A
basic, competitive, aggressive, warring human nature is assumed, and
those who wish to outlaw war or outlaw competitiveness merely try to
find new and less socially destructive ways in which these biologically
given aspects of man's nature can find expression. Then there are those
who take the second view: warfare is the inevitable concomitant of the
development of the state, the struggle for land and natural resources of
class societies springing, not from the nature of man, but from the nature of history. War is nevertheless inevitable unless we change our
social system and outlaw classes, the struggle for power, and possessions; and in the event of our success warfare would disappear, as a
symptom vanishes when the disease is cured.

One may hold a compromise position between these two extremes;
one may claim that all aggression springs from the frustration of man's
biologically determined drives and that, since all forms of culture are
frustrating, it is certain each new generation will be aggressive and the
aggression will find its natural and inevitable expression in race war,
class war, nationalistic war, and so on.

All three positions are very popular today among those who think
seriously about the problems of war and its possible prevention, but I
wish to urge another point of view, less defeatist perhaps than the first
and third, and more accurate than the second: that is, that warfare, by
which I mean organized conflict between two groups *as groups,* in which
each group puts an army (even if the army is only fifteen Pygmies) into
the field to fight and kill, if possible, some of the members of the army
of the other group—that warfare of this sort is an invention like any
other of the inventions in terms of which we order our lives, such as
writing, marriage, cooking our food instead of eating it raw, trial by
jury, or burial of the dead, and so on. Some of this list any one will
grant are inventions: trial by jury is confined to very limited portions

of the globe; we know that there are tribes that do not bury their dead but instead expose or cremate them; and we know that only part of the human race has had a knowledge of writing as its cultural inheritance. But, whenever a way of doing things is found universally, such as the use of fire or the practice of some form of marriage, we tend to think at once that it is not an invention at all but an attribute of humanity itself. And yet even such universals as marriage and the use of fire are inventions like the rest, very basic ones, inventions which were perhaps necessary if human history was to take the turn it has taken, but nevertheless inventions. At some point in his social development man was undoubtedly without the institution of marriage or the knowledge of the use of fire.

The case for warfare is much clearer because there are peoples even today who have no warfare. Of these the Eskimo are perhaps the most conspicuous example, but the Lepchas of Sikkim are an equally good one. Neither of these peoples understands war, not even defensive warfare. The idea of warfare is lacking, and this idea is as essential to carrying on war as an alphabet or a syllabary is to writing. But whereas the Lepchas are a gentle, unquarrelsome people, and the advocates of other points of view might argue that they are not full human beings or that they had never been frustrated and so had no aggression to expend in warfare, the Eskimo case gives no such possibility of interpretation. The Eskimo are not a mild and meek people; many of them are turbulent and troublesome. Fights, theft of wives, murder, cannibalism occur among them—all outbursts of passionate men goaded by desire or intolerable circumstance. Here are men faced with hunger, men faced with loss of their wives, men faced with the threat of extermination by other men, and here are orphan children, growing up miserably with no one to care for them, mocked and neglected by those about them. The personality necessary for war, the circumstances necessary to goad men to desperation are present, but there is no war. When a traveling Eskimo entered a settlement he might have to fight the strongest man in the settlement to establish his position among them, but this was a test of strength and bravery, not war. The idea of warfare, of one *group* organizing against another *group* to maim and wound and kill them, was absent. And without that idea passions might rage but there was no war.

But, it may be argued, isn't this because the Eskimo have such a low and undeveloped form of social organization? They own no land, they move from place to place, camping, it is true, season after season on the same site, but this is not something to fight for as the modern nations of the world fight for land and raw materials. They have no permanent possessions that can be looted, no towns that can be burned. They have no social classes to produce stress and strains within the society which might force it to go to war outside. Doesn't the absence of war among the Eskimo, while disproving the biological necessity of

5

war, just go to confirm the point that it is the state of development of the society which accounts for war, and nothing else?

We find the answer among the Pygmy peoples of the Andaman Islands in the Bay of Bengal. The Andamans also represent an exceedingly low level of society: they are a hunting and food-gathering people; they live in tiny hordes without any class stratification; their houses are simpler than the snow houses of the Eskimo. But they knew about warfare. The army might contain only fifteen determined pygmies marching in a straight line, but it was the real thing none the less. Tiny army met tiny army in open battle, blows were exchanged, casualties suffered, and the state of warfare could only be concluded by a peacemaking ceremony.

Similarly, among the Australian aborigines, who built no permanent dwellings but wandered from water hole to water hole over their almost desert country, warfare—and rules of "international law"—were highly developed. The student of social evolution will seek in vain for his obvious causes of war, struggle for lands, struggle for power of one group over another, expansion of population, need to divert the minds of a populace restive under tyranny, or even the ambition of a successful leader to enhance his own prestige. All are absent, but warfare as a practice remained, and men engaged in it and killed one another in the course of a war because killing is what is done in wars.

From instances like these it becomes apparent that an inquiry into the causes of war misses the fundamental point as completely as does an insistence upon the biological necessity of war. If a people have an idea of going to war and the idea that war is the way in which certain situations, defined within their society, are to be handled, they will sometimes go to war. If they are a mild and unaggressive people, like the Pueblo Indians, they may limit themselves to defensive warfare; but they will be forced to think in terms of war because there are peoples near them who have warfare as a pattern, and offensive, raiding, pillaging warfare at that. When the pattern of warfare is known, people like the Pueblo Indians will defend themselves, taking advantage of their natural defenses, the *mesa* village site, and people like the Lepchas, having no natural defenses and no idea of warfare, will merely submit to the invader. But the essential point remains the same. There is a way of behaving which is known to a given people and labeled as an appropriate form of behavior. A bold and warlike people like the Sioux or the Maori may label warfare as desirable as well as possible; a mild people like the Pueblo Indians may label warfare as undesirable; but to the minds of both peoples the possibility of warfare is present. Their thoughts, their hopes, their plans are oriented about this idea, that warfare may be selected as the way to meet some situation.

So simple peoples and civilized peoples, mild peoples and violent, assertive peoples, will all go to war if they have the invention, just as those peoples who have the custom of dueling will have duels and peoples who have the pattern of vendetta will indulge in vendetta. And, conversely, peoples who do not know of dueling will not fight duels, even though their wives are seduced and their daughters ravished; they may on occasion commit murder but they will not fight duels. Cultures which lack the idea of the vendetta will not meet every quarrel in this way. A people can use only the forms it has. So the Balinese have their special way of dealing with a quarrel between two individuals; if the two feel that the causes of quarrel are heavy they may go and register their quarrel in the temple before the gods, and, making offerings, they may swear never to have anything to do with each other again. Under the Dutch government they registered such mutual "not-speaking" with the Dutch government officials. But in other societies, although individuals might feel as full of animosity and as unwilling to have any further contact as do the Balinese, they cannot register their quarrel with the gods and go on quietly about their business because registering quarrels with the gods is not an invention of which they know.

Yet, if it be granted that warfare is after all an invention, it may   10
nevertheless be an invention that lends itself to certain types of personality, to the exigent needs of autocrats, to the expansionist desires of crowded peoples, to the desire for plunder and rape and loot which is engendered by a dull and frustrating life. What, then, can we say of this congruence between warfare and its uses? If it is a form which fits so well, is not this congruence the essential point? But even here the primitive material causes us to wonder, because there are tribes who go to war merely for glory, having no quarrel with the enemy, suffering from no tyrant within their boundaries, anxious neither for land nor loot nor women, but merely anxious to win prestige which within that tribe has been declared obtainable only by war and without which no young man can hope to win his sweetheart's smile of approval. But if, as was the case with the Bush Negroes of Dutch Guiana, it is artistic ability which is necessary to win a girl's approval, the same young man would have to be carving rather than going out on a war party.

In many parts of the world, war is a game in which the individual can win counters—counters which bring him prestige in the eyes of his own sex or of the opposite sex; he plays for these counters as he might, in our society, strive for a tennis championship. Warfare is a frame for such prestige-seeking merely because it calls for the display of certain skills and certain virtues; all of these skills—riding straight, shooting straight, dodging the missiles of the enemy and sending one's own straight to the mark—can be equally well exercised in some other framework and, equally, the virtues—endurance, bravery, loyalty, steadfastness—can be displayed in other contexts. The tie-up between proving oneself a man and proving this by a success in organized killing is due to a definition which many societies have made of manliness. And often, even in those societies which counted success in warfare a proof of human worth, strange turns were given to the idea, as when the Plains Indians gave their highest awards to the man who touched a live enemy rather than to the man who brought in a scalp—from a dead enemy—because killing a man was less risky. Warfare is just an invention known to the majority of human societies by which they permit their young men either to accumulate prestige or avenge their honor or acquire loot or wives or slaves or sago lands or cattle or appease the blood lust of their gods or the restless souls of the recently dead. It is just an invention, older and more widespread than the jury system, but none the less an invention.

But, once we have said this, have we said anything at all? Despite a few instances, dear to the hearts of controversialists, of the loss of the useful arts, once an invention is made which proves congruent with human needs or social forms, it tends to persist. Grant that war is an invention, that it is not a biological necessity nor the outcome of certain special types of social forms, still, once the invention is made, what are we to do about it? The Indian who had been subsisting on the buffalo for generations because with his primitive weapons he could slaughter only a limited number of buffalo did not return to his primitive weapons when he saw that the white man's more efficient weapons were exterminating the buffalo. A desire for the white man's cloth may mortgage the South Sea Islander to the white man's plantation, but he does not return to making bark cloth, which would have left him free. Once an invention is known and accepted, men do not easily relinquish it. The skilled workers may smash the first steam looms which they feel are to be their undoing, but they accept them in the end, and no movement which has insisted upon the mere abandonment of usable inventions has ever had much success. Warfare is here, as part of our thought; the deeds of warriors are immortalized in the words of our poets; the toys of our children are modeled upon the weapons of the soldier; the frame of reference within which our statesmen and our diplomats work always contains war. If we know that it is not inevitable, that it is due to historical accident that warfare is one of the ways in which we think of behaving, are we given any hope by that? What hope is there of persuading nations to abandon war, nations so thoroughly imbued with the idea that resort to war is, if not actually desirable and noble, at least inevitable whenever certain defined circumstances arise?

In answer to this question I think we might turn to the history of other social inventions, inventions which must once have seemed as firmly entrenched as warfare. Take the methods of trial which preceded the jury system: ordeal and trial by combat. Unfair, capricious, alien as they are to our feeling today, they were once the only methods open to individuals accused of some offense. The invention of trial by jury gradually replaced these methods until only witches, and finally not even witches, had to resort to the ordeal. And for a long time the jury system seemed the one best and finest method of settling legal disputes, but today new inventions, trial before judges only or before commissions, are replacing the jury system. In each case the old method was replaced by a new social invention; the ordeal did not go out because people thought it unjust or wrong, it went out because a method more congruent with the institutions and feelings of the period was invented. And, if we despair over the way in which war seems such an ingrained habit of most of the human race, we can take comfort from the fact that a poor invention will usually give place to a better invention.

For this, two conditions at least are necessary. The people must recognize the defects of the old invention, and some one must make a new one. Propaganda against warfare, documentation of its terrible cost in human suffering and social waste, these prepare the ground by teaching people to feel that warfare is a defective social institution. There is further needed a belief that social invention is possible and the invention of new methods which will render warfare as out-of-date as the tractor is making the plow, or the motor car the horse and buggy. A form of behavior becomes out-of-date only when something else takes its place, and in order to invent forms of behavior which will make war obsolete, it is a first requirement to believe that an invention is possible.

LINES OF INQUIRY
"Warfare: An Invention —Not a Biological Necessity"

Mead argues in this essay that warfare is "an invention—not a biological necessity" or an inevitable outgrowth of social development. In what respects is warfare "an invention"? Have you ever heard it referred to in that way? What evidence and logic does she use to support her claim that warfare is an invention? What kind of evidence and logic does she use to challenge the views of her opponents? In what respects do you find her arguments most convincing? In what respects do you find them least convincing?

Given her claim that warfare is an invention, she also believes that a better invention can replace it, "which will make war obsolete." What kind of invention do you think she has in mind as being sufficient to put an end to war? What kinds of inventions do you know of that have been tried as alternatives to war? Why do you suppose they failed to make war obsolete?

For another essay about the origin, nature, and significance of war, read Thoreau's "War of the Ants." What view of war seems uppermost in each piece? What strategy does each author use to present his or her idea of war? How do you account for the strikingly different modes of presentation that each author uses in his or her piece about war?

N. SCOTT MOMADAY

1 9 3 4 –

*I want you to see the very many deep colors of the distance. I want
you to live, to be for an hour or a day more completely alive in me
than you have ever been. There are moments in that time when I
live so intensely in myself that I wonder how it is possible to keep
from flying apart. I want you to feel that, too, the vibrant ecstasy
of so much being—to know beyond any doubt that it is only the
merely happy accident that you can hold together at all in the
exhilaration of such wonder. The wonder: I want to tell you of it;
I want to speak and to write it all out for you.*

In this passage from his au-
tobiography, *The Names,* Scott Momaday invokes the sense of wonder
and intensity at the heart of all his writing. Though reminiscent of
Annie Dillard's often ecstatic sense of the natural world, Momaday's
wonder is inspired most of all by his experience of growing up a Kiowa
Indian, steeped in the legends of his people and deeply influenced by the
example and presence of his elders. His wonder, therefore, is often
expressed in Indian myths and tribal stories—in narratives and accounts that vividly appeal to the imagination. But his wonder is also
deeply rooted in the experience of the natural landscape, in the aura and
color and feel and image of the Southwestern deserts and mountains
and prairie—of living on the earth, in particular landscapes, shaped by
a particular weather and light.

Momaday (whose last name is a condensed version of his grandfather's sole name, Mammedatty) was born in Oklahoma, homeland of
the Kiowa tribe—his father a full-blooded Kiowa, his mother part-
Cherokee, part-descendant of American pioneers. During the course of
his childhood, he lived in various Indian communities and observed the
ways of different Indian tribes—Kiowa, Navajo, and Jemez—as his
parents moved from one Southwestern village to another, in search of
better employment. During most of his adolescence, he lived among the
Jemez Indians in the canyon and mountain country of New Mexico,
where his father, an artist and teacher, and his mother, a writer and
teacher, found work at a special Indian high school. But throughout his
years of growing up, Momaday's parents deliberately sought to instruct
him in the history, legend, myth, and spirit of his father's Kiowa forbears, while at the same time educating him in the language and literature of his mother's Anglo-American forbears. So, not surprisingly, his
writing and his view of experience are deeply influenced by the two
radically different cultures of which he is a product. Looking back on
his bicultural upbringing and education, Momaday says he "never experienced the kind of segregation that a lot of Indian students do. I went

to Indian schools, but my position in all of those schools was ambiguous . . . . I had the best of both worlds when I was growing up.

After spending his last year of high school at a military academy in Virginia, Momaday enrolled at the University of New Mexico, where he received a B.A. in political science in 1958. During his undergraduate years he also spent a couple of semesters in the law program at the University of Virginia, where he met William Faulkner, whose culturally complex fiction and compelling personal presence evidently contributed to Momaday's subsequent decision to pursue a career in writing. After graduation from New Mexico and a year of teaching at an Indian school in northeastern New Mexico, Momaday applied to the graduate writing program at Stanford University, where he came under the influence of the West Coast poet and literary critic Yvor Winters, as well as the novelist Wallace Stegner. Though he had planned to spend only a couple of years at Stanford, working toward a Master of Fine Arts in writing, Winters convinced him to go on for a Ph.D. which he received in 1963. So, by the time he left Stanford to teach at the University of California at Santa Barbara, Momaday had become not only an accomplished poet and fiction writer, but also a literary scholar and critic, particularly of nineteenth century American poetry. He has also taught at Stanford University, the University of California at Berkeley, the University of Moscow in Russia, and most recently at the University of Arizona.

Momaday's richly varied literary talent and training are reflected in the range of different works he has produced during the past twenty-five years. His first published book was his doctoral dissertation, *The Complete Poems of Frederick Goddard Tuckerman* (1965). His first creative work, the Pulitzer Prize-winning novel, *House Made of Dawn* (1968), bears witness to the difficulty that its Indian hero experiences as a result of attempting to live in the radically different worlds of Indians and Anglos. His next book, *The Way to Rainy Mountain* (1969), which many critics consider to be his finest, weaves Kiowa legends and myths together with historical accounts of the tribe together with autobiographical accounts of how Momaday discovered and learned about his Kiowa heritage, in order to evoke the complex life and collective experience of the Kiowa people. During 1972 and 1973, Momaday produced eighty-six short essays on a wide range of topics for *Viva, Northern New Mexico's Sunday Magazine.* His next two works were both collections of poems, *Angle of Geese* (1974) and *The Gourd Dancer* (1976), the latter of which includes samples of the drawing, painting, and sketching that have occupied much of his creative energy during the past fifteen years. In *Names: A Memoir* (1976), he produced an unusual blend of autobiography and biography, that explores both sides of his familial heritage—a work that has justly been called an American Indian version of *Roots.* During the past several years, he has written a number of personal, descriptive, and travel essays, evoking the Southwestern landscape and Native American experience. Most recently, he has come out with another novel, *The Ancient Child* (1991).

Varied as they are, most of these works celebrate not just the Native American heritage, but the idea of heritage itself and the abiding human need for it. Momaday's belief in the centrality of heritage comes through quite clearly in a recent interview:

> The non-Indian writers of today are culturally deprived, I think, in the sense that they don't have the same sense of heritage that the Indian has. I'm told this time and time again by my students, who say, "Oh, I wish I knew more about my grandparents: I wish I knew more about my ancestors and where they came from and what they did." I've come to believe them. It seems to me that the Indian writer ought to make use of that advantage. One of his subjects ought certainly to be his cultural investment in the world. It is a unique and complete experience, and it is a great subject itself.

The other central theme of Momaday's work is the importance of being connected to the land. "The events of one's life take place," he says, "*take place,*" by which he evidently means to suggest that the experiences of people "have meaning in relation to the things around them." Momaday's own life has been so deeply rooted in the mountains and deserts of the Southwest that he thinks of his "existence" as being "indivisible" from that landscape. But his involvement with the Southwestern landscape, like his commitment to Native American experience, grows out of what he believes to be an abiding human need:

> Once in his life a man ought to concentrate his mind upon the remembered earth, I believe. He ought to give himself up to a particular landscape in his experience, to look at it from as many angles as he can, to wonder about it, to dwell upon it. He ought to imagine that he touches it with his hands at every season and listens to the sounds that are made upon it. He ought to imagine the creatures that are there and all the faintest motions of the wind. He ought to recollect the glare of noon and all the colors of the dawn and dusk.

Whether he is explaining a Kiowa legend, telling about his last visit with his blind grandmother, or describing the topography of a sacred landscape, Momaday's style is at once spare and poetic, matter of fact and highly evocative, exactingly detailed and suggestively vague:

> One day in late afternoon I walked about among the headstones at Rainy Mountain Cemetary. The shadows were very long; there was a deep blush on the sky, and the dark red earth seemed to glow with the setting sun. For a few moments, at that particular time of day, there is deep silence. Nothing moves, and it does not occur to you to make any sound. Something is going on there in the shadows. Everything has slowed to a stop in order that the sun might take leave of the land. And then there is the sudden, piercing call of a bobwhite. The whole world is startled by it.

In such plain words and plainly constructed sentences, Momaday echoes the oral rhythms of Kiowa story-telling. In such plain words and plainly constructed sentences, there is a strong sense that he is not just describing nature but invoking it, dramatically bringing it to life in the visible images of sky, earth, and sun, or the audible sound of the bobwhite, as well as in the invisible, inaudible, and intangible presences that create a sense of mystery, that convey the impression of "something . . . going on there in the shadows."

MY HORSE AND I

I sometimes think of what it means that in their heyday—in 1830, say—the Kiowas owned more horses *per capita* than any other tribe on the Great Plains, that the Plains Indian culture, the last culture to evolve in North America, is also known as "the horse culture" and "the centaur culture," that the Kiowas tell the story of a horse that died of shame after its owner committed an act of cowardice, that I am a Kiowa, that therefore there is in me, as there is in the Tartars, an old, sacred notion of the horse. I believe that at some point in my racial life, this notion must needs be expressed in order that I may be true to my nature.

It happened so: I was thirteen years old, and my parents gave me a horse. It was a small nine-year-old gelding of that rare, soft color that is called strawberry roan. This my horse and I came to be, in the course of our life together, in good understanding, of one mind, a true story and history of that large landscape in which we made the one entity of whole motion, one and the same center of an intricate, pastoral composition, evanescent, ever changing. And to this my horse I gave the name Pecos.

On the back of my horse I had a different view of the world. I could see more of it, how it reached away beyond all the horizons I had ever seen; and yet it was more concentrated in its appearance, too, and more accessible to my mind, my imagination. My mind loomed upon the farthest edges of the earth, where I could feel the full force of the planet whirling into space. There was nothing of the air and light that was not pure exhilaration, and nothing of time and eternity. Oh, Pecos, *un poquito mas!* Oh, my hunting horse! Bear me away, bear me away!

It was appropriate that I should make a long journey. Accordingly I set out one early morning, traveling light. Such a journey must begin in the nick of time, on the spur of the moment, and one must say to himself at the outset: Let there be wonderful things along the way; let me hold to the way and be thoughtful in my going; let this journey be made in beauty and belief.

I sang in the sunshine and heard the birds call out on either side.   5
Bits of down from the cottonwoods drifted across the air, and butterflies fluttered in the sage. I could feel my horse under me, rocking at my legs, the bobbing of the reins in my hand; I could feel the sun on my face and the stirring of a little wind at my hair. And through the hard hooves, the slender limbs, the supple shoulders, the fluent back of my horse I felt the earth under me. Everything was under me, buoying me up; I rode across the top of the world. My mind soared; time and again I

saw the fleeting shadow of my mind moving about me as it went winding upon the sun.

When the song, which was a song of riding, was finished, I had Pecos pick up the pace. Far down on the road to San Ysidro I overtook my friend Pasqual Fragua. He was riding a rangy, stiff-legged black and white stallion, half wild, which horse he was breaking for the rancher Cass Goodner. The horse skittered and blew as I drew up beside him. Pecos began to prance, as he did always in the company of another horse. "Where are you going?" I asked in the Jemez language. And he replied, "I am going down the road." The stallion was hard to manage, and Pasqual had to keep his mind upon it; I saw that I had taken him by surprise. "You know," he said after a moment, "when you rode up just now I did not know who you were." We rode on for a time in silence, and our horses got used to each other, but still they wanted their heads. The longer I looked at the stallion the more I admired it, and I suppose that Pasqual knew this, for he began to say good things about it: that it was a thing of good blood, that it was very strong and fast, that it felt very good to ride it. The thing was this: that the stallion was half wild, and I came to wonder about the wild half of it; I wanted to know what its wildness was worth in the riding. "Let us trade horses for a while," I said, and, well, all right, he agreed. At first it was exciting to ride the stallion, for every once in a while it pitched and bucked and wanted to run. But it was heavy and raw-boned and full of resistance, and every step was a jolt that I could feel deep down in my bones. I saw soon enough that I had made a bad bargain, and I wanted my horse back, but I was ashamed to admit it. There came a time in the late afternoon, in the vast plain far south of San Ysidro, after thirty miles, perhaps, when I no longer knew whether it was I who was riding the stallion or the stallion who was riding me. "Well, let us go back now," said Pasqual at last. "No, I am going on; and I will have my horse back, please," I said, and he was surprised and sorry to hear it, and we said goodbye. "If you are going south or east," he said, "look out for the sun, and keep your face in the shadow of your hat. *Vaya con Dios.*" And I went on my way alone then, wiser and better mounted, and thereafter I held on to my horse. I saw no one for a long time, but I saw four falling stars and any number of jackrabbits, roadrunners, and coyotes, and once, across a distance, I saw a bear, small and black, lumbering in a ravine. The mountains drew close and withdrew and drew close again, and after several days I swung east.

Now and then I came upon settlements. For the most part they were dry, burnt places with Spanish names: Arroyo Seco, Las Piedras, Tres Casas. In one of these I found myself in a narrow street between high adobe walls. Just ahead, on my left, was a door in the wall. As I approached the door was flung open, and a small boy came running out, rolling a hoop. This happened so suddenly that Pecos shied very sharply, and I fell to the ground, jamming the thumb of my left hand. The little boy looked very worried and said that he was sorry to have caused such an accident. I waved the matter off, as if it were nothing; but as a matter of fact my hand hurt so much that tears welled up in my eyes. And the pain lasted for many days. I have fallen many times from a horse, both before and after that, and a few times I fell from a running horse on dangerous ground, but that was the most painful of them all.

In another settlement there were some boys who were interested in racing. They had good horses, some of them, but their horses were not so good as mine, and I won easily. After that, I began to think of ways in which I might even the odds a little, might give some advantage to my competitors. Once or twice I gave them a head start, a reasonable head start of, say, five or ten yards to the hundred, but that was too simple, and I won anyway. Then it came to me that I might try this: we should all line up in the usual way, side by side, but my competitors should be mounted and I should not. When the signal was given I should then have to get up on my horse while the others were breaking away; I should have to mount my horse during the race. This idea appealed to me greatly, for it was both imaginative and difficult, not to mention dangerous; Pecos and I should have to work very closely together. The first few times we tried this I had little success, and over a course of a hundred yards I lost four races out of five. The principal problem was that Pecos simply could not hold still among the other horses. Even before they broke away he was hard to manage, and when they were set running nothing could hold him back, even for an instant. I could not get my foot in the stirrup, but I had to throw myself up across the saddle on my stomach, hold on as best I could, and twist myself into position, and all this while racing at full speed. I could ride well enough to accomplish this feat, but it was a very awkward and inefficient business. I had to find some way to use the whole energy of my horse, to get it all into the race. Thus far I had managed only to break his motion, to divert him from his purpose and mine. To correct this I took Pecos away and worked with him through the better part of a long afternoon on a broad reach of level ground beside an irrigation ditch. And it was hot, hard work. I began by teaching him to run straight away while I ran beside him a few steps, holding on to the saddle horn, with no pressure on the reins. Then, when we had mastered this trick, we proceeded to the next one, which was this: I placed my weight on my arms, hanging from the saddle horn, threw my feet out in front of me, struck them to the ground, and sprang up against the saddle. This I did again and again, until Pecos came to expect it and did not flinch or lose his stride. I sprang a little higher each time. It was in all a slow process of trial and error, and after two or three hours both

Pecos and I were covered with bruises and soaked through with perspi-
ration. But we had much to show for our efforts, and at last the moment
came when we must put the whole performance together. I had not yet
leaped into the saddle, but I was quite confident that I could now do so;
only I must be sure to get high enough. We began this dress rehearsal
then from a standing position. At my signal Pecos lurched and was
running at once, straight away and smoothly. And at the same time I
sprinted forward two steps and gathered myself up, placing my weight
precisely at my wrists, throwing my feet out and together, perfectly. I
brought my feet down sharply to the ground and sprang up hard, as
hard as I could, bringing my legs astraddle of my horse—and everything was just right, except that I sprang too high. I vaulted all the way
over my horse, clearing the saddle by a considerable margin, and came
down into the irrigation ditch. It was a good trick, but it was not the
one I had in mind, and I wonder what Pecos thought of it after all.
Anyway, after a while I could mount my horse in this way and so well
that there was no challenge in it, and I went on winning race after race.

I went on, farther and farther into the wide world. Many things
happened. And in all this I knew one thing: I knew where the journey
was begun, that it was itself a learning of the beginning, that the
beginning was infinitely worth the learning. The journey was well
undertaken, and somewhere in it I sold my horse to an old Spanish man
of Vallecitos. I do not know how long Pecos lived. I had used him hard
and well, and it may be that in his last days an image of me like thought
shimmered in his brain.

LINES OF INQUIRY
"My Horse and I"

Momaday declares in paragraph 1 that "there is in me . . . an old sacred notion of the horse" and "this notion must needs be expressed in order
that I may be true to my nature." How did Momaday express this "sacred
notion" in his adventures with Pecos? How does he express this "sacred notion" in writing about Pecos and himself? What special language and figures of speech does he use in the piece, what particular details does he
report to convey the sacredness he attributes to the horse? Given Momaday's
professed belief in this sacred notion, how do you account for his abandonment of Pecos, which he openly and unapologetically reports in the last
three sentences of the piece.

Most of this piece is given over to Momaday's account of "a long journey" that he took with Pecos, a journey that he introduces in paragraph 4 as
if it were a sacred rite. What special language and figures of speech does
Momaday use in paragraph 4 to convey the sacredness of the journey? What
language and figures of speech does he use in subsequent paragraphs to
convey the sacredness of the journey? What experiences does Momaday

undergo, what activities does he perform, what insights does he gain that demonstrate the sacredness of his journey? Why do you suppose that Momaday considers this journey to be so important as he claims in the final paragraph of the piece?

Think about an important journey that you took during your teens or early twenties, a journey that you regard as having been especially significant, if not sacred. What means of travel did you use on your journey? Who, if anyone, accompanied you? Where did you go on your journey? What special things did you do? What insights did you gain from the journey? How did you change as a result of the journey?

THE WAY TO
RAINY MOUNTAIN

A single knoll rises out of the plain in Oklahoma, north and west of the Wichita range. For my people, the Kiowas, it is an old landmark, and they gave it the name Rainy Mountain. The hardest weather in the world is there. Winter brings blizzards, hot tornadic winds arise in the spring, and in summer the prairie is an anvil's edge. The grass turns brittle and brown, and it cracks beneath your feet. There are green belts along the rivers and creeks, linear groves of hickory and pecan, willow and witch hazel. At a distance in July or August the steaming foliage seems almost to writhe in fire. Great green and yellow grasshoppers are everywhere in the tall grass, popping up like corn to sting the flesh, and tortoises crawl about on the red earth, going nowhere in the plenty of time. Loneliness is an aspect of the land. All things in the plain are isolate; there is no confusion of objects in the eye, but *one* hill or *one* tree or *one* man. To look upon that landscape in the early morning, with the sun at your back, is to lose the sense of proportion. Your imagination comes to life, and this, you think, is where Creation was begun.

I returned to Rainy Mountain in July. My grandmother had died in the spring, and I wanted to be at her grave. She had lived to be very old and at last infirm. Her only living daughter was with her when she died, and I was told that in death her face was that of a child.

I like to think of her as a child. When she was born, the Kiowas were living the last great moment of their history. For more than a hundred years they had controlled the open range from the Smoky Hill River to the Red, from the headwaters of the Canadian to the fork of the Arkansas and Cimarron. In alliance with the Comanches, they had ruled the whole of the Southern Plains. War was their sacred business, and they were the finest horsemen the world has ever known. But warfare for the Kiowas was pre-eminently a matter of disposition rather than of survival, and they never understood the grim, unrelenting advance of the U.S. Cavalry. When at last, divided and ill provisioned, they were driven onto the Staked Plains in the cold of autumn, they fell into panic. In Palo Duro Canyon they abandoned their crucial stores to pillage and had nothing then but their lives. In order to save themselves, they surrendered to the soldiers at Fort Sill and were imprisoned in the old stone corral that now stands as a military museum. My grandmother was spared the humiliation of those high gray walls by eight or ten years, but she must have known from birth the affliction of defeat, the dark brooding of old warriors.

Her name was Aho, and she belonged to the last culture to evolve in North America. Her forbears came down from the high country in western Montana nearly three centuries ago. They were a mountain people, a mysterious tribe of hunters whose language has never been classified in any major group. In the late seventeenth century they began a long migration to the south and east. It was a journey toward the dawn, and it led to a golden age. Along the way the Kiowas were befriended by the Crows, who gave them the culture and religion of the Plains. They acquired horses, and their ancient nomadic spirit was suddenly free of the ground. They acquired Tai-me, the sacred sundance doll, from that moment the object and symbol of their worship, and so shared in the divinity of the sun. Not least, they acquired the sense of destiny, therefore courage and pride. When they entered upon the Southern Plains they had been transformed. No longer were they slaves to the simple necessity of survival; they were a lordly and dangerous society of fighters and thieves, hunters and priests of the sun. According to their origin myth, they entered the world through a hollow log. From one point of view, their migration was the fruit of an old prophecy, for indeed they emerged from a sunless world.

Though my grandmother lived out her long life in the shadow of   5
Rainy Mountain, the immense landscape of the continental interior lay like memory in her blood. She could tell of the Crows, whom she had never seen, and of the Black Hills, where she had never been. I wanted to see in reality what she had seen more perfectly in the mind's eye, and drove fifteen hundred miles to begin my pilgrimage.

A dark mist lay over the Black Hills, and the land was like iron. At the top of a ridge I caught sight of Devil's Tower upthrust against the gray sky as if in the birth of time the core of the earth had broken through its crust and the motion of the world was begun. There are things in nature that engender an awful quiet in the heart of man; Devil's Tower is one of them. Two centuries ago, because of their need to explain it, the Kiowas made a legend at the base of the rock. My grandmother said:

"Eight children were there at play, seven sisters and their brother. Suddenly the boy was struck dumb; he trembled and began to run upon his hands and feet. His fingers became claws, and his body was covered with fur. There was a bear where the boy had been. The sisters were terrified; they ran, and the bear after them. They came to the stump of a great tree, and the tree spoke to them. It bade them climb upon it, and as they did so, it began to rise into the air. The bear came to kill them, but they were just beyond its reach. It reared against the tree and scored the bark all around with its claws. The seven sisters were borne into the sky, and they became the stars of the Big Dipper." From that moment, and so long at the legend lives, the Kiowas have kinsmen in the night sky. Whatever they were in the mountains, they could be no more. However tenuous their well-being, however much they had suffered and would suffer again, they had found a way out of the wilderness.

My grandmother had a reverence for the sun, a holy regard that now is all but gone out of mankind. There was a wariness in her, and an ancient awe. She was a Christian in her later years, but she had come a long way about, and she never forgot her birthright. As a child she had been to the sun dances; she had taken part in that annual rite, and by it she had learned the restoration of her people in the presence of Tai-me. She was about seven when the last Kiowa sun dance was held in 1887 on the Washita River above Rainy Mountain Creek. The buffalo were gone. In order to consummate the ancient sacrifice—to impale the head of a buffalo bull upon the Tai-me tree—a delegation of old men journeyed into Texas, there to beg and barter for an animal from the Goodnight herd. She was ten when the Kiowas came together for the last time as a living sun-dance culture. They could find no buffalo; they had to hang an old hide from the sacred tree. Before the dance could begin, a company of soldiers rode out from Fort Sill under orders to disperse the tribe. Forbidden without cause the essential act of their faith, having seen the wild herds slaughtered and left to rot upon the ground, the Kiowas backed away forever from the tree. That was July 20, 1890, at the great bend of the Washita. My grandmother was there. Without bitterness, and for as long as she lived, she bore a vision of deicide.

Now that I can have her only in memory, I see my grandmother in the several postures that were peculiar to her: standing at the wood stove on a winter morning and turning meat in a great iron skillet; sitting at the south window, bent above her beadwork, and afterwards, when her vision failed, looking down for a long time into the fold of her hands; going out upon a cane, very slowly as she did when the weight of age came upon her; praying. I remember her most often at prayer. She made long, rambling prayers out of suffering and hope, having seen many things. I was never sure that I had the right to hear, so exclusive were they of all mere custom and company. The last time I saw her she prayed standing by the side of her bed at night, naked to the waist, the light of a kerosene lamp moving upon her dark skin. Her long black hair, always drawn and braided in the day, lay upon her shoulders and against her breasts like a shawl. I do not speak Kiowa, and I never understood her prayers, but there was something inherently sad in the sound, some merest hesitation upon the syllables of sorrow. She began in a high and descending pitch, exhausting her breath to silence; then again and again—and always the same intensity of effort, of something that is, and is not, like urgency in the human voice. Transported so in the dancing light among the shadows of her room, she seemed beyond the reach of time. But that was illusion; I think I knew then that I should not see her again.

Houses are like sentinels in the plain, old keepers of the weather watch. There, in a very little while, wood takes on the appearance of great age. All colors wear soon away in the wind and rain, and then the wood is burned gray and the grain appears and the nails turn red with rust. The window panes are black and opaque; you imagine there is nothing within, and indeed there are many ghosts, bones given up to the land. They stand here and there against the sky, and you approach them for a longer time than you expect. They belong in the distance; it is their domain.

Once there was a lot of sound in my grandmother's house, a lot of coming and going, feasting and talk. The summers there were full of excitement and reunion. The Kiowas are a summer people; they abide the cold and keep to themselves, but when the season turns and the land becomes warm and vital they cannot hold still; an old love of going returns upon them. The aged visitors who came to my grandmother's house when I was a child were made of lean and leather, and they bore themselves upright. They wore great black hats and bright ample shirts that shook in the wind. They rubbed fat upon their hair and wound their braids with strips of colored cloth. Some of them painted their faces and carried the scars of old and cherished enmities. They were an old council of warlords, come to remind and be reminded of who they were. Their wives and daughters served them well. The women might indulge themselves; gossip was at once the mark and compensation of their servitude. They made loud and elaborate talk among themselves, full of jest and gesture, fright and false alarm. They went abroad in fringed and flowered shawls, bright beadwork and German silver. They were at home in the kitchen, and they prepared meals that were banquets.

There were frequent prayer meetings, and nocturnal feasts. When I was a child I played with my cousins outside, where the lamplight fell upon the ground and the singing of the old people rose up around us and carried away into the darkness. There were a lot of good things to eat, a lot of laughter and surprise. And afterwards, when the quiet returned, I lay down with my grandmother and could hear the frogs away by the river and feel the motion of the air.

Now there is a funereal silence in the rooms, the endless wake of some final word. The walls have closed in upon my grandmother's house. When I returned to it in mourning, I saw for the first time in my life how small it was. It was late at night, and there was a white moon, nearly full. I sat for a long time on the stone steps by the kitchen door. From there I could see out across the land; I could see the long row of trees by the creek, the low light upon the rolling plains, and the stars of the Big Dipper. Once I looked at the moon and caught sight of a strange thing. A cricket had perched upon the handrail, only a few inches away. My line of vision was such that the creature filled the moon like a fossil. It had gone there, I thought, to live and die, for there, of all places, was its small definition made whole and eternal. A warm wind rose up and purled like the longing within me.

The next morning, I awoke at dawn and went out on the dirt road to Rainy Mountain. It was already hot, and the grasshoppers began to fill the air. Still, it was early in the morning, and birds sang out of the shadows. The long yellow grass on the mountain shone in the bright light, and a scissortail hied above the land. There, where it ought to be, at the end of a long and legendary way, was my grandmother's grave. She had at last succeeded to that holy ground. Here and there on the dark stones were ancestral names. Looking back once, I saw the mountain and came away.

LINES OF INQUIRY
"The Way to Rainy Mountain"

This essay consists of four separate sections, each focusing on a different subject or set of subjects. How do you account for Momaday's organization of the four sections? For example, what is the effect of his beginning with a description of Rainy Mountain, then moving to a brief account of his grandmother's death, then to a history of the Kiowa people, then to a brief account of his grandmother's memories, then to a detailed account of a Kiowa legend as told to him by his grandmother, and so on? Try some different ways of arranging the sections or the material they contain. How does each of your rearrangements affect the pacing, the buildup, and the overall significance of the piece?

Momaday tells about several different journeys that several different people took to or from Rainy Mountain at several different times. Identify each of the journeys, the journeyers, the times of their journeys, and their destinations. Which of the journeys do you think is of primary interest to Momaday? In what ways are these journeys related to each other? In what ways are they similar to each other? What do you think Momaday is trying to convey by writing about all of these journeys and experiences within the space of this relatively brief essay?

Think of a place that is special not only to you, but also to your family, as well as to your community or to some other group of people with whom you identify yourself. What do you know about the place from your own first hand observation of it? What stories have you heard about it from others? What have you learned about it from your reading? Based on all that you know about the place, what significance does it have for you and for others?

SACRED AND
ANCESTRAL GROUND

There is great good in re-
turning to a landscape that has had extraordinary meaning in one's life.
It happens that we return to such places in our minds irresistibly. There
are certain villages and towns, mountains and plains that, having seen
them, walked in them, lived in them, even for a day, we keep forever in
the mind's eye. They become indispensable to our well-being; they
define us, and we say: I am who I am because I have been there, or there.
There is good, too, in actual, physical return.

Some years ago I made a pilgrimage into the heart of North Amer-
ica. I began the journey proper in western Montana. From there I
traveled across the high plains of Wyoming into the Black Hills, then
southward to the southern plains, to a cemetery at Rainy Mountain, in
Oklahoma. It was a journey made by my Kiowa ancestors long before.
In the course of their migration they became a people of the Great
Plains, and theirs was the last culture to evolve in North America.
They had been for untold generations a mountain tribe of hunters.
Their ancient nomadism, which had determined their way of life even
before they set foot on this continent, perhaps 30,000 years ago, was
raised to its highest level of expression when they entered upon the
Great Plains and acquired horses. Their migration brought them to a
Golden Age. At the beginning of their journey they were a people of
hard circumstances, often hungry and cold, fighting always for sheer
survival. At its end, and for a hundred years, they were the lords of the
land, a daring race of centaurs and buffalo hunters whose love of freedom and space was profound.

Recently I returned to the old migration route of the Kiowas. I had in
me a need to behold again some of the principal landmarks of that long,
prehistoric quest, to descend again from the mountain to the plain.

With my close friend Charles, a professor of American literature at
a South Dakota university, I headed north to the Montana-Wyoming
border. I wanted to intersect the Kiowa migration route at the Bighorn
Medicine Wheel, high in the Bighorn Mountains. We ascended to
8,000 feet gradually, on a well-maintained but winding highway. Then
we climbed sharply, bearing upon the timberline. Although the plain
below had been comfortable, even warm at midday, the mountain air
was cold, and much of the ground was covered with snow. We turned
off the pavement, on a dirt road that led three miles to the Medicine
Wheel. The road was forbidding, it was narrow and winding, and the

grades were steep and slippery; here and there the shoulders fell away into deep ravines. But at the same time something wonderful happened: we crossed the line between civilization and wilderness. Suddenly the earth persisted in its original being. Directly in front of us a huge white-tailed buck crossed our path, ambling without haste into a thicket of pines. As we drove over his tracks we saw four does above on the opposite bank, looking down at us, their great black eyes bright and benign, curious. There seemed no wariness, nothing of fear or alienation. Their presence was a good omen, we thought; somehow in their attitude they bade us welcome to their sphere of wilderness.

There was a fork in the road, and we took the wrong branch. At a   5
steep, hairpin curve we got out of the car and climbed to the top of a peak. An icy wind whipped at us; we were among the bald summits of the Bighorns. Great flumes of sunlit snow erupted on the ridges and dissolved in spangles on the sky. Across a deep saddle we caught sight of the Medicine Wheel. It was perhaps two miles away.

When we returned to the car we saw another vehicle approaching. It was a very old Volkswagen bus, in much need of repair, cosmetic repair, at least. Out stepped a thin, bearded young man in thick glasses. He wore a wool cap, a down parka, jeans and well-worn hiking boots. "I am looking for Medicine Wheel," he said, having nodded to us. He spoke softly, with a pronounced accent. His name was Jürg, and he was from Switzerland; he had been traveling for some months in Canada and the United States. Chuck and I shook his hand and told him to follow us, and we drove down into the saddle. From there we climbed on foot to the Medicine Wheel.

The Medicine Wheel is a ring of stones, some 80 feet in diameter. Stone spokes radiate from the center to the circumference. Cairns are placed at certain points on the circumference, one in the center and one just outside the ring to the southwest. We do not know as a matter of fact who made this wheel or to what purpose. It has been proposed that it was an astronomical observatory, a solar calendar and the ground design of a Kiowa sun dance lodge. What we know without doubt is that it is a sacred expression, an equation of man's relation to the cosmos.

There was a great calm upon that place. The hard, snowbearing wind that had burned our eyes and skin only minutes before had died away altogether. The sun was warm and bright, and there was a profound silence. On the wire fence that had been erected to enclose and protect the wheel were fixed offerings, small prayer bundles. Chuck and Jürg and I walked about slowly, standing for long moments here and there, looking into the wheel or out across the great distances. We did not say much; there was little to be said. But we were deeply moved by the spirit of that place. The silence was such that it must be observed. To the north we could see down to the timberline, to the snowfields and draws that marked the black planes of forest among the peaks of the Bighorns. To the south and west the mountains fell abruptly to the plains. We could see thousands of feet down and a hundred miles across the dim expanse.

When we were about to leave, I took from my pocket an eagle-bone whistle that my father had given me, and I blew it in the four directions. The sound was very high and shrill, and it did not break the essential silence. As we were walking down we saw far below, crossing our path, a coyote sauntering across the snow into a wall of trees. It was just there, a wild being to catch sight of, and then it was gone. The wilderness which had admitted us with benediction, with benediction let us go.

When we came within a stone's throw of the highway, Chuck and   10
I said goodbye to Jürg, but not before Jürg had got out his camp stove and boiled water for tea. There in the dusk we enjoyed a small ceremonial feast of tea and crackers. The three of us had become friends. Only later did I begin to understand the extraordinary character of that friendship. It was the friendship of those who come together in recognition of the sacred. If we never meet again, I thought, we shall not forget this day.

On the plains the fences and roads and windmills and houses seemed almost negligible, all but overwhelmed by the earth and sky. It is a landscape of great clarity; its vastness is that of the ocean. It is the near revelation of infinity. Antelope were everywhere in the grassy folds, grazing side by side with horses and cattle. Hawks sailed above, and crows scattered before us. The place names were American— Tensleep, Buffalo, Dull Knife, Crazy Woman, Spotted Horse.

The Black Hills are an isolated and ancient group of mountains in South Dakota and Wyoming. They lie very close to both the geographic center of the United States (including Alaska and Hawaii) and the geographic center of the North American continent. They form an island, an elliptical area of nearly 6,000 square miles, in the vast sea of grasses that is the northern Great Plains. The Black Hills form a calendar of geologic time that is truly remarkable. The foundation rocks of these mountains are older than much of the sedimentary layer of which the Americas are primarily composed. An analysis of this foundation, made in 1975, indicates an age of between two billion and three billion years.

A documented record of exploration in this region is found in the Lewis and Clark journals, 1804–6. The first white party known definitely to have entered the Black Hills proper was led by Jedediah Smith in 1823. The diary of this expedition, kept by one James Clyman, is notable. Clyman reports a confrontation between Jedediah Smith and a grizzly bear, in which Smith lost one of his ears. There is also reported the discovery of a petrified ("putrified," as Clyman has it) forest, where petrified birds sing petrified songs.

Toward the end of the century, after rumors of gold had made the Black Hills a name known throughout the country, Gen. (then Lieut. Col.) George Armstrong Custer led an expedition from Fort Abraham Lincoln into the Black Hills in July and August, 1874. The Custer expedition traveled 600 miles in 60 days. Custer reported proof of gold, but he had an eye to other things as well:

> Every step of our march that day was amid flowers of the most exquisite colors and perfume. So luxuriant in growth were they that men plucked them without dismounting from the saddle. . . . It was a strange sight to glance back at the advancing columns of cavalry and behold the men with beautiful bouquets in their hands, while the headgear of the horses was decorated with wreaths of flowers fit to crown a queen of May. Deeming it a most fitting appellation, I named this Floral Valley.

In the evening of that same day, siting at mess in a meadow, the officers competed to see how many different flowers could be picked by each man, without leaving his seat. Seven varieties were gathered so. Some 50 different flowers were blooming then in Floral Valley.   15

The Lakota, or Teton Sioux, called these mountains Paha Sapa, "Hills That Are Black." Other tribes, besides the Kiowa and the Sioux, thought of the Black Hills as sacred ground, a place crucial in their past. The Arapaho lived here. So did the Cheyenne. Bear Butte, near Sturgis, S.D., on the northeast edge of the Black Hills, is the Cheyenne's sacred mountain. It remains, like the Medicine Wheel, a place of the greatest spiritual intensity. So great was thought to be the power inherent in the Black Hills that the Indians did not camp there. It was a place of rendezvous, a hunting ground, but above all inviolate, a place of thunder and lightning, a dwelling place of the gods.

On the edge of the Black Hills nearest the Bighorn Mountains is Devils Tower, the first of our National Monuments. The Lakotas called it Mateo Tepee, "Grizzly Bear Lodge." The Kiowas called it Tsoai, "Rock Tree." Devils Tower is a great monolith that rises high above the timber of the Black Hills. In conformation it closely resembles the stump of a tree. It is a cluster of rock columns (phonolite porphyry) 1,000 feet across at the base and 275 feet across the top. It rises 865 feet above the high ground on which it stands and 1,280 feet above the Belle Fourche River, in the valley below.

It has to be seen to be believed. "There are things in nature that engender an awful quiet in the heart of man; Devils Tower is one of them." I wrote these words almost 20 years ago. They remain true to my experience. Each time I behold this Tsoai, I am more than ever in awe of it.

Two hundred years ago, more or less, the Kiowas came upon this place. They were moved to tell a story about it:

Eight children were there at play, seven sisters and their brother.   20
Suddenly the boy was struck dumb; he trembled and began to run upon
his hands and feet. His fingers became claws and his body was covered
with fur. Directly there was a bear where the boy had been. The sisters
were terrified; they ran, and the bear ran after them. They came to the
stump of a great tree, and the tree spoke to them. It bade them climb
upon it, and as they did so it began to rise into the air. The bear came to
kill them, but they were just beyond its reach. It reared against the tree
and scored the bark all around with its claws. The seven sisters were
borne into the sky, and they became the stars of the Big Dipper.

This story, which I have known from the time I could first understand language, exemplifies the sacred for me. The storyteller, that
anonymous, illiterate man who told the story for the first time, succeeded in raising the human condition to the level of universal significance. Not only did he account for the existence of the rock tree, but in
the process he related his human race to the stars.

When Chuck and I had journeyed over this ground together, when
we were about to go our separate ways, I reminded him of our friend
Jürg, knowing well enough that I needn't have: Jürg was on our minds.
He had touched us deeply with his trust, not unlike that of the wild
animals we had seen. I can't account for it. Jürg had touched us deeply
with his generosity of spirit, his concern to see beneath the surface of
things, his attitude of free, direct, disinterested kindness.

"Did he tell us what he does?" I asked. "Does he have a profession?"
"I don't think he said," Chuck replied. "I think he's a pilgrim."
"Yes."   25
"Yes."

LINES OF INQUIRY
"Sacred and Ancestral Ground"

Within the scope of this brief essay, Momaday tells about several different journeys that several different people took to several different places in
"the heart of North America." Identify each of the journeys, the journeyers,
the times of their journeys, and their exact destinations. In what ways are
these journeyers and journeys most importantly different from each other?
In what ways are they most significantly similar to each other? What do
you think Momaday is trying to convey by writing about all of these journeys?

In the course of this piece, Momaday not only tells about several different journeys "into the heart of North America," but also describes specific
places in that area. Examine each of the descriptive passages, with an eye to
noting the kinds of places he describes, as well as the particular creatures,
images, scenes, and vistas that he emphasizes at each place. What similarities do you notice in the places he describes, the details he emphasizes, and

the moods or experiences he evokes in each of these passages? What do you think Momaday is trying to convey about these places through his descriptions of them?

In this essay as in "The Way to Rainy Mountain," which he produced some twenty years earlier, Momaday writes about the experience of visiting "sacred and ancestral ground." Examine the two essays carefully, with an eye to noting the most striking differences and similarities you can find in the structure, style, content, and detailing of each. In what respect(s) do you think his conception and presentation of these sacred places have changed? In what respect(s) do you think his conception and presentation of them have remained the same? How do you account for the differences? How
do you account for the similarities? Which of the pieces do you think is more effective in conveying the sacredness and significance of these ancestral places?

EVERETT RUESS: THE DARK TRAIL INTO MYTH

*Alone I will follow the dark
trail, black void on one side
and unattainable heights on
the other, darkness before
and behind me, darkness that
pulses and flows and is
felt. . . .*
                    Everett Ruess

Of all the myths that pervade the American landscape, none is more pervasive than that of the solitary man whose destiny it is to achieve a communion with nature so nearly absolute as to be irrevocable. It is the act of dying into the wilderness, actually or metaphorically. When Everett Ruess disappeared in the Escalante wilderness of Utah in November 1934, he succeeded to that mythic ideal; he became one with the wild earth.

Everett Ruess was born March 28, 1914, in Oakland, California. He was last seen by a sheepherder near Davis Gulch, Utah, on November 19, 1934. He was not quite twenty-one years old. Very little objective information concerning Everett Ruess's life has been published. The principal resources are the letters he wrote to his parents, his brother, and to various friends and acquaintances, and the diaries he kept on his travels in 1932 and 1933. Beyond these, there are a few poems and essays, some photographs, and some graphic art, notably blockprints. Everett Ruess was not an accomplished artist, of course, but he might have become one, had he been given the time to develop his talents. The descriptive elements in his writing are often strong and lyrical. The composition of the blockprints is generally impressive, and the stark features of the landscape—monoliths and trees, especially—are rendered with a fine dramatic force. There can be little doubt that when Everett Ruess trained his eyes upon the physical world, the world of nature, he saw what was there. It might be argued indeed that he saw more than he could say, more than words or pictures can express; he seemed always at grips with the ineffable.

Perhaps his mother was the single most influential person in his life. Stella Knight Ruess dedicated herself to the arts. The daughter of a California pioneer, she established herself firmly in the art world of Los Angeles. She studied art at the University of Southern California and at Columbia University, and she taught courses in drawing. She wrote and published poetry. And she was an active member of several art and literary societies. She was obviously concerned to involve her family in the pursuit of artistic distinction. In booklets entitled the *Ruess Quartette* she printed poems and essays written by her husband, her two sons, and herself. She designed a family seal which bore the legend "Glorify the Hour," and she had imprinted on her stationery "The House of Ruess."

Everett's father Christopher was a graduate of Harvard and of Harvard Divinity School. Although he wrote an occasional poem, he was more deeply interested in philosophy than in poetry, and he brought to the family a certain pragmatic energy that must have served Everett well in his wilderness sojourns. He believed in the principle of preparedness, and he wanted his sons to become educated men. He could only have been disappointed when Everett dropped out of the University of California at Los Angeles after one semester.

Waldo, Everett's older brother and now the only surviving member of the family, made a successful career as an international businessman, living in a number of countries in Europe and Asia and traveling all over the world. Though seemingly much closer in taste and temperament to his father than to his mother, and therefore the opposite of his younger brother, he supported Everett in his quests without hesitation. It was one for all and all for one in "The House of Ruess."

W. L. Rusho, in *Everett Ruess: A Vagabond for Beauty* (Peregrine Smith Books, 1983), writes:

> Everett's greatest talent was his ability to see, and then articulate, the magnitude, color, and changing moods of nature. If he was good at describing the high Sierras (and he was), he was superlative in his descriptions of the red rock deserts of northern Arizona and southern Utah. His astonishing ability to awake in a reader those feelings one has when confronting the land, coupled with the mystery of his vanishing, have prompted the suggestion that he might have been a mystic. (page 5)

Remarkably, we know nothing more of Everett Ruess's disappearance now than we did half a century ago. It is not unlikely that he was murdered and that his remains were buried in a place so remote and inaccessible that it is no wonder that they have never been discovered. The Escalante country is of course remote and inaccessible to begin with, but to be sure there were those who knew that terrain, especially Navajos who had lived all their lives in the region, far better than Ruess and far better than any of the outsiders who searched for him. A renegade Navajo, Jack Crank, confessed to the murder of Everett Ruess, but his confession was never substantiated, and he was apparently not a man to be taken at his word. Nonetheless, Ruess's parents believed that Crank killed their son. Christopher Ruess wrote to Randolph Jenks (who had known Everett in 1931) on August 7, 1952:

He [Crank] was a sort of outlaw among his people even. He was probably drunk when he did the deed. . . . For us, this seems to solve the riddle. (*Everett Ruess,* page 206)

But the murder theory is simply that, a theory. Even now, there are those who believe that Everett Ruess may still be alive. It is intriguing that Ruess himself seemed to encourage the formation of his own legend, the formation of a "riddle." As early as May 1931, he wrote: "I intend to do everything possible to broaden my experiences and allow myself to reach the fullest development. Then, and before physical deterioration obtrudes, I shall go on some last wilderness trip, to a place I have known and loved. I shall not return." In the summer before his disappearance he made the prophetic statement, "When I go, I leave no trace." Alec W. Anderson, a retired librarian, reported that Ruess had visited his home in Covina, California, early in 1934. When he left for Arizona, Ruess told Anderson, "And I don't think you will ever see me again, for I intend to disappear."

"I intend to disappear." One cannot be more explicit than that. Are we to take him seriously in this, literally? Did he in fact effect his disappearance like a magician on the stage? In the final analysis it matters very little what Ruess's intentions might have been, I think. More important are, first, the fact of his disappearance, then the myth-making process itself: the way in which we ascribe meaning to the apparently meaningless, or how we apply our collective imagination to the unknown. Outside that process the story of Everett Ruess is severely limited. He was born, he ventured into the wilderness, he vanished. We are confounded because our principal character has stepped out of the story too soon, and are frustrated. But within the process the story is boundless; when we focus the imagination upon this simple formula, we perceive implications, consequent meanings, possibilities, all with the richness of legend. Everett Ruess, then, was a man (scarcely a man, a boy) whose love and perception of nature were profound, and in his example we can find something of our own sacred commitment to the American landscape.

I can't help thinking of another legend of the American West. From the time I was a small boy, growing up in New Mexico, I have been fascinated with the legend of Billy the Kid. Everett Ruess and Henry McCarty (which was likely Billy the Kid's real name) were not at all alike, of course, on the surface. And yet one can make comparisons that are revealing of our imagination. Everett Ruess disappeared in the Utah wilderness at the age of twenty. Billy the Kid was killed at Fort Sumner, New Mexico, at the age of twenty-one. Both were irrevocably involved in the landscape of the Southwest, and both were engaging personalities, each in his own way. Notwithstanding that one was a

poet and artist and a devout lover of nature in the tradition of the
English Romantics and the other was an unscrupulous outlaw, very
likely a psychopathic killer, they both exemplify crucial attitudes in
our understanding of the Wild West. This is to say that Everett Ruess,
like Billy the Kid, perpetuates the myth of the dying cowboy, that
lonely, heroic figure who bravely confronts his destiny because he
must. The confrontation ends in his demise; but he has achieved the
communion; he has become one with the infinite universe, which in a
large dimension of the popular imagination is the Western Wilderness.
From "Streets of Laredo" to Aaron Copland's great ballet "Billy the
Kid," through a thousand movies and television programs, this notion
predominates: the handsome young man is cut down before his great
promise can be realized; he dies into landscape and legend; and he is
greatly mourned.

> There's many a man with a face fine and fair,
> Who starts out in life with a chance to be square,
> But just like poor Billy he wanders astray
> And loses his life in the very same way.
> (John A. Lomax, *American Ballads and Folk Songs,*
> "Billy the Kid" [Macmillan, 1934], page 136.)

Everett Ruess, of course, cannot be said to have gone "astray" in any but
the most literal sense. Indeed, he was as upstanding and "square" as one
could ask of a young man of his time and place. He is too young and too
late to be a Mountain Man, but the Mountain Man expresses his spirit.
He is a cross between the Mountain Man and the Eagle Scout,
combining the one's nomadism and fearlessness and instinct for survival and the other's moral purpose and strength of character.

The thing that sets Everett Ruess forever apart from the popular   10
myth is what F. Scott Fitzgerald called the "capacity for wonder." In
Ruess this talent amounted to a passion almost overwhelming. In this
respect he is much closer to Albert Bierstadt and John Muir and Ansel
Adams than he is to Billy the Kid and the Mountain Men.

In 1934 he wrote to a friend from Chilchinbetoh, Arizona:

> So here too I have been leading a life of strange contrasts, violent indeed
> when considered separately, yet flowing naturally enough into one another.
> There has been deep peace, vast calm and fury, strange comradeships and
> intimacies, and many times my life and all my possessions have tottered on
> the far side of the balance, but as yet, from each such encounter I have in the
> end come away, unharmed, and even toughened.
>
> But much as I love people, the most important thing to me is still the
> nearly unbearable beauty of what I see. I won't wish that you could see it,
> for you might not find it easy to bear either, but yet I do sincerely wish for
> you a little at least of the impossible. (*Everett Ruess,* page 145)

On the same day he wrote to another friend:

> Once more I am roaring drunk with the lust of life and adventure and unbearable beauty. I have the devil's own conception of a perfect time; adventure seems to beset me on all quarters without my even searching of it; I find gay comradeships and lead the wild, free life wherever I am. And yet, there is always an undercurrent of restlessness and wild longing; "the wind is in my hair, there's a fire in my heels," and I shall always be a rover, I know. Always I'll be able to scorn the worlds I've known like half-burnt candles when the sun is rising, and sally forth to others now unknown. I'm game; I've passed my own rigorous tests, and I know that I can take it. And I'm lucky too, or have been. Time and again, my life or all my possessions have swung on the far side of the balance, and always thus far I've come out on top and unharmed, even toughened by the chances I've taken. (*Everett Ruess,* pages 145–46)

The repetitions are significant, I believe. Ruess wrote the same letter a hundred times over, in effect. His verse, his letters, his journal entries all speak to the same witness of nearly unbearable beauty, of being intensely alive and alone in the incomparable landscape, sensible of dangers all about, sensitive to the extraordinary risks involved.

Everett Ruess was one who made poems and blockprints. He made friends easily, and he left an abiding impression upon them. He seemed not uncomfortable in the drawing rooms of Los Angeles and San Francisco, and he associated with such well-known personalities as Edward Weston and Dorothea Lange. But he was more at home, perhaps, in an abandoned hogan in Monument Valley or Canyon de Chelly. Certainly there was his inspiration, and Everett Ruess was singularly inspired. His very best art consists in his occasional writing, in letters and journal entries and familiar essays.

> I wandered through the Painted Desert and spent days serene and tempestuous in Canyon de Chelly, then traveled up Canyon del Muerto in the shadow of sheer, incurving cliffs, breathtakingly chiseled and gloriously colored. I passed the last Navajo encampments and stopped for a space in an abandoned hogan constructed of smooth clean-limbed cottonwood, with singing water at the door and sighing leaves overhead. Tall, gracefully arched trees screened the turquoise sky with a glistening pattern of dappled green; above and beyond were the gorgeous vermilion cliffs. (*Everett Ruess,* page 81)

There may be one or two extraneous adjectives here, but the description, as such, is first-rate, and anyone who has entered deep into Canyon del Muerto will know it to be true and precise.

Had Everett Ruess lived three-quarters of a century earlier, he   15 might have been in the first rank of American Transcendentalists. He might have found his credo in Emerson's *Nature.* One supposes that he might have wanted to be a mystic, as Emerson did, and his writing indicates that he came closer to a mystical experience than most of us do. But at last he was not a mystic, and however close spiritually, he was geographically and philosophically far removed from the Transcendentalists.

He was a young man intensely in love with the beauty of the American West, whose capacity for wonder was very great. From the time of the Greeks, at least, we have been baffled and disturbed and fascinated by the passing of young men. Everett Ruess took up the dark trail and followed it steadily in the direction of myth. And his achievement is the achievement of myth.

LINES OF INQUIRY
"Everett Ruess: The Dark Trail into Myth"

At several points in this essay, Momaday quotes extensively from Ruess's diaries and letters. What specific aspects of Ruess's character and inclinations does Momaday attempt to reveal by citing these passages? Look carefully at each of these passages yourself. What kind of person do *you* see in them? What does Ruess reveal about his attitudes and inclinations in these passages? In what respect(s) do Ruess's letters suggest that he might have been the mythic figure that Momaday makes him out to be? In what respect(s) do his letters make him seem to you to be less than a mythic figure?

In paragraph 1, Momaday asserts that Ruess achieved the stature of a mythic figure by virtue of "dying into the wilderness," by becoming "one with the wild earth." What does Momaday mean by "dying into the wilderness"? How does such a death qualify one for mythic status as "the solitary man whose destiny it is to achieve communion with nature so nearly absolute as to be irrevocable"? Given what you know about Ruess, how does he compare with other such mythic figures that Momaday discusses? How does he compare with mythically solitary men or women that you have heard about or read about yourself?

For other essays about persons who have led heroically solitary lives in a close communion with nature, look at Didion's "Georgia O'Keeffe" or E.B. White's piece on Thoreau, "A Slight Sound at Evening," or Thoreau's pieces about his life at Walden, "My House," and "Where I Lived and What I Lived For." What similarities—and differences—do you see between Ruess and O'Keeffe or Ruess and Thoreau? In what respect(s) do you think O'Keeffe or Thoreau might qualify for the mythic status that Momaday attributes to Ruess? In what respect(s) do you think they would fail to achieve that status?

MICHEL DE MONTAIGNE

1 5 3 3 — 1 5 9 2

*It is an absolute perfection and virtually divine to know how to
enjoy our being fully. We seek other conditions because we do not
understand the use of our own, and go outside of ourselves because
we do not know what it is like inside. Yet there is no use our
mounting on stilts, for on stilts we must still walk on our own
legs. And on the loftiest throne in the world we are still sitting
only on our own rump.*

In this wryly humorous passage from his essay, "Of Education," Montaigne expresses the common-sense, down-to-earth view of human nature and conduct that animates many of his essays. Given his awareness of human limitations, Montaigne took a deeply skeptical view of elaborate projects for the betterment of the human condition or grand philosophical quests for ultimate truths about existence, Instead, he sought the apparently more modest but actually no less challenging goal of self-knowledge. In order to pursue that goal, he created and developed a highly flexible form of writing—the essay—by means of which he could explore himself and his thoughts, as his mind ranged freely over an extraordinary range of subjects—from smells to sleep to vain subtleties to virtue. His intellectual curiosity, his commitment to self-knowledge, and his awareness of human limits are best epitomized in the hauntingly skeptical question that he took as his motto—"What do I know?"

Michel Eyquem, seigneur de Montaigne, the son of a wealthy merchant, was born at the chateau Montaigne, the home which his grandfather had bought and from which his family derived its title. The third of nine children, Montaigne became the head of the family after the death of his two elder brothers, and thus inherited the chateau when his father died in 1568. As a baby his father put him out to nurse with a peasant woman and gave him peasant godparents, so that he would learn to be at ease with people of that class. As a young child he was educated according to another of his father's schemes, in this case to have him tutored by servants who spoke Latin but not French, so that by the time he was six the youthful Montaigne had acquired Latin as a native language. A more elaborate scheme to teach him Greek evidently failed, but by the time he was seven and attending the College du Guyenne at Bordeaux, Montaigne had become so fluent in Latin that he rivalled his schoolmasters in the language. At thirteen he went on to study law at the university, probably at Toulouse, and at twenty-one he became a counsellor in the *parlement* of Bordeaux, a position he worked at dutifully but unenthusiastically for the next thirteen years.

During his years in Bordeaux, Montaigne travelled frequently to Paris and the royal court, partly for pleasure, partly in the hope of finding a better position, but evidently nothing better came his way. His work in the *parlement* did, however, lead to a close friendship with a talented young poet and public servant, Etienne La Boétie—a relationship that Montaigne later celebrated in his essay, "Of Friendship." But La Boétie's premature death in 1563 left Montaigne even more depressed with his personal situation. His work as a counsellor had evidently led him to have serious doubts about the effectiveness of the law and of other civic institutions as well. So after marrying in 1565, selling his position in *parlement* in 1567, and spending some time in Paris, where he arranged for the publication of La Boétie's works, Montaigne retired to his family estate in 1571. The seriousness with which he undertook so early a retirement is reflected in a Latin inscription that he placed on the wall of his study commemorating his withdrawal from public life:

> In the year of Christ 1571, at the age of thirty-eight, on the last day of February, his birthday, Michel de Montaigne, long weary of the servitude of the court and of public employments, while still entire, retired to the bosom of the learned virgins, where in calm and freedom from all cares he will spend what little remains of his life, now more than half run out. If the fates permit, he will complete this abode, this sweet ancestral retreat, and he has consecrated it to his freedom, tranquillity, and leisure.

Despite that firm resolve, public duties still called him—to the king's chamber, to the battlefield, to the mayorship of Bordeaux, a position he did not seek but that he was named to by four of the most powerful figures in France—Catherine de'Medici, Henry III, Henry of Navarre, and Margaret of Valois. In this important political position, which he held from 1582 to 1586, Montaigne's tactful mediations helped to keep communications open between the Catholic and Protestant forces, whose civil wars had started when he was in his twenties and continued intermittently throughout the rest of his life.

Though often distracted by the civil wars, the plague, his public duties, and his weakened physical condition, Montaigne persistently devoted himself to the book of essays that he began writing in his early retirement and that he continued writing and expanding throughout the remaining twenty years of his life. (The superscript letter A, B, or C in the text indicates material published before 1588, added in 1588, or added after 1588 respectively.) When Montaigne started work on his essays, he was evidently looking for a kind of writing that would be free of the elaborate strictures and structures that governed the scholastic treatises of his time. He wanted to try out his ideas on a variety of subjects. He wanted to explore himself and his thoughts about human experience. He wanted to put his personal observations and reflections in a tentative rather than definitive form. Thus he called his works essays, a word derived from the French verb *essayer,* which literally means to try or to attempt.

Montaigne's commitment to pursuing a freer, more open kind of writing is reflected in the repcated comments he makes on his composing process, which he describes in various essays as proceeding "without a plan and without a promise," "without any system." Given his insistence on writing "without definitions, without divisions, without conclusions," one might even say that he systematically wrote "without any system," because he wanted to let his mind and his ideas take their own direction, without being hemmed in by the boundaries of a rigidly prescribed form. He proudly declares, for example, that "My style and mind alike go roaming"; "I let my thoughts run on, weak and lowly as they are, as I have produced them, without plastering and sewing up the flaws."

Though such declarations of stylistic independence might suggest that Montaigne was completely undisciplined in his writing, a reading of his essays reveals that they are usually focused upon a particular subject and that they reflect a coherent body of ideas, even if the continuity is not always immediately clear, or the connections are not always tight, or the thoughts sometimes take surprising and apparently contradictory turns. As Montaigne himself said of his writing, "I go out of my way, but rather by license than carelessness. My ideas follow one another, but sometimes it is from a distance, and look at each other, but with a sidelong glance."

Ultimately, Montaigne's approach to writing, his concept of the essay, is an expression of his deeply held convictions about the instability of things—convictions that led him to see not only the world but also himself as being constantly in flux: "The world is but a perennial movement. All things in it are in constant motion—the earth, the rocks of the Caucasus, the pyramids of Egypt—both with the common motion and their own." Given the changeableness of everything, including himself—"I may presently change, not only by chance, but also by intention"—Montaigne felt compelled to produce a kind of writing whose very form would bear witness to the necessary instability of his thoughts: "If my mind could gain a firm footing, I would not make essays; I would make decisions; but it is always in apprenticeship and on trial."

The irony of Montaigne's writing is that despite his professed tentativeness, his essays repeatedly include statements that ring out not only because they are strikingly phrased, but also because they are strikingly true: "We can grasp virtue in such a way that it will be vicious, if we embrace it with too sharp and violent a desire"; "If falsehood, like truth, had only one face, we would be in better shape"; "The thing I fear most is fear"; "Our greatest and glorious masterpiece is to live appropriately"; "Only the fools are certain and assured." So, while his essays may not offer a single, overarching truth about existence, they do contain the insights of a mind continuously in motion, "always in apprenticeship and on trial."

OF IDLENESS

^AJust as we see that fallow land, if rich and fertile, teems with a hundred thousand kinds of wild and useless weeds, and that to set it to work we must subject it and sow it with certain seeds for our service; and as we see that women, all alone, produce mere shapeless masses and lumps of flesh, but that to create a good and natural offspring they must be made fertile with a different kind of seed; so it is with minds. Unless you keep them busy with some definite subject that will bridle and control them, they throw themselves in disorder hither and yon in the vague field of imagination.

> ^BThus, in a brazen urn, the water's light
> Trembling reflects the sun's and moon's bright rays,
> And, darting here and there in aimless flight,
> Rises aloft, and on the ceiling plays.
> *Virgil*

^AAnd there is no mad or idle fancy that they do not bring forth in this agitation:

> Like a sick man's dreams,
> They form vain visions.
> *Horace*

The soul that has no fixed goal loses itself; for as they say, to be everywhere is to be nowhere:

> ^BHe who dwells everywhere, Maximus, nowhere dwells.
> *Martial*

^ALately when I retired to my home, determined so far as possible to bother about nothing except spending the little life I have left in rest and seclusion, it seemed to me I could do my mind no greater favor than to let it entertain itself in full idleness and stay and settle in itself, which I hoped it might do more easily now, having become weightier and riper with time. But I find—

> Ever idle hours breed wandering thoughts
> *Lucan*

—that, on the contrary, like a runaway horse, it gives itself a hundred times more trouble than it took for others, and gives birth to so many chimeras and fantastic monsters, one after another, without order or purpose, that in order to contemplate their ineptitude and strangeness at my pleasure, I have begun to put them in writing, hoping in time to make my mind ashamed of itself.

LINES OF INQUIRY
"Of Idleness"

In the first paragraph, Montaigne uses several analogies and metaphors to suggest the dangers of an idle mind. Make a list of *all* the analogies and metaphors you can find, not only in Montaigne's comments but also in the passages that he quotes. What specific dangers are suggested by each analogy or metaphor? What common danger is implied by all the analogies and metaphors? Why do you suppose Montaigne doesn't just come right out and straightforwardly explain what he considers to be the perils of idleness?

In the second paragraph, Montaigne tells a little story about a period of mental idleness in his own life. How does this story develop the theme that he has announced in his first paragraph? Make a list of *all* the analogies and metaphors you can find in his story. Note all the echoes or similarities you can detect between these analogies or metaphors and the ones in the first paragraph. Which of the analogies and metaphors stands out most prominently and emphatically? What specific aspects of idleness do you think Montaigne is trying to emphasize in this highly metaphoric story about himself?

Montaigne concludes his essay by indicating that he has decided to record his "wandering thoughts" as a form of penance, "hoping in time to make my mind ashamed of itself." How wandering do you think he has been in this essay? How ashamed do you think he should be of what his mind has produced in this piece? How wandering have your own thoughts been in the process of reading this essay and thinking about it? When you find your thoughts wandering, what do you do to control their movement? What do you do to make use of your wandering thoughts?

OF SMELLS

^AIt is said of some, as of
Alexander the Great, that their sweat emitted a sweet odor, owing to
some rare and extraordinary constitution of theirs, of which Plutarch
and others seek the cause. But the common make-up of bodies is the
opposite, and the best condition they may have is to be free of smell.
The sweetness even of the purest breath has nothing more excellent
about it than to be without any odor that offends us, as is that of very
healthy children. That is why, says Plautus,

> A woman smells good when she does not smell.

The most perfect smell for a woman is to smell of nothing, ^Bas they say
that her actions smell best when they are imperceptible and mute. ^AAnd
perfumes are rightly considered suspicious in those who use them, and
thought to be used to cover up some natural defect in that quarter.
Whence arise these nice sayings of the ancient poets: To smell good is
to stink:

> You laugh at us because we do not smell.
> I'd rather smell of nothing than smell sweet.
> *Martial*

And elsewhere:

> Men who smell always sweet, Posthumus, don't smell good.
> *Martial*

^BHowever, I like very much to be surrounded with good smells, and
I hate bad ones beyond measure, and detect them from further off than
anyone else:

> My scent will sooner be aware
> Where goat-smells, Polypus, in hairy arm-pits lurk,
> Than keen hounds scent a wild boar's lair.
> *Horace*

^CThe simplest and most natural smells seem to me the most agree-
able. And this concern chiefly affects the ladies. Amid the densest
barbarism, the Scythian women, after washing, powder and plaster
their whole body and face with a certain odoriferous drug that is native

to their soil; and having removed this paint to approach the men, they find themselves both sleek and perfumed.

[B]Whatever the odor is, it is a marvel how it clings to me and how apt my skin is to imbibe it. He who complains of nature that she has left man without an instrument to convey smells to his nose is wrong, for they convey themselves. But in my particular case my mustache, which is thick, performs that service. If I bring my gloves or my handkerchief near it, the smell will stay there a whole day. It betrays the place I come from. The close kisses of youth, savory, greedy, and sticky, once used to adhere to it and stay there for several hours after. And yet, for all that, I find myself little subject to epidemics, which are caught by communication and bred by the contagion of the air; and I have escaped those of my time, of which there have been many sorts in our cities and our armies. [C]We read of Socrates that though he never left Athens during many recurrences of the plague which so many times tormented that city, he alone never found himself the worse for it.

[B]The doctors might, I believe, derive more use from odors than they do; for I have often noticed that they make a change in me and work upon my spirits according to their properties; which makes me approve of the idea that the use of incense and perfumes in churches, so ancient and widespread in all nations and religions, was intended to delight us and arouse and purify our senses to make us more fit for contemplation.

[C]I should like, in order to judge of it, to have shared the art of those cooks who know how to add a seasoning of foreign odors to the savor of foods, as was particularly remarked in the service of the king of Tunis, who in our time landed at Naples to confer with the Emperor Charles. They stuffed his foods with aromatic substances, so sumptuously that one peacock and two pheasants came to a hundred ducats to dress them in that manner; and when they were carved, they filled not only the dining hall but all the rooms in his palace, and even the neighboring houses, with sweet fumes which did not vanish for some time.

[B]The principal care I take in my lodgings is to avoid heavy, stinking air. Those beautiful cities Venice and Paris weaken my fondness for them by the acrid smell of the marshes of the one and of the mud of the other.

LINES OF INQUIRY
"Of Smells"

The first version of this essay consists only of the material following the superscript A—that is, only the first four and one-half sentences in paragraph 1 and the last three sentences in paragraph 1. What idea(s) about smell does Montaigne express in this version of his piece? What kinds of details, examples, and illustrations does he use in this version to define his ideas and express them persuasively?

The second version of this essay consists only of the material following the superscript A plus the material following the superscript B; the third version consists of the material following A plus B plus C—that is, the entire piece. What new ideas about smell does Montaigne introduce in the second version? In the third version? What new kinds of details, examples, and illustrations does he use in the second version? In the third version? How consistent does Montaigne seem to be in his thinking and writing from one version to the next?

As you can see from this essay and Montaigne's other pieces in this collection, he revised his work primarily by adding new material to what he had previously written. What do you consider to be the benefits and the limitations of this approach to revision? What techniques do you use in revising your own work? What benefits and limitations do you see in your own ways of revising?

OF THE INCONSISTENCY OF OUR ACTIONS

^AThose who make a practice of comparing human actions are never so perplexed as when they try to see them as a whole and in the same light; for they commonly contradict each other so strangely that it seems impossible that they have come from the same shop. One moment young Marius is a son of Mars, another moment a son of Venus. Pope Boniface VIII, they say, entered office like a fox, behaved in it like a lion, and died like a dog. And who would believe that it was Nero, that living image of cruelty, who said, when they brought him in customary fashion the sentence of a condemned criminal to sign: "Would to God I had never learned to write!" So much his heart was wrung at condemning a man to death!

Everything is so full of such examples—each man, in fact, can supply himself with so many—that I find it strange to see intelligent men sometimes going to great pains to match these pieces; seeing that irresolution seems to me the most common and apparent defect of our nature, as witness that famous line of Publilius, the farce writer:

> Bad is the plan that never can be changed.
> *Publilius Syrus*

^BThere is some justification for basing a judgment of a man on the most ordinary acts of his life; but in view of the natural instability of our conduct and opinions, it has often seemed to me that even good authors are wrong to insist on fashioning a consistent and solid fabric out of us. They choose one general characteristic, and go and arrange and interpret all a man's actions to fit their picture; and if they cannot twist them enough, they go and set them down to dissimulation. Augustus has escaped them; for there is in this man throughout the course of his life such an obvious, abrupt, and continual variety of actions that even the boldest judges have had to let him go, intact and unsolved. Nothing is harder for me than to believe in men's consistency, nothing easier than to believe in their inconsistency. He who would judge them in detail ^Cand distinctly, bit by bit, ^Bwould more often hit upon the truth.

^AIn all antiquity it is hard to pick out a dozen men who set their lives to a certain and constant course, which is the principal goal of wisdom. For, to comprise all wisdom in a word, says an ancient [Seneca], and to embrace all the rules of our life in one, it is "always to

will the same things, and always to oppose the same things." I would not deign, he says, to add "provided the will is just"; for if it is not just, it cannot always be whole.

In truth, I once learned that vice is only unruliness and lack of   5
moderation, and that consequently consistency cannot be attributed to it. It is a maxim of Demosthenes, they say, that the beginning of all virtue is consultation and deliberation; and the end and perfection, consistency. If it were by reasoning that we settled on a particular course of action, we would choose the fairest course—but no one has thought of that:

> He spurns the thing he sought, and seeks anew
> What he just spurned; he seethes, his life's askew.
> *Horace*

Our ordinary practice is to follow the inclinations of our appetite, to the left, to the right, uphill and down, as the wind of circumstance carries us. We think of what we want only at the moment we want it, and we change like that animal which takes the color of the place you set it on. What we have just now planned, we presently change, and presently again we retrace our steps: nothing but oscillation and inconsistency:

> Like puppets we are moved by outside strings.
> *Horace*

We do not go; we are carried away, like floating objects, now gently, now violently, according as the water is angry or calm:

> BDo we not see all humans unaware
> Of what they want, and always searching everywhere,
> And changing place, as if to drop the load they bear?
> *Lucretius*

AEvery day a new fancy, and our humors shift with the shifts in the weather:

> Such are the minds of men, as is the fertile light
> That Father Jove himself sends down to make earth bright.
> *Homer*

CWe float between different states of mind; we wish nothing freely, nothing absolutely, nothing constantly. AIf any man could prescribe and establish definite laws and a definite organization in his head, we should see shining throughout his life an evenness of habits, an order, and an infallible relation between his principles and his practice.

ᶜEmpedocles noticed this inconsistency in the Agrigentines, that they abandoned themselves to pleasures as if they were to die on the morrow, and built as if they were never to die.

ᴬThis man[1] would be easy to understand, as is shown by the example of the younger Cato: he who has touched one chord of him has touched all; he is a harmony of perfectly concordant sounds, which cannot conflict. With us, it is the opposite: for so many actions, we need so many individual judgments. The surest thing, in my opinion, would be to trace our actions to the neighboring circumstances, without getting into any further research and without drawing from them any other conclusions.

During the disorders of our poor country,[2] I was told that a girl,   10
living near where I then was, had thrown herself out of a high window to avoid the violence of a knavish soldier quartered in her house. Not killed by the fall, she reasserted her purpose by trying to cut her throat with a knife. From this she was prevented, but only after wounding herself gravely. She herself confessed that the soldier had as yet pressed her only with requests, solicitations, and gifts; but she had been afraid, she said, that he would finally resort to force. And all this with such words, such expressions, not to mention the blood that testified to her virtue, as would have become another Lucrece. Now, I learned that as a matter of fact, both before and since, she was a wench not so hard to come to terms with. As the story says: Handsome and gentlemanly as you may be, when you have had no luck, do not promptly conclude that your mistress is inviolably chaste; for all you know, the mule driver may get his will with her.

Antigonus, having taken a liking to one of his soldiers for his virtue and valor, ordered his physicians to treat the man for a persistent internal malady that had long tormented him. After his cure, his master noticed that he was going about his business much less warmly, and asked him what had changed him so and made him such a coward. "You yourself, Sire," he answered, "by delivering me from the ills that made my life indifferent to me." A soldier of Lucullus who had been robbed of everything by the enemy made a bold attack on them to get revenge. When he had retrieved his loss, Lucullus, having formed a good opinion of him, urged him to some dangerous exploit with all the fine expostulations he could think of,

> With words that might have stirred a coward's heart.
> *Horace*

---

[1] The disciplined man in the sentence before last.
[2] The religious civil wars between Catholics and Protestants, which lasted intermittently from 1562 to 1594.

"Urge some poor soldier who has been robbed to do it," he replied;

> Though but a rustic lout,
> "That man will go who's lost his money," he called out;
> *Horace*

and resolutely refused to go.

^CWe read that Sultan Mohammed outrageously berated Hassan, leader of his Janissaries, because he saw his troops giving way to the Hungarians and Hassan himself behaving like a coward in the fight. Hassan's only reply was to go and hurl himself furiously—alone, just as he was, arms in hand—into the first body of enemies that he met, by whom he was promptly swallowed up; this was perhaps not so much self-justification as a change of mood, nor so much his natural valor as fresh spite.

^AThat man whom you saw so adventurous yesterday, do not think it strange to find him just as cowardly today: either anger, or necessity, or company, or wine, or the sound of a trumpet, had put his hart in his belly. His was a courage formed not by reason, but by one of these circumstances; it is no wonder if he has now been made different by other, contrary circumstances.

^CThese supple variations and contradictions that are seen in us have made some imagine that we have two souls, and others that two powers accompany us and drive us, each in its own way, one toward good, the other toward evil; for such sudden diversity cannot well be reconciled with a simple subject.

^BNot only does the wind of accident move me at will, but, besides, I am moved and disturbed as a result merely of my own unstable posture; and anyone who observes carefully can hardly find himself twice in the same state. I give my soul now one face, now another, according to which direction I turn it. If I speak of myself in different ways, that is because I look at myself in different ways. All contradictions may be found in me by some twist and in some fashion. Bashful, insolent; ^Cchaste, lascivious; ^Btalkative, taciturn; tough, delicate; clever, stupid; surly, affable; lying, truthful; ^Clearned, ignorant; liberal, miserly, and prodigal: ^Ball this I see in myself to some extent according to how I turn; and whoever studies himself really attentively finds in himself, yes, even in his judgment, this gyration and discord. I have nothing to say about myself absolutely, simply, and solidly, without confusion and without mixture, or in one word. *Distinguo* is the most universal member of my logic.

^AAlthough I am always minded to say good of what is good, and inclined to interpret favorably anything that can be so interpreted, still it is true that the strangeness of our condition makes it happen that we

are often driven to do good by vice itself—were it not that doing good is judged by intention alone.

Therefore one courageous deed must not be taken to prove a man valiant; a man who was really valiant would be so always and on all occasions. If valor were a habit of virtue, and not a sally, it would make a man equally resolute in any contingency, the same alone as in company, the same in single combat as in battle; for, whatever they say, there is not one valor for the pavement and another for the camp. As bravely would he bear an illness in his bed as a wound in camp, and he would fear death no more in his home than in an assault. We would not see the same man charging into the breach with brave assurance, and later tormenting himself, like a woman, over the loss of a lawsuit or a son. ^CWhen, though a coward against infamy, he is firm against poverty; when, though weak against the surgeons' knives, he is steadfast against the enemy's swords, the action is praiseworthy, not the man.

Many Greeks, says Cicero, cannot look at the enemy, and are brave in sickness; the Cimbrians and Celtiberians, just the opposite; *for nothing can be uniform that does not spring from a firm principle* [Cicero].

^BThere is no more extreme valor of its kind than Alexander's; but it is only of one kind, and not complete and universal enough. ^CIncomparable though it is, it still has its blemishes; ^Bwhich is why we see him worry so frantically when he conceives the slightest suspicion that his men are plotting against his life, and why he behaves in such matters with such violent and indiscriminate injustice and with a fear that subverts his natural reason. Also superstition, with which he was so strongly tainted, bears some stamp of pusillanimity. ^CAnd the excessiveness of the penance he did for the murder of Clytus is also evidence of the unevenness of his temper.

^AOur actions are nothing but a patchwork—^C*they despise pleasure, but are too cowardly in pain; they are indifferent to glory, but infamy breaks their spirit* [Cicero]—^Aand we want to gain honor under false colors. Virtue will not be followed except for her own sake; and if we sometimes borrow her mask for some other purpose, she promptly snatches it from our face. It is a strong and vivid dye, once the soul is steeped in it, and will not go without taking the fabric with it. That is why, to judge a man, we must follow his traces long and carefully. If he does not maintain consistency for its own sake, ^C*with a way of life that has been well considered and preconcerted* [Cicero]; ^Aif changing circumstances make him change his pace (I mean his path, for his pace may be hastened or slowed), let him go: that man goes before the wind, as the motto of our Talbot says.

It is no wonder, says an ancient [Seneca], that chance has so much power over us, since we live by chance. A man who has not directed his life as a whole toward a definite goal cannot possibly set his particular actions in order. A man who does not have a picture of the whole in his head cannot possibly arrange the pieces. What good does it do a man to lay in a supply of paints if he does not know what he is to paint? No one makes a definite plan of his life; we think about it only piecemeal. The archer must first know what he is aiming at, and then set his hand, his bow, his string, his arrow, and his movements for that goal. Our plans go astray because they have no direction and no aim. No wind works for the man who has no port of destination.

I do not agree with the judgment given in favor of Sophocles, on the strength of seeing one of his tragedies, that it proved him competent to manage his domestic affairs, against the accusation of his son. ᶜNor do I think that the conjecture of the Parians sent to reform the Milesians was sufficient ground for the conclusion they drew. Visiting the island, they noticed the best-cultivated lands and the best-run country houses, and noted down the names of their owners. Then they assembled the citizens in the town and appointed these owners the new governors and magistrates, judging that they, who were careful of their private affairs, would be careful of those of the public.

ᴬWe are all patchwork, and so shapeless and diverse in composition that each bit, each moment, plays its own game. And there is as much difference between us and ourselves as between us and others. ᶜ*Consider it a great thing to play the part of one single man* [Seneca]. ᴬAmbition can teach men valor, and temperance, and liberality, and even justice. Greed can implant in the heart of a shop apprentice, brought up in obscurity and idleness, the confidence to cast himself far from hearth and home, in a frail boat at the mercy of the waves and angry Neptune; it also teaches discretion and wisdom. Venus herself supplies resolution and boldness to boys still subject to discipline and the rod, and arms the tender hearts of virgins who are still in their mothers' laps:

> ᴮFurtively passing sleeping guards, with Love as guide,
> Alone by night the girl comes to the young man's side.
> *Tibullus*

ᴬIn view of this, a sound intellect will refuse to judge men simply by their outward actions; we must probe the inside and discover what springs set men in motion. But since this is an arduous and hazardous undertaking, I wish fewer people would meddle with it.

LINES OF INQUIRY
"Of the Inconsistency of Our Actions"

Some of Montaigne's examples stand out much more prominently than others, because he develops them in much more detail than the others. Identify the four most detailed examples in the piece, and consider what is distinctive or unique in the way that each one develops or illustrates Montaigne's reflections on the inconsistency of human actions. What similarities do you find among the three lengthy examples that are grouped together? Why do you suppose that Montaigne doesn't distribute them throughout the piece? In what respect(s) does the fourth example differ so significantly from the other three as to warrant being located separately from them?

Montaigne seeks not only to illustrate the pervasiveness of human inconsistency, but also to reveal and explore the various circumstances that produce it. Make a list of all the causes that Montaigne perceives as leading to human inconsistency, and arrange the causes from the most to the least influential, according to the relative importance that Montaigne seems to give to them. Given the passages he quotes and the examples he cites, which of these causes do you believe to be most important.

Montaigne's reflections in paragraph 15 on his inconsistencies implicitly invite readers to explore their own inconsistencies. So, consider your behavior over the last few hours or days or weeks, with an eye to noting the most flagrant instances in which your behavior has been changeable, contradictory, inconsistent, unstable. What conditions in yourself or your environment do you think have been most influential in producing your inconsistency? How does your own behavior seem to compare with the examples that Montaigne cites in his essay?

OF PRACTICE

^AReasoning and education, though we are willing to put our trust in them, can hardly be powerful enough to lead us to action, unless besides we exercise and form our soul by experience to the way we want it to go; otherwise, when it comes to the time for action, it will undoubtedly find itself at a loss. That is why, among the philosophers, those who have wanted to attain some greater excellence have not been content to await the rigors of Fortune in shelter and repose, for fear she might surprise them inexperienced and new to the combat; rather they have gone forth to meet her and have flung themselves deliberately into the test of difficulties. Some of them have abandoned riches to exercise themselves in a voluntary poverty; others have sought labor and a painful austerity of life to toughen themselves against toil and trouble; others have deprived themselves of the most precious parts of the body, such as sight and the organs of generation, for fear that their services, too pleasant and easy, might relax and soften the firmness of their soul.

But for dying, which is the greatest task we have to perform, practice cannot help us. A man can, by habit and experience, fortify himself against pain, shame, indigence, and such other accidents; but as for death, we can try it only once: we are all apprentices when we come to it.

In ancient times there were men who husbanded their time so excellently that they tried to taste and savor it even at the point of death, and strained their minds to see what this passage was; but they have not come back to tell us news of it:

> No man awakes
> Whom once the icy end of living overtakes.
> *Lucretius*

Canius Julius, a Roman nobleman of singular virtue and firmness, after being condemned to death by that scoundrel Caligula, gave this among many prodigious proofs of his resoluteness. As he was on the point of being executed, a philosopher friend of his asked him: "Well, Canius, how stands your soul at this moment? What is it doing? What are your thoughts?" "I was thinking," he replied, "about holding myself ready and with all my powers intent to see whether in that instant of death, so short and brief, I shall be able to perceive any dislodgment of the soul, and whether it will have any feeling of its departure; so that, if I learn anything about it, I may return later, if I can, to give the information to my friends." This man philosophizes not only unto death, but even in death itself. What assurance it was, and what proud courage, to want his death to serve as a lesson to him, and to have leisure to think about other things in such a great business!

> ^BSuch sway he had over his dying soul.
> *Lucan*

^AIt seems to me, however, that there is a certain way of familiar-   5
izing ourselves with death and trying it out to some extent. We can have an experience of it that is, if not entire and perfect, at least not useless, and that makes us more fortified and assured. If we cannot reach it, we can approach it, we can reconnoiter it; and if we do not penetrate as far as its fort, at least we shall see and become acquainted with the approaches to it.

It is not without reason that we are taught to study even our sleep for the resemblance it has with death. ^CHow easily we pass from waking to sleeping! With how little sense of loss we lose consciousness of the light and of ourselves! Perhaps the faculty of sleep, which deprives us of all action and all feeling, might seem useless and contrary to nature, were it not that thereby Nature teaches us that she has made us for dying and living alike, and from the start of life presents to us the eternal state that she reserves for us after we die, to accustom us to it and take away our fear of it.

^ABut those who by some violent accident have fallen into a faint and lost all sensation, those, in my opinion, have been very close to seeing death's true and natural face. For as for the instant and point of passing away, it is not to be feared that it carries with it any travail or pain, since we can have no feeling without leisure. Our sufferings need time, which in death is so short and precipitate that it must necessarily be imperceptible. It is the approaches that we have to fear; and these may fall within our experience.

Many things seem to us greater in imagination than in reality. I have spent a good part of my life in perfect and entire health; I mean not merely entire, but even blithe and ebullient. This state, full of verdure and cheer, made me find the thought of illnesses so horrible that when I came to experience them I found their pains mild and easy compared with my fears.

^BHere is what I experience every day: if I am warmly sheltered in a nice room during a stormy and tempestuous night, I am appalled and distressed for those who are then in the open country; if I am myself outside, I do not even wish to be anywhere else.

^AThe mere idea of being always shut up in a room seemed to me   10
unbearable. Suddenly I had to get used to being there a week, or a month, full of agitation, alteration, and weakness. And I have found

that in time of health I used to pity the sick much more than I now think I deserve to be pitied when I am sick myself; and that the power of my apprehension made its object appear almost half again as fearful as it was in its truth and essence. I hope that the same thing will happen to me with death, and that it is not worth the trouble I take, the many preparations that I make, and all the many aids that I invoke and assemble to sustain the shock of it. But at all events, we can never be well enough prepared.

During our third civil war, or the second (I do not quite remember which), I went riding one day about a league from my house, which is situated at the very hub of all the turmoil of the civil wars of France. Thinking myself perfectly safe, and so near my home that I needed no better equipage, I took a very easy but not very strong horse. On my return, when a sudden occasion came up for me to use this horse for a service to which it was not accustomed, one of my men, big and strong, riding a powerful work horse who had a desperately hard mouth and was moreover fresh and vigorous—this man, in order to show his daring and get ahead of his companions, spurred his horse at full speed up the path behind me, came down like a colossus on the little man and little horse, and hit us like a thunderbolt with all his strength and weight, sending us both head over heels. So that there lay the horse bowled over and stunned, and I ten or twelve paces beyond, dead, stretched on my back, my face all bruised and skinned, my sword, which I had had in my hand, more than ten paces away, my belt in pieces, having no more motion or feeling than a log. It is the only swoon that I have experienced to this day.

Those who were with me, after having tried all the means they could to bring me round, thinking me dead, took me in their arms and were carrying me with great difficulty to my house, which was about half a French league from there. On the way, and after I had been taken for dead for more than two full hours, I began to move and breathe; for so great an abundance of blood had fallen into my stomach that nature had to revive its forces to discharge it. They set me up on my feet, where I threw up a whole bucketful of clots of pure blood, and several times on the way I had to do the same thing. In so doing I began to recover a little life, but it was bit by bit and over so long a stretch of time that my first feelings were much closer to death than to life:

> [B]Because the shaken soul, uncertain yet
> Of its return, is still not firmly set.
> *Tasso*

[A]This recollection, which is strongly implanted on my soul, showing me the face and idea of death so true to nature, reconciles me to it somewhat.

When I began to see anything, it was with a vision so blurred, weak, and dead, that I still could distinguish nothing but the light,

As one 'twixt wakefulness and doze,
Whose eyes now open, now again they close.
Tasso

As for the functions of the soul, they were reviving with the same progress as those of the body. I saw myself all bloody, for my doublet was stained all over with the blood I had thrown up. The first thought that came to me was that I had gotten a harquebus shot in the head; indeed several were being fired around us at the time of the accident. It seemed to me that my life was hanging only by the tip of my lips; I closed my eyes in order, it seemed to me, to help push it out, and took pleasure in growing languid and letting myself go. It was an idea that was only floating on the surface of my soul, as delicate and feeble as all the rest, but in truth not only free from distress but mingled with that sweet feeling that people have who let themselves slide into sleep.

I believe that this is the same state in which people find themselves whom we see fainting with weakness in the agony of death; and I maintain that we pity them without cause, supposing that they are agitated by grievous pains or have their soul oppressed by painful thoughts. This has always been my view, against the opinion of many, and even of Etienne de La Boétie, concerning those whom we see thus prostrate and comatose as their end approaches, or overwhelmed by the length of the disease, or by a stroke of apoplexy, or by epilepsy—

[B]This do we often see:
A man, struck, as by lightning, by some malady,
Falls down all foaming at the mouth, shivers and rants;
He moans under the torture, writhes his muscles, pants,
And in fitful tossing exhausts his weary limbs
Lucretius

—[A]or wounded in the head: When we hear them groan and from time to time utter poignant sighs, or see them make certain movements of the body, we seem to see signs that they still have some consciousness left; but I have always thought, I say, that their soul and body were buried in sleep.

[B]He lives, and is unconscious of his life.
Ovid

[A]And I could not believe that with so great a paralysis of the limbs, and so great a failing of the senses, the soul could maintain any force within by which to be conscious of itself; and so I believed that they had no reflections to torment them, nothing able to make them judge and feel the misery of their condition, and that consequently they were not much to be pitied.

^BI can imagine no state so horrible and unbearable for me as to have   15
my soul alive and afflicted, without means to express itself. I should say the same of those who are sent to execution with their tongue cut out, were it not that in this sort of death the most silent seems to be the most becoming, if it goes with a firm, grave countenance; and the same of those miserable prisoners who fall into the hands of the villainous murdering soldiers of these days, who torture them with every kind of cruel treatment to force them to pay some excessive and impossible ransom, keeping them meanwhile in a condition and in a place where they have no means whatever of expressing or signifying their thoughts and their misery.

^AThe poets have portrayed some gods as favorable to the deliverance of those who thus drag out a lingering death:

> I bear to Pluto, by decree,
> This lock of hair, and from your body set you free.
> *Virgil*

Nonetheless, the short and incoherent words and replies that are extorted from them by dint of shouting about their ears and storming at them, or the movements that seem to have some connection with what is asked them, are not evidence that they are alive, at least fully alive. So it happens to us in the early stages of sleep, before it has seized us completely, to sense as in a dream what is happening around us, and to follow voices with a blurred and uncertain hearing which seems to touch on only the edges of the soul; and following the last words spoken to us, we make answers that are more random than sensible.

Now I have no doubt, now that I have tried this out by experience, that I judged this matter rightly all along. For from the first, while wholly unconscious, I was laboring to rip open my doublet with my nails (for I was not in armor); and yet I know that I felt nothing in my imagination that hurt me; for there are many movements of ours that do not come from our will:

> ^BAnd half-dead fingers writhe and seize the sword again.
> *Virgil*

^AThus those who are falling throw out their arms in front of them, by a natural impulse which makes our limbs lend each other their services and have stirrings apart from our reason:

They say that chariots bearing scythes will cut so fast
That severed limbs are writhing on the ground below
Before the victim's soul and strength can ever know
Or even feel the pain, so swift has been the hurt.
                                                    Lucretius

[A]My stomach was oppressed with the clotted blood; my hands flew to it of their own accord, as they often do where we itch, against the intention of our will.

There are many animals, and even men, whose muscles we can see contract and move after they are dead. Every man knows by experience that there are parts that often move, stand up, and lie down, without his leave. Now these passions which touch only the rind of us cannot be called ours. To make them ours, the whole man must be involved; and the pains which the foot or the hand feel while we are asleep are not ours.

As I approached my house, where the alarm of my fall had already come, and the members of my family had met me with the outcries customary in such cases, not only did I make some sort of answer to what was asked me, but also (they say) I thought of ordering them to give a horse to my wife, whom I saw stumbling and having trouble on the road, which is steep and rugged. It would seem that this consideration must have proceeded from a wide-awake soul; yet the fact is that I was not there at all. These were idle thoughts, in the clouds, set in motion by the sensations of the eyes and ears; they did not come from within me. I did not know, for all that, where I was coming from or where I was going, nor could I weigh and consider what I was asked. These are slight effects which the senses produce of themselves, as if by habit; what the soul contributed was in a dream, touched very lightly, and merely licked and sprinkled, as it were, by the soft impression of the senses.

Meanwhile my condition was, in truth, very pleasant and peaceful; I felt no affliction either for others or for myself; it was a languor and an extreme weakness, without any pain. I saw my house without recognizing it. When they had put me to bed, I felt infinite sweetness in this repose, for I had been villainously yanked about by those poor fellows, who had taken the pains to carry me in their arms over a long and very bad road, and had tired themselves out two or three times in relays. They offered me many remedies, of which I accepted none, holding it for certain that I was mortally wounded in the head. It would, in truth, have been a very happy death; for the weakness of my understanding kept me from having any judgment of it, and that of my body from having any feeling of it. I was letting myself slip away so gently, so gradually and easily, that I hardly ever did anything with less of a feeling of effort.

When I came back to life and regained my powers,

^BWhen my senses at last regained their strength,
Ovid

^Awhich was two or three hours later, I felt myself all of a sudden caught up again in the pains, my limbs being all battered and bruised by my fall; and I felt so bad two or three nights after that I thought I was going to die all over again, but by a more painful death; and I still feel the effect of the shock of that collision.

I do not want to forget this, that the last thing I was able to re-   20
cover was the memory of this accident; I had people repeat to me several times where I was going, where I was coming from, at what time it had happened to me, before I could take it in. As for the manner of my fall, they concealed it from me and made up other versions for the sake of the man who had been the cause of it. But a long time after, and the next day, when my memory came to open up and picture to me the state I had been in at the instant I had perceived that horse bearing down on me (for I had seen him at my heels and thought I was a dead man, but that thought had been so sudden that I had no time to be afraid), it seemed to me that a flash of lightning was striking my soul with a violent shock, and that I was coming back from the other world.

This account of so trivial an event would be rather pointless, were it not for the instruction that I have derived from it for myself; for in truth, in order to get used to the idea of death, I find there is nothing like coming close to it. Now as Pliny says, each man is a good education to himself, provided he has the capacity to spy on himself from close up. What I write here is not my teaching, but my study; it is not a lesson for others, but for me.

^CAnd yet it should not be held against me if I publish what I write. What is useful to me may also by accident be useful to another. Moreover, I am not spoiling anything, I am using only what is mine. And if I play the fool, it is at my expense and without harm to anyone. For it is a folly that will die with me, and will have no consequences. We have heard of only two or three ancients who opened up this road, and even of them we cannot say whether their manner in the least resembled mine, since we know only their names. No one since has followed their lead. It is a thorny undertaking, and more so than it seems, to follow a movement so wandering as that of our mind, to penetrate the opaque depths of its innermost folds, to pick out and immobilize the innumerable flutterings that agitate it. And it is a new and extraordinary amusement, which withdraws us from the ordinary occupations of the world, yes, even from those most recommended.

It is many years now that I have had only myself as object of my thoughts, that I have been examining and studying only myself; and if I study anything else, it is in order promptly to apply it to myself, or rather within myself. And it does not seem to me that I am making a mistake if—as is done in the other sciences, which are incomparably less useful—I impart what I have learned in this one, though I am hardly satisfied with the progress I have made in it. There is no description equal in difficulty, or certainly in usefulness, to the description of oneself. Even so one must spruce up, even so one must present oneself in an orderly arrangement, if one would go out in public. Now, I am constantly adorning myself, for I am constantly describing myself.

Custom has made speaking of oneself a vice, and obstinately forbids it out of hatred for the boasting that seems always to accompany it. Instead of blowing the child's nose, as we should, this amounts to pulling it off.

> Flight from a fault will lead us into crime.
>> *Horace*

I find more harm than good in this remedy. But even if it were true that it is presumptuous, no matter what the circumstances, to talk to the public about oneself, I still must not, according to my general plan, refrain from an action that openly displays this morbid quality, since it is in me; nor may I conceal this fault, which I not only practice but profess. However, to say what I think about it, custom is wrong to condemn wine because many get drunk on it. We can misuse only things which are good. And I believe that the rule against speaking of oneself applies only to the vulgar form of this failing. Such rules are bridles for calves, with which neither the saints, whom we hear speaking so boldly about themselves, nor the philosophers, nor the theologians curb themselves. Nor do I, though I am none of these. If they do not write about themselves expressly, at least when the occasion leads them to it they do not hesitate to put themselves prominently on display. What does Socrates treat of more fully than himself? To what does he lead his disciples' conversation more often than to talk about themselves, not about the lesson of their book, but about the essence and movement of their soul? We speak our thoughts religiously to God, and to our confessor, as our neighbors[1] do to the whole people. But, someone will answer, we speak only our self-accusations. Then we speak everything: for our very virtue is faulty and fit for repentance.

My trade and my art is living. He who forbids me to speak about it according to my sense, experience, and practice, let him order the architect to speak of buildings not according to himself but according to his neighbor; according to another man's knowledge, not according to his own. If it is vainglory for a man himself to publish his own merits,

25

---

[1] The Protestants.

why doesn't Cicero proclaim the eloquence of Hortensius, Hortensius that of Cicero?

Perhaps they mean that I should testify about myself by works and deeds, not by bare words. What I chiefly portray is my cogitations, a shapeless subject that does not lend itself to expression in actions. It is all I can do to couch my thoughts in this airy medium of words. Some of the wisest and most devout men have lived avoiding all noticeable actions. My actions would tell more about fortune than about me. They bear witness to their own part, not to mine, unless it be by conjecture and without certainty: they are samples which display only details. I expose myself entire: my portrait is a cadaver on which the veins, the muscles, and the tendons appear at a glance, each part in its place. One part of what I am was produced by a cough, another by a pallor or a palpitation of the heart—in any case dubiously. It is not my deeds that I write down; it is myself, it is my essence.

I hold that a man should be cautious in making an estimate of himself, and equally conscientious in testifying about himself—whether he rates himself high or low makes no difference. If I seemed to myself good and wise or nearly so, I would shout it out at the top of my voice. To say less of yourself than is true is stupidity, not modesty. To pay yourself less than you are worth is cowardice and pusillanimity, according to Aristotle. No virtue is helped by falsehood, and truth is never subject to error. To say more of yourself than is true is not always presumption; it too is often stupidity. To be immoderately pleased with what you are, to fall therefore into an undiscerning self-love, is in my opinion the substance of this vice. The supreme remedy to cure it is to do just the opposite of what those people prescribe who, by prohibiting talking about oneself, even more strongly prohibit thinking about oneself. The pride lies in the thought; the tongue can have only a very slight share in it.

It seems to them that to be occupied with oneself means to be pleased with oneself, that to frequent and associate with oneself means to cherish oneself too much. That may be. But this excess arises only in those who touch themselves no more than superficially; who observe themselves only after taking care of their business; who call it daydreaming and idleness to be concerned with oneself, and making castles in Spain to furnish and build oneself; who think themselves something alien and foreign to themselves.

If anyone gets intoxicated with his knowledge when he looks beneath him, let him turn his eyes upward toward past ages, and he will lower his horns, finding there so many thousands of minds that trample him underfoot. If he gets into some flattering presumption about his valor, let him remember the lives of the two Scipios, so many armies, so many nations, all of whom leave him so far behind them. No particular quality will make a man proud who balances it against the many weaknesses and imperfections that are also in him, and, in the end, against the nullity of man's estate.

Because Socrates alone had seriously digested the precept of   30
his god—to know himself—and because by that study he had come to despise himself, he alone was deemed worthy of the name *wise.* Whoever knows himself thus, let him boldly make himself known by his own mouth.

LINES OF INQUIRY
"Of Practice"

In paragraphs 11 through 22, Montaigne tells a detailed story of coming near to death in order to prepare himself (and others) for death. Consider the various ways in which this story might help someone "get used to the idea of death." What does the story suggest about the sensations, feelings, and desires that are actually experienced by someone on the verge of dying? How do these compare with what the story suggests about the apparent sensations, feelings, and desires of a person on the verge of dying? What new insight(s), if any, did you get into death and dying from reading Montaigne's story?

In the last nine paragraphs of this essay, Montaigne digresses so completely from his prior concern with death that he never again returns to the subject. Look closely at the end of paragraph 22 and the beginning of paragraph 23 to see if you can discover any particular thoughts or line of thinking that might have led him into his extended reflections on writing, particularly on writing about himself and his thoughts. Can you think of any respect(s) in which his reflections on writing might be related to his thoughts about dying, or to his thoughts about the general subject "of practice"?

Montaigne is not the only essayist in this collection to write about the actual versus the supposed nature of dying, as you can see by looking at Lewis Thomas's "On Natural Death." In fact, Thomas refers to Montaigne's essay in the course of his own reflections on dying. What new information or experience does Thomas have to offer on the subject? In what respect(s), if any, does Thomas's material corroborate Montaigne's personal reflections. In what respect(s), if any, does Thomas's material shed new light on the subject?

JOYCE CAROL OATES

1938 –

*Uplifting endings and resolutely cheery world views are
appropriate to television commercials but insulting elsewhere.
It is not only wicked to pretend otherwise, it is futile.*

In this uncompromising assertion from an essay in the *New York Times Sunday Book Review,* Joyce Carol Oates reflects the tenor of her many essays, short stories, novels, poems, and plays. Her work is often infused with a sense of anxiety and terror, often focused on violence and perversion, often gothic in content and tone. "We are stimulated to emotional response," she believes, "not by works that confirm our sense of the world, but by works that challenge it." Oates always challenges conventional or comfortable views of the world, compelling her readers to reflect on the social and cultural conditions that lead to violence and suffering.

Oates was born in Lockport, N. Y., a small town in western New York, and grew up in a rural area that she has often reflected in her writing, as she explains in "My Father, My Fiction." The oldest of three children of stable, hard-working parents, she was evidently favored by her father, a tool-and-die maker, who took her flying in two-seater planes, introduced her to boxing, and exposed her to other worlds of experience that were then considered the domain of men. A legacy of poverty and violence in prior generations of her family also exposed her to the convulsive and "malnourished circumstances" that often beset the lives of her fictional characters. As a child she attended a one-room schoolhouse, where she began pouring out stories and constructing books. By the time she was fifteen, in fact, she had already submitted her first novel to a publisher. "She was always so hard-working, a perfectionist at everything," according to her mother.

After graduating Phi Beta Kappa in English from Syracuse University in 1960, she went on for her Masters in English at the University of Wisconsin, where she met her husband, who was working on his Ph.D. in English. They were married in 1961 and then moved to Beaumont, Texas, where he had his first teaching job, and where she began to work full time on her writing. She had planned to study for a Ph.D. in English at Rice University in Houston, but when she saw one of her pieces cited as an honorable mention in Foley's *Best American Short Stories,* she decided that "maybe I could be a writer." In 1962, she and her husband acquired university teaching positions in Detroit, a city whose turbulent life evidently had a powerful impact on her writing— "Detroit, my 'great' subject, made me the person I am, consequently the writer I am, for better or worse." She taught at the University of Detroit until 1967, then moved across the Detroit River to the University of

Windsor in Ontario, where she taught until 1978. Since that time she has been on the faculty of Princeton University, first as a writer in residence, more recently as a Distinguished Professor of Writing.

Though continuously engaged in teaching, her output as a writer during the last thirty years has been astonishing—at last count, 24 novels, 24 short story collections, 13 volumes of poetry, 3 books of literary criticism, 3 essay collections, 2 nonfiction books, 3 plays, and numerous book reviews. Her output amazes, even offends, some of her critics. But she responds by saying that "if you are a writer, you locate yourself behind a wall of silence and no matter what you are doing, driving a car or walking or doing housework, which I love, you can still be writing, because you have that space." In other words, she is always writing, the words always flowing out, though the act of writing is in no sense easy for her. She has always followed a rigorous schedule, seldom going out, and now she says, "As I get older, I find I can't write as fast, and I have to rewrite again and again, sometimes as much as 17 times."

Oates is best known, of course, for her extensive body of fictional writing, which has won her many honors, including the National Book Award for *them,* a saga-like novel about the lives and experience of a lower middle class Detroit family, beginning in the thirties and culminating in the 1967 race riots. Whether she is writing realistic, surrealistic, or gothic fiction, her narratives are invariably marked by the meticulousness of her historical documentation and the complexity of her psychological portraits. A similarly painstaking attention to detail is also evident in her essays, whether she is writing about personal experience, popular culture, or literary texts. In part, of course, her attention to detail is the mark of her intense commitment to vividly representing the fictional and nonfictional worlds of which she writes. But beyond mere vividness, she is driven by a preoccupation with the significance of those details, which reflect the disturbing circumstances of contemporary culture and the psychic trauma that it produces in the lives of individuals. "I am concerned with only one thing," she has said, "the moral and social conditions of my generation." Thus whether she writes about farmworkers, slum-dwellers, yuppies, poets, professors, or religious fanatics, she is invariably interested in the way their lives are marked by the convulsions and tensions of contemporary culture. So, too, whether she writes about young, middle-aged, or older women, of the nineteenth or twentieth centuries, she is invariably concerned with the disturbing predicament of women in a male-dominated world.

Though she is widely recognized for the spectacularly varied cast of women characters who populate her fiction, as well as for her penetrating essays about women's experience and women's writing, she is probably most well known for the violence in her work—for the depravity that dominates such a novel as *Wonderland* (1971) or for the brutal world that preoccupies her in her recent works on boxing. Indeed, she has been asked so often about the violence of which she writes that she finally wrote an essay about it, "Why is Your Writing So Violent?" In answering that question, she reminds her readers of the serious purpose that informs what might otherwise seem to be sensationalist writing:

> Since it is commonly understood that serious writers, as distinct from entertainers or propagandists, take for their natural subjects the complexity of the world, its evils as well as its goods, it is always an insulting question; and it is always sexist. The serious writer, after all, bears witness.

Oates "bears witness" to violence and suffering, because that is what she sees in her culture, and her object as a writer is to describe and critique that culture, to write about the large social evils rather than simply creating some "small, tidy, perfect work of art."

Ultimately, her theme as an essayist and novelist is the inseparability of individuals from the culture in which they exist. In this respect, she is an anti-romantic, skeptical about visions of the isolated hero escaping artificial limits. Indeed, her view of the human situation is aggressively deterministic: "Man is trapped within a temporal, physical world," she says in an essay on Shakespeare, "and his rhetoric, his poetry, even his genius cannot free him." Or in another context, she declares that "man is locked in the historical and the immediate." Her object as a writer, therefore, is to describe those historical and immediate realities, with as much detail and vividness as possible, and to witness their profound influence on the characters and persons of whom she writes.

Though her vision of the contemporary situation may be intensely disturbing, Oates herself believes that "literature is wonderfully optimistic, because it so often demonstrates how human beings get through things, maneuver themselves through chaos, and then *write about it.*" So one might say that Oates's capacity to write about cruelty and suffering with such immediacy is itself a gesture of affirmation. The power of her language is an emblem of the human ability to transform painful experience into meaning, and in that way at least, in some small measure, to transcend it.

BLOOD, NEON, AND FAILURE IN THE DESERT

Other than boxing, everything is so boring.
Mike Tyson

Las Vegas, Nevada. 7 March 1987. In a ring still stained with blood from the desperately fought heavyweight match that preceded it, Mike Tyson, World Boxing Council champion, at twenty the youngest heavyweight titleholder in boxing history, brings the fight for unification of the title to James "Bonecrusher" Smith, World Boxing Association champion, at thirty-three an aging athlete, and, yet more telling, the only heavyweight titleholder in boxing history to have graduated from college—but Smith will have none of it. He clinches, he backs away, he walks away, he clinches again, hugging his frustrated and increasingly infuriated opponent like a drowning man hugging something—anything—that floats. Referee Mills Lane calls "Break!" repeatedly during the twelve long rounds of this very long fight but Smith seems not to hear; or, hearing, will not obey. For the most part his expression is blank, with the blankness of fear, a stark unmitigated fear without shame, yet shameful to witness. "Fight!" the crowd shouts. "Do something!" In the ringside seats close by me Smith's fellow boxers Trevor Berbick (former WBC heavyweight champion) and Edwin Rosario (WBA lightweight champion) are particularly vocal, as if in an agony of professional discomfort. For it seems that the superbly conditioned Smith, who had performed so dramatically only three months ago in Madison Square Garden, knocking out Tim Witherspoon in the first round of his WBA title defense, is now, suddenly, not a boxer: though in that elevated and garishly spotlighted ring with another man, contracted for $1 million to fight him, performing in front of a crowd of some 13,600 people in the Hilton's newly erected outdoor stadium, and how many millions of television viewers, he cannot or will not fight. His instinct is merely to survive—to get through twelve rounds with no injuries more serious than a bleeding left eye and a bad swelling on the right side of his face; and to go back, professionally disgraced, to his wife, family, and plans for the future ("Being a champion opens lots of doors—I'd like to get a real estate license, maybe sell insurance") in Magnolia, North Carolina.

Berbick writhes in the folding chair beside me, muttering, laughing, derisive, very nearly as frustrated as Mike Tyson, and clearly resentful—after all, he is the man who fought Tyson here last November, and so spectacularly (and humiliatingly) lost to him, and in the third minute of the second round of that fight. He too had tried to clinch with Tyson, had gripped the young man's arms and gloves in an effort to hold him back, slow him down, frustrate him, but Berbick had also fought him, or made a game attempt—"I wanted to prove my manhood," he said afterward, ruefully, "that was my mistake." In this match Smith's manhood is not evidently an issue. He has no "machismo" to display or defend; if he is a boxer it must be by default. Minute follows minute, round follows grinding round, as Tyson tries to get inside to throw the rapid-fire combinations for which he is famous, and Smith falls upon him and hugs him, clumsily, defiantly, desperately. Mills Lane, exasperated, penalizes Smith by deducting points from him after rounds two and eight. ("I could have deducted a point from him after each round," he said afterward, "but you don't like to do that in a title fight.") The 6-foot-4-inch 233-pound Smith is a zombie tonight, a parody of a boxer, so resistant to boxing's visible and invisible rules, that complex of mores that make boxing at once the most primitive and the most sophisticated of contact sports, it is fascinating to watch him—to a degree.

"I wasn't prepared for how strong Tyson is, how fast," Smith will say after the fight. "Tyson has a devastating left hook." And, defensively: "I did the best I could." Of current heavyweights Smith has invariably been the most erratic in performance, the most unpredictable—capable, under pressure, of boxing well, yet strangely and unprofessionally susceptible to vagaries of mood. Perhaps because he has no real vocation as a boxer—and no more instinct for fighting than one might expect from a man with a B.A. in business administration (from Shaw College, North Carolina)—he is easily demoralized in the ring, allowing childlike expressions of triumph, hurt, bewilderment, and acute unhappiness to show on his face, as boxers so rarely do; he boxes as an intelligent man might box whose intelligence is his only weapon in an action in which "intelligence" must be subordinated to something more fundamental. He draws upon no deeper reserves of self—no energy, imagination, emotion—beyond those of consciousness.

As for Tyson: unlike Dempsey, Marciano, and Frazier, those famously aggressive fighters to whom he is often compared, Tyson is not a reckless boxer; he is not willing, as so many boxer-fighters are, to take four or five punches in order to throw a punch of his own. His training is defensive and cautious—hence the peek-a-boo stance, a Cus D'Amato signature: for is not boxing primarily the art of self-defense? of hitting your man, and scoring points, without being hit in return? For two years, which must have been very long years, D'Amato trained Tyson to bob, weave, slip punches from sparring partners without throwing a single punch in response—a conditioning that has made Tyson an anomaly in the ring. His reputation is for power, speed, and aggression, but his defensive skills are as remarkable, if less dramatic. Confronted with an opponent like "Bonecrusher" Smith, who violates the decorum of the ring by not fighting, Tyson is at a loss; he hits his man after the bell, in an adolescent display of frustration; he exchanges insults with him during the fight, makes jeering faces; pushes, shoves, laces the cut over Smith's eye during a clinch; betrays those remnants of his Brooklyn street-fighting days (Tyson, as a child of ten, was one of the youngest members of a notorious gang called the Jolly Stompers) his training as a boxer should have overcome. In short, his inexperience shows.

So the pattern of the fight is immediately established: in the en- 5 tire twelve rounds virtually nothing will happen that does not happen in the first thirty seconds of the first round. The spectator is gripped by stasis itself, by the perversity of the expectation that, against all expec- tation, something will happen. If this is theater, and boxing is always theater, we are in the slyly teasing anti-worlds of Jarry, Ionesco, Beck- ett; the aesthetics is that of fanatic tedium, as in John Cage and Andy Warhol. While my press colleagues to a man will report the match boring—"Two interior decorators could have done each other more damage" (*Los Angeles Times*)—I find it uniquely tense, and exhausting; not unlike the first Spinks/Holmes fight in which the frustrated Holmes carried his right glove for round after round, a talismanic club waiting to be swung. Poor Holmes! Poor Lear! This is the very poetry of masculine frustration—the failure of psychic closure. Such fights end, and are funny, in retrospect; but are never resolved.

Tyson's predicament vis-à-vis "Bonecrusher" Smith brings to mind Jack Dempsey, similarly frustrated in his matches with Tunney, shout- ing at his retreating opponent, "Come on and fight!" But, for all his renown, Dempsey was not a strategic boxer of the sort Tyson has been meticulously trained to be; his ring style was virtually nonstop offense with very little defense, which means that he was willing to take punches in the hope of throwing his own. Outboxed by the more cau- tious and more intelligent Tunney, he eventually lost both fights. In the Tyson/Smith match there is no question that Tyson is the superior boxer; he will win every round unanimously in what is in fact one of the easiest fights of his two-year career as a professional. But this is hardly the dramatic public performance he'd hoped to give, and the fight's promoters had hoped to present. No knockout—none of the dazzling combinations of blows for which he is known; very little of what D'Amato taught his protégés was the boxer's primary responsibility to his audience: to entertain. Winning too can be a kind of failure.

The fight recalls several previous fights of Tyson's with opponents who, out of fear or cunning, or both, refused to fight him; yet more wor- risomely it recalls Joe Louis's predicament as heavyweight champion in those years when, after having cleared the heavyweight division of all serious contenders, he was reduced to fighting mere opponents— "Bums-of-the-Month" as the press derisively called them. Worse, Louis's reputation as a puncher, a machine for hitting, so intimidated opponents that they were frightened to enter the ring with him. ("Enter the ring? My man had to be helped down the aisle," one manager is said to have said.) For a sport routinely attacked for its brutality boxing has had its share of historically shameful episodes: Louis's title defense against a long-forgotten challenger named Pastor, whom he chased for ten dreary rounds of running and clutching, running and clutching, is invariably cited. While Rocky Marciano/Jersey Joe Walcott I (September 1952) was notable for both fighters' courage—this was the fight that gave Marciano the heavyweight title—the rematch eight months later ended with the first punch thrown by Marciano: Walcott sat on the canvas and made no effort to get up as he was counted out. ("After twenty-three years as a professional fighter, the former champion went out in a total disgrace that no excuses can relieve"—Red Smith, a former admirer of Walcott.) Both Muhammad Ali/Sonny Liston title matches were memorable for Liston's surprising behavior: in the first, in which Liston was defending his title, he refused to continue fighting after the sixth round, claiming a shoulder injury; in the second, he went down with mysterious alacrity at one minute forty-eight seconds of the first round, struck by a devastating, if invisible, blow to the head. (This defeat disgraced Liston and effectively ended his career: he was never to be offered another championship fight. Even the circumstances of his death some years later at the age of thirty-eight were suspicious.) There was Dempsey's notorious fight with Tommy Gibbons in Shelby, Montana, in 1923, which made money for Dempsey and his promoter, Kearns, while nearly bankrupting the town; there was the bizarre "Slapsie" Maxey Rosenbloom, world light-heavyweight champion of the early 1930s, a sort of pacifist of boxing, whose strategy was to hit (or slap, gloves open) and run—a boxing style as exciting to watch, it is said, as the growth of tree rings. While no one has ever questioned Marvelous Marvin Hagler's integrity, his defense of his middleweight title against Roberto Durán some years ago left many observers skeptical—the usually aggressive Hagler seemed oddly solicitous of his opponent. But the most scandalous boxing incident of modern times still remains Durán's decision, two minutes and forty-four seconds into the eighth round of his welterweight title defense with Sugar Ray Leonard in 1980, to simply quit the fight—"¡No màs!" No more! Leonard had been outboxing him, making a fool of him, and Durán had had enough. Machismo punctures easily.

Though most of Mike Tyson's twenty-eight fights have ended with knockouts, often in early rounds, and once (with Joe Frazier's hapless son Marvis) within thirty seconds of the first round, several opponents have slowed him down as "Bonecrusher" Smith has done, and made him appear baffled, thwarted, intermittently clumsy. "Quick" Tillis and Mitch Green come most readily to mind; and, though Tyson eventually knocked him out, in the final round of a ten-round fight, José Ribalta.

Perhaps the ugliest fight of Tyson's career was with Jesse Ferguson, who, in a performance anticipating Smith's, held onto him with such desperation after Tyson had broken his nose that even the referee could not free the men. (Ferguson was disqualified and the fight was ruled a TKO for Tyson.) Such performances do not constitute boxing at its finest moments, nor do they presage well for Tyson's future: to be a great champion one must have great opponents.

*   *   *

Incongruity, like vulgarity, is not a concept in Las Vegas. This fantasy-land for adults, with its winking neon skyline, its twenty-four-hour clockless casinos, its slots, craps, Keno, roulette, baccarat, blackjack et al., created by fiat when the Nevada legislature passed a law legalizing gambling in 1931, exists as a counterworld to our own. There is no day here—the enormous casinos are pure interiority, like the inside of a skull. Gambling, as François Mauriac once said, is continuous suicide: if suicide, yet continuous. There is no past, no significant future, only an eternal and always optimistic present tense. Vegas is our exemplary American city, a congeries of hotels in the desert, shrines of chance in which, presumably, we are all equal as we are not equal before the law, or God, or one another. One sees in the casinos, especially at the slot machines, those acres and acres of slot machines, men and women of all ages, races, types, degrees of probable or improbable intelligence, as hopefully attentive to their machines as writers and academicians are to their word processors. If one keeps on, faithfully, obsessively, one will surely hit The Jackpot. (You know it's The Jackpot when your machine lights up, a goofy melody ensues, and a flood of coins like a lascivious Greek god comes tumbling into your lap.) The reedy dialects of irony—the habitual tone of the cultural critic in twentieth-century America—are as foreign here as snow, or naturally green grass.

So it is hardly incongruous that boxing matches are held in the   10
Las Vegas Hilton and Caesar's Palace, VIP tickets at $1,000 or more (and the cheapest tickets, at $75, so remote from the ring that attendance at a fight is merely nominal, or symbolic); it is not incongruous that this most physical of sports, like the flipping of cards or the throw of dice, is most brilliantly realized as a gambling opportunity. In the elaborately equipped sports rooms of the big casinos, where television screens monitor various sporting events, sans sound, and betting statistics are constantly being posted, like stock market reports, one can bet on virtually any sport provided it is "professional" and not "amateur." The favorites are naturally baseball, football, basketball, boxing, and, of course, horseracing, the sport that seems to have been invented purely for gambling purposes. In these semidarkened rooms gamblers sit entranced, or comatose, drinks in hand, staring up at the television monitors and the hundreds, or is it thousands, of postings. Red numerals

against a black background. A dozen or more television screens in an electronic collage. The upcoming "fight of the century"—Marvelous Marvin Hagler/Sugar Ray Leonard for Hagler's undisputed middleweight title, 6 April 1987 at Caesar's Palace—is the casinos' dream: as of 7 March odds are posted −3.25 Hagler, +2.25 Leonard, with these propositions: (1) the fight does not go twelve rounds; (2) Hagler by KO; (3) Hagler by decision; (4) Leonard by KO; (5) Leonard by decision. The Mike Tyson/"Bonecrusher" Smith odds are Tyson −7.00, Smith +5.00, which means that you would make a good deal of money betting on Smith, if Smith would only win. Since Tyson's victory is a foregone conclusion the bookmakers offer only one proposition: that the fight does, or does not, go four rounds. (Which accounts for the outburst of ecstatic cheering, the only cheering of the fight, when the bell rings sounding the end of round four and Smith, bleeding down the left side of his face, freshly admonished by Mills Lane for holding and refusing to break, nonetheless walks to his corner.)

While in the antebellum American South white slaveowners frequently pitted their Negro slaves against each other in fights of spectacular savagery, and made bets on the results, in Las Vegas the descendants of these slaves, and their black kinsmen from the West Indies, Africa, and elsewhere, freely fight one another for purses of gratifying generosity: the highest paid athletes in the world are American boxers, and the highest paying fights are always in Vegas. Marvin Hagler, for instance, earned a minimum of $7.5 million for his April 1985 title defense against Thomas Hearns, who earned $7 million; in April 1987 he is guaranteed a minimum of $11 million against Leonard's $10 million in a fight that boxing promoters anticipate will make more money than any boxing match in history. ("I'm sure there will be $100,000 bets on both fighters," says a casino proprietor, "and we'll be right here to take them.") Mike Tyson will earn a minimum of $1.5 million for his fight with Smith (to Smith's $1 million) and if his spectacular career continues as everyone predicts, he will soon be earning as much as Hagler and Leonard, if not more. Though Tyson lacks Muhammad Ali's inspired narcissism, he is not handicapped by Ali's brash black politics and Ali's penchant for antagonizing whites: for all his reserve, his odd, even eerie combination of shyness and aggression, his is a wonderfully *marketable* image. (See the iconic "Mike Tyson" of billboard and newspaper ads, a metallic man, no twenty-year-old but a robot of planes, angles, inhuman composure: "Iron Mike" Tyson.)

Yet how subdued the real Tyson appeared, following the inglorious fight, and the noisy press conference in a candy-striped tent in a corner of the Hilton's parking lot: one caught glimpses of him that night at the jammed victory party on the thirtieth floor of the hotel, being interviewed, photographed, televised, and, later, being led through the hotel's crowded lobby, surrounded by publicity people, still being televised, wearing his preposterously ornate WBC champion's belt around his waist and his newly acquired WBA belt slung over his shoulder, his expression vague, dim, hooded, very possibly embarrassed ("It was a long, boring fight—twelve rounds"), like one of those captive demigods or doomed kings recorded in Frazer's *Golden Bough*.

What is "taboo" except that aspect of us that lies undefined, and inaccessible to consciousness: the core of impersonality within the carefully nurtured and jealously prized "personality" with which we are identified, by ourselves and others. In his speculative essay *Totem and Taboo* Freud meditated upon the ambivalent nature of taboo: its association with the sacred and consecrated, and with the dangerous, uncanny, forbidden, and unclean. All that one can say with certitude about taboo is that it stands in perennial opposition to the ordinary—to the quotidian. Taboo has to do with the numinous, with the ineffable, with utter indefinable mystery: with something not us. Or so we tell ourselves.

To the boxing aficionado the sport's powerful appeal is rarely exponible. It seems to be rooted in its paradoxical nature—the savagery that so clearly underlies, yet is contained by, its myriad rules, regulations, traditions, and superstitions. It seems to make the quotidian that which is uncanny, dangerous, forbidden, and unclean: it ritualizes violence, primarily male violence, to the degree to which violence becomes an aesthetic principle. In this, men's bodies (or, rather, their highly trained employment of their bodies) are instruments and not mere flesh like our own. That a man is a boxer is an action, and no longer a man, or not significantly a "man," puzzles those of us who feel ourselves fully defined in any of our actions. The romantic principles of Existentialism in its broadest, most vernacular sense have much to do with one's volition and one's will in creating oneself as an ethical being by way of a freely chosen action. Boxing, more than most contemporary American sports, clearly inhabits a dimension of human behavior one might call metaethical or meta-existential. There is no evident relationship between the man outside the ring and the man inside the ring—the boxer who is, like Mike Tyson (or Joe Louis, or Rocky Marciano, or any number of other boxers of distinction), "courteous," "soft-spoken," "gentle," in private life, and, in the ring, once the bell has sounded, "brutal," "awesome," "murderous," "devastating," "a young bull"— and the rest. The aim is not to kill one's opponent, for one's opponent is after all one's brother: the aim is to render him temporarily incapacitated, in a simulation of death. "It's unbelievable," Mike Tyson has said of boxing. "It's like a drug; I thrive on it. It's the excitement of the event, and now I need that excitement all the time."

When the boxer enters the ring, ceremonially disrobes, and answers the summons to fight, he ceases being an individual with all that implies of a socially regulated ethical bond with other individuals; he   15 becomes a boxer, which is to say an action. It might be argued that America's fascination with sports—if "fascination" is not too weak a word for such frenzied devotion, weekend after weekend, season after season, in the lives of a majority of men—has to do not only with the power of taboo to violate, or transcend, or render obsolete conventional categories of morality, but with the dark, denied, muted, eclipsed, and wholly unarticulated underside of America's religion of success. Sports is only partly about winning; it is also about losing. Failure, hurt, ignominy, disgrace, physical injury, sometimes even death—these are facts of life, perhaps the very bedrock of lives, which the sports-actor, or athlete, must dramatize in the flesh; and always against his will. Boxing as dream-image, or nightmare, pits self against self, identical twin against twin, as in the womb itself where "dominancy," that most mysterious of human hungers, is first expressed. Its most characteristic moments of ecstasy—the approach to the knockout, the knockout, the aftermath of the knockout, and, by way of television replays, the entire episode retraced in slow motion *as in the privacy of a dream*—are indistinguishable from obscenity, horror. In the words of middleweight Sugar Ray Seales, 1972 Olympic Gold Medalist, a veteran of more than four hundred amateur and professional fights who went blind as a consequence of ring injuries: "I went into the wilderness, and fought the animals there, and when I came back I was blind."

In Clifford Geertz's classic anthropological essay of 1972, "Deep Play: Notes on the Balinese Cockfight," the point is made that, in Bali, the now-illegal cockfighting obsession is wholly male, and masculine: the "cock" is the male organ, as the Balinese freely acknowledge, but it is more than merely that—it is the man, the maleness, codified, individualized, in a context of other individuals: which is to say, society. The cockfight is utterly mindless, bloody, savage, *animal*—and ephemeral: though a Balinese loves his fighting cock, and treats him tenderly, once the cock is dead it is dead, and quickly forgotten. (Sometimes, in a paroxysm of disappointment and rage, Geertz notes, cock-owners dismember their own cocks after the cocks are killed.) Boxing in the United States is far more complex a cultural phenomenon than the Balinese cockfight— it has much to do, for example, with immigrant succession, and with the ever-shifting tensions of race—but some of the principles Geertz isolates in the cockfight are surely operant: men are fascinated by boxing because it suggests that masculinity is measured solely in terms of other men, and not in terms of women; and because, in its very real dangers, it is a species of "deep play" (an action in which stakes are so high that it is, from a utilitarian standpoint, irrational for men to engage in it at all) that seems to demonstrate the way the world really is and not the way it is said, or wished, or promised to be. The boxer is consumed in action, and has no significant identity beyond action; the fight is a convulsion of a kind, strictly delimited in space (a meticulously squared circle bounded, like an animal pen, by ropes) and time. (Jack Dempsey, in whose honor the term "killer instinct" was coined, once remarked that he wasn't the fighter he might have been, with so many rules and regulations governing the sport: "You're in there for three-minute rounds with gloves on and a referee. That's not real fighting.") The passions it arouses are always in excess of its "utilitarian" worth since in fact it has none. As the bloody, repetitious, and ephemeral cockfight is a Balinese reading of Balinese experience, a story Balinese men tell themselves about themselves, so too is the American boxing match a reading of American experience, unsentimentalized and graphic. Yes, one thinks, you have told us about civilized values; you have schooled us in the virtues, presumably Christian, of turning the other cheek; of meekness as a prerequisite for inheriting the earth—the stratagems (manipulative? *feminine?*) of indirection. But the boxing match suggests otherwise, and it is that reading of life that we prefer. The boxers make visible what is invisible in us, thereby defining us, and themselves, in a single consecrated action. As Rocky Graziano once said, "The fight for survival is the fight."

LINES OF INQUIRY
"Blood, Neon, and Failure in the Desert"

Oates has divided this essay about boxing into two main sections, separated from each other by the asterisks between paragraphs 7 and 8; and each of these sections is, in turn, broken down into two segments, separated from each other by a bit of extra space. What images, aspects, and implications of boxing does she emphasize in each of the main sections; what images, aspects, and implications of boxing does she focus on in each of the shorter segments? Why do you suppose she has arranged the four segments as they presently stand? Consider reversing segments 2 and 3. How does this rearrangement affect the pacing, the buildup, the clarity, and the pointedness of the piece?

In the next to last sentence of the essay, Oates claims that "The boxers make visible what is invisible in us, thereby defining us, and themselves." What is Oates referring to when she speaks of "what is invisible in us"? How do boxers "make visible what is invisible in us"? How, for example, does the Tyson-Smith fight that she describes "make visible what is invisible in us"? And in what sense(s) does the revelation of "what is invisible" constitute a definition of "us, and themselves"? Who is Oates referring to when she speaks of "us"? In what respects do you think Oates might consider herself one of "us"? In what respects might you be considered one of "us"?

Five years have passed since the Tyson-Smith fight that Oates writes about in this essay, so it might be interesting to see what has happened to Mike Tyson during the intervening years. Consult a computer-based or printed list of articles about contemporary persons in the news, in order to locate pieces that have been written about Tyson since his fight with Smith. What has happened in his boxing career during the past five years? What has happened in his personal life during the past five years? What, if anything, has become visible in Tyson that might have been invisible five years ago?

MY FATHER, MY FICTION

A November day, 1988, and I am sitting in my study in our house in Princeton, N.J., as dusk comes on, listening to my father playing the piano in another wing of the house. Flawlessly, he's moving through the *presto agitato* of Schubert's "Erl King," striking the nightmarish sequence of notes firmly but rapidly. There's a shimmering quality to the sound, and I'm thinking how the mystery of music is a paradigm of the mystery of personality: most of us "know" family members exclusive of statistical information, sometimes in defiance of it, in the way that we "know" familiar pieces of music without having the slightest comprehension of their thematic or structural composition. We recognize them after a few notes, that's all. The powerful appeal of music is inexplicable, forever mysterious, like the subterranean urgings of the soul, and so too the powerful appeal of certain personalities in our lives. We are rarely aware of the gravitational forces we embody for others, but we are keenly aware of the gravitational forces certain others embody for us. To say *my father, my mother* is for me to name but in no way to approach one of the central mysteries of my life.

How did the malnourished circumstances of my parents' early lives allow them to grow, to blossom, into the exemplary people they have become?—is there no true relationship between personal history and personality?—*is* character, bred in the bone, absolute fate? And what are facts, that we should imagine they have the power to explain the world to us? On the contrary, it is facts that must be explained.

HERE ARE FACTS:

My father's father, Joseph Carlton Oates, left his wife and son when my father, an only child, was 2 or 3 years old. Abandoned them, to be specific: they were very poor. Twenty-eight years later, Joseph Carlton reappeared to seek out his son, Frederic . . . arrived at a country tavern in Millersport, N.Y., one night about 1944, not to ask forgiveness of his son for his selfishness as a father, not even to be reconciled with him, or to explain himself. He had come, he announced, to beat up his son.

It seems that Joseph Carlton had heard rumors that Frederic had long held a grudge against him, wanted to fight him. Thus Joseph Carlton sought him out to bring the fight to him, so to speak. He'd been living not far away (which might mean, in those days, as close as 20 miles), totally out of contact with his ex-wife, my grandmother. But when the drunk, belligerent Joseph Carlton confronted Frederic, the one in his early 50's, the other a young married man of 30, it turned out that the younger man had in fact no special grudge against the older and did not care to fight him, though challenged.

"I couldn't bring myself to hit someone that old," my father says. 5

Joseph Carlton Oates and Frederic Oates are said to have resembled each other dramatically. But though I resemble both my father and my long-deceased grandfather, I never saw this grandfather's face, not even in a photograph. Joseph Carlton—of whom my grandmother would say, simply, whenever she was asked of him, "he was no good"—became one of those phantom beings, no doubt common in family histories, who did not exist.

Suppose Joseph Carlton Oates had not abandoned his wife and young son in 1916. Suppose he'd continued to live with them. It is likely that, given his penchant for drinking and for aggressive behavior, he might very well have been abusive to his wife and to my father, would surely have "beaten him up" many times—so infecting him, if we are to believe current theories of the etiology of domestic violence, with a similar predisposition toward violence. So abandoning his young family was perhaps the most generous gesture Joseph Carlton Oates could have made, though that was not the man's intention.

My father was born in 1914 in Lockport, N.Y., a small city approximately 20 miles north of Buffalo and 15 miles south of Lake Ontario, in Niagara County; its distinctive feature is the steep rock-sided Erie Canal that runs literally through its core. Because they were poor, my grandmother (the former Blanche Morgenstern) frequently moved with her son from one low-priced rental to another. But after he grew up and married my mother (the former Carolina Bush), my father came to live in my mother's adoptive parents' farmhouse in Millersport; and has remained on that land ever since.

My mother has lived on this attractive rural property at the northern edge of Erie County, by the Tonawanda Creek, in the old farmhouse (built 1888) and then in the newer, smaller house in which my parents now live (wood frame, white aluminum siding and brown trim, built in 1961 largely by way of my father's efforts), virtually all her life. This is over 70 years: Carolina Bush was born Nov. 8, 1916, the youngest of a large farm family, given to her aunt as an infant when her father suddenly died and left the family impoverished. (Is "die" too circumspect a term? In fact, my maternal grandfather was killed in a tavern brawl.)

In time, Frederic and Carolina had three children: I was born in 10
1938 (on Bloomsday: June 16), my brother Fred ("Robin" for most of our childhood, thus to me Robin forever) was born in 1943, my sister Lynn (who has been institutionalized as autistic since early adolescence) in 1956.

The generation that preceded my parents' is vanished, of course. First-generation Americans, many of them; or immigrants from

Hungary, Ireland, Germany. My father's mother, Blanche, whom I knew as Grandmother Woodside (she remarried after her early, dissolved marriage), the person whom of all the world I loved most after my parents, died in 1970, after a lengthy illness.

When his mother died, my father was deeply grieved, heartbroken; but according to my mother, he kept most of his sorrow to himself.

For both my parents their marriage is surely the supreme fact of their lives: they married young, seem never to have loved or been seriously involved with others. Yet when their 50th wedding anniversary rolled around in 1987 they chose to keep the date a secret and refused to celebrate.

(My father's wish, surely. He is the sort of man not inclined to "make too much of things." Which is no doubt what the composing of this memoir constitutes. When I was growing up, Daddy was conspicuously and often humorously bored with his birthday, and even more with Christmas; and from him, for better or worse, I seem to have inherited similar prejudices. Thoreau's remark "Beware of all enterprises that require new clothes" speaks eloquently to this temperament.)

Facts: the property my parents shared with my Bush grandparents was a small farm with a fruit orchard, some cherry trees, some apple trees, primarily Bartlett pears. My memories are of chickens, Rhode Island reds, pecking obsessively in the dirt . . . for what is a chicken's life but pecking obsessively in the dirt? Chicken duties (feeding, egg gathering) seem to have fallen within a specifically female province, meaning my Grandmother Bush, my mother and me; fruit picking, especially the harvest of hundreds of bushel baskets of pears, fell to my father, when he wasn't working in Lockport at Harrison Radiator. For a brief fevered interim, there were pigs—pigs that broke free of their enclosure in the barn, and were desperately chased by my father, pigs that sickened and died, or, worse yet, were successfully slaughtered but somehow imperfectly cured, so that their meat, the point after all of so much comical despair, was inedible.

Now, decades later, nothing remains of the Bush farm. My childhood seems to have been plowed under, gone subterranean as a dream. The old house was razed years ago when the country highway was widened, the old barn was dismantled, all of the fruit orchard has vanished. *My* lilac tree near the back door, *my* apple tree at the side of the house, *my* cherry tree . . . long uprooted, gone. Fields once planted in corn, in potatoes, in tomatoes, in strawberries . . . gone. Looking at the property now from the road you would not be able to guess that it was once a farm.

I wonder if it is evident how painfully difficult it has been for me to write this seemingly informal memoir?—as if I were staring into a dazzling beacon of light, yet expected to see?

All children mythologize their parents, who are to them after all giants of the landscape of early childhood; and I'm sure I am no exception.

And yet . . . and *yet:* it does seem to me that my parents are remarkable people, both in themselves, as pèrsons, "personalities," and as representatives and survivors of a world so harsh and so repetitive in its harshness as to defy evocation, except perhaps in art.

Though frequently denounced and often misunderstood by a some-   20 what genteel literary community, my writing is, at least in part, an attempt to memorialize my parents' vanished world; my parents' lives. Sometimes directly, sometimes in metaphor. Of my recent novels, "Marya: A Life" (1986) is an admixture of my mother's early life, some of my own adolescent and young-adult experience, and fiction: reading "Marya," as they read everything I write, they immediately recognized the setting—for of course it *is* the setting—that rural edge of Erie County just across the Tonawanda Creek from Niagara County, not far from the Erie Canal (and the Canal Road where Marya lives). The quintessential world of my fiction. "You Must Remember This" (1987) is set in a mythical western New York city that is an amalgam of Buffalo and Lockport, but primarily Lockport: the novel could not have been imaginatively launched without the Erie Canal, vertiginously steep-walled, cutting through its core. And though my father is not present in the fictional world of "You Must Remember This," his shadow falls over it; it's a work in which I tried consciously to synthesize my father's and my own "visions" of an era now vanished. Felix Stevick is not my father except in his lifelong fascination with boxing and with what I consider the romance of violence, which excludes women; that conviction that there is a mysterious and terrible brotherhood of men by way of violence.

But it is in an early novel, "Wonderland" (1971), that my parents actually make an appearance. My beleaguered young hero Jesse stops his car in Millersport, wanders about my parents' property, happens to see, with a stab of envy, my young mother and me (a child of 3 or 4) swinging in our old wooden swing; and when my father notices Jesse watching he stares at him with a look of hostility. So I envisioned my father as a young man of 27—tall, husky, with black hair, intent on protecting his family against possible intrusion. "In such a way," thinks my fatherless hero, "does a man, a normal man, exclude the rest of the world."

Memory is a transcendental function. Its objects may be physical bodies, faces, "characteristic" expressions of faces, but these are shot with luminosity; they possess an interior radiance that transfixes the imagination like the radiance in medieval and Renaissance religious paintings—that signal that Time has been stopped and Eternity prevails. So, though we can't perceive "soul" or "spirit" first-hand, it seems to me that this is precisely the phenomenon we summon back by way of an exercise of memory. And why the exercise of memory at certain times in our lives is almost too powerful to be borne.

From a letter of my father's, written Oct. 8, 1988:

> Your postcard asking about my history came the day after I phoned so I don't quite know how to give you what you want because I have no school records like you and Fred—all I can do is guess.
>
> Born in Lockport 3/30/14. Parents separated when I was two or 25 three years old. Started violin lessons in sixth grade (class instruction) then began private lessons with money earned peddling newspapers. My mother bought my violin for me otherwise I would have had to quit because the one I used in class belonged to the school. I played in the high school symphony orchestra as a freshman. My mechanical drawing teacher got me a job with Schine Theaters in Lockport in the sign shop working after school. At summer vacation I worked full time at the job and quit school in my second year. Worked at the theater until I was about 17 when the sign shop closed and I went into production advertising.
>
> Got a job in local commercial sign shop when I was about 18 and bought a car. After about 4 years of this work I got a job at Harrison Radiator in the punch press department, and, thinking I had a steady job, I learned to fly, got married, then found myself laid off for extended periods so I had to continue working at the sign shop until the second world war began when I was able to get transferred into the engineering tool room and learned the tool and die making trade, later on was able, after going to night school to learn trig and related subjects, started tool and die design. At about fifty years of age, I took piano lessons for about four years at which time I was operated on to remove herniated disc material and was out of commission for six months then worked about ten more years and retired. Took a course in stained glass as a hobby, a class in painting, then four years ago I started classes in English Literature and music at SUNY which I hope to continue for a few more years.

From my journal, May 20, 1986:

> Last week, my parents' visit. And it was splendid. And it went by with painful swiftness. They arrived on Wednesday, left on Saturday afternoon, immediately the house is too large, empty, quiet, unused. . . . My mother brought me a dress she'd sewed for me, blue print, quite feminine one might say; long-sleeved, full-skirted. "Demure"—to suit my image.
>
> Another family secret revealed, with a disarming casualness. Perhaps because of their ages my parents don't want to keep secrets? Not that they are *old* at seventy or seventy-one. My father told of how his grandfather Morgenstern tried to kill his grandmother in a fit of rage, then killed himself—gun barrel placed under his chin, trigger pulled, with my grandmother Blanche close by. My father was about fifteen at the time. They were all living in a single household evidently. . . . A sordid tale. Yet grimly comical: I asked what occupation my great-grandfather had, was told he was a gravedigger.
>
> Family secrets! So many! Or, no, not so very many, I suppose; but unnerving. And I think of my sweet Grandmother Woodside who nearly witnessed her own father's violent suicide. . . . She had come home to

find the house locked. Her father was beating her mother upstairs in their bedroom. Hearing her at the door, he came downstairs with his gun, and for some reason (frustration, drunkenness, madness?) he went into the basement and shot himself. Several times I said to my father, dazed, but you never told me any of this! and my father said, with the air of utter placidity. Didn't I?—I'm sure I did. This is a countertheme of sorts. The secret is at last revealed, after decades; but it's revealed with the accompanying claim that it had been revealed a long time ago and isn't therefore a secret. . . .

One of my most deeply imprinted memories of childhood is of being taken up in a small plane by my father: tightly buckled in the front seat of a two-seater Piper Cub as my father in the cockpit behind me taxis us along the bumpy runway of a small country airport outside Lockport. Suddenly, the rattling plane leaves the ground, lifts above a line of trees at the end of the runway, climbing, banking, miraculously riding the air currents until the roaring noise of the engine seems to subside and we're airborne, and below is a familiar landscape made increasingly exotic as we climb. Transit Road and its traffic . . . farmland, wooded land, hedgerows . . . houses, barns, pastureland, intersecting roads . . . creeks and streams . . . and the sky opening above us oceanic, unfathomable.

My father has always been a happy, energetic, imaginative man, but never more so than when airborne, riding the waves of invisible currents of air. For what is flying your own plane but defying the laws of nature and of logic? Transcending space and time and the contours of the familiar world in which you work a minimum of 40 hours a week, own property in constant need of repair, have a family for whom you are the sole breadwinner? What is flying but the control of an alien, mysterious element that can at any moment turn killer— the air?

My father began flying lessons in 1935, when he was 21 years old, made his first solo flight in 1937, and, over the decades, logged approximately 200 hours of flying time. It was during the 1940's, especially after the end of World War II when Army Air Forces training planes came into private ownership, that he flew most frequently, on weekends, out of small country airports near our home. What a romance of the air! He took members of the family, including his very young daughter Joyce, up in Piper Cubs, Cessnas, Stinsons; he flew a sporty Waco biplane; the most powerful aircraft in his experience was a Vultee basic trainer, 450 horsepower, which was an Air Force trainer with a canopy, which flew at more than 10,000 feet. Intense excitement—unless it was something beyond excitement—has blurred my precise memory of the flight we once made, my father and me, in a 175-horsepower Fairchild primary trainer. I wore a helmet and goggles, but no parachute, for the very good reason that I wouldn't have known how to use a parachute.

Flying is safer than driving a car, my father has always insisted.

In these planes my father and his flying buddies performed loops, turns, split-S's, slow rolls, spins. Possessed of a brash sense of humor, as it might have been called, my father sometimes flew low to buzz friends' and neighbors' houses. Upon a number of daring occasions he flew gliders—if "flew" is the correct expression—borne up to 1,500 feet by a plane, then released. A few years ago when a West German film crew came to interview him and my mother in preparing a film on "Joyce Carol Oates" for German public television, the program director paid for renting a plane so that he could fly the director and a cameraman (in a Cessna 182 single-propeller plane) over the terrain of my childhood: and it's as if, eerily, seeing this footage, I have come full circle, seeing again these exotic-familiar sights, my father in the cockpit.

How many times I've stared at a newspaper photograph, recently reprinted for novelty's sake in The Lockport Union-Sun and Journal, of 60 employees of Department 11, Press Room, of the Harrison Radiator Division, Washburn Street plant, Aug. 11, 1941. There, in the second row, looking not just young, but boyish, coltish, dramatically handsome, with a thick springy head of black hair, is my father, Frederic Oates.

My father, 27 years old.

At which time my mother would have been 24, and I 3.   35

So long ago!—in another lifetime, it seems; and irretrievable.

I have been speaking of my father's avocational life, his "personal" life, but most of the actual hours of his (waking) life were spent at work. For 40 years he was an employee of Harrison Radiator of Lockport, N.Y.; since the early 1940's he was a dues-paying member of the United Automobile Workers of America. It has always seemed that Frederic Oates's temperament and intelligence might have better suited him for some sort of artistic or theoretical or even teacherly career, but, born in the circumstances in which he was, and coming of age during the Depression, he shared the collective fate of so many. Schooling even through high school was not an option.

(So when it is said of me that I am the first member of my family to graduate from high school, still less college, this is another misleading fact: only chance saved me and others of my generation from the work-oriented lives of our parents. At the time of this writing my father is a student at the State University of New York at Buffalo—the kind of deeply engaged "older" student whom professors, and I speak as one, dearly appreciate in their classes.)

In the old days at Harrison Radiator, as at all nonunion factories, plants, mills, shops, "sweatshops," it was not uncommon that workers might arrive for work in the morning only to be told cursorily that they weren't needed that day, and that there was no promise of when, or if, they might be needed again. Management owed nothing to labor; not even simple courtesy. A few weeks after I was born in 1938 my father reported to work and was told there was no work, some of the press room employees were laid off indefinitely. I have to wonder what a young husband tells his wife when he returns home so early in the day—what the words are, what the tone of voice. About all my father will say of such episodes is, "They were hard." He has never been a person given to self-pity, nor yet to a nostalgic reinvention of the past.

If there was anger it's long since buried, plowed under, to be resurrected in his daughter's writing, as fuel and ballast. *How to evoke that world, that America, rapidly passing from memory.*   40

One definite advantage of my father's shaky economic situation was that he developed a second career of sorts, i.e. sign painting, at which he was very good. (For decades, my father's signs were immediately recognizable in the area. I can "see" the distinctive style of their lettering even now.) And he acquired a habitude of busyness, a predilection for work, for using his hands and his brain, not so much in gainful employment as in useful employment; a trait everyone in my family shares. This is not puritanism, but something less abstract, perhaps even visceral: we love to work because work gives us genuine happiness, the positing and solving of problems, the joyful exercise of the imagination.

I spoke of anger, and, yes, it's a "class" anger as well, but I want to make clear that this is a personal anger, not one I have inherited from my family.

A few days ago, my husband and I took my parents for lunch on the Delaware River (they are visiting us here in Princeton for a week), to one of those "historic" inns for which the region is famous, and while we sat contemplating the antique furnishings of the Black Bass Inn— the tables in the dining room are made of old sewing machines—the subject turned to Harrison's, to the old days, in the 1930's. And after a while my mother said, as so often she sums up an era, and a theme, in a single succinct remark, "I guess we were poor, but it didn't seem that way at the time. Somehow, we always managed."

The old farmhouse in Millersport was razed in 1960, yet there is a dream of mine in which I wake yet again to find myself there, in my old room—the first of the countless rooms of my life. I open my eyes in astonishment to see the square half-window overhead, the child's bureau at the foot of my bed and the child's desk facing it and, through the doorway (no door, only a curtain), in the farthest right-hand corner of the living room the upright piano my father played and on which in time I would practice my piano lessons. A musical instrument is a mysterious thing, inhabiting a complex sort of space: it is both an ordinary three-dimensional object and a portal to another world; it exists as a physical entity solely so that it—and, indeed, physicality—can be transcended.

Thus my father's old upright in that long-vanished living room inhabits its luminous space in my memory.

For nearly his entire life my father has played, and loved playing, 45 the piano: classical music, popular music, Scott Joplin, jazz. He is a precise sight-reader of music but he can also play by ear and improvise, neither of which I can do; he is far more naturally musical than I, though I have inherited from him a temperament that must be called "musical." People like us are always involved in music no matter what we're doing.

If we aren't actually sitting at the piano and playing, our fingers are going through the phantom motions of playing; if we aren't singing or humming out loud, we are singing or humming silently. We are captivated by Mozart, Chopin, Schubert, Beethoven, Bach, but just as readily by "St. James Infirmary," "As Time Goes By," one or another old Hoagy Carmichael tune. For people like us music is a matter of a pulsebeat, melody and rhythm and occasional lyrics, a constant interior beat in a counterpoint of sorts to the world's exterior beat. It must be a way of defining ourselves to ourselves, or perhaps it's purely pleasure, to no purpose. If from my father Frederic Oates I'd inherited nothing more palpable than a habit of singing to myself, I'd say this was more than enough.

So I sit listening to my father playing piano in another wing of the house—now he's playing Satie's elegant "Gnossiennes"—and I think these things. How to write a memoir of him? How even to begin? I spoke of mystery, and it's primarily mystery I feel when I contemplate my father, indeed, both my father and my mother. The quality of personality they embody, their unfailing magnanimity of spirit, is so oddly matched with their origins and with the harsh and unsentimental world out of which they emerged. I can bear a prolonged consideration of that world only in my writing, and there it is transmogrified as writing—as fiction. To consider it head-on, not as art but as historical reality, leaves me weak and bewildered.

If there is one general trait I seem to have inherited from both of my parents it's their instinct for rejoicing in the life in which they have found themselves. They remain models for me, they go far beyond me, I can only hope to continue to learn from them. *Happiness is a kind of genius,* Colete shrewdly observed, and in this genius my parents abound.

LINES OF INQUIRY
"My Father, My Fiction"

Oates begins and ends this essay with the image of herself sitting in her study, at dusk, listening to her "father playing the piano in another wing of the house." What impressions do you get of Oates and her father from this framing image? Why do you suppose she frames her essay with this image, but does not mention it elsewhere in the piece? Elsewhere in the piece, in fact, she jumps around quite a bit, from one time or place to another, rather than telling about her father and her family in a straightforward chronological order. Why do you suppose she organizes her piece in this apparently disorganized way? Can you detect a process or pattern of movement from one segment to the next? What impressions do you get of Oates and her father as you move through the shifting times and places of her essay?

In the next to last paragraph of the essay, Oates says that "it's primarily mystery I feel when I contemplate my father." What do you suppose she means by "mystery" in this context? In what sense(s) does her father seem to be a mystery to her? In what sense(s) does he strike you as a mystery? In what respects is he not a mystery? What kind of person does he seem to be from the facts she reports about his early life (and the lives of his parents), from her own childhood memories of him, from the facts she reports about his adult life, from her most recent impressions of him? What else would you like to know about her father that Oates does not include in this piece?

In the opening paragraph of the essay, Oates says that "most of us 'know' family members exclusive of statistical information, sometimes in defiance of it, in the way that we 'know' familiar pieces of music without having the slightest comprehension of their thematic or structural composition. We recognize them after a few notes, that's all." Think of a person in your immediate family whom you know like a familiar piece of music. What are the "few notes" by which you immediately "recognize" that person? What do you know about that person's "thematic or structural composition"? What "statistical information" do you know about them? What do you not know about them that you wish you knew? In what sense(s) does that person remain a mystery to you?

AGAINST NATURE

*We soon get through with Nature. She excites an expectation
which she cannot satisfy.*

Thoreau, Journal, *1854*

*Sir, if a man has experienced the inexpressible, he is under no
obligation to attempt to express it.*

Samuel Johnson

The writer's resistance to Nature.

It has no sense of humor: in its beauty, as in its ugliness, or its
neutrality, there is no laughter.

It lacks a moral purpose.

It lacks a satiric dimension, registers no irony.

Its pleasures lack resonance, being accidental; its horrors, even when
premeditated, are equally perfunctory, "red in tooth and claw," et
cetera.

It lacks a symbolic subtext—excepting that provided by man.

It has no (verbal) language.

It has no interest in ours.

It inspires a painfully limited set of responses in "nature writers"—
REVERENCE, AWE, PIETY, MYSTICAL ONENESS.

It eludes us even as it prepares to swallow us up, books and all.

I was lying on my back in the dirt gravel of the towpath beside the
Delaware and Raritan Canal, Titusville, New Jersey, staring up at
the sky and trying, with no success, to overcome a sudden attack of
tachycardia that had come upon me out of nowhere—such attacks are
always "out of nowhere," that's their charm—and all around me Nature
thrummed with life, the air smelling of moisture and sunlight, the
canal reflecting the sky, red-winged blackbirds testing their spring
calls; the usual. I'd become the jar in Tennessee, a fictitious center, or
parenthesis, aware beyond my erratic heartbeat of the numberless heart-
beats of the earth, its pulsing, pumping life, sheer life, incalculable.
Struck down in the midst of motion—I'd been jogging a minute before—I was "out of time" like a fallen, stunned boxer, privileged (in an
abstract manner of speaking) to be an involuntary witness to the random, wayward, nameless motion on all sides of me.

Paroxysmal tachycardia can be fatal, but rarely; if the heartbeat
accelerates to 250–270 beats a minute you're in trouble, but the average
attack is about 100–150 beats and mine seemed about average; the trick

now was to prevent it from getting worse. Brainy people try brainy strategies, such as thinking calming thoughts, pseudo-mystic thoughts, *If I die now it's a good death,* that sort of thing, *if I die this is a good place and good time;* the idea is to deceive the frenzied heartbeat that, really, you don't care: you hadn't any other plans for the afternoon. The important thing with tachycardia is to prevent panic! you must prevent panic! otherwise you'll have to be taken by ambulance to the closest emergency room, which is not so very nice a way to spend the afternoon, really. So I contemplated the blue sky overhead. The earth beneath my head. Nature surrounding me on all sides; I couldn't quite see it but I could hear it, smell it, sense it, there is something *there,* no mistake about it. Completely oblivious to the predicament of the individual but that's only "natural," after all, one hardly expects otherwise.

When you discover yourself lying on the ground, limp and unresisting, head in the dirt, and, let's face it, helpless, the earth seems to shift forward as a presence; hard, emphatic, not mere surface but a genuine force—there is no other word for it but *presence.* To keep in motion is to keep in time, and to be stopped, stilled, is to be abruptly out of time, in another time dimension perhaps, an alien one, where human language has no resonance. Nothing to be said about it expresses it, nothing touches it, it's an absolute against which nothing human can be measured. . . . Moving through space and time by way of your own volition you inhabit an interior consciousness, a hallucinatory consciousness, it might be said, so long as breath, heartbeat, the body's autonomy hold; when motion is stopped you are jarred out of it. The interior is invaded by the exterior. The outside wants to come in, and only the self's fragile membrane prevents it.

The fly buzzing at Emily's death.

Still, the earth *is* your place. A tidy grave site measured to your size. Or, from another angle of vision, one vast democratic grave. 5

Let's contemplate the sky. Forget the crazy hammering heartbeat, don't listen to it, don't start counting, remember that there is a clever way of breathing that conserves oxygen as if you're lying below the surface of a body of water breathing through a very thin straw but you *can* breathe through it if you're careful, if you don't panic; one breath and then another and then another, isn't that the story of all lives? careers? Just a matter of breathing. Of course it is. But contemplate the sky, it's there to be contemplated. A mild shock to see it so blank, blue, a thin airy ghostly blue, no clouds to disguise its emptiness. You are beginning to feel not only weightless but near-bodiless, lying on the earth like a scrap of paper about to be blown off. Two dimensions and you'd imagined you were three! And there's the sky rolling away forever, into infinity—if "infinity" can be "rolled into"—and the forlorn truth is, that's where you're going too. And the lovely blue isn't even blue, is it? isn't even there, is it? a mere optical illusion, isn't it? no matter what art has urged you to believe.

Early Nature memories. Which it's best not to suppress.

. . . Wading, as a small child, in Tonawanda Creek near our house, and afterward trying to tear off, in a frenzy of terror and revulsion, the sticky fat black bloodsuckers that had attached themselves to my feet, particularly between my toes.

. . . Coming upon a friend's dog in a drainage ditch, dead for several days, evidently the poor creature had been shot by a hunter and left to die, bleeding to death, and we're stupefied with grief and horror but can't resist sliding down to where he's lying on his belly, and we can't resist squatting over him, turning the body over.

. . . The raccoon, mad with rabies, frothing at the mouth and tearing at his own belly with his teeth, so that his intestines spill out onto the ground . . . a sight I seem to remember though in fact I did not see. I've been told I did not see.

Consequently, my chronic uneasiness with Nature mysticism; Nature adoration; Nature-as-(moral)-instruction-for-mankind. My doubt that one can, with philosophical validity, address "Nature" as a single coherent noun, anything other than a Platonic, hence discredited, is-ness. My resistance to "Nature writing" as a genre, except when it is brilliantly fictionalized in the service of a writer's individual vision—Thoreau's books and *Journal,* of course, but also, less known in this country, the miniaturist prose poems of Colette (*Flowers and Fruit*) and Ponge (*Taking the Side of Things*)—in which case it becomes yet another, and ingenious, form of storytelling. The subject is *there* only by the grace of the author's language.

Nature has no instructions for mankind except that our pool beleaguered humanist-democratic way of life, our fantasies of the individual's high worth, our sense that the weak, no less than the strong, have a right to survive, are absurd. When Edmund of *King Lear* said excitedly, "Nature, be thou my goddess!" he knew whereof he spoke.

In any case, where *is* Nature, one might (skeptically) inquire. Who has looked upon her/its face and survived?

But isn't this all exaggeration, in the spirit of rhetorical contentiousness? Surely Nature is, for you, as for most reasonably intelligent people, a "perennial" source of beauty, comfort, peace, escape from the delirium of civilized life; a respite from the ego's ever-frantic strategies of self-promotion, as a way of ensuring (at least in fantasy) some small measure of immortality? Surely Nature, as it is understood in the usual slapdash way, as human, if not dilettante, *experience* (hiking in a national park, jogging on the beach at dawn, even tending, with the usual comical frustrations, a suburban garden), is wonderfully consoling; a place where, when you go there, it has to take you in?—a palimpsest of sorts you choose to read, layer by layer, always with care, always cautiously, in proportion to your psychological strength?

Nature: as in Thoreau's upbeat Transcendentalist mode ("The   10 indescribable innocence and beneficence of Nature,—such health, such cheer, they afford forever! and such sympathy have they ever with our race, that all Nature would be affected . . . if any man should ever for a just cause grieve"), and not in Thoreau's grim mode ("Nature is hard to be overcome but she must be overcome").

Another way of saying, not *Nature-in-itself* but *Nature-as-experience.*

The former, Nature-in-itself, is, to allude slantwise to Melville, a blankness ten times blank; the latter is what we commonly, or perhaps always, mean, when we speak of Nature as a noun, a single entity— something of *ours.* Most of the time it's just an activity, a sort of hobby, a weekend, a few days, perhaps a few hours, staring out the window at the mind-dazzling autumn foliage of, say, northern Michigan, being rendered speechless—temporarily—at the sight of Mt. Shasta, the Grand Canyon, Ansel Adams's West. Or Nature writ small, contained in the back yard. Nature filtered through our optical nerves, our "senses," our fiercely romantic expectations. Nature that pleases us because it mirrors our souls, or gives the comforting illusion of doing so.

Nature as the self's (flattering) mirror, but not ever, no, never, Nature-in-itself.

Nature is mouths, or maybe a single mouth. Why glamorize it, romanticize it?—well, yes, but we must, we're writers, poets, mystics (of a sort) aren't we, precisely what else are we to do but glamorize and romanticize and generally exaggerate the significance of anything we focus the white heat of our "creativity" upon? And why not Nature, since it's there, common property, mute, can't talk back, allows us the possibility of transcending the human condition for a while, writing prettily of mountain ranges, white-tailed deer, the purple crocuses outside this very window, the thrumming dazzling "life force" we imagine we all support. Why not?

Nature *is* more than a mouth—it's a dazzling variety of mouths.   15 And it pleases the senses, in any case, as the physicists' chill universe of numbers certainly does not.

Oscar Wilde, on our subject:

> Nature is no great mother who has borne us. She is our creation. It is in our brain that she quickens to life. Things are because we see them, and what we see, and how we see it, depends on the Arts that have influenced us. To look

at a thing is very different from seeing a thing. . . . At present, people see fogs, not because there are fogs, but because poets and painters have taught them the mysterious loveliness of such effects. There may have been fogs for centuries in London. I dare say there were. But no one saw them. They did not exist until Art had invented them. . . . Yesterday evening Mrs. Arundel insisted on my going to the window and looking at the glorious sky, as she called it. And so I had to look at it. . . . And what was it? It was simply a very second-rate Turner, a Turner of a bad period, with all the painter's worst faults exaggerated and over-emphasized.

"The Decay of Lying," 1889

(If we were to put it to Oscar Wilde that he exaggerates, his reply might well be, "Exaggeration? I don't know the meaning of the word.")

Walden, that most artfully composed of prose fictions, concludes, in the rhapsodic chapter "Spring," with Henry David Thoreau's contemplation of death, decay, and regeneration as it is suggested to him, or to his protagonist, by the spectacle of vultures feeding off carrion. There is a dead horse close by his cabin, and the stench of its decomposition, in certain winds, is daunting. Yet "the assurance it gave me of the strong appetite and inviolable health of Nature was my compensation for this. I love to see that Nature is so rife with life that myriads can be afforded to be sacrificed and suffered to prey upon one another; that tender organizations can be so serenely squashed out of existence like pulp,— tadpoles which herons gobble up, and tortoises and toads run over in the road; and that sometimes it has rained flesh and blood! . . . The impression made on a wise man is that of universal innocence."

Come off it, Henry David. You've grieved these many years for your elder brother, John, who died a ghastly death of lockjaw; you've never wholly recovered from the experience of watching him die. And you know, or must know, that you're fated too to die young of consumption. . . . But this doctrinaire Transcendentalist passage ends *Walden* on just the right note. It's as impersonal, as coolly detached, as the Oversoul itself: a "wise man" filters his emotions through his brain.

Or through his prose.

Nietzsche: "We all pretend to ourselves that we are more simple-minded than we are: that is how we get a rest from our fellow men."

> Once out of nature I shall never take
> My bodily form from any natural thing,
> But such a form as Grecian goldsmiths make
> Of hammered gold and gold enamelling
> To keep a drowsy Emperor awake;
> Or set upon a golden bough to sing
> To lords and ladies of Byzantium
> Of what is past, or passing, or to come.
>   *William Butler Yeats,* Sailing to Byzantium

Yet even the golden bird is a "bodily form [taken from a] natural thing." No, it's impossible to escape!

The writer's resistance to Nature.

Wallace Stevens: "In the presence of extraordinary actuality, consciousness takes the place of imagination."

Once, years ago, in 1972 to be precise, when I seemed to have been another person, related to the person I am now as one is related, tangentially, sometimes embarrassingly, to cousins not seen for decades—once, when we were living in London, and I was very sick, I had a mystical vision. That is, I "had" a "mystical vision"—the heart sinks: such pretension—or something resembling one. A fever dream, let's call it. It impressed me enormously and impresses me still, though I've long since lost the capacity to see it with my mind's eye, or even, I suppose, to believe in it. There is a statute of limitations on "mystical visions," as on romantic love.

I was very sick, and I imagined my life as a thread, a thread of breath, or heartbeat, or pulse, or light—yes, it was light, radiant light; I was burning with fever and I ascended to that plane of serenity that might be mistaken for (or *is,* in fact) Nirvana, where I had a waking dream of uncanny lucidity:

> My body is a tall column of light and heat.
> My body is not "I" but "it."
> My body is not one but many.

My body, which "I" inhabit, is inhabited as well by other creatures, unknown to me, imperceptible—the smallest of them mere sparks of light. 20

My body, which I perceive as substance, is in fact an organization of infinitely complex, overlapping, imbricated structures, radiant light their manifestation, the "body" a tall column of light and blood heat, a temporary agreement among atoms, like a high-rise building with numberless rooms, corridors, corners, elevator shafts, windows. . . . In this fantastical structure the "I" is deluded as to its sovereignty, let alone its autonomy in the (outside) world; the most astonishing secret is that the "I" doesn't exist!—but it behaves as if it does, as if it were one and not many.

In any case, without the "I" the tall column of light and heat would die, and the microscopic life particles would die with it . . . will die with it. The "I," which doesn't exist, is everything.

But Dr. Johnson is right, the inexpressible need not be expressed.

And what resistance, finally? There is none.

This morning, an invasion of tiny black ants. One by one they appear, out of nowhere—that's their charm too!—moving single file across the white Parsons table where I am sitting, trying without much success to write a poem. A poem of only three or four lines is what I want, something short, tight, mean; I want it to hurt like a white-hot wire up the nostrils, small and compact and turned in upon itself with the density of a hunk of rock from the planet Jupiter. . . .

But here come the black ants: harbingers, you might say, of spring. One by one by one they appear on the dazzling white table and one by one I kill them with a forefinger, my deft right forefinger, mashing each against the surface of the table and then dropping it into a wastebasket at my side. Idle labor, mesmerizing, effortless, and I'm curious as to how long I can do it—sit here in the brilliant March sunshine killing ants with my right forefinger—how long I, and the ants, can keep it up.

After a while I realize that I can do it a long time. And that 25
I've written my poem.

LINES OF INQUIRY
"Against Nature"

In the second segment, Oates gives a vividly detailed account of herself "overcome" by "a sudden attack of tachycardia"; and in the final segment she gives an equally vivid account of herself "killing ants with my right forefinger." Why do you suppose she frames her essay with these segments? What similarities—what differences—do you notice about her condition, her behavior, and her relationship to nature in each segment? What similarities, what differences, do you notice between the images of herself she conveys in these segments and the image of herself she conveys in the "mystical vision" she tells about in the eleventh segment? How do the images in these three segments help to illustrate Oates's reasons for being "against nature"?

In the first segment, Oates lists several reasons for "the writer's resistance to Nature." Why do you suppose that writers in general and Oates in particular would consider these important reasons for being "against Nature"? What overarching assumptions, beliefs, or values are implicit in all of these reasons? Which of these reasons do you think is most important in determining the ideas that Oates expresses about nature in segments four through eight? What do these reasons have in common with the single additional reason she cites in segment 10 for "the writer's resistance to Nature"? Why do you suppose she doesn't include this additional reason in her opening segment?

Annie Dillard in "Living like Weasels," Loren Eiseley in "The Hidden Teacher," Edward Hoagland in "Spring," and Henry David Thoreau in "The War of the Ants" are clearcut instances of nature-writers whom Oates would probably be inclined to attack for their "Nature mysticism," or "Nature adoration," or "Nature-as-(moral)-instruction-for-mankind." Based on your reading of two or three of these essays, how do you think the essayists you've read would defend themselves or respond to Oates's attack on their work? How would you respond to her attack on their work?

(WOMAN) WRITER:
THEORY AND PRACTICE

*To you I am neither man nor woman. I come before you as an
author only. It is the sole standard by which you have a right to
judge me—the sole ground on which I accept your judgment.*
                    Charlotte Brontë, to a critic

I.

*W*hat is the ontological status of the writer *who is also a woman?*

She is likely to experience herself, from within, as a writer primarily:
perhaps even a writer exclusively. She does not inevitably view herself as
an object, a category, an essence—in short, as "representative." The individual, to the individual, is never a type. And in the practice of her craft
she may well become bodiless and invisible, defined to herself fundamentally as what she thinks, dreams, plots, constructs. To paraphrase Emerson, life consists of what a person is thinking day by day.

It would follow, then, that when the writer is alone with language
and with the challenging discipline of creating an art by way of language alone, she is not defined to herself as "she." Does the writer
require the specification of gender? Is memory gender-bound? Are impressions filtered through the prism of gender? Is there a distinctly
female voice?—or even a conspicuously feminine voice? Or is "gender"
in this sense an ontological category imposed upon us from without,
for the convenience of others? If so, it is likely to be a category that
dissolves the uniquely individual in the abstract. The private drama
becomes, in Melville's words, a "hideous, intolerable Allegory."

It has been said by Gide that the artist requires a special, secret
world to which he (she?) alone has the key; and it is surely true that an
unreasoned faith underlies all motives for sustained creativity. If the
ideal reader experiences the classic "enlargement of sympathies" by
way of serious fiction, it is to be assumed that the writer, immersed in
realizing these sympathies, experiences a similar enlargement of vision: at least so long as she is immersed in her art and not subjected to
others' assessments of it, and of her.

In a passage in *Speak, Memory,* his autobiography "revisited,"   5
Vladimir Nabokov meditates upon the secret motive for art; or, at any
rate, the secret motive for his art:

> Whenever I start thinking of my love for a person, I am in the habit of
> immediately drawing radii from my love—from my heart, from the tender

nucleus of a personal matter—to monstrously remote points of the universe. Something impels me to measure the consciousness of my love against such unimaginable and incalculable things as the behavior of nebulae (whose very remoteness seems a form of insanity), the dreadful pitfalls of eternity, the unknowledgeable beyond the unknown, the helplessness, the cold, the sickening involutions and interpenetrations of space and time. . . . When that slow-motion silent explosion of love takes place in me, unfolding its melting fringes and overwhelming me with the sense of something much vaster . . . then my mind cannot help but pinch itself to see if it is really awake. I have to make a rapid inventory of the universe just as a man in a dream tries to condone the absurdity of his position by making sure he is dreaming. I have to have all space and all time participate in my emotion, in my mortal love, so that the edge of its mortality is taken off, thus helping me to fight the fact of having developed an infinity of sensation and thought within a finite existence.[1]

Who has spoken more frankly, and more eloquently, of the mysterious motive for metaphor?—of the subterranean connection between private emotion and the impulse for art, the making of something permanent out of love with its "edge of mortality"? Writing out of such motives is a purely human, which is to say genderless, activity. It is always bound up with love, though the specific object of the love is hidden—indeed, subterranean. The composing of fiction is not antithetical to "experience" and certainly not an escape from experience; it *is* experience.

And it is directed, ideally, toward the future. The faith of the present is that the effort of *now* will endure *then*.

So the days pass and I ask myself sometimes whether one is not hypnotized, as a child by a silver globe, by life; and whether this is living. It's very quick, bright, exciting. But superficial perhaps. I should like to take the globe in my hands and feel it quietly, round, smooth, heavy, and so hold it, day after day.

This insatiable desire to write something before I die, this ravaging sense of the shortness and feverishness of life, make me cling, like a man on a rock, to my one anchor.[2]

There are writers, born women, who rarely think of themselves, when they write, as women; there are other writers, similarly born women, who believe their writing to be conditioned at all times by their gender. ("I am never as female as when I write," says Marguerite Duras.) A good deal has been made in recent years by French feminists and their American counterparts (see essays on *L'Écriture féminine* by Hélène Cixous and others) of the phenomenon of the specifically female voice,

---

[1] Vladimir Nabokov, *Speak, Memory: An Autobiography Revisited* (New York: Pyramid Books, 1968), p. 219.

[2] Virginia Woolf, excerpted in *A Writer's Diary*, edited by Leonard Woolf (New York: Harcourt Brace Jovanovich, 1954), p. 135.

without regard for the fact that voice can only mean voices, if we are being attentive to subtleties of pitch and nuance. And what of subject matter? Is there a distinctly female subject, in contrast to a distinctly masculine subject? (Childbirth clearly the province of the one, war and "adventure" the province of the other?) But subject matter is clearly culture-determined, not gender-determined. And the imagination, in itself genderless, allows us all things.

Our immediate response to a book, which we might succinctly define as an artful assemblage of words, is a response to language, not to a (hypothesized) person. Where can personal identity, let alone personality, reside, in so neuter a phenomenon as *words*? Yet more crucially, where can gender reside? The reader cannot be predisposed to "like" or "dislike" a work of art because its creator (distant, legendary, perhaps long dead) was identified, during his or her lifetime, as *male* or *female*. And what, considering the evidence of moldering bones in remote graves, does *male* or *female* now mean?

Our faith in the craft of writing is that it is a form of sympathy. And, being mimetic, being bodiless, consisting solely of words, it demands no displacement or intrusion in the world; it exults in its own being.

II.

A woman is a Muse or she is nothing.
Robert Graves

In revenge and in love, woman is more
barbaric than man.
Friedrich Nietzsche

LUXURY OF BEING DESPISED

The sneering shout in the street, the anatomical female
stretched wide across the billboard: St. Paul's contempt.

Montaigne instructs us that poetry belongs to women—
a wanton and subtle art, ornate and verbose,
all pleasure
and all show: like themselves.
And Freud, that women have little sense of justice.
And De Kooning, in these angry swaths of paint:
monster-mother women!

The fiery sightless eye which is your own.
The booming breasts, the maniac wink.
All is heat, fecundity, secret seeping blood.
Flesh is here: nor are we out of it.

And yet what bliss, to be so despised:
the closed thighs all muscle,

the Church fathers' contempt,
the Protestant chill, what freedom
in possessing no souls!—
what strange delight.

The angry swaths of flesh which are your own.
The blank stare,
the cartoon heart.
Virginity a mallet.
Mad grin worn like a bonnet.[3]

Though it is true that the writer in his (or her) art is bodiless, 10
and transformed by craft into invisibility, what of the writer, born a
woman, in the eyes of others? Does the (woman) writer occupy a significantly different space? What is the objective, as opposed to the
subjective, nature of her ontological existence?

A woman who writes is a writer by her own definition; but she is a
woman writer by others' definitions. (Among these others are, of
course, women.) The books she writes are assemblages of words but her
sexual identity is not thereby dissolved or transcended, unless she
writes under a male pseudonym and keeps her identity secret. Books
are neuter objects, *its;* writers are *he* or *she.* "A woman's writing is
always feminine; it cannot help being feminine; at its best it is most
feminine; the only difficulty lies in defining what we mean by feminine"—as Virginia Woolf has wittily said.

The irony, of course, is that while there are "women writers" there
are not, and have never been, "men writers." This is an empty category,
a class without specimens; for the noun "writer"—the very verb
"writing"—always implies masculinity. (Hence the double-edged
praise that befalls the woman writer when she is told, by men, that she
writes "like a man." Which man? I always ask.)

The woman writer thus finds herself—and the usage is deliberate:
she does not will, or wish, or invent herself, but *is found*—in a depersonalized category that is her birthright for life. Women can't write,
women can't paint—so Lily Briscoe of Virginia Woolf's *To the Lighthouse* has been hypnotized by male authority, against which she, like
Woolf, must struggle. "Language conceals an invisible adversary," says
Hélène Cixous, "because it is the language of men and their grammar."
Of course not all women are despised by all men, at least not all of the
time, but it is a commonplace dilemma that a man's quarrel with the
feminine in his own nature will be a quarrel with women: the impulse
may be abstract and psychological but its fruition is always concrete.

---

[3] This poem of mine originally appeared in *Bennington Review,* in a slightly
different version, and is included in *Luxury of Sin,* a special limited edition
published by Lord John Press (Northridge, Calif.: 1984).

One need not consider the misogyny of the ages—for one thing, it is too familiar, and too depressing—for there are always examples close at hand, in even the most well-intentioned of literary forums. For instance, the *Harvard Guide to Contemporary American Writing,* published in 1979, is divided into chapters with the titles "Intellectual Background," "Literary Criticism," "Experimental Fiction," "Drama," etc., and "Women's Literature"—the last-named a potpourri of virtually anyone who writes and is female, with the inevitable emphasis on those writers who write about "female subjects." Being so ghettoized seems insulting until the (woman) writer stops to realize that a ghetto, after all, is a place in which to live; raze it, and she may find herself homeless altogether.

The old prejudice dies hard, that a woman is a muse or nothing—that is, an inspiration to the (male) artist; never an artist in her own terms. As a young writer Charlotte Brontë was assured by Robert Southey, Poet Laureate of England, that "Literature cannot be the business of a woman's life, and it ought not to be"—a remark that has subsequently become famous, though not as Southey might have anticipated. Even if, like Emily Dickinson, she succeeds in creating a remarkable body of work, she is still vulnerable to dismissal by dint of her gender: R. P. Blackmur spoke condescendingly of Dickinson as a woman poet who seemed to have taken up verse in the way that other women of her time took up needlepoint or quilting; Gerard Manley Hopkins states dogmatically that "the male quality *is* the creative gift." Anthony Burgess once dismissed Jane Austen's writing because it "lacks a strong male thrust," and William Gass once said that literary women "lack that blood congested genital drive which energizes every great style." Is this sexual contempt or sexual anxiety? one wonders. Some years ago Norman Mailer acknowledged that, though there were probably some excellent women writers in America, he would not read their work: *could* not, in fact. Even excellence isn't enough to compensate for being female.

And here is John Berryman in a slapstick Dream Song: 15

> Them lady poets must not marry, pal.
> Miss Dickinson—fancy in Amherst bedding her.
> Fancy a lark with Sappho,
> a tumble in the bushes with Miss Moore,
> a spoon with Emily, while Charlotte glare.
> Miss Bishop's too noble-O.
>
> That was the lot. And two of them are here
> as yet, and—and: Sylvia Plath is not.
> She—she her credentials
> has handed in, leaving alone two tots

and widower to what he makes of it—
surviving guy. . . .[4]

That was the lot. Centuries of women poets are dismissed in a drunk's baby prattle, and those who are considered worthy of special attention are nonetheless "lady poets" the (male) poet would not want to "bed." (And would the objects of Berryman's boozy sexual interest want to "bed" him? A question the poet seems not to consider.)

The recent publication of the monumental *Norton Anthology of Literature by Women,* edited by Sandra Gilbert and Susan Gubar, had the perhaps unanticipated effect of polarizing women writers into two contending camps: those who denied the claims of gender and those who acknowledged them. The anthology was not seen, in some quarters, as complementing existing anthologies (consisting mainly of work by men) but as challenging them; the revisionist work of feminist scholars and critics was judged threatening, dangerous, and subversive. And some of this reaction has been by women writers whose sense of themselves is "genderless," though their writing has been aimed toward a specifically female audience and their literary reputations nourished, in part, by feminist support.

Yet the (woman) writer who imagines herself assimilated into the mainstream of literature, the literature of men, is surely mistaken, given the evidence of centuries, and the ongoing, by now perplexing, indifference of male critics to female effort. Alfred Kazin's recent *An American Procession: The Major American Writers 1830–1930* contains only one woman writer, Emily Dickinson, whom Kazin could hardly overlook. (Kazin has written elsewhere about Edith Wharton, yet excludes her pointedly from the "procession.") A recent essay by Guy Davenport—"Claiming Kin: Artist, Critic, and Scholar as Family"[5]— contains only fleeting references to women writers (Gertrude Stein, Eudora Welty, H.D., Margaret Mitchell), though it considers, often in meticulous detail, centuries of literary endeavor, from Homer through Shakespeare to O. Henry and Louis Zukofsky. "The principle [sic] concern binding the scholar, the critic, and the artist is the vital one of continuity," Davenport says, but he means only male scholars, male critics, male artists; his "family" consists, mysteriously, of no women, rather like the Christian Trinity. Similarly, Harold Bloom's romantic theory of the psychodynamics of literary influence concerns itself exclusively with father-poets and their "misreading" sons: since women

---

[4] In *The Dream Songs* (New York: Farrar, Straus & Giroux, 1969), p. 206.
[5] In *Shenandoah,* Volume XXXVI, No. 1 (1985–86).

do not exist in the critic's theoretical equation, their texts must be ignored, as if they do not exist either.

As Virginia Woolf predicted in "Women and Fiction," in 1929, the male reader is disposed to dismiss women's writing as offering "not merely a difference of view, but a view that is weak, trivial, or sentimental, because it differs from his own." But even when the (woman) writer's point of view is indistinguishable from the (man) writer's, and she manages to attain some distinction during her lifetime, it frequently happens that she is likely to be devalued and forgotten following her death. Literary scholarship and history, as practiced by homosocial critics like Kazin, Davenport, Bloom, and numberless others, makes no effort to preserve her. For she does not finally belong to the "family" of Man.

Better to be despised, then, than to be ignored; or damned with condescending praise. There is a luxury after all in being despised if it frees energy away from the self and into the work; away from the distractions of visibility and into the permanence of art.

So the (woman) writer has faith in the high worth of the craft to which she has dedicated herself, but she should not be deceived in gauging her relative position within it. Power does not reside with women—no more in the literary world than in the world of politics and finance—and power is never under the obligation to act justly. A writer may be afflicted by any number of demons, real or imagined, but only the (woman) writer is afflicted by her own essential identity.

How can the paradox be accommodated? one asks, and some answers might be: with resilience, with a sense of humor, with stubbornness, with anger, with hope.

LINES OF INQUIRY
"(Woman) Writer: Theory and Practice"

Oates's title for this essay raises several interesting questions about what she is up to in the piece. Why does she put the word "woman" in parentheses? What do the parentheses imply about the focus and topic of her essay? What would be the implication(s) of removing the parentheses? In the essay itself, she sometimes puts gender specifications within parentheses, sometimes not. Note all of the instances in which she refers to woman or male writers or artists, and see if you can account for why she does or does not use parentheses in each case.

This essay is clearly divided into two separately numbered sections, each with its own epigraph or set of epigraphs. What ideas does each section convey about the relationship of gender and writing? What similarities, what differences, do you notice between section one and section two in Oates's approach to the topic of gender and writing? What similarities, what differences, do you notice in her thoughts about gender and writing from one section to the next? How do you account for the differences? Given the differences or apparent contradictions, where do you think Oates stands on the matter? Suppose that the two sections had appeared in reverse order? How do you think such a re-arrangement might have affected your perception of the issues and of her thinking about them?

Oates is not the only woman in this collection to be concerned with the relationship of gender and writing, as you can see by looking at Mairs's "Carnal Acts," or Woolf's "Women and Fiction." Read one of these essays and consider what similarities, what differences, you find between its approach and Oates's approach to gender and writing. Also consider what points of agreement, what points of disagreement, you find between the two pieces. Which of the two comes closer to your own thoughts about gender and writing?

GEORGE ORWELL

(ERIC ARTHUR BLAIR)

1903 – 50

This is a political age. War, Fascism, concentration camps, rubber truncheons, atomic bombs, etc., are what we daily think about, and therefore to a great extent what we write about, even when we do not name them openly. We cannot help this. When you are on a sinking ship, your thoughts will be about sinking ships.

Eric Blair (who took the pen name of George Orwell in 1933) stands out as one of the most politically conscious writers in an age of political writing. As he makes clear in this passage, written in 1948, his intensely political concern was aroused not by trivial issues, but by the globally disastrous conditions of his age—"War, Fascism, concentration camps, rubber truncheons, atomic bombs . . . " During his brief career as a journalist, novelist, satirist, and essayist, he devoted himself almost wholly to writing with a "political purpose," but " 'political' in the widest sense of the word"— with a "desire to push the world in a certain direction, to alter other people's idea of the kind of society they should strive after." Driven by that desire, he managed—despite the affliction of tuberculosis—to produce three documentary books, six novels, a book-length collection of essays, and more than seven hundred journalistic articles and reviews.

Born in Bengal, then a province of British India, Orwell was the second of three children of a minor colonial officer in the Indian Civil Service. In keeping with the social ambitions of his family, he was raised and educated in England, at a convent school in Henley-on-Thames, then at St. Cyprians, a prep school on the south coast, and finally at Eton. At St. Cyprians he first encountered the "snobbish" world "of the English upper and upper-middle classes," a world in which "a glittering car, a title, or a horde of servants was mixed up in people's minds with the idea of actual moral virtue." At Eton he was for a time "both a snob and a revolutionary." After failing to win a university scholarship, he entered the Indian Imperial Police in 1922 and served as a police officer at various posts throughout Burma until he resigned in 1927, "partly because the climate had ruined my health, partly because I already had vague ideas of writing books, but mainly because I could not go on any longer serving an imperialism I had come to regard as very largely a racket."

Orwell moved to Paris in 1928 and worked unsuccessfully at his writing until he ran out of money and was forced to support himself as a dishwasher, an experience that made him realize how little he knew "about working class conditions," about unemployment, and about poverty. So when he returned to England at the end of 1929, he deliberately chose to immerse himself in the world of "social outcasts: tramps, beggars, criminals, prostitutes." His experiences "among the oppressed" provided the material for his first documentary book, *Down and Out in Paris and London* (1933). His experiences in Burma provided the material for his first novel, *Burmese Days* (1934), which expressed the disgust with British imperialism that he was to convey once again in "Shooting an Elephant" (1936). Early in 1936, he accepted the invitation of a socialist group to observe the plight of unemployed coal miners in the north of England and to write about their impoverished situation, as he did in *The Road to Wigan Pier* (1937), a documentary work that also includes several autobiographical chapters about the political and social transformation he underwent between his time in the Imperial Indian Police and his subsequent work as a chronicler of the oppressed. In June 1936 he was married, and in late 1936 he went to observe and take part in the Spanish Civil War.

Though he stayed in Spain only for six months, fighting on the Republican side until he was shot in the throat by a Fascist sniper, his experiences there "turned the scale" for him. From then on "every line of serious work" that he produced was "written, directly or indirectly, *against* totalitarianism and *for* democratic socialism." Fighting and living in the Spanish countryside and then in revolutionary Barcelona, Orwell had glimpsed, however briefly, what appeared to be the ideal of a classless socialist society, only to see it undermined by the devious "efforts of the Russian Government to prevent revolution in Spain." His account of the war in *Homage to Catalonia* (1938) reveals that the political situation was far more complex than he had originally supposed. The difficulty of understanding that situation, as he makes clear in "Looking Back on the Spanish Civil War" (1943), was compounded by the widespread distortion of truth, both in outright political propaganda and in "newspaper reports which did not bear any relation to the facts." From that disturbing experience he developed the passionate commitment to clear and honest writing that he later expressed in "Politics and the English Language" (1946).

During the last ten years of his life, Orwell produced his two most well-known political novels, the beast fable of *Animal Farm* (1945) and the nightmarish political vision of *1984* (1949), which together convey what he perceived to be the special horrors of totalitarianism—the brutality, the lies, the corruption of language, the thought control, the overwhelming tyranny of the state. During the same period, though increasingly weakened by his tubercular condition, he also gave voice to his political concerns in articles, book reviews, columns, letters, and essays for a broad range of magazines and newspapers. In virtually all of this work, "directly or indirectly" he sought "to push the world" in the direction of decency, honesty, liberty, and human well-being. Given his intense concern with the dangers of propaganda, of party lines, he never let himself become too closely aligned with any political position, not even with socialism. Indeed, he was at last too individualistic, too intellectually curious, too devoted to getting at the truth of things ever to let himself be strictly hemmed in by any political position.

Orwell's concern for clear and truthful writing is reflected in the very direct style of his own prose—in the familiar words, the straight-forward sentences, the vividly detailed images, scenes and events through which he expresses his thoughts. He is equally straightforward whether he is writing about the beauty of toads or the horror of capital punishment:

> I mention the spawning of toads because it is one of the phenomena of spring that most deeply appeal to me, and because the toad, unlike the skylark and the primose, has never had much of a boost from the poets.

> When I saw the prisoner step aside to avoid the puddle, I saw the mystery, the unspeakable wrongness, of cutting a life short when it is in full tide.

Here as elsewhere, his style is forceful because he follows his own advice of "using the fewest and shortest words that will cover one's meaning." Ultimately his prose is forceful because he is always true to his commitment "to see things as they are," and to present things as he sees them, no matter how painful the vision might be:

> I thought of a rather cruel trick I once played on a wasp. He was sucking jam on my plate, and I cut him in half. He paid no attention, merely went on with his meal, while a tiny stream of jam trickled out of his severed oesophagus. Only when he tried to fly away did he grasp the dreadful thing that had happened to him. It is the same with modern man. The thing that has been cut away is his soul, and there was a period—twenty years, perhaps—during which he did not notice it.

A HANGING

It was in Burma, a sodden morning of the rains. A sickly light, like yellow tinfoil, was slanting over the high walls into the jail yard. We were waiting outside the condemned cells, a row of sheds fronted with double bars, like small animal cages. Each cell measured about ten feet by ten and was quite bare within except for a plank bed and a pot for drinking water. In some of them brown, silent men were squatting at the inner bars, with their blankets draped round them. These were the condemned men, due to be hanged within the next week or two.

One prisoner had been brought out of his cell. He was a Hindu, a puny wisp of a man, with a shaven head and vague liquid eyes. He had a thick, sprouting moustache, absurdly too big for his body, rather like the moustache of a comic man on the films. Six tall Indian warders were guarding him and getting him ready for the gallows. Two of them stood by with rifles and fixed bayonets, while the others hand-cuffed him, passed a chain through his handcuffs and fixed it to their belts, and lashed his arms tight to his sides. They crowded very close about him, with their hands always on him in a careful, caressing grip, as though all the while feeling him to make sure he was there. It was like men handling a fish which is still alive and may jump back into the water. But he stood quite unresisting, yielding his arms limply to the ropes, as though he hardly noticed what was happening.

Eight o'clock struck and a bugle call, desolately thin in the wet air, floated from the distant barracks. The superintendent of the jail, who was standing apart from the rest of us, moodily prodding the gravel with his stick, raised his head at the sound. He was an army doctor, with a grey toothbrush moustache and a gruff voice. "For God's sake hurry up, Francis," he said irritably. "The man ought to have been dead by this time. Aren't you ready yet?"

Francis, the head jailer, a fat Dravidian in a white drill suit and gold spectacles, waved his black hand. "Yes sir, yes sir," he bubbled. "All iss satisfactorily prepared. The hangman iss waiting. We shall proceed."

"Well, quick march, then. The prisoners can't get their breakfast till this job's over." 5

We set out for the gallows. Two warders marched on either side of the prisoner, with their rifles at the slope; two others marched close against him, gripping him by arm and shoulder, as though at once pushing and supporting him. The rest of us, magistrates and the like, followed behind. Suddenly, when we had gone ten yards, the procession stopped short without any order or warning. A dreadful thing had happened—a dog, come goodness knows whence, had appeared in the yard. It came bounding among us with a loud volley of barks and leapt round us wagging its whole body, wild with glee at finding so many human beings together. It was a large woolly dog, half Airedale, half pariah. For a moment it pranced round us, and then, before anyone could stop it, it had made a dash for the prisoner, and jumping up tried to lick his face. Everybody stood aghast, too taken aback even to grab the dog.

"Who let that bloody brute in here?" said the superintendent angrily. "Catch it, someone!"

A warder detached from the escort, charged clumsily after the dog, but it danced and gambolled just out of his reach, taking everything as part of the game. A young Eurasian jailer picked up a handful of gravel and tried to stone the dog away, but it dodged the stones and came after us again. Its yaps echoed from the jail walls. The prisoner, in the grasp of the two warders, looked on incuriously, as though this was another formality of the hanging. It was several minutes before someone managed to catch the dog. Then we put my handkerchief through its collar and moved off once more, with the dog still straining and whimpering.

It was about forty yards to the gallows. I watched the bare brown back of the prisoner marching in front of me. He walked clumsily with his bound arms, but quite steadily, with that bobbing gait of the Indian who never straightens his knees. At each step his muscles slid neatly into place, the lock of hair on his scalp danced up and down, his feet printed themselves on the wet gravel. And once, in spite of the men who gripped him by each shoulder, he stepped slightly aside to avoid a puddle on the path.

It is curious, but till that moment I had never realized what it means   10
to destroy a healthy, conscious man. When I saw the prisoner step aside to avoid the puddle I saw the mystery, the unspeakable wrongness, of cutting a life short when it is in full tide. This man was not dying, he was alive just as we are alive. All the organs of his body were working—bowels digesting food, skin renewing itself, nails growing, tissues forming—all toiling away in solemn foolery. His nails would still be growing when he stood on the drop, when he was falling through the air with a tenth-of-a-second to live. His eyes saw the yellow gravel and the grey walls, and his brain still remembered, foresaw, reasoned—even about puddles. He and we were a party of men walking together, seeing, hearing, feeling, understanding the same world; and in two minutes, with a sudden snap, one of us would be gone—one mind less, one world less.

The gallows stood in a small yard, separate from the main grounds of the prison, and overgrown with tall prickly weeds. It was a brick erection like three sides of a shed, with planking on top, and above that two beams and a crossbar with the rope dangling. The hangman, a grey-haired convict in the white uniform of the prison, was waiting beside his machine. He greeted us with a servile crouch as we entered. At a word from Francis the two warders, gripping the prisoner more closely than ever, half led, half pushed him to the gallows and helped him clumsily up the ladder. Then the hangman climbed up and fixed the rope round the prisoner's neck.

We stood waiting, five yards away. The warders had formed in a rough circle round the gallows. And then, when the noose was fixed, the prisoner began crying out to his god. It was a high, reiterated cry of "Ram! Ram! Ram! Ram!" not urgent and fearful like a prayer or cry for help, but steady, rhythmical, almost like the tolling of a bell. The dog answered the sound with a whine. The hangman, still standing on the gallows, produced a small cotton bag like a flour bag and drew it down over the prisoner's face. But the sound, muffled by the cloth, still persisted, over and over again: "Ram! Ram! Ram! Ram! Ram!"

The hangman climbed down and stood ready, holding the lever. Minutes seemed to pass. The steady, muffled crying from the prisoner went on and on, "Ram! Ram! Ram!" never faltering for an instant. The superintendent, his head on his chest, was slowly poking the ground with his stick; perhaps he was counting the cries, allowing the prisoner a fixed number—fifty, perhaps, or a hundred. Everyone had changed colour. The Indians had gone grey like bad coffee, and one or two of the bayonets were wavering. We looked at the lashed, hooded man on the drop, and listened to his cries—each cry another second of life; the same thought was in all our minds: oh, kill him quickly, get it over, stop that abominable noise!

Suddenly the superintendent made up his mind. Throwing up his head he made a swift motion with his stick. "Chalo!" he shouted almost fiercely.

There was a clanking noise, and then dead silence. The prisoner had vanished, and the rope was twisting on itself. I let go of the dog, and it galloped immediately to the back of the gallows; but when it got there it stopped short, barked, and then retreated into a corner of the yard, where it stood among the weeds, looking timorously out at us. We went round the gallows to inspect the prisoner's body. He was dangling with his toes pointed straight downwards, very slowly revolving, as dead as a stone.

The superintendent reached out with his stick and poked the bare brown body; it oscillated slightly. "*He's* all right," said the superintendent. He backed out from under the gallows, and blew out a deep breath. The moody look had gone out of his face quite suddenly. He glanced at his wrist-watch. "Eight minutes past eight. Well, that's all for this morning, thank God."

15

The warders unfixed bayonets and marched away. The dog, sobered and conscious of having misbehaved itself, slipped after them. We walked out of the gallows yard, past the condemned cells with their waiting prisoners, into the big central yard of the prison. The convicts, under the command of warders armed with lathis, were already receiving their breakfast. They squatted in long rows, each man holding a tin pannikin, while two warders with buckets marched round ladling out rice; it seemed quite a homely, jolly scene, after the hanging. An enormous relief had come upon us now that the job was done. One felt an impulse to sing, to break into a run, to snigger. All at once everyone began chattering gaily.

The Eurasian boy walking beside me nodded towards the way we had come, with a knowing smile: "Do you know, sir, our friend (he meant the dead man), when he heard his appeal had been dismissed, he pissed on the floor of his cell. From fright. Kindly take one of my cigarettes, sir. Do you not admire my new silver case, sir? From the boxwallah, two rupees eight annas. Classy European style."

Several people laughed—at what, nobody seemed certain.

Francis was walking by the superintendent, talking garrulously: "Well, 20 sir, all hass passed off with the utmost satisfactoriness. It was all finished—flick! like that. It iss not always so—oah, no! I have known cases where the doctor wass obliged to go beneath the gallows and pull the prissoner's legs to ensure decease. Most disagreeable!"

"Wriggling about, eh? That's bad," said the superintendent.

"Ach, sir, it iss worse when they become refractory! One man, I recall, clung to the bars of hiss cage when we went to take him out. You will scarcely credit, sir, that it took six warders to dislodge him, three pulling at each leg. We reasoned with him. 'My dear fellow,' we said, 'think of all the pain and trouble you are causing to us!' But no, he would not listen! Ach, he wass very troublesome!"

I found that I was laughing quite loudly. Everyone was laughing. Even the superintendent grinned in a tolerant way. "You'd better all come out and have a drink," he said quite genially. "I've got a bottle of whisky in the car. We could do with it."

We went through the big double gates of the prison into the road. "Pulling at his legs!" exclaimed a Burmese magistrate suddenly, and burst into a loud chuckling. We all began laughing again. At that moment Francis' anecdote seemed extraordinarily funny. We all had a drink together, native and European alike, quite amicably. The dead man was a hundred yards away.

1931

LINES OF INQUIRY
"A Hanging"

In a pointed story such as Orwell's, every character presumably contributes something to the meaning of the essay. Given this premise, what particular significance do you attribute to the dog and to the reactions of the other characters to its behavior? Why do you suppose that Orwell devotes so much attention to describing the dog's behavior? At one point, the dog is referred to as "having misbehaved itself." In what sense has it misbehaved? How do the dog's reactions to the prisoner and to the hanging compare to the reactions of the other witnesses?

Midway through this essay, Orwell expresses what many people have taken to be the point of his story about the hanging, namely "the unspeakable wrongness of cutting a life short when it is in full tide." If this statement against capital punishment is the point of the story, why doesn't Orwell end the story and his essay at this point? What is the purpose of all the material that follows this statement? What other issues does the essay deal with that are developed in the remainder of the story?

In this essay, as in "Shooting an Elephant," Orwell presents himself in a distinctly unpleasant light by showing how he went along with a deed that went against his own moral judgment. Why do you suppose that he depicts himself in each piece in so unfavorable a way? How did his personal moral compromise affect your reaction to him and to the ideas that he is trying to convey in each piece?

SHOOTING AN ELEPHANT

In Moulmein, in lower Burma, I was hated by large numbers of people—the only time in my life that I have been important enough for this to happen to me. I was sub-divisional police officer of the town, and in an aimless, petty kind of way anti-European feeling was very bitter. No one had the guts to raise a riot, but if a European woman went through the bazaars alone somebody would probably spit betel juice over her dress. As a police officer I was an obvious target and was baited whenever it seemed safe to do so. When a nimble Burman tripped me up on the football field and the referee (another Burman) looked the other way, the crowd yelled with hideous laughter. This happened more than once. In the end the sneering yellow faces of young men that met me everywhere, the insults hooted after me when I was at a safe distance, got badly on my nerves. The young Buddhist priests were the worst of all. There were several thousands of them in the town and none of them seemed to have anything to do except stand on street corners and jeer at Europeans.

All this was perplexing and upsetting. For at that time I had already made up my mind that imperialism was an evil thing and the sooner I chucked up my job and got out of it the better. Theoretically—and secretly, of course—I was all for the Burmese and all against their oppressors, the British. As for the job I was doing, I hated it more bitterly than I can perhaps make clear. In a job like that you see the dirty work of Empire at close quarters. The wretched prisoners huddling in the stinking cages of the lock-ups, the gray, cowed faces of the long-term convicts, the scarred buttocks of the men who had been flogged with bamboos—all these oppressed me with an intolerable sense of guilt. But I could get nothing into perspective. I was young and ill educated and I had had to think out my problems in the utter silence that is imposed on every Englishman in the East. I did not even know that the British Empire is dying, still less did I know that it is a great deal better than the younger empires that are going to supplant it. All I knew was that I was stuck between my hatred of the empire I served and my rage against the evil-spirited little beasts who tried to make my job impossible. With one part of my mind I thought of the British Raj as an unbreakable tyranny, as something clamped down, in *saecula saeculorum,* upon the will of prostrate peoples; with another part I thought that the greatest joy in the world would be to drive a bayonet into a Buddhist priest's guts. Feelings like these are the normal by-products of imperialism; ask any Anglo-Indian official, if you can catch him off duty.

One day something happened which in a roundabout way was enlightening. It was a tiny incident in itself; but it gave me a better glimpse
than I had had before of the real nature of imperialism—the real motives for which despotic governments act. Early one morning the sub-
inspector at a police station the other end of the town rang me up on
the 'phone and said that an elephant was ravaging the bazaar. Would I
please come and do something about it? I did not know what I could
do, but I wanted to see what was happening and I got on to a pony
and started out. I took my rifle, an old .44 Winchester and much too
small to kill an elephant, but I thought the noise might be useful *in
terrorem*. Various Burmans stopped me on the way and told me about
the elephant's doings. It was not, of course, a wild elephant, but a tame
one which had gone "must." It had been chained up, as tame elephants
always are when their attack of "must" is due, but on the previous
night it had broken its chain and escaped. Its mahout, the only person
who could manage it when it was in that state, had set out in pursuit,
but had taken the wrong direction and was now twelve hours' journey
away, and in the morning the elephant had suddenly reappeared in the
town. The Burmese population had no weapons and were quite helpless against it. It had already destroyed somebody's bamboo hut, killed
a cow and raided some fruit-stalls and devoured the stock; also it had
met the municipal rubbish van and, when the driver jumped out
and took to his heels, had turned the van over and inflicted violences
upon it.

The Burmese sub-inspector and some Indian constables were waiting for me in the quarter where the elephant had been seen. It was a
very poor quarter, a labyrinth of squalid bamboo huts, thatched with
palm-leaf, winding all over a steep hillside. I remember that it was a
cloudy, stuffy morning at the beginning of the rains. We began questioning the people as to where the elephant had gone and, as usual,
failed to get any definite information. That is invariably the case in the
East; a story always sounds clear enough at a distance, but the nearer
you get to the scene of events the vaguer it becomes. Some of the
people said that the elephant had gone in one direction, some said that
he had gone in another, some professed not even to have heard of any
elephant. I had almost made up my mind that the whole story was a
pack of lies, when we heard yells a little distance away. There was a
loud, scandalized cry of "Go away, child! Go away this instant!" and
an old woman with a switch in her hand came round the corner of a
hut, violently shooing away a crowd of naked children. Some more
women followed, clicking their tongues and exclaiming; evidently there
was something that the children ought not to have seen. I rounded the
hut and saw a man's dead body sprawling in the mud. He was an Indian, a black Dravidian coolie, almost naked, and he could not have
been dead many minutes. The people said that the elephant had come

suddenly upon him round the corner of the hut, caught him with its trunk, put its foot on his back and ground him into the earth. This was the rainy season and the ground was soft, and his face had scored a trench a foot deep and a couple of yards long. He was lying on his belly with arms crucified and head sharply twisted to one side. His face was coated with mud, the eyes wide open, the teeth bared and grinning with an expression of unendurable agony. (Never tell me, by the way, that the dead look peaceful. Most of the corpses I have seen looked devilish.) The friction of the great beast's foot had stripped the skin from his back as neatly as one skins a rabbit. As soon as I saw the dead man I sent an orderly to a friend's house nearby to borrow an elephant rifle. I had already sent back the pony, not wanting it to go mad with fright and throw me if it smelt the elephant.

The orderly came back in a few minutes with a rifle and five cartridges, and meanwhile some Burmans had arrived and told us that the elephant was in the paddy fields below, only a few hundred yards away. As I started forward practically the whole population of the quarter flocked out of the houses and followed me. They had seen the rifle and were all shouting excitedly that I was going to shoot the elephant. They had not shown much interest in the elephant when he was merely ravaging their homes, but it was different now that he was going to be shot. It was a bit of fun to them, as it would be to an English crowd; besides they wanted the meat. It made me vaguely uneasy. I had no intention of shooting the elephant—I had merely sent for the rifle to defend myself if necessary—and it is always unnerving to have a crowd following you. I marched down the hill, looking and feeling a fool, with the rifle over my shoulder and an ever-growing army of people jostling at my heels. At the bottom, when you got away from the huts, there was a metalled road and beyond that a miry waste of paddy fields a thousand yards across, not yet ploughed but soggy from the first rains and dotted with coarse grass. The elephant was standing eight yards from the road, his left side toward us. He took not the slightest notice of the crowd's approach. He was tearing up bunches of grass, beating them against his knees to clean them, and stuffing them into his mouth.

I had halted on the road. As soon as I saw the elephant I knew with perfect certainty that I ought not to shoot him. It is a serious matter to shoot a working elephant—it is comparable to destroying a huge and costly piece of machinery—and obviously one ought not to do it if it can possibly be avoided. And at that distance, peacefully eating, the elephant looked no more dangerous than a cow. I thought then and I think now that his attack of "must" was already passing off; in which case he would merely wander harmlessly about until the mahout came back and caught him. Moreover, I did not in the least want to shoot him. I decided that I would watch him for a little while to make sure that he did not turn savage again, and then go home.

But at that moment I glanced round at the crowd that had followed me. It was an immense crowd, two thousand at the least and growing every minute. It blocked the road for a long distance on either side. I looked at the sea of yellow faces above the garish clothes—faces all happy and excited over this bit of fun, all certain that the elephant was going to be shot. They were watching me as they would watch a conjurer about to perform a trick. They did not like me, but with the magical rifle in my hands I was momentarily worth watching. And suddenly I realized that I should have to shoot the elephant after all. The people expected it of me and I had got to do it; I could feel their two thousand wills pressing me forward, irresistibly. And it was at this moment, as I stood there with the rifle in my hands, that I first grasped the hollowness, the futility of the white man's dominion in the East. Here was I, the white man with his gun, standing in front of the unarmed native crowd—seemingly the leading actor of the piece; but in reality I was only an absurd puppet pushed to and fro by the will of those yellow faces behind. I perceived in this moment that when the white man turns tyrant it is his own freedom that he destroys. He becomes a sort of hollow, posing dummy, the conventionalized figure of a sahib. For it is the condition of his rule that he shall spend his life in trying to impress the "natives," and so in every crisis he has got to do what the "natives" expect of him. He wears a mask, and his face grows to fit it. I had got to shoot the elephant. I had committed myself to doing it when I sent for the rifle. A sahib has got to act like a sahib; he has got to appear resolute, to know his own mind and do definite things. To come all that way, rifle in hand, with two thousand people marching at my heels, and then to trail feebly away, having done nothing— no, that was impossible. The crowd would laugh at me. And my whole life, every white man's life in the East, was one long struggle not to be laughed at.

But I did not want to shoot the elephant. I watched him beating his bunch of grass against his knees with that preoccupied grandmotherly air that elephants have. It seemed to me that it would be murder to shoot him. At that age I was not squeamish about killing animals, but I had never shot an elephant and never wanted to. (Somehow it always seems worse to kill a *large* animal.) Besides, there was the beast's owner to be considered. Alive, the elephant was worth at least a hundred pounds; dead, he would only be worth the value of his tusks, five pounds, possibly. But I had got to act quickly. I turned to some experienced-looking Burmans who had been there when we arrived, and asked them how the elephant had been behaving. They all said the same thing: he took no notice of you if you left him alone, but he might charge if you went too close to him.

It was perfectly clear to me what I ought to do. I ought to walk up to within, say, twenty-five yards of the elephant and test his behavior.

If he charged, I could shoot; if he took no notice of me, it would be safe to leave him until the mahout came back. But also I knew that I was going to do no such thing. I was a poor shot with a rifle and the ground was soft mud into which one would sink at every step. If the elephant charged and I missed him, I should have about as much chance as a toad under a steam-roller. But even then I was not thinking particularly of my own skin, only of the watchful yellow faces behind. For at that moment, with the crowd watching me, I was not afraid in the ordinary sense, as I would have been if I had been alone. A white man mustn't be frightened in front of "natives"; and so, in general, he isn't frightened. The sole thought in my mind was that if anything went wrong those two thousand Burmans would see me pursued, caught, trampled on, and reduced to a grinning corpse like that Indian up the hill. And if that happened it was quite probable that some of them would laugh. That would never do. There was only one alternative. I shoved the cartridges into the magazine and lay down on the road to get a better aim.

The crowd grew very still, and a deep, low, happy sigh, as of people who see the theater curtain go up at last, breathed from innumerable throats. They were going to have their bit of fun after all. The rifle was a beautiful German thing with crosshair sights. I did not then know that in shooting an elephant one would shoot to cut an imaginary bar running from ear-hole to ear-hole. I ought, therefore, as the elephant was sideways on, to have aimed straight at his ear-hole; actually I aimed several inches in front of this, thinking the brain would be further forward.

When I pulled the trigger I did not hear the bang or feel the kick—one never does when a shot goes home—but I heard the devilish roar of glee that went up from the crowd. In that instant, in too short a time, one would have thought, even for the bullet to get there, a mysterious terrible change had come over the elephant. He neither stirred, nor fell, but every line of his body had altered. He looked suddenly stricken, shrunken, immensely old, as though the frightful impact of the bullet had paralyzed him without knocking him down. At last, after what seemed a long time—it might have been five seconds, I dare say—he sagged flabbily to his knees. His mouth slobbered. An enormous senility seemed to have settled upon him. One could have imagined him thousands of years old. I fired again into the same spot. At the second shot he did not collapse but climbed with desperate slowness to his feet and stood weakly upright, with legs sagging and head drooping. I fired a third time. That was the shot that did for him. You could see the agony of it jolt his whole body and knock the last remnant of strength from his legs. But in falling he seemed for a moment to rise, for as his hind legs collapsed beneath him he seemed to tower upward like a huge rock toppling, his trunk reaching skyward like a tree. He

10

trumpeted, for the first and only time. And then down he came, his belly toward me, with a crash that seemed to shake the ground even where I lay.

I got up. The Burmans were already racing past me across the mud. It was obvious that the elephant would never rise again, but he was not dead. He was breathing very rhythmically with long rattling gasps, his great mound of a side painfully rising and falling. His mouth was wide open—I could see far down into caverns of pale pink throat. I waited a long time for him to die, but his breathing did not weaken. Finally I fired my two remaining shots into the spot where I thought his heart must be. The thick blood welled out of him like red velvet, but still he did not die. His body did not even jerk when the shots hit him, the tortured breathing continued without a pause. He was dying, very slowly and in great agony, but in some world remote from me where not even a bullet could damage him further. I felt that I had got to put an end to that dreadful noise. It seemed dreadful to see the great beast lying there, powerless to move and yet powerless to die, and not even to be able to finish him. I sent back for my small rifle and poured shot after shot into his heart and down his throat. They seemed to make no impression. The tortured gasps continued as steadily as the ticking of a clock.

In the end I could not stand it any longer and went away. I heard later that it took him half an hour to die. Burmans were bringing dahs and baskets even before I left, and I was told they had stripped his body almost to the bones by the afternoon.

Afterward, of course, there were endless discussions about the shooting of the elephant. The owner was furious, but he was only an Indian and could do nothing. Besides, legally I had done the right thing, for a mad elephant has to be killed, like a mad dog, if its owner fails to control it. Among the Europeans opinion was divided. The older men said I was right, the younger men said it was a damn shame to shoot an elephant for killing a coolie, because an elephant was worth more than any damn Coringhee coolie. And afterward I was very glad that the coolie had been killed; it put me legally in the right and it gave me a sufficient pretext for shooting the elephant. I often wondered whether any of the others grasped that I had done it solely to avoid looking a fool.

1936

LINES OF INQUIRY
"Shooting an Elephant"

Throughout this essay, Orwell is remarkably frank not only in telling about his actions and experiences, but also in revealing his personal thoughts and feelings. What did you discover about Orwell as a result of his frankness? Did you ever find yourself being offended either by his frankly confessional manner or by what he revealed about himself? Why do you suppose that he chose to be so frank about himself?

Orwell refers to his experience of shooting the elephant as an "enlightening . . . incident" that gave him a "better glimpse" than he "had had before of the real nature of imperialism." What in particular did Orwell discover about imperialism from the experience of shooting the elephant, and at what point during the experience did he make his discoveries? What did you discover about imperialism from reading the essay, and at what point(s) in the essay did you make your discoveries?

Think about a time in your life when an unpleasant incident that you were involved in, or that you witnessed, helped you to discover something important about "the real nature" of social or political tyranny. What did you discover? When did you make your discovery—during the incident or sometime later? Did you find yourself, like Orwell, to be divided in your loyalties and confused about what to think or do? Or did you have a clear-cut view of the situation from beginning to end? How has your discovery affected your subsequent political or social outlook?

MARRAKECH

As the corpse went past the flies left the restaurant table in a cloud and rushed after it, but they came back a few minutes later.

The little crowd of mourners—all men and boys, no women—threaded their way across the market-place between the piles of pomegranates and the taxis and the camels, wailing a short chant over and over again. What really appeals to the flies is that the corpses here are never put into coffins, they are merely wrapped in a piece of rag and carried on a rough wooden bier on the shoulders of four friends. When the friends get to the burying-ground they hack an oblong hole a foot or two deep, dump the body in it and fling over it a little of the dried-up, lumpy earth, which is like broken brick. No gravestone, no name, no identifying mark of any kind. The burying-ground is merely a huge waste of hummocky earth, like a derelict building-lot. After a month or two no one can even be certain where his own relatives are buried.

When you walk through a town like this—two hundred thousand inhabitants, of whom at least twenty thousand own literally nothing except the rags they stand up in—when you see how the people live, and still more how easily they die, it is always difficult to believe that you are walking among human beings. All colonial empires are in reality founded upon that fact. The people have brown faces—besides, there are so many of them! Are they really the same flesh as yourself? Do they even have names? Or are they merely a kind of undifferentiated brown stuff, about as individual as bees or coral insects? They rise out of the earth, they sweat and starve for a few years, and then they sink back into the nameless mounds of the graveyard and nobody notices that they are gone. And even the graves themselves soon fade back into the soil. Sometimes, out for a walk, as you break your way through the prickly pear, you notice that it is rather bumpy underfoot, and only a certain regularity in the bumps tells you that you are walking over skeletons.

I was feeding one of the gazelles in the public gardens.

Gazelles are almost the only animals that look good to eat when they are still alive, in fact, one can hardly look at their hindquarters without thinking of mint sauce. The gazelle I was feeding seemed to know that this thought was in my mind, for though it took the piece of bread I was holding out it obviously did not like me. It nibbled rapidly at the bread, then lowered its head and tried to butt me, then took another nibble and then butted again. Probably its idea was that if it could drive me away the bread would somehow remain hanging in mid-air.

An Arab navvy working on the path nearby lowered his heavy hoe and sidled towards us. He looked from the gazelle to the bread and from the bread to the gazelle, with a sort of quiet amazement, as though he had never seen anything quite like this before. Finally he said shyly in French:

"I could eat some of that bread."

I tore off a piece and he stowed it gratefully in some secret place under his rags. This man is an employee of the Municipality.

When you go through the Jewish quarters you gather some idea of what the medieval ghettoes were probably like. Under their Moorish rulers the Jews were only allowed to own land in certain restricted areas, and after centuries of this kind of treatment they have ceased to bother about overcrowding. Many of the streets are a good deal less than six feet wide, the houses are completely windowless, and sore-eyed children cluster everywhere in unbelievable numbers, like clouds of flies. Down the centre of the street there is generally running a little river of urine.

In the bazaar huge families of Jews, all dressed in the long black 10
robe and little black skull-cap, are working in dark fly-infested booths that look like caves. A carpenter sits cross-legged at a prehistoric lathe, turning chair-legs at lightning speed. He works the lathe with a bow in his right hand and guides the chisel with his left foot, and thanks to a lifetime of sitting in this position his left leg is warped out of shape. At his side his grandson, aged six, is already starting on the simpler parts of the job.

I was just passing the coppersmiths' booths when somebody noticed that I was lighting a cigarette. Instantly, from the dark holes all round, there was a frenzied rush of Jews, many of them old grandfathers with flowing grey beards, all clamouring for a cigarette. Even a blind man somewhere at the back of one of the booths heard a rumour of cigarettes and came crawling out, groping in the air with his hand. In about a minute I had used up the whole packet. None of these people, I suppose, works less than twelve hours a day, and every one of them looks on a cigarette as a more or less impossible luxury.

As the Jews live in self-contained communities they follow the same trades as the Arabs, except for agriculture. Fruit-sellers, potters, silversmiths, blacksmiths, butchers, leather-workers, tailors, water-carriers, beggars, porters—whichever way you look you see nothing but Jews. As a matter of fact there are thirteen thousand of them, all living in the space of a few acres. A good job Hitler isn't here. Perhaps he is on his way, however. You hear the usual dark rumours about the Jews, not only from the Arabs but from the poorer Europeans.

"Yes, *mon vieux,* they took my job away from me and gave it to a Jew. The Jews! They're the real rulers of this country, you know. They've got all the money. They control the banks, finance—everything."

"But," I said, "isn't it a fact that the average Jew is a labourer working for about a penny an hour?"

"Ah, that's only for show! They're all moneylenders really. They're   15 cunning, the Jews."

In just the same way, a couple of hundred years ago, poor old women used to be burned for witchcraft when they could not even work enough magic to get themselves a square meal.

All people who work with their hands are partly invisible, and the more important the work they do, the less visible they are. Still, a white skin is always fairly conspicuous. In northern Europe, when you see a labourer ploughing a field, you probably give him a second glance. In a hot country, anywhere south of Gibraltar or east of Suez, the chances are that you don't even see him. I have noticed this again and again. In a tropical landscape one's eye takes in everything except the human beings. It takes in the dried-up soil, the prickly pear, the palm-tree and the distant mountain, but it always misses the peasant hoeing at his patch. He is the same colour as the earth, and a great deal less interesting to look at.

It is only because of this that the starved countries of Asia and Africa are accepted as tourist resorts. No one would think of running cheap trips to the Distressed Areas. But where the human beings have brown skins their poverty is simply not noticed. What does Morocco mean to a Frenchman? An orange-grove or a job in government service. Or to an Englishman? Camels, castles, palm-trees, Foreign Legionnaires, brass trays and bandits. One could probably live here for years without noticing that for nine-tenths of the people the reality of life is an endless, back-breaking struggle to wring a little food out of an eroded soil.

Most of Morocco is so desolate that no wild animal bigger than a hare can live on it. Huge areas which were once covered with forest have turned into a treeless waste where the soil is exactly like broken-up brick. Nevertheless a good deal of it is cultivated, with frightful labour. Everything is done by hand. Long lines of women, bent double like inverted capital Ls, work their way slowly across the field, tearing up the prickly weeds with their hands, and the peasant gathering lucerne for fodder pulls it up stalk by stalk instead of reaping it, thus saving an inch or two on each stalk. The plough is a wretched wooden thing, so frail that one can easily carry it on one's shoulder, and fitted underneath with a rough iron spike which stirs the soil to a depth of about four inches. This is as much as the strength of the animals is equal to. It is usual to plough with a cow and a donkey yoked together. Two donkeys would not be quite strong enough, but on the other hand two cows would cost a little more to feed. The peasants possess no harrows, they merely plough the soil several times over in different directions, finally leaving it in rough furrows, after which the whole field has to be shaped with hoes into small oblong patches, to conserve water. Except for a day or two after the rare rainstorms there is never enough water. Along the edges of the fields channels are hacked out to a depth of thirty or forty feet to get at the tiny trickles which run through the subsoil.

Every afternoon a file of very old women passes down the road   20 outside my house, each carrying a load of firewood. All of them are mummified with age and the sun, and all of them are tiny. It seems to be generally the case in primitive communities that the women, when they get beyond a certain age, shrink to the size of children. One day a poor old creature who could not have been more than four feet tall crept past me under a vast load of wood. I stopped her and put a five-sou piece (a little more than a farthing) into her hand. She answered with a shrill wail, almost a scream, which was partly gratitude but mainly surprise. I suppose that from her point of view, by taking any notice of her, I seemed almost to be violating a law of nature. She accepted her status as an old woman, that is to say as a beast of burden. When a family is travelling it is quite usual to see a father and a grown-up son riding ahead on donkeys, and an old woman following on foot, carrying the baggage.

But what is strange about these people is their invisibility. For several weeks, always at about the same time of day, the file of old women had hobbled past the house with their firewood, and though they had registered themselves on my eyeballs I cannot truly say that I had seen them. Firewood was passing—that was how I saw it. It was only that one day I happened to be walking behind them, and the curious up-and-down motion of a load of wood drew my attention to the human being underneath it. Then for the first time I noticed the poor old earth-coloured bodies, bodies reduced to bones and leathery skin, bent double under the crushing weight. Yet I suppose I had not been five minutes on Moroccan soil before I noticed the overloading of the donkeys and was infuriated by it. There is no question that the donkeys are damnably treated. The Moroccan donkey is hardly bigger than a St Bernard dog, it carries a load which in the British army would be considered too much for a fifteen-hands mule, and very often its pack-saddle is not taken off its back for weeks together. But what is peculiarly pitiful is that it is the most willing creature on earth, it follows its master like a dog and does not need either bridle or halter. After a dozen years of devoted work it suddenly drops dead, whereupon its master tips it into the ditch and the village dogs have torn its guts out before it is cold.

This kind of thing makes one's blood boil, whereas—on the whole—the plight of the human beings does not. I am not commenting, merely pointing to a fact. People with brown skins are next door to invisible.

Anyone can be sorry for the donkey with its galled back, but it is generally owing to some kind of accident if one even notices the old woman under her load of sticks.

As the storks flew northward the Negroes were marching southward—a long, dusty column, infantry, screw-gun batteries and then more infantry, four or five thousand men in all, winding up the road with a clumping of boots and a clatter of iron wheels.

They were Senegalese, the blackest Negroes in Africa, so black that sometimes it is difficult to see whereabouts on their necks the hair begins. Their splendid bodies were hidden in reach-me-down khaki uniforms, their feet squashed into boots that looked like blocks of wood, and every tin hat seemed to be a couple of sizes too small. It was very hot and the men had marched a long way. They slumped under the weight of their packs and the curiously sensitive black faces were glistening with sweat.

As they went past a tall, very young Negro turned and caught my   25
eye. But the look he gave me was not in the least the kind of look you might expect. Not hostile, not contemptuous, not sullen, not even inquisitive. It was the shy, wide-eyed Negro look, which actually is a look of profound respect. I saw how it was. This wretched boy, who is a French citizen and has therefore been dragged from the forest to scrub floors and catch syphilis in garrison towns, actually has feelings of reverence before a white skin. He has been taught that the white race are his masters, and he still believes it.

But there is one thought which every white man (and in this connection it doesn't matter twopence if he calls himself a Socialist) thinks when he sees a black army marching past. "How much longer can we go on kidding these people? How long before they turn their guns in the other direction?"

It was curious, really. Every white man there has this thought stowed somewhere or other in his mind. I had it, so had the other onlookers, so had the officers on their sweating chargers and the white NCOs marching in the ranks. It was a kind of secret which we all knew and were too clever to tell; only the Negroes didn't know it. And really it was almost like watching a flock of cattle to see the long column, a mile or two miles of armed men, flowing peacefully up the road, while the great white birds drifted over them in the opposite direction, glittering like scraps of paper.

1939

LINES OF INQUIRY
"Marrakech"

Orwell's essay consists of five distinctly separate sections. How do you account for Orwell's organization of the five sections? For example, what is the effect of his beginning with the funeral procession, then moving to the incident with the gazelle and the navvy in the public garden, then depicting the scene in the Jewish ghetto, and so on. Try some different ways of arranging the five sections. How does each of your rearrangements affect the pacing, the buildup, the climax, and the overall significance of the piece?

Each of the five sections offers a vividly detailed picture, somewhat like a snapshot, of a particular scene or happening in Marrakech. What kinds of details, images, and scenes does Orwell emphasize in these snapshots? What do you suppose is his primary purpose in focusing on such scenes? What do you suppose is his main purpose in writing about Marrakech?

The title of this piece suggests that it will provide an informative description of Marrakech. What did you discover about the place from reading Orwell's piece about it? About its size, its geography, its commerce, its history, its social makeup, its inhabitants? What more would you like to have known about Marrakech that Orwell does not consider in his essay? Do some research in the library to find out what Marrakech is like today. In what ways has Marrakech (and the world that it symbolizes) changed since Orwell wrote his essay? In what respects has it remained the same?

SOME THOUGHTS ON THE COMMON TOAD

Before the swallow, before the daffodil, and not much later than the snowdrop, the common toad salutes the coming of spring after his own fashion, which is to emerge from a hole in the ground, where he has lain buried since the previous autumn, and crawl as rapidly as possible towards the nearest suitable patch of water. Something—some kind of shudder in the earth, or perhaps merely a rise of a few degrees in the temperature—has told him that it is time to wake up: though a few toads appear to sleep the clock round and miss out a year from time to time—at any rate, I have more than once dug them up, alive and apparently well, in the middle of the summer.

At this period, after his long fast, the toad has a very spiritual look, like a strict Anglo-Catholic toward the end of Lent. His movements are languid but purposeful, his body is shrunken, and by contrast his eyes look abnormally large. This allows one to notice, what one might not at another time, that a toad has about the most beautiful eye of any living creature. It is like gold, or more exactly it is like the golden-colored semi-precious stone which one sometimes sees in signet rings, and which I think is called a chrysoberyl.

For a few days after getting into the water the toad concentrates on building up his strength by eating small insects. Presently he has swollen to his normal size again, and then he goes through a phase of intense sexiness. All he knows, at least if he is a male toad, is that he wants to get his arms round something, and if you offer him a stick, or even your finger, he will cling to it with surprising strength and take a long time to discover that it is not a female toad. Frequently one comes upon shapeless masses of ten or twenty toads rolling over and over in the water, one clinging to another without distinction of sex. By degrees, however, they sort themselves out into couples, with the male duly sitting on the female's back. You can now distinguish males from females, because the male is smaller, darker and sits on top, with his arms tightly clasped round the female's neck. After a day or two the spawn is laid in long strings which wind themselves in and out of the reeds and soon become invisible. A few more weeks, and the water is alive with masses of tiny tadpoles which rapidly grow larger, sprout hind legs, then forelegs, then shed their tails: and finally, about the middle of the summer, the new generation of toads, smaller than one's thumb-nail but perfect in every particular, crawl out of the water to begin the game anew.

I mention the spawning of the toads because it is one of the phenomena of spring which most deeply appeal to me, and because the toad, unlike the skylark and the primrose, has never had much of a boost from the poets. But I am aware that many people do not like reptiles or amphibians, and I am not suggesting that in order to enjoy the spring you have to take an interest in toads. There are also the crocus, the missel thrush, the cuckoo, the blackthorn, etc. The point is that the pleasures of spring are available to everybody, and cost nothing. Even in the most sordid street the coming of spring will register itself by some sign or other, if it is only a brighter blue between the chimney pots or the vivid green of an elder sprouting on a blitzed site. Indeed it is remarkable how Nature goes on existing unofficially, as it were, in the very heart of London. I have seen a kestrel flying over the Deptford gasworks, and I have heard a first-rate performance by a black bird in the Euston Road. There must be some hundreds of thousands, if not millions, of birds living inside the four-mile radius, and it is rather a pleasing thought that none of them pays a half-penny of rent.

As for spring, not even the narrow and gloomy streets round the 5 Bank of England are quite able to exclude it. It comes seeping in everywhere, like one of those new poison gases which pass through all filters. The spring is commonly referred to as "a miracle," and during the past five or six years this worn-out figure of speech has taken on a new lease of life. After the sort of winters we have had to endure recently, the spring does seem miraculous, because it has become gradually harder and harder to believe that it is actually going to happen. Every February since 1940 I have found myself thinking that this time winter is going to be permanent. But Persephone, like the toads, always rises from the dead at about the same moment. Suddenly, toward the end of March, the miracle happens and the decaying slum in which I live is transfigured. Down in the square the sooty privets have turned bright green, the leaves are thickening on the chestnut trees, the daffodils are out, the wallflowers are budding, the policeman's tunic looks positively a pleasant shade of blue, the fish-monger greets his customers with a smile, and even the sparrows are quite a different color, having felt the balminess of the air and nerved themselves to take a bath, their first since last September.

Is it wicked to take a pleasure in spring, and other seasonal changes? To put it more precisely, is it politically reprehensible, while we are all groaning, under the shackles of the capitalist system, to point out that life is frequently more worth living because of a blackbird's song, a yellow elm tree in October, or some other natural phenomenon which does not cost money and does not have what the editors of the left-wing newspapers call a class angle? There is no doubt that many people think so. I know by experience that a favorable reference to "Nature" in one of my articles is liable to bring me abusive letters, and though the keyword in these letters is usually "sentimental," two ideas seem to be mixed up in them. One is that any pleasure in the actual process of life encourages a sort of political quietism. People, so the thought runs, ought to be discontented, and it is our job to multiply our wants and not simply to increase our enjoyment of the things we have already. The other idea is that this is the age of machines and that to dislike the machine, or even to want to limit its domination, is backward-looking, reactionary, and slightly ridiculous. This is often backed up by the statement that a love of Nature is a foible of urbanized people who have no notion what Nature is really like. Those who really have to deal with the soil, so it is argued, do not love the soil, and do not take the faintest interest in birds or flowers, except from a strictly utilitarian point of view. To love the country one must live in the town, merely taking an occasional week-end ramble at the warmer times of year.

This last idea is demonstrably false. Medieval literature, for instance, including the popular ballads, is full of an almost Georgian enthusiasm for Nature, and the art of agricultural peoples such as the Chinese and Japanese centers always round trees, birds, flowers, rivers, mountains. The other idea seems to me to be wrong in a subtler way. Certainly we ought to be discontented, we ought not simply to find out ways of making the best of a bad job, and yet if we kill all pleasure in the actual process of life, what sort of future are we preparing for ourselves? If a man cannot enjoy the return of spring, why should he be happy in a labor-saving Utopia? What will he do with the leisure that the machine will give him? I have always suspected that if our economic and political problems are ever really solved, life will become simpler instead of more complex, and that the sort of pleasure one gets from finding the first primrose will loom larger than the sort of pleasure one gets from eating an ice to the tune of a Wurlitzer. I think that by retaining one's childhood love of such things as trees, fishes, butterflies, and—to return to my first instance—toads, one makes a peaceful and decent future a little more probable, and that by preaching the doctrine that nothing is to be admired except steel and concrete, one merely makes it a little surer that human beings will have no outlet for their surplus energy except in hatred and leader-worship.

At any rate, spring is here, even in London, N.1, and they can't stop you enjoying it. This is a satisfying reflection. How many a time have I stood watching the toads mating, or a pair of hares having a boxing match in the young corn, and thought of all the important persons who would stop me enjoying this if they could. But luckily they can't. So long as you are not actually ill, hungry, frightened, or immured in a prison or a holiday camp, spring is still spring. The atom bombs are piling up in the factories, the police are prowling through the cities, the lies are streaming from the loudspeakers, but the earth is still going round the sun, and neither the dictators nor the bureaucrats, deeply as they disapprove of the process, are able to prevent it.

1946

LINES OF INQUIRY
"Some Thoughts on the Common Toad"

Though the title of this essay might lead one to expect that it is primarily, even exclusively, concerned with "the common toad," Orwell focuses on the toad only in the opening section of his essay. In the remaining two sections, he does not discuss toads any longer, but merely alludes to them four or five times. Why do you suppose he features "the common toad" in his title? In what sense does the toad figure in the piece even when Orwell is not discussing it explicitly? In what sense does the significance of the toad remain constant from one section to the next? In what senses, if any, does it change?

Given Orwell's commitment to writing with a political purpose, how do you account for his decision to write an essay such as this one, which seems far more interested in the spawning of toads, the coming of spring, and the pleasures of nature than it is in any specific political issue? Or, might it be argued that despite all of his talk about toads and spring and nature (indeed, by means of focusing on such things), Orwell is actually exploring some serious political issues, such as the nature of the good life, the implications of a machine-age culture, and the perils of thought control? If so, which of these concerns do you think is uppermost in his mind?

Other essayists in this collection have also used natural creatures as a focus for meditations about some aspect of experience, as you can see by looking at Dillard's "Living Like Weasels," Eiseley's "The Bird and the Machine," or Woolf's "The Death of the Moth." After reading or rereading one of these pieces, think about how it compares to Orwell's essay in its descriptive and meditative techniques.

POLITICS AND THE ENGLISH LANGUAGE

Most people who bother with the matter at all would admit that the English language is in a bad way, but it is generally assumed that we cannot by conscious action do anything about it. Our civilization is decadent and our language—so the argument runs—must inevitably share in the general collapse. It follows that any struggle against the abuse of language is a sentimental archaism, like preferring candles to electric light or hansom cabs to aeroplanes. Underneath this lies the half-conscious belief that language is a natural growth and not an instrument which we shape for our own purposes.

Now, it is clear that the decline of a language must ultimately have political and economic causes: it is not due simply to the bad influence of this or that individual writer. But an effect can become a cause, reinforcing the original cause and producing the same effect in an intensified form, and so on indefinitely. A man may take to drink because he feels himself to be a failure, and then fail all the more completely because he drinks. It is rather the same thing that is happening to the English language. It becomes ugly and inaccurate because our thoughts are foolish, but the slovenliness of our language makes it easier for us to have foolish thoughts. The point is that the process is reversible. Modern English, especially written English, is full of bad habits which spread by imitation and which can be avoided if one is willing to take the necessary trouble. If one gets rid of these habits one can think more clearly, and to think clearly is a necessary first step toward political regeneration: so that the fight against bad English is not frivolous and is not the exclusive concern of professional writers. I will come back to this presently, and I hope that by that time the meaning of what I have said here will have become clearer. Meanwhile, here are five specimens of the English language as it is now habitually written.

These five passages have not been picked out because they are especially bad—I could have quoted far worse if I had chosen—but because they illustrate various of the mental vices from which we now suffer. They are a little below the average, but are fairly representative samples. I number them so that I can refer back to them when necessary:

(1) I am not, indeed, sure whether it is not true to say that the Milton who once seemed not unlike a seventeenth-century Shelley had not become, out of an experience ever more bitter in each year, more alien [sic]

to the founder of that Jesuit sect which nothing could induce him to tolerate.

Professor Harold Laski
(Essay in *Freedom of Expression*)

(2) Above all, we cannot play ducks and drakes with a native battery of idioms which prescribes such egregious collocations of vocables as the basic *put up with* for *tolerate* or *put at a loss* for *bewilder*.

Professor Lancelot Hogben (*Interglossa*)

(3) On the one side we have the free personality: by definition it is not neurotic, for it has neither conflict nor dream. Its desires, such as they are, are transparent, for they are just what institutional approval keeps in the forefront of consciousness; another institutional pattern would alter their number and intensity; there is little in them that is natural, irreducible, or culturally dangerous. But *on the other side,* the social bond itself is nothing but the mutual reflection of these self-secure integrities. Recall the definition of love. Is not this the very picture of a small academic? Where is there a place in this hall of mirrors for either personality or fraternity?

Essay on psychology in *Politics* (New York)

(4) All the "best people" from the gentlemen's clubs, and all the frantic fascist captains, united in common hatred of Socialism and bestial horror of the rising tide of the mass revolutionary movement, have turned to acts of provocation, to foul incendiarism, to medieval legends of poisoned wells, to legalize their own destruction of proletarian organizations, and rouse the agitated petty-bourgeoisie to chauvinistic fervor on behalf of the fight against the revolutionary way out of the crisis.

Communist pamphlet

(5) If a new spirit *is* to be infused into this old country, there is one thorny and contentious reform which must be tackled, and that is the humanization and galvanization of the B.B.C. Timidity here will bespeak canker and atrophy of the soul. The heart of Britain may be sound and of strong beat, for instance, but the British lion's roar at present is like that of Bottom in Shakespeare's *Midsummer Night's Dream*—as gentle as any sucking dove. A virile new Britain cannot continue indefinitely to be traduced in the eyes, or rather ears, of the world by the effete languors of Langham Place, brazenly masquerading as "standard English." When the Voice of Britain is heard at nine o'clock, better far and infinitely less ludicrous to hear aitches honestly dropped than the present priggish, inflated, inhibited, school-ma'amish arch braying of blameless bashful mewing maidens!

Letter in *Tribune*

Each of these passages has faults of its own, but, quite apart from avoidable ugliness, two qualities are common to all of them. The first is staleness of imagery; the other is lack of precision. The writer either has a meaning and cannot express it, or he inadvertently says something else, or he is almost indifferent as to whether his words mean anything or not. This mixture of vagueness and sheer incompetence is the most marked characteristic of modern English prose, and especially of any kind of political writing. As soon as certain topics are raised, the concrete melts into the abstract and no one seems able to think of turns of speech that are not hackneyed: prose consists less and less of *words* chosen for the sake of their meaning, and more and more of *phrases* tacked together like the sections of a prefabricated henhouse. I list below, with notes and examples, various of the tricks by means of which the work of prose-construction is habitually dodged:

Dying metaphors. A newly invented metaphor assists thought by evoking a visual image, while on the other hand a metaphor which is technically "dead" (e.g. *iron resolution*) has in effect reverted to being an ordinary word and can generally be used without loss of vividness. But in between these two classes there is a huge dump of worn-out metaphors which have lost all evocative power and are merely used because they save people the trouble of inventing phrases for themselves. Examples are: *Ring the changes on, take up the cudgels for, toe the line, ride roughshod over, stand shoulder to shoulder with, play into the hands of, no axe to grind, grist to the mill, fishing in troubled waters, on the order of the day, Achilles' heel, swan song, hotbed.* Many of these are used without knowledge of their meaning (what is a "rift," for instance?), and incompatible metaphors are frequently mixed, a sure sign that the writer is not interested in what he is saying. Some metaphors now current have been twisted out of their original meaning without those who use them ever being aware of the fact. For example, *toe the line* is sometimes written *tow the line.* Another example is *the hammer and the anvil,* now always used with the implication that the anvil gets the worst of it. In real life it is always the anvil that breaks the hammer, never the other way about: a writer who stopped to think what he was saying would be aware of this, and would avoid perverting the original phrase.

Operators or *verbal false limbs.* These save the trouble of picking out appropriate verbs and nouns, and at the same time pad each sentence with extra syllables which give it an appearance of symmetry. Characteristic phrases are *render inoperative, militate against, make contact with, be subjected to, give rise to, give grounds for, have the effect of, play a leading part (role) in, make itself felt, take effect, exhibit a tendency to, serve the purpose of,* etc., etc. The key-note is the elimination of simple verbs. Instead of being a single word, such as *break, stop, spoil, mend, kill,* a verb becomes a *phrase,* made up of a noun or adjective tacked on to some general-purpose verb such as *prove, serve, form, play, render.* In addition, the passive voice is wherever possible used in preference to the active, and noun constructions are used instead of gerunds (*by examination of* instead of *by examining*). The range of verbs is further cut down by means of the *-ize* and *de-* formations, and the banal statements are given an appearance of profundity by means of the *not un-* formation. Simple conjunctions and prepositions are replaced by such phrases as *with respect to, having regard to, the fact that, by dint of, in view of, in the interests of, on the hypothesis that;* and the ends of sentences are saved from anticlimax by such resounding commonplaces as *greatly to be desired, cannot be left out of account, a development to be expected in the near future, deserving of serious consideration, brought to a satisfactory conclusion,* and so on and so forth.

Pretentious diction. Words like *phenomenon, element, individual* (as noun), *objective, categorical, effective, virtual, basic, primary, promote, constitute, exhibit, exploit, utilize, eliminate, liquidate,* are used to dress up simple statements and give an air of scientific impartiality to biased judgments. Adjectives like *epoch-making, epic, historic, unforgettable, triumphant, age-old, inevitable, inexorable, veritable,* are used to dignify the sordid process of international politics, while writing that aims at glorifying war usually takes on an archaic color, its characteristic words being: *realm, throne, chariot, mailed fist, trident, sword, shield, buckler, banner, jackboot, clarion.* Foreign words and expressions such as *cul de sac, ancien régime, deus ex machina, mutatis mutandis, status quo, gleichschaltung, weltanschauung,* are used to give an air of culture and elegance. Except for the useful abbreviations *i.e., e.g.,* and *etc.,* there is no real need for any of the hundreds of foreign phrases now current in English. Bad writers, and especially scientific, political, and sociological writers, are nearly always haunted by the notion that Latin or Greek words are grander than Saxon ones, and unnecessary words like *expedite, ameliorate, predict, extraneous, deracinated, clandestine, subaqueous,* and hundreds of others constantly gain ground from their Anglo-Saxon opposite numbers.[1] The jargon peculiar to Marxist writing (*hyena, hangman, cannibal, petty bourgeois, these gentry, lackey, flunkey, mad dog, White Guard,* etc.) consists largely of words and phrases translated from Russian, German, or French; but the normal way of coining a new word is to use a Latin or Greek root with the appropriate affix and, where necessary, the –ize formation. It is often easier to make up words of this kind (*deregionalize, impermissible, extramarital, nonfragmentary* and so forth) than to think up the English words that will cover one's meaning. The result, in general, is an increase in slovenliness and vagueness.

---

[1] An interesting illustration of this is the way in which the English flower names which were in use till very recently are being ousted by Greek ones, *snapdragon* becoming *antirrhinum, forget-me-not* becoming *myosotis,* etc. It is hard to see any practical reason for this change of fashion: it is probably due to an instinctive turning away from the more homely word and a vague feeling that the Greek word is scientific.

Meaningless words. In certain kinds of writing, particularly in art criticism and literary criticism, it is normal to come across long passages
which are almost completely lacking in meaning.[2] Words like *romantic,*
plastic, values, human, dead, sentimental, natural, vitality, as used in art
criticism, are strictly meaningless, in the sense that they not only do
not point to any discoverable object, but are hardly ever expected to do
so by the reader. When one critic writes, "The outstanding feature of
Mr. X's work is its living quality," while another writes, "The immediately striking thing about Mr. X's work is its peculiar deadness," the
reader accepts this as a simple difference of opinion. If words like *black*
and *white* were involved, instead of the jargon words *dead* and *living,* he
would see at once that language was being used in an improper way.
Many political words are similarly abused. The word *Fascism* has now
no meaning except in so far as it signifies "something not desirable."
The words *democracy, socialism, freedom, patriotic, realistic, justice,* have
each of them several different meanings which cannot be reconciled with
one another. In the case of a word like *democracy,* not only is there no
agreed definition, but the attempt to make one is resisted from all sides.
It is almost universally felt that when we call a country democratic we
are praising it: consequently the defenders of every kind of régime claim
that it is a democracy, and fear that they might have to stop using the
word if it were tied down to any one meaning. Words of this kind are
often used in a consciously dishonest way. That is, the person who uses
them has his own private definition, but allows his hearer to think he
means something quite different. Statements like *Marshal Pétain was a*
true patriot, The Soviet press is the freest in the world, The Catholic Church
is opposed to persecution, are almost always made with intent to deceive.
Other words used in variable meanings, in most cases more or less
dishonestly, are: *class, totalitarian, science, progressive, reactionary, bour-*
geois, equality.

Now that I have made this catalogue of swindles and perversions,
let me give another example of the kind of writing that they lead to.
This time it must of its nature be an imaginary one. I am going to
translate a passage of good English into modern English of the worst
sort. Here is a well-known verse from *Ecclesiastes:*

> I returned and saw under the sun, that the race is not to the swift,
> nor the battle to the strong, neither yet bread to the wise, nor yet riches

---

[2]Example: "Comfort's catholicity of perception and image, strangely Whit-
manesque in range, almost the exact opposite in aesthetic compulsion, continues to evoke that trembling atmospheric accumulative hinting at a cruel, an
inexorably serene timelessness. . . . Wrey Gardiner scores by aiming at simple
bull's-eyes with precision. Only they are not so simple, and through this contented sadness runs more than the surface bittersweet of resignation." (*Poetry*
Quarterly.)

to men of understanding, nor yet favor to men of skill; but time and chance happeneth to them all.

Here it is in modern English: 10

Objective consideration of contemporary phenomena compels the conclusion that success or failure in competitive activities exhibits no tendency to be commensurate with innate capacity, but that a considerable element of the unpredictable must invariably be taken into account.

This is a parody, but not a very gross one. Exhibit (3), above, for instance, contains several patches of the same kind of English. It will be seen that I have not made a full translation. The beginning and ending of the sentence follow the original meaning fairly closely, but in the middle the concrete illustration—race, battle, bread—dissolve into the vague phrase "success or failure in competitive activities." This had to be so, because no modern writer of the kind I am discussing—no one capable of using phrases like "objective consideration of contemporary phenomena"—would ever tabulate his thoughts in that precise and detailed way. The whole tendency of modern prose is away from concreteness. Now analyze these two sentences a little more closely. The first contains forty-nine words but only sixty syllables, and all its words are those of everyday life. The second contains thirty-eight words of ninety syllables: eighteen of its words are from Latin roots and one from Greek. The first sentence contains six vivid images, and only one phrase ("time and chance") that could be called vague. The second contains not a single fresh, arresting phrase, and in spite of its ninety syllables it gives only a shortened version of the meaning contained in the first. Yet without a doubt it is the second kind of sentence that is gaining ground in modern English. I do not want to exaggerate. This kind of writing is not yet universal, and outcrops of simplicity will occur here and there in the worst-written page. Still, if you or I were told to write a few lines on the uncertainty of human fortunes, we should probably come much nearer to my imaginary sentence than to the one from *Ecclesiastes*.

As I have tried to show, modern writing at its worst does not consist in picking out words for the sake of their meaning and inventing images in order to make the meaning clearer. It consists in gumming together long strips of words which have already been set in order by someone else, and making the results presentable by sheer humbug. The attraction of this way of writing is that it is easy. It is easier—even quicker, once you have the habit—to say *In my opinion it is not an unjustifiable assumption that* than to say *I think*. If you use ready-made phrases, you not only don't have to hunt about for words; you also don't have to bother with the rhythms of your sentences, since these phrases are generally so arranged as to be more or less euphonious. When you are composing in a hurry—when you are dictating to a stenographer, for instance, or making a public speech—it is natural to fall into a pretentious, Latinized style. Tags like *a consideration which we should do well to bear in mind* or *a conclusion to which all of us would readily assent* will save many a sentence from coming down with a bump. By using stale metaphors, similes, and idioms, you save much mental effort, at the cost of leaving your meaning vague, not only for your reader but for yourself. This is the significance of mixed metaphors. The sole aim of a metaphor is to call up a visual image. When these images clash—as in *The Fascist octopus has sung its swan song, the jackboot is thrown into the melting pot*—it can be taken as certain that the writer is not seeing a mental image of the objects he is naming; in other words he is not really thinking. Look again at the examples I gave at the beginning of this essay. Professor Laski (1) uses five negatives in fifty-three words. One of these is superfluous, making nonsense of the whole passage, and in addition there is the slip—*alien* for akin—making further nonsense, and several avoidable pieces of clumsiness which increase the general vagueness. Professor Hogben (2) plays ducks and drakes with a battery which is able to write prescriptions, and, while disapproving of the everyday phrase *put up with,* is unwilling to look *egregious* up in the dictionary and see what it means; (3), if one takes an uncharitable attitude towards it, is simply meaningless: probably one could work out its intended meaning by reading the whole of the article in which it occurs. In (4), the writer knows more or less what he wants to say, but an accumulation of stale phrases chokes him like tea leaves blocking a sink. In (5), words and meaning have almost parted company. People who write in this manner usually have a general emotional meaning— they dislike one thing and want to express solidarity with another—but they are not interested in the detail of what they are saying. A scrupulous writer, in every sentence that he writes, will ask himself at least four questions, thus: What am I trying to say? What words will express it? What image or idiom will make it clearer? Is this image fresh enough to have an effect? And he will probably ask himself two more: Could I put it more shortly? Have I said anything that is avoidably ugly? But you are not obliged to go to all this trouble. You can shirk it by simply throwing your mind open and letting the ready-made phrases come crowding in. They will construct your sentences for you—even think your thoughts for you, to a certain extent—and at need they will perform the important service of partially concealing your meaning even from yourself. It is at this point that the special connection between politics and the debasement of language becomes clear.

In our time it is broadly true that political writing is bad writing. Where it is not true, it will generally be found that the writer is some kind of rebel, expressing his private opinions and not a "party line."

Orthodoxy, of whatever color, seems to demand a lifeless, imitative style. The political dialects to be found in pamphlets, leading articles, manifestoes, White Papers and the speeches of undersecretaries do, of course, vary from party to party, but they are all alike in that one almost never finds in them a fresh, vivid, home-made turn of speech. When one watches some tired hack on the platform mechanically repeating the familiar phrases—*bestial atrocities, iron heel, bloodstained tyranny, free peoples of the world, stand shoulder to shoulder*—one often has a curious feeling that one is not watching a live human being but some kind of dummy: a feeling which suddenly becomes stronger at moments when the light catches the speaker's spectacles and turns them into blank discs which seem to have no eyes behind them. And this is not altogether fanciful. A speaker who uses that kind of phraseology has gone some distance towards turning himself into a machine. The appropriate noises are coming out of his larynx, but his brain is not involved as it would be if he were choosing his words for himself. If the speech he is making is one that he is accustomed to make over and over again, he may be almost unconscious of what he is saying, as one is when one utters the responses in church. And this reduced state of consciousness, if not indispensable, is at any rate favorable to political conformity.

In our time, political speech and writing are largely the defense of the indefensible. Things like the continuance of British rule in India, the Russian purges and deportations, the dropping of the atom bombs on Japan, can indeed be defended, but only by arguments which are too brutal for most people to face, and which do not square with the professed aims of political parties. Thus political language has to consist largely of euphemism, question-begging and sheer cloudy vagueness. Defenseless villages are bombarded from the air, the inhabitants driven out into the countryside, the cattle machine-gunned, the huts set on fire with incendiary bullets: this is called *pacification*. Millions of peasants are robbed of their farms and sent trudging along the roads with no more than they can carry: this is called *transfer of population* or *rectification of frontiers*. People are imprisoned for years without trial, or shot in the back of the neck or sent to die of scurvy in Arctic lumber camps: this is called *elimination of unreliable elements*. Such phraseology is needed if one wants to name things without calling up mental pictures of them. Consider for instance some comfortable English professor defending Russian totalitarianism. He cannot say outright, "I believe in killing off your opponents when you can get good results by doing so." Probably, therefore, he will say something like this:

"While freely conceding that the Soviet régime exhibits certain features which the humanitarian may be inclined to deplore, we must, I think, agree that a certain curtailment of the right to political opposition is an unavoidable concomitant of transitional periods, and that the

15

rigors which the Russian people have been called upon to undergo have been amply justified in the sphere of concrete achievement."

The inflated style is itself a kind of euphemism. A mass of Latin words falls upon the facts like soft snow, blurring the outlines and covering up all the details. The great enemy of clear language is insincerity. When there is a gap between one's real and one's declared aims, one turns as it were instinctively to long words and exhausted idioms, like a cuttlefish squirting out ink. In our age there is no such thing as "keeping out of politics." All issues are political issues, and politics itself is a mass of lies, evasions, folly, hatred and schizophrenia. When the general atmosphere is bad, language must suffer. I should expect to find—this is a guess which I have not sufficient knowledge to verify—that the German, Russian, and Italian languages have all deteriorated in the last ten or fifteen years, as a result of dictatorship.

But if thought corrupts language, language can also corrupt thought. A bad usage can spread by tradition and imitation, even among people who should and do know better. The debased language that I have been discussing is in some ways very convenient. Phrases like *a not unjustifiable assumption, leaves much to be desired, would serve no good purpose, a consideration which we should do well to bear in mind,* are a continuous temptation, a packet of aspirins always at one's elbow. Look back through this essay, and for certain you will find that I have again and again committed the very faults I am protesting against. By this morning's post I have received a pamphlet dealing with conditions in Germany. The author tells me that he "felt impelled" to write it. I open it at random, and here is almost the first sentence that I see: "[The Allies] have an opportunity not only of achieving a radical transformation of Germany's social and political structure in such a way as to avoid a nationalistic reaction in Germany itself, but at the same time of laying the foundations of a co-operative and unified Europe." You see, he "feels impelled" to write—feels, presumably, that he has something new to say—and yet his words, like cavalry horses answering the bugle, group themselves automatically into the familiar dreary pattern. This invasion of one's mind by ready-made phrases (*lay the foundations, achieve a radical transformation*) can only be prevented if one is constantly on guard against them, and every such phrase anaesthetizes a portion of one's brain.

I said earlier that the decadence of our language is probably curable. Those who deny this would argue, if they produced an argument at all, that language merely reflects existing social conditions, and that we cannot influence its development by any direct tinkering with words and constructions. So far as the general tone or spirit of a language goes, this may be true, but it is not true in detail. Silly words and expressions have often disappeared, not through any evolutionary process but owing to the conscious action of a minority. Two recent examples were *explore every avenue* and *leave no stone unturned,* which were killed by the jeers of a few journalists. There is a long list of flyblown metaphors which could similarly be got rid of if enough people would interest themselves in the job; and it should also be possible to laugh the *not un-*formation out of existence,[3] to reduce the amount of Latin and Greek in the average sentence, to drive out foreign phrases and strayed scientific words, and, in general, to make pretentiousness unfashionable. But all these are minor points. The defense of the English language implies more than this, and perhaps it is best to start by saying what it does *not* imply.

To begin with it has nothing to do with archaism, with the salvaging of obsolete words and turns of speech, or with the setting up of a "standard English" which must never be departed from. On the contrary, it is especially concerned with the scrapping of every word or idiom which has outworn its usefulness. It has nothing to do with correct grammar and syntax, which are of no importance so long as one makes one's meaning clear, or with the avoidance of Americanisms, or with having what is called a "good prose style." On the other hand it is not concerned with fake simplicity and the attempt to make written English colloquial. Nor does it even imply in every case preferring the Saxon word to the Latin one, though it does imply using the fewest and shortest words that will cover one's meaning. What is above all needed is to let the meaning choose the word, and not the other way about. In prose, the worst thing one can do with words is to surrender to them. When you think of a concrete object, you think wordlessly, and then, if you want to describe the thing you have been visualizing you probably hunt about till you find the exact words that seem to fit it. When you think of something abstract you are more inclined to use words from the start, and unless you make a conscious effort to prevent it, the existing dialect will come rushing in and do the job for you, at the expense of blurring or even changing your meaning. Probably it is better to put off using words as long as possible and get one's meaning as clear as one can through pictures or sensations. Afterward one can choose—not simply *accept*—the phrases that will best cover the meaning, and then switch round and decide what impression one's words are likely to make on another person. This last effort of the mind cuts out all stale or mixed images, all prefabricated phrases, needless repetitions, and humbug and vagueness generally. But one can often be in doubt about the effect of a word or a phrase, and one needs rules that one can rely on when instinct fails. I think the following rules will cover most cases:

---

[3] One can cure oneself of the *not un-* formation by memorizing this sentence: *A not unblack dog was chasing a not unsmall rabbit across a not ungreen field.*

(i) Never use a metaphor, simile, or other figure of speech which you are used to seeing in print.
(ii) Never use a long word where a short one will do.
(iii) If it is possible to cut a word out, always cut it out.
(iv) Never use the passive where you can use the active.
(v) Never use a foreign phrase, a scientific word, or a jargon word if you can think of an everyday English equivalent.
(vi) Break any of these rules sooner than say anything outright barbarous.

These rules sound elementary, and so they are, but they demand a deep change of attitude in anyone who has grown used to writing in the style now fashionable. One could keep all of them and still write bad English, but one could not write the kind of stuff that I quoted in those five specimens at the beginning of this article.

I have not here been considering the literary use of language, but merely language as an instrument for expressing and not for concealing or preventing thought. Stuart Chase and others have come near to claiming that all abstract words are meaningless, and have used this as a pretext for advocating a kind of political quietism. Since you don't know what Fascism is, how can you struggle against Fascism? One need not swallow such absurdities as this, but one ought to recognize that the present political chaos is connected with the decay of language, and that one can probably bring about some improvement by starting at the verbal end. If you simplify your English, you are freed from the worst follies of orthodoxy. You cannot speak any of the necessary dialects, and when you make a stupid remark its stupidity will be obvious, even to yourself. Political language—and with variations this is true of all political parties, from Conservatives to Anarchists—is designed to make lies sound truthful and murder respectable, and to give an appearance of solidity to pure wind. One cannot change this all in a moment, but one can at least change one's own habits, and from time to time one can even, if one jeers loudly enough, send some worn-out and useless phrase—some *jackboot, Achilles' heel, hotbed, melting pot, acid test, veritable inferno,* or other lump of verbal refuse—into the dustbin where it belongs.

1946

LINES OF INQUIRY
"Politics and the English Language"

Given his attack on "inflated" writing, Orwell presumably must have taken considerable pains to avoid any "kind of euphemism" in his own prose, so that this essay itself would be a model of politically responsible English. How effective is Orwell in fulfilling his own standards? In his diction? In his sentence structure? In his analogies and metaphors?

At the beginning of paragraph 16, Orwell says that "the inflated style is itself a kind of euphemism." What does Orwell mean by "the inflated style"? Why does he consider it to be "a kind of euphemism"? In paragraphs 5–8, Orwell identifies and illustrates four different kinds of stylistic "tricks by means of which the work of prose-construction is habitually dodged." In what sense is each of these tricks "a kind of euphemism"? In what sense might the euphemistic impulse be considered the root of all the problems that Orwell discusses in his essay? In what senses might it not?

Forty-five years have passed since Orwell made his "catalogue of swindles and perversions," so an updating of his work is certainly in order. Find four or five passages from current American writing that you consider to be representative of what is worst about the way people are writing today. In what respects do these passages exhibit the same basic problems that Orwell was attacking? In what respects do they reflect what you consider to be new problems? How would you categorize, define, and account for these new problems?

WHY I WRITE

From a very early age, perhaps the age of five or six, I knew that when I grew up I should be a writer. Between the ages of about seventeen and twenty-four I tried to abandon this idea, but I did so with the consciousness that I was outraging my true nature and that sooner or later I should have to settle down and write books.

I was the middle child of three, but there was a gap of five years on either side, and I barely saw my father before I was eight. For this and other reasons I was somewhat lonely, and I soon developed disagreeable mannerisms which made me unpopular throughout my schooldays. I had the lonely child's habit of making up stories and holding conversations with imaginary persons, and I think from the very start my literary ambitions were mixed up with the feeling of being isolated and undervalued. I knew that I had a facility with words and a power of facing unpleasant facts, and I felt that this created a sort of private world in which I could get my own back for my failure in everyday life. Nevertheless the volume of serious—i.e., seriously intended—writing which I produced all through my childhood and boyhood would not amount to half a dozen pages. I wrote my first poem at the age of four or five, my mother taking it down to dictation. I cannot remember anything about it except that it was about a tiger and the tiger had "chair-like teeth"—a good enough phrase, but I fancy the poem was a plagiarism of Blake's "Tiger, Tiger." At eleven, when the war of 1914–18 broke out, I wrote a patriotic poem which was printed in the local newspaper, as was another, two years later, on the death of Kitchener. From time to time, when I was a bit older, I wrote bad and usually unfinished "nature poems" in the Georgian style. I also, about twice, attempted a short story which was a ghastly failure. That was the total of the would-be serious work that I actually set down on paper during all those years.

However, throughout this time I did in a sense engage in literary activities. To begin with there was the made-to-order stuff which I produced quickly, easily and without much pleasure to myself. Apart from school work, I wrote *vers d'occasion,* semi-comic poems which I could turn out at what now seems to me astonishing speed—at fourteen I wrote a whole rhyming play, in imitation of Aristophanes, in about a week—and helped to edit school magazines, both printed and in manuscript. These magazines were the most pitiful burlesque stuff that you could imagine, and I took far less trouble with them than I now would with the cheapest journalism. But side by side with all this, for fifteen years or more, I was carrying out a literary exercise of a quite different kind: this was the making up of a continuous "story" about myself, a sort of diary existing only in the mind. I believe this is a common habit of children and adolescents. As a very small child I used to imagine that I was, say, Robin Hood, and picture myself as the hero of thrilling adventures, but quite soon my "story" ceased to be narcissistic in a crude way and became more and more a mere description of what I was doing and the things I saw. For minutes at a time this kind of thing would be running through my head: "He pushed the door open and entered the room. A yellow beam of sunlight, filtering through the muslin curtains, slanted on to the table, where a matchbox, half open, lay beside the inkpot. With his right hand in his pocket he moved across to the window. Down in the street a tortoiseshell cat was chasing a dead leaf," etc etc. This habit continued till I was about twenty-five, right through my non-literary years. Although I had to search, and did search, for the right words, I seemed to be making this descriptive effort almost against my will, under a kind of compulsion from outside. The "story" must, I suppose, have reflected the styles of the various writers I admired at different ages, but so far as I remember it always had the same meticulous descriptive quality.

When I was about sixteen I suddenly discovered the joy of mere words, i.e., the sounds and associations of words. The lines from *Paradise Lost,*

> So hee with difficulty and labour hard
> Moved on: with difficulty and labour hee,

which do not now seem to me so very wonderful, sent shivers down my backbone; and the spelling "hee" for "he" was an added pleasure. As for the need to describe things, I knew all about it already. So it is clear what kind of books I wanted to write, in so far as I could be said to want to write books at that time. I wanted to write enormous naturalistic novels with unhappy endings, full of detailed descriptions and arresting similes, and also full of purple passages in which words were used partly for the sake of their sound. And in fact my first completed novel, *Burmese Days,* which I wrote when I was thirty but projected much earlier, is rather that kind of book.

I give all this background information because I do not think one   5 can assess a writer's motives without knowing something of his early development. His subject matter will be determined by the age he lives in—at least this is true in tumultuous, revolutionary ages like our own— but before he ever begins to write he will have acquired an emotional attitude from which he will never completely escape. It is his job, no doubt, to discipline his temperament and avoid getting stuck at some immature stage, or in some perverse mood: but if he escapes from his early influences altogether, he will have killed his impulse to write. Putting aside the need to earn a living, I think there are four great motives for writing, at any rate for writing prose. They exist in different degrees in every writer, and in any one writer the proportions will vary from time to time, according to the atmosphere in which he is living. They are:

1. Sheer egoism. Desire to seem clever, to be talked about, to be remembered after death, to get your own back on grown-ups who snubbed you in childhood, etc. etc. It is humbug to pretend that this is not a motive, and a strong one. Writers share this characteristic with scientists, artists, politicians, lawyers, soldiers, successful businessmen—in short, with the whole top crust of humanity. The great mass of human beings are not acutely selfish. After the age of about thirty they abandon individual ambition—in many cases, indeed, they almost abandon the sense of being individuals at all—and live chiefly for others, or are simply smothered under drudgery. But there is also the minority of gifted, wilful people who are determined to live their own lives to the end, and writers belong in this class. Serious writers, I should say, are on the whole more vain and self-centered than journalists, though less interested in money.

2. Aesthetic enthusiasm. Perception of beauty in the external world, or, on the other hand, in words and their right arrangement. Pleasure in the impact of one sound on another, in the firmness of good prose or the rhythm of a good story. Desire to share an experience which one feels is valuable and ought not to be missed. The aesthetic motive is very feeble in a lot of writers, but even a pamphleteer or a writer of textbooks will have pet words and phrases which appeal to him for non-utilitarian reasons; or he may feel strongly about typography, width of margins, etc. Above the level of a railway guide, no book is quite free from aesthetic considerations.

3. Historical impulse. Desire to see things as they are, to find out true facts and store them up for the use of posterity.

4. Political purpose—using the word "political" in the widest possible sense. Desire to push the world in a certain direction, to alter other people's idea of the kind of society that they should strive after. Once again, no book is genuinely free from political bias. The opinion that art should have nothing to do with politics is itself a political attitude.

It can be seen how these various impulses must war against one another, and how they must fluctuate from person to person and from time to time. By nature—taking your "nature" to be the state you have attained when you are first adult—I am a person in whom the first three motives would outweigh the fourth. In a peaceful age I might have written ornate or merely descriptive books, and might have remained almost unaware of my political loyalties. As it is I have been forced into becoming a sort of pamphleteer. First I spent five years in an unsuitable profession (the Indian Imperial Police, in Burma), and then I underwent

10

poverty and the sense of failure. This increased my natural hatred of authority and made me for the first time fully aware of the existence of the working classes, and the job in Burma had given me some understanding of the nature of imperialism: but these experiences were not enough to give me an accurate political orientation. Then came Hitler, the Spanish civil war, etc. By the end of 1935 I had still failed to reach a firm decision. I remember a little poem that I wrote at that date, expressing my dilemma:

> A happy vicar I might have been
> Two hundred years ago,
> To preach upon eternal doom
> And watch my walnuts grow;
>
> But born, alas, in an evil time,
> I missed that pleasant haven,
> For the hair has grown on my upper lip
> And the clergy are all clean-shaven.
>
> And later still the times were good,
> We were so easy to please,
> We rocked our troubled thoughts to sleep
> On the bosoms of the trees.
>
> All ignorant we dared to own
> The joys we now dissemble;
> The greenfinch on the apple bough
> Could make my enemies tremble.
>
> But girls' bellies and apricots,
> Roach in a shaded stream,
> Horses, ducks in flight at dawn,
> All these are a dream.
>
> It is forbidden to dream again;
> We maim our joys or hide them;
> Horses are made of chromium steel
> And little fat men shall ride them.
>
> I am the worm who never turned,
> The eunuch without a harem;
> Between the priest and the commissar
> I walk like Eugene Aram;
>
> And the commissar is telling my fortune
> While the radio plays,
> But the priest has promised an Austin Seven,
> For Duggie always pays.
>
> I dreamed I dwelt in marble halls,
> And woke to find it true;
> I wasn't born for an age like this;
> Was Smith? Was Jones? Were you?

The Spanish war and other events in 1936–37 turned the scale and thereafter I knew where I stood. Every line of serious work that I have written since 1936 has been written, directly or indirectly, *against* totalitarianism and *for* democratic Socialism, as I understand it. It seems to me nonsense, in a period like our own, to think that one can avoid writing of such subjects. Everyone writes of them in one guise or another. It is simply a question of which side one takes and what approach one follows. And the more one is conscious of one's political bias, the more chance one has of acting politically without sacrificing one's aesthetic and intellectual integrity.

What I have most wanted to do throughout the past ten years is to make political writing into an art. My starting point is always a feeling of partisanship, a sense of injustice. When I sit down to write a book, I do not say to myself, "I am going to produce a work of art." I write it because there is some lie that I want to expose, some fact to which I want to draw attention, and my initial concern is to get a hearing. But I could not do the work of writing a book, or even a long magazine article, if it were not also an aesthetic experience. Anyone who cares to examine my work will see that even when it is downright propaganda it contains much that a full-time politician would consider irrelevant. I am not able, and I do not want, completely to abandon the world-view that I acquired in childhood. So long as I remain alive and well I shall continue to feel strongly about prose style, to love the surface of the earth, and to take pleasure in solid objects and scraps of useless information. It is no use trying to suppress that side of myself. The job is to reconcile my ingrained likes and dislikes with the essentially public, non-individual activities that this age forces on all of us.

It is not easy. It raises problems of construction and language, and it raises in a new way the problem of truthfulness. Let me give just one example of the cruder kind of difficulty that arises. My book about the Spanish civil war, *Homage to Catalonia,* is, of course, a frankly political book, but in the main it is written with a certain detachment and regard for form. I did try very hard in it to tell the whole truth without violating my literary instincts. But among other things it contains a long chapter, full of newspaper quotations and the like, defending the Trotskyists who were accused of plotting with Franco. Clearly such a chapter, which after a year or two would lose its interest for any ordinary reader, must ruin the book. A critic whom I respect read me a lecture about it. "Why did you put in all that stuff?" he said. "You've turned what might have been a good book into journalism." What he said was true, but I could not have done otherwise. I happened to know, what very few people in England had been allowed to know, that innocent men were being falsely accused. If I had not been angry about that I should never have written the book.

In one form or another this problem comes up again. The problem of language is subtler and would take too long to discuss. I will only say that of late years I have tried to write less picturesquely and more exactly. In any case I find that by the time you have perfected any style of writing, you have always outgrown it. *Animal Farm* was the first book in which I tried, with full consciousness of what I was doing, to fuse political purpose and artistic purpose into one whole. I have not written a novel for seven years, but I hope to write another fairly soon. It is bound to be a failure, every book is a failure, but I know with some clarity what kind of book I want to write.

Looking back through the last page or two, I see that I have made it appear as though my motives in writing were wholly public-spirited. I don't want to leave that as the final impression. All writers are vain, selfish and lazy, and at the very bottom of their motives there lies a mystery. Writing a book is a horrible, exhausting struggle, like a long bout of some painful illness. One would never undertake such a thing if one were not driven on by some demon whom one can neither resist nor understand. For all one knows that demon is simply the same instinct that makes a baby squall for attention. And yet it is also true that one can write nothing readable unless one constantly struggles to efface one's own personality. Good prose is like a window pane. I cannot say with certainty which of my motives are the strongest, but I know which of them deserve to be followed. And looking back through my work, I see that it is invariably where I lacked a *political* purpose that I wrote lifeless books and was betrayed into purple passages, sentences without meaning, decorative adjectives and humbug generally.

1946

LINES OF INQUIRY
"Why I Write"

Given the title and purpose of this piece, why do you suppose that Orwell does not restrict himself to listing, defining, illustrating, and explaining the four reasons for writing that he enumerates in paragraphs 6–9? How is the material that precedes and follows these paragraphs related to the purpose of his essay? How in particular is the surrounding material related to the points that he makes in these paragraphs?

After listing his four reasons for writing, Orwell says (at the beginning of paragraph 10) that "it can be seen how these various impulses must war against another, and how they must fluctuate from person to person and from time to time." Why does he believe they must war against one another? Why does he believe they must fluctuate from person to person and from time to time? Have you ever experienced conflicting impulses in your own writing? Have your reasons for writing fluctuated from time to time?

Which of the four reasons that Orwell lists do you consider to be the most important purpose for writing? What other reasons for writing can you think of beyond those that Orwell has defined? Why do you suppose he has not included them in his list? What are your reasons for writing? How do they compare with Orwell's?

CYNTHIA OZICK

1928 –

*In life I am simply a rationalist. I don't pursue the illogical, and
I regard anything smacking of occultism as plain illusory folly.
Superstitions of every kind make me lose patience. But in
storytelling I am attracted to magic and mysticism and
irrationalism and the strange vagaries of obsessiveness.*

In this forthright state-
ment about herself, Cynthia Ozick defines a major conflict that has
shaped her life. Though she is committed to a rational way of being in
the world, to intellectual inquiry, and the pursuit of ideas, she is equally
attracted to the realm of mystery and the fantastic, governed by the
creative power of the imagination. Reconciling the tensions between
those two realms has not been an easy matter, especially for someone
whose Jewish heritage leads her to worry that the imagination's capacity
for making images might be an insidious form of idolatry. So, in carrying on her storytelling, Ozick is concerned that she might be betraying
her commitment to monotheism and the Judaic tradition. Yet the seduc-
tions of the creative life, whatever their dangers, have been irresistible
to her; whether writing "is God's work or Satan's work, I will do it."
Asked why, she replies, simply: "Willfulness."

Ozick was born in Pelham Bay, the Bronx, at a time when it was
still almost a rural suburb of New York. Her parents, both Russian
Jewish immigrants, jointly operated a corner drugstore, and the family,
which included Ozick's brother and grandmother, not only lived above
the store but also focussed its life on the activities of the store. From an
early age, Ozick helped out delivering prescriptions, which her father
the pharmacist prepared, while her mother worked behind the drug
counter or soda fountain, struggling to keep the family business afloat.

From her early days at public school in the Bronx, Ozick remembers
being "hurt" by her teachers, because they "made me believe I was
stupid and inferior." She also remembers her schoolmates taunting her
because of her Jewishness. Thus her intense sense of being an outsider
was formed early by her heightened consciousness of being the daughter of immigrant Jews in an established Gentile culture. Her home-life,
by contrast, was a haven of warmth and security, enriched with stories
told by her grandmother, by the neighbors in the drugstore, by her
parents over tea at night after the drugstore closed. Above all, her life at
home was enriched by her obsession with reading, which led her into a
world where language was supreme. She describes herself still as being
afflicted with "word-besottedness."

"Even at age six—no, as soon as I was conscious of being alive—I
knew I was a writer," she says. Her mother's brother, a Hebrew poet of
considerable reputation, made it seem natural that she enter into what

she has called "the secular world of literature." Her gender likewise made such a "frivolous" vocation acceptable:

> My father loved me. But I think one of the reasons I felt free from earliest childhood that I was going to be a writer is that if I had been a boy, I would have had to go be something else.

It seems, in fact, that writing for Ozick was not and has not ever been a matter of choice. Indeed, she speaks of herself even in childhood as being "possessed" by the desire to write: "The beginning was almost physiological in its ecstatic pursuits. . . . I am thinking back to the delectable excitement, the *waiting-to-be-born-excitement,* of longing to write. I suppose it is a kind of parallel Eros."

Other aspects of Ozick's personal and professional identity were also born during her childhood in the Bronx. She dates her feminism to the day when she was five and a half, and the rabbi refused to enroll her in Hebrew school: "Take her home," he said, "a girl doesn't have to study." The next day, Ozick's grandmother took her back to the school and insisted that her granddaughter be accepted. She was a model pupil, and her feminism, like her Jewish identity, has persisted strongly to this day. She was an early contributor to the women's movement during its rebirth in the late 1960s and early 1970s, protesting against the limitations imposed on women artists in her well-known essays of that period, such as "The Hole/Birth Catalogue" and "Women and Creativity: The Demise of the Dancing Dog." More recently, she has argued against the elements in contemporary feminism that insist on studying and celebrating women writers as a separate category, deploring what she calls "the Ovarian Theory of Literature" and envisioning a world in which gender is irrelevant.

After receiving her B.A. from New York University in 1949, Ozick earned a master's degree in English from Ohio State University, but decided against staying on for a doctorate. Art, not scholarship, was her passion. She returned to New York after a brief sojourn in Boston, married, and settled down to the task of writing. For the next fourteen years she served an isolated and painful apprenticeship, working on two long novels, the first of which, *Trust* (1966) was finally published when she was in her mid-thirties. Of that period in her life, she says, "I was fixed, transfixed. It was Literature every breathing moment. I had no 'ordinary life.' I despised ordinary life: I had contempt for it. What a *meshugas!*"

The publication of *Trust* coincided closely with the birth of her only child, Rachel: "I had the baby and the galleys together." That happy combination, along with the fact that some of her stories and essays began to be published around the same time, pulled Ozick out of her solitary obsessions and set her on the way to being a writer with a strong public identity. Of *Trust,* she says, "I began as an American novelist and ended as a Jewish novelist. I Judaized myself as I wrote it." Ozick's view of herself is echoed by the critics, one of whom has written that "her most characteristic and compelling themes are Jewish identity, Jewish history, and Jewish art." Another has declared that "Cynthia Ozick's is the most provocative of contemporary Jewish-American voices."

Though Ozick's short stories, published steadily in collections over the past twenty years, have probably earned her the greatest critical acclaim, she is also widely recognized for her essays. They have appeared in numerous magazines and newspapers, such as *Harper's, McCall's, Ms.,* and *The New York Times,* as well as being noted in the *Best American Essays* series. They have been collected in two volumes: *Art and Ardor* (1983) and *Metaphor and Memory* (1989). Like others in this anthology who have written both fiction and essays—Virginia Woolf, George Orwell, James Baldwin, Joan Didion, and Edward Hoagland—Ozick brings to her writing of essays an intense concern with the verbal and narrative art of literary nonfiction. Indeed, one reviewer has noted that "As an essayist, Cynthia Ozick is a very good storyteller." And Ozick herself, in the foreword to *Metaphor and Memory,* has gone so far as to insist upon a fundamental set of parallels between the essay and the story:

> A story is a hypothesis, a tryout of human nature under the impingement of certain given materials; so is an essay. After which, the mind moves on. Nearly every essay, like every story, is an experiment, not a credo.
>
> Or, to put it more stringently: an essay, like a story or novel, is a fiction.

By "fiction," of course, Ozick does not mean to imply that she considers the essay to be wholly an invention of the imagination. Most of her own essays, after all, are unmistakably rooted in her personal experience or based on her rigorously informed thinking about aspects of literature and culture. But she does quite clearly believe that the essay is always a carefully crafted piece of prose, something "made up," as she puts it, and not a literal replica of experience or thought, even though it may seem to be so:

> What is fictitious about the essay is that it is pretending not to be made up—so that reading an essay may be more dangerous than reading a story.

Thus she reminds readers that the essay, as she practices it, is always "a bewitched contraption."

MY GRANDMOTHER'S PENNIES

I keep in my dresser drawer an unusual heirloom. When people speak of heirlooms, they mean, I suppose, grand old clocks with brass pendulums and carved oak cases, or perhaps a ribboned bundle of weighty Victorian silver. There are houses that are heirlooms, too, lived in by the same family for generations, and antique lockets with ancestral ringlets in them, and fine old bridal lace, and cracked-leather chairs like hereditary thrones.

Our heirloom is different. It is made of rags, and if you tried to price it, it would fetch no more than 18 cents. Every darkening December, as the evening before the 25th day of the Hebrew month of Kislev approaches, my daughter and I take out our heirloom and renew our familiarity with its shapes and parts.

The first shape we see is an elongated cheesecloth bag, more yellowed now than white, knotted at the top. The seams are machine-sewn and hardy; it is the kind of homely sack in which, long ago, a whole cheese used to be packed.

We lift out of it a drawstring bag. Now, without warning, we are in the presence of something royal: This second bag is of a resplendent crimson velvet, hand-sewn with large, precise stitches in a broad green double thread. The neck of it, housing the drawstring, is green and white; tiny blossoms winding over a meadow. The colors are as fresh and bright as the day my grandmother cut out the fabric, a month or so before my first Hanukkah. The velvet is as deep and thick as the day my grandmother embroidered on its face the Hebrew letters that my daughter and I now begin to read together.

The first letters spell out a surprise: my daughter's own name! 5 There it is, embroidered in a brilliant blue on the blazing velvet: *Rachel.* Yet how can this be? Rachel is 13, and the bag was sewn almost half a century ago. Instantly, there is the crackle of a magical connection— my grandmother, my daughter's great-grandmother, was also named Rachel. She sewed the letters of her own name into the velvet. Did she know that one day this rich sack and its homely contents would come into the hands of another Rachel?

Ah, she knew. Among Jews of eastern European origin, it is a nearly universal practice to name children in memoriam, to bring alive one's nearest forebears on one's daily tongue. "I am never lonely," my grandmother Rachel used to say to me when I was still very young. "I have my mother and father with me always." She meant my brother and me;

he is (in Hebrew) Judah, and I am (in Hebrew) Susannah; we are named for our great-grandparents, Judah and Susannah. So my grandmother knew, when she emblazoned her name, that in time there would surely be another Rachel to read it and claim it as her own inheritance. The first Rachel was born in 1861; the second, in 1965. The blue embroidery binds them.

And so does the Hebrew language. At Hanukkah last year the younger Rachel came to the traditional age of bat mitzvah, which means "daughter of the Commandments," and signifies a ripening into moral, religious and communal responsibility. All of this implies, of course, a scholarly obligation to the language of the Bible. The Hebrew name *Rachel,* glowing on this velvet sack, flows backward not only to the Rachel born into Czarist Russia, but back and back and back to, at last, the Rachel of the Bible who is the mother of the Jewish people. All the history of the Children of Israel flickers in the blue strands my grandmother sewed one winter night long ago.

And now the younger Rachel takes up the velvet heirloom sack and reads the simple Hebrew legend embroidered under her name:

> The gifts of Hanukkah
> An inheritance
> Let it not pass

Let it not pass! My mother sews Hanukkah *baytelakh* for Rachel, and I will sew them for Rachel's children, and Rachel for her grandchildren, and so on into history-to-come, and it will not pass, this dedicated old task. But what, after all, does the velvet sack hold? Rachel stretches open its drawstring neck and spills out the contents. Onto the kitchen table there falls a small hill of colorful smaller sacks, each with its drawstring. In Yiddish—the language my grandmother and I used to converse in—the little sacks are called *baytelakh.*

We count them, there are only ten, because my grandmother died in the summer after my 11th birthday, months before Hanukkah. She had not yet sewn the eleventh. The *baytelakh* are made mostly of motley scraps of silk and reminiscence—here is a bit of redolent old shawl, and a fragment of unforgotten dress (how I used to bury my head in its lap!), and still another vivid swatch of someone's skirt, and here is a little sack of red and purple, material bought on purpose for making *baytelakh.* Each Hanukkah my grandmother sewed 22 *baytelakh,* one for each grandchild.

And all the while my grandmother was stitching, stitching—I see her worn, creased hands and the lightning glint of the needle—Hitler was thumping his fists, and his soldiers were thumping their boots, and Jewish life in Europe was growing dimmer and dimmer, passing, passing into ash; and my grandmother's needle flashed its defiant light.

10

Then it was 1939, and something called the British White Paper sent its terrible flashes into our kitchen, and my grandmother sat weeping over her Yiddish newspaper, beating her breast with a crumpled hand, because the British were turning back to Hitler's death-ridden Germany ships packed with Jewish orphans coming to seek refuge in the Holy Land.

In the kitchen now, it is time for the younger Rachel to open her great-grandmother's *baytelakh*. Inside are the gifts of Hanukkah—what will they be? Out of each miniature sack there tumbles, still shiny, 18 pennies!

It is a night in dark December. All of America is occupied with gifts—the stores are giddy with shoppers, mountains of boxes rise in closets and behind doors, cascades of brilliant wrapping paper wind themselves around tantalizing shapes, rivers of ribbons curl into bows. Gifts, gifts, gifts everywhere—toys and things to wear, bicycles and perfumes, cameras and television sets; in an American December the gifts ascend. But in our kitchen at Hanukkah, from Rachel to Rachel, there are only the bags of 18 pennies, some old enough to show their Indian heads, all as shiny as the day they were slipped into a little silken sack cut from a worn-out shawl.

There are 18 pennies because in Hebrew (as with Roman numerals) the letters of the alphabet also stand for numbers. The Hebrew letters that make up the number 18 are *khet* and *yud* (the latter is the *jot* of the Gospels: *Till heaven and earth pass, one jot or one tittle shall in no wise pass from the law,* says Jesus), and *khet* and *yud* together spell the Hebrew word *khai,* which means life. So there are 18 symbolic pennies for Hanukkah *gelt*—Hanukkah money—not because of the gift of "buying power," but because of the powerful gift of life. My grandmother Rachel, who died in 1939, the year Hitler swarmed over Europe like a death's-head, calls to her unknown-but-known great-granddaughter Rachel: Choose life, life!

We set up the menorah, a candelabrum with eight candle holders—   15
nine, counting the kindling candle. We recite the blessings and sing the hymn. We fry potato pancakes (latkes, these are called in Yiddish) in oil—the reason for the oil will soon emerge—and eat them by the dozens, with sour cream or apple sauce. We play a game called dreydl, a four-sided wooden top spun for a prize of nuts. The sides of the dreydl are engraved with the Hebrew letters that stand for the word *A Great Miracle Happened There.* We light the candles, recite the blessings and sing the hymn for eight days—a matter of a few minutes each afternoon at dusk. And that, in all its simplicity and fun, is the whole of the Hanukkah celebration. In our family, because of grandmother Rachel's lightning needle and the foresight of her embroidery, the 18 pennies come in *baytelakh*. Other families give Hanukkah *gelt* in other ways—

but always in units of 18, to remember life. And the candles blaze, like trees of life.

Choosing life is the theme of Hanukkah—as it is the cry of Jewish history—because again and again oppressors have tried to snuff out the lives of Jews, lives made witness to dedication ever since God spoke to Abraham, the first Jew. Only three and a half decades ago six million Jews were gassed and incinerated by Hitler. But Hanukkah began more than two thousand years ago, when there arose in Greek culture an ancient precursor of Hitler, a rapacious persecutor called Antiochus. His troops marched into Jerusalem and raised up idols everywhere. In the Temple on Mount Zion Antiochus's men tore apart the altar, poured pigs' blood over the scrolls of Scripture and then set fire to them; and in the charred and desolated Temple they set up a vast idol, a towering statue of Zeus. Jewish practices and customs were outlawed, and the study of Scripture was decreed a crime punishable by death. All Jews, Antiochus declared, had to bow before Zeus and a host of other gods, or die. They had to look, eat and behave like Greeks, or die. Blood ran in all the villages of Israel; even when the fearful Jews obeyed, they were killed. The Greek soldiers went from town to town all over the land, killing Jews and burning books. Antiochus's army was in the thousands. The Jews, an occupied people, had no army, and were only a handful of anguished citizens. But the handful of Jews fought back, inspired by the cry, "Whoever is for the Lord, come!"—and won.

Hanukkah marks the first time in the history of the world that a people struggled for freedom of religion.

Stuffed with pancakes, we roll out of the kitchen, settle down on the hall floor and begin spinning the dreydl. It's my turn. The dreydl whirls, then falls on the letter *Hey*, for Half. I take six out of the 12 walnuts in the pot. It's Rachel's turn. She lands on *Gimel*, for Get-All—all my winnings!

It's such an easy game—even though suspenseful—that we can make up another game while we're busy with this one. The game we invent is based on the letter *Nun*. When the dreydl rolls *Nun*, for Nothing, nobody gets anything.

The *Nun* game asks this question: If Israel had lost to Antiochus over two thousand years ago, if Judaism had been extinguished—and how close it came to that!—160 years before the birth of Jesus, what would our civilization be like now?

Answer: *Nun*. Nothing.

The Ten Commandments would not have been inherited by the nations of the world.

There would be no Christianity or Islam.

There would now be no Christmas to light the dark of an American December.

The pagan way would have won out over the centuries.   25

A scary game!

The Hanukkah candles are still spilling their radiance on the windowsill. Across the street the neighbors' electric Christmas lights are winking on strings along all the porches.

The two kinds of lights appear to be paired, if only by the darkness.

But the two *events* are not paired, except by a coincidence of the calendar. Hanukkah is by no means what some negligently call it, "the Jewish Christmas" (any more than Christmas is the Christian Hanukkah!). The two celebrations—the great one of multitudinous lights and abundant gifts and the modest one of eight lights and 18 pennies—have not a jot or tittle in common, and certainly ought not to be observed in tandem. And yet Christmas is joined to Hanukkah by a single vital bond. If Judaism had not been preserved against the onslaught of Antiochus, there would have been no Jewish family to give birth to Jesus, and no Jewish Jesus to give birth to Christianity.

But look, a wonder among the walnuts! The last four throws of   30
the dreydl have come out in order! Rachel throws *Nun.* I throw *Gimel.* She gets *Hey.* I land on *Shin.* The walnuts are scattered everywhere, the game's in disarray—the dreydl has, unbidden, spelled out its historic reminder: *Nes Gadol Hayah Sham.*

A Great Miracle Happened There.

But why, after all, "great"? It was, in fact, as miracles go, a very modest one.

This is how it happened:

When at last the Jewish citizen-soldiers of Jerusalem entered the defiled Temple their jubilation at their courageous victory was shadowed by signs of hatred and vandalism all around. They got rid of the idol and began to clean up. They swept up the debris, washed away the dried pigs' blood, put up new curtains, rebuilt broken walls and doors. And then they began to look around for some oil to light the candelabrum with, to show that the Temple was renewed and rededicated to the idea of the One Creator.

But Antiochus's soldiers had spilled out nearly all the stock of   35
consecrated oil, and only one jar was left. All it held was a few drops, enough to burn for one day.

Now comes the miracle (and notice how modest it is!): The few drops of oil burned for eight full days, long enough for a fresh supply of oil to be secured for the candelabrum.

This is the miracle that Hanukkah records and celebrates, and that is why Hanukkah lasts for eight days, beginning with the lighting of a single candle, until, on the eighth night, by the addition of a new candle daily, the glory has grown and all eight candles are afire at once.

The rabbis who first began to mark Hanukkah—which means dedication—thought this small miracle more important than any victory, even a victory for freedom of religion, even a victory over a brutal oppressor. We can understand why the rabbis emphasized the miracle of the little bit of oil that lasted and lasted, and endured beyond all expectation. The oil reminds us of the burning bush that burned and burned and was not consumed, and out of which the Voice of the Lord was heard. The oil reminds us of the Children of Israel—the saving remnant of the Jewish people—who are often endangered, but who live and live and will always live, eternally choosing freedom.

On the Sabbath that occurs during the eight days of Hanukkah, a special cycle of Psalms is sung in the synagogue, and these words from the prophet Zechariah are recited:

Not by might, nor by power, but by my Spirit, saith the Lord . . .   40

I think this must be what my grandmother Rachel continues to tell her great-granddaughter Rachel each year at Hanukkah, when we read the words her precious old fingers embroidered into our unusual heirloom. A message written in a remnant, not from a far-off time but from the future: *Let it not pass.* Hanukkah and life. The inheritance they bring is freedom.

LINES OF INQUIRY
"My Grandmother's Pennies"

This essay was first published in *McCall's* in December 1978—that is, the month when Hanukkah takes place. Thus it was probably intended mainly to explain Hanukkah to a large audience of readers, of various religious beliefs. Why, then, do you suppose that Ozick doesn't begin right off by listing the traditional activities connected with Hanukkah, telling about the historical background of Hanukkah, and explaining the major Hanukkah ritual of lighting the menorah? Why does she hold off that basic information until paragraphs 17–38? In other words, why do you think that Ozick begins her piece with the story of the heirloom from her grandmother? Why do you think she devotes so much attention to the heirloom—in the title, in the first fifteen paragraphs, and in the final paragraph?

The heirloom from Ozick's grandmother is, of course, a very personal part of the Hanukkah ritual for Ozick and her daughter. What aspects of the heirloom seem unique to Ozick's family? What aspects of it pertain to the Hanukkah festivities? In what respect(s) is the heirloom symbolic of basic Jewish beliefs and values? In what respect(s) is the heirloom symbolic of Jewish history or ideals distinctly connected with Hanukkah? In what respect(s) is the heirloom a symbol uniquely meaningful to Ozick and her family alone?

Think of an heirloom in your family that is connected with a specific religious or national holiday. Who did it come from—that is, who made it or procured it? How long has it been in your family? Who presently owns it? Who will it pass to next? Exactly how does it figure in the holiday celebrations? In what special way(s) is it meaningful to you and your family? In what ways is it symbolic of religious beliefs or national ideals?

THE SEAM OF THE SNAIL

In my Depression childhood, whenever I had a new dress, my cousin Sarah would get suspicious. The nicer the dress was, and especially the more expensive it looked, the more suspicious she would get. Finally she would lift the hem and check the seams. This was to see if the dress had been bought or if my mother had sewed it. Sarah could always tell. My mother's sewing had elegant outsides, but there was something catch-as-catch-can about the insides. Sarah's sewing, by contrast, was as impeccably finished inside as out; not one stray thread dangled.

My uncle Jake built meticulous grandfather clocks out of rosewood; he was a perfectionist, and sent to England for the clockworks. My mother built serviceable radiator covers and a serviceable cabinet, with hinged doors, for the pantry. She built a pair of bookcases for the living room. Once, after I was grown and in a house of my own, she fixed the sewer pipe. She painted ceilings, and also landscapes; she reupholstered chairs. One summer she planted a whole yard of tall corn. She thought herself capable of doing anything, and did everything she imagined. But nothing was perfect. There was always some clear flaw, never visible head-on. You had to look underneath, where the seams were. The corn thrived, though not in rows. The stalks elbowed one another like gossips in a dense little village.

"Miss Brrrrooooaker," my mother used to mock, rolling her Russian r's, whenever I crossed a t she had left uncrossed, or corrected a word she had misspelled, or became impatient with a v that had tangled itself up with a w in her speech. ("Vvventriloquist," I would say. "Vvventriloquist," she would obediently repeat. And the next time it would come out "wiolinist.") Miss Brubaker was my high school English teacher, and my mother invoked her name as an emblem of raging finical obsession. "Miss Brrrrooooaker," my mother's voice hoots at me down the years, as I go on casting and recasting sentences in a tiny handwriting on monomaniacally uniform paper. The loops of my mother's handwriting—it was the Palmer Method—were as big as soup bowls, spilling generous splashy ebullience. She could pull off, at five minutes' notice, a satisfying dinner for ten concocted out of nothing more than originality and panache. But the napkin would be folded a little off center, and the spoon might be on the wrong side of the knife. She was an optimist who ignored trifles; for her, God was not in the details but in the intent. And all these culinary and agricultural efflorescences were extracurricular, accomplished in the crevices and niches of a fourteen-hour business day. When she scribbled out her family memoirs, in heaps of dog-eared notebooks, or on the backs of old bills, or on the margins of last year's calendar, I would resist typing them; in the speed of the chase she often omitted words like "the," "and," "will." The same flashing and bountiful hand fashioned and fired ceramic pots, and painted brilliant autumn views and vases of imaginary flowers and ferns, and decorated ordinary Woolworth platters with lavish enameled gardens. But bits of the painted petals would chip away.

Lavish: my mother was as lavish as nature. She woke early and saturated the hours with work and inventiveness, and read late into the night. She was all profusion, abundance, fabrication. Angry at her children, she would run after us whirling the cord of the electric iron, like a lasso or a whip; but she never caught us. When, in seventh grade, I was afraid of failing the Music Appreciation final exam because I could not tell the difference between "To a Wild Rose" and "Barcarole," she got the idea of sending me to school with a gauze sling rigged up on my writing arm, and an explanatory note that was purest fiction. But the sling kept slipping off. My mother gave advice like mad—she boiled over with so much passion for the predicaments of strangers that they turned into permanent cronies. She told intimate stories about people I had never heard of.

Despite the gargantuan Palmer loops (or possibly because of them),   5 I have always known that my mother's was a life of—intricately abashing word!—excellence: insofar as excellence means ripe generosity. She burgeoned, she proliferated; she was endlessly leafy and flowering. She wore red hats, and called herself a gypsy. In her girlhood she marched with the suffragettes and for Margaret Sanger and called herself a Red. She made me laugh, she was so varied: like a tree on which lemons, pomegranates, and prickly pears absurdly all hang together. She had the comedy of prodigality.

My own way is a thousand times more confined. I am a pinched perfectionist, the ultimate fruition of Miss Brubaker; I attend to crabbed minutiae and am self-trammeled through taking pains. I am a kind of human snail, locked in and condemned by my own nature. The ancients believed that the moist track left by the snail as it crept was the snail's own essence, depleting its body little by little; the farther the snail toiled, the smaller it became, until it finally rubbed itself out. That is how perfectionists are. Say to us Excellence, and we will show you how we use up our substance and wear ourselves away, while making scarcely any progress at all. The fact that I am an exacting perfectionist in a narrow strait only, and nowhere else, is hardly to the point, since nothing matters to me so much as a comely and muscular sentence. It is my narrow strait, this snail's road; the track of the sentence I am writing now; and when I have eked out the wet substance, ink or blood, that is its mark, I will begin the next sentence. Only in treading out sentences am I perfectionist; but then there is nothing else I know how to do, or take much interest in. I miter every pair of abutting sentences as scrupulously as Uncle Jake fitted one strip of rosewood against another. My mother's worldly and bountiful hand has escaped me. The sentence I am writing is my cabin and my shell, compact, self-sufficient. It is the burnished horizon—a merciless planet where flawlessness is the single standard, where even the inmost seams, however hidden from a laxer eye, must meet perfection. Here "excellence" is not strewn casually from a tipped cornucopia, here disorder does not account for charm, here trifles rule like tyrants.

I measure my life in sentences pressed out, line by line, like the lustrous ooze on the underside of the snail, the snail's secret open seam, its wound, leaking attar. My mother was too mettlesome to feel the force of a comma. She scorned minutiae. She measured her life according to what poured from the horn of plenty, which was her own seamless, ample, cascading, elastic, susceptible, inexact heart. My narrower heart rides between the tiny twin horns of the snail, dwindling as it goes.

And out of this thinnest thread, this ink-wet line of words, must rise a visionary fog, a mist, a smoke, forging cities, histories, sorrows, quagmires, entanglements, lives of sinners, even the life of my furnace-hearted mother: so much wilderness, waywardness, plenitude on the head of the precise and impeccable snail, between the horns. (Ah, if this could be!)

LINES OF INQUIRY
"The Seam of the Snail"

In paragraph five, Ozick claims that "I miter every pair of abutting sentences as scrupulously as Uncle Jake fitted one strip of rosewood against another." Check over the sentences in this paragraph and a couple of others to see whether her claim is valid, whether she has, in fact, mitered her "abutting sentences . . . scrupulously." What techniques does she use to miter them? Consider also whether she has mitered her abutting paragraphs scrupulously. What techniques does she use to miter them? Given that the first half of this essay is about her mother and the last half is about Ozick herself, what techniques has Ozick used to miter these differently focused halves to each other? What verbal, imagistic, and metaphoric connections do you find between the first half and the second half of the essay?

Ozick clearly differentiates between her mother's excellence and her own. What kind of excellence does her mother embody? What kind of excellence does Ozick herself embody? What defects, or limitations, or problems does she associate with each kind of excellence? Given the way(s) that she discusses each kind of excellence in the essay, which kind do you suppose that she favors? Which of the two kinds do you favor?

Consider an area of your own life in which you think of yourself as excellent (or nearly so), and consider an aspect of your mother's or father's life in which you consider either of them to be excellent. What kind of excellence do you associate with yourself? How did you acquire it? What problems do you associate with your kind of excellence? What kind of excellence do you associate with your parent? How does it compare with your own? How do you account for the similarities and/or differences? How do the similarities and/or differences affect the way you get on with each other?

THE SHOCK OF TEAPOTS

One morning in Stockholm, after rain and just before November, a mysteriously translucent shadow began to paint itself across the top of the city. It skimmed high over people's heads, a gauzy brass net, keeping well above the streets, skirting everything fabricated by human arts—though one or two steeples were allowed to dip into it, like pens filling their nibs with palest ink. It made a sort of watermark over Stockholm, as if a faintly luminous river ran overhead, yet with no more weight or gravity than a vapor.

This glorious strangeness—a kind of crystalline wash—was the sunlight of a Swedish autumn. The sun looked *new:* it had a lucidity, a texture, a tincture, a position across the sky that my New York gape had never before taken in. The horizontal ladder of light hung high up, higher than any sunlight I had ever seen, and the quality of its glow seemed thinner, wanner, more tentatively morning-brushed; or else like gold leaf beaten gossamer as tissue—a lambent skin laid over the spired marrow of the town.

"Ah yes, the sun *does* look a bit different this time of year," say the Stockholmers in their perfect English (English as a second first language), but with a touch of ennui. Whereas I, under the electrified rays of my whitening hair, stand drawn upward to the startling sky, restored to the clarity of childhood. The Swedes have known a Swedish autumn before; I have not.

Travel returns us in just this way to sharpness of notice; and to be saturated in the sight of what is entirely new—the sun at an unaccustomed slope, stretched across the northland, separate from the infiltrating dusk that always seems about to fall through clear gray Stockholm—is to revisit the enigmatically lit puppet-stage outlines of childhood: those mental photographs and dreaming woodcuts or engravings that we retain from our earliest years. What we remember from childhood we remember forever—permanent ghosts, stamped, imprinted, eternally seen. Travelers regain this ghost-seizing brightness, eeriness, firstness.

They regain it because they have cut themselves loose from their own society, from every society; they are, for a while, floating vagabonds, like astronauts out for a space walk on a long free line. They are subject to preternatural exhilarations, absurd horizons, unexpected forms and transmutations: the matter-of-fact (a battered old stoop, say, or the shape of a door) appears beautiful; or a stone that at home would not merit the blink of your eye here arrests you with its absolute particularity—just because it is what your hand already intimately knows. You think: a stone, a stone! They have stones here too! And you think: how uncannily the planet is girdled, as stone-speckled in Sweden as in New York. For the vagabond-voyeur (and for travelers voyeurism is irresistible), nothing is not for notice, nothing is banal, nothing is ordinary: not a rock, not the shoulder of a passerby, not a teapot.

Plenitude assaults; replication invades. Everything known has its spooky shadow and Doppelgänger. On my first trip anywhere—it was 1957 and I landed in Edinburgh with the roaring of the plane's four mammoth propellers for days afterward embedded in my ears—I rode in a red airport bus to the middle of the city, out of which ascended its great castle. It is a fairy-book castle, dreamlike, Arthurian, secured in the long-ago. But the shuddery red bus—hadn't I been bounced along in an old bus before, perhaps not so terrifically red as this one?—the red bus was not within reach of plain sense. Every inch of its interior streamed with unearthliness, with an undivulged and consummate witchery. It put me in the grip of a wild Elsewhere. This unexceptional vehicle, with its bright forward snout, was all at once eclipsed by a rush of the abnormal, the unfathomably Martian. It was the bus, not the phantasmagorical castle, that clouded over and bewildered our reasoned humanity. The red bus was what I intimately knew: only I had never seen it before. A reflected flicker of the actual. A looking-glass bus. A Scottish ghost.

This is what travelers discover: that when you sever the links of normality and its claims, when you break off from the quotidian, it is the teapots that truly shock. Nothing is so awesomely unfamiliar as the familiar that discloses itself at the end of a journey. Nothing shakes the heart so much as meeting—far, far away—what you last met at home. Some say that travelers are informal anthropologists. But it is ontology—the investigation of the nature of being—that travelers do. Call it the flooding-in of the real.

There is, besides, the flooding-in of character. Here one enters not landscapes or streetlit night scenes, but fragments of drama: splinters of euphoria that catch you up when you are least deserving. Sometimes it is a jump into a pop-up book, as when a cockney cabdriver, of whom you have asked directions while leaning out from the curb, gives his native wink of blithe goodwill. Sometimes it is a mazy stroll into a toy theater, as when, in a museum, you suddenly come on the intense little band following the lecturer on Mesopotamia, or the lecturer on genre painting, and the muse of civilization alights on these rapt few. What you are struck with then—one of those mental photographs that go on sticking to the retina—is not what lies somnolently in the glass case or hangs romantically on the wall, but the enchantment of a minutely idiosyncratic face shot into your vision with indelible singularity, delivered over forever by your own fertile gaze. When travelers stare at heads and ears and necks and beads and mustaches, they are—in the encapsuled force of the selection—making art: portraits, voice sonatinas, the quick haiku of a strictly triangular nostril.

Traveling is seeing; it is the implicit that we travel by. Travelers are fantasists, conjurers, seers—and what they finally discover is that every round object everywhere is a crystal ball: stone, teapot, the marvelous globe of the human eye.

LINES OF INQUIRY
"The Shock of Teapots"

Throughout this piece, Ozick attempts to show how travel leads people to see familiar things in "awesomely unfamiliar" ways. What images does she focus on, what metaphors does she offer, to show how familiar things become "unfamiliar"? What descriptive, narrative, and stylistic techniques does she use to evoke the surprising and awesome experience of seeing familiar things in unfamiliar ways? Given the title of her piece, why do you suppose that Ozick mentions teapots just three times, and then only in passing, without describing or discussing them at all?

Throughout this essay, Ozick takes the very unusual position of claiming that travelers are bewitched by familiar rather than unfamiliar images and experiences—"It was the bus, not the phantasmagorical castle, that clouded over and bewildered our reasoned humanity." How does she explain this unusual position? According to her, what aspects of travel cause people to be shocked or enchanted by such familiar things as a bus, a stone, the sun, or a teapot? Why does she think familiar things are more surprising to travelers than such unusual sights as a strange city or a "fairy-book castle"? Does she believe that unfamiliarity has no role at all in creating the enchantment of travel?

Consider your own experience as a traveler by thinking about some especially memorable things you've seen or experienced while away from home. To what extent were you, like Ozick, enchanted by such familiar things as a bus, a stone, the sunlight, or a teapot? To what extent were you enchanted by such unfamiliar things as a castle? To what extent were you enchanted by a combination of the familiar and the unfamiliar?

THE FIRST DAY OF SCHOOL: WASHINGTON SQUARE, 1946

This portion of New York appears to many persons the most delectable. It has a kind of established repose which is not of frequent occurrence in other quarters of the long, shrill city; it has a riper, richer, more honorable look than any of the upper ramifications of the great longitudinal thoroughfare—the look of having had something of a social history.

Henry James, Washington Square

I first came down to Washington Square on a colorless February morning in 1946. I was seventeen and a half years old and was carrying my lunch in a brown paper bag, just as I had carried it to high school only a month before. It was—I thought it was—the opening day of spring term at Washington Square College, my initiation into my freshman year at New York University. All I knew of NYU then was that my science-minded brother had gone there; he had written from the army that I ought to go there too. With master-of-ceremonies zest he described the Browsing Room on the second floor of the Main Building as a paradisal chamber whose bookish loungers leafed languidly through magazines and exchanged high-principled witticisms between classes. It had the sound of a carpeted Olympian club in Oliver Wendell Holmes's Boston, Hub of the Universe, strewn with leather chairs and delectable old copies of *The Yellow Book.*

On that day I had never heard of Oliver Wendell Holmes or *The Yellow Book,* and Washington Square was a faraway bower where wounded birds fell out of trees. My brother had once brought home from Washington Square Park a baby sparrow with a broken leg, to be nurtured back to flight. It died instead, emitting in its last hours melancholy faint cheeps, and leaving behind a dense recognition of the minute explicitness of mortality. All the same, in the February grayness Washington Square had the allure of the celestial unknown. A sparrow might die, but my own life was luminously new: I felt my youth like a nimbus.

Which dissolves into the dun gauze of a low and sullen city sky. And here I am flying out of the Lexington Avenue subway at Astor Place, just a few yards from Wanamaker's, here I am turning a corner past a secondhand bookstore and a union hall; already late, I begin walking very fast toward the park. The air is smoky with New York winter grit, and on clogged Broadway a mob of trucks shifts squawking gears. But there, just ahead, crisscrossed by paths under high branches, is Washington Square; and on a single sidewalk, three clear omens—or call them riddles, intricate and redolent. These I will disclose in a moment, but before you must push open the heavy brass-and-glass doors of the Main Building and come with me, at a hard and panting pace, into the lobby of Washington Square College on the earliest morning of my freshman year.

On the left, a bank of elevators. Straight ahead, a long burnished corridor, spooky as a lit tunnel. And empty, all empty. I can hear my solitary footsteps reverberate, as in a radio mystery drama: they lead me up a short staircase into a big dark ghost-town cafeteria. My brother's letter, along with his account of the physics and chemistry laboratories (I will never see them), has already explained that this place is called Commons—and here my heart will learn to shake with the merciless newness of life. But not today; today there is nothing. Tables and chairs squat in dead silhouette. I race back through a silent maze of halls and stairways to the brass-and-glass doors—there stands a lonely guard. From the pocket of my coat I retrieve a scrap with a classroom number on it and ask the way. The guard announces in a sly croak that the first day of school is not yet; come back tomorrow, he says.

A dumb bad joke: I'm humiliated. I've journeyed the whole way   5 down from the end of the line—Pelham Bay, in the northeast Bronx— to find myself in desolation, all because of a muddle: Tuesday isn't Wednesday. The nimbus of expectation fades. The lunch bag in my fist takes on a greasy sadness. I'm not ready to dive back into the subway— I'll have a look around.

Across the street from the Main Building, the three omens. First, a pretzel man with a cart. He's wearing a sweater, a cap that keeps him faceless—he's nothing but the shadows of his creases—and wool gloves with the fingertips cut off. He never moves; he might as well be made of papier-mâché, set up and left out in the open since spring. There are now almost no pretzels for sale, and this gives me a chance to inspect the construction of his bare pretzel-poles. The pretzels are hooked over a column of gray cardboard cylinders, themselves looped around a stick, the way horseshoes drop around a post. The cardboard cylinders are the insides of toilet paper rolls.

The pretzel man is rooted between a Chock Full O' Nuts (that's the second omen) and a newsstand (that's the third).

The Chock Full: the doors are like fans, whirling remnants of conversation. *She will marry him. She will not marry him.* Fragrance of coffee and hot chocolate. *We can prove that the senses are partial and unreliable vehicles of information, but who is to say that reason is not equally a product of human limitation?* Powdered doughnut sugar on their lips.

Attached to a candy store, the newsstand. Copies of *Partisan Review:* the table of the gods. Jean Stafford, Mary McCarthy, Elizabeth

Hardwick, Irving Howe, Delmore Schwartz, Alfred Kazin, Clement Greenberg, Stephen Spender, William Phillips, John Berryman, Saul Bellow, Philip Rahv, Richard Chase, Randall Jarrell, Simone de Beauvoir, Karl Shapiro, George Orwell! I don't know a single one of these names, but I feel their small conflagration flaming in the gray street: the succulent hotness of their promise. I mean to penetrate every one of them. Since all the money I have is my subway fare—a nickel—I don't buy a copy (the price of *Partisan* in 1946 is fifty cents); I pass on.

I pass on to the row of houses on the north side of the square. 10 Henry James was born in one of these, but I don't know that either. Still, they are plainly old, though no longer aristocratic: haughty last-century shabbies with shut eyelids, built of rosy-ripe respectable brick, down on their luck. Across the park bulks Judson Church, with its squat squarish bell tower; by the end of the week I will be languishing at the margins of a basketball game in its basement, forlorn in my blue left-over-from-high-school gym suit and mooning over Emily Dickinson:

> There's a certain Slant of light,
> Winter Afternoons—
> That oppresses, like the Heft
> Of Cathedral Tunes—

There is more I don't know. I don't know that W. H. Auden lives just down *there,* and might at any moment be seen striding toward home under his tall rumpled hunch; I don't know that Marianne Moore is only up the block, her doffed tricorn resting on her bedroom dresser. It's Greenwich Village—I know *that*—no more than twenty years after Edna St. Vincent Millay has sent the music of her name (her best, perhaps her only, poem) into these bohemian streets: bohemia, the honeypot of poets.

On that first day in the tea-leafed cup of the town I am ignorant, ignorant! But the three riddle-omens are soon to erupt, and all of them together will illumine Washington Square.

Begin with the benches in the park. Here, side by side with students and their looseleafs, lean or lie the shadows of the pretzel man, his creased ghosts or doubles: all those pitiables, half-women and half-men, neither awake nor asleep; the discountable, the repudiated, the unseen. No more notice is taken of any of them than of a scudding fragment of newspaper in the path. Even then, even so long ago, the benches of Washington Square are pimpled with this hell-tossed crew, these Mad Margarets and Cokey Joes, these volcanic coughers, shakers, groaners, tremblers, droolers, blasphemers, these public urinators with vomitous breath and rusted teeth stumps, dead-eyed and self-abandoned, dragging their makeshift junkyard shoes, their buttonless layers of raggedy ratfur. The pretzel man with his toilet paper rolls conjures and spews them all—he is a loftier brother to these citizens of the lower pox, he is guardian of the garden of the jettisoned. They rattle along all the seams of Washington Square. They are the pickled city, the true and universal City-Below-Cities, the wolfish vinegar-Babylon that dogs the spittled skirts of bohemia. The toilet paper rolls are the temple columns of this sacred grove.

Next, the whirling doors of Chock Full O'Nuts. Here is the marketplace of Washington Square, its bazaar, its roiling gossip-parlor, its matchmaker's office and arena—the outermost wing, so to speak, evolved from the Commons. On a day like today, when the Commons is closed, the Chock Full is thronged with extra power, a cello making up a missing viola. Until now, the fire of my vitals has been for the imperious tragedians of the *Aeneid;* I have lived in the narrow throat of poetry. Another year or so of this oblivion, until at last I am hammerstruck with the shock of Europe's skull, the bled planet of death camp and war. Eleanor Roosevelt has not yet written her famous column announcing the discovery of Anne Frank's diary. The term *cold war* is new. The Commons, like the college itself, is overcrowded, veterans in their pragmatic thirties mingling with the reluctant dreamy young. And the Commons is convulsed with politics: a march to the docks is organized, no one knows by whom, to protest the arrival of Walter Gieseking, the German musician who flourished among Nazis. The Communists—two or three readily recognizable cantankerous zealots—stomp through with their daily leaflets and sneers. There is even a Monarchist, a small poker-faced rectangle of a man with secretive tireless eyes who, when approached for his views, always demands, in perfect Bronx tones, the restoration of his king. The engaged girls—how many of them there seem to be!—flash their rings and tangle their ankles in their long New Look skirts. There is no feminism and no feminists: I am, I think, the only one. The Commons is a tide: it washes up the cold war, it washes up the engaged girls' rings, it washes up the several philosophers and the numerous poets. The philosophers are all existentialists; the poets are all influenced by *The Waste Land.* When the Commons overflows, the engaged girls cross the street to show their rings at the Chock Full.

Call it density, call it intensity, call it continuity: call it, finally, 15 society. The Commons belongs to the satirists. Here, one afternoon, is Alfred Chester, holding up a hair, a single strand, before a crowd. (He will one day write stories and novels. He will die young.) "What is that hair?" I innocently ask, having come late on the scene. "A pubic hair," he replies, and I feel as Virginia Woolf did when she declared human nature to have "changed in or about December 1910"—soon after her sister Vanessa explained away a spot on her dress as "semen."

In or about February 1946 human nature does not change; it keeps on. On my bedroom wall I tack—cut out from *Life* magazine—the wildest Picasso I can find: a face that is also a belly. Mr. George E. Mutch, a lyrical young English teacher still in his twenties, writes on the blackboard: "When lilacs last in the dooryard bloom'd," and "Bare, ruined choirs, where late the sweet birds sang," and "A green thought in a green shade"; he tells us to burn, like Pater, with a hard, gemlike flame. Another English teacher—older and crustier—compares Walt Whitman to a plumber; the next year he is rumored to have shot himself in a wood. The initial letters of Washington Square College are a device to recall three of the seven deadly sins: Wantonness, Sloth, Covetousness. In the Commons they argue the efficacy of the orgone box. Eda Lou Walton, sprightly as a bird, knows all the Village bards, and is a Village bard herself. Sidney Hook is an intellectual rumble in the logical middle distance. Homer Watt, chairman of the English department, is the very soul who, in a far-off time of bewitchment, hired Thomas Wolfe.

And so, in February 1946, I make my first purchase of a "real" book—which is to say, not for the classroom. It is displayed in the window of the secondhand bookstore between the Astor Place subway station and the union hall, and for weeks I have been coveting it: *Of Time and the River.* I am transfigured; I am pierced through with rapture; skipping gym, I sit among morning mists on a windy bench a foot from the stench of Mad Margaret, sinking into that cascading syrup:

> Man's youth is a wonderful thing: It is so full of anguish and of magic and he never comes to know it as it is, until it is gone from him forever. . . . And what is the essence of that strange and bitter miracle of life which we feel so poignantly, so unutterably, with such a bitter pain and joy, when we are young?

Thomas Wolfe, lost, and by the wind grieved, ghost, come back again! In Washington Square I am appareled in the "numb exultant secrecies of fog, fog-numb air filled with solemn joy of nameless and impending prophecy, an ancient yellow light, the old smoke-ochre of the morning . . ."

The smoke-ochre of the morning. Ah, you who have flung Thomas Wolfe, along with your strange and magical youth, onto the ash-heap of juvenilia and excess, myself among you, isn't this a lovely phrase still? It rises out of the old pavements of Washington Square as delicately colored as an eggshell.

The veterans in their pragmatic thirties are nailed to Need; they have families and futures to attend to. When Mr. George E. Mutch exhorts them to burn with a hard, gemlike flame, and writes across the blackboard the line that reveals his own name,

20

> The world is too much with us; late and soon,
> Getting and spending, we lay waste our powers,

one of the veterans heckles, "What about getting a Buick, what about spending a buck?" Chester, at sixteen, is a whole year younger than I; he has transparent eyes and a rosebud mouth, and is in love with a poet named Diana. He has already found his way to the Village bars, and keeps in his wallet Truman Capote's secret telephone number. We tie our scarves tight against the cold and walk up and down Fourth Avenue, winding in and out of the rows of secondhand bookshops crammed one against the other. The proprietors sit reading their wares and never look up. The books in all their thousands smell sleepily of cellar. Our envy of them is speckled with longing; our longing is sick with envy. We are the sorrowful literary young.

Every day, month after month, I hang around the newsstand near the candy store, drilling through the enigmatic pages of *Partisan Review.* I still haven't bought a copy; I still can't understand a word. I don't know what cold war means. Who is Trotsky? I haven't read *Ulysses;* my adolescent phantoms are rowing in the ablative absolute with *pius* Aeneas. I'm in my mind's cradle, veiled by the exultant secrecies of fog.

Washington Square will wake me. In a lecture room in the Main Building, Dylan Thomas will cry his webwork syllables. Afterward he'll warm himself at the White Horse Tavern. Across the corridor I will see Sidney Hook plain. I will read the Bhagavad-Gita and Catullus and Lessing, and, in Hebrew, a novel eerily called *Whither?* It will be years and years before I am smart enough, worldly enough, to read Alfred Kazin and Mary McCarthy.

In the spring, all of worldly Washington Square will wake up to the luster of little green leaves.

LINES OF INQUIRY
"The First Day of School: Washington Square, 1946"

Though this essay is presumably concerned with "the first day of school," Ozick has very little to say about her first day of classes and much more to tell about Washington Square, especially about the "three omens" that she first mentions in paragraph 3. What are those three omens? Why do you think she refers to them as "riddles"? Why do you suppose that she changes the tense of her narrative from past to present tense in the same paragraph that she first mentions the riddles? What significance(s) did the three omens have for her when she first saw them? What significance(s) do they have for her as she looks back upon them some forty years later?

In paragraph twelve, Ozick proclaims that "On that first day in the tea-leafed cup of the town I am ignorant, ignorant." In what sense(s) does she believe she was ignorant? What sorts of things was she ignorant of? In other words, what kinds of knowledge does she value in this essay, and how does she show herself to have been ignorant of them? To what extent does her first day of classes at NYU help her to overcome her ignorance? To what extent does her first day in Washington Square help her to overcome her ignorance? What other sorts of experiences helped her to overcome her ignorance?

Consider your own first day of college. What were you ignorant of that day, and to what extent were you then aware of your ignorance? What were you ignorant of that first day that you only realized you were ignorant of somewhat later? In what ways did your first day of classes help you to overcome your ignorance or make you aware of your ignorance? To what extent did places and people outside of classes help you to overcome your ignorance or at least become aware of it? What kinds of knowledge do you most value and how have you come to acquire them since your first day at college?

LEWIS THOMAS

1913 –

It is no good standing on dignity in a situation like this, and better not to try. It is a mystery.

The mystery that Thomas affirms in this passage from *The Lives of a Cell* is the behavior of the submicroscopic mitochondria that inhabit the cells of his own body and those of every living thing on earth, producing and regulating the use of oxygen. Mitochondria are not the only natural things that have puzzled and fascinated him. Though an accomplished biochemist and cell biologist who has published over two hundred scientific articles, Thomas repeatedly celebrates in his essays the "astonishments," the "mysteries," of nature, from the intricate unities of a single cell to the complex ecologies of the earth as a whole. Often with wry humor and wit, sometimes with a poetic lyricism, Thomas demonstrates that much in our experience remains "unflattened by science," and he insists that this should encourage us: to respect our limits, to respect each other, to respect the world we inhabit and have the power to destroy.

Born in Flushing, New York, to a general practitioner and a former nurse, he grew up admiring his father's hard work and devotion to his patients. In *The Youngest Science* (1983), both an autobiography and a reflection on the recent history of medicine, Thomas portrays his father's dedication as representative of the medical profession at a time when it was "turning into a science, but the old art was still in place." Intent on becoming a doctor himself, he entered Princeton University, where he says he "turned into a moult of dullness and laziness, average or below average in the courses requiring real work," although an advanced course in biology his senior year awakened his interest in science. With the help of a family friend he was admitted to Harvard Medical School. After an internship at Boston City Hospital and residency at the Neurological Institute in New York, he was called into the Navy in 1941, for a tour of duty that led him into research on the origins of tropical diseases. After the war Thomas continued his research in the fields of immunology and pathology as a faculty member in the medical schools at Johns Hopkins, Tulane, and the University of Minnesota, gradually establishing a reputation as one of the premier cell biologists in the world. He has also established himself as a distinguished university and hospital administrator, first at New York University Medical School, then at Yale Medical School, and since 1973 at the Memorial Sloan-Kettering Cancer Center in New York, where he is currently chancellor.

Throughout his career as a scientist and researcher, Thomas has maintained an interest in literature and writing. At Princeton, the poetry of Eliot and Pound moved him to publish poems in the college literary magazine. While an intern and resident he published poems in the *Atlantic, Harper's Bazaar,* and *The Saturday Evening Post,* and he has continued writing poetry—"good bad verse" as he calls it. In *The Youngest Science* he admits that stylistically the scientific papers he wrote earlier in his career seem "hideous" as he reads them today, composed, as they had to be, "in the relentlessly flat style required for absolute unambiguity in every word."

In 1971 Thomas was given the opportunity to free himself from that style when he was invited to do an open-ended monthly column of 1200 words for one of the bastions of that style, *The New England Journal of Medicine.* Writing late at night, "usually on the weekend two days after [he'd] already passed the deadline," never outlining "or planning in advance," he started producing informal, personal essays, using scientific knowledge, particularly from the world of cell biology, as a source of metaphors for exploring relationships throughout the world of nature and human experience. The grace and humaneness of the column attracted such a large following outside the medical profession that a collection of them was published in 1974, *The Lives of a Cell,* which subsequently won the National Book Award. Two other collections followed, *The Medusa and the Snail* (1979) and *Late Night Thoughts on Listening to Mahler's Ninth Symphony* (1983).

As an essayist, Thomas' habit is to read the behavior of all organisms—mitochondria, sea slugs and jelly fish, ants, bees, beavers and otters—as metaphors of relationship and cooperation. "Every creature," Thomas says in *The Lives of a Cell,* "is, in some sense, connected to and dependent on the rest." Microbes "live together in dense, interdependent communities"; bacteria "live by collaboration, accommodation, exchange, and barter"—are "social animals." Human beings are part of this ecology, equally dependent upon other things, existing in various symbiotic relationships with microorganisms, animals, each other, the earth itself. For Thomas, in other words, nature is a cause for optimism, for celebration, although he worries throughout his essays about the ways in which human beings may violate the unity of nature. In the end he offers anthills and protozoan parasites and the generosity of mitochondria as hopeful alternatives to the suspicion, the violence, and the warfare of human beings. "There is something intrinsically good-natured about all symbiotic relations."

Nature is also, perhaps most of all, a cause of wonder. Though Thomas values the knowledge that science can bring us and insists on the integrity of the scientific method, symbiosis is only his favorite example of the mysteries science can never fully understand. "Things that used to seem clear and rational, matters of absolute certainty," he says, "have slipped through our fingers, and we are left with a new set of gigantic puzzles, cosmic uncertainties, ambiguities." So, like other essayists in the American naturalist tradition—such as Thoreau, White, Eiseley, Dillard, and Hoagland—Thomas's attitude is often one of wonder and amazement, of pleased astonishment. "The mind of a cat is an inscrutable mystery, beyond reach"; "bees are filled with astonishments, confounding anyone who studies them." In his view we understand almost nothing fully in our experience, from DNA, to language, to music, to our own behavior, to the ecological symmetry of the whole earth, functioning somehow as a giant cell, a "marvel." So, "illumination," according to Thomas, "comes in small bits, only from time to time, not ever in broad, bright flashes of public comprehension, and there can be no promise that we will ever emerge from the great depths of the mystery of being."

In the face of these mysteries and wonders, Thomas' stance as a writer is tentative, exploratory, personal, in the classic tradition of the essay. He tells about the events and experiences and places that stimulate his thinking—the music of Mahler, the behavior of germs, the physiology of warts—then tells about the ebb and flow of his thinking itself, digressing, juxtaposing images and ideas, seeming to revise as he goes, exclaiming, his language often down to earth and homey, often rich, textured, and evocative:

> I have been trying to think of the earth as a kind of organism, but it is no go. I cannot think of it this way. It is too big, too complex, with too many working parts lacking visible connections. The other night driving through a hilly, wooded part of southern New England, I wondered about this. If not like an organism, what is it like, what is it *most* like? Then satisfactorily for that moment, it came to me: it is *most* like a single cell.

Here as elsewhere, Thomas admits that he doesn't have the answers. So he lets us in on the drama of his thinking, sharing with us its origins and uncertainty. Like the essays of his hero and model Montaigne, Thomas' essays give the illusion of being "the easiest of conversations with a very old friend"—but they are conversations that challenge us even as they include us, that cause us to stop and consider both the wonders and the dangers around us.

essays
the catalog → dialogic
vs the
books

(the essay addresses the
premise of these books, starting won
para. 3.

ON NATURAL DEATH

traditional
title —
defensional

Contemporary
comfort

There are so many new
books about dying that there are now special shelves set aside for them
in bookshops, along with the health-diet and home-repair paperbacks
and the sex manuals. Some of them are so packed with detailed information and step-by-step instructions for performing the function that
you'd think this was a new sort of skill which all of us are now required
to learn. The strongest impression the casual reader gets, leafing
through, is that proper dying has become an extraordinary, even an
exotic experience, something only the specially trained get to do.

free mod.

Also, you could be led to believe that we are the only creatures
capable of the awareness of death, that when all the rest of nature is
being cycled through dying, one generation after another, it is a different kind of process, done automatically and trivially, more "natural," as
we say.

an issue
is raised,
a Q.

An elm in our backyard caught the blight this summer and dropped
stone dead, leafless, almost overnight. One weekend it was a normal-
looking elm, maybe a little bare in spots but nothing alarming, and the
next weekend it was gone, passed over, departed, taken. Taken is right,
for the tree surgeon came by yesterday with his crew of young helpers
and their cherry picker, and took it down branch by branch and carted it
off in the back of a red truck, everyone singing.

a catalog
begins

The dying of a field mouse, at the jaws of an amiable household cat,
is a spectacle I have beheld many times. It used to make me wince. Early
in life I gave up throwing sticks at the cat to make him drop the mouse,
because the dropped mouse regularly went ahead and died anyway, but
I always shouted unaffections at the cat to let him know the sort of
animal he had become. Nature, I thought, was an abomination.

a change of mind
Q:

Recently I've done some thinking about that mouse, and I wonder   5
if his dying is necessarily all that different from the passing of our elm.
The main difference, if there is one, would be in the matter of pain. I do
not believe that an elm tree has pain receptors, and even so, the blight
seems to me a relatively painless way to go even if there were nerve
endings in a tree, which there are not. But the mouse dangling tail-
down from the teeth of a gray cat is something else again, with pain
beyond bearing, you'd think, all over his small body.

There are now some plausible reasons for thinking it is not like that
at all, and you can make up an entirely different story about the mouse
and his dying if you like. At the instant of being trapped and penetrated
by teeth, peptide hormones are released by cells in the hypothalamus
and the pituitary gland; instantly these substances, called endorphins,

science-
talk

are attached to the surface of other cells responsible for pain perception; the hormones have the pharmacologic properties of opium; there is no pain. Thus it is that the mouse seems always to dangle so languidly from the jaws, lies there so quietly when dropped, dies of his injuries without a struggle. If a mouse could shrug, he'd shrug.

I do not know if this is true or not, nor do I know how to prove it if it is true. Maybe if you could get in there quickly enough and administer naloxone, a specific morphine antagonist, you could turn off the endorphins and observe the restoration of pain, but this is not something I would care to do or see. I think I will leave it there, as a good guess about the dying of a cat-chewed mouse, perhaps about dying in general.

Montaigne had a hunch about dying, based on his own close call in a riding accident. He was so badly injured as to be believed dead by his companions, and was carried home with lamentations, "all bloody, stained all over with the blood I had thrown up." He remembers the entire episode, despite having been "dead, for two full hours," with wonderment:

> It seemed to me that my life was hanging only by the tip of my lips. I closed my eyes in order, it seemed to me, to help push it out, and took pleasure in growing languid and letting myself go. It was an idea that was only floating on the surface of my soul, as delicate and feeble as all the rest, but in truth not only free from distress but mingled with that sweet feeling that people have who have let themselves slide into sleep. I believe that this is the same state in which people find themselves whom we see fainting in the agony of death, and I maintain that we pity them without cause. . . . In order to get used to the idea of death, I find there is nothing like coming close to it.

Later, in another essay, Montaigne returns to it:

> If you know not how to die, never trouble yourself; Nature will in a moment fully and sufficiently instruct you; she will exactly do that business for you; take you no care for it.

The worst accident I've ever seen was in Okinawa, in the early days of the invasion, when a jeep ran into a troop carrier and was crushed nearly flat. Inside were two young MPs, trapped in bent steel, both mortally hurt, with only their heads and shoulders visible. We had a conversation while people with the right tools were prying them free. Sorry about the accident, they said. No, they said, they felt fine. Is everyone else okay, one of them said. Well, the other one said, no hurry now. And then they died.

Pain is useful for avoidance, for getting away when there's time to get away, but when it is end game, and no way back, pain is likely to be turned off, and the mechanisms for this are wonderfully precise and quick. If I had to design an ecosystem in which creatures had to live off each other and in which dying was an indispensable part of living, I could not think of a better way to manage. *he decides*

LINES OF INQUIRY
"On Natural Death"

In the course of his reflections on dying, Thomas tells about the death of his elm tree, the dying of field mice at the jaws of a cat, the near death of Montaigne, and the actual death of two soldiers that he observed in Okinawa. Why do you suppose that he tells about all of these cases? Why doesn't he just confine himself to the soldiers at Okinawa and possibly the story of Montaigne, since these are the only cases which bear directly on his main point—that when human beings are on the verge of dying "pain is likely to be turned off"? What purposes are served by his telling about the tree and the field mice? And why does he tell about them before he takes up Montaigne and the soldiers?

The first passage by Montaigne ends with the assertion that "In order to get used to the idea of death, I find there is nothing like coming close to it." But the gist of Thomas's essay is that human beings don't need to worry about getting ready for death, since nature has already endowed them with chemical mechanisms that make it "wonderfully quick and precise." How do you account for this disagreement between Thomas and Montaigne? Why do you suppose that he doesn't directly acknowledge it? Or do you suppose that Thomas doesn't consider Montaigne's statements to be at odds with his own? Do you see any other respects in which Montaigne's story might not exactly fit the point that Thomas is trying to make?

Montaigne's complete story of his near fatal accident is quite fascinating and vividly detailed, as you can see by looking at his essay, "Of Practice," which is included in this collection (pp. 466–475). Based on Montaigne's account, how painless does the process of dying appear to be? How "precise and quick" does the mechanism seem to have been working in his case? What similarities, what differences, do you notice between Montaigne's experience and Thomas's hypothesis of how the endorphins work in the case of a dying mouse? What similarities, what differences, do you notice between Montaigne's experience and Thomas's story of the dying soldiers on Okinawa? Whose depiction of death and dying do you find most convincing?

ON CLONING A HUMAN BEING

It is now theoretically possible to recreate an identical creature from any animal or plant, from the DNA contained in the nucleus of any somatic cell. A single plant root-tip cell can be teased and seduced into conceiving a perfect copy of the whole plant; a frog's intestinal epithelial cell possesses the complete instructions needed for a new, same frog. If the technology were further advanced, you could do this with a human being, and there are now startled predictions all over the place that this will in fact be done, someday, in order to provide a version of immortality for carefully selected, especially valuable people.

The cloning of humans is on most of the lists of things to worry about from Science, along with behavior control, genetic engineering, transplanted heads, computer poetry, and the unrestrained growth of plastic flowers.

Cloning is the most dismaying of prospects, mandating as it does the elimination of sex with only a metaphoric elimination of death as compensation. It is almost no comfort to know that one's cloned, identical surrogate lives on, especially when the living will very likely involve edging one's real, now aging self off to the side, sooner or later. It is hard to imagine anything like filial affection or respect for a single, unmated nucleus; harder still to think of one's new, self-generated self as anything but an absolute, desolate orphan. Not to mention the complex interpersonal relationship involved in raising one's self from infancy, teaching the language, enforcing discipline, instilling good manners, and the like. How would you feel if you became an incorrigible juvenile delinquent by proxy, at the age of fifty-five?

The public questions are obvious. Who is to be selected, and on what qualifications? How to handle the risks of misused technology, such as self-determined cloning by the rich and powerful but socially objectionable, or the cloning by governments of dumb, docile masses for the world's work? What will be the effect on all the uncloned rest of us of human sameness? After all, we've accustomed ourselves through hundreds of millennia to the continual exhilaration of uniqueness; each of us is totally different, in a fundamental sense, from all the other four billion. Selfness is an essential fact of life. The thought of human non-selfness, precise sameness, is terrifying, when you think about it.

Well, don't think about it, because it isn't a probable possibility, not even as a long shot for the distant future, in my opinion. I agree 5 that you might clone some people who would look amazingly like their parental cell donors, but the odds are that they'd be almost as different as you or me, and certainly more different than any of today's identical twins.

The time required for the experiment is only one of the problems, but a formidable one. Suppose you wanted to clone a prominent, spectacularly successful diplomat, to look after the Middle East problems of the distant future. You'd have to catch him and persuade him, probably not very hard to do, and extirpate a cell. But then you'd have to wait for him to grow up through embryonic life and then for at least forty years more, and you'd have to be sure all observers remained patient and unmeddlesome through his unpromising, ambiguous childhood and adolescence.

Moreover, you'd have to be sure of recreating his environment, perhaps down to the last detail. "Environment" is a word which really means people, so you'd have to do a lot more cloning than just the diplomat himself.

This is a very important part of the cloning problem, largely overlooked in our excitement about the cloned individual himself. You don't have to agree all the way with B. F. Skinner to acknowledge that the environment does make a difference, and when you examine what we really mean by the word "environment" it comes down to other human beings. We use euphemisms and jargon for this, like "social forces," "cultural influences," even Skinner's "verbal community," but what is meant is the dense crowd of nearby people who talk to, listen to, smile or frown at, give to, withhold from, nudge, push, caress, or flail out at the individual. No matter what the genome says, these people have a lot to do with shaping a character. Indeed, if all you had was the genome, and no people around, you'd grow a sort of vertebrate plant, nothing more.

So, to start with, you will undoubtedly need to clone the parents. No question about this. This means the diplomat is out, even in theory, since you couldn't have gotten cells from both his parents at the time when he was himself just recognizable as an early social treasure. You'd have to limit the list of clones to people already certified as sufficiently valuable for the effort, with both parents still alive. The parents would need cloning and, for consistency, their parents as well. I suppose you'd also need the usual informed-consent forms, filled out and signed, not easy to get if I know parents, even harder for grandparents.

But this is only the beginning. It is the whole family that really   10
influences the way a person turns out, not just the parents, according to current psychiatric thinking. Clone the family.

Then what? The way each member of the family develops has already been determined by the environment set around him, and this environment is more people, people outside the family, schoolmates, acquaintances, lovers, enemies, car-pool partners, even in special circumstances, peculiar strangers across the aisle on the subway. Find them, and clone them.

But there is no end to the protocol. Each of the outer contacts has his own surrounding family, and his and their outer contacts. Clone them all.

To do the thing properly, with any hope of ending up with a genuine duplicate of a single person, you really have no choice. You must clone the world, no less.

We are not ready for an experiment of this size, nor, I should think, are we willing. For one thing, it would mean replacing today's world by an entirely identical world to follow immediately, and this means no new, natural, spontaneous, random, chancy children. No children at all, except for the manufactured doubles of those now on the scene. Plus all those identical adults, including all of today's politicians, all seen double. It is too much to contemplate.

Moreover, when the whole experiment is finally finished, fifty years   15
or so from now, how could you get a responsible scientific reading on the outcome? Somewhere in there would be the original clonee, probably lost and overlooked, now well into middle age, but everyone around him would be precise duplicates of today's everyone. It would be today's same world, filled to overflowing with duplicates of today's people and their same, duplicated problems, probably all resentful at having had to go through our whole thing all over, sore enough at the clonee to make endless trouble for him, if they found him.

And obviously, if the whole thing were done precisely right, they would still be casting about for ways to solve the problem of universal dissatisfaction, and sooner or later they'd surely begin to look around at each other, wondering who should be cloned for his special value to society, to get us out of all this. And so it would go, in regular cycles, perhaps forever.

I once lived through a period when I wondered what Hell could be like, and I stretched my imagination to try to think of a perpetual sort of damnation. I have to confess, I never thought of anything like this.

I have an alternative suggestion, if you're looking for a way out. Set cloning aside, and don't try it. Instead, go in the other direction. Look for ways to get mutations more quickly, new variety, different songs. Fiddle around, if you must fiddle, but never with ways to keep things the same, no matter who, not even yourself. Heaven, somewhere ahead, has got to be a change.

LINES OF INQUIRY
"On Cloning a Human Being"

Throughout this piece, Thomas often uses familiar, even conversational language, such as "all over the place," "things to worry about," and "long shot." What impression of Thomas do you get from such words and phrases? Is there a relationship between this impression and the kind of argument that Thomas is making here against cloning? What is the overall effect of mixing such down-to-earth language with the scientific terminology that Thomas also uses?

Thomas suggests that we should use the techniques of genetic engineering to "go in the other direction" from cloning, creating new mutations, "new variety, different songs." What exactly is he getting at in this alternative vision? Can you see any problems with it? What kind of world would result from his desire to "go in the other direction"? How consistent is his method of argument in this piece with the kind of world he argues for?

Many forces in our culture seem to work toward making people behave and think similarly if not identically. What pressures toward uniformity have you experienced within your own family? Within your home community? Within the school you're presently attending? Within your present writing course? What resources have you found in your studies—and in yourself—to resist such pressures?

THE TUCSON ZOO

Science gets most of its information by the process of reductionism, exploring the details, then the details of the details, until all the smallest bits of the structure, or the smallest parts of the mechanism, are laid out for counting and scrutiny. Only when this is done can the investigation be extended to encompass the whole organism or the entire system. So we say.

Sometimes it seems that we take a loss, working this way. Much of today's public anxiety about science is the apprehension that we may forever be overlooking the whole by an endless, obsessive preoccupation with the parts. I had a brief, personal experience of this misgiving one afternoon in Tucson, where I had time on my hands and visited the zoo, just outside the city. The designers there have cut a deep pathway between two small artificial ponds, walled by clear glass, so when you stand in the center of the path you can look into the depths of each pool, and at the same time you can regard the surface. In one pool, on the right side of the path, is a family of otters; on the other side, a family of beavers. Within just a few feet from your face, on either side, beavers and otters are at play, underwater and on the surface, swimming toward your face and then away, more filled with life than any creatures I have ever seen before, in all my days. Except for the glass, you could reach across and touch them.

I was transfixed. As I now recall it, there was only one sensation in my head: pure elation mixed with amazement at such perfection. Swept off my feet, I floated from one side to the other, swiveling my brain, staring astounded at the beavers, then at the otters. I could hear shouts across my corpus callosum, from one hemisphere to the other. I remember thinking, with what was left in charge of my consciousness, that I wanted no part of the science of beavers and otters; I wanted never to know how they performed their marvels; I wished for no news about the physiology of their breathing, the coordination of their muscles, their vision, their endocrine systems, their digestive tracts. I hoped never to have to think of them as collections of cells. All I asked for was the full hairy complexity, then in front of my eyes, of whole, intact beavers and otters in motion.

It lasted, I regret to say, for only a few minutes, and then I was back in the late twentieth century, reductionist as ever, wondering about the details by force of habit, but not, this time, the details of otters and beavers. Instead, me. Something worth remembering had happened in my mind, I was certain of that; I would have put it somewhere in the brain stem; maybe this was my limbic system at work. I became a behavioral scientist, an experimental psychologist, an ethologist, and in the instant I lost all the wonder and the sense of being overwhelmed. I was flattened.

But I came away from the zoo with something, a piece of news   5 about myself: I am coded, somehow, for otters and beavers. I exhibit instinctive behavior in their presence, when they are displayed close at hand behind glass, simultaneously below water and at the surface. I have receptors for this display. Beavers and otters possess a "release" for me, in the terminology of ethology, and the releasing was my experience. What was released? Behavior. What behavior? Standing, swiveling flabbergasted, feeling exultation and a rush of friendship. I could not, as the result of the transaction, tell you anything more about beavers and otters than you already know. I learned nothing new about them. Only about me, and I suspect also about you, maybe about human beings at large: we are endowed with genes which code out our reaction to beavers and otters, maybe our reaction to each other as well. We are stamped with stereotyped, unalterable patterns of response, ready to be released. And the behavior released in us, by such confrontations, is, essentially, a surprised affection. It is compulsory behavior and we can avoid it only by straining with the full power of our conscious minds, making up conscious excuses all the way. Left to ourselves, mechanistic and autonomic, we hanker for friends.

Everyone says, stay away from ants. They have no lessons for us; they are crazy little instruments, inhuman, incapable of controlling themselves, lacking manners, lacking souls. When they are massed together, all touching, exchanging bits of information held in their jaws like memoranda, they become a single animal. Look out for that. It is a debasement, a loss of individuality, a violation of human nature, an unnatural act.

Sometimes people argue this point of view seriously and with deep thought. Be individuals, solitary and selfish, is the message. Altruism, a jargon word for what used to be called love, is worse than weakness, it is sin, a violation of nature. Be separate. Do not be a social animal. But this is a hard argument to make convincingly when you have to depend on language to make it. You have to print up leaflets or publish books and get them bought and sent around, you have to turn up on television and catch the attention of millions of other human beings all at once, and then you have to say to all of them, all at once, all collected and paying attention: be solitary; do not depend on each other. You can't do this and keep a straight face.

Maybe altruism is our most primitive attribute, out of reach, beyond our control. Or perhaps it is immediately at hand, waiting to be released, disguised now, in our kind of civilization, as affection or friendship or attachment. I don't see why it should be unreasonable for all human beings to have strands of DNA coiled up in chromosomes, coding out instincts for usefulness and helpfulness. Usefulness may turn out to be the hardest test of fitness for survival, more important than aggression, more effective, in the long run, than grabbiness. If this is the sort of information biological science holds for the future, applying to us as well as to ants, then I am all for science.

One thing I'd like to know most of all: when those ants have made the Hill, and are all there, touching and exchanging, and the whole mass begins to behave like a single huge creature, and *thinks,* what on earth is that thought? And while you're at it, I'd like to know a second thing: when it happens, does any single ant know about it? Does his hair stand on end?

LINES OF INQUIRY
"The Tucson Zoo"

In paragraphs 3 and 4 of this essay, Thomas tells how his mind was "transfixed," as he watched the beavers and otters at play. Why does he let us in on his private thoughts like this, rather than simply presenting us with the polished and finished conclusions that he comes to in this piece? What is the effect of his telling us, as he does, about the ebb and flow of his thoughts on that occasion? Exactly how does this method of presentation differ from the scientific method that Thomas describes in the first paragraph?

Look closely at the different stages that Thomas goes through in the process of perceiving and reacting to the beavers and otters in paragraphs 2–5. Exactly what does he learn from looking at this display of the beavers and the otters? How does this knowledge challenge or confirm his identity as a scientist? Does Thomas end up in favor of scientific inquiry, or is he finally against such analysis? Or does he somehow arrive at a third position or no position at all?

In this essay Thomas describes what the romantic poet William Wordsworth called "a spot of time" or what the modern novelist James Joyce called an "piphany"—an intense, private experience that stands out, because it involves a significant and memorable insight. Think about an epiphany that you've had. What was the occasion, the place, and the time? What happened to you on that occasion? What went on in your mind? What insight(s) did you have? Did your "hair stand on end"?

THE CORNER OF THE EYE

There are some things that human beings can see only out of the corner of the eye. The niftiest examples of this gift, familiar to all children, are small, faint stars. When you look straight at one such star, it vanishes; when you move your eyes to stare into the space nearby, it reappears. If you pick two faint stars, side by side, and focus on one of the pair, it disappears and now you can see the other in the corner of your eye, and you can move your eyes back and forth, turning off the star in the center of your retina and switching the other one on. There is a physiological explanation for the phenomenon: we have more rods, the cells we use for light perception, at the periphery of our retinas, more cones, for perceiving color, at the center.

Something like this happens in music. You cannot really hear certain sequences of notes in a Bach fugue unless at the same time there are other notes being sounded, dominating the field. The real meaning in music comes from tones only audible in the corner of the mind.

I used to worry that computers would become so powerful and sophisticated as to take the place of human minds. The notion of Artificial Intelligence used to scare me half to death. Already, a large enough machine can do all sorts of intelligent things beyond our capacities: calculate in a split second the answers to mathematical problems requiring years for a human brain, draw accurate pictures from memory, even manufacture successions of sounds with a disarming resemblance to real music. Computers can translate textbooks, write dissertations of their own for doctorates, even speak in machine-tooled, inhuman phonemes any words read off from a printed page. They can communicate with one another, holding consultations and committee meetings of their own in networks around the earth.

Computers can make errors, of course, and do so all the time in small, irritating ways, but the mistakes can be fixed and nearly always are. In this respect they are fundamentally inhuman, and here is the relaxing thought: computers will not take over the world, they cannot replace us, because they are not designed, as we are, for ambiguity.

Imagine the predicament faced by a computer programmed to make   5
language, not the interesting communication in sounds made by vervets or in symbols by brilliant chimpanzee prodigies, but real human talk. The grammar would not be too difficult, and there would be no problem in constructing a vocabulary of etymons, the original, pure, unambiguous words used to name real things. The impossibility would

come in making the necessary mistakes we humans make with words instinctively, intuitively, as we build our kinds of language, changing the meanings to imply quite different things, constructing and elaborating the varieties of ambiguity without which speech can never become human speech.

Look at the record of language if you want to glimpse the special qualities of the human mind that lie beyond the reach of any machine. Take, for example, the metaphors we use in everyday speech to tell ourselves who we are, where we live, and where we come from.

The earth is a good place to begin. The word "earth" is used to name the ground we walk on, the soil in which we grow plants or dig clams, and the planet itself; we also use it to describe all of humanity ("the whole earth responds to the beauty of a child," we say to each other).

The earliest word for earth in our language was the Indo-European root *dhghem,* and look what we did with it. We turned it, by adding suffixes, into *humus* in Latin; today we call the complex polymers that hold fertile soil together "humic" acids, and somehow or other the same root became "humility." With another suffix the word became "human." Did the earth become human, or did the human emerge from the earth? One answer may lie in that nice cognate word "humble." "Humane" was built on, extending the meaning of both the earth and ourselves. In ancient Hebrew, *adamha* was the word for earth, *adam* for man. What computer could run itself through such manipulations as those?

We came at the same system of defining ourselves from the other direction. The word *wiros* was the first root for man; it took us in our vanity on to "virile" and "virtue," but also turned itself into the Germanic word *weraldh,* meaning the life of man, and thence in English to our word "world."

There is a deep hunch in this kind of etymology. The world of man 10 derives from this planet, shares origin with the life of the soil, lives in humility with all the rest of life. I cannot imagine programming a computer to think up an idea like that, not a twentieth-century computer, anyway.

The world began with what it is now the fashion to call the "Big Bang." Characteristically, we have assigned the wrong words for the very beginning of the earth and ourselves, in order to evade another term that would cause this century embarrassment. It could not, of course, have been a bang of any sort, with no atmosphere to conduct the waves of sound, and no ears. It was something else, occurring in the most absolute silence we can imagine. It was the Great Light.

We say it had been chaos before, but it was not the kind of place we use the word "chaos" for today, things tumbling over each other and bumping around. Chaos did not have that meaning in Greek; it simply meant empty.

We took it, in our words, from chaos to cosmos, a word that simply meant order, cosmetic. We perceived the order in surprise, and our cosmologists and physicists continue to find new and astonishing aspects of the order. We made up the word "universe" from the whole affair, meaning literally turning everything into one thing. We used to say it was a miracle, and we still permit ourselves to refer to the whole universe as a marvel, holding in our unconscious minds the original root meaning of these two words, miracle and marvel—from the ancient root word *smei,* signifying a smile. It immensely pleases a human being to see something never seen before, even more to learn something never known before, most of all to think something never thought before. The rings of Saturn are the latest surprise. All my physicist friends are enchanted by this phenomenon, marveling at the small violations of the laws of planetary mechanics, shocked by the unaccountable braids and spokes stuck there among the rings like graffiti. It is nice for physicists to see something new and inexplicable; it means that the laws of nature are once again about to be amended by a new footnote.

The greatest surprise of all lies within our own local, suburban solar system. It is not Mars; Mars was surprising in its way but not flabbergasting; it was a disappointment not to find evidences of life, and there was some sadness in the pictures sent back to earth from the Mars Lander, that lonely long-legged apparatus poking about with its jointed arm, picking up sample after sample of the barren Mars soil, looking for any flicker of life and finding none; the only sign of life on Mars was the Lander itself, an extension of the human mind all the way from earth to Mars, totally alone.

Nor is Saturn the great surprise, nor Jupiter, nor Venus, nor Mercury, nor any of the glimpses of the others.   15

The overwhelming astonishment, the queerest structure we know about so far in the whole universe, the greatest of all cosmological scientific puzzles, confounding all our efforts to comprehend it, is the earth. We are only now beginning to appreciate how strange and splendid it is, how it catches the breath, the loveliest object afloat around the sun, enclosed in its own blue bubble of atmosphere, manufacturing and breathing its own oxygen, fixing its own nitrogen from the air into its own soil, generating its own weather at the surface of its rain forests, constructing its own carapace from living parts: chalk cliffs, coral reefs, old fossils from earlier forms of life now covered by layers of new life meshed together around the globe, Troy upon Troy.

Seen from the right distance, from the corner of the eye of an extraterrestrial visitor, it must surely seem a single creature, clinging to the round warm stone, turning in the sun.

LINES OF INQUIRY
"The Corner of the Eye"

This essay begins with a clear thesis statement and then provides a paragraph of examples which support that thesis, followed by a paragraph that illustrates the same point by analogy. What strategies of diction, sentence rhythm, and organization does Thomas use to keep this initially straightforward organization and mode of presentation from becoming too mechanical and predictable? In other words, what makes this essay different from a strict and straightforward thesis–illustration type of theme? How does Thomas create in the form of this essay itself a sense of the "surprise" that he celebrates in nature?

In paragraphs 7–9, Thomas devotes himself primarily to discussing the derivation of various words. What leads him into this kind of etymological discussion? Do you notice any pattern or motif in the words that he chooses to discuss, or in their root meanings? What does this etymological exercise have to do with the overriding theme of this essay, namely with seeing things out of the corner of the eye?

Thomas says that "the record of language" reflects "the special qualities of the human mind that lie beyond the reach of any machine." If this statement is true, how is it possible that we can use computers to produce writing? Likewise, how is it possible that we can use computers to learn to read and write? Are there certain qualities of writing that cannot be grasped by computers, that can be seen, as it were, only out of the corner of the eye? If so, how can anyone learn to capture those qualities?

HENRY DAVID THOREAU

1817 – 62

If a man does not keep pace with his companions, perhaps it is because he hears a different drummer.

In this resonant and famous sentence from *Walden,* Thoreau might well have been thinking of himself, for his life and his writing bear the marks of someone who evidently did hear "a different drummer." Indeed, he stands out as one of the most independent-minded figures of his time—and one of the most vigorous cultural critics to be heard from at any time in American history. As a critic of American culture, especially of its materialistic values, he is best known for *Walden, or Life in the Woods,* the work that grew out of his two-year experiment in living close to nature to "see if I could not learn what it had to teach, and not, when I came to die, discover that I had not lived." But long before the book appeared in 1854, or before the spring of 1845 when Thoreau "borrowed an axe and went down to the woods by Walden Pond," it was clear to all who knew him that his temperament, his inclinations, and his beliefs set him apart from most of his contemporaries.

He was born and grew up in Concord, Massachusetts. In fact, he spent almost his entire life in Concord, except for the four years of his undergraduate study at Harvard (1833–37), and for brief excursions to Canada, Cape Cod, Long Island, the Maine woods, Minnesota, and New Hampshire. He was "content," as he wrote his mother during one of those excursions, "to sit at the back door in Concord, under the poplar tree, henceforth forever." So he never really left home, and he never married. And though he worked sporadically in his father's pencil manufacturing business, he never did hold a regular job. Yet he was far from being idle or reclusive.

After graduating from Harvard, where he read widely in English poetry, classical literature, and mystical writing, he turned to teaching—briefly at the Concord town school during the fall of 1837, and then from 1838 to 1841 at a private school that he jointly founded and developed with his brother John. He had quit the town school because he objected to what was then the standard practice of disciplining students with a whip. So the school that he started up in his father's home was a counter-cultural enterprise—the first of many such ventures that he was to engage in throughout his life. Thoreau's school was radical not only in its gentle form of discipline but also in its enterprising way of teaching students about nature by taking them on field trips to observe it firsthand, a form of instruction that was then entirely new to American education.

The act of observing nature was hardly something new to Thoreau. From his childhood on, he had roamed the countryside around Concord—first looking for places to fish and hunt, then looking more closely at things with the eye of a naturalist and the spirit of a transcendentalist. His youthful attraction to nature had made him homesick throughout his years at Harvard. His scientific interest in it subsequently led him to carry out highly original studies in the succession of trees and in the ecology of lakes and rivers. Indeed, his fascination with nature gave rise to almost all of his major works. In 1839, for example, Thoreau and his brother John took a two-week canoe trip down the Concord River and then up the Merrimack River, which Thoreau transformed into his first published book, *A Week on the Concord and Merrimack Rivers* (1849). Then, as noted earlier, his two-year stay at Walden Pond led to *Walden, or Life in the Woods* (1854). Finally, his several excursions to other points of interest around the northeast provided the material for his posthumously published books, *The Maine Woods* (1864), *Cape Cod* (1865), and *A Yankee in Canada* (1866).

Whether he reports on his bean field or describes the eye of a fish, an exacting sense of detail always marks Thoreau's writing about nature. Thoreau achieved that sense of detail not only by observing nature carefully, but by keeping a meticulous written record of his observations. He logged his perceptions in a journal that he began in 1834 as a student at Harvard and that he maintained throughout the remaining twenty-eight years of his life. In it he kept notes on his reading, personal reflections, and experiences, as well as records of his scientific observations and investigations. Thus his journal, which ran to fourteen volumes when it was first published in 1906, served him as the principal source for most of his essays, lectures, and books. Indeed, Thoreau's journal might well be considered the major occupation of his life.

Committed as he was to preserving and understanding the natural world, Thoreau was just as intensely concerned with the quality of life that prevailed among his neighbors in Concord and by extension among his countrymen throughout the United States. Even during his two years at Walden Pond, he did not by any means withdraw completely from human companionship; in fact he received visitors at his cabin, and made visits to friends and relatives in Concord. So *Walden* is not just a paean to nature, but is an invocation to his countrymen, meant "to wake my neighbors up . . . to a higher life than we fell asleep from."

Thoreau himself had come to awareness of "a higher life," a world of transcendent moral and spiritual values, through his extensive reading in mystical literature, especially Hindu writing, and through his close friendship with Ralph Waldo Emerson, the leading member of a group of Concord intellectuals, known as transcendentalists, who aspired to reshape the beliefs and values of their time. In keeping with these aspirations, Thoreau went to Walden, not simply to observe nature, but to engage in philosophic meditation and to lead a life whose integrity and simplicity might constitute a challenge to the materialism of the times. Throughout *Walden* Thoreau's descriptions of nature are often resonant with philosophic implications—a lake "is earth's eye; looking into which the beholder measures the depth of his own nature." And his musings, in turn, often have social or political ramifications.

But the stands he took on the most pressing national issues of his time best reveal Thoreau's political consciousness. In 1845, the summer he went to settle at Walden, he refused to pay his poll tax as a form of protest against the Mexican War and against slavery. His protest landed him in jail, and the experience led him to write an essay, "Civil Disobedience" (1849), which came to be a guiding document for such eminent proponents of passive resistance as Mohandas K. Gandhi and Martin Luther King, Jr. In the early 1850s, he assisted fugitive slaves in escaping to Canada. In 1854, he delivered a passionate speech against the slavery in his home state of Massachusetts. And in 1859, his unyielding opposition to slavery gained him national attention when he became the first person to speak out in defense of the political martyr Captain John Brown. After the John Brown affair, he spent much of his time bedridden with tuberculosis, working on manuscripts of the several books that were published after his death.

As he lived, so he wrote in a style that was deliberately meant to awaken his readers, to get them to think about his ideas by expressing them in a provocative or surprising way. Thus, Thoreau's writing is always animated by a surprising play of language, by an arresting turn of speech. Sometimes the surprise comes from a striking allusion, sometimes from an unusual image or metaphor, sometimes from the power of a single word and the meanings that can be wrung out of it:

> I fear chiefly lest my expression may not be *extra-vagant* enough, may not wander far enough beyond the narrow limits of my daily experience, to be adequate to the truth of which I have been convinced. *Extra-vagance!* it depends on how you are yarded. The migrating buffalo, which seeks new pastures in another latitude, is not extravagant like the cow which kicks over the pail, leaps the cowyard fence, and runs after her calf, in

milking time. I desire to speak somewhere *without* bounds; like a man in a waking moment, to men in their waking moments; for I am convinced that I cannot exaggerate enough to lay the foundation of a true expression.

In this passage from *Walden,* the key word is "extravagant," and Thoreau playfully calls attention to it by putting it in italics and breaking it down into its Latin roots, *"extra-vagant,"* which mean literally "to wander outside." Then as if to confirm and emphasize this root meaning of the word, Thoreau repeatedly echoes it in such expressions as "may not wander far enough beyond" and *"without* bounds," as well as in such images as the "migrating buffalo" and the cow "which kicks over the pail, leaps the cowyard fence, and runs after her calf, in milking time." Thoreau's "expression" is not always so outlandish. But it usually does go beyond the "narrow limits" of standard usage and daily experience, inviting us to kick over a pail and leap a fence or two ourselves.

MY HOUSE

Near the end of March, 1845, I borrowed an axe and went down to the woods by Walden Pond, nearest to where I intended to build my house, and began to cut down some tall arrowy white pines, still in their youth, for timber. It is difficult to begin without borrowing, but perhaps it is the most generous course thus to permit your fellow-men to have an interest in your enterprise. The owner of the axe, as he released his hold on it, said that it was the apple of his eye; but I returned it sharper than I received it. It was a pleasant hillside where I worked, covered with pine woods, through which I looked out on the pond, and a small open field in the woods where pines and hickories were springing up. The ice in the pond was all dark colored and saturated with water. There were some slight flurries of snow during the days that I worked there; but for the most part when I came out on to the railroad, on my way home, its yellow sand heap stretched away gleaming in the hazy atmosphere, and the rails shone in the spring sun, and I heard the lark and pewee and other birds already come to commence another year with us. They were pleasant spring days, in which the winter of man's discontent was thawing as well as the earth, and the life that had lain torpid began to stretch itself. One day, when my axe had come off and I had cut a green hickory for a wedge, driving it with a stone, and had placed the whole to soak in a pond hole in order to swell the wood, I saw a striped snake run into the water, and he lay on the bottom, apparently without inconvenience, as long as I staid there, or more than a quarter of an hour, perhaps because he had not yet fairly come out of the torpid state. It appeared to me that for a like reason men remain in their present low and primitive condition; but if they should feel the influence of the spring of springs arousing them, they would of necessity rise to a higher and more ethereal life. I had previously seen the snakes in frosty mornings in my path with portions of their bodies still numb and inflexible, waiting for the sun to thaw them. On the 1st of April it rained and melted the ice, and in the early part of the day, which was very foggy, I heard a stray goose groping about over the pond and cackling as if lost, or like the spirit of the fog.

So I went on for some days cutting and hewing timber, and also studs and rafters, all with my narrow axe, not having many communicable or scholar-like thoughts, singing to myself—

Men say they know many things;
But lo! they have taken wings,—

> The arts and sciences,
> And a thousand appliances;
> The wind that blows
> Is all that any body knows.

I hewed the main timbers six inches square, most of the studs on two sides only, and the rafters and floor timbers on one side, leaving the rest of the bark on, so that they were just as straight and much stronger than sawed ones. Each stick was carefully mortised or tenoned by its stump, for I had borrowed other tools by this time. My days in the woods were not very long ones; yet I usually carried my dinner of bread and butter, and read the newspaper in which it was wrapped, at noon, sitting amid the green pine boughs which I had cut off, and to my bread was imparted some of the fragrance, for my hands were covered with a thick coat of pitch. Before I had done I was more the friend than the foe of the pine tree, though I had cut down some of them, having become better acquainted with it. Sometimes a rambler in the wood was attracted by the sound of my axe, and we chatted pleasantly over the chips which I had made.

By the middle of April, for I made no haste in my work, but rather made the most of it, my house was framed and ready for the raising. I had already bought the shanty of James Collins, an Irishman who worked on the Fitchburg Railroad, for boards. James Collins' shanty was considered an uncommonly fine one. When I called to see it he was not at home. I walked about the outside, at first unobserved from within, the window was so deep and high. It was of small dimensions, with a peaked cottage roof, and not much else to be seen, the dirt being raised five feet all around as if it were a compost heap. The roof was the soundest part, though a good deal warped and made brittle by the sun. Doorsill there was none, but a perennial passage for the hens under the door board. Mrs. C. came to the door and asked me to view it from the inside. The hens were driven in by my approach. It was dark, and had a dirt floor for the most part, dank, clammy, and aguish, only here a board and there a board which would not bear removal. She lighted a lamp to show me the inside of the roof and the walls, and also that the board floor extended under the bed, warning me not to step into the cellar, a sort of dust hole two feet deep. In her own words, they were "good boards overhead, good boards all around and a good window,"—of two whole squares originally, only the cat had passed out that way lately. There was a stove, a bed, and a place to sit, an infant in the house where it was born, a silk parasol, gilt-framed looking-glass, and patent new coffee mill nailed to an oak sapling, all told. The bargain was soon concluded, for James had in the meanwhile returned. I to pay four dollars and twenty-five cents tonight, he to vacate at five tomorrow morning, selling to nobody else meanwhile: I to take possession at six. It were well, he said, to be there early, and anticipate certain indistinct but wholly unjust claims on the score of ground rent and fuel. This he assured me was the only encumbrance. At six I passed him and his family on the road. One large bundle held their all,—bed, coffee-mill, looking glass, hens,—all but the cat, she took to the woods and became a wild cat, and, as I learned afterward, trod in a trap set for woodchucks, and so became a dead cat at last.

I took down this dwelling the same morning, drawing the nails, and removed it to the pond side by small cart-loads, spreading the boards on the grass there to bleach and warp back again in the sun. One early thrush gave me a note or two as I drove along the woodland path. I was informed treacherously by a young Patrick that neighbor Seeley, an Irishman, in the intervals of the carting, transferred the still tolerable, straight, and drivable nails, staples, and spikes to his pocket and then stood when I came back to pass the time of day, and look freshly up, unconcerned, with spring thoughts, at the devastation; there being a dearth of work, as he said. He was there to represent spectatordom, and help make this seemingly insignificant event one with the removal of the gods of Troy.

I dug my cellar in the side of a hill sloping to the south, where a woodchuck had formerly dug his burrow, down through sumach and blackberry roots, and the lowest stain of vegetation, six feet square by seven deep, to a fine sand where potatoes would not freeze in any winter. The sides were left shelving, and not stoned; but the sun having never shone on them, the sand still keeps its place. It was but two hours' work. I took particular pleasure in this breaking of ground, for in almost all latitudes men dig into the earth for an equable temperature. Under the most splendid house in the city is still to be found the cellar where they store their roots as of old, and long after the superstructure has disappeared posterity remark its dent in the earth. The house is still but a sort of porch at the entrance of a burrow.

At length, in the beginning of May, with the help of some of my acquaintances, rather to improve so good an occasion for neighborliness than from any necessity, I set up the frame of my house. No man was ever more honored in the character of his raisers than I. They are destined, I trust, to assist at the raising of loftier structures one day. I began to occupy my house on the 4th of July, as soon as it was boarded and roofed, for the boards were carefully feather-edged and lapped, so that it was perfectly impervious to rain; but before boarding I laid the foundation of a chimney at one end, bringing two cartloads of stones up the hill from the pond in my arms. I built the chimney after my hoeing in the fall, before a fire became necessary for warmth, doing my cooking in the mean while out of doors on the ground, early in the morning: which mode I still think is in some respects more convenient and agreeable than the usual one. When it stormed before my bread was baked, I fixed a few boards over the fire, and sat under them to watch my loaf, and passed some pleasant hours in that way. In those days, when my hands were much employed, I read but little, but the least scraps of paper which lay on the ground, my holder, or table-cloth, afforded me as much entertainment, in fact answered the same purpose as the Iliad.

It would be worth the while to build still more deliberately than I did, considering, for instance, what foundation a door, a window, a cellar, a garret, have in the nature of man, and perchance never raising any superstructure until we found a better reason for it than our temporal necessities even. There is some of the same fitness in a man's building his own house that there is in a bird's building its own nest. Who knows but if men constructed their dwellings with their own hands, and provided food for themselves and families simply and honestly enough, the poetic faculty would be universally developed, as birds universally sing when they are so engaged? But alas! we do like cow-birds and cuckoos, which lay their eggs in nests which other birds have built, and cheer no traveller with their chattering and unmusical notes. Shall we forever resign the pleasure of construction to the carpenter? What does architecture amount to in the experience of the mass of men? I never in all my walks came across a man engaged in so simple and natural an occupation as building his house. We belong to the community. It is not the tailor alone who is the ninth part of a man, it is as much the preacher, and the merchant, and the farmer. Where is this division of labor to end? and what object does it finally serve? No doubt another *may* also think for me; but it is not therefore desirable that he should do so to the exclusion of my thinking for myself.

True, there are architects so called in this country, and I have heard of one at least possessed with the idea of making architectural orna-ments have a core of truth, a necessity, and hence a beauty, as if it were a revelation to him. All very well perhaps from his point of view, but only a little better than the common dilettantism. A sentimental re-former in architecture, he began at the cornice, not at the foundation. It was only how to put a core of truth within the ornaments, that every sugar plum in fact might have an almond or caraway seed in it,—though I hold that almonds are most wholesome without the sugar—and not how the inhabitant, the indweller, might build truly within and with-out, and let the ornaments take care of themselves. What reasonable man ever supposed that ornaments were something outward and in the skin merely,—that the tortoise got his spotted shell, or the shellfish its mother-o'-pearl tints by such a contract as the inhabitants of Broadway their Trinity Church? But a man has no more to do with the style of architecture of his house than a tortoise with that of its shell: nor need the soldier be so idle as to try to paint the precise *color* of his virtue on his standard. The enemy will find it out. He may turn pale when the trial comes. This man seemed to me to lean over the cornice, and timidly whisper his half truth to the rude occupants who really knew it better than he. What of architectural beauty I now see, I know has gradually grown from within outward, out of the necessities and character of the indweller, who is the only builder—out of some unconscious truthfulness, and nobleness, without ever a thought for the appearance; and whatever additional beauty of this kind is destined to be produced will be preceded by a like unconscious beauty of life. The most interesting dwellings in this country, as the painter knows, are the most unpretending, humble log huts and cottages of the poor commonly; it is the life of the inhabitants whose shells they are, and not any peculiarity in their surfaces, merely, which makes them *picturesque;* and equally interesting will be the citizen's suburban box, when his life shall be as simple and as agreeable to the imagination, and there is as little straining after effect in the style of his dwelling. A great proportion of architectural ornaments are literally hollow, and a September gale would strip them off, like borrowed plumes, without injury to the substantials. They can do without *architecture* who have no olives nor wines in the cellar. What if an equal ado were made about the ornaments of style in literature, and the architects of our bibles spent as much time about their cornices as the architects of our churches do? So are made the *belles-lettres* and the *beaux-arts* and their professors. Much it concerns a man, forsooth, how a few sticks are slanted over him or under him and what colors are daubed upon his box. It would signify somewhat, if, in any earnest sense, *he* slanted them and daubed it; but the spirit having departed out of the tenant, it is of a piece with constructing his own coffin,—the architecture of the grave, and "carpenter," is but another name for "coffin-maker." One man says, in his despair or indifference to life, take up a handful of the earth at your feet, and paint your house that color. Is he thinking of his last and narrow house? Toss up a copper for it as well. What an abundance of leisure he must have! Why do you take up a handful of dirt? Better paint your house your own complexion; let it turn pale or blush for you. An enterprise to improve the style of cottage architecture! When you have got my ornaments ready I will wear them.

Before winter I built a chimney, and shingled the sides of my house, which were already impervious to rain, with imperfect and sappy shingles made of the first slice of the log, whose edges I was obliged to straighten with a plane.

I have thus a tight shingled and plastered house, ten feet wide by   10
fifteen long, and eight-feet posts, with a garret and a closet, a large window on each side, two trap doors, one door at the end, and a brick fireplace opposite. The exact cost of my house, paying the usual price for such materials as I used, but not counting the work, all of which

was done by myself, was as follows; and I give the details because very few are able to tell exactly what their houses cost, and fewer still, if any, the separate cost of the various materials which compose them:—

Boards	$8 03½,	mostly shanty boards.
Refuse shingles for roof and sides,	4 00	
Laths,	1 25	
Two second-hand windows with glass,	2 43	
One thousand old brick,	4 00	
Two casks of lime,	2 40	That was high.
Hair,	0 31	More than I needed.
Mantle-tree iron,	0 15	
Nails,	3 90	
Hinges and screws,	0 14	
Latch,	0 10	
Chalk,	0 01	
Transportation,	1 40	I carried a good part on my back.
In all,	$28 12½	

These are all the materials excepting the timber, stones and sand, which I claimed by squatter's right. I have also a small wood-shed adjoining made chiefly of the stuff which was left after building the house.

I intend to build me a house which will surpass any on the main street in Concord in grandeur and luxury, as soon as it pleases me as much and will cost me no more than my present one.

I thus found that the student who wishes for a shelter can obtain one for a lifetime at an expense not greater than the rent which he now pays annually. If I seem to boast more than is becoming, my excuse is that I brag for humanity rather than for myself; and my shortcomings and inconsistencies do not affect the truth of my statement. Notwithstanding much cant and hypocrisy,—chaff which I find it difficult to separate from my wheat, but for which I am sorry as any man,—I will breathe freely and stretch myself in this respect, it is such a relief to both the moral and physical system; and I am resolved that I will not through humility become the devil's attorney. I will endeavor to speak a good word for the truth. At Cambridge College the mere rent of a student's room, which is only a little larger than my own, is thirty dollars each year, though the corporation had the advantage of building thirty-two side by side and under one roof, and the occupant suffers the inconvenience of many and noisy neighbors, and perhaps a residence in the fourth story. I cannot but think that if we had more true wisdom in these respects, not only less education would be needed,

because, forsooth, more would already have been acquired, but the pecuniary expense of getting an education would in a great measure vanish. Those conveniences which the student requires at Cambridge or
elsewhere cost him or somebody else ten times as great a sacrifice of
life as they would with proper management on both sides. Those things
for which the most money is demanded are never the things which the
student most wants. Tuition, for instance, is an important item in the
term bill, while for the far more valuable education which he gets by
associating with the most cultivated of his contemporaries no charge is
made. The mode of founding a college is, commonly, to get up a subscription of dollars, and cents, and then following blindly the principles
of a division of labor to its extreme, a principle which should never be
followed but with circumspection,—to call in a contractor who makes
this a subject of speculation, and he employs Irishmen or other opera-
tives actually to lay the foundation, while the students that are to be are
said to be fitting themselves for it; and for these oversights successive
generations have to pay. I think that it would be *better than this,* for the
students, or those who desire to be benefited by it, even to lay the
foundation themselves. The student who secures his coveted leisure and
retirement by systematically shirking any labor necessary to man obtains but an ignoble and unprofitable leisure, defrauding himself of the
experience which alone can make leisure fruitful. "But," says one, "you
do not mean that the students should go to work with their hands instead of their heads?" I do not mean that exactly, but I mean something
which he might think a good deal like that; I mean that they should not
play life, or *study* it merely, while the community supports them at this
expensive game, but earnestly *live* it from beginning to end. How could
youths better learn to live than by at once trying the experiment of
living? Methinks this would exercise their minds as much as mathematics. If I wished a boy to know something about the arts and sciences, for instance, I would not pursue the common course, which is
merely to send him into the neighborhood of some professor, where
any thing is professed and practised but the art of life;—to survey the
world through a telescope or a microscope, and never with his natural
eye; to study chemistry, and not learn how his bread is made, or mechanics, and not learn how it is earned; to discover new satellites to
Neptune, and not detect the motes in his eyes, or to what vagabond he
is a satellite himself; or to be devoured by the monsters that swarm all
around him, while contemplating the monsters in a drop of vinegar.
Which would have advanced the most at the end of a month,—the boy
who had made his own jackknife from the ore which he had dug and
smelted, reading as much as would be necessary for this,—or the boy
who had attended the lectures on metallurgy at the Institute in the mean
while, and had received a Rogers' penknife from his father? Which would
be most likely to cut his fingers? . . . To my astonishment I was

informed on leaving college that I had studied navigation!—why, if I had taken one turn down the harbor I should have known more about it. Even the *poor* student studies and is taught only *political* economy, while that economy of living which is synonymous with philosophy is not even sincerely professed in our colleges. The consequence is, that while he is reading Adam Smith, Ricardo, and Say, he runs his father in debt irretrievably.

LINES OF INQUIRY
"My House"

Throughout this piece about building his house, Thoreau repeatedly digresses from his account, sometimes briefly, sometimes lengthily, to tell about or reflect upon other topics. Why do you suppose he doesn't keep himself focused entirely on the report of his house-building? Make a note of all the points at which he digresses. What seems to trigger each of these digressions? How does he move back and forth between his account and these other topics without losing an overall sense of continuity?

How are these digressions related to each other? How are they related to Thoreau's house-building account? For example, what is the relationship between his lengthy reflections on architecture and college education, and how are these, in turn, related to the detailed financial record of his house-building costs that comes in between them? What point do you think Thoreau is trying to convey through the interplay between the account of his house and the other topics he discusses?

At the end of this piece, Thoreau criticizes the scientific teaching in his own time. For other views of scientific teaching, look at Eiseley's "The Hidden Teacher" or Baker's "The Cruelest Month." Based on your own experience in science courses, whose view of scientific instruction is most relevant to the problems you have observed?

WHERE I LIVED, AND WHAT I LIVED FOR

When first I took up my abode in the woods, that is, began to spend my nights as well as days there, which, by accident, was on Independence Day, or the Fourth of July, 1845, my house was not finished for winter, but was merely a defence against the rain, without plastering or chimney, the walls being of rough, weather-stained boards, with wide chinks, which made it cool at night. The upright white hewn studs and freshly planed door and window casings gave it a clean and airy look, especially in the morning, when its timbers were saturated with dew, so that I fancied that by noon some sweet gum would exude from them. To my imagination it retained throughout the day more or less of this auroral character, reminding me of a certain house on a mountain which I had visited a year before. This was an airy and unplastered cabin, fit to entertain a travelling god, and where a goddess might trail her garments. The winds which passed over my dwelling were such as sweep over the ridges of mountains, bearing the broken strains, or celestial parts only, of terrestrial music. The morning wind forever blows, the poem of creation is uninterrupted; but few are the ears that hear it. Olympus is but the outside of the earth everywhere.

The only house I had been the owner of before, if I except a boat, was a tent, which I used occasionally when making excursions in the summer, and this is still rolled up in my garret; but the boat, after passing from hand to hand, has gone down the stream of time. With this more substantial shelter about me, I had made some progress toward settling in the world. This frame, so slightly clad, was a sort of crystallization around me, and reacted on the builder. It was suggestive somewhat as a picture in outlines. I did not need to go out of doors to take the air, for the atmosphere within had lost none of its freshness. It was not so much within doors as being a door where I sat, even in the rainiest weather. The Harivansa[1] says, "An abode without birds is like a meat without seasoning." Such was not my abode, for I found myself suddenly neighbor to the birds; not by having imprisoned one, but having caged myself near them. I was not only nearer to some of those which commonly frequent the garden and the orchard, but to those wilder and more thrilling songsters of the forest which never, or rarely, serenade a villager,—the wood-thrush, the veery, the scarlet tanager, the field-sparrow, the whippoorwill, and many others.

---

[1] A fifth-century Hindu epic.

I was seated by the shore of a small pond, about a mile and half south of the village of Concord and somewhat higher than it, in the midst of an extensive wood between that town and Lincoln, and about two miles south of that our only field known to fame, Concord Battle Ground; but I was so low in the woods that the opposite shore, half a mile off, like the rest, covered with wood, was my most distant horizon. For the first week, whenever I looked out on the pond it impressed me like a tarn high up on the side of a mountain, its bottom far above the surface of other lakes, and, as the sun arose, I saw it throwing off its nightly clothing of mist, and here and there, by degrees, its soft ripples or its smooth reflecting surface was revealed, while the mists, like ghosts, were stealthily withdrawing in every direction into the woods, as at the breaking up of some nocturnal conventicle. The very dew seemed to hang upon the trees later into the day than usual, as on the sides of mountains.

This small lake was of most value as a neighbor in the intervals of a gentle rain-storm in August, when, both air and water being perfectly still, but the sky overcast, mid-afternoon had all the serenity of evening, and the wood thrush sang around, and was heard from shore to shore. A lake like this is never smoother than at such a time; and the clear portion of the air above it being shallow and darkened by clouds, the water, full of light and reflections, becomes a lower heaven itself so much the more important. From a hilltop near by, where the wood had been recently cut off, there was a pleasing vista southward across the pond, through a wide indentation in the hills which form the shore there, where their opposite sides sloping toward each other suggested a stream flowing out in that direction through a wooded valley, but stream there was none. That way I looked between and over the near green hills to some distant and higher ones in the horizon, tinged with blue. Indeed, by standing on tiptoe I could catch a glimpse of some of the peaks of the still bluer and more distant mountain ranges in the northwest, those true-blue coins from heaven's own mint, and also of some portion of the village. But in other directions, even from this point, I could not see over or beyond the woods which surrounded me. It is well to have some water in your neighborhood, to give buoyancy to and float the earth. One value even of the smallest well is, that when you look into it you see that earth is not continent but insular. This is as important as that it keeps butter cool. When I looked across the pond from this peak toward the Sudbury meadows, which in time of flood I distinguished elevated perhaps by a mirage in their seething valley, like a coin in a basin, all the earth beyond the pond appeared like a thin crust insulated and floated even by this small sheet of intervening water, and I was reminded that this on which I dwelt was but *dry land*.

Though the view from my door was still more contracted, I did not feel crowded or confined in the least. There was pasture enough for my   5 imagination. The low shrub oak plateau to which the opposite shore arose stretched away toward the prairies of the West and the steppes of Tartary, affording ample room for all the roving families of men. "There are none happy in the world but beings who enjoy freely a vast horizon,"—said Damodara,[2] when his herds required new and larger pastures.

Both place and time were changed, and I dwelt nearer to those parts of the universe and to those eras in history which had most attracted me. Where I lived was as far off as many a region viewed nightly by astronomers. We are wont to imagine rare and delectable places in some remote and more celestial corner of the system, behind the constellation of Cassiopeia's Chair, far from noise and disturbance. I discovered that my house actually had its site in such a withdrawn, but forever new and unprofaned, part of the universe. If it were worth the while to settle in those parts near to the Pleiades or the Hyades, to Aldebaran or Altair,[3] then I was really there, or at an equal remoteness from the life which I had left behind, divided and twinkling with as fine a ray to my nearest neighbor, and to be seen only in moonless nights by him. Such was that part of creation where I had squatted;—

> "There was a shepherd that did live,
>   And held his thoughts as high
> As were the mounts whereon his flocks
>   Did hourly feed him by."

What should we think of the shepherd's life if his flocks always wandered to higher pastures than his thoughts?

Every morning was a cheerful invitation to make my life of equal simplicity, and I may say innocence, with Nature herself. I have been as sincere a worshipper of Aurora[4] as the Greeks. I got up early and bathed in the pond; that was a religious exercise, and one of the best things which I did. They say that characters were engraven on the bathing tub of King Tchingthang[5] to this effect—"Renew thyself completely each day; do it again, and again, and forever again." I can understand that. Morning brings back the heroic ages. I was as much affected by the faint hum of a mosquito making its invisible and unimaginable tour through my apartment at earliest dawn, when I was sitting with door and windows open, as I could be by any trumpet that ever sang of fame. It was Homer's requiem; itself an Iliad and Odyssey in the air, singing its own wrath and wanderings. There was something

---

[2]Krishna, in the Hindu religion, is the incarnation of the God Vishnu.
[3]Names of stars and constellations.
[4]The classical goddess of dawn.
[5]Confucius (551–479 B.C.) was China's greatest sage.

cosmical about it; a standing advertisement, till forbidden, of the everlasting vigor and fertility of the world. The morning, which is the most memorable season of the day, is the awakening hour. Then there is least somnolence in us; and for an hour, at least, some part of us awakes which slumbers all the rest of the day and night. Little is to be expected of that day, if it can be called a day, to which we are not awakened by our Genius, but by the mechanical nudgings of some servitor, are not awakened by our own newly acquired force and aspirations from within, accompanied by the undulations of celestial music, instead of factory bells, and a fragrance filling the air—to a higher life than we fell asleep from; and thus the darkness bear its fruit, and prove itself to be good, no less than the light. The man who does not believe that each day contains an earlier, more sacred, and auroral hour than he has yet profaned, has despaired of life, and is pursuing a descending and darkening way. After a partial cessation of his sensuous life, the soul of man, or its organs rather, are reinvigorated each day, and his Genius tries again what noble life it can make. All memorable events, I should say, transpire in morning time and in a morning atmosphere. The Vedas[6] say, "All intelligences awake with the morning." Poetry and art, and the fairest and most memorable of the actions of men, date from such an hour. All poets and heroes, like Memmon,[7] are the children of Aurora, and emit their music at sunrise. To him whose elastic and vigorous thought keeps pace with the sun, the day is a perpetual morning. It matters not what the clocks say or the attitudes and labors of men. Morning is when I am awake and there is a dawn in me. Moral reform is the effort to throw off sleep. Why is it that men give so poor an account of their day if they have not been slumbering? They are not such poor calculators. If they had not been overcome with drowsiness, they would have performed something. The millions are awake enough for physical labor; but only one in a million is awake enough for effective intellectual exertion, only one in a hundred millions to a poetic or divine life. To be awake is to be alive. I have never yet met a man who was quite awake. How could I have looked him in the face?

We must learn to reawaken and keep ourselves awake, not by mechanical aids, but by an infinite expectation of the dawn, which does not forsake us in our soundest sleep. I know of no more encouraging fact than the unquestionable ability of man to elevate his life by a conscious endeavor. It is something to be able to paint a particular picture, or to carve a statue, and so to make a few objects beautiful; but it is far more glorious to carve and paint the very atmosphere and medium through which we look, which morally we can do. To affect the qual-

---

[6] Ancient Hindu scriptures.
[7] At Thebes the statue of Memmon was said to emit music at dawn.

ity of the day, that is the highest of arts. Every man is tasked to make his life, even in its details, worthy of the contemplation of his most elevated and critical hour. If we refused, or rather used up, such paltry information as we get, the oracles would distinctly inform us how this might be done.

I went to the woods because I wished to live deliberately, to front only the essential facts of life, and see if I could not learn what it had to teach, and not, when I came to die, discover that I had not lived. I did not wish to live what was not life, living is so dear, nor did I wish to practice resignation, unless it was quite necessary. I wanted to live deep and suck out all the marrow of life, to live so sturdily and Spartan-like as to put to rout all that was not life, to cut a broad swath and shave close, to drive life into a corner, and reduce it to its lowest terms, and, if it proved to be mean, why then to get the whole and genuine meanness of it, and publish its meanness to the world; or it if were sublime, to know it by experience, and be able to give a true account of it in my next excursion. For most men, it appears to me, are in a strange uncertainty about it, whether it is of the devil or of God and have *somewhat hastily* concluded that it is the chief end of man here to "glorify God and enjoy him forever."

Still we live meanly, like ants; though the fable tells us that we were   10 long ago changed into men; like pygmies we fight with cranes; it is error upon error, and clout upon clout, and our best virtue has for its occasion a superfluous and evitable wretchedness. Our life is frittered away by detail. An honest man has hardly need to count more than his ten fingers, or in extreme cases he may add his ten toes, and lump the rest. Simplicity, simplicity, simplicity! I say, let your affairs be as two or three, and not a hundred or a thousand; instead of a million count half a dozen, and keep your accounts on your thumb-nail. In the midst of this chopping sea of civilized life, such are the clouds and storms and quicksands and thousand-and-one items to be allowed for, that a man has to live, if he would not founder and go to the bottom and not make his port at all, by dead reckoning, and he must be a great calculator indeed who succeeds. Simplify, simplify. Instead of three meals a day, if it be necessary eat but one; instead of a hundred dishes, five; and reduce other things in proportion. Our life is like a German Confeder-acy, made up of petty states, with its boundary forever fluctuating, so that even a German cannot tell you how it is bounded at any moment. The nation itself, with all its so-called internal improvements, which, by the way, are all external and superficial, is just such an unwieldy and overgrown establishment, cluttered with furniture and tripped up by its own traps, ruined by luxury and heedless expense, by want of calcula-tion and a worthy aim, as the million households in the land; and the only cure for it, as for them, is in a rigid economy, a stern and more than Spartan simplicity of life and elevation of purpose. It lives too fast.

Men think that it is essential that the *Nation* have commerce, and export ice, and talk through a telegraph, and ride thirty miles an hour, without a doubt, whether *they* do or not; but whether we should live like baboons or like men, is a little uncertain. If we do not get out sleepers,[8] and forge rails, and devote days and nights to the work, but go to tinkering upon our *lives* to improve *them,* who will build railroads? And if railroads are not built, how shall we get to Heaven in season? But if we stay at home and mind our business, who will want railroads? We do not ride on the railroad; it rides upon us. Did you ever think what those sleepers are that underlie the railroad? Each one is a man, an Irishman, or a Yankee man. The rails are laid on them, and they are covered with sand, and the cars run smoothly over them. They are sound sleepers, I assure you. And every few years a new lot is laid down and run over; so that, if some have the pleasure of riding on a rail, others have the misfortune to be ridden upon. And when they run over a man that is walking in his sleep, a supernumerary sleeper in the wrong position, and wake him up, they suddenly stop the cars, and make a hue and cry about it, as if this were an exception. I am glad to know that it takes a gang of men for every five miles to keep the sleepers down and level in their beds as it is, for this is a sign that they may sometime get up again.

Why should we live with such hurry and waste of life? We are determined to be starved before we are hungry. Men say that a stitch in time saves nine, and so they take a thousand stitches to-day to save nine tomorrow. As for *work,* we haven't any of any consequence. We have the Saint Vitus' dance, and cannot possibly keep our heads still. If I should only give a few pulls at the parish bell-rope, as for a fire, that is, without setting the bell, there is hardly a man on his farm in the outskirts of Concord, notwithstanding that press of engagements which was his excuse so many times this morning, nor a boy, nor a woman, I might almost say, but would forsake all and follow that sound, not mainly to save property from the flames, but, if we will confess the truth, much more to see it burn, since burn it must, and we, be it known, did not set it on fire,—or to see it put out, and have a hand in it, if that is done as handsomely; yes, even if it were the parish church itself. Hardly a man takes a half-hour's nap after dinner, but when he wakes he holds up his head and asks, "What's the news?" as if the rest of mankind had stood his sentinels. Some give directions to be waked every half-hour, doubtless for no other purpose; and then, to pay for it, they tell what they have dreamed. After a night's sleep the news is as indispensable as the breakfast. "Pray tell me anything new that has happened to a man anywhere on this globe,"—and he reads it over his

---

[8]Railroad ties.

coffee and rolls, that a man has had his eyes gouged out this morning on the Wachito River, never dreaming the while that he lives in the dark unfathomed mammoth cave of this world, and has but the rudiment of an eye himself.

For my part, I could easily do without the post-office. I think that there are very few important communications made through it. To speak critically, I never received more than one or two letters in my life—I wrote this some years ago—that were worth the postage. The penny-post is, commonly, an institution through which you seriously offer a man that penny for his thoughts which is so often safely offered in jest. And I am sure that I never read any memorable news in a newspaper. If we read of one man robbed, or murdered, or killed by accident, or one house burned, or one vessel wrecked, or one steamboat blown up, or one cow run over on the Western Railroad, or one mad dog killed, or one lot of grasshoppers in the winter,—we never read of another. One is enough. If you are acquainted with the principle, what do you care for a myriad instances and applications? To a philosopher all *news,* as it is called, is gossip and they who edit and read it are old women over their tea. Yet not a few are greedy after this gossip. There was such a rush, as I hear, the other day at one of the offices to learn the foreign news by the last arrival, that several large squares of plate glass belonging to the establishment were broken by the pressure,—news which I seriously think a ready wit might write a twelvemonth, or twelve years, beforehand with sufficient accuracy. As for Spain, for instance, if you know how to throw in Don Carlos and the Infanta, and Don Pedro and Seville and Granada, from time to time in the right proportions,—they may have changed the names a little since I saw the papers,—and serve up a bull-fight when other entertainments fail, it will be true to the letter, and give us as good an idea of the exact state of ruin of things in Spain as the most succinct and lucid reports under this head in the newspapers: and as for England, almost the last significant scrap of news from that quarter was the revolution of 1649,[9] and if you have learned the history of her crops for an average year, you never need attend to that thing again, unless your speculations are of a merely pecuniary character. If one may judge who rarely looks into the newspapers, nothing new does ever happen in foreign parts, a French revolution not excepted.

What news! how much more important to know what that is which was never old! "Kieou-he-yu (great dignitary of the state of Wei) sent a man to Khoung-tseu to know his news. Khoung-tseu caused the messenger to be seated near him, and questioned him in these terms: What

---

[9]The English monarchy was overthrown and Charles I executed by the Puritans in 1649.

is your master doing? The messenger answered with respect: My master desires to diminish the number of his faults, but he cannot come to the end of them. The messenger being gone, the philosopher remarked: 'What a worthy messenger! What a worthy messenger!' " The preacher, instead of vexing the ears of drowsy farmers on their day of rest at the end of the week,—for Sunday is the fit conclusion of an ill-spent week, and not the fresh and brave beginning of a new one,—with this one other draggle-tail of a sermon, should shout with thundering voice, "Pause! Avast! Why so seeming fast, but deadly slow?"

Shams and delusions are esteemed for soundest truths, while reality is fabulous. If men would steadily observe realities only, and not allow themselves to be deluded, life, to compare it with such things as we know, would be like a fairy tale and the Arabian Nights' Entertainments. If we respected only what is inevitable and has a right to be, music and poetry would resound along the streets. When we are unhurried and wise, we perceive that only great and worthy things have any permanent and absolute existence, that petty fears and petty pleasures are but the shadow of the reality. This is always exhilarating and sublime. By closing the eyes and slumbering, and consenting to be deceived by shows, men establish and confirm their daily life of routine and habit everywhere, which still is built on purely illusory foundations. Children, who play life, discern its true law and relations more clearly than men, who fail to live it worthily, but who think that they are wiser by experience, that is, by failure. I have read in a Hindoo book, that "there was a king's son, who, being expelled in infancy from his native city, was brought up by a forester, and growing up to maturity in that state, imagined himself to belong to the barbarous race with which he lived. One of his father's ministers having discovered him, revealed to him what he was, and the misconception of his character was removed, and he knew himself to be a prince. So soul," continues the Hindoo philosopher, "from the circumstances in which it is placed, mistakes its own character, until the truth is revealed to it by some holy teacher, and then it knows itself to be *Brahma*." I perceive that we inhabitants of New England live this mean life that we do because our vision does not penetrate the surface of things. We think that that *is* which *appears* to be. If a man should walk through this town and see only the reality, where, think you, would the "Mill-dam" go to? If he should give us an account of the realities he beheld there, we should not recognize the place in his description. Look at a meeting-house, or a court-house, or a jail, or a shop, or a dwelling-house, and say what that thing really is before a true gaze, and they would all go to pieces in your account of them. Men esteem truth remote, in the outskirts of the system, behind the farthest star, before Adam and after the last man. In eternity there is indeed something true and sublime. But all these times and places and occasions are now and here. God himself culminates in the present moment, and will never be more divine in the lapse of all the ages. And we are enabled to apprehend at all what is sublime and noble only by the perpetual instilling and drenching of the reality that surrounds us. The universe constantly and obediently answers to our conceptions; whether we travel fast or slow, the track is laid for us. Let us spend our lives in conceiving then. The poet or the artist never yet had so fair and noble a design but some of his posterity at least could accomplish it.

Let us spend one day as deliberately as Nature, and not be thrown off the track by every nutshell and mosquito's wing that falls on the rails. Let us rise early and fast, or break fast, gently and without perturbation; let company come and let company go, let the bells ring and the children cry,—determined to make a day of it. Why should we knock under and go with the stream? Let us not be upset and overwhelmed in that terrible rapid and whirlpool called a dinner, situated in the meridian shallows. Weather this danger and you are safe, for the rest of the way is down hill. With unrelaxed nerves, with morning vigor, sail by it, looking another way, tied to the mast like Ulysses. If the engine whistles, let it whistle till it is hoarse for its pains. If the bell rings, why should we run? We will consider what kind of music they are like. Let us settle ourselves, and work and wedge our feet downward through the mud and slush of opinion, and prejudice, and tradition, and delusion, and appearance, that alluvion which covers the globe, through Paris and London, through New York and Boston and Concord, through Church and State, through poetry and philosophy and religion, till we come to a hard bottom and rocks in place, which we can call *reality,* and say, This is, and no mistake; and then begin, having a *point d'appui,*[10] below freshet and frost and fire, a place where you might found a wall or a state, or set a lamp-post safely, or perhaps a gauge, not a Nilometer,[11] but a Realometer, that future ages might know how deep a freshet of shams and appearances had gathered from time to time. If you stand right fronting and face to face to a fact, you will see the sun glimmer on both its surfaces, as if it were a cimeter,[12] and feel its sweet edge dividing you through the heart and marrow, and so you will happily conclude your mortal career. Be it life or death, we crave only reality. If we are really dying, let us hear the rattle in our throats and feel cold in the extremities; if we are alive, let us go about our business.

Time is but the stream I go a-fishing in. I drink at it; but while I drink I see the sandy bottom and detect how shallow it is. Its thin

15

---

[10] A point of support or foundation.
[11] A device to measure the water level in the Nile River.
[12] A curved sword.

current slides away, but eternity remains. I would drink deeper; fish in the sky, whose bottom is pebbly with stars. I cannot count one. I know not the first letter of the alphabet. I have always been regretting that I was not as wise as the day I was born. The intellect is a cleaver; it discerns and rifts its way into the secret of things. I do not wish to be any more busy with my hands than is necessary. My head is hands and feet. I feel all my best faculties concentrated in it. My instinct tells me that my head is an organ for burrowing, as some creatures use their snout and fore paws, and with it I would mine and burrow my way through these hills. I think that the richest vein is somewhere hereabouts; so by the divining-rod and thin rising vapors I judge; and here I will begin to mine.

LINES OF INQUIRY
"Where I Lived, and What I Lived For"

In this piece, Thoreau contrasts his life in the woods with life elsewhere in mid-nineteenth-century America. Notice the various ways in which he organizes and develops this contrast. What kinds of details does he focus on in the first half of the piece when he describes his life in the woods; what kinds does he focus on in the second half when he describes life elsewhere? How would you characterize his style, tone of voice, and attitude in the first half? In the second half?

Notice all the instances in which "life," "to live," or some other form of these words appears in this piece, particularly in the second half. What do these words mean to Thoreau? What does he mean, for example, when he says, "I wished to live deliberately, to front only the essential facts of life, and see if I could not learn what it had to teach, and not, when I came to die, discover that I had not lived. I did not wish to live what was not life, living is so dear"? In other words, what is Thoreau's idea of life? What is his idea of not living?

This piece from the second chapter of *Walden* clearly relates to the previous piece about Thoreau's house-building from the first chapter of *Walden,* if only because his house in the woods figures in both selections. In what respects are they concerned with related topics and ideas, in what respects with different topics and ideas? In what respects do they involve similar styles of writing and modes of presentation, and in what respects different styles and modes of presentation? How do you account for the differences?

THE WAR OF THE ANTS

One day when I went out to my wood-pile, or rather my pile of stumps, I observed two large ants, the one red, the other much larger, nearly half an inch long, and black, fiercely contending with one another. Having once got hold they never let go, but struggled and wrestled and rolled on the chips incessantly. Looking farther, I was surprised to find that the chips were covered with such combatants, that it was not a *duellum,* but a *bellum,* a war between two races of ants, the red always pitted against the black, and frequently two red ones to one black. The legions of these Myrmidons covered all the hills and vales in my wood-yard, and the ground was already strewn with the dead and dying, both red and black. It was the only battle which I have ever witnessed, the only battle-field I ever trod while the battle was raging; internecine war; the red republicans on the one hand, and the black imperialists on the other. On every side they were engaged in deadly combat, yet without any noise that I could hear, and human soldiers never fought so resolutely. I watched a couple that were fast locked in each other's embraces, in a little sunny valley amid the chips, now at noonday prepared to fight till the sun went down, or life went out. The smaller red champion had fastened himself like a vise to his adversary's front, and through all the tumblings on that field never for an instant ceased to gnaw at one of his feelers near the root, having already caused the other to go by the board; while the stronger black one dashed him from side to side, and, as I saw on looking nearer, had already divested him of several of his members. They fought with more pertinacity than bulldogs. Neither manifested the least disposition to retreat. It was evident that their battle-cry was "Conquer or die." In the meanwhile there came along a single red ant on the hillside of this valley, evidently full of excitement, who either had despatched his foe, or had not yet taken part in the battle; probably the latter, for he had lost none of his limbs; whose mother had charged him to return with his shield or upon it. Or perchance he was some Achilles, who had nourished his wrath apart, and had now come to avenge or rescue his Patroclus. He saw this unequal combat from afar,—for the blacks were nearly twice the size of the red,—he drew near with rapid pace till he stood on his guard within half an inch of the combatants; then, watching his opportunity, he sprang upon the black warrior, and commenced his operations near the root of his right fore leg, leaving the foe to select among his own members; so there were three united for life, as if a new kind of attraction had been invented which put all other locks and cements to shame. I should not have wondered by this time to find that they had their respective musical bands stationed on some eminent chip, and playing their national airs the while, to excite the slow and cheer the dying combatants. I was myself excited somewhat even as if they had been men. The more you think of it, the less the difference. And certainly there is not the fight recorded in Concord history, at least, if in the history of America, that will bear a moment's comparison with this, whether for the numbers engaged in it, or for the patriotism and heroism displayed. For numbers and for carnage it was an Austerlitz or Dresden. Concord fight! Two killed on the patriots' side, and Luther Blanchard wounded! Why here every ant was a Buttrick,—"Fire! for God's sake fire!"—and thousands shared the fate of Davis and Hosmer. There was not one hireling there. I have no doubt that it was a principle they fought for, as much as our ancestors, and not to avoid a three-penny tax on their tea; and the results of this battle will be as important and memorable to those whom it concerns as those of the battle of Bunker Hill, at least.

I took up the chip on which the three I have particularly described were struggling, carried it into my house, and placed it under a tumbler on my window-sill, in order to see the issue. Holding a microscope to the first-mentioned red ant, I saw that, though he was assiduously gnawing at the near fore leg of his enemy, having severed his remaining feeler, his own breast was all torn away, exposing what vitals he had there to the jaws of the black warrior, whose breastplate was apparently too thick for his to pierce; and the dark carbuncles of the sufferer's eyes shone with ferocity such as war only could excite. They struggled half an hour longer under the tumbler, and when I looked again the black soldier had severed the heads of his foes from their bodies, and the still living heads were hanging on either side off him like ghastly trophies at his saddle-bow, still apparently as firmly fastened as ever, and he was endeavoring with feeble struggles, being without feelers, and with only the remnant of a leg, and I know not how many other wounds, to divest himself of them; which at length, after half an hour or more, he accomplished. I raised the glass, and he went off over the window-sill in that crippled state. Whether he finally survived that combat, and spent the remainder of his days in some Hôtel des Invalides, I do not know; but I thought that his industry would not be worth much thereafter. I never learned which party was victorious, nor the cause of the war; but I felt for the rest of that day as if I had had my feelings excited and harrowed by witnessing the struggle, the ferocity and carnage, of a human battle before my door.

Kirby and Spence tell us that the battles of ants have long been celebrated and the date of them recorded, though they say that Huber is the only modern author who appears to have witnessed them. "Æneas Sylvius," say they, "after giving a very circumstantial account of one contested with great obstinacy by a great and small species on the trunk of a pear tree," adds that " 'this action was fought in the pontificate of Eugenius the Fourth, in the presence of Nicholas Pistoriensis, an eminent lawyer, who related the whole history of the battle with the greatest fidelity.' A similar engagement between great and small ants is recorded by Olaus Magnus, in which the small ones, being victorious, are said to have buried the bodies of their own soldiers, but left those of their giant enemies a prey to the birds. This event happened previous to the expulsion of the tyrant Christiern the Second from Sweden." The battle which I witnessed took place in the Presidency of Polk, five years before the passage of Webster's Fugitive-Slave Bill.

LINES OF INQUIRY
"The War of the Ants"

Throughout this piece, Thoreau repeatedly compares the conflict among the ants to human warfare, alluding in the process to a variety of wars and warriors, from classical Greek literature to colonial American history. Examine the piece carefully in order to identify all of the words and phrases that contribute implicitly or explicitly to this extended analogy. What do you think he wanted to convey through this extended analogy? Why do you think he ends this piece about the ants by referring to other written accounts of warfare among ants?

Brief though it is, this piece on the ants offers a highly detailed description of conflict among creatures who are ordinarily considered to be highly social beings. What do you suppose was Thoreau's main purpose in making so detailed a description of the conflict? Do you think he was primarily concerned with making an observation about the behavior of ants? Or about the nature of war? Or about racial conflict? Or do you suppose he had some other subject uppermost in mind? Whatever you take his primary subject to be, what do you think he was trying to say about it through this description?

This essay-like piece is actually an excerpt from Chapter 12 of Thoreau's *Walden*. Read that chapter, and you will see that it includes detailed descriptions of activities not only among ants, but also among several other natural creatures—squirrels, otters, partridges, cats, and loons. Based on your reading of that chapter, what do you believe to be Thoreau's main purpose for describing the ants in the context of these other creatures?

CIVIL DISOBEDIENCE[1]

I heartily accept the motto, "That government is best which governs least"; and I should like to see it acted up to more rapidly and systematically. Carried out, it finally amounts to this, which also I believe,—"That government is best which governs not at all"; and when men are prepared for it, that will be the kind of government which they will have. Government is at best but an expedient; but most governments are usually, and all governments are sometimes, inexpedient. The objections which have been brought against a standing army, and they are many and weighty, and deserve to prevail, may also at last be brought against a standing government. The standing army is only an arm of the standing government. The government itself, which is only the mode which the people have chosen to execute their will, is equally liable to be abused and perverted before the people can act through it. Witness the present Mexican war, the work of comparatively a few individuals using the standing government as their tool; for, in the outset, the people would not have consented to this measure.

This American government,—what is it but a tradition, though a recent one, endeavoring to transmit itself unimpaired to posterity, but each instant losing some of its integrity? It has not the vitality and force of a single living man; for a single man can bend it to his will. It is a sort of wooden gun to the people themselves. But it is not the less necessary for this; for the people must have some complicated machinery or other, and hear its din, to satisfy that idea of government which they have. Governments show thus how successfully men can be imposed on, even impose on themselves, for their own advantage. It is excellent, we must all allow. Yet this government never of itself furthered any enterprise, but by the alacrity with which it got out of its way. *It* does not keep the country free. *It* does not settle the West. *It* does not educate. The character inherent in the American people has done all that has been accomplished; and it would have done somewhat more, if the government had not sometimes got in its way. For government is an expedient by which men would fain succeed in letting one another alone; and, as has been said, when it is most expedient, the

---

[1]The episode that prompted this essay occurred in the summer of 1846. Thoreau had not paid his poll tax since 1841, apparently to make a test case of the poll-tax law, but his Aunt Maria paid the tax for him, so the only case left to Thoreau was rhetorical.—Ed.

governed are most let alone by it. Trade and commerce, if they were not made of india-rubber, would never manage to bounce over the obstacles which legislators are continually putting in their way; and, if one were to judge these men wholly by the effects of their actions and not partly by their intentions, they would deserve to be classed and punished with those mischievous persons who put obstructions on the railroads.

But, to speak practically and as a citizen, unlike those who call themselves no-government men, I ask for, not at once no government, but *at once* a better government. Let every man make known what kind of government would command his respect, and that will be one step toward obtaining it.

After all, the practical reason why, when the power is once in the hands of the people, a majority are permitted, and for a long period continue, to rule is not because they are most likely to be in the right, nor because this seems fairest to the minority, but because they are physically the strongest. But a government in which the majority rule in all cases cannot be based on justice, even as far as men understand it. Can there not be a government in which majorities do not virtually decide right and wrong, but conscience?—in which majorities decide only those questions to which the rule of expediency is applicable? Must the citizen ever for a moment, or in the least degree, resign his conscience to the legislator? Why has every man a conscience, then? I think that we should be men first, and subjects afterward. It is not desirable to cultivate a respect for the law, so much as for the right. The only obligation which I have a right to assume is to do at any time what I think right. It is truly enough said that a corporation has no conscience; but a corporation of conscientious men is a corporation *with* a conscience. Law never made men a whit more just; and, by means of their respect for it, even the well-disposed are daily made the agents of injustice. A common and natural result of an undue respect for law is, that you may see a file of soldiers, colonel, captain, corporal, privates, powder-monkeys, and all, marching in admirable order over hill and dale to the wars, against their wills, ay, against their common sense and consciences, which makes it very steep marching indeed, and produces a palpitation of the heart. They have no doubt that it is a damnable business in which they are concerned; they are all peaceably inclined. Now, what are they? Men at all? or small movable forts and magazines, at the service of some unscrupulous man in power? Visit the Navy-Yard, and behold a marine, such a man as an American government can make, or such as it can make a man with its black arts,—a mere shadow and reminiscence of humanity, a man laid out alive and standing, and already, as one may say, buried under arms with funeral accompaniments, though it may be,—

"Not a drum was heard, not a funeral note,
  As his corse to the rampart we hurried;
Not a soldier discharged his farewell shot
  O'er the grave where our hero we buried."

The mass of men serve the state thus, not as men mainly, but as machines, with their bodies. They are the standing army, and the militia, jailers, constables, *posse comitatus,* etc. In most cases there is no free exercise whatever of the judgment or of the moral sense; but they put themselves on a level with wood and earth and stones; and wooden men can perhaps be manufactured that will serve the purpose as well. Such command no more respect than men of straw or a lump of dirt. They have the same sort of worth only as horses and dogs. Yet such as these even are commonly esteemed good citizens. Others—as most legislators, politicians, lawyers, ministers, and office-holders—serve the state chiefly with their heads; and, as they rarely make any moral distinctions, they are as likely to serve the devil, without *intending* it, as God. A very few—as heroes, patriots, martyrs, reformers in the great sense, and *men*—serve the state with their consciences also, and so necessarily resist it for the most part; and they are commonly treated as enemies by it. A wise man will only be useful as a man, and will not submit to be "clay," and "stop a hole to keep the wind away," but leave that office to his dust at least:—

"I am too high-born to be propertied,
  To be a secondary at control,
  Or useful serving-man and instrument
To any sovereign state throughout the world."

He who gives himself entirely to his fellow-men appears to them useless and selfish; but he who gives himself partially to them is pronounced a benefactor and philanthropist.

How does it become a man to behave toward this American government to-day? I answer, that he cannot without disgrace be associated with it. I cannot for an instant recognize that political organization as *my* government which is the *slave*'s government also.

All men recognize the right of revolution; that is, the right to refuse allegiance to, and to resist, the government, when its tyranny or its inefficiency are great and unendurable. But almost all say that such is not the case now. But such was the case, they think, in the Revolution of '75. If one were to tell me that this was a bad government because it taxed certain foreign commodities brought to its port, it is most probable that I should not make an ado about it, for I can do without them. All machines have their friction; and possibly this does enough good to counterbalance the evil. At any rate, it is a great evil to make a stir about it. But when the friction comes to have its machine, and oppression and robbery are organized, I say, let us not have such a machine any longer. In other words, when a sixth of the population of a nation which has undertaken to be the refuge of liberty are slaves, and a whole country is unjustly overrun and conquered by a foreign army, and subjected to military law, I think that it is not too soon for honest men to rebel and revolutionize. What makes this duty the more urgent is the fact that the country so overrun is not our own, but ours is the invading army.

Paley, a common authority with many on moral questions, in his chapter on the "Duty of Submission to Civil Government," resolves all civil obligation into expediency; and he proceeds to say that

> so long as the interest of the whole society requires it, that is, so long as the established government cannot be resisted or changed without public inconveniency, it is the will of God . . . that the established government be obeyed,—and no longer. This principle being admitted, the justice of every particular case of resistance is reduced to a computation of the quantity of the danger and grievance on the one side, and of the probability and expense of redressing it on the other.

Of this, he says, every man shall judge for himself. But Paley appears never to have contemplated those cases to which the rule of expediency does not apply, in which a people, as well as an individual, must do justice, cost what it may. If I have unjustly wrested a plank from a drowning man, I must restore it to him though I drown myself. This, according to Paley, would be inconvenient. But he that would save his life, in such a case, shall lose it. This people must cease to hold slaves, and to make war on Mexico, though it cost them their existence as a people.

In their practice, nations agree with Paley; but does any one think   10
that Massachusetts does exactly what is right at the present crisis?

> "A drab of state, a cloth-o'-silver slut,
>   To have her train borne up, and her soul trail in the dirt."

Practically speaking, the opponents to a reform in Massachusetts are not a hundred thousand politicians at the South, but a hundred thousand merchants and farmers here, who are more interested in commerce and agriculture than they are in humanity, and are not prepared to do justice to the slave and to Mexico, *cost what it may*. I quarrel not with far-off foes, but with those who, near at home, cooperate with, and do the bidding of, those far away, and without whom the latter would be harmless. We are accustomed to say, that the mass of men are unprepared; but improvement is slow, because the few are not materially wiser or better than the many. It is not so important that many should be as good as you, as that there be some absolute goodness somewhere;

for that will leaven the whole lump. There are thousands who are *in opinion* opposed to slavery and to the war, who yet in effect do nothing to put an end to them; who, esteeming themselves children of Washington and Franklin, sit down with their hands in their pockets, and say that they know not what to do, and do nothing; who even postpone the question of freedom to the question of free trade, and quietly read the prices-current along with the latest advices from Mexico, after dinner, and, it may be, fall asleep over them both. What is the price-current of an honest man and patriot to-day? They hesitate, and they regret, and sometimes they petition; but they do nothing in earnest and with effect. They will wait, well disposed, for others to remedy the evil, that they may no longer have it to regret. At most, they give only a cheap vote, and a feeble countenance and God-speed, to the right, as it goes by them. There are nine hundred and ninety-nine patrons of virtue to one virtuous man. But it is easier to deal with the real possessor of a thing than with the temporary guardian of it.

All voting is a sort of gaming, like checkers or backgammon, with a slight moral tinge to it, a playing with right and wrong, with moral questions; and betting naturally accompanies it. The character of the voters is not staked. I cast my vote, perchance, as I think right; but I am not vitally concerned that that right should prevail. I am willing to leave it to the majority. Its obligation, therefore, never exceeds that of expediency. Even voting *for the right* is *doing* nothing for it. It is only expressing to men feebly your desire that it should prevail. A wise man will not leave the right to the mercy of chance, nor wish it to prevail through the power of the majority. There is but little virtue in the action of masses of men. When the majority shall at length vote for the abolition of slavery, it will be because they are indifferent to slavery, or because there is but little slavery left to be abolished by their vote. *They* will then be the only slaves. Only *his* vote can hasten the abolition of slavery who asserts his own freedom by his vote.

I hear of a convention to be held at Baltimore, or elsewhere, for the selection of a candidate for the Presidency, made up chiefly of editors, and men who are politicians by profession; but I think, what is it to any independent, intelligent, and respectable man what decision they may come to? Shall we not have the advantage of his wisdom and honesty, nevertheless? Can we not count upon some independent votes? Are there not many individuals in the country who do not attend conventions? But no: I find that the respectable man, so called, has immediately drifted from his position, and despairs of his country, when his country has more reason to despair of him. He forthwith adopts one of the candidates thus selected as the only *available* one, thus proving that he is himself *available* for any purposes of the demagogue. His vote is of no more worth than that of any unprincipled foreigner or hireling native, who may have been bought. O for a man who is a *man,* and, as my neighbor says, has a bone in his back which you cannot pass your hand through! Our statistics are at fault: the population has been returned too large. How many *men* are there to a square thousand miles in this country? Hardly one. Does not America offer any inducement for men to settle here? The American has dwindled into an Odd Fellow,—one who may be known by the development of his organ of gregariousness, and a manifest lack of intellect and cheerful self-reliance; whose first and chief concern, on coming into the world, is to see that the almshouses are in good repair; and, before yet he has lawfully donned the virile garb, to collect a fund for the support of the widows and orphans that may be; who, in short, ventures to live only by the aid of the Mutual Insurance company, which has promised to bury him decently.

It is not a man's duty, as a matter of course, to devote himself to the eradication of any, even the most enormous, wrong; he may still properly have other concerns to engage him; but it is his duty, at least, to wash his hands of it, and, if he gives it no thought longer, not to give it practically his support. If I devote myself to other pursuits and contemplations, I must first see, at least, that I do not pursue them sitting upon another man's shoulders. I must get off him first, that he may pursue his contemplations too. See what gross inconsistency is tolerated. I have heard some of my townsmen say, "I should like to have them order me out to help put down an insurrection of the slaves, or to march to Mexico;—see if I would go"; and yet these very men have each, directly by their allegiance, and so indirectly, at least, by their money, furnished a substitute. The soldier is applauded who refuses to serve in an unjust war by those who do not refuse to sustain the unjust government which makes the war; is applauded by those whose own act and authority he disregards and sets at naught; as if the state were penitent to that degree that it hired one to scourge it while it sinned, but not to that degree that it left off sinning for a moment. Thus, under the name of Order and Civil Government, we are all made at last to pay homage to and support our own meanness. After the first blush of sin comes its indifference; and from immoral it becomes, as it were, *un*moral, and not quite unnecessary to that life which we have made.

The broadest and most prevalent error requires the most disinterested virtue to sustain it. The slight reproach to which the virtue of patriotism is commonly liable, the noble are most likely to incur. Those who, while they disapprove of the character and measures of a government, yield to it their allegiance and support are undoubtedly its most conscientious supporters, and so frequently the most serious obstacles to reform. Some are petitioning the State to dissolve the Union, to disregard the requisitions of the President. Why do they not dissolve it themselves,—the union between themselves and the State,—and refuse to pay their quota into its treasury? Do not they stand in the same relation to the State that the State does to the Union? And have not the same reasons prevented the State from resisting the Union which have prevented them from resisting the State?

How can a man be satisfied to entertain an opinion merely, and   15
enjoy *it?* Is there any enjoyment in it, if his opinion is that he is aggrieved? If you are cheated out of a single dollar by your neighbor, you do not rest satisfied with knowing that you are cheated, or with saying that you are cheated, or even with petitioning him to pay you your due, but you take effectual steps at once to obtain the full amount, and see that you are never cheated again. Action from principle, the perception and the performance of right, changes things and relations; it is essentially revolutionary, and does not consist wholly with anything which was. It not only divides States and churches, it divides families; ay, it divides the *individual,* separating the diabolical in him from the divine.

Unjust laws exist: shall we be content to obey them, or shall we endeavor to amend them, and obey them until we have succeeded, or shall we transgress them at once? Men generally, under such a government as this, think that they ought to wait until they have persuaded the majority to alter them. They think that, if they should resist, the remedy would be worse than the evil. But it is the fault of the government itself that the remedy *is* worse than the evil. *It* makes it worse. Why is it not more apt to anticipate and provide for reform? Why does it not cherish its wise minority? Why does it cry and resist before it is hurt? Why does it not encourage its citizens to be on the alert to point out its faults, and *do* better than it would have them? Why does it always crucify Christ, and excommunicate Copernicus and Luther, and pronounce Washington and Franklin rebels?

One would think, that a deliberate and practical denial of its authority was the only offence never contemplated by government; else, why has it not assigned its definite, its suitable and proportionate, penalty? If a man who has no property refuses but once to earn nine shillings for the State, he is put in prison for a period unlimited by any law that I know, and determined only by the discretion of those who placed him there; but if he should steal ninety times nine shillings from the State, he is soon permitted to go at large again.

If the injustice is part of the necessary friction of the machine of government, let it go, let it go: perchance it will wear smooth,—certainly the machine will wear out. If the injustice has a spring, or a pulley, or a rope, or a crank, exclusively for itself, then perhaps you may consider whether the remedy will not be worse than the evil; but if it is of such a nature that it requires you to be the agent of injustice to another, then, I say, break the law. Let your life be a counter-friction to stop the machine. What I have to do is to see, at any rate, that I do not lend myself to the wrong which I condemn.

As for adopting the ways which the State has provided for remedying the evil, I know not of such ways. They take too much time, and a man's life will be gone. I have other affairs to attend to. I came into this world, not chiefly to make this a good place to live in, but to live in it, be it good or bad. A man has not everything to do, but something; and because he cannot do *everything,* it is not necessary that he should do *something* wrong. It is not my business to be petitioning the Governor or the Legislature any more than it is theirs to petition me; and if they should not hear my petition, what should I do then? But in this case the State has provided no way: its very Constitution is the evil. This may seem to be harsh and stubborn and unconciliatory; but it is to treat with the utmost kindness and consideration the only spirit that can appreciate or deserves it. So is all change for the better, like birth and death, which convulse the body.

I do not hesitate to say, that those who call themselves Abolitionists 20 should at once effectually withdraw their support, both in person and property, from the government of Massachusetts, and not wait till they constitute a majority of one, before they suffer the right to prevail through them. I think that it is enough if they have God on their side, without waiting for that other one. Moreover, any man more right than his neighbors constitutes a majority of one already.

I meet this American government, or its representative, the State government, directly, and face to face, once a year—no more—in the person of its tax-gatherer; this is the only mode in which a man situated as I am necessarily meets it; and it then says distinctly, Recognize me; and the simplest, the most effectual, and, in the present posture of affairs, the indispensablest mode of treating with it on this head, of expressing your little satisfaction with and love for it, is to deny it then. My civil neighbor, the tax-gatherer, is the very man I have to deal with,—for it is, after all, with men and not with parchment that I quarrel,—and he has voluntarily chosen to be an agent of the government. How shall he ever know well what he is and does as an officer of the government, or as a man, until he is obliged to consider whether he shall treat me, his neighbor, for whom he has respect, as a neighbor and well-disposed man, or as a maniac and disturber of the peace, and see if he can get over this obstruction to his neighborliness without a ruder and more impetuous thought or speech corresponding with his action. I know this well, that if one thousand, if one hundred, if ten men whom I could name,—if ten *honest* men only,—ay, if *one* HONEST man, in this State of Massachusetts, *ceasing to hold slaves,* were actually to withdraw from this copartnership, and be locked up in the county jail therefor, it would be the abolition of slavery in America. For it matters not how small the beginning may seem to be: what is once well done is done forever. But we love better to talk about it: that we say is our mission. Reform keeps many scores of newspapers in its service, but not one man. If my esteemed neighbor, the State's ambassador, who will devote his days to the settlement of the question of human rights in the Council Chamber, instead of being threatened with the prisons of Carolina, were to sit down the prisoner of Massachusetts, that State which is so anxious to foist the sin of slavery upon her sister,—though at present she can discover only an act of inhospitality to be the ground of a quarrel with her,—the Legislature would not wholly waive the subject the following winter.

Under a government which imprisons any unjustly, the true place for a just man is also a prison. The proper place to-day, the only place which Massachusetts has provided for her freer and less desponding spirits, is in her prisons, to be put out and locked out of the State by her own act, as they have already put themselves out by their principles. It is there that the fugitive slave, and the Mexican prisoner on parole, and the Indian come to plead the wrongs of his race should find them; on that separate, but more free and honorable, ground, where the State places those who are not *with* her, but *against* her,—the only house in a slave State in which a free man can abide with honor. If any think that their influence would be lost there, and their voices no longer afflict the ear of the State, that they would not be as an enemy within its walls, they do not know by how much truth is stronger than error, nor how much more eloquently and effectively he can combat injustice who has experienced a little in his own person. Cast your whole vote, not a strip of paper merely, but your whole influence. A minority is powerless while it conforms to the majority; it is not even a minority then; but it is irresistible when it clogs by its whole weight. If the alternative is to keep all just men in prison, or give up war and slavery, the State will not hesitate which to choose. If a thousand men were not to pay their tax-bills this year, that would not be a violent and bloody measure, as it would be to pay them, and enable the State to commit violence and shed innocent blood. This is, in fact, the definition of a peaceable revolution, if any such is possible. If the tax-gatherer, or any other public officer, asks me, as one has done, "But what shall I do?" my answer is, "If you really wish to do anything, resign your office." When the subject has refused allegiance, and the officer has resigned his office, then the revolution is accomplished. But even suppose blood should flow. Is there not a sort of blood shed when the conscience is wounded? Through this wound a man's real manhood and immortality flow out, and he bleeds to an everlasting death. I see this blood flowing now.

I have contemplated the imprisonment of the offender, rather than the seizure of his goods,—though both will serve the same purpose,—

because they who assert the purest right, and consequently are most dangerous to a corrupt State, commonly have not spent much time in accumulating property. To such the State renders comparatively small service, and a slight tax is wont to appear exorbitant, particularly if they are obliged to earn it by special labor with their hands. If there were one who lived wholly without the use of money, the State itself would hesitate to demand it of him. But the rich man—not to make any invidious comparison—is always sold to the institution which makes him rich. Absolutely speaking, the more money, the less virtue; for money comes between a man and his objects, and obtains them for him; and it was certainly no great virtue to obtain it. It puts to rest many questions which he would otherwise be taxed to answer; while the only new question which it puts is the hard but superfluous one, how to spend it. Thus his moral ground is taken from under his feet. The opportunities of living are diminished in proportion as what are called the "means" are increased. The best thing a man can do for his culture when he is rich is to endeavor to carry out those schemes which he entertained when he was poor. Christ answered the Herodians according to their condition. "Show me the tribute money," said he,— and one took a penny out of his pocket;—if you use money which has the image of Caesar on it, and which he has made current and valuable, that is, *if you are men of the State,* and gladly enjoy the advantages of Caesar's government, then pay him back some of his own when he demands it. "Render therefore to Caesar that which is Caesar's, and to God those things which are God's,"—leaving them no wiser than before as to which was which; for they did not wish to know.

When I converse with the freest of my neighbors, I perceive that, whatever they may say about the magnitude and seriousness of the question, and their regard for the public tranquillity, the long and the short of the matter is, that they cannot spare the protection of the existing government, and they dread the consequences to their property and families of disobedience to it. For my own part, I should not like to think that I ever rely on the protection of the State. But, if I deny the authority of the State when it presents its tax-bill, it will soon take and waste all my property, and so harass me and my children without end. This is hard. This makes it impossible for a man to live honestly, and at the same time comfortably, in outward respects. It will not be worth the while to accumulate property; that would be sure to go again. You must hire or squat somewhere, and raise but a small crop, and eat that soon. You must live within yourself, and depend upon yourself always tucked up and ready for a start, and not have many affairs. A man may grow rich in Turkey even, if he will be in all respects a good subject of the Turkish government. Confucius said: "If a state is governed by the principles of reason, poverty and misery are subjects of shame; if a state is not governed by the principles of reason, riches and honors are the subjects of shame." No: until I want the protection of Massachusetts to be extended to me in some distant Southern port, where my liberty is endangered, or until I am bent solely on building up an estate at home by peaceful enterprise, I can afford to refuse allegiance to Massachusetts, and her right to my property and life. It costs me less in every sense to incur the penalty of disobedience to the State than it would to obey. I should feel as if I were worth less in that case.

Some years ago, the State met me in behalf of the Church, and   25 commanded me to pay a certain sum toward the support of a clergyman whose preaching my father attended, but never I myself. "Pay," it said, "or be locked up in the jail." I declined to pay. But, unfortunately, another man saw fit to pay it. I did not see why the schoolmaster should be taxed to support the priest, and not the priest the schoolmaster; for I was not the State's schoolmaster, but I supported myself by voluntary subscription. I did not see why the lyceum should not present its tax-bill, and have the State to back its demand, as well as the Church. However, at the request of the selectmen, I condescended to make some such statement as this in writing:—"Know all men by these presents, that I, Henry Thoreau, do not wish to be regarded as a member of any incorporated society which I have not joined." This I gave to the town clerk; and he has it. The State, having thus learned that I did not wish to be regarded as a member of that church, has never made a like demand on me since; though it said that it must adhere to its original presumption that time. If I had known how to name them, I should then have signed off in detail from all the societies which I never signed on to; but I did not know where to find a complete list.

I have paid no poll-tax for six years. I was put into a jail once on this account, for one night; and, as I stood considering the walls of solid stone, two or three feet thick, the door of wood and iron, a foot thick, and the iron grating which strained the light, I could not help being struck with the foolishness of that institution which treated me as if I were mere flesh and blood and bones, to be locked up. I wondered that it should have concluded at length that this was the best use it could put me to, and had never thought to avail itself of my services in some way. I saw that, if there was a wall of stone between me and my townsmen, there was a still more difficult one to climb or break through before they could get to be as free as I was. I did not for a moment feel confined, and the walls seemed a great waste of stone and mortar. I felt as if I alone of all my townsmen had paid my tax. They plainly did not know how to treat me, but behaved like persons who are underbred. In every threat and in every compliment there was a blunder; for they thought that my chief desire was to stand the other side of that stone wall. I could not but smile to see how industriously they locked the door on my meditations, which followed them out again without let or hindrance, and *they* were really all that was dangerous. As they could not reach me, they had resolved to punish my body; just as boys, if they cannot come at some person against whom they have a spite, will abuse his dog. I saw that the State was half-witted, that it was timid as a lone woman with her silver spoons, and that it did not know its friends from its foes, and I lost all my remaining respect for it, and pitied it.

Thus the State never intentionally confronts a man's sense, intellectual or moral, but only his body, his senses. It is not armed with superior wit or honesty, but with superior physical strength. I was not born to be forced. I will breathe after my own fashion. Let us see who is the strongest. What force has a multitude? They only can force me who obey a higher law than I. They force me to become like themselves. I do not hear of *men* being *forced* to live this way or that by masses of men. What sort of life were that to live? When I meet a government which says to me, "Your money or your life," why should I be in haste to give it my money? It may be in a great strait, and not know what to do: I cannot help that. It must help itself; do as I do. It is not worth the while to snivel about it. I am not responsible for the successful working of the machinery of society. I am not the son of the engineer. I perceive that, when an acorn and a chestnut fall side by side, the one does not remain inert to make way for the other, but both obey their own laws, and spring and grow and flourish as best they can, till one, perchance, overshadows and destroys the other. If the plant cannot live according to its nature, it dies; and so a man.

The night in prison was novel and interesting enough. The prisoners in their shirt-sleeves were enjoying a chat and the evening air in the doorway, when I entered. But the jailer said, "Come, boys, it is time to lock up"; and so they dispersed, and I heard the sound of their steps returning into the hollow apartments. My room-mate was introduced to me by the jailer as "a first-rate fellow and a clever man." When the door was locked, he showed me where to hang my hat, and how he managed matters there. The rooms were whitewashed once a month; and this one, at least, was the whitest, most simply furnished, and probably the neatest apartment in the town. He naturally wanted to know where I came from, and what brought me there; and, when I had told him, I asked him in my turn how he came there, presuming him to be an honest man, of course; and, as the world goes, I believe he was. "Why," said he, "they accuse me of burning a barn; but I never did it." As near as I could discover, he had probably gone to bed in a barn when drunk, and smoked his pipe there; and so a barn was burnt. He had the reputation of being a clever man, had been there some three months waiting for his trial to come on, and would have to wait as much longer; but he was quite domesticated and contented, since he got his board for nothing, and thought that he was well treated.

He occupied one window, and I the other; and I saw that if one stayed there long, his principal business would be to look out the window. I had soon read all the tracts that were left there, and examined where former prisoners had broken out, and where a grate had been sawed off, and heard the history of the various occupants of that room; for I found that even here there was a history and a gossip which never circulated beyond the walls of the jail. Probably this is the only house in the town where verses are composed, which are afterward printed in a circular form, but not published. I was shown quite a long list of verses which were composed by some young men who had been detected in an attempt to escape, who avenged themselves by singing them.

I pumped my fellow-prisoner as dry as I could, for fear I should   30
never see him again; but at length he showed me which was my bed, and left me to blow out the lamp.

It was like traveling into a far country, such as I had never expected to behold, to lie there for one night. It seemed to me that I never had heard the town clock strike before, nor the evening sounds of the village; for we slept with the windows open, which were inside the grating. It was to see my native village in the light of the Middle Ages, and our Concord was turned into a Rhine stream, and visions of knights and castles passed before me. They were the voices of old burghers that I heard in the streets. I was an involuntary spectator and auditor of whatever was done and said in the kitchen of the adjacent village inn,— a wholly new and rare experience to me. It was a closer view of my native town. I was fairly inside of it. I never had seen its institutions before. This is one of its peculiar institutions; for it is a shire town. I began to comprehend what its inhabitants were about.

In the morning, our breakfasts were put through the hole in the door, in small oblong-square tin pans, made to fit, and holding a pint of chocolate, with brown bread, and an iron spoon. When they called for the vessels again, I was green enough to return what bread I had left; but my comrade seized it, and said that I should lay that up for lunch or dinner. Soon after he was let out to work at haying in a neighboring field, whither he went every day, and would not be back till noon; so he bade me good-day, saying that he doubted if he should see me again.

When I came out of prison,—for some one interfered, and paid that tax,—I did not perceive that great changes had taken place on the common, such as he observed who went in a youth and emerged a tottering and gray-headed man; and yet a change had to my eyes come over the scene,—the town, and State, and country,—greater than any that mere time could effect. I saw yet more distinctly the State in which I lived. I saw to what extent the people among whom I lived could be trusted as good neighbors and friends; that their friendship was for summer weather only; that they did not greatly propose to do right; that they were a distinct race from me by their prejudices and superstitions, as the Chinamen and Malays are; that in their sacrifices to humanity they ran no risks, not even to their property; that after all they were not so noble but they treated the thief as he had treated them, and hoped, by a certain outward observance and a few prayers, and by walking in a particular straight though useless path from time to time, to save their souls. This may be to judge my neighbors harshly; for I believe that many of them are not aware that they have such an institution as the jail in their village.

It was formerly the custom in our village, when a poor debtor came out of jail, for his acquaintances to salute him, looking through their fingers, which were crossed to represent the grating of a jail window, "How do ye do?" My neighbors did not thus salute me, but first looked at me, and then at one another, as if I had returned from a long journey. I was put into jail as I was going to the shoemaker's to get a shoe which was mended. When I was let out the next morning, I proceeded to finish my errand, and, having put on my mended shoe, joined a huckleberry party, who were impatient to put themselves under my conduct; and in half an hour,—for the horse was soon tackled,—was in the midst of a huckleberry field, on one of our highest hills, two miles off, and then the State was nowhere to be seen.

This is the whole history of "My Prisons." 35

I have never declined paying the highway tax, because I am as desirous of being a good neighbor as I am of being a bad subject; and as for supporting schools, I am doing my part to educate my fellow-countrymen now. It is for no particular item in the tax-bill that I refuse to pay it. I simply wish to refuse allegiance to the State, to withdraw and stand aloof from it effectually. I do not care to trace the course of my dollar, if I could, till it buys a man or a musket to shoot one with,— the dollar is innocent,—but I am concerned to trace the effects of my allegiance. In fact, I quietly declare war with the State, after my fashion, though I will still make what use and get what advantage of her I can, as is usual in such cases.

If others pay the tax which is demanded of me, from a sympathy with the State, they do but what they have already done in their own case, or rather they abet injustice to a greater extent than the State requires. If they pay the tax from a mistaken interest in the individual taxed, to save his property, or prevent his going to jail, it is because they have not considered wisely how far they let their private feelings interfere with the public good.

This, then, is my position at present. But one cannot be too much on his guard in such a case, lest his action be biased by obstinacy or an undue regard for the opinions of men. Let him see that he does only what belongs to himself and to the hour.

I think sometimes, Why, this people mean well, they are only ignorant; they would do better if they knew how: why give your neighbors this pain to treat you as they are not inclined to? But I think again, This is no reason why I should do as they do, or permit others to suffer much greater pain of a different kind. Again, I sometimes say to myself, When many millions of men, without heat, without ill will, without personal feeling of any kind, demand of you a few shillings only, without the possibility, such is their constitution, of retracting or altering their present demand, and without the possibility, on your side, of appeal to any other millions, why expose yourself to this overwhelming brute force? You do not resist cold and hunger, the winds and the waves, thus obstinately; you quietly submit to a thousand similar necessities. You do not put your head into the fire. But just in proportion as I regard this as not wholly a brute force, but partly a human force, and consider that I have relations to those millions as to so many millions of men, and not of mere brute or inanimate things, I see that appeal is possible, first and instantaneously, from them to the Maker of them, and, secondly, from them to themselves. But if I put my head deliberately into the fire, there is no appeal to fire or to the Maker of fire, and I have only myself to blame. If I could convince myself that I have any right to be satisfied with men as they are, and to treat them accordingly, and not according, in some respects, to my requisitions and expectations of what they and I ought to be, then, like a good Mussulman and fatalist, I should endeavor to be satisfied with things as they are, and say it is the will of God. And, above all, there is this difference between resisting this and a purely brute or natural force, that I can resist this with some effect; but I cannot expect, like Orpheus, to change the nature of the rocks and trees and beasts.

I do not wish to quarrel with any man or nation. I do not wish to split hairs, to make fine distinctions, or set myself up as better than my neighbors. I seek rather, I may say, even an excuse for conforming to the laws of the land. I am but too ready to conform to them. Indeed, I have reason to suspect myself on this head; and each year, as the taxgatherer comes round, I find myself disposed to review the acts and position of the general and State governments, and the spirit of the people, to discover a pretext for conformity.

> "We must affect our country as our parents,
> And if at any time we alienate
> Our love or industry from doing it honor,
> We must respect effects and teach the soul
> Matter of conscience and religion,
> And not desire of rule or benefit."

I believe that the State will soon be able to take all my work of this sort out of my hands, and then I shall be no better a patriot than my fellow-countrymen. Seen from a lower point of view, the Constitution, with all its faults, is very good; the law and the courts are very respectable; even this State and this American government are, in many respects, very admirable, and rare things, to be thankful for, such as a great many have described them; but seen from a point of view a little higher, they are what I have described them; seen from a higher still, and the highest, who shall say what they are, or that they are worth looking at or thinking of at all?

However, the government does not concern me much, and I shall bestow the fewest possible thoughts on it. It is not many moments that I live under a government, even in this world. If a man is thought-free, fancy-free, imagination-free, that which *is not* never for a long time appearing *to be* to him, unwise rulers or reformers cannot fatally interrupt him.

I know that most men think differently from myself; but those whose lives are by profession devoted to the study of these or kindred subjects content me as little as any. Statesmen and legislators, standing so completely within the institution, never distinctly and nakedly behold it. They speak of moving society; but have no resting-place without it. They may be men of a certain experience and discrimination, and have no doubt invented ingenious and even useful systems, for which we sincerely thank them; but all their wit and usefulness lie within certain not very wide limits. They are wont to forget that the world is not governed by policy and expediency. Webster never goes behind government, and so cannot speak with authority about it. His words are wisdom to those legislators who contemplate no essential reform in the existing government; but for thinkers, and those who legislate for all time, he never once glances at the subject. I know of those whose serene and wise speculations on this theme would soon reveal the limits of his mind's range and hospitality. Yet, compared with the cheap professions of most reformers, and the still cheaper wisdom and eloquence of politicians in general, his are almost the only sensible and valuable words, and we thank Heaven for him. Comparatively, he is always strong, original, and, above all, practical. Still, his quality is not wisdom, but prudence. The lawyer's truth is not Truth, but consistency or a consistent expediency. Truth is always in harmony with herself, and is not concerned chiefly to reveal the justice that may consist with wrong-doing. He well deserves to be called, as he has been called, the Defender of the Constitution. There are really no blows to be given by him but defensive ones. He is not a leader, but a follower. His leaders are the men of '87. "I have never made an effort," he says, "and never propose to make an effort; I have never countenanced an effort, and never mean to countenance an effort, to disturb the arrangement as originally made, by which the various States came into the Union." Still thinking of the sanction which the Constitution gives to slavery,

he says, "Because it was a part of the original compact,—let it stand."
Notwithstanding his special acuteness and ability, he is unable to take a
fact out of its merely political relations, and behold it as it lies absolutely to be disposed of by the intellect,—what, for instance, it be-
hooves a man to do here in America to-day with regard to slavery,—
but ventures, or is driven, to make some such desperate answer as the
following, while professing to speak absolutely, and as a private man,—
from which what new and singular code of social duties might be inferred? "The manner," says he,

> in which the governments of those States where slavery exists are to reg-
> ulate it is for their own consideration, under their responsibility to their
> constituents, to the general laws of propriety, humanity, and justice, and
> to God. Associations formed elsewhere, springing from a feeling of hu-
> manity, or any other cause, have nothing whatever to do with it. They
> have never received any encouragement from me, and they never will.[2]

They who know of no purer sources of truth, who have traced up
its stream no higher, stand, and wisely stand, by the Bible and the
Constitution, and drink at it there with reverence and humility; but
they who behold where it comes trickling into this lake or that pool,
gird up their loins once more, and continue their pilgrimage toward its
fountain-head.

No man with a genius for legislation has appeared in America. They
are rare in the history of the world. There are orators, politicians, and
eloquent men, by the thousand; but the speaker has not yet opened his
mouth to speak who is capable of settling the much-vexed questions of
the day. We love eloquence for its own sake, and not for any truth
which it may utter, or any heroism it may inspire. Our legislators have
not yet learned the comparative value of free trade and of freedom, of
union, and of rectitude, to a nation. They have no genius or talent for
comparatively humble questions of taxation and finance, commerce and
manufactures and agriculture. If we were left solely to the wordy wit
of legislators in Congress for our guidance, uncorrected by the season-
able experience and the effectual complaints of the people, America could
not long retain her rank among the nations. For eighteen hundred years,
though perchance I have no right to say it, the New Testament has
been written; yet where is the legislator who has wisdom and practical
talent enough to avail himself of the light which it sheds on the science
of legislation?

The authority of government, even such as I am willing to submit 　45
to,—for I will cheerfully obey those who know and can do better than
I, and in many things even those who neither know nor can do so

---

[2] These extracts have been inserted since the lecture was read.

well,—is still an impure one: to be strictly just, it must have the sanction and consent of the governed. It can have no pure right over my person and property but what I concede to it. The progress from an absolute to a limited monarchy, from a limited monarchy to a democracy, is a progress toward a true respect for the individual. Even the Chinese philosopher was wise enough to regard the individual as the basis of the empire. Is a democracy, such as we know it, the last improvement possible in government? Is it not possible to take a step further toward recognizing and organizing the rights of man? There will never be a really free and enlightened State until the State comes to recognize the individual as a higher and independent power, from which all its own power and authority are derived, and treats him accordingly. I please myself with imagining a State at last which can afford to be just to all men, and to treat the individual with respect as a neighbor; which even would not think it inconsistent with its own repose if a few were to live aloof from it, not meddling with it, nor embraced by it, who fulfilled all the duties of neighbors and fellowmen. A State which bore this kind of fruit, and suffered it to drop off as fast as it ripened, would prepare the way for a still more perfect and glorious State, which also I have imagined, but not yet anywhere seen.

LINES OF INQUIRY
"Civil Disobedience"

Thoreau considers several issues in the course of this piece. How do you account for the selection and organization of material that he discusses? For example, why do you suppose that he begins by affirming the idea of a government "which governs least," when he makes clear in paragraph 3 that he is not a "no-government man"? Why does he discuss the issue of voting in paragraphs 11 and 12 rather than doing so immediately after paragraph 19, as one of "the ways which the State has provided for remedying the evil"? Why does he tell the lengthy story of his night in jail? Why does he single out Webster for attack near the end of the essay?

What exactly is Thoreau's idea of "civil disobedience"? For example, what assumptions does it entail about the relationship of citizens to the government? Under what type of circumstances does Thoreau believe that civil disobedience is necessary? Why does he consider other remedies inferior to it? Under what type of circumstances does he believe it is not required? What are the basic elements in any act of civil disobedience?

How does Thoreau's idea of civil disobedience relate to King's idea of nonviolent resistance as explained in "An Experiment in Love" and "A Letter from Birmingham Jail"? In what respects are these similar ideas, in what respects different?

MARK TWAIN

(SAMUEL LANGHORNE CLEMENS)

1835 – 1910

The most permanent lessons in morals are those which come not of booky teaching, but of experience.

Samuel Clemens (who took the pen name of Mark Twain in 1862) was undoubtedly moved to this observation by the force of his own firsthand experience, for his experiences were extraordinarily wide-ranging, and he drew on them throughout his career as a journalist, humorist, lecturer, novelist, and essayist. In fact, by the time he wrote this maxim in 1880, Mark Twain not only had worked his way around much of the United States, Hawaii (then an independent monarchy), and Europe, but also had turned his adventures into four remarkably successful books. So it is hardly surprising that he came to think of experience as "an author's most valuable asset . . . the thing that puts the muscle and the breath and the warm blood into the book he writes."

The itch to travel came early—from his boyhood in the river town of Hannibal, Missouri, where his family moved when he was four years old. There on the Mississippi, in the heyday of river traffic, he grew up with the steamboat whistle sounding in his ears, and the steamboat pilots, the riverboat gamblers, the adventurers, and the speculators passing before his eyes. There, too, when he was twelve years old and his father had just died, he dropped out of school and became a "printer's devil" for the local newspaper. At eighteen he left Hannibal and for the next fifteen years traveled around the country trying his hand at a variety of occupations—journeyman printer, steamboat pilot, secretary, and gold miner—before turning once again to the newspaper business in 1862, but this time as a reporter for the Virginia City *Territorial Enterprise* in Nevada.

The job of reporting, especially in a frontier mining town, brought out his natural talent for humorous storytelling, and Twain refined it when he moved to San Francisco in 1864 and met up with a group of humorous writers and lecturers, most notably Artemus Ward, from whom he learned the "high and delicate art" of "how a story ought to be told." His mastery of that art in "The Celebrated Jumping Frog of Calaveras County" (1865) brought him widespread attention, and the attention brought him further opportunities to display it—as a roving reporter in Hawaii for the Sacramento *Union,* as a public lecturer on the west coast, in the Rocky Mountains, and in New York City, and as a reporter on a tour of Europe and the Holy Land for the San Francisco *Alta California.* His vividly detailed and amusing travel stories, which he later incorporated in *Innocents Abroad* (1869) and *Roughing It* (1872), were so widely read and distributed that soon after he returned from his Mediterranean tour in 1867 he had become one of the most popular authors in America.

In 1870, he married Olivia Langdon, the socially cultivated daughter of a well-to-do mine owner from upstate New York, and in 1872 they moved to Hartford, where Twain made his home for most of the next thirty years. During that period, he continued to lecture and travel extensively throughout Europe and the United States, yet he also managed to produce virtually all of his major works, most notably *The Adventures of Tom Sawyer* (1876), *The Prince and the Pauper* (1882), *Life on the Mississippi* (1883), *The Adventures of Huckleberry Finn* (1884), and *A Connecticut Yankee in King Arthur's Court* (1889). During that period, too, he invested heavily in several business ventures, among them a publishing house and a typesetting machine, all of which failed, leaving him bankrupt and badly in debt by the early 1890s. Though he managed to work off the debt by lecturing around the world and recording his experiences in *Following the Equator* (1897), the last ten years of his life were darkened by the deaths of his wife and two of his daughters.

Well before the misfortunes of his later years, Twain began to develop a distinctly cynical set of views about human nature and religious belief, epitomized by his reference to the "damned human race." In an essay on "The Character of Man" (1885), for example, he described man as "the most detestable" [of all the creatures], "the only one—the solitary one—that possesses malice." Thus, in one of the sardonic maxims that opens each chapter of *Following the Equator,* he was moved to observe that "Man is the Only Animal that blushes. Or needs to." In the years that followed, his increasingly pessimistic and deterministic views were embodied in *The Man That Corrupted Hadleyburg* (1900), *What Is Man?* (privately printed, 1906), and other writings so philosophically somber and so much at odds with the prevailing view of him as a humorist that he chose not to publish them during his lifetime.

Given the reach of his experience and the length of his career, Twain's essays cover a wide range of subject matter—personal, literary, social, political, religious, and philosophical. Whatever their subject, his essays typically reflect his interest in story telling, whether a brief anecdote or a full-fledged account. The style of his essays reflects his experience as a lecturer, keenly aware that a good "talker" can "persuade a fish to come out and take a walk with him." His language, in turn, is meant for the ear, so it generally stays close to the American idiom of his time. The "right word," as he knew, "tastes as tart and crisp and good as the autumn butter that creams the sumac berry." But above all, his essays, no matter how serious their subject, are almost always tinged with humor, for humor, as he believed, "is the great thing, the saving thing, after all."

"S-T-E-A-M-BOAT A-COMIN'!"

When I was a boy there was but one permanent ambition among my comrades in our village[1] on the west bank of the Mississippi River. That was to be a steamboatman. We had transient ambitions of other sorts but they were only transient. When a circus came and went, it left us all burning to become clowns; the first Negro minstrel show that ever came to our section left us all suffering to try that kind of life; now and then we had a hope that, if we lived and were good, God would permit us to be pirates. These ambitions faded out, each in its turn; but the ambition to be a steamboatman always remained.

Once a day a cheap, gaudy packet arrived upward from St Louis, and another downward from Keokuk. Before these events, the day was glorious with expectancy; after them, the day was a dead and empty thing. Not only the boys but the whole village felt this. After all these years I can picture that old time to myself now, just as it was then: the white town drowsing in the sunshine of a summer's morning; the streets empty or pretty nearly so; one or two clerks sitting in front of the Water Street stores, with their splint-bottomed chairs tilted back against the walls, chins on breasts, hats slouched over their faces, asleep—with shingle-shavings enough around to show what broke them down; a sow and a litter of pigs loafing along the sidewalk, doing a good business in watermelon rinds and seeds; two or three lonely little freight piles scattered about the "levee"; a pile of "skids" on the slope of the stone-paved wharf, and the fragrant town drunkard asleep in the shadow of them; two or three wood flats at the head of the wharf but nobody to listen to the peaceful lapping of the wavelets against them; the great Mississippi, the majestic, the magnificent Mississippi, rolling its mile-wide tide along, shining in the sun; the dense forest away on the other side; the "point" above the town, and the "point" below, bounding the river-glimpse and turning it into a sort of sea, and withal a very still and brilliant and lonely one. Presently a film of dark smoke appears above one of those remote "points"; instantly a Negro drayman, famous for his quick eye and prodigious voice, lifts up the cry, "S-t-e-a-m-boat a-comin'!" and the scene changes! The town drunkard stirs, the clerks wake up, a furious clatter of drays follows, every house and store

---

[1] Hannibal, Missouri.

pours out a human contribution, and all in a twinkling the dead town is alive and moving. Drays, carts, men, boys, all go hurrying from many quarters to a common center, the wharf. Assembled there, the people fasten their eyes upon the coming boat as upon a wonder they are seeing for the first time. And the boat *is* rather a handsome sight, too. She is long and sharp and trim and pretty; she has two tall, fancy-topped chimneys, with a gilded device of some kind swung between them; a fanciful pilot-house, all glass and "gingerbread," perched on top of the "texas" deck behind them; the paddle-boxes are gorgeous with a picture or with gilded rays above the boat's name; the boiler-deck, the hurricane-deck, and the texas deck are fenced and ornamented with clean white railings; there is a flag gallantly flying from the jack-staff; the furnace doors are open and the fires glaring bravely; the upper decks are black with passengers; the captain stands by the big bell, calm, imposing, the envy of all; great volumes of the blackest smoke are rolling and tumbling out of the chimneys—a husbanded grandeur created with a bit of pitch-pine just before arriving at a town; the crew are grouped on the forecastle; the broad stage is run far out over the port bow and an envied deck-hand stands picturesquely on the end of it with a coil of rope in his hand; the pent steam is screaming through the gauge-cocks; the captain lifts his hand, a bell rings, the wheels stop; then they turn back, churning the water to foam, and the steamer is at rest. Then such a scramble as there is to get aboard and to get ashore, and to take in freight and to discharge freight, all at one and the same time; and such a yelling and cursing as the mates facilitate it all with! Ten minutes later the steamer is under way again, with no flag on the jack-staff and no black smoke issuing from the chimneys. After ten more minutes the town is dead again and the town drunkard asleep by the skids once more.

LINES OF INQUIRY
"'S-t-e-a-m-boat a-comin'!'"

The fourth and eighth sentences of paragraph 2 each run on for an extraordinarily long time, each accumulating quite a few details along the way. What effects are produced in each case by including all of those details in a single sentence, rather than in a series of shorter ones? How does Twain keep each sentence moving clearly and emphatically from beginning to end? How has he selected the organized details in the fourth sentence to lead up to the coming of the steamboat? How has he selected and organized details in the eighth sentence to give a comprehensive, vivid, and dramatic impression of the steamboat?

Immediately after the steamboat is announced, "the scene changes," according to Twain, as if to suggest that the arrival and departure of the steamboat are something like a dramatic production. In what particular ways does

Twain depict these events as being like a theatrical performance and the towns-people like theatrical spectators? What does this analogy imply about Twain's attitude toward the steamboat? Toward the quality of life in the village?

For a description of life in a different kind of village culture, look at Mead's "A Day in Samoa." What similarities, what differences, do you notice in the ways that Mead and Twain select, organize, and present details about life in each village? How do you account for both the similarities and the differences in their methods of description?

CORN-PONE OPINIONS

Fifty years ago, when I was a boy of fifteen and helping to inhabit a Missourian village on the banks of the Mississippi, I had a friend whose society was very dear to me because I was forbidden by my mother to partake of it. He was a gay and impudent and satirical and delightful young black man—a slave—who daily preached sermons from the top of his master's woodpile, with me for sole audience. He imitated the pulpit style of the several clergymen of the village, and did it well, and with fine passion and energy. To me he was a wonder. I believed he was the greatest orator in the United States, and would some day be heard from. But it did not happen; in the distribution of rewards he was overlooked. It is the way, in this world.

He interrupted his preaching, now and then, to saw a stick of wood; but the sawing was a pretence—he did it with his mouth; exactly imitating the sound the buck-saw makes in shrieking its way through the wood. But it served its purpose: it kept his master from coming out to see how the work was getting along. I listened to the sermons from the window of a lumber-room at the back of our house. One of his texts was this:

"You tell me whar a man gits his corn-pone, en I'll tell you what his 'pinions is."

I can never forget it. It was deeply impressed upon me. By my mother. Not upon my memory, but elsewhere. She had slipped in upon me while I was absorbed and not watching. The black philosopher's idea was, that a man is not independent, and cannot afford views which might interfere with his bread and butter. If he would prosper, he must train with the majority; in matters of large moment, like politics and religion, he must think and feel with the bulk of his neighbors, or suffer damage in his social standing and in his business prosperities. He must restrict himself to corn-pone opinions—at least on the surface. He must get his opinions from other people; he must reason out none for himself; he must have no first-hand views.

I think Jerry was right, in the main, but I think he did not go far enough.   5

1. It was his idea that a man conforms to the majority-view of his locality by calculation and intention. This happens, but I think it is not the rule.

2. It was his idea that there is such a thing as a first-hand opinion; an original opinion; an opinion which is coldly reasoned out in a man's head, by a searching analysis of facts involved, with the heart uncon-

sulted, and the jury-room closed against outside influences. It may be that such an opinion has been born somewhere, at some time or other, but I suppose it got away before they could catch it and stuff it and put it in the museum.

I am persuaded that a coldly thought-out and independent verdict upon a fashion in clothes, or manners, or literature, or politics, or religion, or any other matter that is projected into the field of our notice and interest, is a most rare thing—if it has indeed ever existed.

A new thing in costume appears—the flaring hoop-skirt, for example—and the passers-by are shocked, and the irreverent laugh. Six months later everybody is reconciled; the fashion has established itself; it is admired, now, and no one laughs. Public opinion resented it before, public opinion accepts it now, and is happy in it. Why? Was the resentment reasoned out? Was the acceptance reasoned out? No. The instinct that moves to conformity did the work. It is our nature to conform; it is a force which not many can successfully resist. What is its seat? The inborn requirement of Self-Approval. We all have to bow to that; there are no exceptions. Even the woman who refuses from first to last to wear the hoop-skirt comes under that law and is its slave; she could not wear the skirt and have her own approval; and that she *must* have, she cannot help herself. But as a rule our self-approval has its source in but one place and not elsewhere—the approval of other people. A person of vast consequence can introduce any kind of novelty in dress and the general world will presently adopt it—moved to do it, in the first place, by the natural instinct to passively yield to that vague something recognized as authority, and in the second place by the human instinct to train with the multitude and have its approval. An Empress introduced the hoop-skirt, and we know the result. A nobody introduced the bloomer, and we know the result. If Eve should come again, in her ripe renown, and reintroduce her quaint styles—well, we know what would happen. And we should be cruelly embarrassed, along at first.

The hoop-skirt runs its course, and disappears. Nobody reasons about it. One woman abandons the fashion; her neighbor notices this and follows her lead; this influences the next woman; and so on and so on, and presently the skirt has vanished out of the world, no one knows how nor why; nor cares, for that matter. It will come again, by and by; and in due course will go again.

Twenty-five years ago, in England, six or eight wine glasses stood grouped by each person's plate at a dinner party, and they were used, not left idle and empty; to-day there are but three or four in the group, and the average guest sparingly uses about two of them. We have not adopted this new fashion yet, but we shall do it presently. We shall not think it out, we shall merely conform, and let it go at that. We get our

notions and habits and opinions from outside influences, we do not
have to study them out.

Our table manners, and company manners, and street manners change
from time to time, but the changes are not reasoned out; we merely
notice and conform. We are creatures of outside influences; as a rule we
do not think, we only imitate. We cannot invent standards that will
stick; what we mistake for standards are only fashions, and perishable.
We may continue to admire them, but we drop the use of them. We
notice this in literature. Shakespeare is a standard, and fifty years ago
we used to write tragedies which he couldn't tell from—from somebody else's; but we don't do it any more, now. Our prose standard,
three-quarters of a century ago, was ornate and diffuse; some authority
or other changed it in the direction of compactness and simplicity, and
conformity followed, without argument. The historical novel starts up
suddenly, and sweeps the land. Everybody writes one, and the nation
is glad. We had historical novels before; but nobody read them, and the
rest of us conformed—without reasoning it out. We are conforming in
the other way, now, because it is another case of everybody.

The outside influences are always pouring in upon us, and we are
always obeying their orders and accepting their verdicts. The Smiths
like the new play; the Joneses go to see it, and they copy the Smith
verdict. Morals, religions, politics, get their following from surrounding influences and atmospheres, almost entirely; not from study, not
from thinking. A man must and will have his own approval first of all,
in each and every moment and circumstance of his life—even if he must
repent of a self-approved act the moment after its commission, in order
to get his self-approval *again;* but, speaking in general terms, a man's
self-approval, in the large concerns of life, has its source in the approval
of the people about him, and not in a searching personal examination
of the matter. Mohammedans are Mohammedans because they are born
and reared among that sect, not because they have thought it out and
can furnish sound reasons for being Mohammedans; we know why
Catholics are Catholics; why Presbyterians are Presbyterians; why Baptists are Baptists; why Mormons are Mormons; why thieves are thieves;
why monarchists are monarchists; why republicans are republicans, and
democrats democrats. We know it is a matter of association and sympathy, not reasoning and examination; that hardly a man in the world
has an opinion upon morals, politics or religion which he got otherwise
than through his associations and sympathies. Broadly speaking, there
are none but corn-pone opinions. And broadly speaking, Corn-Pone
stands for Self-Approval. Self-approval is acquired mainly from the approval of other people. The result is Conformity. Sometimes Conformity has a sordid business interest—the bread-and-butter interest—but
not in most cases, I think. I think that in the majority of cases it is

unconscious and not calculated; that it is born of the human being's natural yearning to stand well with his fellows, and have their inspiring approval and praise—a yearning which is commonly so strong and so insistent that it cannot be effectually resisted, and must have its way.

A political emergency brings out the corn-pone opinion in fine force in its two chief varieties—the pocket-book variety, which has its origin in self-interest, and the bigger variety, the sentimental variety—the one which can't bear to be outside the pale; can't bear to be in disfavor; can't endure the averted face and the cold shoulder; wants to stand well with the friends, wants to be smiled upon, wants to be welcome, wants to hear the precious words *"he's* on the right track!" Uttered, perhaps, by an ass, but still an ass of high degree, an ass whose approval is gold and diamonds to a smaller ass, and confers glory, and honor and happiness, and membership in the herd. For these gauds many a man will dump his life-long principles into the street, and his conscience along with them. We have seen it happen. In some millions of instances.

Men think they think upon great political questions, and they do; but they think with their party, not independently; they read its literature, but not that of the other side; they arrive at convictions, but they are drawn from a partial view of the matter in hand and are of no particular value. They swarm with their party, they feel with their party, they are happy in their party's approval; and where the party leads they will follow, whether for right and honor, or through blood and dirt and a mush of mutilated morals.   15

In our late canvas half of the nation passionately believed that in silver lay salvation, the other half as passionately believed that that way lay destruction. Do you believe that a tenth part of the people, on either side, had any rational excuse for having an opinion about the matter at all? I studied that mighty question to the bottom—and came out empty. Half of our people passionately believe in high tariff, the other half believe otherwise. Does this mean study and examination, or only feeling? The latter, I think. I have deeply studied that question, too—and didn't arrive. We all do no end of feeling, and we mistake it for thinking. And out of it we get an aggregation which we consider a Boon. Its name is Public Opinion. It is held in reverence. It settles everything. Some think it the Voice of God. Pr'aps.

I suppose that in more cases than we should like to admit, we have two sets of opinions: one private, the other public; one secret and sincere, the other corn-pone, and more or less tainted.

1901

LINES OF INQUIRY
"Corn-Pone Opinions"

Twain begins this piece about public opinion with a detailed little story of himself and Jerry, a slave. Why doesn't he begin, instead, with a more direct statement of his topic and point, such as appears in paragraph 9? In what respects is the story particularly relevant to his point about the power of public opinion? How does your view of this story compare with the comments that Hoagland makes about it in "What I Think, What I Am"?

Twain views public opinion quite negatively. What kinds of evidence does he offer to support his contention about the rareness of original opinion? What assumptions about human nature, human behavior, and human motives does Twain bring to the discussion in support of his contention about public opinion and belief? In what respects does Twain seem more concerned with voicing his ideas about the weakness of human nature than with arguing his point about the rarity of original ideas?

According to Twain, public opinion exerts its dominating influence in all areas of human existence—in clothes, manners, morals, art, politics, and religion. In which of these respects does he seem most convincing? In which respects, least convincing? What do you suppose would be the most effective way(s) of challenging Twain's contentions about public opinion and human nature?

WAS THE WORLD MADE FOR MAN?

*"Alfred Russell Wallace's revival of the theory that this earth is
at the centre of the stellar universe, and is the only habitable globe,
has aroused great interest in the world."*—Literary Digest.

*"For ourselves we do thoroughly believe that man, as he lives
just here on this tiny earth, is in essence and possibilities the most
sublime existence in all the range of non-divine being—the chief
love and delight of God."*—Chicago "Interior," (Presb.)

I seem to be the only sci-
entist and theologian still remaining to be heard from on this important
matter of whether the world was made for man or not. I feel that it is
time for me to speak.

I stand almost with the others. They believe the world was made
for man, I believe it likely that it was made for man; they think there
is proof, astronomical mainly, that it was made for man, I think there
is evidence only, not proof, that it was made for him. It is too early,
yet, to arrange the verdict, the returns are not all in. When they are all
in, I think they will show that the world was made for man; but we
must not hurry, we must patiently wait till they are all in.

Now as far as we have got, astronomy is on our side. Mr. Wallace[1]
has clearly shown this. He has clearly shown two things: that the world
was made for man, and that the universe was made for the world—to
stiddy it, you know. The astronomy part is settled, and cannot
be challenged.

We come now to the geological part. This is the one where the
evidence is not all in, yet. It is coming in, hourly, daily, coming in all
the time, but naturally it comes with geological carefulness and deliberation, and we must not be impatient, we must not get excited, we
must be calm, and wait. To lose our tranquillity will not hurry geology; nothing hurries geology.

It takes a long time to prepare a world for man, such a thing is not   5
done in a day. Some of the great scientists, carefully ciphering the evidences furnished by geology, have arrived at the conviction that our
world is prodigiously old, and they may be right, but Lord Kelvin[2] is
not of their opinion. He takes a cautious, conservative view, in order

---

[1] *Mr. Wallace:* Alfred Russell Wallace, English naturalist, 1823–1913
[2] *Lord Kelvin:* William Thomson Kelvin, British mathematician and physicist, 1824–1907.

to be on the safe side, and feels sure it is not so old as they think. As Lord Kelvin is the highest authority in science now living, I think we must yield to him and accept his view. He does not concede that the world is more than a hundred million years old. He believes it is that old, but not older. Lyell[3] believed that our race was introduced into the world 31,000 years ago, Herbert Spencer[4] makes it 32,000. Lord Kelvin agrees with Spencer.

Very well. According to these figures it took 99,968,000 years to prepare the world for man, impatient as the Creator doubtless was to see him and admire him. But a large enterprise like this has to be conducted warily, painstakingly, logically. It was foreseen that man would hav: to have the oyster. Therefore the first preparation was made for the oyster. Very well, you cannot make an oyster out of whole cloth, you must make the oyster's ancestor first. This is not done in a day. You must make a vast variety of invertebrates, to start with—belemnites, trilobites, jebusites, amalekites, and that sort of fry, and put them to soak in a primary sea, and wait and see what will happen. Some will be a disappointment—the belemnites, the ammonites and such; they will be failures, they will die out and become extinct, in the course of the 19,000,000 years covered by the experiment, but all is not lost, for the amalekites will fetch the home-stake; they will develop gradually into encrinites, and stalactites, and blatherskites, and one thing and another as the mighty ages creep on and the Archaean and the Cambrian Periods pile their lofty crags in the primordial seas, and at last the first grand stage in the preparation of the world for man stands completed, the Oyster is done. An oyster has hardly any more reasoning power than a scientist has; and so it is reasonably certain that this one jumped to the conclusion that the nineteen-million years was a preparation for *him;* but that would be just like an oyster, which is the most conceited animal there is, except man. And anyway, this one could not know, at that early date, that he was only an incident in a scheme, and that there was some more to the scheme, yet.

The oyster being achieved, the next thing to be arranged for in the preparation of the world for man, was fish. Fish, and coal—to fry it with. So the Old Silurian seas were opened up to breed the fish in, and at the same time the great work of building Old Red Sandstone mountains 80,000 feet high to cold-storage their fossils in was begun. This latter was quite indispensable, for there would be no end of failures again, no end of extinctions—millions of them—and it would be cheaper and less trouble to can them in the rocks than keep tally of them in a book. One does not build the coal beds and 80,000 feet of perpendicular Old

---

[3] *Lyell:* Sir Charles Lyell, British geologist, 1797–1875.
[4] *Spencer:* Herbert Spencer, English philosopher, 1820–1903.

Red Sandstone in a brief time—no, it took twenty million years. In the first place, a coal bed is a slow and troublesome and tiresome thing to construct. You have to grow prodigious forests of tree-ferns and reeds and calamites and such things in a marshy region; then you have to sink them under out of sight and let them rot; then you have to turn the streams on them, so as to bury them under several feet of sediment, and the sediment must have time to harden and turn to rock; next you must grow another forest on top, then sink it and put on another layer of sediment and harden it; then more forest and more rock, layer upon layer, three miles deep—ah, indeed it is a sickening slow job to build a coal-measure and do it right!

So the millions of years drag on; and meantime the fish-culture is lazying along and frazzling out in a way to make a person tired. You have developed ten thousand kinds of fishes from the oyster; and come to look, you have raised nothing but fossils, nothing but extinctions. There is nothing left alive and progressive but a ganoid or two and perhaps half a dozen asteroids. Even the cat wouldn't eat such.

Still, it is no great matter; there is plenty of time, yet, and they will develop into something tasty before man is ready for them. Even a ganoid can be depended on for that, when he is not going to be called on for sixty million years.

The Palaeozoic time-limit having now been reached, it was necessary to begin the next stage in the preparation of the world for man, by opening up the Mesozoic Age and instituting some reptiles. For man would need reptiles. Not to eat, but to develop himself from. This being the most important detail of the scheme, a spacious liberality of time was set apart for it—thirty million years. What wonders followed! From the remaining ganoids and asteroids and alkaloids were developed by slow and steady and pains-taking culture those stupendous saurians that used to prowl about the steamy world in those remote ages, with their snaky heads reared forty feet in the air and sixty feet of body and tail racing and thrashing after. All gone, now, alas—all extinct, except the little handful of Arkansawrians left stranded and lonely with us here upon this far-flung verge and fringe of time.

Yes, it took thirty million years and twenty million reptiles to get one that would stick long enough to develop into something else and let the scheme proceed to the next step.

Then the Pterodactyl burst upon the world in all his impressive solemnity and grandeur, and all Nature recognized that the Cainozoic threshold was crossed and a new Period open for business, a new stage begun in the preparation of the globe for man. It may be that the Pterodactyl thought the thirty million years had been intended as a preparation for himself, for there was nothing too foolish for a Pterodactyl to imagine, but he was in error, the preparation was for man. Without doubt the Pterodactyl attracted great attention, for even the least observant could see that there was the making of a bird in him. And so it turned out. Also the makings of a mammal, in time. One thing we have to say to his credit, that in the matter of picturesqueness he was the triumph of his Period; he wore wings and had teeth, and was a starchy and wonderful mixture altogether, a kind of long-distance premonitory symptom of Kipling's marine:

> 'E isn't one o' the reg'lar Line, nor 'e isn't one of the crew,
> 'E's a kind of a giddy harumfrodite—soldier an' sailor too!

From this time onward for nearly another thirty million years the preparation moved briskly. From the Pterodactyl was developed the bird; from the bird the kangaroo, from the kangaroo the other marsupials; from these the mastodon, the megatherium, the giant sloth, the Irish elk, and all that crowd that you make useful and instructive fossils out of—then came the first great Ice Sheet, and they all retreated before it and crossed over the bridge at Behring's strait and wandered around over Europe and Asia and died. All except a few, to carry on the preparation with. Six Glacial Periods with two million years between Periods chased these poor orphans up and down and about the earth, from weather to weather—from tropic swelter at the poles to Arctic frost at the equator and back again and to and fro, they never knowing what kind of weather was going to turn up next; and if ever they settled down anywhere the whole continent suddenly sank under them without the least notice and they had to trade places with the fishes and scramble off to where the seas had been, and scarcely a dry rag on them; and when there was nothing else doing a volcano would let go and fire them out from wherever they had located. They led this unsettled and irritating life for twenty-five million years, half the time afloat, half the time aground, and always wondering what it was all for, they never suspecting, of course, that it was a preparation for man and had to be done just so or it wouldn't be any proper and harmonious place for him when he arrived.

And at last came the monkey, and anybody could see that man wasn't far off, now. And in truth that was so. The monkey went on developing for close upon 5,000,000 years, and then turned into a man—to all appearances.

Such is the history of it. Man has been here 32,000 years. That it took a hundred million years to prepare the world for him is proof that that is what it was done for. I suppose it is. I dunno. If the Eiffel tower were now representing the world's age, the skin of paint on the pinnacle-knob at its summit would represent man's share of that age; and anybody would perceive that that skin was what the tower was built for. I reckon they would, I dunno.

1903

LINES OF INQUIRY
"Was the World Made for Man?"

The speaker in this piece refers to himself as a "scientist and theologian." How scientific and theological do his information and ideas seem to be in paragraphs 6 and 7, when he explains what was required "to prepare the world for man"? How scientific and theological does his style seem to be in those same paragraphs—in such expressions as "make an oyster out of whole cloth" or "the amalekites will fetch the home-stake"? How would you describe the style of such expressions or characterize the personality that comes across as a result of them? To what extent do you associate that personality with Twain?

The story of geological, natural, and human evolution that comes across in this piece is quite preposterous. In what respect(s), if any, does it seem intended to mock scientific theories of evolution? Or theological explanations of evolution? What exactly do you think is the point of Twain's mock story of evolution? What is the point of his analogy in the final paragraph between the world and the Eiffel tower?

For another story of evolution, look at Eiseley's "How Flowers Changed the World." What similarities, what differences, do you notice between these two explanations? Assuming that you did not know of Twain and of his typically humorous and satiric approach to experience, and that you did not know about Eiseley and his scientific background, how would you know to take one piece humorously and the other straight-forwardly? What do you suppose Twain would think about Eiseley's story of how flowers changed the world? What do you think Eiseley would think about Twain's story?

"THE TURNING POINT OF MY LIFE"

If I understand the idea, the *Bazar* invites several of us to write upon the above text. It means the change in my life's course which introduced what must be regarded by me as the most *important* condition of my career. But it also implies— without intention, perhaps—that that turning point was *itself,* individually, the creator of the new condition. This gives it too much distinction, too much prominence, too much credit. It is only the *last* link in a very long chain of turning points commissioned to produce the weighty result; it is not any more important than the humblest of its ten thousand predecessors. Each of the ten thousand did its appointed share, on its appointed date, in forwarding the scheme, and they were all necessary; to have let out any one of them would have defeated the scheme and brought about *some other* result. I know we have a fashion of saying "such and such an event was *the* turning point of my life," but we shouldn't say it. We should merely grant that its place as *last* link in the chain makes it the most *conspicuous* link; in real importance it has no advantage over any one of its predecessors.

Perhaps the most celebrated turning point recorded in history was the crossing of the Rubicon. Suetonius says:

> Coming up with his troops on the banks of the Rubicon, he halted for a while, and, revolving in his mind the importance of the step he was on the point of taking, he turned to those about him and said, "We may still retreat; but if we pass this little bridge, nothing is left for us but to fight it out in arms."

This was a stupendously important moment. And all the incidents, big and little, of Caesar's previous life had been leading up to it, stage by stage, link by link. This was the *last* link—merely the last one, and no bigger than the others; but as we gaze back at it through the inflating mists of our imagination, it looks as big as the orbit of Neptune.

You, the reader, have a *personal* interest in that link, and so have I; so has the rest of the human race. It was one of the links in your life-chain, and it was one of the links in mine. We may wait, now, with bated breath, while Caesar reflects. Your fate and mine are involved in his decision.

> While he was thus hesitating, the following incident occurred. A person remarkable for his noble mien and graceful aspect, appeared close at hand,

sitting and playing upon a pipe. When not only the shepherds, but a number of soldiers also, flocked to listen to him, and some trumpeters among them, he snatched a trumpet from one of them, ran to the river with it, and sounding the advance with a piercing blast, crossed to the other side. Upon this, Caesar exclaimed, "Let us go whither the omens of the gods and the iniquity of our enemies call us. *The die is cast.*"

So he crossed—and changed the future of the whole human race, 5 for all time. But that stranger was a link in Caesar's life-chain, too; and a necessary one. We don't know his name, we never hear of him again, he was very casual, he acts like an accident; but he was no accident, he was there by compulsion of *his* life-chain, to blow the electrifying blast that was to make up Caesar's mind for him, and thence go piping down the aisles of history forever.

If the stranger hadn't been there! But he *was.* And Caesar crossed. With such results! Such vast events—each a link in the *human race's* life-chain; each event producing the next one, and that one the next one, and so on: the destruction of the republic; the founding of the empire; the breaking up of the empire; the rise of Christianity upon its ruins; the spread of the religion to other lands—and so on: link by link took its appointed place at its appointed time, the discovery of America being one of them; our Revolution another; the inflow of English and other immigrants another; their drift westward (my ancestors among them) another; the settlement of certain of them in Missouri—which resulted in *me.* For I was one of the unavoidable results of the crossing of the Rubicon. If the stranger, with his trumpet blast, had stayed away (which he *couldn't,* for he was an appointed link), Caesar would not have crossed. What would have happened, in that case, we can never guess. We only know that the things that did happen would not have happened. They might have been replaced by equally prodigious things, of course, but their nature and results are beyond our guessing. But the matter that interests me personally is, that I would not be *here,* now, but somewhere else; and probably black—there is no telling. Very well, I am glad he crossed. And very really and thankfully glad, too, though I never cared anything about it before.

II

To me, the most important feature of my life is its literary feature. I have been professionally literary something more than forty years. There have been many turning points in my life, but the one that was the last link in the chain appointed to conduct me to the literary guild is the most *conspicuous* link in that chain. *Because* it was the last one. It was not any more important than its predecessors. All the other links have an inconspicuous look, except the crossing of the Rubicon; but as factors in making me literary they are all of the one size, the crossing of the Rubicon included.

I know how I came to be literary, and I will tell the steps that led up to it and brought it about.

The crossing of the Rubicon was not the first one, it was hardly even a recent one; I should have to go back ages before Caesar's day to find the first one. To save space I will go back only a couple of generations, and start with an incident of my boyhood. When I was twelve and a half years old, my father died. It was in the spring. The summer came, and brought with it an epidemic of measles. For a time, a child died almost every day. The village was paralysed with fright, distress, despair. Children that were not smitten with the disease were imprisoned in their homes to save them from the infection. In the homes there were no cheerful faces, there was no music, there was no singing but of solemn hymns, no voice but of prayer, no romping was allowed, no noise, no laughter, the family moved spectrally about on tiptoe, in a ghostly hush. I was a prisoner. My soul was steeped in this awful dreariness—and in fear. At some time or other every day and every night a sudden shiver shook me to the marrow, and I said to myself, "There, I've got it! and I shall die." Life on these miserable terms was not worth living, and at last I made up my mind to get the disease and have it over, one way or the other. I escaped from the house and went to the house of a neighbor where a playmate of mine was very ill with the malady. When the chance offered I crept into his room and got into bed with him. I was discovered by his mother and sent back into captivity. But I had the disease; they could not take that from me. I came near to dying. The whole village was interested, and anxious, and sent for news for me every day; and not only once a day, but several times. Everybody believed I would die; but on the fourteenth day a change came for the worse and they were disappointed.

This was a turning point of my life. (Link number one.) For when   10
I got well my mother closed my school career and apprenticed me to a printer. She was tired of trying to keep me out of mischief, and the adventure of the measles decided her to put me into more masterful hands than hers.

I became a printer, and began to add one link after another to the chain which was to lead me into the literary profession. A long road, but I could not know that; and as I did not know what its goal was, or even that it had one, I was indifferent. Also contented.

A young printer wanders around a good deal, seeking and finding work; and seeking again, when necessity commands. N. B. Necessity is a *Circumstance;* Circumstance is man's master—and when Circumstance commands, he must obey; he may argue the matter—that is his privilege, just as it is the honorable privilege of a falling body to argue with the attraction of gravitation—but it won't do any good, he must *obey.* I wandered for ten years, under the guidance and dictatorship of Circumstance, and finally arrived in a city of Iowa, where I worked several months. Among the books that interested me in those days was one about the Amazon. The traveler told an alluring tale of his long voyage up the great river from Para to the sources of the Madeira, through the heart of an enchanted land, a land wastefully rich in tropical wonders, a romantic land where all the birds and flowers and animals were of the museum varieties, and where the alligator and the crocodile and the monkey seemed as much at home as if they were in the Zoo. Also, he told an astonishing tale about *coca,* a vegetable product of miraculous powers; asserting that it was so nourishing and so strength-giving that the native of the mountains of the Madeira region would tramp up-hill and down all day on a pinch of powdered coca and require no other sustenance.

I was fired with a longing to ascend the Amazon. Also with a longing to open up a trade in coca with all the world. During months I dreamed that dream, and tried to contrive ways to get to Para and spring that splendid enterprise upon an unsuspecting planet. But all in vain. A person may *plan* as much as he wants to, but nothing of consequence is likely to come of it until the magician *Circumstance* steps in and takes the matter off his hands. At last Circumstance came to my help. It was in this way. Circumstance, to help or hurt another man, made him lose a fifty-dollar bill in the street; and to help or hurt me, made me find it. I advertised the find, and left for the Amazon the same day. This was another turning point, another link.

Could Circumstance have ordered another dweller in that town to go to the Amazon and open up a world-trade in coca on a fifty-dollar basis and been obeyed? No, I was the only one. There were other fools there—shoals and shoals of them—but they were not of my kind. I was the only one of my kind.

Circumstance is powerful, but it cannot work alone, it has to have a partner. Its partner is man's *temperament*—his natural disposition. His temperament is not his invention, it is *born* in him, and he has no authority over it, neither is he responsible for its acts. He cannot change it, nothing can change it, nothing can modify it,—except temporarily. But it won't stay modified. It is permanent; like the color of the man's eyes and the shape of his ears. Blue eyes are gray, in certain unusual lights; but they resume their natural color when that stress is removed. 15

A Circumstance that will coerce one man, will have no effect upon a man of a different temperament. If Circumstance had thrown the bank note in Caesar's way, his temperament would not have made him start for the Amazon. His temperament would have compelled him to do something with the money, but not that. It might have made him advertise the note—and *wait*. We can't tell. Also, it might have made him go to New York and buy into the government; with results that would leave Tweed nothing to learn when it came his turn.

Very well, Circumstance furnished the capital, and my temperament told me what to do with it. Sometimes a temperament is an ass.

When that is the case the owner of it is an ass, too, and is going to remain one. Training, experience, association, can temporarily so elevate him that people will think he is a mule, but they will be mistaken. Artificially he *is* a mule, for the time being, but at bottom he is an ass yet, and will remain one.

By temperament I was the kind of person that *does* things. Does them, and reflects afterwards. So I started for the Amazon, without reflecting, and without asking any questions. That was more than fifty years ago. In all that time my temperament has not changed, by even a shade. I have been punished many and many a time, and bitterly, for doing things first and reflecting afterward, but these tortures have been of no value to me; I still do the thing commanded by Circumstance and Temperament, and reflect afterward. Always violently. When I am reflecting, on those occasions, even deaf persons can hear me think.

I went by the way of Cincinnati, and down the Ohio and Mississippi. My idea was to take ship, at New Orleans, for Para. In New Orleans I inquired, and found there was no ship leaving for Para. Also, that there never had *been* one leaving for Para. I reflected. A policeman came and asked me what I was doing, and I told him. He made me move on; and said if he caught me reflecting in the public street again he would run me in.

After a few days I was out of money. Then Circumstance arrived, 20 with another turning point of my life—a new link. On my way down, I had made the acquaintance of a pilot; I begged him to teach me the river, and he consented. I became a pilot.

By and by Circumstance came again—introducing the Civil War, this time, in order to push me ahead a stage or two toward the literary profession. The boats stopped running, my livelihood was gone.

Circumstance came to the rescue with a new turning point and a fresh link. My brother was appointed secretary to the new Territory of Nevada, and he invited me to go with him and help him in his office. I accepted.

In Nevada, Circumstance furnished me the silver fever and I went into the mines to make a fortune and enter the ministry. As I supposed; but that was not the idea. The idea was, to move me another step toward literature. For amusement I scribbled things for the Virginia City *Enterprise*. One isn't a printer ten years without setting up acres of good and bad literature, and learning—unconsciously at first, consciously later—to discriminate between the two, within his mental limitations; and meantime he is unconsciously acquiring what is called a "style." One of my efforts attracted attention, and the *Enterprise* sent for me, and put me on its staff.

And so I became a journalist—another link. By and by Circumstance and the Sacramento *Union* sent me to the Sandwich Islands for five or six months, to write up sugar. I did it; and threw in a good deal of extraneous matter that hadn't anything to do with sugar. But it was this extraneous matter that helped me to another link.

It made me notorious, and San Francisco invited me to lecture. Which 25 I did. And profitably. I had long had a desire to travel and see the world, and now the platform had furnished me the means. So I joined the "Quaker City Excursion."

When I returned to America, Circumstance was waiting on the pier— with the *last* link: I was asked to *write a book,* and I did it, and called it *The Innocents Abroad.* Thus at last I became a member of the literary guild. That was forty-two years ago, and I have been a member ever since. Leaving the Rubicon incident away back where it belongs, I can say with truth that the reason I am in the literary profession is because I had the measles when I was twelve years old.

III

Now what interests me, as regards these details, is not the details themselves, but the fact that none of them was foreseen by me, none of them was planned by me, I was the author of none of them. Circumstance, working in harness with my temperament, created them all and compelled them all. I often offered help, and with the best intentions, but it was rejected: as a rule, uncourteously. I could never plan a thing and get it to come out the way I planned it. It came out some other way— some way I had not counted upon.

And so I do not admire the human being—as an intellectual marvel—as much as I did when I was young, and got him out of books, and did not know him personally. When I used to read that such and such a general did a certain brilliant thing, I believed it. Whereas it was not so. Circumstance did it, by help of his temperament. The circumstances would have failed of effect with a general of another temperament: he might see the chance, but lose the advantage by being by nature too slow or too quick or too doubtful. Once General Grant was asked a question about a matter which had been much debated by the public and the newspapers; he answered the question without any hesitancy: "General, who planned the march through Georgia?" "The enemy!" He added that the enemy usually makes your plans for you. He meant that the enemy, by neglect or through force of circumstances, leaves an opening for you, and you see your chance and take advantage of it.

Circumstances do the planning for us all, no doubt, by help of our temperaments. I see no great difference between a man and a watch, except that the man is conscious and the watch isn't, and the man *tries* to plan things and the watch doesn't. The watch doesn't wind itself, and doesn't regulate itself—these things are done exteriorly. Outside influences, outside circumstances, wind the *man* and regulate him. Left to himself he wouldn't get regulated at all, and the sort of time he would keep would not be valuable. Some rare men are wonderful watches, with gold case, compensation balance, and all those things, and some men are only simple and sweet and humble Waterburys. I am a Waterbury. A Waterbury of that kind, some say.

A nation is only an individual, multiplied. It makes plans, and Circumstance comes and upsets them—or enlarges them. A gang of patriots throws the tea overboard; it destroys a Bastile. The plans stop there; then Circumstance comes in, quite unexpectedly, and turns these modest riots into a revolution.

And there was poor Columbus. He elaborated a deep plan to find a new route to an old country. Circumstance revised his plan for him, and he found a new *world*. And *he* gets the credit of it, to this day. He hadn't anything to do with it.

Necessarily the scene of the real turning point of my life (and of yours) was the Garden of Eden. It was there that the first link was forged of the chain that was ultimately to lead to the emptying of me into the literary guild. Adam's *temperament* was the first command the Deity ever issued to a human being on this planet. And it was the only command Adam would *never* be able to disobey. It said, "Be weak, be water, be characterless, be cheaply persuadable." The later command, to let the fruit alone, was certain to be disobeyed. Not by Adam himself, but by his *temperament*—which he did not create and had no authority over. For the *temperament* is the man; the thing tricked out with clothes and named Man, is merely its Shadow, nothing more. The law of the tiger's temperament is, Thou shalt kill; the law of the sheep's temperament is, Thou shalt not kill. To issue later commands requiring the tiger to let the fat stranger alone, and requiring the sheep to imbue its hands in the blood of the lion is not worth while, for those commands *can't* be obeyed. They would invite to violations of the law of *temperament,* which is supreme, and takes precedence of all other authorities. I cannot help feeling disappointed in Adam and Eve. That is, in their temperaments. Not in *them,* poor helpless young creatures—afflicted with temperaments made out of butter; which butter was commanded to get into contact with fire and *be melted*. What I cannot help wishing is, that Adam and Eve had been postponed, and Martin Luther and Joan of Arc put in their place—that splendid pair equipped with temperaments not made of butter, but of asbestos. By neither sugary persuasions nor by hellfire could Satan have beguiled *them* to eat the apple.

There would have been results! Indeed yes. The apple would be intact to-day: there would be no human race; there would be no *you;* there would be no *me*. And the old, old creation-dawn scheme of ultimately launching me into the literary guild would have been defeated.

1910

LINES OF INQUIRY
"'The Turning Point of My Life'"

Twain claims that no single event in a person's life is of more "real importance" than "any one of its predecessors," yet he tells what he considers to be
the most important events that led to his becoming a writer. How do you
account for this apparent contradiction? Given his mocking attitude towards the
idea of a turning point in life, why doesn't he confine himself instead to the
story of Caesar crossing the Rubicon? Or to the story of Adam and Eve? What
purpose is served by telling the story of his life from the age of twelve to thirty-
four? What purposes are served by preceding it with the story of Caesar and
following it with the story of Adam?

From the beginning to the end of this piece, Twain states several of his
beliefs concerning the course of human affairs. Note down or underline the
ones that seem to be most important in his thinking, and then try to produce
an outline showing how these ideas are logically interrelated. Check your analysis
of his ideas against the essay as a whole in order to determine what you consider to be the major idea that he is trying to convey in this piece.

In this essay, Twain considers "Circumstance" to be the decisive influence
in human affairs, whereas in"Corn-Pone Opinions," he regards "Conformity"
as the decisive influence. How do you make sense of this apparent contradiction? Which of these influences do you consider to be most decisive in human
affairs? Which one has been most influential in your own life?

ALICE WALKER

1944 –

I believe that the truth about any subject only comes when all the sides of the story are put together, and all their different meanings make one new one. Each writer writes the missing parts to the other writer's story. And the whole story is what I'm after.

Alice Walker's contribution to American writing has been to add a black woman's "side of the story" and to challenge any version of the American experience that has pretended to be the "whole story" but which has, in fact, been constructed around the silence of that "missing part." As a writer, she has consistently supported the interests of her "affinity groups," black people and women, yet her work has never been narrowly political. Ultimately, her artistic quest is also a spiritual one: "One thing I try to have in my life and my fiction is an awareness of and openness to mystery, which, to me, is deeper than any politics, race, or geographical location."

The youngest of eight children, Walker was born in Eatonton, Georgia, a town "which passes for the Walker ancestral home." Her "four-greats" grandmother on her father's side had been forced in the early nineteenth century to walk all the way from Virginia to Georgia, a baby on each hip, and Walker has chosen to keep and use her family name to honor this grandmother and that walk. By the time she was born, Walker's father, a sharecropper, was a defeated, sickly, and emotionally distant man. But her mother was a "large, soft, loving-eyed woman" who "adorned with flowers whatever shabby house we were forced to live in" and sustained her large family with her patient industry. In addition to teaching by example the "womanist" tradition of black women who grow up knowing they can "do anything," Walker's mother gave her three symbolically significant gifts: a sewing machine, suggesting "independence and self-sufficiency"; a suitcase, representing "permission to travel"; and a typewriter, supporting her interest in writing.

Throughout her childhood, Walker read avidly: "Books became my world because the world I was in was very hard." From the age of eight, when she was accidentally blinded in her right eye, Walker kept a detailed personal notebook. While in many ways profoundly connected to her family, she felt herself to be also profoundly different:

> Sometimes I thought I'd gotten into the family by mistake. I always seemed to need more peace and quiet than anybody else. Th t's very difficult when you're living with ten people in three or four rooms. So I found what privacy I had by walking in the fields. We had to get our water from a spring, so that was a time to be alone, too.

Walker's early love affair with nature was also an escape from the harsh reality of her hometown, where before integration blacks were not permitted to swim in the public pool, where they could enter the local drug store to buy ice cream but were not allowed to stay inside to eat it, and where stories of lynchings and other forms of racial violence perpetually filled the air. Completely segregated from the white population, in schools as in neighborhoods, blacks took care of each other's needs, fostering the education of the young, nursing the sick, sharing food and clothes, burying the dead. That interdependence gave Walker a rich experience of community, but "I was an exile in my own town," she writes, "and grew to despise its white citizens as much as I loved the Georgia countryside where I fished and swam and walked through fields of black-eyed Susans. . . ."

Walker struggled with the hatred, and like James Baldwin and Martin Luther King before her, came to realize that it would finally destroy not her enemies but herself: "Once spread about . . . [hatred] becomes a web in which I would sit caught and paralyzed like the fly who stepped into the parlor." Walker has said that King gave the South back to its black sons and daughters and inspired her to hope rather than hate. Nevertheless, the memory of her poverty-stricken and racially oppressed heritage remains vivid: "It is memory, more than anything else, that sours the sweetness of what has been accomplished in the South. What we cannot forget and will never forget."

Walker left home in 1961 to attend Spelman College for black women in Atlanta, but after two years became frustrated with its strict social rules and regulations, so in search of greater "freedom" she transferred to Sarah Lawrence, an academically elite, predominantly white woman's college, where she graduated in 1965. While in college she traveled to the Soviet Union, Europe, and Africa on fellowships, and began to develop the global consciousness that has characterized her later writing. And at Sarah Lawrence, encouraged by her writing teachers, particularly the poet Muriel Rukeyser, she completed her first book, *Once,* a collection of poems that was published in 1968.

After graduating from college, Walker married an activist lawyer in 1967 (from whom she was divorced in 1976) and moved with him to

Mississippi, where he went to take part in the civil rights movement. Back in the South, she taught black studies at Jackson State College, and she thus came to discover a wealth of black literature of which her education had left her ignorant. So, she entered "still another college," this one "simply a college of books," and became acquainted with her literary forbears. Having read widely in the work of white writers throughout her school years, she sought to correct the imbalance by immersing herself in the work of black poets and novelists, many of them out of print and forgotten. Her discoveries inspired her to begin a crusade to restore black writing into the mainstream of American literature. In her essays she has repeatedly made known the work of black American and African writers, and she has also written a children's biography of Langston Hughes, as well as having edited a collection of works by Zora Neale Hurston.

Walker herself has been a prolific writer, publishing thirteen books—novels, short stories, poems, and essays—and numerous magazine pieces since 1968. Her work has won her wide recognition and many awards, though she is probably best known for her novel of southern black experience. *The Color Purple* (1983), which received both the Pulitzer Prize and the National Book Award before being made into a highly successful motion picture. She has served for a number of years as a contributing editor of *Ms* magazine, as well as having taught writing and literature at schools in Mississippi, Boston, and New York, before settling in California, where she lives with her family in the countryside near San Francisco.

Her essays have been collected in two volumes, *In Search of Our Mothers' Gardens* (1983) and *Living by the Word* (1988), both of which represent significant contributions to the self-defining process of her race and her gender. Her growing vision, though, has led her increasingly to resist race as a category for definition:

> I have not labeled myself yet. I would like to call myself revolutionary, for I am always changing, and growing, it is hoped for the good of more black people. I do call myself black when it seems necessary to call myself anything, especially since I believe one's work rather than one's appearance adequately labels one.

In this respect, Walker follows the precedent of Baldwin, among others, in calling into question the designations of "white" and "black." Indeed, in her most recent essays, Walker has pressed on her readers a mystical vision of oneness, not only of all the world's people but also of humankind with everything else in creation. Following in the tradition of ancient African and Native American belief, she celebrates a vision affirming that "everything is inhabited by spirit." So, in historical times filled with doubt and with the fear of annihilation, she has taken upon herself the task of urging the need for the "survival whole" of the human race and the planet which is its home. "The truest and most enduring impulse I have is simply to write," she says, and she is clear about what it is she hopes to accomplish through her writing:

> I am trying to arrive at that place where black music already is; to arrive at that unself-conscious sense of collective oneness; that naturalness, that (even when anguished) grace.

BEAUTY: WHEN THE OTHER DANCER IS THE SELF

It is a bright summer day in 1947. My father, a fat, funny man with beautiful eyes and a subversive wit, is trying to decide which of his eight children he will take with him to the county fair. My mother, of course, will not go. She is knocked out from getting most of us ready: I hold my neck stiff against the pressure of her knuckles as she hastily completes the braiding and then beribboning of my hair.

My father is the driver for the rich old white lady up the road. Her name is Miss Mey. She owns all the land for miles around, as well as the house in which we live. All I remember about her is that she once offered to pay my mother thirty-five cents for cleaning her house, raking up piles of her magnolia leaves, and washing her family's clothes, and that my mother—she of no money, eight children, and a chronic earache—refused it. But I do not think of this in 1947. I am two and a half years old. I want to go everywhere my daddy goes. I am excited at the prospect of riding in a car. Someone has told me fairs are fun. That there is room in the car for only three of us doesn't faze me at all. Whirling happily in my starchy frock, showing off my biscuit-polished patent-leather shoes and lavender socks, tossing my head in a way that makes my ribbons bounce, I stand, hands on hips, before my father. "Take me, Daddy," I say with assurance; "I'm the prettiest!"

Later, it does not surprise me to find myself in Miss Mey's shiny black car, sharing the back seat with the other lucky ones. Does not surprise me that I thoroughly enjoy the fair. At home that night I tell the unlucky ones all I can remember about the merry-go-round, the man who eats live chickens, and the teddy bears, until they say: that's enough, baby Alice. Shut up now, and go to sleep.

It is Easter Sunday, 1950. I am dressed in a green, flocked, scalloped-hem dress (handmade by my adoring sister, Ruth) that has its own smooth satin petticoat and tiny hot-pink roses tucked into each scallop. My shoes, new T-strap patent leather, again highly biscuit-polished. I am six years old and have learned one of the longest Easter speeches to be heard that day, totally unlike the speech I said when I was two: "Easter lilies/pure and white/blossom in/the morning light." When I rise to give my speech I do so on a great wave of love and pride and expectation. People in the church stop rustling their new crinolines. They seem to hold their breath. I can tell they admire my dress, but it is my spirit, bordering on sassiness (womanishness), they secretly applaud.

"That girl's a little *mess*," they whisper to each other, pleased.   5

Naturally I say my speech without stammer or pause, unlike those who stutter, stammer, or, worst of all, forget. This is before the word "beautiful" exists in people's vocabulary, but "Oh, isn't she the *cutest* thing!" frequently floats my way. "And got so much sense!" they gratefully add . . . for which thoughtful addition I thank them to this day.

It was great fun being cute. But then, one day, it ended.

I am eight years old and a tomboy. I have a cowboy hat, cowboy boots, checkered shirt and pants, all red. My playmates are my brothers, two and four years older than I. Their colors are black and green, the only difference in the way we are dressed. On Saturday nights we all go to the picture show, even my mother; Westerns are her favorite kind of movie. Back home, "on the ranch," we pretend we are Tom Mix, Hopalong Cassidy, Lash LaRue (we've even named one of our dogs Lash LaRue); we chase each other for hours rustling cattle, being outlaws, delivering damsels from distress. Then my parents decide to buy my brothers guns. These are not "real" guns. They shoot "BBs," copper pellets my brothers say will kill birds. Because I am a girl, I do not get a gun. Instantly I am relegated to the position of Indian. Now there appears a great distance between us. They shoot and shoot at everything with their new guns. I try to keep up with my bow and arrows.

One day while I am standing on top of our makeshift "garage"— pieces of tin nailed across some poles—holding my bow and arrow and looking out toward the fields, I feel an incredible blow in my right eye. I look down just in time to see my brother lower his gun.

Both brothers rush to my side. My eye stings, and I cover it with   10
my hand. "If you tell," they say, "we will get a whipping. You don't want that to happen, do you?" I do not. "Here is a piece of wire," says the older brother, picking it up from the roof; "say you stepped on one end of it and the other flew up and hit you." The pain is beginning to start. "Yes," I say. "Yes, I will say that is what happened." If I do not say this is what happened, I know my brothers will find ways to make me wish I had. But now I will say anything that gets me to my mother.

Confronted by our parents we stick to the lie agreed upon. They place me on a bench on the porch and I close my left eye while they examine the right. There is a tree growing from underneath the porch that climbs past the railing to the roof. It is the last thing my right eye sees. I watch as its trunk, its branches, and then its leaves are blotted out by the rising blood.

I am in shock. First there is intense fever, which my father tries to break using lily leaves bound around my head. Then there are chills: my mother tries to get me to eat soup. Eventually, I do not know how, my parents learn what has happened. A week after the "accident" they take me to see a doctor. "Why did you wait so long to come?" he asks, looking into my eye and shaking his head. "Eyes are sympathetic," he says. "If one is blind, the other will likely become blind too."

This comment of the doctor's terrifies me. But it is really how I look that bothers me most. Where the BB pellet struck there is a glob of whitish scar tissue, a hideous cataract, on my eye. Now when I stare at people—a favorite pastime, up to now—they will stare back. Not at the "cute" little girl, but at her scar. For six years I do not stare at anyone, because I do not raise my head.

Years later, in the throes of a mid-life crisis, I ask my mother and sister whether I changed after the "accident." "No," they say, puzzled. "What do you mean?"

What do I mean?   15

I am eight, and, for the first time, doing poorly in school, where I have been something of a whiz since I was four. We have just moved to the place where the "accident" occurred. We do not know any of the people around us because this is a different county. The only time I see the friends I knew is when we go back to our old church. The new school is the former state penitentiary. It is a large stone building, cold and drafty, crammed to overflowing with boisterous, ill-disciplined children. On the third floor there is a huge circular imprint of some partition that has been torn out.

"What used to be here?" I ask a sullen girl next to me on our way past it to lunch.

"The electric chair," says she.

At night I have nightmares about the electric chair, and about all the people reputedly "fried" in it. I am afraid of the school, where all the students seem to be budding criminals.

"What's the matter with your eye?" they ask, critically.   20

When I don't answer (I cannot decide whether it was an "accident" or not), they shove me, insist on a fight.

My brother, the one who created the story about the wire, comes to my rescue. But then brags so much about "protecting" me, I become sick.

After months of torture at the school, my parents decide to send me back to our old community, to my old school. I live with my grandparents and the teacher they board. But there is no room for Phoebe, my cat. By the time my grandparents decide there *is* room, and I ask for my cat, she cannot be found. Miss Yarborough, the boarding teacher, takes me under her wing, and begins to teach me to play the piano. But soon she marries an African—a "prince," she says—and is whisked away to his continent.

At my old school there is at least one teacher who loves me. She is the teacher who "knew me before I was born" and bought my first baby clothes. It is she who makes life bearable. It is her presence that finally helps me turn on the one child at the school who continually calls me "one-eyed bitch." One day I simply grab him by his coat and beat him until I am satisfied. It is my teacher who tells me my mother is ill.

My mother is lying in bed in the middle of the day, something I have never seen. She is in too much pain to speak. She has an abscess in her ear. I stand looking down on her, knowing that if she dies, I cannot live. She is being treated with warm oils and hot bricks held against her cheek. Finally a doctor comes. But I must go back to my grandparents' house. The weeks pass but I am hardly aware of it. All I know is that my mother might die, my father is not so jolly, my brothers still have their guns, and I am the one sent away from home.

"You did not change," they say.   25

Did I imagine the anguish of never looking up?

I am twelve. When relatives come to visit I hide in my room. My cousin Brenda, just my age, whose father works in the post office and whose mother is a nurse, comes to find me. "Hello," she says. And then she asks, looking at my recent school picture, which I did not want taken, and on which the "glob," as I think of it, is clearly visible, "You still can't see out of that eye?"

"No," I say, and flop back on the bed over my book.

That night, as I do almost every night, I abuse my eye. I rant and rave at it, in front of the mirror. I plead with it to clear up before morning. I tell it I hate and despise it. I do not pray for sight. I pray for beauty.

"You did not change," they say.   30

I am fourteen and baby-sitting for my brother Bill, who lives in Boston. He is my favorite brother and there is a strong bond between us. Understanding my feelings of shame and ugliness he and his wife take me to a local hospital, where the "glob" is removed by a doctor named O. Henry. There is still a small bluish crater where the scar tissue was, but the ugly white stuff is gone. Almost immediately I become a different person from the girl who does not raise her head. Or so I think. Now that I've raised my head I win the boyfriend of my dreams. Now that I've raised my head I have plenty of friends. Now that I've raised my head classwork comes from my lips as faultlessly as Easter speeches did, and I leave high school as valedictorian, most popular student, and *queen,* hardly believing my luck. Ironically, the girl who was voted most beautiful in our class (and was) was later shot twice through the chest by a male companion, using a "real" gun, while she was pregnant. But that's another story in itself. Or is it?

"You did not change," they say.

It is now thirty years since the "accident." A beautiful journalist comes to visit and to interview me. She is going to write a cover story for her magazine that focuses on my latest book. "Decide how you want to look on the cover," she says. "Glamorous, or whatever."

Never mind "glamorous," it is the "whatever" that I hear. Suddenly all I can think of is whether I will get enough sleep the night before the photography session: if I don't, my eye will be tired and wander, as blind eyes will.

At night in bed with my lover I think up reasons why I should not appear on the cover of a magazine. "My meanest critics will say I've sold out," I say. "My family will now realize I write scandalous books." 35

"But what's the real reason you don't want to do this?" he asks.

"Because in all probability," I say in a rush, "my eye won't be straight."

"It will be straight enough," he says. Then, "Besides, I thought you'd made your peace with that."

And I suddenly remember that I have.

I remember: 40

I am talking to my brother Jimmy, asking if he remembers anything unusual about the day I was shot. He does not know I consider that day the last time my father, with his sweet home remedy of cool lily leaves, chose me, and that I suffered and raged inside because of this. "Well," he says, "all I remember is standing by the side of the highway with Daddy, trying to flag down a car. A white man stopped, but when Daddy said he needed somebody to take his little girl to the doctor, he drove off."

I remember:

I am in the desert for the first time. I fall totally in love with it. I am so overwhelmed by its beauty, I confront for the first time, consciously, the meaning of the doctor's words years ago: "Eyes are sympathetic. If one is blind, the other will likely become blind too." I realize I have dashed about the world madly, looking at this, looking at that, storing up images against the fading of the light. *But I might have missed seeing the desert!* The shock of that possibility—and gratitude for over twenty-five years of sight—sends me literally to my knees. Poem after poem comes—which is perhaps how poets pray.

ON SIGHT

I am so thankful I have seen
The Desert
And the creatures in the desert
And the desert Itself.

The desert has its own moon
Which I have seen
With my own eye.
There is no flag on it.

Trees of the desert have arms
All of which are always up
That is because the moon is up
The sun is up
Also the sky
The stars
Clouds
None with flags.

If there *were* flags, I doubt
the trees would point.
Would you?

But mostly, I remember this:

I am twenty-seven, and my baby daughter is almost three. Since   40
her birth I have worried about her discovery that her mother's eyes are
different from other people's. Will she be embarrassed? I think. What
will she say? Every day she watches a television program called "Big
Blue Marble." It begins with a picture of the earth as it appears from
the moon. It is bluish, a little battered-looking, but full of light, with
whitish clouds swirling around it. Every time I see it I weep with love,
as if it is a picture of Grandma's house. One day when I am putting
Rebecca down for her nap, she suddenly focuses on my eye. Something
inside me cringes, gets ready to try to protect myself. All children are
cruel about physical differences, I know from experience, and that they
don't always mean to be is another matter. I assume Rebecca will be
the same.

But no-o-o-o. She studies my face intently as we stand, her inside
and me outside her crib. She even holds my face maternally between
her dimpled little hands. Then, looking every bit as serious and law-
yerlike as her father, she says, as if it may just possibly have slipped
my attention: "Mommy, there's a *world* in your eye." (As in, "Don't
be alarmed, or do anything crazy.") And then, gently, but with great
interest: "Mommy, where did you *get* that world in your eye?"

For the most part, the pain left then. (So what if my brothers grew
up to buy even more powerful pellet guns for their sons and to carry
real guns themselves. So what, if a young "Morehouse man" once nearly

fell off the steps of Trevor Arnett Library because he thought my eyes were blue.) Crying and laughing I ran to the bathroom, while Rebecca mumbled and sang herself off to sleep. Yes indeed, I realized, looking into the mirror. There *was* a world in my eye. And I saw that it was possible to love it: that in fact, for all it had taught me of shame and anger and inner vision, I *did* love it. Even to see it drifting out of orbit in boredom, or rolling up out of fatigue, not to mention floating back at attention in excitement (bearing witness, a friend has called it), deeply suitable to my personality, and even characteristic of me.

That night I dream I am dancing to Stevie Wonder's song "Always" (the name of the song is really "As," but I hear it as "Always"). As I dance, whirling and joyous, happier than I've ever been in my life, another bright-faced dancer joins me. We dance and kiss each other and hold each other through the night. The other dancer has obviously come through all right, as I have done. She is beautiful, whole and free. And she is also me.

1983

LINES OF INQUIRY
"Beauty: When the Other Dancer Is the Self"

In this narrative essay, Walker tells her story in a number of unusual ways. For example, what do you consider to be the effect(s) of her telling about the past in present tense? Why do you suppose she divides the story into a series of short segments, separated from each other by some extra space, rather than telling it and presenting it on the page in a continuously connected manner? And why does she depart from chronological order in the last two segments, first telling about a time "thirty years since the 'accident'" and then about an episode when she was twenty-seven? Imagine how the piece might work out if these episodes were reversed.

Though Walker never announces the point of this essay, it seems clear that she is not just telling about herself because she wants to divulge an aspect of her private life. So, what do you infer about the significance of this piece from her unusual ways of telling her story? What do you infer about the significance of the piece from the lines that she has singled out for emphasis either by italics or by indentation, such as her poem "On Sight"? What do you infer about the significance of the piece from the title and the echoes of it throughout the essay, particularly in the final paragraph?

Think about an especially painful accident or loss that you suffered earlier in your life that has been difficult for you to come to terms with. What was the nature of your accident or loss? In what specific way(s) did it affect you and your attitude towards yourself? At what points in your subsequent life can you remember being particularly troubled by its effects or at ease with them? What has been most helpful for you in coming to terms with it? In what respects, if any, did your reading about Walker's experience help to shed light on your own?

THE CIVIL RIGHTS MOVEMENT: WHAT GOOD WAS IT?[1]

Someone said recently to an old black lady from Mississippi, whose legs had been badly mangled by local police who arrested her for "disturbing the peace," that the Civil Rights Movement was dead, and asked, since it was dead, what she thought about it. The old lady replied, hobbling out of his presence on her cane, that the Civil Rights Movement was like herself, "if it's dead, it shore ain't ready to lay down!"

This old lady is a legendary freedom fighter in her small town in the Delta. She has been severely mistreated for insisting on her rights as an American citizen. She has been beaten for singing Movement songs, placed in solitary confinement in prisons for talking about freedom, and placed on bread and water for praying aloud to God for her jailers' deliverance. For such a woman the Civil Rights Movement will never be over as long as her skin is black. It also will never be over for twenty million others with the same "affliction," for whom the Movement can never "lay down," no matter how it is killed by the press and made dead and buried by the white American public. As long as one black American survives, the struggle for equality with other Americans must also survive. This is a debt we owe to those blameless hostages we leave to the future, our children.

Still, white liberals and deserting Civil Rights sponsors are quick to justify their disaffection from the Movement by claiming that it is all over. "And since it is over," they will ask, "would someone kindly tell me what has been gained by it?" They then list statistics supposedly showing how much more advanced segregation is now than ten years ago—in schools, housing, jobs. They point to a gain in conservative politicians during the last few years. They speak of ghetto riots and of the survey that shows that most policemen are admittedly too anti-Negro to do their jobs in ghetto areas fairly and effectively. They speak

---

[1] I wrote the following essay in the winter of 1966–67 while sharing one room above Washington Square Park in New York with a struggling young Jewish law student who became my husband. It was my first published essay and won the three-hundred-dollar first prize in the annual *American Scholar* essay contest. The money was almost magically reassuring to us in those days of dissaffected parents, outraged friends, and one-item meals, and kept us in tulips, peonies, daisies, and lamb chops for several months.

of every area that has been touched by the Civil Rights Movement as somehow or other going to pieces.

They rarely talk, however, about human attitudes among Negroes that have undergone terrific changes just during the past seven to ten years (not to mention all those years when there was a Movement and only the Negroes knew about it). They seldom speak of changes in personal lives because of the influence of people in the Movement. They see general failure and few, if any, individual gains.

They do not understand what it is that keeps the Movement from   5 "laying down" and Negroes from reverting to their former *silent* second-class status. They have apparently never stopped to wonder why it is always the white man—on his radio and in his newspaper and on his television—who says that the Movement is dead. If a Negro were audacious enough to make such a claim, his fellows might hanker to see him shot. The Movement is dead to the white man because it no longer interests him. And it no longer interests him because he can afford to be uninterested: he does not have to live by it, with it, or for it, as Negroes must. He can take a rest from the news of beatings, killings, and arrests that reach him from North and South—if his skin is white. Negroes cannot now and will never be able to take a rest from the injustices that plague them, for they—not the white man—are the target.

Perhaps it is naïve to be thankful that the Movement "saved" a large number of individuals and gave them something to live for, even if it did not provide them with everything they wanted. (Materially, it provided them with precious little that they wanted.) When a movement awakens people to the possibilities of life, it seems unfair to frustrate them by then denying what they had thought was offered. But what was offered? What was promised? What was it all about? What good did it do? Would it have been better, as some have suggested, to leave the Negro people as they were, unawakened, unallied with one another, unhopeful about what to expect for their children in some future world?

I do not think so. If knowledge of my condition is all the freedom I get from a "freedom movement," it is better than unawareness, forgottenness, and hopelessness, the existence that is like the existence of a beast. Man only truly lives by knowing; otherwise he simply performs, copying the daily habits of others, but conceiving nothing of his creative possibilities as a man, and accepting someone else's superiority and his own misery.

When we are children, growing up in our parents' care, we await the spark from the outside world. Sometimes our parents provide it— if we are lucky—sometimes it comes from another source far from home. We sit, paralyzed, surrounded by our anxiety and dread, hoping we will not have to grow up into the narrow world and ways we see about us. We are hungry for a life that turns us on; we yearn for a knowledge of living that will save us from our innocuous lives that resemble death. We look for signs in every strange event; we search for heroes in every unknown face.

It was just six years ago that I began to be alive. I had, of course, been living before—for I am now twenty-three—but I did not really know it. And I did not know it because nobody told me that I—a pensive, yearning, typical high-school senior, but Negro—existed in the minds of others as I existed in my own. Until that time my mind was locked apart from the outer contours and complexion of my body as if it and the body were strangers. The mind possessed both thought and spirit—I wanted to be an author or a scientist—which the color of the body denied. I had never seen myself and existed as a statistic exists, or as a phantom. In the white world I walked, less real to them than a shadow; and being young and well hidden among the slums, among people who also did not exist—either in books or in films or in the government of their own lives—I waited to be called to life. And, by a miracle, I was called.

There was a commotion in our house that night in 1960. We had   10
managed to buy our first television set. It was battered and overpriced, but my mother had gotten used to watching the afternoon soap operas at the house where she worked as maid, and nothing could satisfy her on days when she did not work but a continuation of her "stories." So she pinched pennies and bought a set.

I remained listless throughout her "stories," tales of pregnancy, abortion, hypocrisy, infidelity, and alcoholism. All these men and women were white and lived in houses with servants, long staircases that they floated down, patios where liquor was served four times a day to "relax" them. But my mother, with her swollen feet eased out of her shoes, her heavy body relaxed in our only comfortable chair, watched each movement of the smartly coiffed women, heard each word, pounced upon each innuendo and inflection, and for the duration of these "stories" she saw herself as one of them. She placed herself in every scene she saw, with her braided hair turned blond, her two hundred pounds compressed into a sleek size-seven dress, her rough dark skin smooth and *white*. Her husband became "dark and handsome," talented, witty, urbane, charming. And when she turned to look at my father sitting near her in his sweat shirt with his smelly feet raised on the bed to "air," there was always a tragic look of surprise on her face. Then she would sigh and go out to the kitchen looking lost and unsure of herself. My mother, a truly great woman who raised eight children of her own and half a dozen of the neighbors' without a single complaint, was convinced that she did not exist compared to "them." She subordinated her soul to theirs and became a faithful and timid supporter of the

"Beautiful White People." Once she asked me, in a moment of vicarious pride and despair, if I didn't think that "they" were "jest naturally smarter, prettier, better." My mother asked this: a woman who never got rid of any of her children, never cheated on my father, was never a hypocrite if she could help it, and never even tasted liquor. She could not even bring herself to blame "them" for making her believe what they wanted her to believe: that if she did not look like them, think like them, be sophisticated and corrupt-for-comfort's sake like them, she was a nobody. Black was not a color on my mother; it was a shield that made her invisible.

Of course, the people who wrote the soap-opera scripts always made the Negro maids in them steadfast, trusty, and wise in a home-remedial sort of way; but my mother, a maid for nearly forty years, never once identified herself with the scarcely glimpsed black servant's face beneath the ruffled cap. Like everyone else, in her daydreams at least, she thought she was free.

Six years ago, after half-heartedly watching my mother's soap operas and wondering whether there wasn't something more to be asked of life, the Civil Rights Movement came into my life. Like a good omen for the future, the face of Dr. Martin Luther King, Jr., was the first black face I saw on our new television screen. And, as in a fairy tale, my soul was stirred by the meaning for me of his mission—at the time he was being rather ignominiously dumped into a police van for having led a protest march in Alabama—and I fell in love with the sober and determined face of the Movement. The singing of "We Shall Overcome"—that song betrayed by nonbelievers in it—rang for the first time in my ears. The influence that my mother's soap operas might have had on me became impossible. The life of Dr. King, seeming bigger and more miraculous than the man himself, because of all he had done and suffered, offered a pattern of strength and sincerity I felt I could trust. He had suffered much because of his simple belief in nonviolence, love, and brotherhood. Perhaps the majority of men could not be reached through these beliefs, but because Dr. King kept trying to reach them in spite of danger to himself and his family, I saw in him the hero for whom I had waited so long.

What Dr. King promised was not a ranch-style house and an acre of manicured lawn for every black man, but jail and finally freedom. He did not promise two cars for every family, but the courage one day for all families everywhere to walk without shame and unafraid on their own feet. He did not say that one day it will be us chasing prospective buyers out of our prosperous well-kept neighborhoods, or in other ways exhibiting our snobbery and ignorance as all other ethnic groups before us have done; what he said was that we had a right to live anywhere in this country we chose, and a right to a meaningful well-paying job to provide us with the upkeep of our homes. He did not say we had to become carbon copies of the white American middle class; but he did say we had the right to become whatever we wanted to become.

Because of the Movement, because of an awakened faith in the   15
newness and imagination of the human spirit, because of "black and white together"—for the first time in our history in some human relationship on and off TV—because of the beatings, the arrests, the hell of battle during the past years, I have fought harder for my life and for a chance to be myself, to be something more than a shadow or a number, than I had ever done before in my life. Before, there had seemed to be no real reason for struggling beyond the effort for daily bread. Now there was a chance at that other that Jesus meant when He said we could not live by bread alone.

I have fought and kicked and fasted and prayed and cursed and cried myself to the point of existing. It has been like being born again, literally. Just "knowing" has meant everything to me. Knowing has pushed me out into the world, into college, into places, into people.

Part of what existence means to me is knowing the difference between what I am now and what I was then. It is being capable of looking after myself intellectually as well as financially. It is being able to tell when I am being wronged and by whom. It means being awake to protect myself and the ones I love. It means being a part of the world community, and being *alert* to which part it is that I have joined, and knowing how to change to another part if that part does not suit me. To know is to exist: to exist is to be involved, to move about, to see the world with my own eyes. This, at least, the Movement has given me.

The hippies and other nihilists would have me believe that it is all the same whether the people in Mississippi have a movement behind them or not. Once they have their rights, they say, they will run all over themselves trying to be just like everybody else. They will be well fed, complacent about things of the spirit, emotionless, and without that marvelous humanity and "soul" that the Movement has seen them practice time and time again. "What has the Movement done," they ask, "with the few people it has supposedly helped?" "Got them white-collar jobs, moved them into standardized ranch houses in white neighborhoods, given them nondescript gray flannel suits?" "What are these people now?" they ask. And then they answer themselves, "Nothings!"

I would find this reasoning—which I have heard many, many times from hippies and nonhippies alike—amusing if I did not also consider it serious. For I think it is a delusion, a cop-out, an excuse to disassociate themselves from a world in which they feel too little has been changed or gained. The real question, however, it appears to me, is not whether poor people will adopt the middle-class mentality once they are well fed; rather, it is whether they will ever be well fed enough to be able to choose whatever mentality they think will suit them. The lack of a movement did not keep my mother from *wishing* herself bourgeois in her daydreams.

There is widespread starvation in Mississippi. In my own state of 20 Georgia there are more hungry families than Lester Maddox would like to admit—or even see fed. I went to school with children who ate red dirt. The Movement has prodded and pushed some liberal senators into pressuring the government for food so that the hungry may eat. Food stamps that were two dollars and out of the reach of many families not long ago have been reduced to fifty cents. The price is still out of the reach of some families, and the government, it seems to a lot of people, could spare enough free food to feed its own people. It angers people in the Movement that it does not; they point to the billions in wheat we send free each year to countries abroad. Their government's slowness while people are hungry, its unwillingness to believe that there are Americans starving, its stingy cutting of the price of food stamps, make many Civil Rights workers throw up their hands in disgust. But they do not give up. They do not withdraw into the world of psychedelia. They apply what pressure they can to make the government give away food to hungry people. They do not plan so far ahead in their disillusionment with society that they can see these starving families buying identical ranch-style houses and sending their snobbish children to Bryn Mawr and Yale. They take first things first and try to get them fed.

They do not consider it their business, in any case, to say what kind of life the people they help must lead. How one lives is, after all, one of the rights left to the individual—when and if he has opportunity to choose. It is not the prerogative of the middle class to determine what is worthy of aspiration. There is also every possibility that the middle-class people of tomorrow will turn out ever so much better than those of today. I even know some middle-class people of today who are not *all* bad.

I think there are so few Negro hippies because middle-class Negroes, although well fed, are not careless. They are required by the treacherous world they live in to be clearly aware of whoever or whatever might be trying to do them in. They are middle class in money and position, but they cannot afford to be middle class in complacency. They distrust the hippie movement because they know that it can do nothing for Negroes as a group but "love" them, which is what all paternalists claim to do. And since the only way Negroes can survive (which they cannot do, unfortunately, on love alone) is with the support of the group, they are wisely wary and stay away.

A white writer tried recently to explain that the reason for the relatively few Negro hippies is that Negroes have built up a "super-cool" that cracks under LSD and makes them have a "bad trip." What this writer doesn't guess at is that Negroes are needing drugs less than ever these days for any kind of trip. While the hippies are "tripping," Negroes are going after power, which is so much more important to their survival and their children's survival than LSD and pot.

Everyone would be surprised if the Israelis ignored the Arabs and took up "tripping" and pot smoking. In this country we are the Israelis. Everybody who can do so would like to forget this, of course. But for us to forget it for a minute would be fatal. "We Shall Overcome" is just a song to most Americans, *but we must do it.* Or die.

What good was the Civil Rights Movement? If it had just given this country Dr. King, a leader of conscience, for once in our lifetime, it would have been enough. If it had just taken black eyes off white television stories, it would have been enough. If it had fed one starving child, it would have been enough.

If the Civil Rights Movement is "dead," and if it gave us nothing else, it gave us each other forever. It gave some of us bread, some of us shelter, some of us knowledge and pride, all of us comfort. It gave us our children, our husbands, our brothers, our fathers, as men reborn and with a purpose for living. It broke the pattern of black servitude in this country. It shattered the phony "promise" of white soap operas that sucked away so many pitiful lives. It gave us history and men far greater than Presidents. It gave us heroes, selfless men of courage and strength, for our little boys and girls to follow. It gave us hope for tomorrow. It called us to life.

Because we live, it can never die.

1967

LINES OF INQUIRY
"The Civil Rights Movement: What Good Was It?"

In the course of this piece, Walker tells stories not only about herself, but also about her mother and about "an old black lady from Mississippi." Why doesn't she focus just on her own behavior and experience? Why does she tell about those other two women and go into such detail about her mother? In the course of this piece she also talks about the behavior of "white liberals and deserting Civil Rights sponsors," as well as about "hippies and other nihilists," but she never refers to any one of them specifically. Why do you suppose she concentrates on individuals in one case and groups in the other? Why do you suppose she begins by attacking one pair of groups but ends by attacking a different pair?

In trying to make clear "what good was" served by the movement, Walker explicitly pits her value system against some others. Define her value system and explain how it differs from the others that she attacks. Why do you think she attacks those other systems? Why doesn't she just answer the question that she puts in the title by telling directly what good she thinks the movement did? According to Walker, what was its greatest good?

Here, as in "Beauty: When the Other Dancer Is the Self," Walker writes about herself and her mother, but the tone she takes in each piece and the way her personality comes across in each piece is quite different. How would you describe her style and characterize the way she comes across in each piece? How do you account for the differences?

THE BLACK WRITER AND THE SOUTHERN EXPERIENCE

My mother tells of an incident that happened to her in the thirties during the Depression. She and my father lived in a small Georgia town and had half a dozen children. They were sharecroppers, and food, especially flour, was almost impossible to obtain. To get flour, which was distributed by the Red Cross, one had to submit vouchers signed by a local official. On the day my mother was to go into town for flour she received a large box of clothes from one of my aunts who was living in the North. The clothes were in good condition, though well worn, and my mother needed a dress, so she immediately put on one of those from the box and wore it into town. When she reached the distribution center and presented her voucher she was confronted by a white woman who looked her up and down with marked anger and envy.

"What'd you come up here for?" the woman asked.

"For some flour," said my mother, presenting her voucher.

"Humph," said the woman, looking at her more closely and with unconcealed fury. "Anybody dressed up as good as you don't need to come here *begging* for food."

"I ain't begging," said my mother; "the government is giving away   5
flour to those that need it, and I need it. I wouldn't be here if I didn't. And these clothes I'm wearing was given to me." But the woman had already turned to the next person in line, saying over her shoulder to the white man who was behind the counter with her, "The *gall* of niggers coming in here dressed better than me!" This thought seemed to make her angrier still, and my mother, pulling three of her small children behind her and crying from humiliation, walked sadly back into the street.

"What did you and Daddy do for flour that winter?" I asked my mother.

"Well," she said, "Aunt Mandy Aikens lived down the road from us and she got plenty of flour. We had a good stand of corn so we had plenty of meal. Aunt Mandy would swap me a bucket of flour for a bucket of meal. We got by all right."

Then she added thoughtfully, "And that old woman that turned me off so short got down so bad in the end that she was walking on two sticks." And I knew she was thinking, though she never said it, "... day, my eight children healthy and grown and three ... and me with hardly a sick day for years. Ain't Je...

In this small story is revealed the condition and strength of a people. Outcasts to be used and humiliated by the larger society, the Southern black sharecropper and poor farmer clung to his own kind and to a religion that had been given to pacify him as a slave but which he soon transformed into an antidote against bitterness. Depending on one another, because they had nothing and no one else, the sharecroppers often managed to come through "all right." And when I listen to my mother tell and retell this story I find that the white woman's vindictiveness is less important than Aunt Mandy's resourceful generosity or my mother's ready stand of corn. For their lives were not about that pitiful example of Southern womanhood, but about themselves.

What the black Southern writer inherits as a natural right is a sense   10 of *community*. Something simple but surprisingly hard, especially these days, to come by. My mother, who is a walking history of our community, tells me that when each of her children was born the midwife accepted as payment such home-grown or homemade items as a pig, a quilt, jars of canned fruits and vegetables. But there was never any question that the midwife would come when she was needed, whatever the eventual payment for her services. I consider this each time I hear of a hospital that refuses to admit a woman in labor unless she can hand over a substantial sum of money, cash.

Nor am I nostalgic, as a French philosopher once wrote, for lost poverty. I am nostalgic for the solidarity and sharing a modest existence can sometimes bring. We knew, I suppose, that we were poor. Somebody knew; perhaps the landowner who grudgingly paid my father three hundred dollars a year for twelve months' labor. But we never considered ourselves to be poor, unless, of course, we were deliberately humiliated. And because we never believed we were poor, and therefore worthless, we could depend on one another without shame. And always there were the Burial Societies, the Sick-and-Shut-in Societies, that sprang up out of spontaneous need. And no one seemed terribly upset that black sharecroppers were ignored by white insurance companies. It went without saying, in my mother's day, that birth and death required assistance from the community, and that the magnitude of these events was lost on outsiders.

As a college student I came to reject the Christianity of my parents, and it took me years to realize that though they had been force-fed a white man's palliative, in the form of religion, they had made it into something at once simple and noble. True, even today, they can never successfully picture a God who is not white, and that is a major cruelty, but their lives testify to a greater comprehension of the teachings of Jesus than the lives of people who sincerely believe a God *must* have a color and that there can be such a phenomenon as a "white" church.

The richness of the black writer's experience in the South can be remarkable, though some people might not think so. Once, while in college, I told a white middle-aged Northerner that I hoped to be a poet. In the nicest possible language, which still made me as mad as I've ever been, he suggested that a "farmer's daughter" might not be the stuff of which poets are made. On one level, of course, he had a point. A shack with only a dozen or so books is an unlikely place to discover a young Keats. But it is narrow thinking, indeed, to believe that a Keats is the only kind of poet one would want to grow up to be. One wants to write poetry that is understood by one's people, not by the Queen of England. Of course, should she be able to profit by it too, so much the better, but since that is not likely, catering to her tastes would be a waste of time.

For the black Southern writer, coming straight out of the country, as Wright did—Natchez and Jackson are still not as citified as they like to think they are—there is the world of comparisons; between town and country, between the ugly crowding and griminess of the cities and the spacious cleanliness (which actually seems impossible to dirty) of the country. A country person finds the city confining, like a too tight dress. And always, in one's memory, there remain all the rituals of one's growing up: the warmth and vividness of Sunday worship (never mind that you never quite believed) in a little church hidden from the road, and houses set so far back into the woods that at night it is impossible for strangers to find them. The daily dramas that evolve in such a private world are pure gold. But this view of a strictly private and hidden existence, with its triumphs, failures, grotesqueries, is not nearly as valuable to the socially conscious black Southern writer as his double vision is. For not only is he in a position to see his own world, and its close community ("Homecomings" on First Sundays, barbecues to raise money to send to Africa—one of the smaller ironies—the simplicity and eerie calm of a black funeral, where the beloved one is buried way in the middle of a wood with nothing to mark the spot but perhaps a wooden cross already coming apart), but also he is capable of knowing, with remarkably silent accuracy, the people who make up the larger world that surrounds and suppresses his own.

It is a credit to a writer like Ernest J. Gaines, a black writer who   15
writes mainly about the people he grew up with in rural Louisiana, that he can write about whites and blacks exactly as he sees them and *knows* them, instead of writing of one group as a vast malignant lump and of the other as a conglomerate of perfect virtues.

In large measure, black Southern writers owe their clarity of vision to parents who refused to diminish themselves as human beings by succumbing to racism. Our parents seemed to know that an extreme negative emotion held against other human beings for reasons they do not control can be blinding. Blindness about other human beings, especially for a writer, is equivalent to death. Because of this blindness, which is, above all, racial, the works of many southern writers have died. Much that we read today is fast expiring.

My own slight attachment to William Faulkner was rudely broken by realizing, after reading statements he made in *Faulkner in the University,* that he believed whites superior morally to blacks; that whites had a duty (which at their convenience they would assume) to "bring blacks along" politically, since blacks, in Faulkner's opinion, were "not ready" yet to function properly in a democratic society. He also thought that a black man's intelligence is directly related to the amount of white blood he has.

For the black person coming of age in the sixties, where Martin Luther King stands against the murderers of Goodman, Chaney, and Schwerner, there appears no basis for such assumptions. Nor was there any in Garvey's day, or in Du Bois's or in Douglass's or in Nat Turner's. Nor at any other period in our history, from the very founding of the country; for it was hardly incumbent upon slaves to be slaves and saints too. Unlike Tolstoy, Faulkner was not prepared to struggle to change the structure of the society he was born in. One might concede that in his fiction he did seek to examine the reasons for its decay, but unfortunately, as I have learned while trying to teach Faulkner to black students, it is not possible, from so short a range, to separate the man from his works.

One reads Faulkner knowing that his "colored" people had to come through "Mr. William's" back door, and one feels uneasy, and finally enraged that Faulkner did not burn the whole house down. When the provincial mind starts out *and continues* on a narrow and unprotesting course, "genius" itself must run on a track.

Flannery O'Connor at least had the conviction that "reality" is at best superficial and that the puzzle of humanity is less easy to solve than that of race. But Miss O'Connor was not so much of Georgia, as in it. The majority of Southern writers have been too confined by prevailing social customs to probe deeply into mysteries that the Citizens Councils insist must never be revealed.

Perhaps my Northern brothers will not believe me when I say there is a great deal of positive material I can draw from my "underprivileged" background. But they have never lived, as I have, at the end of a long road in a house that was faced by the edge of the world on one side and nobody for miles on the other. They have never experienced the magnificent quiet of a summer day when the heat is intense and one is so very thirsty, as one moves across the dusty cotton fields, that one learns forever that water is the essence of all life. In the cities it cannot be so clear to one that he is a creature of the earth, feeling the soil between the toes, smelling the dust thrown up by the rain, loving the earth so much that one longs to taste it and sometimes does.

Nor do I intend to romanticize the Southern black country life. I can recall that I hated it, generally. The hard work in the fields, the shabby houses, the evil greedy men who worked my father to death and almost broke the courage of that strong woman, my mother. No, I am simply saying that Southern black writers, like most writers, have a heritage of love and hate, but that they also have enormous richness and beauty to draw from. And, having been placed, as Camus says, "halfway between misery and the sun," they, too, know that "though all is not well under the sun, history is not everything."

No one could wish for a more advantageous heritage than that bequeathed to the black writer in the South: a compassion for the earth, a trust in humanity beyond our knowledge of evil, and an abiding love of justice. We inherit a great responsibility as well, for we must give voice to centuries not only of silent bitterness and hate but also of neighborly kindness and sustaining love.

1970

LINES OF INQUIRY
"The Black Writer and the Southern Experience"

Walker opens this piece with a vividly detailed story about her mother, a story that she offers to illustrate "the condition and strength of a people." Though she does not refer specifically to the story later on in her essay, she clearly intends it to echo throughout the remainder of the essay. What details does she use, what assertions does she make, that echo in the story? In what respects might it also be said that Walker's own way of thinking and talking in this piece echoes the behavior of her mother?

The "black Southern writer" is uniquely endowed, according to Walker, by virtue of inheriting "a sense of *community*." What exactly does she mean by community that makes it so special? In what respect(s) does she believe that the black Southern writer's sense of community differs from that of anyone else? Why does she believe that this sense of community is so important to a writer? To what extent do you think she displays that sense of community in her own writing?

A sense of community, particularly the kind of community that prevails in a rural or village setting, might also be seen in Baker's "A Visit with the Folks" or Baldwin's "Stranger in the Village" or Mead's "A Day in Samoa" or Momaday's "The Way to Rainy Mountain" or Twain's "S-t-e-a-m-boat a-comin'!" Read or reread a couple of these pieces, and then consider whether the communities depicted in them share any qualities with the community Walker portrayed.

AM I BLUE?

"Ain't these tears in these eyes tellin' you?"[1]

For about three years my companion and I rented a small house in the country that stood on the edge of a large meadow that appeared to run from the end of our deck straight into the mountains. The mountains, however, were quite far away, and between us and them there was, in fact, a town. It was one of the many pleasant aspects of the house that you never really were aware of this.

It was a house of many windows, low, wide, nearly floor to ceiling in the living room, which faced the meadow, and it was from one of these that I first saw our closest neighbor, a large white horse, cropping grass, flipping its mane, and ambling about—not over the entire meadow, which stretched well out of sight of the house, but over the five or so fenced-in acres that were next to the twenty-odd that we had rented. I soon learned that the horse, whose name was Blue, belonged to a man who lived in another town, but was boarded by our neighbors next door. Occasionally, one of the children, usually a stocky teen-ager, but sometimes a much younger girl or boy, could be seen riding Blue. They would appear in the meadow, climb up on his back, ride furiously for ten or fifteen minutes, then get off, slap Blue on the flanks, and not be seen again for a month or more.

There were many apple trees in our yard, and one by the fence that Blue could almost reach. We were soon in the habit of feeding him apples, which he relished, especially because by the middle of summer the meadow grasses—so green and succulent since January—had dried out from lack of rain, and Blue stumbled about munching the dried stalks half-heartedly. Sometimes he would stand very still just by the apple tree, and when one of us came out he would whinny, snort loudly, or stamp the ground. This meant, of course: I want an apple.

It was quite wonderful to pick a few apples, or collect those that had fallen to the ground overnight, and patiently hold them, one by one, up to his large, toothy mouth. I remained as thrilled as a child by his flexible dark lips, huge, cubelike teeth that crunched the apples, core and all, with such finality, and his high, broad-breasted *enormity*; beside which, I felt small indeed. When I was a child, I used to ride horses, and was especially friendly with one named Nan until the day I was riding and my brother deliberately spooked her and I was thrown, head first, against the trunk of a tree. When I came to, I was in bed and my mother was bending worriedly over me; we silently agreed that perhaps horseback riding was not the safest sport for me. Since then I have walked, and prefer walking to horseback riding—but I had forgotten the depth of feeling one could see in horses' eyes.

I was therefore unprepared for the expression in Blue's. Blue was   5
lonely. Blue was horribly lonely and bored. I was not shocked that this should be the case; five acres to tramp by yourself, endlessly, even in the most beautiful of meadows—and his was—cannot provide many interesting events, and once rainy season turned to dry that was about it. No, I was shocked that I had forgotten that human animals and nonhuman animals can communicate quite well; if we are brought up around animals as children we take this for granted. By the time we are adults we no longer remember. However, the animals have not changed. They are in fact *completed* creations (at least they seem to be, so much more than we) who are not likely *to* change; it is their nature to express themselves. What else are they going to express? And they do. And, generally speaking, they are ignored.

After giving Blue the apples, I would wander back to the house, aware that he was observing me. Were more apples not forthcoming then? Was that to be his sole entertainment for the day? My partner's small son had decided he wanted to learn how to piece a quilt; we worked in silence on our respective squares as I thought . . .

Well, about slavery: about white children, who were raised by black people, who knew their first all-accepting love from black women, and then, when they were twelve or so, were told they must "forget" the deep levels of communication between themselves and "mammy" that they knew. Later they would be able to relate quite calmly, "My old mammy was sold to another good family." "My old mammy was——
——." Fill in the blank. Many more years later a white woman would say: "I can't understand these Negroes, these blacks. What do they want? They're so different from us."

And about the Indians, considered to be "like animals" by the "set-tlers" (a very benign euphemism for what they actually were), who did not understand their description as a compliment.

And about the thousands of American men who marry Japanese, Korean, Filipina, and other non-English-speaking women and of how happy they report they are, "*blissfully,*" until their brides learn to speak English, at which point the marriages tend to fall apart. What then did the men see, when they looked into the eyes of the women they married, before they could speak English? Apparently only their own reflections.

I thought of society's impatience with the young. "Why are they   10
playing the music so loud?" Perhaps the children have listened to much

of the music of oppressed people their parents danced to before they were born, with its passionate but soft cries for acceptance and love, and they have wondered why their parents failed to hear.

I do not know how long Blue had inhabited his five beautiful, boring acres before we moved into our house; a year after we had arrived—and had also traveled to other valleys, other cities, other worlds— he was still there.

But then, in our second year at the house, something happened in Blue's life. One morning, looking out the window at the fog that lay like a ribbon over the meadow, I saw another horse, a brown one, at the other end of Blue's field. Blue appeared to be afraid of it, and for several days made no attempt to go near. We went away for a week. When we returned, Blue had decided to make friends and the two horses ambled or galloped along together, and Blue did not come nearly as often to the fence underneath the apple tree.

When he did, bringing his new friend with him, there was a different look in his eyes. A look of independence, of self-possession, of inalienable *horse*ness. His friend eventually became pregnant. For months and months there was, it seemed to me, a mutual feeling between me and the horses of justice, of peace. I fed apples to them both. The look in Blue's eyes was one of unabashed "this is *it*ness."

It did not, however, last forever. One day, after a visit to the city, I went out to give Blue some apples. He stood waiting, or so I thought, though not beneath the tree. When I shook the tree and jumped back from the shower of apples, he made no move. I carried some over to him. He managed to half-crunch one. The rest he let fall to the ground. I dreaded looking into his eyes—because I had of course noticed that Brown, his partner, had gone—but I did look. If I had been born into slavery, and my partner had been sold or killed, my eyes would have looked like that. The children next door explained that Blue's partner had been "put with him' (the same expression that old people used, I had noticed, when speaking of an ancestor during slavery who had been impregnated by her owner) so that they could mate and she conceive. Since that was accomplished, she had been taken back by her owner, who lived somewhere else.

Will she be back? I asked.   15

They didn't know.

Blue was like a crazed person. Blue *was*, to me, a crazed person. He galloped furiously, as if he were being ridden, around and around his five beautiful acres. He whinnied until he couldn't. He tore at the ground with his hooves. He butted himself against his single shade tree. He looked always and always toward the road down which his partner had gone. And then, occasionally, when he came up for apples, or I took apples to him, he looked at me. It was a look so piercing, so full of grief, a look so *human*, I almost laughed (I felt too sad to cry) to think there are people who do not know that animals suffer. People like me who have forgotten, and daily forget, all that animals try to tell us. "Everything you do to us will happen to you; we are your teachers, as you are ours. We are one lesson" is essentially it, I think. There are those who never once have even considered animals' rights: those who have been taught that animals actually want to be used and abused by us, as small children "love" to be frightened, or women "love" to be mutilated and raped. . . . They are the great-grandchildren of those who honestly thought, because someone taught them this: "Women can't think," and "niggers can't faint." But most disturbing of all, in Blue's large brown eyes was a new look, more painful than the look of despair: the look of disgust with human beings, with life; the look of hatred. And it was odd what the look of hatred did. It gave him, for the first time, the look of a beast. And what that meant was that he had put up a barrier within to protect himself from further violence; all the apples in the world wouldn't change that fact.

And so Blue remained, a beautiful part of our landscape, very peaceful to look at from the window, white against the grass. Once a friend came to visit and said, looking out on the soothing view: "And it *would* have to be a *white* horse; the very image of freedom." And I thought, yes, the animals are forced to become for us merely "images" of what they once so beautifully expressed. And we are used to drinking milk from containers showing "contented" cows, whose real lives we want to hear nothing about, eating eggs and drumsticks from "happy" hens, and munching hamburgers advertised by bulls of integrity who seem to command their fate.

As we talked of freedom and justice one day for all, we sat down to steaks. I am eating misery, I thought, as I took the first bite. And spit it out.

1986

LINES OF INQUIRY
"Am I Blue?"

Notice the descriptive and narrative techniques that Walker uses to make her point in this essay. For example, what descriptive details does she emphasize and endow with special significance? Why does she interrupt her description of Blue, first to tell about her childhood horseback riding accident, then to tell about the thoughts that ran through her mind as she was quilting with the son of her partner? What do these apparent digressions have to do with her initial description of Blue, with the subsequent story of Blue, or with the point of her piece? Why doesn't she focus just on the story of Blue and Brown?

Why do you think Walker focuses as she does on Blue? To what extent do you think she intends him to be suggestive of the mistreated and misunderstood persons that she thinks about in the middle of her piece? To what extent do you think she intends him to be a symbol of the inhumane treatment of animals? To what extent do you think she is concerned with the interdependency of animals and human beings and thus with inhumanity in general? Or is she concerned with some other issue?

The situation of animals and their relationship to human beings is also explored in Dillard's "The Deer at Providencia," in Eiseley's "The Bird and the Machine," in Hoagland's "The Courage of Turtles," and in Momaday's "My Horse and I." Read or reread one of these and consider what ideas and concerns Walker shares with that essayist, as well as what issues are of special interest to her alone.

E.B. WHITE

1899 – 1985

The whole duty of a writer is to please and satisfy himself, and the true writer always plays to an audience of one. Let him start sniffing the air, or glancing at the Trend Machine, and he is as good as dead, although he may make a nice living.

Throughout his career, E. B. White remained just as staunchly self-reliant as he is in this uncompromising statement of principle. Yet in writing "to please and satisfy himself," he attracted an audience of millions. His readers followed him through a surprisingly varied body of writing, for White was not willing either to glance at the "Trend Machine" or to work in a single, narrowly established vein. Indeed, during his most active years as a professional writer, from 1920 to 1970, he won recognition for his witty poems and sketches, his personal essays, his reflections on world government, his children's stories, and his advice to young writers. Varied as it is, White's writing embodies a clear-cut and persistent set of values that can be seen in his "intoxication" with nature, his "love affair" with freedom, his desire for world peace, and his belief "in the truth and worth of the scrawl."

The youngest of six children of a wealthy piano manufacturer, Elwyn Brooks White was born and raised in the New York City suburb of Mount Vernon. There, in his father's stable, in his friends' backyards, and in the nearby woods and ponds, he first experienced his long felt "sense of living somewhat freely in a natural world," a feeling that that was intensified for him at the "large and undisturbed lake" in Maine where his family vacationed each August. As a youngster, he also started keeping a daily journal—a record of his experiences, observations, and early literary efforts—that he maintained for the next twenty years. As a teenager, he not only wrote for the school literary journal, but also entered and won a handful of national magazine contests for aspiring writers.

White's commitment to writing grew even stronger during his undergraduate days at Cornell University. Throughout his four years there (1917–21), he worked on the *Cornell Daily Sun*, first as a reporter, finally as editor-in-chief. So, too, one of his favorite professors was William Strunk, whose lessons in how to be "clear, brief, bold" touched White so deeply that forty years later he resurrected Strunk's writing manual, *The Elements of Style*, and turned it into a best-selling textbook. After graduation, he turned halfheartedly to the world of practical writing, but the business of getting out news reports, press releases, and advertising copy was evidently far less interesting to White than the pleasure of writing his own witty poems and sketches. Far less interesting, too, than a cross-country trip in his Model T Ford during the spring and summer of 1922, or a one-way ticket on a cruise ship to Alaska and Siberia in the summer of 1923.

Not until 1925, when *The New Yorker* magazine was launched, did White find a publication congenial to the witty writing that he had been working at for several years. From 1926 to 1937, he was continuously affiliated with *The New Yorker*, bringing to it a wryly humorous voice and a common-sensical view of affairs for which the magazine came to be very well known. White's wide-ranging contributions during those years included not only editorials and sketches in its "Talk of the Town" section, but also poems, cartoon captions, and witty taglines that appeared elsewhere in the magazine. During those years, he also published several humorous books, most notably *Is Sex Necessary? or Why You Feel the Way You Do* (1929), a parody of various sexual studies, done jointly with his office mate and fellow humorist, James Thurber.

But by the mid-thirties, the complex pressures of "the weekly gaiety field" and the complex pressures, too, of living amid "the spiky ruins of New York" had begun to weigh heavily upon White. So, in the spirit of Thoreau, he decided "to simplify" his life by giving up his full-time job at *The New Yorker* and moving his family to a saltwater farm in Maine. Though he continued to do occasional work for *The New Yorker*, the bulk of his writing between 1938 and 1943 was devoted to a monthly column that he produced for *Harper's Magazine* under the general heading of "One Man's Meat." As its title suggests, the column was "a personal record," a "description or narration" based on his experience in Maine, or wherever else he happened to be. His personal experience, in turn, invariably provided him with an occasion to reflect upon a broad range of ideas, issues, and concerns—from "A Shepherd's Life" to "The World of Tomorrow," from "Children's Books" to the "Second World War."

"One Man's Meat," by his own admission, "turned out to be one of the luckiest things that ever happened" to White, for it gave him the opportunity to write in "the first person singular." Given the freedom and directness of that perspective, White achieved a rare blend of description and reflection, of seriousness and humor, of personal and public testimony that gradually led to his being widely recognized as the most distinguished American essayist of his time. But by 1943, White's desire to be more directly and frequently involved in writing about the war—and about the need for world government after the war—led him to give up his monthly column at *Harper's* and devote himself once again to writing weekly editorials for *The New Yorker*. His "Notes and Comments" about war, peace, and the politics of world government were subsequently collected and published in *The Wild Flag* (1946).

Busy as he was at *The New Yorker*, as well as in moving back and forth between an apartment in New York City and his farm in Maine, he managed during the forties and early-fifties to produce two best-selling children's books—*Stuart Little* (1945) and *Charlotte's Web* (1952). In these classic works, as in his numerous essays about the barnyard life on his farm, White drew on his affection for animals, transforming them into enchanting characters whose experiences embody his personal ideas about life and human experience. By the mid-fifties, the weekly deadlines at *The New Yorker* had once again become too much of a burden both for White and for his wife, Katherine Angell, who for many years had been fiction editor of the magazine. So in 1957, they both resigned their positions and returned to their permanent home in Maine. Between the mid-fifties and the mid-seventies, White wrote occasional "Letters" to *The New Yorker*, very much in the manner of his pieces for "One Man's Meat," and in 1970 his last children's book appeared, *The Trumpet of the Swan*.

White's wide-ranging essays, editorials, and sketches can be found in several collections, most notably *One Man's Meat* (1944), *The Second Tree from the Corner* (1954), *The Points of My Compass* (1962), *Essays of E. B. White* (1977), and *Poems and Sketches of E. B. White* (1981). Given the variety of his subjects and moods, his essays present him in an equally wide array of "attitudes or poses"—as "philosopher, scold, jester, raconteur, confidant, pundit, devil's advocate, enthusiast." Each of his essays "differs from the last," if only because each is a "new excursion," "a new 'attempt' " that "takes him into a new country." Still, in all of his writing he remains true to his first principles—"to please and satisfy himself." So, he never wavers from his personal convictions. So, too, he never wavers from his personal voice, which above all else remains true to his belief in the value of "plainness, simplicity, orderliness, sincerity."

ONCE MORE TO THE LAKE

One summer, along about 1904, my father rented a camp on a lake in Maine and took us all there for the month of August. We all got ringworm from some kittens and had to rub Pond's Extract on our arms and legs at night and morning, and my father rolled over in a canoe with all his clothes on; but outside of that the vacation was a success and from then on none of us ever thought there was any place in the world like that lake in Maine. We returned summer after summer—always on August 1 for one month. I have since become a salt-water man, but sometimes in summer there are days when the restlessness of the tides and the fearful cold of the sea water and the incessant wind that blows across the afternoon and into the evening make me wish for the placidity of a lake in the woods. A few weeks ago this feeling got so strong I bought myself a couple of bass hooks and a spinner and returned to the lake where we used to go, for a week's fishing and to revisit old haunts.

I took along my son, who had never had any fresh water up his nose and who had seen lily pads only from train windows. On the journey over to the lake I began to wonder what it would be like. I wondered how time would have marred this unique, this holy spot—the coves and streams, the hills that the sun set behind, the camps and the paths behind the camps. I was sure that the tarred road would have found it out, and I wondered in what other ways it would be desolated. It is strange how much you can remember about places like that once you allow your mind to return into the grooves that lead back. You remember one thing, and that suddenly reminds you of another thing. I guess I remembered clearest of all the early mornings, when the lake was cool and motionless, remembered how the bedroom smelled of the lumber it was made of and of the wet woods whose scent entered through the screen. The partitions in the camp were thin and did not extend clear to the top of the rooms, and as I was always the first up I would dress softly so as not to wake the others, and sneak out into the sweet outdoors and start out in the canoe, keeping close along the shore in the long shadows of the pines. I remembered being very careful never to rub my paddle against the gunwale for fear of disturbing the stillness of the cathedral.

The lake had never been what you would call a wild lake. There were cottages sprinkled around the shores, and it was in farming country although the shores of the lake were quite heavily wooded. Some of the cottages were owned by nearby farmers, and you would live at the shore and eat your meals at the farmhouse. That's what our family did. But although it wasn't wild, it was a fairly large and undisturbed lake and there were places in it that, to a child at least, seemed infinitely remote and primeval.

I was right about the tar: it led to within half a mile of the shore. But when I got back there, with my boy, and we settled into a camp near a farmhouse and into the kind of summertime I had known, I could tell that it was going to be pretty much the same as it had been before—I knew it, lying in bed the first morning, smelling the bedroom and hearing the boy sneak quietly out and go off along the shore in a boat. I began to sustain the illusion that he was I, and therefore, by simple transposition, that I was my father. This sensation persisted, kept cropping up all the time we were there. It was not an entirely new feeling, but in this setting it grew much stronger. I seemed to be living a dual existence. I would be in the middle of some simple act, I would be picking up a bait box or laying down a table fork, or I would be saying something, and suddenly it would be not I but my father who was saying the words or making the gesture. It gave me a creepy sensation.

We went fishing the first morning. I felt the same damp moss cov-   5
ering the worms in the bait can, and saw the dragonfly alight on the tip of my rod as it hovered a few inches from the surface of the water. It was the arrival of this fly that convinced me beyond any doubt that everything was as it always had been, that the years were a mirage and that there had been no years. The small waves were the same, chucking the rowboat under the chin as we fished at anchor, and the boat was the same boat, the same color green and the ribs broken in the same places, and under the floorboards the same fresh-water leavings and débris—the dead helgramite, the wisps of moss, the rusty discarded fishhook, the dried blood from yesterday's catch. We stared silently at the tips of our rods, at the dragonflies that came and went. I lowered the tip of mine into the water, tentatively, pensively dislodging the fly, which darted two feet away, poised, darted two feet back, and came to rest again a little farther up the rod. There had been no years between the ducking of this dragonfly and the other one—the one that was part of memory. I looked at the boy, who was silently watching his fly, and it was my hands that held his rod, my eyes watching. I felt dizzy and didn't know which rod I was at the end of.

We caught two bass, hauling them in briskly as though they were mackerel, pulling them over the side of the boat in a businesslike manner without any landing net, and stunning them with a blow on the back of the head. When we got back for a swim before lunch, the lake was exactly where we had left it, the same number of inches from the dock, and there was only the merest suggestion of a breeze. This seemed an utterly enchanted sea, this lake you could leave to its own devices for a few hours and come back to, and find that it had not stirred, this constant and trustworthy body of water. In the shallows, the dark, water-soaked sticks and twigs, smooth and old, were undulating in clusters on the bottom against the clean ribbed sand, and the track of the mussel was plain. A school of minnows swam by, each minnow with its small individual shadow, doubling the attendance, so clear and sharp in the sunlight. Some of the other campers were in swimming, along the shore, one of them with a cake of soap, and the water felt thin and clear and unsubstantial. Over the years there had been this person with the cake of soap, this cultist, and here he was. There had been no years.

Up to the farmhouse to dinner through the teeming, dusty field, the road under our sneakers was only a two-track road. The middle track was missing, the one with the marks of the hooves and the splotches of dried, flaky manure, There had been three tracks to choose from in choosing which track to walk in; now the choice was narrowed down to two. For a moment I missed terribly the middle alternative. But the way led past the tennis court, and something about the way it lay there in the sun reassured me; the tape had loosened along the backline, the alleys were green with plantains and other weeds, and the net (installed in June and removed in September) sagged in the dry noon, and the whole place steamed with midday heat and hunger and emptiness. There was a choice of pie for dessert, and one was blueberry and one was apple, and the waitresses were the same country girls, there having been no passage of time, only the illusion of it as in a dropped curtain—the waitresses were still fifteen; their hair had been washed, that was the only difference—they had been to the movies and seen the pretty girls with clean hair.

Summertime, oh, summertime, pattern of life indelible, the fade-proof lake, the woods unshatterable, the pasture with the sweetfern and the juniper forever and ever, summer without end; this was the background, and the life along the shore was the design, the cottagers with their innocent and tranquil design, their tiny docks with the flagpole and the American flag floating against the white clouds in the blue sky, the little paths over the roots of the trees leading from camp to camp and the paths leading back to the outhouses and the can of lime for sprinkling, and at the souvenir counters at the store the miniature birch-bark canoes and the postcards that showed things looking a little better than they looked. This was the American family at play, escaping the city heat, wondering whether the newcomers in the camp at the head of the cove were "common" or "nice," wondering whether it was true that the people who drove up for Sunday dinner at the farmhouse were turned away because there wasn't enough chicken.

It seemed to me, as I kept remembering all this, that those times and those summers had been infinitely precious and worth saving. There had been jollity and peace and goodness. The arriving (at the beginning of August) had been so big a business in itself, at the railway station the farm wagon drawn up, the first smell of the pine-laden air, the first glimpse of the smiling farmer, and the great importance of the trunks and your father's enormous authority in such matters, and the feel of the wagon under you for the long ten-mile haul, and at the top of the last long hill catching the first view of the lake after eleven months of not seeing this cherished body of water. The shouts and cries of the other campers when they saw you, and the trunks to be unpacked, to give up their rich burden. (Arriving was less exciting nowadays, when you sneaked up in your car and parked it under a tree near the camp and took out the bags and in five minutes it was all over, no fuss, no loud wonderful fuss about trunks.)

Peace and goodness and jollity. The only thing that was wrong now, really, was the sound of the place, an unfamiliar nervous sound of the outboard motors. This was the note that jarred, the one thing that would sometimes break the illusion and set the years moving. In those other summertimes all motors were inboard; and when they were at a little distance, the noise they made was a sedative, an ingredient of summer sleep. They were one-cylinder and two-cylinder engines, and some were make-and-break and some were jump-spark, but they all made a sleepy sound across the lake. The one-lungers throbbed and fluttered, and the twin-cylinder ones purred and purred, and that was a quiet sound, too. But now the campers all had outboards. In the daytime, in the hot mornings, these motors made a petulant, irritable sound; at night, in the still evening when the afterglow lit the water, they whined about one's ears like mosquitoes. My boy loved our rented outboard, and his great desire was to achieve single-handed mastery over it, and authority, and he soon learned the trick of choking it a little (but not too much), and the adjustment of the needle valve. Watching him I would remember the things you could do with the old one-cylinder engine with the heavy flywheel, how you could have it eating out of your hand if you got really close to it spiritually. Motorboats in those days didn't have clutches, and you would make a landing by shutting off the motor at the proper time and coasting in with a dead rudder. But there was a way of reversing them, if you learned the trick, by cutting the switch and putting it on again exactly on the final dying revolution of the flywheel, so that it would kick back against compression and begin reversing. Approaching a dock in a strong following breeze, it was difficult to slow up sufficiently by the ordinary coasting method, and if a boy felt he had complete mastery over his motor, he was tempted to keep it running beyond its time and then reverse it a few feet from the dock. It took a cool nerve, because if you threw the switch a twentieth of a second too soon you would catch the flywheel when it still had speed enough to go up past center, and the boat would leap ahead, charging bull-fashion at the dock.

We had a good week at the camp. The bass were biting well and the sun shone endlessly, day after day. We would be tired at night and lie down in the accumulated heat of the little bedrooms after the long

10

hot day and the breeze would stir almost imperceptibly outside and the smell of the swamp drift in through the rusty screens. Sleep would come easily and in the morning the red squirrel would be on the roof, tapping out his gay routine. I kept remembering everything, lying in bed in the mornings—the small steamboat that had a long rounded stern like the lip of a Ubangi, and how quietly she ran on the moonlight sails, when the older boys played their mandolins and the girls sang and we ate doughnuts dipped in sugar, and how sweet the music was on the water in the shining night, and what it had felt like to think about girls then. After breakfast we would go up to the store and the things were in the same place—the minnows in a bottle, the plugs and spinners disarranged and pawed over by the youngsters from the boys' camp, the Fig Newtons and the Beeman's gum. Outside, the road was tarred and cars stood in front of the store. Inside, all was just as it had always been, except there was more Coca-Cola and not so much Moxie and root beer and birch beer and sarsaparilla. We would walk out with the bottle of pop apiece and sometimes the pop would backfire up our noses and hurt. We explored the streams, quietly, where the turtles slid off the sunny logs and dug their way into the soft bottom; and we lay on the town wharf and fed worms to the tame bass. Everywhere we went I had trouble making out which was I, the one walking at my side, the one walking in my pants.

One afternoon while we were there at that lake a thunderstorm came up. It was like the revival of an old melodrama that I had seen long ago with childish awe. The second-act climax of the drama of the electrical disturbance over a lake in America had not changed in any important respect. This was the big scene, still the big scene. The whole thing was so familiar, the first feeling of oppression and heat and a general air around camp of not wanting to go very far away. In mid-afternoon (it was all the same) a curious darkening of the sky, and a lull in everything that had made life tick; and then the way the boats suddenly swung the other way at their moorings with the coming of a breeze out of the new quarter, and the premonitory rumble. Then the kettle drum, then the snare, then the bass drum and cymbals, then crackling light against the dark, and the gods grinning and licking their chops in the hills. Afterward the calm, the rain steadily rustling in the calm lake, the return of light and hope and spirits, and the campers running out in joy and relief to go swimming in the rain, their bright cries perpetuating the deathless joke about how they were getting simply drenched, and the children screaming with delight at the new sensation of bathing in the rain, and the joke about getting drenched linking the generations in a strong indestructible chain. And the comedian who waded in carrying an umbrella.

When the others went swimming, my son said he was going in, too. He pulled his dripping trunks from the line where they had hung all through the shower and wrung them out. Languidly, and with no thought of going in, I watched him, his hard little body, skinny and bare, saw him wince slightly as he pulled up around his vitals the small, soggy, icy garment. As he buckled the swollen belt, suddenly my groin felt the chill of death.

August 1941

LINES OF INQUIRY
"Once More to the Lake"

Early in the essay, White remarks that "it is strange how much you can remember about places like that once you allow your mind to return into the grooves that lead back." How does White organize the story of his visit to show the "strange" experience he went through when he allowed his mind to return into the grooves that lead back? How does White organize his material to clarify not only the memories of his past experience but also the details of his present experience, as well as the interplay between the two?

On his journey back to the lake, White "wondered how time would have marred this unique, this holy spot." How do his memories of the place compare with the place as he finds it during the visit with his son? In what ways has it changed? In what ways has it stayed the same? How does the presence of his son affect White's memories and perceptions of the lake, the camps, the cottagers, the surroundings, and himself?

Think about a place that was important during your earlier life and that you revisited after having been away from it for a period of time. In what ways did it change? In what ways did it stay the same? What particular memories about the place stand out for you when you allow your mind to return into the grooves that lead back? Did your visit turn out to be as haunting and disturbing to you as White's was to him, or did it prove to be just an ordinary visit without anything noteworthy to distinguish it? Or did it have a special twist that you associate with the place itself?

THE RING OF TIME

Fiddler Bayou, March 22, 1956

After the lions had returned to their cages, creeping angrily through the chutes, a little bunch of us drifted away and into an open doorway nearby, where we stood for a while in semidarkness, watching a big brown circus horse go harumphing around the practice ring. His trainer was a woman of about forty, and the two of them, horse and woman, seemed caught up in one of those desultory treadmills of afternoon from which there is no apparent escape. The day was hot, and we kibitzers were grateful to be briefly out of the sun's glare. The long rein, or tape, by which the woman guided her charge counterclockwise in his dull career formed the radius of their private circle, of which she was the revolving center; and she, too, stepped a tiny circumference of her own, in order to accommodate the horse and allow him his maximum scope. She had on a short-skirted costume and a conical straw hat. Her legs were bare and she wore high heels, which probed deep into the loose tanbark and kept her ankles in a state of constant turmoil. The great size and meekness of the horse, the repetitious exercise, the heat of the afternoon, all exerted a hypnotic charm that invited boredom; we spectators were experiencing a languor—we neither expected relief nor felt entitled to any. We had paid a dollar to get into the grounds, to be sure, but we had got our dollar's worth a few minutes before, when the lion trainer's whiplash had got caught around a toe of one of the lions. What more did we want for a dollar?

Behind me I heard someone say, "Excuse me, please," in a low voice. She was halfway into the building when I turned and saw her— a girl of sixteen or seventeen, politely threading her way through us onlookers who blocked the entrance. As she emerged in front of us, I saw that she was barefoot, her dirty little feet fighting the uneven ground. In most respects she was like any of two or three dozen showgirls you encounter if you wander about the winter quarters of Mr. John Ringling North's circus, in Sarasota—cleverly proportioned, deeply browned by the sun, dusty, eager, and almost naked. But her grave face and the naturalness of her manner gave her a sort of quick distinction and brought a new note into the gloomy octagonal building where we had all cast our lot for a few moments. As soon as she had squeezed through the crowd, she spoke a word or two to the older woman, whom I took to be her mother, stepped to the ring, and waited while the horse coasted to a stop in front of her. She gave the animal a couple of affectionate swipes on his enormous neck and then swung herself aboard. The horse immediately resumed his rocking canter, the woman goading him on, chanting something that sounded like "Hop! Hop!"

In attempting to recapture this mild spectacle, I am merely acting as recording secretary for one of the oldest of societies—the society of those who, at one time or another, have surrendered, without even a show of resistance, to the bedazzlement of a circus rider. As a writing man, or secretary, I have always felt charged with the safekeeping of all unexpected items of worldly or unworldly enchantment, as though I might be held personally responsible if even a small one were to be lost. But it is not easy to communicate anything of this nature. The circus comes as close to being the world in microcosm as anything I know; in a way, it puts all the rest of show business in the shade. Its magic is universal and complex. Out of its wild disorder comes order; from its rank smell rises the good aroma of courage and daring; out of its preliminary shabbiness comes the final splendor. And buried in the familiar boasts of its advance agents lies the modesty of most of its people. For me the circus is at its best before it has been put together. It is at its best at certain moments when it comes to a point, as through a burning glass, in the activity and destiny of a single performer out of so many. One ring is always bigger than three. One rider, one aerialist, is always greater than six. In short, a man has to catch the circus unawares to experience its full impact and share its gaudy dream.

The ten-minute ride the girl took achieved—as far as I was concerned, who wasn't looking for it, and quite unbeknownst to her, who wasn't even striving for it—the thing that is sought by performers everywhere, on whatever stage, whether struggling in the tidal currents of Shakespeare or bucking the difficult motion of a horse. I somehow got the idea she was just cadging a ride, improving a shining ten minutes in the diligent way all serious artists seize free moments to hone the blade of their talent and keep themselves in trim. Her brief tour included only elementary postures and tricks, perhaps because they were all she was capable of, perhaps because her warmup at this hour was unscheduled and the ring was not rigged for a real practice session. She swung herself off and on the horse several times, gripping his mane. She did a few knee-stands—or whatever they are called—dropping to her knees and quickly bouncing back up on her feet again. Most of the time she simply rode in a standing position, well aft on the beast, her hands hanging easily at her sides, her head erect, her straw-colored ponytail lightly brushing her shoulders, the blood of exertion showing faintly through the tan of her skin. Twice she managed a one-foot stance—a sort of ballet pose, with arms outstretched. At one point the neck strap of her bathing suit broke and she went twice around the ring in the classic attitude of a woman making minor repairs to a garment. The fact that she was standing on the back of a moving horse while doing this invested the matter with a clownish significance that perfectly fitted the spirit of the circus—jocund, yet charming. She just rolled the strap into a neat ball and stowed it inside her bodice while the horse rocked and rolled beneath her in dutiful innocence. The bathing suit proved as self-reliant as its owner and stood up well enough without benefit of strap.

The richness of the scene was in its plainness, its natural condition—   5
of horse, of ring, of girl, even to the girl's bare feet that gripped the bare back of her proud and ridiculous mount. The enchantment grew not out of anything that happened or was performed but out of something that seemed to go round and around and around with the girl, attending her, a steady gleam in the shape of a circle—a ring of ambition, of happiness, of youth. (And the positive pleasures of equilibrium under difficulties.) In a week or two, all would be changed, all (or almost all) lost: the girl would wear makeup, the horse would wear gold, the ring would be painted, the bark would be clean for the feet of the horse, the girl's feet would be clean for the slippers that she'd wear. All, all would be lost.

As I watched with the others, our jaws adroop, our eyes alight, I became painfully conscious of the element of time. Everything in the hideous old building seemed to take the shape of a circle, conforming to the course of the horse. The rider's gaze, as she peered straight ahead, seemed to be circular, as though bent by force of circumstance; then time itself began running in circles, and so the beginning was where the end was, and the two were the same, and one thing ran into the next and time went round and around and got nowhere. The girl wasn't so young that she did not know the delicious satisfaction of having a perfectly behaved body and the fun of using it to do a trick most people can't do, but she was too young to know that time does not really move in a circle at all. I thought: "She will never be as beautiful as this again"—a thought that made me acutely unhappy—and in a flash my mind (which is too much of a busybody to suit me) had projected her twenty-five years ahead, and she was now in the center of the ring, on foot, wearing a conical hat and high-heeled shoes, the image of the older woman, holding the long rein, caught in the treadmill of an afternoon long in the future. "She is at that enviable moment in life [I thought] when she believes she can go once around the ring, make one complete circuit, and at the end be exactly the same age as at the start." Everything in her movements, her expression, told you that for her the ring of time was perfectly formed, changeless, predictable, without beginning or end, like the ring in which she was traveling at this moment with the horse that wallowed under her. And then I slipped back into my trance, and time was circular again—time, pausing quietly with the rest of us, so as not to disturb the balance of a performer.

Her ride ended as casually as it had begun. The older woman stopped the horse, and the girl slid to the ground. As she walked toward us to leave, there was a quick, small burst of applause. She smiled broadly, in surprise and pleasure; then her face suddenly regained its gravity and she disappeared through the door.

It has been ambitious and plucky of me to attempt to describe what is indescribable, and I have failed, as I knew I would. But I have discharged my duty to my society; and besides, a writer, like an acrobat, must occasionally try a stunt that is too much for him. At any rate, it is worth reporting that long before the circus comes to town, its most notable performances have already been given. Under the bright lights of the finished show, a performer need only reflect the electric candle power that is directed upon him; but in the dark and dirty old training rings and in the makeshift cages, whatever light is generated, whatever excitement, whatever beauty, must come from original sources—from internal fires of professional hunger and delight, from the exuberance and gravity of youth. It is the difference between planetary light and the combustion of stars.

The South is the land of the sustained sibilant. Everywhere, for the appreciative visitor, the letter "s" insinuates itself in the scene: in the sound of sea and sand, in the singing shell, in the heat of sun and sky, in the sultriness of the gentle hours, in the siesta, in the stir of birds and insects. In contrast to the softness of its music, the South is also cruel and hard and prickly. A little striped lizard, flattened along the sharp green bayonet of a yucca, wears in its tiny face and watchful eye the pure look of death and violence. And all over the place, hidden at the bottom of their small sandy craters, the ant lions lie in wait for the ant that will stumble into their trap. (There are three kinds of lions in this region: the lions of the circus, the ant lions, and the Lions of the Tampa Lions Club, who roared their approval of segregation at a meeting the other day—all except one, a Lion named Monty Gurwit, who declined to roar and thereby got his picture in the paper.)

The day starts on a note of despair: the sorrowing dove, alone on   10
its telephone wire, mourns the loss of night, weeps at the bright perils of the unfolding day. But soon the mockingbird wakes and begins an early rehearsal, setting the dove down by force of character, running through a few slick imitations, and trying a couple of original numbers into the bargain. The redbird takes it from there. Despair gives way to good humor. The Southern dawn is a pale affair, usually, quite different from our northern daybreak. It is a triumph of gradualism; night turns to day imperceptibly, softly, with no theatrics. It is subtle and undisturbing. As the first light seeps in through the blinds I lie in bed half awake, despairing with the dove, sounding the A for the brothers

Alsop. All seems lost, all seems sorrowful. Then a mullet jumps in the bayou outside the bedroom window. It falls back into the water with a smart smack. I have asked several people why the mullet incessantly jump and I have received a variety of answers. Some say the mullet jump to shake off a parasite that annoys them. Some say they jump for the love of jumping—as the girl on the horse seemed to ride for the love of riding (although she, too, like all artists, may have been shaking off some parasite that fastens itself to the creative spirit and can be got rid of only by fifty turns around a ring while standing on a horse).

In Florida at this time of year, the sun does not take command of the day until a couple of hours after it has appeared in the east. It seems to carry no authority at first. The sun and the lizard keep the same schedule; they bide their time until the morning has advanced a good long way before they come fully forth and strike. The cold lizard waits astride his warming leaf for the perfect moment; the cold sun waits in his nest of clouds for the crucial time.

On many days, the dampness of the air pervades all life, all living. Matches refuse to strike. The towel, hung to dry, grows wetter by the hour. The newspaper, with its headlines about integration, wilts in your hand and falls limply into the coffee and the egg. Envelopes seal themselves. Postage stamps mate with one another as shamelessly as grasshoppers. But most of the time the days are models of beauty and wonder and comfort, with the kind sea stroking the back of the warm sand. At evening there are great flights of birds over the sea, where the light lingers; the gulls, the pelicans, the terns, the herons stay aloft for half an hour after land birds have gone to roost. They hold their ancient formations, wheel and fish over the Pass, enjoying the last of day like children playing outdoors after suppertime.

To a beachcomber from the North, which is my present status, the race problem has no pertinence, no immediacy. Here in Florida I am a guest in two houses—the house of the sun, the house of the State of Florida. As a guest, I mind my manners and do not criticize the customs of my hosts. It gives me a queer feeling, though, to be at the center of the greatest social crisis of my time and see hardly a sign of it. Yet the very absence of signs seems to increase one's awareness. Colored people do not come to the public beach to bathe, because they would not be made welcome there; and they don't fritter away their time visiting the circus, because they have other things to do. A few of them turn up at the ballpark, where they occupy a separate but equal section of the left-field bleachers and watch Negro players on the visiting Braves team using the same bases as the white players, instead of separate (but equal) bases. I have had only two small encounters with "color." A colored woman named Viola, who had been a friend of my wife's sister years ago, showed up one day with some laundry of ours that she had consented to do for us, and with the bundle she brought a bunch of nasturtiums, as a sort of natural accompaniment to the delivery of clean clothes. The flowers seemed a very acceptable thing and I was touched by them. We asked Viola about her daughter, and she said she was at Kentucky State College, studying voice.

The other encounter was when I was explaining to our cook, who is from Finland, the mysteries of bus travel in the American Southland. I showed her the bus stop, armed her with a timetable, and then, as a matter of duty, mentioned the customs of the Romans. "When you get on the bus," I said, "I think you'd better sit in one of the front seats—the seats in back are for colored people." A look of great weariness came into her face, as it does when we use too many dishes, and she replied, "Oh, I know—isn't it silly!"

Her remark, coming as it did all the way from Finland and landing 15 on this sandbar with a plunk, impressed me. The Supreme Court said nothing about silliness, but I suspect it may play more of a role than one might suppose. People are, if anything, more touchy about being thought silly than they are about being thought unjust. I note that one of the arguments in the recent manifesto of Southern Congressmen in support of the doctrine of "separate but equal" was that it had been founded on "common sense." The sense that is common to one generation is uncommon to the next. Probably the first slave ship, with Negroes lying in chains on its decks, seemed commonsensical to the owners who operated it and to the planters who patronized it. But such a vessel would not be in the realm of common sense today. The only sense that is common, in the long run, is the sense of change—and we all instinctively avoid it, and object to the passage of time, and would rather have none of it.

The Supreme Court decision is like the Southern sun, laggard in its early stages, biding its time. It has been the law in Florida for two years now, and the years have been like the hours of the morning before the sun has gathered its strength. I think the decision is as incontrovertible and warming as the sun, and, like the sun, will eventually take charge.

But there is certainly a great temptation in Florida to duck the passage of time. Lying in warm comfort by the sea, you receive gratefully the gift of the sun, the gift of the South. This is true seduction. The day is a circle—morning, afternoon, and night. After a few days I was clearly enjoying the same delusion as the girl on the horse—that I could ride clear around the ring of day, guarded by wind and sun and sea and sand, and be not a moment older.

P.S. (April, 1962).   When I first laid eyes on Fiddler Bayou, it was wild land, populated chiefly by the little crabs that gave it its name, visited by wading birds and by an occasional fisherman. Today, houses ring the bayou, and part of the mangrove shore has been bulkheaded with a concrete wall. Green lawns stretch from patio to water's edge, and sprinklers make rainbows in the light. But despite man's encroachment, Nature manages to hold her own and assert her authority: high tides and high winds in the gulf sometimes send the sea crashing across the sand barrier, depositing its wrack on lawns and ringing everyone's front door bell. The birds and the crabs accommodate themselves quite readily to the changes that have taken place; every day brings herons to hunt around among the roots of the mangroves, and I have discovered that I can approach to within about eight feet of a Little Blue Heron simply by entering the water and swimming slowly toward him. Apparently he has decided that when I'm in the water, I am without guile—possibly even desirable, like a fish.

The Ringling circus has quit Sarasota and gone elsewhere for its hibernation. A few circus families still own homes in the town, and every spring the students at the high school put on a circus, to let off steam, work off physical requirements, and provide a promotional spectacle for Sarasota. At the drugstore you can buy a postcard showing the bed John Ringling slept in. Time has not stood still for anybody but the dead, and even the dead must be able to hear the acceleration of little sports cars and know that things have changed.

From the all-wise *New York Times,* which has the animal kingdom ever in mind, I have learned that one of the creatures most acutely aware of the passing of time is the fiddler crab himself. Tiny spots on his body enlarge during daytime hours, giving him the same color as the mudbank he explores and thus protecting him from his enemies. At night the spots shrink, his color fades, and he is almost invisible in the light of the moon. These changes are synchronized with the tides, so that each day they occur at a different hour. A scientist who experimented with the crabs to learn more about the phenomenon discovered that even when they are removed from their natural environment and held in confinement, the rhythm of their bodily change continues uninterrupted, and they mark the passage of time in their laboratory prison, faithful to the tides in their fashion. 20

LINES OF INQUIRY
"The Ring of Time"

Though this essay consists of two separate sections, and a P.S. that White added several years after its initial publication, anthologizers usually truncate it, reprinting only the first section, which focuses on the scene at the circus. What do you think is lost, what do you think is gained, by reprinting only the first section? What images and themes from the first section are carried over and developed in the second section and the P.S.? What new images and themes are developed in the second section and the P.S.?

At various spots in this essay, White seems to be reflecting on several topics—on the circus, on writing, on artistic performance, on time, on the southern landscape, climate, and culture, on segregation, and on the ways of nature. Which of these do you consider to be White's primary center of interest in this piece? What point do you think White is trying to develop through his focus on this topic? How are his other topics of interest related to the development of this idea?

In this piece as in "Once More to the Lake," White focuses on specific places that are important to him, not just because they are vacation spots, but because they involve images and experiences that are endowed with special significance and value for him. Based on your reading of these two essays, what issues and themes are of special interest to White? What do you consider to be the most striking similarities and differences in the way that White develops and conveys his thoughts in these two pieces?

THE AGE OF DUST

echo   *anti-climax*

Voice shades into a lusher plain style

On a sunny morning last week, I went out and put up a swing for a little girl, age three, under an apple tree—the tree being much older than the girl, the sky being blue, the clouds white. I pushed the little girl for a few minutes, then returned to the house and settled down to an article on death dust, or radiological warfare, in the July *Bulletin of the Atomic Scientists,* Volume VI, No. 7.

near synonyms

voice

The article ended on a note of disappointment. "The area that can be poisoned with the fission products available to us today is disappointingly small; it amounts to not more than two or three major cities per month." At first glance, the sentence sounded satirical, but a rereading convinced me that the scientist's disappointment was real enough—that it had the purity of detachment. The world of the child in the swing (the trip to the blue sky and back again) seemed, as I studied the ABC of death dust, more and more a dream world with no true relation to things as they are or to the real world of discouragement over the slow rate of the disappearance of cities.

voice
he "reads it"
term
cliche
x vs)
mixed voice
Q: what is real?

Probably the scientist-author of the death-dust article, if he were revising his literary labors with a critical eye, would change the wording of that queer sentence. But the fact is, the sentence got written and published. The terror of the atom age is not the violence of the new power but the speed of man's adjustment to it—the speed of his acceptance. Already, bombproofing is on approximately the same level as mothproofing. Two or three major cities per month isn't much of an area, but it is a start. To the purity of science (which hopes to enlarge the area) there seems to be no corresponding purity of political thought, never the same detachment. We sorely need, from a delegate in the Security Council, a statement as detached in its way as the statement of the scientist on death dust. This delegate (and it makes no difference what nation he draws his pay from) must be a man who has not adjusted to the age of dust. He must be a person who still dwells in the mysterious dream world of swings, and little girls in swings. He must be more than a good chess player studying the future; he must be a memoirist remembering the past.

x vs y
Coined word
)-tone
goal
girl as touchstone

I couldn't seem to separate the little girl from radiological warfare— she seemed to belong with it, although inhabiting another sphere. The article kept getting back to her. "This is a novel type of warfare, in that it produces no destruction, except to life." The weapon, said the author, can be regarded as a horrid one, or, on the other hand, it "can be regarded as a remarkably humane one. In a sense, it gives each member

voices back and forth

of the target population [including each little girl] a choice of whether he will live or die." It turns out that the way to live—if that be your choice—is to leave the city as soon as the dust arrives, holding "a folded, dampened handkerchief" over your nose and mouth. I went outdoors again to push the swing some more for the little girl, who is always forgetting her handkerchief. At lunch I watched her try to fold her napkin. It seemed to take forever.

absurd even then

As I lay in bed that night, thinking of cities and target populations, I saw the child again. This time she was with the other little girls in the subway. When the train got to 242nd Street, which is as far as it goes into unreality, the children got off. They started to walk slowly north. Each child had a handkerchief, and every handkerchief was properly moistened and folded neatly—the way it said in the story.

5

the logic of it is played out —

LINES OF INQUIRY
"The Age of Dust"

At the opening of paragraph 4, White says that he "couldn't seem to separate the little girl from radiological warfare—she seemed to belong with it, although inhabiting another sphere." In what sense(s) does she inhabit "another sphere"? Given that White regards her as existing in another sphere, why does he think that "she seemed to belong with radiological warfare"? Consider how this piece might work if it focused exclusively on the article about radiological warfare without any reference to the little girl.

Q

In paragraph 2, White speaks of the sentence that he quotes from the article as being "queer." What exactly is queer about it? How would you "change the wording" of it, so that it would not seem queer? Though White doesn't make any explicit judgments about the sentences that he quotes in paragraph 4, he evidently also considers them to be queer. But are they queer in the same way as the one in paragraph 2? How would you change these sentences to make them less queer? In what sense(s) is the queer wording of the article reflective of the larger problem that concerns White in this piece?

style or into content

White is not the only author in this collection to be concerned with queer language, as you can see by looking at Goodman's "Sinking the Relationship" or Orwell's "Politics and the English Language." In what ways is White's concern with queer language similar to that of Goodman and Orwell? In what ways is it different?

what is White's voice?
persona? style?

is it a familiar style?

A SLIGHT SOUND
AT EVENING

In his journal for July 10–12, 1841, Thoreau wrote: "A slight sound at evening lifts me up by the ears, and makes life seem inexpressibly serene and grand. It may be in Uranus, or it may be in the shutter." The book into which he later managed to pack both Uranus and the shutter was published in 1854, and now, a hundred years having gone by, *Walden,* its serenity and grandeur unimpaired, still lifts us up by the ears, still translates for us that language we are in danger of forgetting, "which all things and events speak without metaphor, which alone is copious and standard."

Walden is an oddity in American letters. It may very well be the oddest of our distinguished oddities. For many it is a great deal too odd, and for many it is a particular bore. I have not found it to be a well-liked book among my acquaintances, although usually spoken of with respect, and one literary critic for whom I have the highest regard can find no reason for anyone's giving *Walden* a second thought. To admire the book is, in fact, something of an embarrassment, for the mass of men have an indistinct notion that its author was a sort of Nature Boy.

I think it is of some advantage to encounter the book at a period in one's life when the normal anxieties and enthusiasms and rebellions of youth closely resemble those of Thoreau in that spring of 1845 when he borrowed an ax, went out to the woods, and began to whack down some trees for timber. Received at such a juncture, the book is like an invitation to life's dance, assuring the troubled recipient that no matter what befalls him in the way of success or failure he will always be welcome at the party—that the music is played for him, too, if he will but listen and move his feet. In effect, that is what the book is—an invitation, unengraved; and it stirs one as a young girl is stirred by her first big party bid. Many think it a sermon; many set it down as an attempt to rearrange society; some think it an exercise in nature-loving; some find it a rather irritating collection of inspirational puffballs by an eccentric show-off. I think it none of these. It still seems to me the best youth's companion yet written by an American, for it carries a solemn warning against the loss of one's valuables, it advances a good argument for traveling light and trying new adventures, it rings with the power of positive adoration, it contains religious feeling without religious images, and it steadfastly refuses to record bad news. Even its pantheistic note is so pure as to be noncorrupting—pure as the flute-note blown across the pond on those faraway summer nights. If our colleges and universities were alert, they would present a cheap pocket edition of the book to every senior upon graduating, along with his sheepskin, or instead of it. Even if some senior were to take it literally and start felling trees, there could be worse mishaps: the ax is older than the Dictaphone and it is just as well for a young man to see what kind of chips he leaves before listening to the sound of his own voice. And even if some were to get no farther than the table of contents, they would learn how to name eighteen chapters by the use of only thirty-nine words and would see how sweet are the uses of brevity.

If Thoreau had merely left us an account of a man's life in the woods or if he had simply retreated to the woods and there recorded his complaints about society, or even if he had contrived to include both records in one essay, *Walden* would probably not have lived a hundred years. As things turned out, Thoreau, very likely without knowing quite what he was up to, took man's relation to Nature and man's dilemma in society and man's capacity for elevating his spirit and he beat all these matters together, in a wild free interval of self-justification and delight, and produced an original omelette from which people can draw nourishment in a hungry day. *Walden* is one of the first of the vitamin-enriched American dishes. If it were a little less good than it is, or even a little less queer, it would be an abominable book. Even as it is, it will continue to baffle and annoy the literal mind and all those who are unable to stomach its caprices and imbibe its theme. Certainly the plodding economist will continue to have rough going if he hopes to emerge from the book with a clear system of economic thought. Thoreau's assault on the Concord society of the mid-nineteenth century has the quality of a modern Western: he rides into the subject at top speed, shooting in all directions. Many of his shots ricochet and nick him on the rebound, and throughout the melee there is a horrendous cloud of inconsistencies and contradictions, and when the shooting dies down and the air clears, one is impressed chiefly by the courage of the rider and by how splendid it was that somebody should have ridden in there and raised all that ruckus.

When he went to the pond, Thoreau struck an attitude and did so   5 deliberately, but his posturing was not to draw the attention of others to him but rather to draw his own attention more closely to himself. "I learned this at least by my experiment: that if one advances confidently in the direction of his dreams, and endeavors to live the life which he has imagined, he will meet with a success unexpected in common hours." The sentence has the power to resuscitate the youth drowning in his sea of doubt. I recall my exhilaration upon reading it, many years ago, in a time of hesitation and despair. It restored me to health. And now in 1954 when I salute Henry Thoreau on the hundredth birthday of his book, I am merely paying off an old score—or an installment on it.

In his journal for May 3–4, 1838—Boston to Portland—he wrote: "Midnight—head over the boat's side—between sleeping and waking—with glimpses of one or more lights in the vicinity of Cape Ann. Bright moonlight—the effect heightened by seasickness." The entry illuminates the man, as the moon the sea on that night in May. In Thoreau the natural scene was heightened, not depressed, by a disturbance of the stomach, and nausea met its match at last. There was a steadiness in at least one passenger if there was none in the boat. Such steadiness (which in some would be called intoxication) is at the heart of *Walden*—confidence, faith, the discipline of looking always at what is to be seen, undeviating gratitude for the life-everlasting that he found growing in his front yard. "There is nowhere recorded a simple and irrepressible satisfaction with the gift of life, any memorable praise of God." He worked to correct that deficiency. *Walden* is his acknowledgement of the gift of life. It is the testament of a man in a high state of indignation because (it seemed to him) so few ears heard the uninterrupted poem of creation, the morning wind that forever blows. If the man sometimes wrote as though all his readers were male, unmarried, and well-connected, it is because he gave his testimony during the callow years. For that matter, he never really grew up. To reject the book because of the immaturity of the author and the bugs in the logic is to throw away a bottle of good wine because it contains bits of the cork.

Thoreau said he required of every writer, first and last, a simple and sincere account of his own life. Having delivered himself of this chesty dictum, he proceeded to ignore it. In his books and even in his enormous journal, he withheld or disguised most of the facts from which an understanding of his life could be drawn. *Walden,* subtitled "Life in the Woods," is not a simple and sincere account of a man's life, either in or out of the woods; it is an account of a man's journey into the mind, a toot on the trumpet to alert the neighbors. Thoreau was well aware that no one can alert his neighbors who is not wide-awake himself, and he went to the woods (among other reasons) to make sure that he would stay awake during his broadcast. What actually took place during the years 1845–47 is largely unrecorded, and the reader is excluded from the private life of the author, who supplies almost no gossip about himself, a great deal about his neighbors and about the universe.

As for me, I cannot in this short ramble give a simple and sincere account of my own life, but I think Thoreau might find it instructive to know that this memorial essay is being written in a house that, through no intent on my part, is the same size and shape as his own domicile on the pond—about ten by fifteen, tight, plainly finished, and at a little distance from my Concord. The house in which I sit this morning was built to accommodate a boat, not a man, but by long experience I have learned that in most respects it shelters me better than the larger dwelling where my bed is, and which, by design, is a manhouse not a boathouse. Here in the boathouse I am a wilder and, it would appear, a healthier man, by a safe margin. I have a chair, a bench, a table, and I can walk into the water if I tire of the land. My house fronts a cove. Two fishermen have just arrived to spot fish from the air—an osprey and a man in a small yellow plane who works for the fish company. The man, I have noticed, is less well equipped than the hawk, who can dive directly on his fish and carry it away, without telephoning. A mouse and a squirrel share the house with me. The building is, in fact, a multiple dwelling, a semidetached affair. It is because I am semidetached while here that I find it possible to transact this private business with the fewest obstacles.

There is also a woodchuck here, living forty feet away under the wharf. When the wind is right, he can smell my house; and when the wind is contrary, I can smell his. We both use the wharf for sunning, taking turns, each adjusting his schedule to the other's convenience. Thoreau once ate a woodchuck. I think he felt he owed it to his readers, and that it was little enough, considering the indignities they were suffering at his hands and the dressing-down they were taking. (Parts of *Walden* are pure scold.) Or perhaps he ate the woodchuck because he believed every man should acquire strict business habits, and the woodchuck was destroying his market beans. I do not know. Thoreau had a strong experimental streak in him. It is probably no harder to eat a woodchuck than to construct a sentence that lasts a hundred years. At any rate, Thoreau is the only writer I know who prepared himself for his great ordeal by eating a woodchuck; also the only one who got a hangover from drinking too much water. (He was drunk the whole time, though he seldom touched wine or coffee or tea.)

Here in this compact house where I would spend one day as deliberately as Nature if I were not being pressed by the editor of a magazine, and with a woodchuck (as yet uneaten) for neighbor, I can feel the companionship of the occupant of the pond-side cabin in Walden woods, a mile from the village, near the Fitchburg right of way. Even my immediate business is no barrier between us: Thoreau occasionally batted out a magazine piece, but was always suspicious of any sort of purposeful work that cut into his time. A man, he said, should take care not to be thrown off the track by every nutshell and mosquito's wing that falls on the rails.

There has been much guessing as to why he went to the pond. To set it down to escapism is, of course, to misconstrue what happened. Henry went forth to battle when he took to the woods, and *Walden* is the report of a man torn by two powerful and opposing drives—the desire to enjoy the world (and not be derailed by a mosquito wing) and the urge to set the world straight. One cannot join these two successfully, but sometimes, in rare cases, something good or even great results from the attempt of the tormented spirit to reconcile them. Henry went forth to battle, and if he set the stage himself, if he fought on his own terms and with his own weapons, it was because it was his nature to do things differently from most men, and to act in a cocky fashion. If the pond and the woods seemed a more plausible site for a house than an in-town location, it was because a cowbell made for him a sweeter sound than a churchbell. *Walden,* the book, makes the sound of a cowbell, more than a churchbell, and proves the point, although both sounds are in it, and both remarkably clear and sweet. He simply preferred his churchbell at a little distance.

I think one reason he went to the woods was a perfectly simple and commonplace one—and apparently he thought so, too. "At a certain season of our life," he wrote, "we are accustomed to consider every spot as the possible site of a house." There spoke the young man, a few years out of college, who had not yet broken away from home. He hadn't married, and he had found no job that measured up to his rigid standards of employment, and like any young man, or young animal, he felt uneasy and on the defensive until he had fixed himself a den. Most young men, of course, casting about for a site, are content merely to draw apart from their kinfolks. Thoreau, convinced that the greater part of what his neighbors called good was bad, withdrew from a great deal more than family: he pulled out of everything for a while, to serve everybody right for being so stuffy, and to try his own prejudices on the dog.

The house-hunting sentence above, which starts the chapter called "Where I Lived, and What I Lived For," is followed by another passage that is worth quoting here because it so beautifully illustrates the offbeat prose that Thoreau was master of, a prose at once strictly disciplined and wildly abandoned. "I have surveyed the country on every side within a dozen miles of where I live," continued this delirious young man. "In imagination I have bought all the farms in succession, for all were to be bought, and I knew their price. I walked over each farmer's premises, tasted his wild apples, discoursed on husbandry with him, took his farm at his price, at any price, mortgaging it to him in my mind; even put a higher price on it—took everything but a deed of it—took his word for his deed, for I dearly love to talk—cultivated it, and him too to some extent, I trust, and withdrew when I had enjoyed it long enough, leaving him to carry it on." A copy-desk man would get a double hernia trying to clean up that sentence for the management, but the sentence needs no fixing, for it perfectly captures the meaning of the writer and the quality of the ramble.

"Wherever I sat, there I might live, and the landscape radiated from me accordingly." Thoreau, the home-seeker, sitting on his hummock with the entire State of Massachusetts radiating from him, is to me the most humorous of the New England figures, and *Walden* the most humorous of the books, though its humor is almost continuously subsurface and there is nothing deliberately funny anywhere, except a few weak jokes and bad puns that rise to the surface like the perch in the pond that rose to the sound of the maestro's flute. Thoreau tended to write in sentences, a feat not every writer is capable of, and *Walden* is, rhetorically speaking, a collection of certified sentences, some of them, it would now appear, as indestructible as they are errant. The book is distilled from the vast journals, and this accounts for its intensity: he picked out bright particles that pleased his eye, whirled them in the kaleidoscope of his content, and produced the pattern that has endured—the color, the form, the light.

On this its hundredth birthday, Thoreau's *Walden* is pertinent and timely. In our uneasy season, when all men unconsciously seek a retreat from a world that has got almost completely out of hand, his house in the Concord woods is a haven. In our culture of gadgetry and the multiplicity of convenience, his cry "Simplicity, simplicity, simplicity!" has the insistence of a fire alarm. In the brooding atmosphere of war and the gathering radioactive storm, the innocence and serenity of his summer afternoons are enough to burst the remembering heart, and one gazes back upon that pleasing interlude—its confidence, its purity, its deliberateness—with awe and wonder, as one would look upon the face of a child asleep.

"This small lake was of most value as a neighbor in the intervals of a gentle rain-storm in August, when, both air and water being perfectly still, but the sky overcast, midafternoon had all the serenity of evening, and the wood-thrush sang around, and was heard from shore to shore." Now, in the perpetual overcast in which our days are spent, we hear with extra perception and deep gratitude that song, tying century to century.

I sometimes amuse myself by bringing Henry Thoreau back to life and showing him the sights. I escort him into a phone booth and let him dial Weather. "This is a delicious evening," the girl's voice says, "when the whole body is one sense, and imbibes delight through every pore." I show him the spot in the Pacific where an island used to be, before some magician made it vanish. "We know not where we are," I murmur. "The light which puts out our eyes is darkness to us. Only that day dawns to which we are awake." I thumb through the latest copy of *Vogue* with him. "Of two patterns which differ only by a few threads more or less of a particular color," I read, "the one will be sold readily, the other lie on the shelf, though it frequently happens that, after the lapse of a season, the latter becomes the most fashionable." Together we go outboarding on the Assabet, looking for what we've lost—a hound, a bay horse, a turtledove. I show him a distracted farmer who is trying to repair a hay baler before the thunder shower breaks. "This farmer," I remark, "is endeavoring to solve the problem of a

livelihood by a formula more complicated than the problem itself. To
get his shoestrings he speculates in herds of cattle."

I take the celebrated author to Twenty-One for lunch, so the wait-
ers may study his shoes. The proprietor welcomes us. "The gross feeder,"
remarks the proprietor, sweeping the room with his arm, "is a man in
the larva stage." After lunch we visit a classroom in one of those schools
conducted by big corporations to teach their superannuated executives
how to retire from business without serious injury to their health. (The
shock to men's systems these days when relieved of the exacting routine of amassing wealth is very great and must be cushioned.) "It is not
necessary," says the teacher to his pupils, "that a man should earn his
living by the sweat of his brow, unless he sweats easier than I do. We
are determined to be starved before we are hungry."

I turn on the radio and let Thoreau hear Winchell beat the red hand
around the clock. "Time is but the stream I go a-fishing in," shouts
Mr. Winchell, rattling his telegraph key. "Hardly a man takes a half
hour's nap after dinner, but when he wakes he holds up his head and
asks, 'What's the news?' If we read of one man robbed, or murdered,
or killed by accident, or one house burned, or one vessel wrecked, or
one steamboat blown up, or one cow run over on the Western Railroad, or one mad dog killed, or one lot of grasshoppers in the winter—
we need never read of another. One is enough."

I doubt that Thoreau would be thrown off balance by the fantastic   20
sights and sounds of the twentieth century. "The Concord nights," he
once wrote, "are stranger than the Arabian nights." A four-engined
airliner would merely serve to confirm his early views on travel. Everywhere he would observe, in new shapes and sizes, the old predicaments
and follies of men—the desperation, the impedimenta, the meanness—
along with the visible capacity for elevation of the mind and soul. "This
curious world which we inhabit is more wonderful than it is convenient; more beautiful than it is useful; it is more to be admired and
enjoyed than used." He would see that today ten thousand engineers
are busy making sure that the world shall be convenient even if it is
destroyed in the process, and others are determined to increase its usefulness even though its beauty is lost somewhere along the way.

At any rate, I'd like to stroll about the countryside in Thoreau's
company for a day, observing the modern scene, inspecting today's
snowstorm, pointing out the sights, and offering belated apologies for
my sins. Thoreau is unique among writers in that those who admire
him find him uncomfortable to live with—a regular hairshirt of a man.
A little band of dedicated Thoreauvians would be a sorry sight indeed:
fellows who hate compromise and have compromised, fellows who love
wildness and have lived tamely, and at their side, censuring them and
chiding them, the ghostly figure of this upright man, who long ago
gave corroboration to impulses they perceived were right and issued

warnings against the things they instinctively knew to be their enemies. I should hate to be called a Thoreauvian, yet I wince every time I walk into the barn I'm pushing before me, seventy-five feet by forty, and the author of *Walden* has served as my conscience through the long stretches of my trivial days.

Hairshirt or no, he is a better companion than most, and I would not swap him for a soberer or more reasonable friend even if I could. I can reread his famous invitation with undiminished excitement. The sad thing is that not more acceptances have been received, that so many decline for one reason or another, pleading some previous engagement or ill health. But the invitation stands. It will beckon as long as this remarkable book stays in print—which will be as long as there are August afternoons in the intervals of a gentle rainstorm, as long as there are ears to catch the faint sounds of the orchestra. I find it agreeable to sit here this morning, in a house of correct proportions, and hear across a century of time his flute, his frogs, and his seductive summons to the wildest revels of them all.

Allen Cove, Summer, 1954

LINES OF INQUIRY
"A Slight Sound at Evening"

White has divided this essay into two sections, marked by a space break between paragraphs 16 and 17. What is the purpose of that second section, in which White imagines himself "bringing Henry Thoreau back to life and showing him the sights"? What relationship, if any, does it have to the first section, in which White is concerned with commemorating the hundredth anniversary of *Walden?* Why doesn't White simply end his essay with paragraph 16, especially since that paragraph ends with a sentence that seems to be a fitting conclusion to the piece as a whole?

In paragraphs 3–7, White lists numerous reasons for his admiration of *Walden*. What connection do you see between all of these reasons and the ones that he cites in paragraphs 15–16, having to do with the contemporary relevance of *Walden?* What overriding values seem to be guiding White in his enumeration of all these reasons? How are these values reflected by White's description in paragraphs 8–10 of the house where he wrote "this memorial essay"?

For another, quite different, essay dealing with Thoreau and *Walden,* you might find it interesting to look at Oates' "Against Nature," which also appears in this collection. What are the most striking differences that you notice between the views that White and Oates offer of Thoreau and his work? How do you account for these differences? Based on your own reading of Thoreau's pieces in this collection, whose view do you think is more reliable?

THE ESSAYIST AND THE ESSAY

The essayist is a self-liberated man, sustained by the childish belief that everything he thinks about, everything that happens to him, is of general interest. He is a fellow who thoroughly enjoys his work, just as people who take bird walks enjoy theirs. Each new excursion of the essayist, each new "attempt," differs from the last and takes him into new country. This delights him. Only a person who is congenitally self-centered has the effrontery and the stamina to write essays.

There are as many kinds of essays as there are human attitudes or poses, as many essay flavors as there are Howard Johnson ice creams. The essayist arises in the morning and, if he has work to do, selects his garb from an unusually extensive wardrobe: he can pull on any sort of shirt, be any sort of person, according to his mood or his subject matter—philosopher, scold jester, raconteur, confidant, pundit, devil's advocate, enthusiast. I like the essay, have always liked it, and even as a child was at work, attempting to inflict my young thoughts and experiences on others by putting them on paper. I early broke into print in the pages of *St. Nicholas.* I tend still to fall back on the essay form (or lack of form) when an idea strikes me, but I am not fooled about the place of the essay in twentieth-century American letters—it stands a short distance down the line. The essayist, unlike the novelist, the poet, and the playwright, must be content in his self-imposed role of second-class citizen. A writer who has his sights trained on the Nobel Prize or other earthly triumphs had best write a novel, a poem, or a play, and leave the essayist to ramble about, content with living a free life and enjoying the satisfactions of a somewhat undisciplined existence. (Dr. Johnson called the essay "an irregular, undigested piece"; this happy practitioner has no wish to quarrel with the good doctor's characterization.)

There is one thing the essayist cannot do, though—he cannot indulge himself in deceit or in concealment, for he will be found out in no time. Desmond MacCarthy, in his introductory remarks to the 1928 E. P. Dutton & Company edition of Montaigne, observes that Montaigne "had the gift of natural candour. . . ." It is the basic ingredient. And even the essayist's escape from discipline is only a partial escape: the essay, although a relaxed form, imposes its own disciplines, raises its own problems, and these disciplines and problems soon become apparent and (we all hope) act as a deterrent to anyone wielding a pen merely because he entertains random thoughts or is in a happy or wandering mood.

I think some people find the essay the last resort of the egoist, a much too self-conscious and self-serving form for their taste; they feel that it is presumptuous of a writer to assume that his little excursions or his small observations will interest the reader. There is some justice in their complaint. I have always been aware that I am by nature self-absorbed and egoistical; to write of myself to the extent I have done indicates a too great attention to my own life, not enough to the lives of others. I have worn many shirts, and not all of them have been a good fit. But when I am discouraged or downcast I need only fling open the door of my closet, and there, hidden behind everything else, hangs the mantle of Michel de Montaigne, smelling slightly of camphor.

LINES OF INQUIRY
"The Essayist and the Essay"

In his second paragraph, White claims that "there are as many kinds of essays as there are human attitudes or poses," and that the essayist can "be any sort of person, according to his mood or his subject matter." What "sort of person" does White appear to be in this piece? How would you characterize his "mood" and his "attitudes"? How is your impression of him shaped by his ideas? By the way he develops his ideas? By the way he words his ideas? What relationship do you see between the kind of person he appears to be and the subject matter he discusses?

In his third paragraph, White maintains that the essayist "cannot indulge himself in deceit or in concealment." How do you square this assertion with his previous statement about all of the "poses" that are available to the essayist? How is it possible to assume a pose in writing without engaging "in deceit or in concealment?" How is it possible to assume a pose while also being "self-centered"? What exactly do you think White believes about the relationship between the sort of person an essayist appears to be in writing and the sort of person an essayist actually is?

White is not the only essayist to be concerned with the personality that comes across in an essay, as you can see by looking at Hoagland's "What I Think, What I Am" and Woolf's "The Modern Essay." How does White's idea about the "poses" of an essayist compare with Hoagland's assertion that "the artful 'I' of an essay can be as chameleon as any narrator in fiction"? How does White's idea compare with Woolf's belief that the "problem" for every essayist is "never to be yourself and yet always" to be yourself? What relationship do you think exists between the sort of person you are and the sort of person you appear to be in your writing? For another point of view on this question, you might find it useful to read Mairs' "Carnal Acts."

TOM WOLFE

1 9 3 1 –

Readers were bored to tears without understanding why. When they came upon that pale beige tone, it began to signal to them, unconsciously, that a well-known bore was here again, "the journalist," a phlegmatic spirit, a faded personality, and there was no way to get rid of the pallid little troll, short of ceasing to read.

In this passage from his essay, "The New Journalism," Tom Wolfe criticizes the "calm," "cultivated," "genteel" voice that characterized nonfiction writing in the early sixties. To avoid such a "beige" and "faded" style in his own writing, Wolfe says, "I would try anything," and he does: imitating the voices of his subjects, inhabiting their minds, stretching sentences to their limits with modifiers and intensifiers—using a whole battery of amplifying strategies that have come to define the "new journalism." For him, these strategies are not simply matters of prose style alone. In his view, only writing with "personality, energy, drive, bravura" can capture the intensity of American experience, particularly the exuberance and excesses of popular culture since the sixties, the object of his most brilliant satire.

Born in Richmond, Virginia, a graduate of Washington and Lee University, Wolfe left the South for graduate school at Yale, where he received a PhD in American Studies in 1957. The atmosphere of Yale was "poisonous," and "morbid," Wolfe says, and he longed to escape it for the "real world" of newspaper reporting. After stints with the *Springfield Union* and *Washington Post,* he left for "the hulking carnival" of New York City and the staffs of *The New York Herald Tribune* and *New York Times Sunday Magazine.* There, working under the pressure of deadlines and the competition of his fellow reporters, Wolfe developed his signature techniques for bringing feature writing alive.

The breakthrough came in 1963 on a story Wolfe was doing for *Esquire* on the custom car culture in California. He'd done all the research but didn't know how to shape or analyze it. "I couldn't pull the thing together," he says, so he just sat down and started "typing away," "recording it all, and inside of a couple of hours, typing along like a madman, I could tell something was beginning to happen." The spontaneity and immediacy of the result impressed the editors at *Esquire,* who published the piece exactly as it was—as "The Kandy-Kolored Tangerine-Flake Streamline Baby"—even though Wolfe intended it to begin simply as a memo noting first impressions. He had found his style, his voice, his way of making things happen in prose.

Since then Wolfe has written a series of controversial social portraits and cultural critiques. In 1965 he published his first collection of essays—also entitled *The Kandy-Kolored Tangerine-Flake Streamline Baby*—revelling in the "freer forms" of popular culture, from the "electronic jollification" of Las Vegas to the down-home heroism of stock car racing to the "marvelous" tackiness of youth culture figures like Murray the K and Muhammed Ali. But Wolfe satirizes even as he celebrates. In *The Electric Kool Aid Acid Test* (1968), he zestfully recreates the manic energy of novelist Ken Kesey and the Merry Pranksters, a group of hippies dedicated to LSD and the psychedelic experience, yet he questions their undisciplined ways and their solemn elevation of a life-style into a "theology," an experience of "the holy." In *Radical Chic and Mau-Mauing the Flak Catchers* (1970), one of his most controversial books, Wolfe caricatures Leonard Bernstein and other "radically chic" liberals who raise money for groups like the Black Panthers at high society cocktail parties. In *The Painted Word* (1975) and *From Bauhaus to Our House* (1981) he satirizes the self-important obscurity of modern painting and architecture. And in his most widely known and highly praised book, *The Right Stuff* (1979), Wolfe offers a detailed study of "the righteous fraternities" of fighter pilots and astronauts in the early years of the American space program. Again, he is attracted by energy and talent and uniqueness, in this case by the "ineffable" quality of "the right stuff," a mysterious amalgam of bravery and skill possessed by every successful pilot. Yet he remains skeptical of the romanticizing, the mystifying, and the pomposity inherent in the very idea of "the right stuff."

Like many other satirists, Wolfe takes as his targets excessiveness and pretentiousness. His concern is that the various trends and consciousness-raising movements of the sixties and seventies oversimplify complex experience. So, he is always on the lookout for the holier-than-thou, for people who take themselves too seriously and look down on everyone else. He also cautions us about the dangers of self-indulgence. In a famous and much quoted essay, "The Me Decade and the Third Great Awakening," he writes with great irony about "the luxury enjoyed by so many millions of middling folk, of dwelling upon the self."

Wolfe's satire is not often so direct. Indeed, he rarely comes out in his own voice and tells us what he thinks. Instead, he relies on the technique of third-person omniscient narration, looking at experience through "the eye sockets" of the people involved, speaking in their own voices, as if he knows their thoughts and feelings. Through the hard work of "saturation reporting," of interviewing and researching and living with the subject, a reporter, he believes, can learn enough about an individual to re-create his or her thoughts accurately and fairly. Saturation reporting is one of the four basic techniques of the "new journalism," according to Wolfe, the one most attacked by other journalists as "subjective" and "biased." Another technique is what Wolfe calls "scene-by-scene reconstruction," "telling the story by moving from scene to scene and resorting as little as possible to sheer historical narrative." A third technique uses "status details," bits and pieces of everyday life—gestures, habits, manners, "modes of behaving"—that help evoke the textures of an experience. The fourth is dialogue, which Wolfe says "involves the reader more completely than any other device." In other words, Wolfe shows, rarely tells. So his essays and books are often hard to distinguish from fiction, made up as they are of stories and events and descriptions of experience.

On the sentence level Wolfe pulls out all the stops. He exclaims, digresses, interrupts, writing often in the present tense, as if the event is happening before our eyes, even as we are reading about it. So his phrases expand and develop excitedly. His punctuation abounds with ellipses, dashes, parentheses, italics. He plays with the sound of words, mimicking, repeating. His goal, he says, "is to give the illusion not only of a person talking but of a person thinking":

> My God—to be a part of Edwards in the late forties and early fifties!— even to be on the ground and hear one of those incredible explosions from 35,000 feet and know that some True Brother had commenced his rocket launch . . . in the X–1, the X–1A, the X–2, the D558–1, the horrible XF–92A, the beautiful D–558–2 . . . and to know that he would seem to be at an altitude, in the thin air at the edge of space, where the stars and the moon came out at noon, in an atmosphere so thin that the ordinary laws of aerodynamics no longer applied and a plane could skid into a flat spin like a cereal bowl on a waxed Formica counter and then start tumbling, not spinning and not diving, but tumbling, end over end like a brick. . . .

Wolfe has said in an interview that he wanted the writing in *The Right Stuff* to appear "buoyant, free and easy, spontaneous," but the paradox is that "creating the effect of spontaneity in writing is one of the most difficult things you can do." It requires revision and discipline. Like the fighter-jocks themselves, who "push the outside of the envelope" whenever they set a new speed or altitude record, Wolfe pushes the outside of the envelope of language, but only through hard work, painstaking control, and the risk of "tumbling, end over end like a brick. . . ."

THE MILD ONES

God knows how many thousands of work-a-daddy citizens of Columbus, Ohio, Tom's own city, drive past the Harley-Davidson agency at 491 West Broad Street every day without ever seeing *Tom's Bomb,* that weird monster in the show window. Yet there are many boys and men, religiosi of a sort, in Los Angeles, Oakland, Chicago, Cleveland, who know of it. They know of this *ecstatic* in Columbus, Tom Reiser—the stud who rides a motorcycle with an automobile engine in it—

Liberation!

Tom's Bomb is up on a platform in one corner of the window. It is a Harley-Davidson 74-XA motorcycle with a Chevrolet V-8 automobile engine in it. Reiser put a whole automobile engine in a motorcycle. He had to put it in crossways, so that half the block sticks out of one side of the bike and half out the other, right out of the frame there, right in front of the rider's legs and just in back of the front wheel. The proportions are like a boulder rammed through a sheet of plywood. The motorcycle frame weighs 300 pounds and the engine weighs 550 pounds, a Chevrolet V-8 with all the headers, the wires, the flywheel, everything showing.

Reiser got the idea from another one of the underground heroes of the motorcycle world, Ed Potter. Ed Potter, in motorcycling, is like what Chuck Berry, Muddy Waters, Hank Williams, or one of these people is in music, a *germinal* folk figure from back 'ere on Route 422 or something. Potter put a whole automobile engine in a motorcycle frame and called the machine the "Bloody Mary." But he didn't have any transmission in it, no gear shift. He couldn't start it off from a dead start and accelerate. He had to go out to the drag strip and get on and have his buddy Jimmy jack the rear wheel up off the ground. Then he would turn the throttle up until the rear wheel was turning at the equivalent of about 110 miles an hour. Then his buddy Jimmy would kick the jack out from under it and—holy jesus—the back wheel would hit the asphalt and shriek like a woman's scream and he would start careening down the strip, fishtailing every way you can think of, including straight into the crowd. There was a true ball buster.

Tom Reiser refined the whole thing. He invented a motorcycle transmission, the kind you operate on the handlebars of the motorcycle, for the Chevrolet V-8 engine. Reiser is a student of the motorcycle. That is one thing people do not generally understand about the motorcycle crowd. The kids who go in for racing, whether drag racing, like Reiser, or oval track racing or long-distance road racing, hill climbing or

5

cross-country racing, are very studious. They develop a priestly passion for speed engineering. They are truly religious men, bound by their devotion to Liberation through the internal-combustion engine. They are sequestered from most secular concerns. They spend practically all their spare time working on the machines. They seldom drink much because it takes up too much time or even smoke much because it gets in the way when you're working on the machine.

Reiser looks a little like Slats in the comic strip, "Abbie and Slats." He is 29 years old, tall, blond, raw-boned, open, outgoing; *Western*-looking, one might say. He is married and has two children. His father, who is retired, was a florist and his mother was a seamstress; he went to South High School in Columbus and later was trained at the Harley-Davidson mechanics school in California. He was always a genius with motorcycles. And courage—raw nerve—it seemed like his priestly passion for the motorcycle, for speed, made it so he would do practically anything to get speed out of a motorcycle. Reiser won the Canadian hill-climbing championship in 1965 and is after the speed record at the Utah salt flats. He put together "Tom's Bomb" in 1961, and thankgod they had just built the superhighway from Columbus west to Cincinnati, Route 71, because that was the chance to try it out.

The federal superhighway program has been a godsend for speed engineering in the state of Ohio. The beautiful time is right after a stretch of highway is built, but before it is opened to cars. Ohio's speed kids, the motorcyclists, the drag racers, both motorcycle and automobile, follow that beautiful superhighway system wherever the road contractors go with it. At night they sneak out onto the great smooth stretches of American superhighway and . . . *go.* Tom Reiser warmed up "Tom's Bomb" out on Route 71 under the moon and then he took it out to the drag strip near Newark, Ohio, for an exhibition. They all saw the machine rolling out toward the starting line, and a shriek went up—

"Well, when I started off," Reiser was saying, "the back wheel bit down so hard it threw me back and it felt like the whole motorcycle was going to go over backward. It was like the whole thing was just going to lift up and go over backward. It was like the whole thing was covered in smoke, me and everything. I couldn't see nothing. The guys thought the engine had exploded or something. It was the rubber burning, but they thought the whole thing was on fire and they were going to have to get me out of there with a fire hose. It was a weird feeling. It started off with a whole row of jerks. I don't know what that was, unless there was so much power, it was just running over the top of itself, and then all of a sudden it shot out of the cloud, and after that there wasn't anything to do but *hang on*—"

By the time he burst out of the cloud, Reiser was already going about 50 miles an hour. By the time he hit 60, he had his head practically down on the handlebars, to lower his body and cut down on the wind resistance. His body was stretched out over the Chevrolet V-8 engine, which was mounted in the frame between the seat and the front wheel. He was stretching more and more flat out with each split second of acceleration until his feet came up off the foot rests and his legs stretched out straight behind—

"When I hit about 90," said Reiser, "it was like the bike wasn't   10 hardly touching the road any more—"

—and when he hit 130, he *knew* it wasn't—

"All of a sudden I was *sailing*—like I wasn't on the ground any more at all. I couldn't hardly see anything or hear anything. There was no gravity or nothing, I was just *sailing*—"

—and as he spoke, I could *see* it, the ultimate vision. I could see his body stretched out and pressing down tighter and tighter upon the V-8 engine until his thoracic cavity was practically bolted onto it. Its fiery combustions were his neural explosions and his neural explosions were its fiery combustions. His body and that roaring engine block were one and the same creature, sailing—at 140—160—180—200 miles an hour—*2,000* miles an hour—sailing!—at last, the winged American centaur, the American dream, at last: soaring over God's own good green Great Plains of America bareback aboard a 300-horsepower Chevrolet V-8 engine!

LINES OF INQUIRY
"The Mild Ones"

In this brief essay, Wolfe uses a widely varied mix of conventional reporting and editorializing methods, as well as new journalistic narrative and stylistic techniques. Examine the essay paragraph by paragraph to see how Wolfe uses and mixes these two different ways of presenting a subject. In what paragraphs does he seem to rely most heavily on conventional methods of presentation? In what paragraphs does he rely most heavily on new journalistic techniques? How do you account for the specific places in which he relies most heavily on one method or the other?

Though this essay is called "The Mild Ones," it is devoted almost entirely to a portrait of Tom Reiser and his extraordinary motorcycle. Why do you suppose that Wolfe chose to give the essay such an unusual, perhaps even misleading, title? What are the implications of the title? In what senses might Reiser be considered a mild one? In what respects is he not a mild one at all? What does the title suggest about Wolfe's attitude toward Reiser and toward others like him?

Given the brevity of this piece, it might be considered a miniaturized version of Wolfe's presentational strategies in other pieces. So, consider this essay in relation to one of the other pieces by Wolfe in this collection. What similarities—what differences—do you notice between the ways that Wolfe presents his subject in each piece? How do you account for the differences?

O ROTTEN GOTHAM—
SLIDING DOWN INTO THE
BEHAVIORAL SINK

I just spent two days with Edward T. Hall, an anthropologist, watching thousands of my fellow New Yorkers short-circuiting themselves into hot little twitching death balls with jolts of their own adrenalin. Dr. Hall says it is overcrowding that does it. Overcrowding gets the adrenalin going, and the adrenalin gets them hyped up. And here they are, hyped up, turning bilious, nephritic, queer, autistic, sadistic, barren, batty, sloppy, hot-in-the-pants, chancred-on-the-flankers, leering, puling, numb—the usual in New York, in other words, and God knows what else. Dr. Hall has the theory that overcrowding has already thrown New York into a state of behavioral sink. Behavioral sink is a term from ethology, which is the study of how animals relate to their environment. Among animals, the sink winds up with a "population collapse" or "massive die-off." O rotten Gotham.

It got to be easy to look at New Yorkers as animals, especially looking down from some place like a balcony at Grand Central at the rush hour Friday afternoon. The floor was filled with the poor white humans, running around, dodging, blinking their eyes, making a sound like a pen full of starlings or rats or something.

"Listen to them skid," says Dr. Hall.

He was right. The poor old etiolate animals were out there skidding on their rubber soles. You could hear it once he pointed it out. They stop short to keep from hitting somebody or because they are disoriented and they suddenly stop and look around, and they skid on their rubber-sole shoes, and a screech goes up. They pour out onto the floor down the escalators from the Pan-Am Building, from 42nd Street, from Lexington Avenue, up out of subways, down into subways, railroad trains, up into helicopters—

"You can also hear the helicopters all the way down here," says Dr. 5 Hall. The sound of the helicopters using the roof of the Pan-Am Building nearly fifty stories up beats right through. "If it weren't for this ceiling"—he is referring to the very high ceiling in Grand Central— "this place would be unbearable with this kind of crowding. And yet they'll probably never 'waste' space like this again."

They screech! And the adrenal glands in all those poor white animals enlarge, micrometer by micrometer, to the size of cantaloupes. Dr. Hall pulls a Minox camera out of a holster he has on his belt and starts shooting away at the human scurry. The Sink!

Dr. Hall has the Minox up to his eye—he is a slender man, calm, 52 years old, young-looking, an anthropologist who has worked with Navajos, Hopis, Spanish-Americans, Negroes, Trukese. He was the most important anthropologist in the government during the crucial years of the foreign aid program, the 1950's. He directed both the Point Four training program and the Human Relations Area Files. He wrote *The Silent Language* and *The Hidden Dimension,* two books that are picking up the kind of "underground" following his friend Marshall McLuhan started picking up about five years ago. He teaches at the Illinois Institute of Technology, lives with his wife, Mildred, in a high-ceilinged town house on one of the last great residential streets in downtown Chicago, Astor Street; has a grown son and daughter, loves good food, good wine, the relaxed, civilized life—but comes to New York with a Minox at his eye to record—perfect!—The Sink.

We really got down in there by walking down into the Lexington Avenue line subway stop under Grand Central. We inhaled those nice big fluffy fumes of human sweat, urine, effluvia, and sebaceous secretions. One old female human was already stroked out on the upper level, on a stretcher, with two policemen standing by. The other humans barely looked at her. They rushed into line. They bellied each other, haunch to paunch, down the stairs. Human heads shone through the gratings. The species North European tried to create bubbles of space around themselves, about a foot and a half in diameter—

"See, he's reacting against the line," says Dr. Hall.

—but the species Mediterranean presses on in. The hell with bubbles of space. The species North European resents that, this male human behind him presses forward toward the booth . . . *breathing* on him, he's disgusted, he pulls out of the line entirely, the species Mediterranean resents him for resenting it, and neither of them realizes what the hell they are getting irritable about exactly. And in all of them the old adrenals grow another micrometer.

Dr. Hall whips out the Minox. Too perfect! The bottom of The Sink.

It is the sheer overcrowding, such as occurs in the business sections of Manhattan five days a week and in Harlem, Bedford-Stuyvesant, southeast Bronx every day—sheer overcrowding is converting New Yorkers into animals in a sink pen. Dr. Hall's argument runs as follows: all animals, including birds, seem to have a built-in, inherited requirement to have a certain amount of territory, space, to lead their lives in. Even if they have all the food they need, and there are no predatory animals threatening them, they cannot tolerate crowding beyond a certain point. No more than two hundred wild Norway rats can survive on a quarter acre of ground, for example, even when they are given all the food they can eat. They just die off.

But why? To find out, ethologists have run experiments on all sorts of animals, from stickleback crabs to Sika deer. In one major experiment, an ethologist named John Calhoun put some domesticated white Norway rats in a pen with four sections to it, connected by ramps. Calhoun knew from previous experiments that the rats tend to split up into groups of ten to twelve and that the pen, therefore, would hold forty to forty-eight rats comfortably, assuming they formed four equal groups. He allowed them to reproduce until there were eighty rats, balanced between male and female, but did not let it get any more crowded. He kept them supplied with plenty of food, water, and nesting materials. In other words, all their more obvious needs were taken care of. A less obvious need—space—was not. To the human eye, the pen did not even look especially crowded. But to the rats, it was crowded beyond endurance.

The entire colony was soon plunged into a profound behavioral sink. "The sink," said Calhoun, "is the outcome of any behavioral process that collects animals together in unusually great numbers. The unhealthy connotations of the term are not accidental: a behavioral sink does act to aggravate all forms of pathology that can be found within a group."

For a start, long before the rat population reached eighty, a status   15
hierarchy had developed in the pen. Two dominant male rats took over the two end sections, acquired harems of eight to ten females each, and forced the rest of the rats into the two middle pens. All the overcrowding took place in the middle pens. That was where the "sink" hit. The aristocrat rats at the ends grew bigger, sleeker, healthier, and more secure the whole time.

In The Sink, meanwhile, nest building, courting, sex behavior, reproduction, social organization, health—all of it went to pieces. Normally, Norway rats have a mating ritual in which the male chases the female, the female ducks down into a burrow and sticks her head up to watch the male. He performs a little dance outside the burrow, then she comes out, and he mounts her, usually for a few seconds. When The Sink set in, however, no more than three males—the dominant males in the middle sections—kept up the old customs. The rest tried everything from satyrism to homosexuality or else gave up on sex altogether. Some of the subordinate males spent all their time chasing females. Three or four might chase one female at the same time, and instead of stopping at the burrow entrance for the ritual, they would charge right in. Once mounted, they would hold on for minutes instead of the usual seconds.

Homosexuality rose sharply. So did bisexuality. Some males would mount anything—males, females, babies, senescent rats, anything. Still other males dropped sexual activity altogether, wouldn't fight and, in fact, would hardly move except when the other rats slept. Occasionally a female from the aristocrat rats' harems would come over the ramps and into the middle sections to sample life in The Sink. When she had had enough, she would run back up the ramp. Sink males would give chase up to the top of the ramp, which is to say, to the very edge of the aristocratic preserve. But one glance from one of the king rats would stop them cold and they would return to The Sink.

The slumming females from the harems had their adventures and then returned to a placid, healthy life. Females in The Sink, however, were ravaged, physically and psychologically. Pregnant rats had trouble continuing pregnancy. The rate of miscarriages increased significantly, and females started dying from tumors and other disorders of the mammary glands, sex organs, uterus, ovaries, and Fallopian tubes. Typically, their kidneys, livers, and adrenals were also enlarged or diseased or showed other signs associated with stress.

Child-rearing became totally disorganized. The females lost the interest or the stamina to build nests and did not keep them up if they did build them. In the general filth and confusion, they would not put themselves out to save offspring they were momentarily separated from. Frantic, even sadistic competition among the males was going on all around them and rendering their lives chaotic. The males began unprovoked and senseless assaults upon one another, often in the form of tailbiting. Ordinarily, rats will suppress this kind of behavior when it crops up. In The Sink, male rats gave up all policing and just looked out for themselves. The "pecking order" among males in The Sink was never stable. Normally, male rats set up a three-class structure. Under the pressure of overcrowding, however, they broke up into all sorts of unstable subclasses, cliques, packs—and constantly pushed, probed, explored, tested one another's power. Anyone was fair game, except for the aristocrats in the end pens.

Calhoun kept the population down to eighty, so that the next stage, "population collapse" or "massive die-off," did not occur. But the autopsies showed that the pattern—as in the diseases among the female rats—was already there.

The classic study of die-off was John J. Christian's study of Sika deer on James Island in the Chesapeake Bay, west of Cambridge, Maryland. Four or five of the deer had been released on the island, which was 280 acres and uninhabited, in 1916. By 1955 they had bred freely into a herd of 280 to 300. The population density was only about one deer per acre at this point, but Christian knew that this was already too high for the Sikas' inborn space requirements, and something would give before long. For two years the number of deer remained 280 to 300. But suddenly, in 1958, over half the deer died; 161 carcasses were recovered. In 1959 more deer died and the population steadied at about 80.

In two years, two-thirds of the herd had died. Why? It was not starvation. In fact, all the deer collected were in excellent condition, with well-developed muscles, shining coats, and fat deposits between the muscles. In practically all the deer, however, the adrenal glands had enlarged by 50 percent. Christian concluded that the die-off was due to "shock following severe metabolic disturbance, probably as a result of prolonged adrenocortical hyperactivity. . . . There was no evidence of infection, starvation, or other obvious cause to explain the mass mortality." In other words, the constant stress of overpopulation, plus the normal stress of the cold of the winter, had kept the adrenalin flowing so constantly in the deer that their systems were depleted of blood sugar and they died of shock.

Well, the white humans are still skidding and darting across the floor of Grand Central. Dr. Hall listens a moment longer to the skidding and the darting noises, and then says, "You know, I've been on commuter trains here after everyone has been through one of these rushes, and I'll tell you, there is enough acid flowing in the stomachs in every car to dissolve the rails underneath."

Just a little invisible acid bath for the linings to round off the day. The ulcers the acids cause, of course, are the one disease people have already been taught to associate with the stress of city life. But overcrowding, as Dr. Hall sees it, raises a lot more hell with the body than just ulcers. In everyday life in New York—just the usual, getting to work, working in massively congested areas like 42nd Street between Fifth Avenue and Lexington, especially now that the Pan-Am Building is set in there, working in cubicles such as those in the editorial offices at Time-Life, Inc., which Dr. Hall cites as typical of New York's poor handling of space, working in cubicles with low ceilings and, often, no access to a window, while construction crews all over Manhattan drive everybody up the Masonite wall with air-pressure generators with noises up to the boil-a-brain decibel levels, then rushing to get home, piling into subways and trains, fighting for time and for space, the usual day in New York—the whole now-normal thing keeps shooting jolts of adrenalin into the body, breaking down the body's defenses and winding up with the work-a-daddy human animal stroked out at the breakfast table with his head apoplexed like a cauliflower out of his $6.95 semispread Pima-cotton shirt, and nosed over into a plate of No-Kloresto egg substitute, signing off with the black thrombosis, cancer, kidney, liver, or stomach failure, and the adrenals ooze to a halt, the size of eggplants in July.

One of the people whose work Dr. Hall is interested in on this score is Rene Dubos at the Rockefeller Institute. Dubos's work indicates that specific organisms, such as the tuberculosis bacillus or a pneumonia virus, can seldom be considered "the cause" of a disease. The germ or virus, apparently, has to work in combination with other things that have already broken the body down in some way—such as the old adrenal hyperactivity. Dr. Hall would like to see some autopsy studies

25

made to record the size of adrenal glands in New York, especially of people crowded into slums and people who go through the full rush-hour-work-rush-hour cycle every day. He is afraid that until there is some clinical, statistical data on how overcrowding actually ravages the human body, no one will be willing to do anything about it. Even in so obvious a thing as air pollution, the pattern is familiar. Until people can actually see the smoke or smell the sulphur or feel the sting in their eyes, politicians will not get excited about it, even though it is well known that many of the lethal substances polluting the air are invisible and odorless. For one thing, most politicians are like the aristocrat rats. They are insulated from The Sink by practically sultanic buffers—limousines, chauffeurs, secretaries, aides-de-camp, doormen, shuttered houses, high-floor apartments. They almost never ride subways, fight rush hours, much less live in the slums or work in the Pan-Am Building.

We took a cab from Grand Central to go up to Harlem, and by 48th Street we were already socked into one of those great, total traffic jams on First Avenue on Friday afternoon. Dr. Hall motions for me to survey the scene, and there they all are, humans, male and female, behind the glass of their automobile windows, soundlessly going through the torture of their own adrenalin jolts. This male over here contracts his jaw muscles so hard that they bunch up into a great cheese Danish pattern. He twists his lips, he bleeds from the eyeballs, he shouts . . . soundlessly behind glass . . . the fat corrugates on the back of his neck, his whole body shakes as he pounds the heel of his hand into the steering wheel. The female human in the car ahead of him whips her head around, she bares her teeth, she screams . . . soundlessly behind glass . . . she throws her hands up in the air, Whaddya expect me—Yah, yuh stupid—and they all sit there, trapped in their own congestion, bleeding hate all over each other, shorting out the ganglia and—goddam it—

Dr. Hall sits back and watches it all. This is it! The Sink! And where is everybody's wandering boy?

Dr. Hall says, "We need a study in which drivers who go through these rush hours every day would wear GSR bands."

GSR?

"Galvanic skin response. It measures the electric potential of the skin, which is a function of sweating. If a person gets highly nervous, his palms begin to sweat. It is an index of tension. There are some other fairly simple devices that would record respiration and pulse. I think everybody who goes through this kind of experience all the time should take his own pulse—not literally—but just be aware of what's happening to him. You can usually tell when stress is beginning to get you physically."

In testing people crowded into New York's slums, Dr. Hall would 30
like to take it one step further—gather information on the plasma hy-
drocortisone level in the blood or the corticosteroids in the urine. Both
have been demonstrated to be reliable indicators of stress, and testing
procedures are simple.

The slums—we finally made it up to East Harlem. We drove into
101st Street, and there was a new, avant-garde little church building,
the Church of the Epiphany, which Dr. Hall liked—and, next to it, a
pile of rubble where a row of buildings had been torn down, and from
the back windows of the tenements beyond several people were busy
"airmailing," throwing garbage out the window, into the rubble, beer
cans, red shreds, the No-Money-Down Eames roller stand for a TV
set, all flying through the air onto the scaggy sump. We drove around
some more in Harlem, and a sequence was repeated, trash, buildings
falling down, buildings torn down, rubble, scaggy sumps or, suddenly,
a cluster of high-rise apartment projects, with fences around the grass.

"You know what this city looks like?" Dr. Hall said. "It looks
bombed out. I used to live at Broadway and 124th Street back in 1946
when I was studying at Columbia. I can't tell you how much Harlem
has changed in twenty years. It looks bombed out. It's broken down.
People who live in New York get used to it and don't realize how filthy
the city has become. The whole thing is typical of a behaviorial sink.
So is something like the Kitty Genovese case—a girl raped and murdered in the courtyard of an apartment complex and forty or fifty people look on from their apartments and nobody even calls the police.
That kind of apathy and anomie is typical of the general psychological
deterioration of The Sink."

He looked at the high-rise housing projects and found them mainly
testimony to how little planners know about humans' basic animal requirements for space.

"Even on the simplest terms," he said, "it is pointless to build one
of these blocks much over five stories high. Suppose a family lives on
the fifteenth floor. The mother will be completely cut off from her
children if they are playing down below, because the elevators are constantly broken in these projects, and it often takes half an hour, literally
half an hour, to get the elevator if it is running. That's very common.
A mother in that situation is just as much a victim of overcrowding as
if she were back in the tenement block. Some Negro leaders have a
bitter joke about how the white man is solving the slum problem by
stacking Negroes up vertically, and there is a lot to that."

For one thing, says Dr. Hall, planners have no idea of the different 35
space requirements of people from different cultures, such as Negroes
and Puerto Ricans. They are all treated as if they were minute, compact
middle-class whites. As with the Sika deer, who are overcrowded at

one per acre, overcrowding is a relative thing for the human animal, as well. Each species has its own feeling for space. The feeling may be "subjective," but it is quite real.

Dr. Hall's theories on space and territory are based on the same information, gathered by biologists, ethologists, and anthropologists, chiefly, as Robert Ardrey's. Ardrey has written two well-publicized books, *African Genesis* and *The Territorial Imperative*. *Life* magazine ran big excerpts from *The Territorial Imperative*, all about how the drive to acquire territory and property and add to it and achieve status is built into all animals, including man, over thousands of centuries of genetic history, etc., and is a more powerful drive than sex. *Life*'s big display prompted Marshall McLuhan to crack, "They see this as a great historic justification for free enterprise and Republicanism. If the birds do it and the stickle-back crabs do it, then it's right for man." To people like Hall and McLuhan, and Ardrey, for that matter, the right or wrong of it is irrelevant. The only thing they find inexcusable is the kind of thinking, by influential people, that isn't even aware of all this. Such as the thinking of most city planners.

"The planners always show you a bird's-eye view of what they are doing," he said. "You've seen those scale models. Everyone stands around the table and looks down and says that's great. It never occurs to anyone that they are taking a bird's-eye view. In the end, these projects do turn out fine, when viewed from an airplane."

As an anthropologist, Dr. Hall has to shake his head every time he hears planners talking about fully integrated housing projects for the year 1980 or 1990, as if by then all cultural groups will have the same feeling for space and will live placidly side by side, happy as the happy burghers who plan all the good clean bird's-eye views. According to his findings, the very fact that every cultural group does have its own peculiar, unspoken feeling for space is what is responsible for much of the uneasiness one group feels around the other.

It is like the North European and the Mediterranean in the subway line. The North European, without ever realizing it, tries to keep a bubble of space around himself, and the moment a stranger invades that sphere, he feels threatened. Mediterranean peoples tend to come from cultures where everyone is much more involved physically, publicly, with one another on a day-to-day basis and feels no uneasiness about mixing it up in public, but may have very different ideas about space inside the home. Even Negroes brought up in America have a different vocabulary of space and gesture from the North European Americans who, historically, have been their models, according to Dr. Hall. The failure of Negroes and whites to communicate well often boils down to things like this: some white will be interviewing a Negro for a job; the Negro's culture has taught him to show somebody you are interested by looking right at him and listening intently to what he has to say. But the species North European requires something more. He expects his listener to nod from time to time, as if to say, "Yes, keep going." If he doesn't get this nodding, he feels anxious, for fear the listener doesn't agree with him or has switched off. The Negro may learn that the white expects this sort of thing, but he isn't used to the precise kind of nodding that is customary, and so he may start overresponding, nodding like mad, and at this point the North European is liable to think he has some kind of stupid Uncle Tom on his hands, and the guy still doesn't get the job.

The whole handling of space in New York is so chaotic, says Dr. 40 Hall, that even middle-class housing now seems to be based on the bird's-eye models for slum projects. He took a look at the big Park West Village development, set up originally to provide housing in Manhattan for families in the middle-income range, and found its handling of space very much like a slum project with slightly larger balconies. He felt the time has come to start subsidizing the middle class in New York on its own terms—namely, the kind of truly "human" spaces that still remain in brownstones.

"I think New York City should seriously consider a program of encouraging the middle-class development of an area like Chelsea, which is already starting to come up. People are beginning to renovate houses there on their own, and I think if the city would subsidize that sort of thing with tax reliefs and so forth, you would be amazed at what would result. What New York needs is a string of minor successes in the housing field, just to show everyone that it can be done, and I think the middle class can still do that for you. The alternative is to keep on doing what you're doing now, trying to lift a very large lower class up by main force almost and finding it a very slow and discouraging process."

"But before deciding how to redesign space in New York," he said, "people must first simply realize how severe the problem already is. And the handwriting is already on the wall."

"A study published in 1962," he said, "surveyed a representative sample of people living in New York slums and found only 18 percent of them free from emotional symptoms. Thirty-eight percent were in need of psychiatric help, and 23 percent were seriously disturbed or incapacitated. Now, this study was published in 1962, which means the work probably went on from 1955 to 1960. There is no telling how bad it is now. In a behavioral sink, crises can develop rapidly."

Dr. Hall would like to see a large-scale study similar to that undertaken by two sociopsychologists, Chombart de Lauwe and his wife, in a French working-class town. They found a direct relationship between crowding and general breakdown. In families where people were crowded into the apartment so that there was less than 86 to 108 square feet per person, social and physical disorders doubled. That would mean that for four people the smallest floor space they could tolerate would be an apartment, say, 12 by 30 feet.

What would one find in Harlem? "It is fairly obvious," Dr. Hall   45 wrote in *The Hidden Dimension,* "that the American Negroes and people of Spanish culture who are flocking to our cities are being very seriously stressed. Not only are they in a setting that does not fit them, but they have passed the limits of their own tolerance of stress. The United States is faced with the fact that two of its creative and sensitive peoples are in the process of being destroyed and like Samson could bring down the structure that houses us all."

Dr. Hall goes out to the airport, to go back to Chicago, and I am coming back in a cab, along the East River Drive. It is four in the afternoon, but already the damned drive is clogging up. There is a 1959 Oldsmobile just to the right of me. There are about eight people in there, a lot of popeyed silhouettes against a leopard-skin dashboard, leopard-skin seats—and the driver is classic. He has a mustache, sideburns down to his jaw socket, and a tattoo on his forearm with a Rossetti painting of Jane Burden Morris with her hair long. All right; it is even touching, like a postcard photo of the main drag in San Pedro, California. But suddenly Sideburns guns it and cuts in front of my cab so that my driver has to hit the brakes, and then hardly 100 feet ahead Sideburns hits a wall of traffic himself and has to hit his brakes, and then it happens. A stuffed white Angora animal, a dog, no, it's a Pekingese cat, is mounted in his rear window—as soon as he hits the brakes its *eyes* light up, Nighttown pink. To keep from ramming him, my driver has to hit the brakes again, too, and so here I am, out in an insane, jammed-up expressway at four in the afternoon, shuddering to a stop while a stuffed Pekingese grows bigger and bigger and brighter in the eyeballs directly in front of me. Jolt! Nighttown pink! Hey—that's me the adrenalin is hitting, *I* am this white human sitting in a projectile heading amid a mass of clotted humans toward a white Angora stuffed goddam leopard-dash Pekingese freaking cat—kill that damned Angora—Jolt!—got me—another micrometer on the old adrenals—

LINES OF INQUIRY
"O Rotten Gotham—Sliding down into the Behavioral Sink"

Wolfe's style differs greatly from that of Edward Hall and the other anthropologists he writes about here. Hall, for example, speaks of "galvanic skin response" in "humans," whereas Wolfe notes that New Yorkers in Grand Central Station "screech" and their adrenal glands enlarge "to the size of cantaloupes." How would you describe such differences in the diction and sentence structure of Wolfe and Hall? What are the effects of these stylistic differences? What are the advantages in Wolfe's style of communicating Hall's idea of "behavioral sink"? What are the disadvantages?

"Behavioral sink" is clearly the most important concept in this piece, so you might find it useful to summarize what it means in your own words. What does this phenomenon have to do with the other concepts that are central in Hall's studies, namely "status hierarchy" and the "territorial imperative"? How does the research of Calhoun, Christian, and Dubos support Hall's theories? How does Wolfe's cab ride illustrate Hall's theories? How does life in a college dormitory illustrate Hall's theories?

New York City, of course, is not the only place where one can find a behavioral sink, as you may have noticed either in your own home community or in the place where you are presently going to school. What experience(s) have you had of living in a behavioral sink or witnessing a sink in action? What similarities—what differences—did you notice between the sink(s) you are familiar with and the one that Wolfe describes in New York City? How do you account for the differences?

THE PUMP HOUSE GANG

Our boys never hair out. The black panther has black feet. Black feet on the crumbling black panther. Pan-thuh. Mee-dah. Pam Stacy, 16 years old, a cute girl here in La Jolla, California, with a pair of orange bell-bottom hip-huggers on, sits on a step about four steps down the stairway to the beach and she can see a pair of revolting black feet without lifting her head. So she says it out loud, "The black panther."

Somebody farther down the stairs, one of the boys with the *major* hair and khaki shorts, says, "The black feet of the black panther."

"Mee-dah," says another kid. This happens to be the cry of a, well, *underground* society known as the Mac Meda Destruction Company.

"The pan-thuh."

"The poon-thuh."   5

All these kids, seventeen of them, members of the Pump House crowd, are lollygagging around the stairs down to Windansea Beach, La Jolla, California, about 11 a.m., and they all look at the black feet, which are a woman's pair of black street shoes, out of which stick a pair of old veiny white ankles, which lead up like a senile cone to a fudge of tallowy, edematous flesh, her thighs, squeezing out of her bathing suit, with old faded yellow bruises on them, which she probably got from running eight feet to catch a bus or something. She is standing with her old work-a-hubby, who has on *sandals:* you know, a pair of navy-blue anklet socks and these sandals with big, wide, new-smelling tan straps going this way and that, *for keeps.* Man, they look like orthopedic sandals, if one can imagine that. Obviously, these people come from Tucson or Albuquerque or one of those hincty adobe towns. All these hincty, crumbling black feet come to La Jolla-by-the-sea from the adobe towns for the weekend. They even drive in cars all full of thermos bottles and mayonnaisey sandwiches and some kind of latticework wooden-back support for the old crock who drives and Venetian blinds on the back window.

"The black panther."

"Pan-thuh."

"Poon-thuh."

"Mee-dah."   10

Nobody says it to the two old crocks directly. God, they must be practically 50 years old. Naturally, they're carrying every piece of garbage imaginable: the folding aluminum chairs, the newspapers, the lending-library book with the clear plastic wrapper on it, the sunglasses, the sun ointment, about a vat of goo—

It is a Mexican standoff. In a Mexican standoff, both parties narrow their eyes and glare but nobody throws a punch. Of course, nobody in the Pump House crowd would ever even jostle these people or say anything right to them; they are too cool for that.

Everybody in the Pump House crowd looks over, even Tom Coman, who is a cool person. Tom Coman, 16 years old, got thrown out of his garage last night. He is sitting up on top of the railing, near the stairs, up over the beach, with his legs apart. Some nice long willowy girl in yellow slacks is standing on the sidewalk but leaning into him with her arms around his body, just resting. Neale Jones, 16, a boy with great lank perfect surfer's hair, is standing nearby with a Band-Aid on his upper lip, where the sun has burnt it raw. Little Vicki Ballard is up on the sidewalk. Her older sister, Liz, is down the stairs by the Pump House itself, a concrete block, 15 feet high, full of machinery for the La Jolla water system. Liz is wearing her great "Liz" styles, a hulking rabbit-fur vest and black-leather boots over her Levis, even though it is about 85 out here and the sun is plugged in up there like God's own dentist lamp and the Pacific is heaving in with some fair-to-middling surf. Kit Tilden is lollygagging around, and Tom Jones, Connie Carter, Roger Johnson, Sharon Sandquist, Mary Beth White, Rupert Fellows, Glenn Jackson, Dan Watson from San Diego, they are all out here, and everybody takes a look at the panthers.

The old guy, one means, you know, he must be practically 50 years old, he says to his wife, "Come on, let's go farther up," and he takes her by her fat upper arm as if to wheel her around and aim her away from here.

But she says, "No! We have just as much right to be here as 15 they do."

"That's *not the point—*"

"Are you going to—"

"*Mrs. Roberts,*" the work-a-hubby says, calling his own wife by her official married name, as if to say she took a vow once and his word is law, even if he is not testing it with the blond kids here—"farther up, *Mrs. Roberts.*"

They start to walk up the sidewalk, but one kid won't move his feet, and, oh, god, her work-a-hubby breaks into a terrible shaking Jello smile as she steps over them, as if to say, Excuse me, sir, I don't mean to make trouble, please, and don't you and your colleagues rise up and jump me, screaming *Gotcha—*

Mee-dah!   20

But exactly! This beach *is* verboten for people practically 50 years old. This is a segregated beach. They can look down on Windansea Beach and see nothing but lean tan kids. It is posted "no swimming" (for safety reasons), meaning surfing only. In effect, it is segregated by age. From Los Angeles on down the California coast, this is an era of age segregation. People have always tended to segregate themselves by age, teenagers hanging around with teenagers, old people with old people, like the old men who sit on the benches up near the Bronx Zoo and smoke black cigars. But before, age segregation has gone on within a larger community. Sooner or later during the day everybody has melted back into the old community network that embraces practically everyone, all ages.

But in California today surfers, not to mention rock 'n' roll kids and the hot-rodders or Hair Boys, named for their fanciful pompadours—all sorts of sets of kids—they don't merely hang around together. They establish whole little societies for themselves. In some cases they live with one another for months at a time. The "Sunset Strip" on Sunset Boulevard used to be a kind of Times Square for Hollywood hot dogs of all ages, anyone who wanted to promenade in his version of the high life. Today "The Strip" is almost completely the preserve of kids from about 16 to 25. It is lined with go-go clubs. One of them, a place called It's Boss, is set up for people 16 to 25 and won't let in anybody over 25, and there are some terrible I'm-dying-a-thousand-deaths scenes when a girl comes up with her boyfriend and the guy at the door at It's Boss doesn't think she looks under 25 and tells her she will have to produce some identification proving she is young enough to come in here and live The Strip kind of life and—she's *had* it, because she can't get up the I.D. and nothing in the world is going to make a woman look stupider than to stand around trying to argue *I'm younger than I look, I'm younger than I look.* So she practically shrivels up like a Peruvian shrunken head in front of her boyfriend and he trundles her off, looking for some place you can get an old doll like this into. One of the few remaining clubs for "older people," curiously, is the Playboy Club. There are apartment houses for people 20 and 30 only, such as the Sheri Plaza in Hollywood and the E'Questre Inn in Burbank. There are whole suburban housing developments, mostly private developments, where only people over 45 or 50 can buy a house. Whole towns, meantime, have become identified as "young": Venice, Newport Beach, Balboa—or "old": Pasadena, Riverside, Coronado Island.

Behind much of it—especially something like a whole nightclub district of a major city, "The Strip," going teenage—is, simply, money. World War II and the prosperity that followed pumped incredible amounts of money into the population, the white population at least, at every class level. All of a sudden here is an area with thousands of people from 16 to 25 who can get their hands on enough money to support a whole nightclub belt and to have the cars to get there and to set up autonomous worlds of their own in a fairly posh resort community like La Jolla—

—Tom Coman's garage. Some old bastard took Tom Coman's garage away from him, and that means eight or nine surfers are out of a place to stay.

"I went by there this morning, you ought to see the guy," Tom Coman says. Yellow Stretch Pants doesn't move. She has him around the waist. "He was out there painting and he had this brush and about a thousand gallons of ammonia. He was really going to scrub me out of there."

"What did he do with the furniture?"

"I don't know. He threw it out."

"What are you going to do?"

"I don't know."

"Where are you going to stay?"

"I don't know. I'll stay on the beach. It wouldn't be the first time. I haven't had a place to stay for three years, so I'm not going to start worrying now."

Everybody thinks that over awhile. Yellow Stretch just hangs on and smiles. Tom Coman, 16 years old, piping fate again. One of the girls says, "You can stay at my place, Tom."

"Um. Who's got a cigarette?"

Pam Stacy says, "You can have these."

Tom Coman lights a cigarette and says, "Let's have a destructo." A destructo is what can happen in a garage after eight or 10 surfers are kicked out of it.

"Mee-dah!"

"Wouldn't that be bitchen?" says Tom Coman. Bitchen is a surfer's term that means "great," usually.

"Bitchen!"

"Mee-dah!"

It's incredible—that old guy out there trying to scour the whole surfing life out of that garage. He's a pathetic figure. His shoulders are hunched over and he's dousing and scrubbing away and the sun doesn't give him a tan, it gives him these . . . *mottles* on the back of his neck. But never mind! The hell with destructo. One only has a destructo spontaneously, a Dionysian . . . *bursting out,* like those holes through the wall during the Mac Meda Destruction Company Convention at Manhattan Beach—Mee-dah!

Something will pan out. It's a magic economy—yes!—all up and down the coast from Los Angeles to Baja California kids can go to one of these beach towns and live the complete surfing life. They take off from home and get to the beach, and if they need a place to stay, well, somebody rents a garage for twenty bucks a month and everybody moves in, girls and boys. Furniture—it's like, one means, you know, one *appropriates* furniture from here and there. It's like the Volkswagen buses a lot of kids now use as beach wagons instead of woodies. Woodies are old station wagons, usually Fords, with wooden bodies, from back before 1953. One of the great things about a Volkswagen bus is that one can . . . *exchange* motors in about three minutes. A good VW motor exchanger can go up to a parked Volkswagen, and a few ratchets of the old wrench here and it's up and out and he has a new motor. There must be a few nice old black panthers around wondering why their nice hubby-mommy VW's don't run so good anymore—but—then—they—are—probably—puzzled—about—a—lot of things. Yes.

Cash—it's practically in the air. Around the beach in La Jolla a guy can walk right out in the street and stand there, stop cars and make the candid move. Mister, I've got a quarter, how about 50 cents so I can get a *large* draft. Or, I need some after-ski boots. And the panthers give one a Jello smile and hand it over. Or a guy who knows how to do it can get $40 from a single night digging clams, and it's nice out there. Or he can go around and take up a collection for a keg party, a keg of beer. Man, anybody who won't kick in a quarter for a keg is a jerk. A couple of good keg collections—that's a trip to Hawaii, which is the surfer's version of a trip to Europe: there is a great surf and great everything there. Neale spent three weeks in Hawaii last year. He got $30 from a girl friend, he scrounged a little here and there and got $70 more and he headed off for Hawaii with $100.02, that being the exact plane fare, and borrowed 25 cents when he got there to . . . blast the place up. He spent the 25 cents in a photo booth, showed the photos to the people on the set of *Hawaii* and got a job in the movie. What's the big orgy about money? It's warm, nobody even wears shoes, nobody is starving.

All right, Mother gets worried about all this, but it is limited worry, as John Shine says. Mainly, Mother says, *Sayonara,* you all, and you head off for the beach.

The thing is, everybody, practically everybody, comes from a good family. Everyone has been . . . *reared well,* as they say. Everybody is very upper-middle, if you want to bring it down to that. It's just that this is a new order. Why hang around in the hubby-mommy household with everybody getting neurotic hang-ups with each other and slamming doors and saying, Why can't they have some privacy? Or, it doesn't mean anything that I have to work for a living, does it? It doesn't mean a thing to you. All of you just lie around here sitting in the big orange easy chair smoking cigarettes. I'd hate for you to have to smoke standing up, you'd probably get phlebitis from it—Listen to me, Sarah—

—why go through all that? It's a good life out here. Nobody is   45 mugging everybody for money and affection. There are a lot of bright people out here, and there are a lot of interesting things. One night there was a toga party in a garage, and everybody dressed in sheets, like togas, boys and girls and they put on the appropriated television set to an old Deanna Durbin movie and turned off the sound and put on Rolling Stones records, and you should have seen Deanna Durbin opening her puckered kumquat mouth with Mick Jagger's voice bawl-ing out, *I ain't got no satisfaction.* Of course, finally everybody started pulling the togas off each other, but that is another thing. And one time they had a keg party down on the beach in Mission Bay and the lights from the amusement park were reflected all over the water and that, the whole design of the thing, those nutty lights, that was part of the party. Liz put out the fire throwing a "sand potion" or some-thing on it. One can laugh at Liz and her potions, her necromancy and everything, but there is a lot of thought going into it, a lot of, well, mysticism.

You can even laugh at mysticism if you want to, but there is a kid like Larry Alderson, who spent two years with a monk, and he learned a lot of stuff, and Artie Nelander is going to spend next summer with some Outer Mongolian tribe; he really means to do that. Maybe the "mysterioso" stuff is a lot of garbage, but still, it is interesting. The surfers around the Pump House use that word, mysterioso, quite a lot. It refers to the mystery of the Oh Mighty Hulking Pacific Ocean and everything. Sometimes a guy will stare at the surf and say, "Myster-ioso." They keep telling the story of Bob Simmons' wipeout, and somebody will say "mysterioso."

Simmons was a fantastic surfer. He was fantastic even though he had a bad leg. He rode the really big waves. One day he got wiped out at Windansea. When a big wave overtakes a surfer, it drives him right to the bottom. The board came in but he never came up and they never found his body. Very mysterioso. The black panthers all talked about what happened to "the Simmons boy." But the mysterioso thing was how he could have died at all. If he had been one of the old pan-thuhs, hell, sure he could have got killed. But Simmons was, well, one's own age, he was the kind of guy who could have been in the Pump House gang, he was . . . *immune,* he was plugged into the whole pattern, he could feel the whole Oh Mighty Hulking Sea, he didn't have to think it out step by step. But he got wiped out and killed. Very mysterioso.

Immune! If one is in the Pump House gang and really keyed in to this whole thing, it's— well, one is . . . *immune,* one is not full of black pan-thuh panic. Two kids, a 14-year-old girl and a 16-year-old boy, go out to Windansea at dawn, in the middle of winter, cold as hell, and take on 12-foot waves all by themselves. The girl, Jackie Haddad, daughter of a certified public accountant, wrote a composition about it, just for herself, called "My Ultimate Journey":

"It was six o'clock in the morning, damp, foggy and cold. We could feel the bitter air biting at our cheeks. The night before, my friend Tommy and I had seen one of the greatest surf films, *Surf Classics.* The film had excited us so much we made up our minds to go surfing the following morning. That is what brought us down on the cold, wet, soggy sand of Windansea early on a December morning.

"We were the first surfers on the beach. The sets were rolling in at 50 eight to 10, filled with occasional 12-footers. We waxed up and waited for a break in the waves. The break came, neither of us said a word, but instantly grabbed our boards and ran into the water. The paddle out was difficult, not being used to the freezing water.

"We barely made it over the first wave of the set, a large set. Suddenly Tommy put on a burst of speed and shot past me. He cleared the biggest wave of the set. It didn't hit me hard as I rolled under it. It dragged me almost 20 yards before exhausting its strength. I climbed on my board gasping for air. I paddled out to where Tommy was resting. He laughed at me for being wet already. I almost hit him but I began laughing, too. We rested a few minutes and then lined up our position with a well known spot on the shore.

"I took off first. I bottom-turned hard and started climbing up the wave. A radical cut-back caught me off balance and I fell, barely hanging onto my board. I recovered in time to see Tommy go straight over the falls on a 10-footer. His board shot nearly 30 feet in the air. Luckily, I could get it before the next set came in, so Tommy didn't have to make the long swim in. I pushed it to him and then laughed. All of a sudden Tommy yelled, 'Outside!'

"Both of us paddled furiously. We barely made it up to the last wave, it was a monster. In precision timing we wheeled around and I took off. I cut left in reverse stance, then cut back, driving hard toward the famous Windansea bowl. As I crouched, a huge wall of energy came down over me, covering me up. I moved toward the nose to gain more speed and shot out of the fast-flowing suction just in time to kick out as the wave closed out.

"As I turned around I saw Tommy make a beautiful drop-in, then the wave peaked and fell all at once. Miraculously he beat the suction. He cut back and did a spinner, which followed with a reverse kick-up.

"Our last wave was the biggest. When we got to shore, we rested, 55 neither of us saying a word, but each lost in his own private world of thoughts. After we had rested, we began to walk home. We were about half way and the rain came pouring down. That night we both had bad colds, but we agreed it was worth having them after the thrill and satisfaction of an extra good day of surfing."

John Shine and Artie Nelander are out there right now. They are just "outside," about one fifth of a mile out from the shore, beyond where the waves start breaking. They are straddling their surfboards with their backs to the shore, looking out toward the horizon, waiting for a good set. Their backs look like some kind of salmon-colored porcelain shells, a couple of tiny shells bobbing up and down as the swells roll under them, staring out to sea like Phrygian sacristans looking for a sign.

John and Artie! They are—they are what one means when one talks about the surfing life. It's like, you know, one means, they have this life all of their own; it's like a glass-bottom boat, and it floats over the "real" world, or the square world or whatever one wants to call it. They are not exactly off in a world of their own, they are and they aren't. What it is, they float right through the real world, but it can't touch them. They do these things, like the time they went to Malibu, and there was this party in some guy's apartment, and there wasn't enough *legal* parking space for everybody, and so somebody went out and painted the red curbs white and everybody parked. Then the cops came. Everybody ran out. Artie and John took an airport bus to the Los Angeles Airport, just like they were going to take a plane, in khaki shorts and T-shirts with Mac Meda Destruction Company stenciled on them. Then they took a helicopter to Disneyland. At Disneyland crazy Ditch had his big raincoat on and a lot of flasks strapped onto his body underneath, Scotch, bourbon, all kinds of stuff. He had plastic tubes from the flasks sticking out of the flyfront of his raincoat and everybody was sipping whiskey through the tubes—

—Ooooo-eeee—Mee-dah! They chant this chant, Mee-dah, in a real fakey deep voice, and it *really bugs people*. They don't know what the hell it is. It is the cry of the Mac Meda Destruction Company. The Mac Meda Destruction Company is . . . an *underground* society that started in La Jolla about three years ago. Nobody can remember exactly how; they have arguments about it. Anyhow, it is mainly something to *bug* people with and organize huge beer orgies with. They have their own complete, bogus phone number in La Jolla. They have Mac Meda Destruction Company decals. They stick them on phone booths, on cars, any place. Some mommy-hubby will come out of the shopping plaza and walk up to his Mustang, which is supposed to make him a hell of a tiger now, and he'll see a sticker on the side of it saying, "Mac Meda Destruction Company," and for about two days or something he'll think the sky is going to fall in.

But the big thing is the parties, the "conventions." Anybody can join, any kid, anybody can come, as long as they've heard about it, and they can only hear about it by word of mouth. One was in the Sorrento Valley, in the gulches and arroyos, and the fuzz came, and so the older guys put the young ones and the basket cases, the ones just too stoned out of their gourds, into the tule grass, and the cops shined their searchlights and all they saw was tule grass, while the basket cases moaned scarlet and oozed on their bellies like reptiles and everybody else ran down the arroyos, yelling Mee-dah.

The last one was at Manhattan Beach, inside somebody's poor hulking house. The party got *very Dionysian* that night and somebody put a hole through one wall, and everybody else decided to see if they could make it bigger. Everybody was stoned out of their hulking gourds, and it got

60

to be about 3:30 a.m. and everybody decided to go see the riots. These were the riots in Watts. The Los Angeles *Times* and the San Diego *Union* were all saying, WATTS NO-MAN'S LAND and STAY WAY FROM WATTS YOU GET YO' SE'F KILLED, but naturally nobody believed that. Watts was a blast, and the Pump House gang was immune to the trembling gourd panic rattles of the L.A. *Times* black panthuhs. Immune!

So John Shine, Artie Nelander and Jerry Sterncorb got in John's VW bus, known as the Hog of Steel, and they went to Watts. Gary Wickham and some other guys ran into an old man at a bar who said he owned a house in Watts and had been driven out by the drunk niggers. So they drove in a car to save the old guy's house from the drunk niggers. Artie and John had a tape recorder and decided they were going to make a record called "Random Sounds from the Watts Riots." They drove right into Watts in the Hog of Steel and there was blood on the streets and roofs blowing off the stores and all these apricot flames and drunk Negroes falling through the busted plate glass of the liquor stores. Artie got a nice recording of a lot of Negroes chanting "Burn, baby, burn." They all got out and talked to some Negro kids in a gang going into a furniture store, and the Negro kids didn't say Kill Whitey or Geed'um or any of that. They just said, Come on, man, it's a party and it's free. After they had been in there for about three hours talking to Negroes and watching drunks collapse in the liquor stores, some cop with a helmet on came roaring up and said, "Get the hell out of here, you kids, we cannot and will not provide protection."

Meantime, Gary Wickham and his friends drove in in a car with the old guy, and a car full of Negroes *did* stop them and say, Whitey, Geed'um, and all that stuff, but one of the guys in Gary's car just draped a pistol he had out the window and the colored guys drove off. Gary and everybody drove the old guy to his house and they all walked in and had a great raunchy time drinking beer and raising hell. A couple of Negroes, the old guy's neighbors, came over and told the old guy to cut out the racket. There were flames in the sky and ashes coming down with little rims of fire on them, like apricot crescents. The old guy got very cocky about all his "protection" and went out on the front porch about dawn and started yelling at some Negroes across the street, telling them "No more drunk niggers in Watts" and a lot of other unwise slogans. So Gary Wickham got up and everybody left. They were there about four hours altogether and when they drove out, they had to go through a National Guard checkpoint, and a lieutenant from the San Fernando Valley told them he could not and would not provide protection.

But exactly! Watts just happened to be what was going on at the time, as far as the netherworld of La Jolla surfing was concerned, and so one goes there and sees what is happening and comes back and tells everybody about it and laughs at the L.A. *Times*. That is what makes it so weird when all these black pan-thuhs come around to pick up "surfing styles," like the clothing manufacturers. They don't know what any of it means. It's like archaeologists discovering hieroglyphics of something, and they say, god, that's neat—Egypt!—but they don't know what the hell it is. They don't know anything about . . . *The Life*. It's great to think of a lot of old emphysematous pan-thuhs in the Garment District in New York City struggling in off the street against a gummy 15-mile-an-hour wind full of soot and coffee-brown snow and gasping in the elevator to clear their old nicotine-phlegm tubes on the way upstairs to make out the invoices on a lot of surfer stuff for 1966, the big nylon windbreakers with the wide, white horizontal competition stripes, nylon swimming trunks with competition stripes, bell-bottom slacks for girls, the big hairy sleeveless jackets, vests, the blue "tennies," meaning tennis shoes, and the . . . *look,* the Major Hair, all this long lank blond hair, the plain face kind of tanned and bleached out at the same time, but with big eyes. It all starts in a few places, a few strategic groups, the Pump House gang being one of them, and then it moves up the beach, to places like Newport Beach and as far up as Malibu.

Well, actually there is a kind of back-and-forth thing with some of the older guys, the old heroes of surfing, like Bruce Brown, John Severson, Hobie Alter and Phil Edwards. Bruce Brown will do one of those incredible surfing movies and he is out in the surf himself filming Phil Edwards coming down a 20-footer in Hawaii, and Phil has on a pair of nylon swimming trunks, which he has had made in Hawaii, because they dry out fast—and it is like a grapevine. Everybody's got to have a pair of nylon swimming trunks, and then the manufacturers move in, and everybody's making nylon swimming trunks, boxer trunk style, and pretty soon every kid in Utica, N.Y., is buying a pair of them, with the competition stripe and the whole thing, and they never heard of Phil Edwards. So it works back and forth—but so what? Phil Edwards is part of it. He may be an old guy, he is 28 years old, but he and Bruce Brown, who is even older, 30, and John Severson, 32, and Hobie Alter, 29, never haired out to the square world even though they make thousands. Hair refers to courage. A guy who "has a lot of hair" is courageous; a guy who "hairs out" is yellow.

Bruce Brown and Severson and Alter are known as the "surfing   65
millionaires." They are not millionaires, actually, but they must be among the top businessmen south of Los Angeles. Brown grossed something around $500,000 in 1965 even before his movie *Endless Summer* became a hit nationally; and he has only about three people working for him.

He goes out on a surfboard with a camera encased in a plastic shell and takes his own movies and edits them himself and goes around showing them himself and narrating them at places like the Santa Monica Civic Auditorium, where 24,000 came in eight days once, at $1.50 a person, and all he has to pay is for developing the film and hiring the hall. John Severson has the big surfing magazine, *Surfer*. Hobie Alter is the biggest surfboard manufacturer, all hand-made boards. He made 5,000 boards in 1965 at $140 a board. He also designed the "Hobie" skate boards and gets 25 cents for every one sold. He grossed between $900,000 and $1 million in 1964.

God, if only everybody could grow up like these guys and know that crossing the horror dividing line, 25 years old, won't be the end of everything. One means, keep on living *The Life* and not get sucked into the ticky-tacky life with some insurance salesman sitting forward in your stuffed chair on your wall-to-wall telling you that life is like a football game and you sit there and take that stuff. The hell with that! Bruce Brown has the money and *The Life*. He has a great house on a cliff about 60 feet above the beach at Dana Point. He is married and has two children, but it is not that hubby-mommy you're-breaking-my-gourd scene. His office is only two blocks from his house and he doesn't even have to go on the streets to get there. He gets on his Triumph scrambling motorcycle and cuts straight across a couple of vacant lots and one can see him . . . *bounding* to work over the vacant lots. The Triumph hits ruts and hummocks and things and Bruce Brown bounces into the air with the motor—*thragggggh*—moaning away, and when he gets to the curbing in front of his office, he just leans back and pulls up the front wheel and hops it and gets off and walks into the office barefooted. *Barefooted;* why not? He wears the same things now that he did when he was doing nothing but surfing. He has on a faded gray sweatshirt with the sleeves cut off just above the elbows and a pair of faded corduroys. His hair is the lightest corn yellow imaginable, towheaded, practically white, from the sun. Even his eyes seem to be bleached. He has a rainbarrel old-apple-tree Tom-Sawyer little-boy roughneck look about him, like Bobby Kennedy.

Sometimes he carries on his business right there at the house. He has a dugout room built into the side of the cliff, about 15 feet down from the level of the house. It is like a big pale green box set into the side of the cliff, and inside is a kind of upholstered bench or settee you can lie down on if you want to and look out at the Pacific. The surf is crashing like a maniac on the rocks down below. He has a telephone in there. Sometimes it will ring, and Bruce Brown says hello, and the surf is crashing away down below, roaring like mad, and the guy on the other end, maybe one of the TV networks calling from New York or some movie hair-out from Los Angeles, says:

"What is all that noise? It sounds like you're sitting out in the surf."

"That's right," says Bruce Brown, "I have my desk out on the beach now. It's nice out here."

The guy on the other end doesn't know what to think. He is an-   70
other Mr. Efficiency who just got back from bloating his colon up at a three-hour executive lunch somewhere and now he is Mr.-Big-Time-Let's-Get-This-Show-on-the-Road.

"On the beach?"

"Yeah. It's cooler down here. And it's good for you, but it's not so great for the desk. You know what I have now? A warped leg."

"A warped leg?"

"Yeah, and this is an $800 desk."

Those nutball California kids—and he will still be muttering that   75
five days after Bruce Brown delivers his film, on time, and Mr. Efficiency is still going through memo thickets or heaving his way into the bar car to Darien—in the very moment that Bruce Brown and Hobie Alter are both on their motorcycles out on the vacant lot in Dana Point. Hobie Alter left his surfboard plant about two in the afternoon because the wind was up and it would be good catamaranning and he wanted to go out and see how far he could tip his new catamaran without going over, and he did tip it over, about half a mile out in high swells and it was hell getting the thing right side up again. But he did, and he got back in time to go scrambling on the lot with Bruce Brown. They are out there, roaring over the ruts, bouncing up in the air, and every now and then they roar up the embankment so they can . . . fly, going up in the air about six feet off the ground as they come up off the embankment—*thraaagggggh*—all these people in the houses around there come to the door and look out. These two . . . nuts are at it again. Well, they can only fool around there for 20 minutes, because that is about how long it takes the cops to get there if anybody gets burned up enough and calls, and what efficient business magnate wants to get hauled off by the Dana Point cops for scrambling on his motorcycle in a vacant lot.

Bruce Brown has it figured out so no one in the whole rubber-bloated black pan-thuh world can trap him, though. He bought a forest in the Sierras. There is nothing on it but trees. His own wilds: no house, no nothing, just Bruce Brown's forest. Beautiful things happen up there. One day, right after he bought it, he was on the edge of his forest, where the road comes into it, and one of these big rancher king moth-eroos with the broad belly and the $70 lisle Safari shirt comes tooling up in a Pontiac convertible with a funnel of dust pouring out behind. He gravels it to a great flashy stop and yells:

"Hey! You!"

Of course, what he sees is some towheaded barefooted kid in a torn-off sweatshirt fooling around the edge of the road.

"Hey! You!"

"Yeah?" says Bruce Brown.   80

"Don't you know this is private property?"

"Yeah," says Bruce Brown.

"Well, then, why don't you get your ass off it?"

"Because it's mine, it's my private property," says Bruce Brown. "Now you get *yours* off it."

And Safari gets a few rays from that old apple-tree rainbarrel don't-   85
cross-that-line look and doesn't say anything and roars off, slipping gravel, the dumb crumbling pan-thuh.

But . . . perfect! It is like, one means, you know, poetic justice for all the nights Bruce Brown slept out on the beach at San Onofre and such places in the old surfing days and would wake up with some old crock's black feet standing beside his head and some phlegmy black rubber voice saying:

"All right, kid, don't you know this is private property?"

And he would prop his head up and out there would be the Pacific Ocean, a kind of shadowy magenta-mauve, and one thing, *that* was nobody's private property—

But how many Bruce Browns can there be? There is a built-in trouble with age segregation. Eventually one *does* reach the horror age of 25, the horror dividing line. Surfing and the surfing life have been going big since 1958, and already there are kids who—well, who aren't kids anymore, they are pushing 30, and they are stagnating on the beach. Pretty soon the California littoral will be littered with these guys, stroked out on the beach like beached white whales, and girls, too, who can't give up the mystique, the mysterioso mystique, Oh Mighty Hulking Sea, who can't *conceive* of living any other life. It is pathetic when they are edged out of groups like the Pump House gang. Already there are some guys who hang around with the older crowd around the Shack who are stagnating on the beach. Some of the older guys, like Gary Wickham, who is 24, are still in *The Life,* they still have it, but even Gary Wickham will be 25 one day and then 26 and then. . . . and then even pan-thuh age. Is one really going to be pan-thuh age one day? Watch those black feet go. And Tom Coman still snuggles with Yellow Slacks, and Liz still roosts moodily in her rabbit fur at the bottom of the Pump House and Pam still sits on the steps contemplating the mysterioso mysteries of Pump House ascension and John and Artie still bob, tiny pink porcelain shells, way out there waiting for godsown bitchen *set,* and godsown sun still turned on like a dentist's lamp and so far—

—the panthers scrape on up the sidewalk. They are at just about the   90
point Leonard Anderson and Donna Blanchard got that day, December 6, 1964, when Leonard said, Pipe it, and fired two shots, one at her

and one at himself. Leonard was 18 and Donna was 21—21!—god, for a girl in the Pump House gang that is almost the horror line right there. But it was all so mysterioso. Leonard was just lying down on the beach at the foot of the Pump House, near the stairs, just talking to John K. Weldon down there, and then Donna appeared at the top of the stairs and Leonard got up and went up the stairs to meet her, and they didn't say anything, they weren't *angry* over anything, they never had been, although the police said they had, they just turned and went a few feet down the sidewalk, away from the Pump House and—blam blam!— these two shots. Leonard fell dead on the sidewalk and Donna died that afternoon in Scripps Memorial Hospital. Nobody knew what to think. But one thing it seemed like—well, it seemed like Donna and Leonard thought they had lived *The Life* as far as it would go and now it was running out. All that was left to do was—but that is an *insane* idea. It can't be like that, *The Life* can't run out, people can't change all that much just because godsown chronometer runs on and the body packing starts deteriorating and the fudgy tallow shows up at the thighs where they squeeze out of the bathing suit—

Tom, boy! John, boy! Gary, boy! Neale, boy! Artie, boy! Pam, Liz, Vickie, Jackie Haddad! After all this—just a pair of bitchen black panther bunions inching down the sidewalk away from the old Pump House stairs?

LINES OF INQUIRY
"*The Pump House Gang*"

Throughout much of this piece, Wolfe mimics the language of the pump house gang, speaking as if he is one of them, recreating the experience from inside their heads. Why do you suppose that he engages in this mimicry? Does it help you to understand the surfers? Does it lead you to sympathize with them? Does it leave you confused about Wolfe's attitude toward them? What do you suppose is his attitude toward them? What words or phrases, what details or scenes, suggest his attitude?

Wolfe says that "there is a built-in trouble with age segregation." What exactly does he mean by "age segregation"? How is this segregation reflected in styles of clothing and language, in patterns of behavior, in values and beliefs? What is the "built-in trouble" with such segregation? Why is such segregation always temporary? Why is it potentially tragic?

Though this essay is rooted in scenes and situations from the sixties, it might be considered in relation to contemporary experience. What recent versions of age segregation have you noticed in American culture? What styles of behavior, what patterns of belief, most clearly reflect such segregation today? Do you think that your generation is more—or less—respectful of age and the values of the "shiny black shoe masses"? Do you think that age segregation is inevitable?

THE RIGHT STUFF

A young man might go into military flight training believing that he was entering some sort of technical school in which he was simply going to acquire a certain set of skills. Instead, he found himself all at once enclosed in a fraternity. And in this fraternity, even though it was military, men were not rated by their outward rank as ensigns, lieutenants, commanders, or whatever. No, herein the world was divided into those who had it and those who did not. This quality, this *it,* was never named, however, nor was it talked about in any way.

As to just what this ineffable quality was . . . well, it obviously involved bravery. But it was not bravery in the simple sense of being willing to risk your life. The idea seemed to be that any fool could do that, if that was all that was required, just as any fool could throw away his life in the process. No, the idea here (in the all-enclosing fraternity) seemed to be that a man should have the ability to go up in a hurtling piece of machinery and put his hide on the line and then have the moxie, the reflexes, the experience, the coolness, to pull it back in the last yawning moment—and then to go up again *the next day,* and the next day, and every next day, even if the series should prove infinite—and, ultimately, in its best expression, do so in a cause that means something to thousands, to a people, a nation, to humanity, to God. Nor was there *a test* to show whether or not a pilot had this righteous quality. There was, instead, a seemingly infinite series of tests. A career in flying was like climbing one of those ancient Babylonian pyramids made up of a dizzy progression of steps and ledges, a ziggurat, a pyramid extraordinarily high and steep; and the idea was to prove at every foot of the way up that pyramid that you were one of the elected and anointed ones who had *the right stuff* and could move higher and higher and even—ultimately, God willing, one day—that you might be able to join that special few at the very top, that elite who had the capacity to bring tears to men's eyes, the very Brotherhood of the Right Stuff itself.

None of this was to be mentioned, and yet it was acted out in a way that a young man could not fail to understand. When a new flight (i.e., a class) of trainees arrived at Pensacola, they were brought into an auditorium for a little lecture. An officer would tell them: "Take a look at the man on either side of you." Quite a few actually swiveled their heads this way and that, in the interest of appearing diligent. Then the officer would say: "One of the three of you is not going to make it!"— meaning, not get his wings. That was the opening theme, the *motif* of primary training. We already know that one-third of you do not have the right stuff—it only remains to find out who.

Furthermore, that was the way it turned out. At every level in one's progress up that staggeringly high pyramid, the world was once more divided into those men who had the right stuff to continue the climb and those who had to be *left behind* in the most obvious way. Some were eliminated in the course of the opening classroom work, as either not smart enough or not hardworking enough, and were left behind. Then came the basic flight instruction in single-engine, propeller-driven trainers, and a few more—even though the military tried to make this stage easy—were washed out and left behind. Then came more demanding levels, one after the other, formation flying, instrument flying, jet training, all-weather flying, gunnery, and at each level more were washed out and left behind. By this point easily a third of the original candidates had been, indeed, eliminated . . . from the ranks of those who might prove to have the right stuff.

In the Navy, in addition to the stages that Air Force trainees went 5 through, the neophyte always had waiting for him, out in the ocean, a certain grim gray slab; namely, the deck of an aircraft carrier; and with it perhaps the most difficult routine in military flying, carrier landings. He was shown films about it, he heard lectures about it, and he knew that carrier landings were hazardous. He first practiced touching down on the shape of a flight deck painted on an airfield. He was instructed to touch down and gun right off. This was safe enough—the shape didn't move, at least—but it could do terrible things to, let us say, the gyroscope of the soul. *That shape!—it's so damned small!* And more candidates were washed out and left behind. Then came the day, without warning, when those who remained were sent out over the ocean for the first of many days of reckoning with the slab. The first day was always a clear day with little wind and a calm sea. The carrier was so steady that it seemed, from up there in the air, to be resting on pilings, and the candidate usually made his first carrier landing successfully, with relief and even *élan*. Many young candidates looked like terrific aviators up to that very point—and it was not until they were actually standing on the carrier deck that they first began to wonder if they had the proper stuff, after all. In the training film the flight deck was a grand piece of gray geometry, perilous, to be sure, but an amazing abstract shape as one looks down upon it on the screen. And yet once the newcomer's two feet were on it . . . *Geometry*—my God, man, this is a . . . skillet! It *heaved,* it moved up and down underneath his feet, it pitched up, it pitched down, it rolled to port (this great beast *rolled!*) and it rolled to starboard, as the ship moved into the wind and, therefore, into the waves, and the wind kept sweeping across, sixty feet up in the air out in the open sea, and there were no railings whatsoever. This was a *skillet!*—a frying pan!—a short-order grill!—not gray but black, smeared with skid marks from one end to the other and glistening with pools of hydraulic fluid and the occasional jet-fuel slick, all of it still hot, sticky, greasy, runny, virulent from God knows what traumas—still ablaze!—consumed in detonations, explosions, flames, combustion, roars, shrieks, whines, blasts, horrible shudders, fracturing impacts, as little men in screaming red and yellow and purple and green shirts with black Mickey Mouse helmets over their ears skittered about on the surface as if for their very lives (you've said it now!), hooking fighter planes onto the catapult shuttles so that they can explode their afterburners and be slung off the deck in a red-mad fury with a *kaboom!* that pounds through the entire deck—a procedure that seems absolutely controlled, orderly, sublime, however, compared to what he is about to watch as aircraft return to the ship for what is known in the engineering stoicisms of the military as "recovery and arrest." To say that an F–4 was coming back onto this heaving barbecue from out of the sky at a speed of 135 knots . . . that might have been the truth in the training lecture, but it did not begin to get across the idea of what the newcomer saw from the deck itself, because it created the notion that perhaps the plane was gliding in. On the deck one knew differently! As the aircraft came closer and the carrier heaved on into the waves and the plane's speed did not diminish and the deck did not grow steady—indeed, it pitched up and down five or ten feet per greasy heave—one experienced a neural alarm that no lecture could have prepared him for: This is not an *airplane* coming toward me, it is a brick with some poor sonofabitch riding it *(someone much like myself!),* and it is not *gliding,* it is *falling,* a thirty-thousand-pound brick, headed not for a stripe on the deck but for *me*— and with a horrible *smash!* it hits the skillet, and with a blur of momentum as big as a freight train's it hurtles toward the far end of the deck— another blinding storm!—another roar as the pilot pushes the throttle up to full military power and another smear of rubber screams out over the skillet—and this is nominal!—quite okay!—for a wire stretched across the deck has grabbed the hook on the end of the plane as it hit the deck tail down, and the smash was the rest of the fifteen-ton brute slamming onto the deck, as it tripped up, so that it is now straining against the wire at full throttle, in case it hadn't held and the plane had "boltered" off the end of the deck and had to struggle up into the air again. And already the Mickey Mouse helmets are running toward the fiery monster . . .

    And the candidate, looking on, begins to *feel* that great heaving sun-blazing deathboard of a deck wallowing in his own vestibular system— and suddenly he finds himself backed up against his own limits. He ends up going to the flight surgeon with so-called conversion symptoms. Overnight he develops blurred vision or numbness in his hands and feet or sinusitis so severe that he cannot tolerate changes in altitude. On one level the symptom is real. He really cannot see too well or use his fingers or stand the pain. But somewhere in his subconscious he knows it is a plea and a beg-off; he shows not the slightest concern (the flight surgeon notes) that the condition might be permanent and affect him in whatever life awaits him outside the arena of the right stuff.

Those who remained, those who qualified for carrier duty—and even more so those who later on qualified for *night* carrier duty—began to feel a bit like Gideon's warriors. *So many have been left behind!* The young warriors were now treated to a deathly sweet and quite unmentionable sight. They could gaze at length upon the crushed and wilted pariahs who had washed out. They could inspect those who did not have that righteous stuff.

The military did not have very merciful instincts. Rather than packing up these poor souls and sending them home, the Navy, like the Air Force and the Marines, would try to make use of them in some other role, such as flight controller. So the washout has to keep taking classes with the rest of his group, even though he can no longer touch an airplane. He sits there in the classes staring at sheets of paper with cataracts of sheer human mortification over his eyes while the rest steal looks at him . . . this man reduced to an ant, this untouchable, this poor sonofabitch. And in what test had he been found wanting? Why, it seemed to be nothing less than *manhood* itself. Naturally, this was never mentioned, either. Yet there it was. *Manliness, manhood, manly courage* . . . there was something ancient, primordial, irresistible about the challenge of this stuff, no matter what a sophisticated and rational age one might think he lived in.

Perhaps because it could not be talked about, the subject began to take on superstititous and even mystical outlines. A man either had it or he didn't! There was no such thing as having *most* of it . Moreover, it could blow at any seam. One day a man would be ascending the pyramid at a terrific clip, and the next—bingo!— he would reach his own limits in the most unexpected way. Conrad and Schirra met an Air Force pilot who had had a great pal at Tyndall Air Force Base in Florida. This man had been the budding ace of the training class; he had flown the hottest fighter-style trainer, the T–38, like a dream; and then he began the routine step of being checked out in the T–33. The T–33 was not nearly as hot an aircraft as the T–38; it was essentially the old P–80 jet fighter. It had an exceedingly small cockpit. The pilot could barely move his shoulders. It was the sort of airplane of which everybody said, "You don't get into it, you *wear* it." Once inside a T–33 cockpit this man, this budding ace, developed claustrophobia of the most paralyzing sort. He tried everything to overcome it. He even went to a psychiatrist, which was a serious mistake for a military officer if his superiors learned of it. But nothing worked. He was shifted over to flying jet transports, such as the C–135. Very demanding and necessary aircraft they were, too, and he was still spoken of as an excellent pilot.

But as everyone knew—and, again, it was never explained in so many words—only those who were assigned to fighter squadrons, the "fighter jocks," as they called each other with a self-satisfied irony, remained in the true fraternity. Those assigned to transports were not humiliated like washouts—*somebody* had to fly those planes—nevertheless, they, too, had been *left behind* for lack of the right stuff.

Or a man could go for a routine physical one fine day, feeling like   10
a million dollars, and be grounded for *fallen arches*. It happened!—just like that! (And try raising them.) Or for breaking his wrist and losing only *part* of its mobility. Or for a minor deterioration of eyesight, or for any of hundreds of reasons that would make no difference to a man in an ordinary occupation. As a result all fighter jocks began looking upon doctors as their natural enemies. Going to see a flight surgeon was a no-gain proposition; a pilot could only hold his own or lose in the doctor's office. To be grounded for a medical reason was no humiliation, looked at objectively. But it was a humiliation, nonetheless!—for it meant you no longer had that indefinable, unutterable, integral stuff. (It could blow at *any* seam.)

All the hot young fighter jocks began trying to test the limits themselves in a superstitious way. They were like believing Presbyterians of a century before who used to probe their own experience to see if they were truly among *the elect*. When a fighter pilot was in training, whether in the Navy or the Air Force, his superiors were continually spelling out strict rules for him, about the use of the aircraft and conduct in the sky. They repeatedly forbade so-called hot-dog stunts, such as outside loops, buzzing, flat-hatting, hedgehopping and flying under bridges. But somehow one got the message that the man who truly *had* it could ignore those rules—not that he should make a point of it, but that he *could*—and that after all there was only one way to find out—and that in some strange unofficial way, peeking through his fingers, his instructor halfway expected him to challenge all the limits. They would give a lecture about how a pilot should never fly without a good solid breakfast—eggs, bacon, toast, and so forth—because if he tried to fly with his blood-sugar level too low, it could impair his alertness. Naturally, the next day every hot dog in the unit would get up and have a breakfast consisting of one cup of black coffee and take off and go up into a vertical climb until the weight of the ship exactly canceled out the upward thrust of the engine and his air speed was zero, and he would hang there for one thick adrenal instant—and then fall like a rock, until one of three things happened: he keeled over nose first and regained his aerodynamics and all was well, he went into a spin and fought his way out of it, or he went into a spin and had to eject or crunch it, which was always supremely possible.

Likewise, "hassling"—mock dogfighting—was strictly forbidden, and so naturally young fighter jocks could hardly wait to go up in, say, a pair of F–100s and start the duel by making a pass at each other at 800 miles an hour, the winner being the pilot who could slip in behind the other one and get locked in on his tail ("wax his tail"), and it was not uncommon for some eager jock to try too tight an outside turn and have his engine flame out, whereupon, unable to restart it, he has to eject . . . and he shakes his fist at the victor as he floats down by parachute and his million-dollar aircraft goes *kaboom!* on the palmetto grass or the desert floor, and he starts thinking about how he can get together with the other guy back at the base in time for the two of them to get their stories straight before the investigation: "I don't know what happened, sir. I was pulling up after a target run, and it just flamed out on me." Hassling was forbidden, and hassling that led to the destruction of an aircraft was a serious court-martial offense, and the man's superiors knew that the engine hadn't *just flamed out,* but every unofficial impulse on the base seemed to be saying: "Hell, we wouldn't give you a nickel for a pilot who hasn't done some crazy rat-racing like that. It's all part of the right stuff."

The other side of this impulse showed up in the reluctance of the young jocks to admit it when they had maneuvered themselves into a bad corner they couldn't get out of. There were two reasons why a fighter pilot hated to declare an emergency. First, it triggered a complex and very public chain of events at the field: all other incoming flights were held up, including many of one's comrades who were probably low on fuel; the fire trucks came trundling out to the runway like yellow toys (as seen from way up there), the better to illustrate one's hapless state; and the bureaucracy began to crank up the paper monster for the investigation that always followed. And second, to declare an emergency, one first had to reach that conclusion in his own mind, which to the young pilot was the same as saying: "A minute ago I still *had* it—now I need your help!" To have a bunch of young fighter pilots up in the air thinking this way used to drive flight controllers crazy. They would see a ship beginning to drift off the radar, and they couldn't rouse the pilot on the microphone for anything other than a few meaningless mumbles, and they would know he was probably out there with engine failure at a low altitude, trying to reignite by lowering his auxilliary generator rig, which had a little propeller that was supposed to spin in the slipstream like a child's pinwheel.

"Whiskey Kilo Two Eight, do you want to declare an emergency?"

This would rouse him!—to say: "Negative, negative, Whiskey Kilo Two Eight is not declaring an emergency."

Kaboom. Believers in the right stuff would rather crash and burn.

One fine day, after he had joined a fighter squadron, it would dawn on the young pilot exactly how the losers in the great fraternal competition were now being left behind. Which is to say, not by instructors or other superiors or by failures at prescribed levels of competence, but

15

by death. At this point the essence of the enterprise would begin to dawn on him. Slowly, step by step, the ante had been raised until he was now involved in what was surely the grimmest and grandest gamble of manhood. Being a fighter pilot—for that matter, simply taking off in a single-engine jet fighter of the Century series, such as an F–102, or any of the military's other marvelous bricks with fins on them—presented a man, on a perfectly sunny day, with more ways to get himself killed than his wife and children could imagine in their wildest fears. If he was barreling down the runway at two hundred miles an hour, completing the takeoff run, and the board started lighting up red, should he (a) abort the takeoff (and try to wrestle with the monster, which was gorged with jet fuel, out in the sand beyond the end of the runway) or (b) eject (and hope that the goddamned human cannonball trick works at zero altitude and he doesn't shatter an elbow or a kneecap on the way out) or (c) continue the takeoff and deal with the problem aloft (knowing full well that the ship may be on fire and therefore seconds away from exploding)? He would have one second to sort out the options and act, and this kind of little workaday decision came up all the time. Occasionally a man would look coldly at the binary problem he was now confronting every day—Right Stuff/Death—and decide it wasn't worth it and voluntarily shift over to transports or reconnaissance or whatever. And his comrades would wonder, for a day or so, what evil virus had invaded his soul . . . as they left him behind. More often, however, the reverse would happen. Some college graduate would enter Navy aviation through the Reserves, simply as an alternative to the Army draft, fully intending to return to civilian life, to some waiting profession or family business; would become involved in the obsessive business of ascending the ziggurat pyramid of flying; and, at the end of his enlistment, would astound everyone back home and very likely himself as well by signing up for another one. What on earth got into him? He couldn't explain it. After all, the very words for it had been amputated. A Navy study showed that two-thirds of the fighter pilots who were rated in the top rungs of their groups—i.e., the hottest young pilots—reenlisted when the time came, and practically all were college graduates. By this point, a young fighter jock was like the preacher in *Moby Dick* who climbs up into the pulpit on a rope ladder and then pulls the ladder up behind him; except the pilot could not use the words necessary to express the vital lessons. Civilian life, and even home and hearth, now seemed not only far away but far *below,* back down many levels of the pyramid of the right stuff.

A fighter pilot soon found he wanted to associate only with other fighter pilots. Who else could understand the nature of the little proposition (right stuff/death) they were all dealing with? And what other subject could compare with it? It was riveting! To talk about it in so many words was forbidden, of course. The very words *death, danger, bravery, fear* were not to be uttered except in the occasional specific instance or for ironic effect. Nevertheless, the subject could be adumbrated in *code* or *by example*. Hence the endless evenings of pilots huddled together talking about flying. On these long and drunken evenings (the bane of their family life) certain theorems would be propounded and demonstrated—and all by *code* and *example*. One theorem was: There are no *accidents* and no fatal flaws in the machines; there are only pilots with the wrong stuff. (I.e., blind Fate can't kill me.) When Bud Jennings crashed and burned in the swamps at Jacksonville, the other pilots in Pete Conrad's squadron said: *How could he have been so stupid?* It turned out that Jennings had gone up in the SNJ with his cockpit canopy opened in a way that was expressly forbidden in the manual, and carbon monoxide had been sucked in from the exhaust, and he passed out and crashed. All agreed that Bud Jennings was a good guy and a good pilot, but his epitaph on the ziggurat was: *How could he have been so stupid?* This seemed shocking at first, but by the time Conrad had reached the end of that bad string at Pax River, he was capable of his own corollary to the theorem: viz., no single factor ever killed a pilot; there was always a chain of mistakes. But what about Ted Whelan, who fell like a rock from 8,100 feet when his parachute failed? Well, the parachute was merely part of the chain: first, someone should have caught the structural defect that resulted in the hydraulic leak that triggered the emergency; second, Whelan did not check out his seat-parachute rig, and the drogue failed to separate the main parachute from the seat; but even after those two mistakes, Whelan had fifteen or twenty seconds, as he fell, to disengage himself from the seat and open the parachute manually. Why just stare at the scenery coming up to smack you in the face! And everyone nodded. (He failed—but I wouldn't have!) Once the theorem and the corollary were understood, the Navy's statistics about one in every four Navy aviators dying meant nothing. The figures were averages, and averages applied to those with average stuff.

A riveting subject, especially if it were one's own hide that was on the line. Every evening at bases all over America, there were military pilots huddled in officers clubs eagerly cutting the right stuff up in coded slices so they could talk about it. What more compelling topic of conversation was there in the world? In the Air Force there were even pilots who would ask the tower for priority landing clearance so that they could make the beer call on time, at 4 p.m. sharp, at the Officers Club. They would come right out and state the reason. The drunken rambles began at four and sometimes went on for ten or twelve hours. Such conversations! They diced that righteous stuff up into little bits, bowed ironically to it, stumbled blindfolded around it, groped, lurched, belched, staggered, bawled, sang, roared, and feinted at it with self-deprecating humor. Nevertheless!—they never mentioned it by name. No, they used the approved codes, such as: "Like a jerk I got myself into a hell of a corner today." They told of how they "lucked out of it." To get across the extreme peril of his exploit, one would use certain oblique cues. He would say, "I looked over at Robinson"—who would be known to the listeners as a non-com who sometimes rode backseat to read radar— "and he wasn't talking any more, he was just staring at the radar, like this, giving it that *zombie* look. Then I *knew* I was in trouble!" Beautiful! Just right! For it would also be known to the listeners that the non-coms advised one another: "*Never* fly with a lieutenant. *Avoid* captains and majors. Hell, man, do yourself a favor: don't fly with anybody below colonel." Which in turn said: "Those young bucks shoot dice with death!" And yet once in the air the non-com had his own standards. He was determined to remain as outwardly cool as the pilot, so that when the pilot did something that truly petrified him, he would say nothing; instead, he would turn silent, catatonic, like a zombie. Perfect! *Zombie.* There you had it, compressed into a single word, all of the foregoing. I'm a hell of a pilot! I shoot dice with death! And now all you fellows know it! And I haven't spoken of that unspoken stuff even once!

The talking and drinking began at the beer call, and then the boys would break for dinner and come back afterward and get more wasted and more garrulous or else more quietly fried, drinking good cheap PX booze until 2 a.m. The night was young! Why not get the cars and go out for a little proficiency run? It seemed that every fighter jock thought himself an ace driver, and he would do anything to obtain a hot car, especially a sports car, and the drunker he was, the more convinced he would be about his driving skills, as if the right stuff, being indivisible, carried over into any enterprise whatsoever, under any conditions. A little proficiency run, boys! (There's only one way to find out!) And they would roar off in close formation from, say, Nellis Air Force Base, down Route 15, into Las Vegas, barreling down the highway, ratracing, sometimes four abreast, jockeying for position, piling into the most listless curve in the desert flats as if they were trying to root each other out of the groove at the Rebel 500—and then bursting into downtown Las Vegas with a rude fraternal roar like the Hell's Angels—and the natives chalked it up to youth and drink and the bad element that the Air Force attracted. They knew nothing about the right stuff, of course.

More fighter pilots died in automobiles than in airplanes. Fortunately, there was always some kindly soul up the chain to certify the papers "line of duty," so that the widow could get a better break on the insurance. That was okay and only proper because somehow the system itself had long ago said *Skol!* and *Quite right!* to the military cycle of Flying & Drinking and Drinking & Driving, as if there were no other way. Every young fighter jock knew the feeling of getting two or three hours' sleep and then waking up at 5:30 a.m. and having a few cups of coffee, a few cigarettes, and then carting his poor quivering liver out to the field for another day of flying. There were those who arrived not merely hungover but still drunk, slapping oxygen tank cones over their faces and trying to burn the alcohol out of their systems, and then going up, remarking later: "I don't *advise* it, you understand, but it *can* be done." (Provided you have the right stuff, you miserable pudknocker.)

Air Force and Navy airfields were usually on barren or marginal stretches of land and would have looked especially bleak and Low Rent to an ordinary individual in the chilly light of dawn. But to a young pilot there was an inexplicable bliss to coming out to the flight line while the sun was just beginning to cook up behind the rim of the horizon, so that the whole field was still in shadow and the ridges in the distance were in silhouette and the flight line was a monochrome of Exhaust Fume Blue, and every little red light on top of the water towers or power stanchions looked dull, shriveled, congealed, and the runway lights, which were still on, looked faded, and even the landing lights on a fighter that had just landed and was taxiing in were no longer dazzling, as they would be at night, and looked instead like shriveled gobs of candlepower out there—and yet it was beautiful, exhilarating!—for he was revved up with adrenalin, anxious to take off before the day broke, to burst up into the sunlight over the ridges before all those thousands of comatose souls down there, still dead to the world, snug in home and hearth, even came to their senses. To take off in an F–100 at dawn and cut in the afterburner and hurtle twenty-five thousand feet up into the sky so suddenly that you felt not like a bird but like a trajectory, yet with full control, full control of *five tons* of thrust, all of which flowed from your will and through your fingertips, with the huge engine right beneath you, so close that it was as if you were riding it bareback, until you leveled out and went supersonic, an event registered on earth by a tremendous cracking boom that shook windows, but up here only by the fact that you now felt utterly free of the earth—to describe it, even to wife, child, near ones and dear ones, seemed impossible. So the pilot kept it to himself, along with an even more indescribable . . . an even more sinfully inconfessable . . . feeling of superiority, appropriate to him and to his kind, lone bearers of the right stuff.

From *up here* at dawn the pilot looked down upon poor hopeless Las Vegas (or Yuma, Corpus Christi, Meridian, San Bernardino, or Dayton) and began to wonder: How can all of them down there, those poor souls who will soon be waking up and trudging out of their minute rectangles and inching along their little noodle highways toward whatever slots and grooves make up their everyday lives—how could they live like that, with such earnestness, if they had the faintest idea of what it was like up here in this righteous zone?

But of course! Not only the washed-out, grounded, and dead pilots had been left behind—but also all of those millions of sleepwalking souls who never even attempted the great gamble. The entire world below . . . *left behind*. Only at this point can one begin to understand just how big, how titanic, the ego of the military pilot could be. The world was used to enormous egos in artists, actors, entertainers of all sorts, in politicians, sports figures, and even journalists, because they had such familiar and convenient ways to show them off. But that slim young man over there in uniform, with the enormous watch on his wrist and the withdrawn look on his face, that young officer who is so shy that he can't even open his mouth unless the subject is flying—that young pilot—well, my friends, his ego is even *bigger!*—so big, it's *breathtaking!* Even in the 1950's it was difficult for civilians to comprehend such a thing, but *all* military officers and many enlisted men tended to feel superior to civilians. It was really quite ironic, given the fact that for a good thirty years the rising business classes in the cities had been steering their sons away from the military, as if from a bad smell, and the officer corps had never been held in lower esteem. Well, career officers returned the contempt in trumps. They looked upon themselves as men who lived by higher standards of behavior than civilians, as men who were the bearers and protectors of the most important values of American life, who maintained a sense of discipline while civilians abandoned themselves to hedonism, who maintained a sense of honor while civilians lived by opportunism and greed. Opportunism and greed: there you had your much-vaunted corporate business world. Khrushchev was right about one thing: when it came time to hang the capitalist West, an American businessman would sell him the rope. When the showdown came—and the showdowns always came—not all the wealth in the world or all the sophisticated nuclear weapons and radar and missile systems it could buy would take the place of those who had the uncritical willingness to face danger, those who, in short, had the right stuff.

In fact, the feeling was so righteous, so exalted, it could become   25
religious. Civilians seldom understood this, either. There was no one to teach them. It was no longer the fashion for serious writers to describe the glories of war. Instead, they dwelt upon its horrors, often with cynicism or disgust. It was left to the occasional pilot with a literary flair to provide a glimpse of the pilot's self-conception in its heavenly or spiritual aspect. When a pilot named Robert Scott flew his P–43 over Mount Everest, quite a feat at the time, he brought his hand up and snapped a salute to his fallen adversary. He thought he had *defeated* the mountain, surmounting all the forces of nature that had made it formidable. And why not? "God is my co-pilot," he said—that became the title of his book—and he meant it. So did the most gifted of all the pilot authors, the Frenchman Antoine de Saint-Exupéry. As he gazed down upon the world . . . from up there . . . during trans-

continental flights, the good Saint-Ex saw civilization as a series of tiny fragile patches clinging to the otherwise barren rock of Earth. He felt like a lonely sentinel, a protector of those vulnerable little oases, ready to lay down his life in their behalf, if necessary; a saint, in short, true to his name, flying up here at the right hand of God. The good Saint-Ex! And he was not the only one. He was merely the one who put it into words most beautifully and anointed himself before the altar of the right stuff.

LINES OF INQUIRY
"The Right Stuff"

Wolfe relies heavily in this piece on a deliberate repetition of the term "the right stuff" and several other key phrases. How often and at what special points does he repeat these phrases? What variations, if any, do you note in his wording of these phrases? Why do you suppose that he engages in such repetitions? How did they affect you?

In his discussion of the right stuff, Wolfe also relies heavily on religious terminology, comparing the test pilots to the righteous "elect" and calling the right stuff itself "mystical" and "ineffable." In what ways, according to Wolfe, do the astronauts behave like members of a religious group or sect? How is their own language religious? Why do you think Wolfe makes these comparisons?

Think about the field or profession that you plan to enter. Does it call just for hard work and preparation or does success depend on some special talent—the right stuff—that you either have or don't have? How do you know when something calls for such a special quality? Do you think that successful writing depends on having the right stuff, or can anyone learn to write well?

VIRGINIA WOOLF

1882 – 1941

But literature is stern; it is no use being charming, virtuous, or even learned and brilliant into the bargain, unless, she seems to reiterate, you fulfill her first condition—to know how to write.

Few writers of her generation were quite so charming, virtuous, learned, and brilliant as Virginia Woolf herself, and few were quite so keenly aware that these admirable qualities do not themselves give rise to literature. Writing for her was evidently a very "stern" and challenging discipline—"each day's work like a fence which I have to ride at. . . ." And the fences she rode at were especially challenging because as a critic, novelist, and essayist she self-consciously sought to alter not only the imaginative world of fiction but also the actual world of women's experience. So while she took great pleasure in entertaining a circle of remarkably gifted artists, writers, and intellectuals, she also realized that "if one wishes to better the world, one must paradoxically enough, withdraw and spend more and more time fashioning one's sentences to perfection in solitude." Though she was self-evidently a perfectionist, she managed over the course of her career to produce nine novels, four collections of short stories, two biographies, two books of feminist commentary, more than three hundred articles, essays, and reviews, six volumes of correspondence, and an extensive diary.

Born and raised in London, she was the third of four children of her father's second marriage. She did not attend school, but was educated at home under the highly cultured influence of her father, Leslie Stephen, a distinguished biographer, critic, editor, and philosopher. From her father she learned "to read what one liked because one liked it . . ." and "to write in the fewest possible words, as clearly as possible, exactly what one meant." From her father, too, she learned that "all the rest must be learnt for oneself." So she immersed herself in his extensive collection of English and classical literature, as well as in his dazzling array of literary acquaintances, and therefore grew up to be an extraordinarily cultured person herself. She also grew up in touch with the life and rhythm of the sea at her father's summer house in Cornwall.

After her father's death in 1904, her mother having died in 1895, she took up residence with her sister, Vanessa, and her brothers, Thoby and Adrian, at a house in the Bloomsbury area of London, conveniently located near the British Museum. Bloomsbury, in turn, soon became a gathering place for Thoby's friends from Cambridge University—a place to carry on the lively discussions of art, literature, politics, and society that had occupied them during their college years. After the death of Thoby and the marriage of Vanessa in 1906, Virginia and Adrian moved to another house in Bloomsbury, where they continued to hold the gatherings that Thoby had started, attracting over the years such well-known figures as the art critic Roger Fry, the biographer and historian Lytton Strachey, the economist John Maynard Keynes, the novelist E. M. Forster, and the political activist Leonard Woolf, whom she married in 1912. This remarkable array of progressive artists and intellectuals, which came to be known as the Bloomsbury Group, provided a uniquely stimulating atmosphere for Woolf, an ambiance that encouraged her to pursue her own progressive literary and social interests.

Shortly after moving to Bloomsbury, she began to pursue her own interests by writing literary reviews and articles, an activity that she was to continue from 1905 through the rest of her life, not simply out of a desire to convey her impressions of individual works, but also out of "an instinct to create . . . a portrait of a man, a sketch of an age, a theory of the art of writing." Her "instinct to create" also provoked her to begin writing her own fiction, which led in 1915 to the publication of her first novel, *The Voyage Out*. Two years later, when she and her husband bought a hand press and started up their own publishing house, the Hogarth Press, her creative instincts found another outlet in the form of literary editing. The Hogarth Press turned out, in fact, to be a very successful business, publishing the writing of such eminent figures as T. S. Eliot, E. M. Forster, Sigmund Freud, Robert Graves, Katherine Mansfield, and H. G. Wells.

The press also gave Woolf the freedom to follow her own creative bent, knowing she would have an outlet for her fiction no matter how experimental it might be. During the last twenty years of her career, she directly challenged the long-standing fictional emphasis on materialistic circumstances—on clear-cut settings, characters, and events—preferring instead to focus on the complex flow of mental experience, which she considered to be the essence of "life itself." "The mind," she believed, "receives a myriad impressions—trivial, fantastic, evanescent, or engraved with the sharpness of steel. From all sides they come, an incessant show of innumerable atoms. . . ." So, she set out "to record the atoms as they fall upon the mind," and she did so in a series of increasingly interiorized novels—*Jacob's Room* (1922), *Mrs. Dalloway*

(1925), *To the Lighthouse* (1927), *The Waves* (1931), *The Years* (1937), and *Between the Acts* (1941). Her focus on the interior life of her characters—on their sensations, associations, memories, and expectations—enabled her, in turn, to explore the complex nature of personal awareness, personal identity, and personal relationships.

Her own personal life was evidently far more complex than it seemed to be to her friends and acquaintances. Though she appeared on most occasions to be a very buoyant and vivacious person, she was, in fact, during most of her life afflicted by periods of severe depression, especially after completing a novel. Whatever the cause of her depressions and nervous breakdowns, she felt "certain" in March 1941 that she was "going mad again," and rather than put herself and her husband "through another of those terrible times," she put an end to her life by drowning herself in the river near the cottage where she had just finished her last novel.

Her personal essays and critical pieces cover a wide range of subjects from the death of a moth to the status of women, from the lives of the obscure to the works of the famous. They also embody a wide range of modes from description, narration, and reflection to explanation, evaluation, and argument. But whatever their subject or mode, they are always marked by "some fierce attachment to an idea . . . something believed in with conviction or seen with precision," which she believed to be the "backbone" of writing. Whatever the source of their backbone, they are always permeated by the sound of a human voice, the sense of a human presence—by the "spirit of personality," which she considered to be "the essayist's most proper but most dangerous and delicate tool."

THE DEATH OF THE MOTH

Moths that fly by day are not properly to be called moths; they do not excite that pleasant sense of dark autumn nights and ivy-blossom which the commonest yellow-underwing asleep in the shadow of the curtain never fails to rouse in us. They are hybrid creatures, neither gay like butterflies nor sombre like their own species. Nevertheless the present specimen, with his narrow hay-coloured wings, fringed with a tassel of the same colour, seemed to be content with life. It was a pleasant morning, mid-September, mild, benignant, yet with a keener breath than that of the summer months. The plough was already scoring the field opposite the window, and where the share had been, the earth was pressed flat and gleamed with moisture. Such vigour came rolling in from the fields and the down beyond that it was difficult to keep the eyes strictly turned upon the book. The rooks too were keeping one of their annual festivities; soaring round the tree tops until it looked as if a vast net with thousands of black knots in it had been cast up into the air; which, after a few moments sank slowly down upon the trees until every twig seemed to have a knot at the end of it. Then, suddenly, the net would be thrown into the air again in a wider circle this time, with the utmost clamour and vociferation, as though to be thrown into the air and settle slowly down upon the tree tops were a tremendously exciting experience.

The same energy which inspired the rooks, the ploughmen, the horses, and even, it seemed, the lean bare-backed downs, sent the moth fluttering from side to side of his square of the window-pane. One could not help watching him. One was, indeed, conscious of a queer feeling of pity for him. The possibilities of pleasure seemed that morning so enormous and so various that to have only a moth's part in life, and a day moth's at that, appeared a hard fate, and his zest in enjoying his meagre opportunities to the full, pathetic. He flew vigorously to one corner of his compartment, and, after waiting there a second, flew across to the other. What remained for him but to fly to a third corner and then to a fourth? That was all he could do, in spite of the size of the downs, the width of the sky, the far-off smoke of houses, and the romantic voice, now and then, of a steamer out at sea. What he could do he did. Watching him, it seemed as if a fibre, very thin, but pure, of the enormous energy of the world had been thrust into his frail and diminutive body. As often as he crossed the pane, I could fancy that a thread of vital light became visible. He was little or nothing but life.

Yet, because he was so small, and so simple a form of the energy that was rolling in at the open window and driving its way through so many narrow and intricate corridors in my own brain and in those of other human beings, there was something marvellous as well as pathetic about him. It was as if someone had taken a tiny bead of pure life and decking it as lightly as possible with down and feathers, had set it dancing and zigzagging to show us the true nature of life. Thus displayed one could not get over the strangeness of it. One is apt to forget all about life, seeing it humped and bossed and garnished and cumbered so that it has to move with the greatest circumspection and dignity. Again, the thought of all that life might have been had he been born in any other shape caused one to view his simple activities with a kind of pity.

After a time, tired by his dancing apparently, he settled on the window ledge in the sun, and, the queer spectacle being at an end, I forgot about him. Then, looking up, my eye was caught by him. He was trying to resume his dancing, but seemed either so stiff or so awkward that he could only flutter to the bottom of the window-pane; and when he tried to fly across it he failed. Being intent on other matters I watched these futile attempts for a time without thinking, unconsciously waiting for him to resume his flight, as one waits for a machine, that has stopped momentarily, to start again without considering the reason of its failure. After perhaps a seventh attempt he slipped from the wooden ledge and fell, fluttering his wings, on to his back on the window sill. The helplessness of his attitude roused me. It flashed upon me that he was in difficulties; he could no longer raise himself; his legs struggled vainly. But, as I stretched out a pencil, meaning to help him to right himself, it came over me that the failure and awkwardness were the approach of death. I laid the pencil down again.

The legs agitated themselves once more. I looked as if for the enemy against which he struggled. I looked out of doors. What had happened there? Presumably it was mid-day, and work in the fields had stopped. Stillness and quiet had replaced the previous animation. The birds had taken themselves off to feed in the brooks. The horses stood still. Yet the power was there all the same, massed outside indifferent, impersonal, not attending to anything in particular. Somehow it was opposed to the little hay-coloured moth. It was useless to try to do anything. One could only watch the extraordinary efforts made by those tiny legs against an oncoming doom which could, had it chosen, have submerged an entire city, not merely a city, but masses of human beings; nothing, I knew, had any chance against death. Nevertheless after a pause of exhaustion the legs fluttered again. It was superb this last protest, and so frantic that he succeeded at last in righting himself. One's sympathies, of course, were all on the side of life. Also, when there was nobody to care or to know, this gigantic effort on the part of an insignificant little moth, against a power of such magnitude, to retain what no one else valued or desired to keep, moved one strangely. Again,

5

somehow, one saw life, a pure bead. I lifted the pencil again, useless though I knew it to be. But even as I did so, the unmistakable tokens of death showed themselves. The body relaxed, and instantly grew stiff. The struggle was over. The insignificant little creature now knew death. As I looked at the dead moth, this minute wayside triumph of so great a force over so mean an antagonist filled me with wonder. Just as life had been strange a few minutes before, so death was now as strange. The moth having righted himself now lay most decently and uncomplainingly composed. O yes, he seemed to say, death is stronger than I am.

LINES OF INQUIRY
"The Death of the Moth"

Woolf begins her essay using a third-person point of view, but in the fourth paragraph she shifts to a predominantly first-person point of view. In the fifth paragraph, she moves back and forth between these two points of view. Why do you suppose that she combines these two very different points of view in a single essay? Why do you suppose that she shifts from one to the other at each point that such a shift occurs? How did the changing point of view affect your thoughts and feelings abut the moth? About Woolf?

Moths are such ordinary creatures that at first thought they seem to be an unlikely subject for an essay. What is it about this particular moth that catches the attention of Woolf? And once she takes note of the creature, why does she become absorbed in following its movements? Why does she come to see the "spectacle" of the moth as being so "queer," so "extraordinary," and so significant?

Virginia Woolf is not the only essayist in this collection to be concerned with the existence of moths, as you can see by looking at Annie Dillard's "The Death of a Moth." Given the very close connection in the titles of Dillard's and Woolf's essays, what other similarities do you see in their pieces? What are the most notable differences in the way they approach the death of a moth?

THE MOMENT:
SUMMER'S NIGHT

The night was falling so that the table in the garden among the trees grew whiter and whiter; and the people round it more indistinct. An owl, blunt, obsolete looking, heavy weighted, crossed the fading sky with a black spot between its claws. The trees murmured. An aeroplane hummed like a piece of plucked wire. There was also, on the roads, the distant explosion of a motor cycle, shooting further and further away down the road. Yet what composed the present moment? If you are young, the future lies upon the present, like a piece of glass, making it tremble and quiver. If you are old, the past lies upon the present, like a thick glass, making it waver, distorting it. All the same, everybody believes that the present is something, seeks out the different elements in this situation in order to compose the truth of it, the whole of it.

To begin with: it is largely composed of visual and of sense impressions. The day was very hot. After heat, the surface of the body is opened, as if all the pores were open and everything lay exposed, not sealed and contracted, as in cold weather. The air wafts cold on the skin under one's clothes. The soles of the feet expand in slippers after walking on hard roads. Then the sense of the light sinking back into darkness seems to be gently putting out with a damp sponge the colour in one's own eyes. Then the leaves shiver now and again, as if a ripple of irresistible sensation ran through them, as a horse suddenly ripples its skin.

But this moment is also composed of a sense that the legs of the chair are sinking through the centre of the earth, passing through the rich garden earth; they sink, weighted down. Then the sky loses its colour perceptibly and a star here and there makes a point of light. Then changes, unseen in the day, coming in succession seem to make an order evident. One becomes aware that we are spectators and also passive participants in a pageant. And as nothing can interfere with the order, we have nothing to do but accept, and watch. Now little sparks, which are not steady, but fitful as if somebody were doubtful, come across the field. Is it time to light the lamp, the farmers' wives are saying: can I see a little longer? The lamp sinks down; then it burns up. All doubt is over. Yes the time has come in all cottages, in all farms, to light the lamps. Thus then the moment is laced about with these weavings to and fro, these inevitable downsinkings, flights, lamp lightings.

But that is the wider circumference of the moment. Here in the centre is a knot of consciousness; a nucleus divided up into four heads, eight legs, eight arms, and four separate bodies. They are not subject to the law of the sun and the owl and the lamp. They assist it. For sometimes a hand rests on the table; sometimes a leg is thrown over a leg. Now the moment becomes shot with the extraordinary arrow which people let fly from their mouths—when they speak.

"He'll do well with his hay."   5

The words let fall this seed, but also, coming from that obscure face, and the mouth, and the hand so characteristically holding the cigarette, now hit the mind with a wad, then explode like a scent suffusing the whole dome of the mind with its incense, flavour; let fall, from their ambiguous envelope, the self-confidence of youth, but also its urgent desire, for praise, and assurance; if they were to say: "But you're no worse looking than many—you're no different—people don't mark you out to laugh at you": that he should be at once so cock-a-hoop and so ungainly makes the moment rock with laughter, and with the malice that comes from overlooking other people's motives; and seeing what they keep hid; and so that one takes sides; he will succeed; or no he won't; and then again, this success, will it mean my defeat; or won't it? All this shoots through the moment, makes it quiver with malice and amusement; and the sense of watching and comparing; and the quiver meets the shore, when the owl flies out, and puts a stop to this judging, this overseeing, and with our wings spread, we too fly, take wing, with the owl, over the earth and survey the quietude of what sleeps, folded, slumbering, arm stretching in the vast dark and sucking its thumb too; the amorous and the innocent; and a sigh goes up. Could we not fly too, with broad wings and with softness; and be all one wing; all embracing, all gathering, and these boundaries, these pryings over hedge into hidden compartments of different colours be all swept into one colour by the brush of the wing; and so visit in splendour, augustly, peaks; and there lie exposed, bare, on the spine, high up, to the cold light of the moon rising, and when the moon rises, single, solitary, behold her, one, eminent over us?

Ah, yes, if we could fly, fly, fly. . . . Here the body is gripped; and shaken; and the throat stiffens; and the nostrils tingle; and like a rat shaken by a terrier one sneezes; and the whole universe is shaken; mountains, snows, meadows; moon; higgledy-piggledy, upside down, little splinters flying; and the head is jerked up, down. "Hay fever—what a noise!—there's no cure. Except spending hay time on a boat. Perhaps worse than the disease, though that's what a man did—crossing and recrossing, all the summer."

Issuing from a white arm, a long shape, lying back, in a film of black and white, under the tree, which, down sweeping, seems a part of that curving, that flowing, the voice, with its ridicule and its sense, reveals to the shaken terrier its own insignificance. No longer part of the snow; no part of the mountain; not in the least venerable to other human

beings; but ridiculous; a little accident; a thing to be laughed at; discrim-
inated out; seen clearly cut out, sneezing, sneezing, judged and compared. Thus into the moment steals self-assertion; ah, the sneeze again;
the desire to sneeze with conviction; masterfully; making oneself heard;
felt; if not pitied, then somebody of importance; perhaps to break away
and go. But no; the other shape has sent from its arrow another fine
binding thread, "Shall I fetch my Vapex?" She, the observant, the discriminating, who keeps in mind always other instances, so that there is
nothing singular in any special case—who refuses to be jumped into
extravagance; and so sceptical withal; cannot believe in miracles; sees
the vanity of effort there; perhaps then it would be well to try here; yet if
she isolates cases from the mists of hugeness, sees what is there all the
more definitely; refuses to be bamboozled; yet in this definite discrimination shows some amplitude. That is why the moment becomes harder,
is intensified, diminished, begins to be stained by some expressed personal juice; with the desire to be loved, to be held close to the other
shape; to put off the veil of darkness and see burning eyes.

Then a light is struck; in it appears a sunburnt face, lean, blue-eyed,
and the arrow flies as the match goes out:

"He beats her every Saturday; from boredom, I should say; not   10
drink; there's nothing else to do."

The moment runs like quicksilver on a sloping board into the cottage parlour; there are the tea things on the table; the hard windsor
chairs; tea caddies on the shelf for ornament; the medal under a glass
shade; vegetable steam curling from the pot; two children crawling on
the floor; and Liz comes in and John catches her a blow on the side of
her head as she slopes past him, dirty, with her hair loose and one
hairpin sticking out about to fall. And she moans in a chronic animal
way; and the children look up and then make a whistling noise to
imitate the engine which they trail across the flags; and John sits
himself down with a thump at the table and carves a hunk of bread and
munches because there is nothing to be done. A steam rises from his
cabbage patch. Let us do something then, something to end this horrible moment, this plausible glistening moment that reflects in its
smooth sides this intolerable kitchen, this squalor; this woman moaning; and the rattle of the toy on the flags, and the man munching. Let us
smash it by breaking a match. There—snap.

And then comes the low of the cows in the field; and another cow to
the left answers; and all the cows seem to be moving tranquilly across
the field and the owl flutes off its watery bubble. But the sun is deep
below the earth. The trees are growing heavier, blacker; no order is
perceptible; there is no sequence in these cries, these movements; they
come from no bodies; they are cries to the left and to the right. Nothing can be seen. We can only see ourselves as outlines, cadaverous,
sculpturesque. And it is more difficult for the voice to carry through

this dark. The dark has stripped the fledge from the arrow—the vibrations that rise red shiver as it passes through us.

Then comes the terror, the exultation; the power to rush out unnoticed, alone; to be consumed; to be swept away to become a rider on the random wind; the tossing wind; the trampling and neighing wind; the horse with the blown-back mane; the tumbling, the foraging; he who gallops forever, nowhither travelling, indifferent; to be part of the eyeless dark, to be rippling and streaming, to feel the glory run molten up the spine, down the limbs, making the eyes glow, burning, bright, and penetrate the buffeting waves of the wind.

"Everything's sopping wet. It's the dew off the grass. Time to go in."

And then one shape heaves and surges and rises, and we pass, trailing coats, down the path towards the lighted windows, the dim glow behind the branches, and so enter the door, and the square draws its lines round us, and here is a chair, a table, glasses, knives, and thus we are boxed and housed, and will soon require a draught of soda-water and to find something to read in bed.   15

LINES OF INQUIRY
"The Moment: Summer's Night"

Though this essay is called "The Moment," it often seems to be telling about an experience that lasted more than a moment. When and where does the experience take place? What goes on during the experience? How long does it actually last? How many people take part in the experience? What are they talking about? What are they thinking about? At what points in the essay did you feel most capable of answering such questions as these? At what points did you feel most incapable of answering them? What aspects of the experience itself might account for the alternating clarity and blurriness of the essay? What aspects of Woolf's narrative technique might account for the wavering clarity and blurriness of the piece?

In the middle of the first paragraph of the essay, Woolf asks "what composed the present moment?" And at the opening of the second, third, and fourth paragraphs, as well as in subsequent paragraphs, she refers to what the moment included or what the moment was like. Examine all of Woolf's explicit references to "the moment," and make a list of all the things she says about it. Taking into account all of Woolf's statements about the moment, what is it "composed of"? What is the nature of this moment? Why do you suppose she lavishes so much detail on it? To what extent do you suppose she might have intended this moment to be seen as typical of other moments in her experience or the experience of other human beings?

For another essay by Woolf about another moment in her life, look at "The Death of the Moth." What similarities—what differences—do you notice in the nature of each moment? What similarities—what differences—do you notice in Woolf's method of telling about each experience? How do you account for the differences in her narrative technique? How were you affected by her differing methods of presentation?

LESLIE STEPHEN

By the time that his children were growing up the great days of my father's life were over. His feats on the river and on the mountains had been won before they were born. Relics of them were to be found lying about the house—the silver cup on the study mantelpiece; the rusty alpenstocks that leant against the bookcase in the corner; and to the end of his days he would speak of great climbers and explorers with a peculiar mixture of admiration and envy. But his own years of activity were over, and my father had to content himself with pottering about the Swiss valleys or taking a stroll across the Cornish moors.

That to potter and to stroll meant more on his lips than on other people's is becoming obvious now that some of his friends have given their own version of those expeditions. He would start off after breakfast alone, or with one companion. Shortly before dinner he would return. If the walk had been successful, he would have out his great map and commemorate a new short-cut in red ink. And he was quite capable, it appears, of striding all day across the moors without speaking more than a word or two to his companion. By that time, too, he had written the *History of English Thought in the Eighteenth Century,* which is said by some to be his masterpiece; and the *Science of Ethics*—the book which interested him most; and *The Playground of Europe,* in which is to be found 'The Sunset on Mont Blanc'—in his opinion the best thing he ever wrote.

He still wrote daily and methodically, though never for long at a time. In London he wrote in the large room with three long windows at the top of the house. He wrote lying almost recumbent in a low rocking chair which he tipped to and fro as he wrote, like a cradle, and as he wrote he smoked a short clay pipe, and he scattered books round him in a circle. The thud of a book dropped on the floor could be heard in the room beneath. And often as he mounted the stairs to his study with his firm, regular tread he would burst, not into song, for he was entirely unmusical, but into a strange rhythmical chant, for verse of all kinds, both 'utter trash', as he called it, and the most sublime words of Milton and Wordsworth, stuck in his memory, and the act of walking or climbing seemed to inspire him to recite whichever it was that came uppermost or suited his mood.

But it was his dexterity with his fingers that delighted his children before they could potter along the lanes at his heels or read his books. He would twist a sheet of paper beneath a pair of scissors and out would drop an elephant, a stag, or a monkey with trunks, horns, and tails delicately and exactly formed. Or, taking a pencil, he would draw beast after beast—an art that he practised almost unconsciously as he read, so that the fly-leaves of his books swarm with owls and donkeys as if to illustrate the 'Oh, you ass!' or 'Conceited dunce', that he was wont to scribble impatiently in the margin. Such brief comments, in which one may find the germ of the more temperate statements of his essays, recall some of the characteristics of his talk. He could be very silent, as his friends have testified. But his remarks, made suddenly in a low voice between the puffs of his pipe, were extremely effective. Sometimes with one word—but his one word was accompanied by a gesture of the hand—he would dispose of the tissue of exaggerations which his own sobriety seemed to provoke. 'There are 40,000,000 unmarried women in London alone!' Lady Ritchie once informed him. 'Oh, Annie, Annie!' my father exclaimed in tones of horrified but affectionate rebuke. But Lady Ritchie, as if she enjoyed being rebuked, would pile it up even higher next time she came.

The stories he told to amuse his children of adventures in the Alps—   5 but accidents only happened, he would explain, if you were so foolish as to disobey your guides—or of those long walks, after one of which, from Cambridge to London on a hot day, 'I drank, I am sorry to say, rather more than was good for me,' were told very briefly, but with a curious power to impress the scene. The things that he did not say were always there in the background. So, too, though he seldom told anecdotes, and his memory for facts was bad, when he described a person—and he had known many people, both famous and obscure—he would convey exactly what he thought of him in two or three words. And what he thought might be the opposite of what other people thought. He had a way of upsetting established reputations and disregarding conventional values that could be disconcerting, and sometimes perhaps wounding, though no one was more respectful of any feeling that seemed to him genuine. But when, suddenly opening his bright blue eyes, and rousing himself from what had seemed complete abstraction, he gave his opinion, it was difficult to disregard it. It was a habit, especially when deafness made him unaware that this opinion could be heard, that had its inconveniences.

'I am the most easily bored of men', he wrote, truthfully as usual: and when, as was inevitable in a large family, some visitor threatened to stay not merely for tea but also for dinner, my father would express his anguish at first by twisting and untwisting a certain lock of hair. Then he would burst out, half to himself, half to the powers above, but quite audibly, 'Why can't he go? Why can't he go?' Yet such is the charm of simplicity—and did he not say, also truthfully, that 'bores are the salt of the earth'?—that the bores seldom went, or, if they did, forgave him and came again.

Too much, perhaps, has been said of his silence; too much stress has been laid upon his reserve. He loved clear thinking, he hated

sentimentality and gush; but this by no means meant that he was cold
and unemotional, perpetually critical and condemnatory in daily life.
On the contrary, it was his power of feeling strongly and of expressing
his feeling with vigour that made him sometimes so alarming as a
companion. A lady, for instance, complained of the wet summer that
was spoiling her tour in Cornwall. But to my father, though he never
called himself a democrat, the rain meant that the corn was being laid;
some poor man was being ruined; and the energy with which he
expressed his sympathy—not with the lady—left her discomfited. He
had something of the same respect for farmers and fishermen that he
had for climbers and explorers. So, too, he talked little of patriotism,
but during the South African War—and all wars were hateful to
him—he lay awake thinking that he heard the guns on the battlefield.
Again, neither his reason nor his cold common sense helped to convince him that a child could be late for dinner without having been
maimed or killed in an accident. And not all his mathematics together
with a bank balance which he insisted must be ample in the extreme,
could persuade him, when it came to signing a cheque, that the whole
family was not 'shooting Niagara to ruin', as he put it. The pictures
that he would draw of old age and the Bankruptcy Court, of ruined
men of letters who have to support large families in small houses at
Wimbledon (he owned a very small house at Wimbledon) might have
convinced those who complain of his understatements that hyperbole
was well within his reach had he chosen.

Yet the unreasonable mood was superficial, as the rapidity with
which it vanished would prove. The cheque-book was shut; Wimbledon and the workhouse were forgotten. Some thought of a humorous
kind made him chuckle. Taking his hat and his stick, calling for his dog
and his daughter, he would stride off into Kensington Gardens, where
he had walked as a little boy, where his brother Fitzjames and he had
made beautiful bows to young Queen Victoria and she had swept them
a curtsy, and so, round the Serpentine, to Hyde Park Corner, where he
had once saluted the great Duke himself; and so home. He was not then
in the least 'alarming'; he was very simple, very confiding; and his
silence, though one might last unbroken from the Round Pond to the
Marble Arch, was curiously full of meaning, as if he were thinking half
aloud, about poetry and philosophy and people he had known.

He himself was the most abstemious of men. He smoked a pipe
perpetually, but never a cigar. He wore his clothes until they were too
shabby to be tolerable; and he held old-fashioned and rather Puritanical
views as to the vice of luxury and the sin of idleness. The relations
between parents and children today have a freedom that would have
been impossible with my father. He expected a certain standard of
behaviour, even of ceremony, in family life. Yet if freedom means the
right to think one's own thoughts and to follow one's own pursuits,

then no one respected and indeed insisted upon freedom more completely than he did. His sons, with the exception of the Army and
Navy, should follow whatever professions they chose; his daughters,
though he cared little enough for the higher education of women,
should have the same liberty. If at one moment he rebuked a daughter
sharply for smoking a cigarette—smoking was not in his opinion a nice
habit in the other sex—she had only to ask him if she might become a
painter, and he assured her that so long as she took her work seriously
he would give her all the help he could. He had no special love for
painting; but he kept his word. Freedom of that sort was worth thousands of cigarettes.

It was the same with the perhaps more difficult problem of lit-   10
erature. Even today there may be parents who would doubt the wisdom
of allowing a girl of fifteen the free run of a large and quite unexpur-
gated library. But my father allowed it. There were certain facts—very
briefly, very shyly he referred to them. Yet 'Read what you like,' he
said, and all his books, 'mangy and worthless', as he called them, but
certainly they were many and various, were to be had without asking.
To read what one liked because one liked it, never to pretend to admire
what one did not—that was his only lesson in the art of reading. To
write in the fewest possible words, as clearly as possible, exactly what
one meant—that was his only lesson in the art of writing. All the rest
must be learnt for oneself. Yet a child must have been childish in the
extreme not to feel that such was the teaching of a man of great learning and wide experience, though he would never impose his own views
or parade his own knowledge. For, as his tailor remarked when he saw
my father walk past his shop up Bond Street, 'There goes a gentleman
that wears good clothes without knowing it.'

In those last years, grown solitary and very deaf, he would sometimes call himself a failure as a writer; he had been 'jack of all trades,
and master of none'. But whether he failed or succeeded as a writer, it is
permissible to believe that he left a distinct impression of himself on
the minds of his friends. Meredith saw him as 'Phoebus Apollo turned
fasting friar' in his earlier days; Thomas Hardy, years later, looked at
the 'spare and desolate figure' of the Schreckhorn and thought of

> him,
> Who scaled its horn with ventured life and limb,
> Drawn on by vague imaginings, maybe,
> Of semblance to his personality
> In its quaint glooms, keen lights, and rugged trim.

But the praise he would have valued most, for though he was an agnos-
tic nobody believed more profoundly in the worth of human relationships, was Meredith's tribute after his death: 'He was the one man to

my knowledge worthy to have married your mother.' And Lowell, when he called him 'L.S., the most lovable of men', has best described the quality that makes him, after all these years, unforgettable.

LINES OF INQUIRY
"Leslie Stephen"

In this essay, Woolf presents a portrait of her father Leslie Stephen, who was an eminent English literary critic and scholar of the late nineteenth and early twentieth centuries. In what ways does Woolf's point of view seem to be influenced by the fact that she is writing about her father? In what ways does her selection and arrangement of details appear to be influenced by the fact that she is writing about her father? What kinds of information does she emphasize in the piece? What kinds of information about him seem to be missing from the piece? What kinds of information would you like to know about Stephen that are not included here? Where do you think you might be able to find more information about him?

Woolf begins her portrait with a sentence that seems to establish an intensely downbeat mood for the portrait to follow—"By the time that his children were growing up the great days of my father's life were over." How closely does she stay with the somber mood and somewhat elegiac tone of this sentence? What kind of person does Stephen appear to have been from his personal habits and activities? From his activities with his children? From his treatment of Woolf? From his behavior towards friends and acquaintances? What aspects of Stephen's behavior and personality come across most clearly, frequently, and prominently in Woolf's portrayal of him.

For another woman essayist's portrait of her father, consider Joyce Carol Oates's "My Father, My Fiction." What similarities—what differences—do you notice between the kind of information that Oates and Woolf include in their portraits? Between the ways they organize their information and structure their portraits? Between the approaches they take to writing about their fathers? How do you account for the differences? How were you affected by the differences?

WOMEN AND FICTION

The title of this article can be read in two ways: it may allude to women and the fiction that they write, or to women and the fiction that is written about them. The ambiguity is intentional, for in dealing with women as writers, as much elasticity as possible is desirable; it is necessary to leave oneself room to deal with other things besides their work, so much has that work been influenced by conditions that have nothing whatever to do with art.

The most superficial inquiry into women's writing instantly raises a host of questions. Why, we ask at once, was there no continuous writing done by women before the eighteenth century? Why did they then write almost as habitually as men, and in the course of that writing produce, one after another, some of the classics of English fiction? And why did their art then, and why to some extent does their art still, take the form of fiction?

A little thought will show us that we are asking questions to which we shall get, as answer, only further fiction. The answer lies at present locked in old diaries, stuffed away in old drawers, half-obliterated in the memories of the aged. It is to be found in the lives of the obscure— in those almost unlit corridors of history where the figures of genera- tions of women are so dimly, so fitfully perceived. For very little is known about women. The history of England is the history of the male line, not of the female. Of our fathers we know always some fact, some distinction. They were soldiers or they were sailors; they filled that office or they made that law. But of our mothers, our grandmothers, our great-grandmothers, what remains? Nothing but a tradition. One was beautiful; one was red-haired; one was kissed by a Queen. We know nothing of them except their names and the dates of their mar- riages and the number of children they bore.

Thus, if we wish to know why at any particular time women did this or that, why they wrote nothing, why on the other hand they wrote masterpieces, it is extremely difficult to tell. Anyone who should seek among those old papers, who should turn history wrong side out and so construct a faithful picture of the daily life of the ordinary woman in Shakespeare's time, in Milton's time, in Johnson's time, would not only write a book of astonishing interest, but would furnish the critic with a weapon which he now lacks. The extraordinary woman depends on the ordinary woman. It is only when we know what were the con- ditions of the average woman's life—the number of her children, whether she had money of her own, if she had a room to herself, whether she had help in bringing up her family, if she had servants, whether part of the housework was her task—it is only when we can measure the way of life and the experience of life made possible to the ordinary woman that we can account for the success or failure of the extraordinary woman as a writer.

Strange spaces of silence seem to separate one period of activity   5 from another. There was Sappho and a little group of women all writing poetry on a Greek island six hundred years before the birth of Christ. They fall silent. Then about the year 1000 we find a certain court lady, the Lady Murasaki, writing a very long and beautiful novel in Japan. But in England in the sixteenth century, when the dramatists and poets were most active, the women were dumb. Elizabethan literature is exclusively masculine. Then, at the end of the eighteenth century and in the beginning of the nineteenth, we find women again writing—this time in England—with extraordinary frequency and success.

Law and custom were of course largely responsible for these strange intermissions of silence and speech. When a woman was liable, as she was in the fifteenth century, to be beaten and flung about the room if she did not marry the man of her parents' choice, the spiritual atmosphere was not favourable to the production of works of art. When she was married without her own consent to a man who thereupon became her lord and master, "so far at least as law and custom could make him," as she was in the time of the Stuarts, it is likely she had little time for writing, and less encouragement. The immense effect of environment and suggestion upon the mind, we in our psychoanalytical age are beginning to realize. Again, with memoirs and letters to help us, we are beginning to understand how abnormal is the effort needed to produce a work of art, and what shelter and what support the mind of the artist requires. Of those facts the lives and letters of men like Keats and Carlyle and Flaubert assure us.

Thus it is clear that the extraordinary outburst of fiction in the beginning of the nineteenth century in England was heralded by innumerable slight changes in law and customs and manners. And women of the nineteenth century had some leisure; they had some education. It was no longer the exception for women of the middle and upper classes to choose their own husbands. And it is significant that of the four great women novelists—Jane Austen, Emily Brontë, Charlotte Brontë, and George Eliot—not one had a child, and two were unmarried.

Yet, though it is clear that the ban upon writing had been removed, there was still, it would seem, considerable pressure upon women to write novels. No four women can have been more unlike in genius and character than these four. Jane Austen can have had nothing in common with George Eliot; George Eliot was the direct opposite of Emily Brontë. Yet all were trained for the same profession; all, when they wrote, wrote novels.

Fiction was, as fiction still is, the easiest thing for a woman to write. Nor is it difficult to find the reason. A novel is the least concentrated form of art. A novel can be taken up or put down more easily than a play or a poem. George Eliot left her work to nurse her father. Charlotte Brontë put down her pen to pick the eyes out of the potatoes. And living as she did in the common sitting-room, surrounded by people, a woman was trained to use her mind in observation and upon the analysis of character. She was trained to be a novelist and not to be a poet.

Even in the nineteenth century, a woman lived almost solely in her home and her emotions. And those nineteenth-century novels, remarkable as they were, were profoundly influenced by the fact that the women who wrote them were excluded by their sex from certain kinds of experience. That experience has a great influence upon fiction is indisputable. The best part of Conrad's novels, for instance, would be destroyed if it had been impossible for him to be a sailor. Take away all that Tolstoi knew of war as a soldier, of life and society as a rich young man whose education admitted him to all sorts of experience, and *War and Peace* would be incredibly impoverished.

Yet *Pride and Prejudice, Wuthering Heights, Villette,* and *Middlemarch* were written by women from whom was forcibly withheld all experience save that which could be met with in a middle-class drawing-room. No first-hand experience of war or seafaring or politics or business was possible for them. Even their emotional life was strictly regulated by law and custom. When George Eliot ventured to live with Mr. Lewes without being his wife, public opinion was scandalized. Under its pressure she withdrew into a suburban seclusion which, inevitably, had the worst possible effects upon her work. She wrote that unless people asked of their own accord to come and see her, she never invited them. At the same time, on the other side of Europe, Tolstoi was living a free life as a soldier, with men and women of all classes, for which nobody censured him and from which his novels drew much of their astonishing breadth and vigour.

But the novels of women were not affected only by the necessarily narrow range of the writer's experience. They showed, at least in the nineteenth century, another characteristic which may be traced to the writer's sex. In *Middlemarch* and in *Jane Eyre* we are conscious not merely of the writer's character, as we are conscious of the character of Charles Dickens, but we are conscious of a woman's presence—of someone resenting the treatment of her sex and pleading for its rights. This brings into women's writing an element which is entirely absent from a man's, unless, indeed, he happens to be a working-man, a negro, or one who for some other reason is conscious of disability. It introduces a distortion and is frequently the cause of weakness. The desire to plead some personal cause or to make a character the mouthpiece of some personal discontent or grievance always has a distressing effect, as if the spot at which the reader's attention is directed were suddenly twofold instead of single.

The genius of Jane Austen and Emily Brontë is never more convincing than in their power to ignore such claims and solicitations and to hold on their way unperturbed by scorn or censure. But it needed a very serene or a very powerful mind to resist the temptation to anger. The ridicule, the censure, the assurance of inferiority in one form or another which were lavished upon women who practised an art, provoked such reactions naturally enough. One sees the effect in Charlotte Brontë's indignation, in George Eliot's resignation. Again and again one finds it in the work of the lesser women writers—in their choice of a subject, in their unnatural self-assertiveness, in their unnatural docility. Moreover, insincerity leaks in almost unconsciously. They adopt a view in deference to authority. The vision becomes too masculine or it becomes too feminine; it loses its perfect integrity and, with that, its most essential quality as a work of art.

The great change that has crept into women's writing is, it would seem, a change of attitude. The woman writer is no longer bitter. She is no longer angry. She is no longer pleading and protesting as she writes. We are approaching, if we have not yet reached, the time when her writing will have little or no foreign influence to disturb it. She will be able to concentrate upon her vision without distraction from outside. The aloofness that was once within the reach of genius and originality is only now coming within the reach of ordinary women. Therefore the average novel by a woman is far more genuine and far more interesting to-day than it was a hundred or even fifty years ago.

But it is still true that before a woman can write exactly as she   15
wishes to write, she has many difficulties to face. To begin with, there is the technical difficulty—so simple, apparently; in reality, so baffling—that the very form of the sentence does not fit her. It is a sentence made by men; it is too loose, too heavy, too pompous for a woman's use. Yet in a novel, which covers so wide a stretch of ground, an ordinary and usual type of sentence has to be found to carry the reader on easily and naturally from one end of the book to the other. And this a woman must make for herself, altering and adapting the current sentence until she writes one that takes the natural shape of her thought without crushing or distorting it.

But that, after all, is only a means to an end, and the end is still to be reached only when a woman has the courage to surmount opposition and the determination to be true to herself. For a novel, after all, is a statement about a thousand different objects—human, natural, divine; it is an attempt to relate them to each other. In every novel of merit these different elements are held in place by the force of the writer's vision. But they have another order also, which is the order imposed upon them by convention. And as men are the arbiters of that convention, as they have established an order of values in life, so too, since fiction is largely based on life, these values prevail·there also to a very great extent.

It is probable, however, that both in life and in art the values of a woman are not the values of a man. Thus, when a woman comes to write a novel, she will find that she is perpetually wishing to alter the established values—to make serious what appears insignificant to a man, and trivial what is to him important. And for that, of course, she will be criticized; for the critic of the opposite sex will be genuinely puzzled and surprised by an attempt to alter the current scale of values, and will see in it not merely a difference of view, but a view that is weak, or trivial, or sentimental, because it differs from his own.

But here, too, women are coming to be more independent of opinion. They are beginning to respect their own sense of values. And for this reason the subject matter of their novels begins to show certain changes. They are less interested, it would seem, in themselves; on the other hand, they are more interested in other women. In the early nineteenth century, women's novels were largely autobiographical. One of the motives that led them to write was the desire to expose their own suffering, to plead their own cause. Now that this desire is no longer so urgent, women are beginning to explore their own sex, to write of women as women have never been written of before; for of course, until very lately, women in literature were the creation of men.

Here again there are difficulties to overcome for, if one may generalize, not only do women submit less readily to observation than men, but their lives are far less tested and examined by the ordinary processes of life. Often nothing tangible remains of a woman's day. The food that has been cooked is eaten; the children that have been nursed have gone out into the world. Where does the accent fall? What is the salient point for the novelist to seize upon? It is difficult to say. Her life has an anonymous character which is baffling and puzzling in the extreme. For the first time, this dark country is beginning to be explored in fiction; and at the same moment a woman has also to record the changes in women's minds and habits which the opening of the professions has introduced. She has to observe how their lives are ceasing to run underground; she has to discover what new colours and shadows are showing in them now that they are exposed to the outer world.

If, then, one should try to sum up the character of women's fiction   20 at the present moment, one would say that it is courageous; it is sincere; it keeps closely to what women feel. It is not bitter. It does not insist upon its femininity. But at the same time, a woman's book is not written as a man would write it. These qualities are much commoner than they were, and they give even to second- and third-rate work the value of truth and the interest of sincerity.

But in addition to these good qualities, there are two that call for a word more of discussion. The change which has turned the English woman from a nondescript influence, fluctuating and vague, to a voter, a wage-earner, a responsible citizen, has given her both in her life and in her art a turn toward the impersonal. Her relations now are not only emotional; they are intellectual, they are political. The old system which condemned her to squint askance at things through the eyes or through the interests of husband or brother, has given place to the direct and practical interests of one who must act for herself, and not merely influence the acts of others. Hence her attention is being directed away from the personal centre which engaged it exclusively in the past to the impersonal, and her novels naturally become more critical of society, and less analytical of individual lives.

We may expect that the office of gadfly to the state, which has been so far a male prerogative, will now be discharged by women also. Their novels will deal with social evils and remedies. Their men and women will not be observed wholly in relation to each other emotionally, but as they cohere and clash in groups and classes and races. That is one change of some importance. But there is another more interesting to those who prefer the butterfly to the gadfly—that is to say, the artist to the reformer. The greater impersonality of women's lives will encourage the poetic spirit, and it is in poetry that women's fiction is still weakest. It will lead them to be less absorbed in facts and no longer content to record with astonishing acuteness the minute details which fall under their own observation. They will look beyond the personal and political relationships to the wider questions which the poet tries to solve—of our destiny and the meaning of life.

The basis of the poetic attitude is of course largely founded upon material things. It depends upon leisure, and a little money, and the chance which money and leisure give to observe impersonally and dispassionately. With money and leisure at their service, women will naturally occupy themselves more than has hitherto been possible with the craft of letters. They will make a fuller and a more subtle use of the instrument of writing. Their technique will become bolder and richer.

In the past, the virtue of women's writing often lay in its divine spontaneity, like that of the blackbird's song or the thrush's. It was untaught; it was from the heart. But it was also, and much more often, chattering and garrulous—mere talk spilt over paper and left to dry in pools and blots. In future, granted time and books and a little space in the house for herself, literature will become for women, as for men, an art to be studied. Women's gift will be trained and strengthened. The novel will cease to be the dumping-ground for the personal emotions. It will become, more than at present, a work of art like any other, and its resources and its limitations will be explored.

From this it is a short step to the practice of the sophisticated arts, 25

hitherto so little practised by women—to the writing of essays and criticism, of history and biography. And that, too, if we are considering
the novel, will be of advantage; for besides improving the quality of
the novel itself, it will draw off the aliens who have been attracted to
fiction by its accessibility while their hearts lay elsewhere. Thus will the
novel be rid of those excrescences of history and fact which, in our
time, have made it so shapeless.

So, if we may prophesy, women in time to come will write fewer
novels, but better novels; and not novels only, but poetry and criticism
and history. But in this, to be sure, one is looking ahead to that golden,
that perhaps fabulous, age when women will have what has so long
been denied them—leisure, and money, and a room to themselves.

March 1929

LINES OF INQUIRY
"Women and Fiction"

In the second paragraph of her essay, Woolf asks a series of pointed questions about "women's writing," but then at the opening of her third paragraph
she says "that we are asking questions to which we shall get, as answer, only
further fiction." What do you think she means by describing the answers as
"only further fiction"? During most of the essay that follows, Woolf gives
herself over to answering those very same questions. In what respects do her
answers seem to be only further fiction? In what respects do they seem to be
something other than fiction, such as fact, or inference, or surmise, or common
sense? In what ways does she manage to give her answers an air of credibility?

In paragraph 6, Woolf notes "how abnormal is the effort needed to produce
a work of art." Later in the same sentence she speaks about the "shelter" and
"support the mind of the artist requires," as if to suggest that these needs are
also "abnormal." Why do you suppose Woolf believes that such an abnormal
state of affairs is necessary to "produce a work of art"? Why does she believe
that this abnormal situation has normally been available to men, but not to
women? What kind of social and economic changes would be necessary to make
this abnormal state of affairs available to women?

In her final paragraph, Woolf imagines a golden age, when women write
"not novels only, but poetry and criticism and history." Given the careers of
the recent women writers represented in this collection, and any others you
may be familiar with, how do you think Woolf would characterize the current
situation? What do you think about the current situation for women's writing?

THE MODERN ESSAY

As Mr. Rhys truly says, it is unnecessary to go profoundly into the history and origin of the essay—whether it derives from Socrates or Siranney the Persian—since, like all living things, its present is more important than its past. Moreover, the family is widely spread; and while some of its representatives have risen in the world and wear their coronets with the best, others pick up a precarious living in the gutter near Fleet Street. The form, too, admits variety. The essay can be short or long, serious or trifling, about God and Spinoza, or about turtles and Cheapside. But as we turn over the pages of these five little volumes,[1] containing essays written between 1870 and 1920, certain principles appear to control the chaos, and we detect in the short period under review something like the progress of history.

Of all forms of literature, however, the essay is the one which least calls for the use of long words. The principle which controls it is simply that it should give pleasure; the desire which impels us when we take it from the shelf is simply to receive pleasure. Everything in an essay must be subdued to that end. It should lay us under a spell with its first word, and we should only wake, refreshed, with its last. In the interval we may pass through the most various experiences of amusement, surprise, interest, indignation; we may soar to the heights of fantasy with Lamb or plunge to the depths of wisdom with Bacon, but we must never be roused. The essay must lap us about and draw its curtain across the world.

So great a feat is seldom accomplished, though the fault may well be as much on the reader's side as on the writer's. Habit and lethargy have dulled his palate. A novel has a story, a poem rhyme; but what art can the essayist use in these short lengths of prose to sting us wide awake and fix us in a trance which is not sleep but rather an intensification of life—a basking, with every faculty alert, in the sun of pleasure? He must know—that is the first essential—how to write. His learning may be as profound as Mark Pattison's, but in an essay it must be so fused by the magic of writing that not a fact juts out, not a dogma tears the surface of the texture. Macaulay in one way, Froude in another, did this superbly over and over again. They have blown more knowledge into us in the course of one essay than the innumerable chapters of a hundred text-books. But when Mark Pattison has to tell

---

[1] *Modern English Essays,* edited by Ernest Rhys, five volumes (Dent).

us, in the space of thirty-five little pages, about Montaigne, we feel that he had not previously assimilated M. Grün. M. Grün was a gentleman who once wrote a bad book. M. Grün and his book should have been embalmed for our perpetual delight in amber. But the process is fa-iguing; it requires more time and perhaps more temper than Pattison had at his command. He served M. Grün up raw, and he remains a crude berry among the cook meats, upon which our teeth must grate for ever. Something of the sort applies to Matthew Arnold and a certain translator of Spinoza. Literal truth-telling and finding fault with a cul-prit for his good are out of place in an essay, where everything should be for our good and rather for eternity than for the March number of the *Fortnightly Review*. But if the voice of the scold should never be heard in this narrow plot, there is another voice which is as a plague of locusts—the voice of a man stumbling drowsily among loose words, clutching aimlessly at vague ideas, the voice, for example, of Mr. Hut-ton in the following passage:

> Add to this that his married life was very brief, only seven years and a half, being unexpectedly cut short, and that his passionate reverence for his wife's memory and genius—in his own words, "a religion"—was one which, as he must have been perfectly sensible, he could not make to appear otherwise than extravagant, not to say an hallucination, in the eyes of the rest of mankind, and yet that he was possessed by an irresistible yearning to attempt to embody it in all the tender and enthusiastic hy-perbole of which it is so pathetic to find a man who gained his fame by his "dry-light" a master, and it is impossible not to feel that the human incidents in Mr. Mill's career are very sad.

A book could take that blow, but it sinks an essay. A biography in two volumes is indeed the proper depositary; for there, where the li-cence is so much wider, and hints and glimpses of outside things make part of the feast (we refer to the old type of Victorian volume), these yawns and stretches hardly matter, and have indeed some positive value of their own. But that value, which is contributed by the reader, per-haps illicitly, in his desire to get as much into the book from all possible sources as he can, must be ruled out here.

There is no room for the impurities of literature in an essay. Some- 5 how or other, by dint of labour or bounty of nature, or both combined, the essay must be pure—pure like water or pure like wine, but pure from dullness, deadness, and deposits of extraneous matter. Of all writ-ers in the first volume, Walter Pater best achieves this arduous task, because before setting out to write his essay ("Notes on Leonardo da Vinci") he has somehow contrived to get his material fused. He is a learned man, but it is not knowledge of Leonardo that remains with us, but a vision, such as we get in a good novel where everything contrib-utes to bring the writer's conception as a whole before us. Only here, in the essay, where the bounds are so strict and facts have to be used in their nakedness, the true writer like Walter Pater makes these limitations yield their own quality. Truth will give it authority; from its narrow limits he will get shape and intensity; and then there is no more fitting place for some of those ornaments which the old writers loved and we, by calling them ornaments, presumably despise. Nowadays nobody would have the courage to embark on the once famous description of Leonardo's lady who has

> learned the secrets of the grave; and has been a diver in deep seas and keeps their fallen day about her; and trafficked for strange webs with Eastern merchants; and, as Leda, was the mother of Helen of Troy, and, as Saint Anne, the mother of Mary . . .

The passage is too thumb-marked to slip naturally into the context. But when we come unexpectedly upon "the smiling of women and the motion of great waters," or upon "full of the refinement of the dead, in sad, earth-coloured raiment, set with pale stones," we suddenly remember that we have ears and we have eyes, and that the English language fills a long array of stout volumes with innumerable words, many of which are of more than one syllable. The only living Englishman who ever looks into these volumes is, of course, a gentleman of Polish extraction. But doubtless our abstention saves us much gush, much rhetoric, much high-stepping and cloud-prancing, and for the sake of the prevailing sobriety and hard-headedness we should be willing to barter the splendour of Sir Thomas Browne and the vigour of Swift.

Yet, if the essay admits more properly than biography or fiction of sudden boldness and metaphor, and can be polished till every atom of its surface shines, there are dangers in that too. We are soon in sight of ornament. Soon the current, which is the life-blood of literature, runs slow; and instead of sparkling and flashing or moving with a quieter impulse which has a deeper excitement, words coagulate together in frozen sprays which, like the grapes on a Christmas-tree, glitter for a single night, but are dusty and garish the day after. The temptation to decorate is great where the theme may be of the slightest. What is there to interest another in the fact that one has enjoyed a walking tour, or has amused oneself by rambling down Cheapside and looking at the turtles in Mr. Sweeting's shop window? Stevenson and Samuel Butler chose very different methods of exciting our interest in these domestic themes. Stevenson, of course, trimmed and polished and set out his matter in the traditional eighteenth-century form. It is admirably done, but we cannot help feeling anxious, as the essay proceeds, lest the material may give out under the craftsman's fingers. The ingot is so small, the manipulation so incessant. And perhaps that is why the peroration—

> To sit still and contemplate—to remember the faces of women without
> desire, to be pleased by the great deeds of men without envy, to be
> everything and everywhere in sympathy and yet content to remain where
> and what you are—

has the sort of insubstantiality which suggests that by the time he got
to the end he had left himself nothing solid to work with. Butler adopted
the very opposite method. Think your own thoughts, he seems to say,
and speak them as plainly as you can. These turtles in the shop window
which appear to leak out of their shells through heads and feet suggest
a fatal faithfulness to a fixed idea. And so, striding unconcernedly from
one idea to the next, we traverse a large stretch of ground; observe that
a wound in the solicitor is a very serious thing; that Mary Queen of
Scots wears surgical boots and is subject to fits near the Horse Shoe in
Tottenham Court Road; take it for granted that no one really cares
about Aeschylus; and so, with many amusing anecdotes and some profound reflections, reach the peroration, which is that, as he had been
told not to see more in Cheapside than he could get into twelve pages
of the *Universal Review,* he had better stop. And yet obviously Butler
is at least as careful of our pleasure as Stevenson; and to write like
oneself and call it not writing is a much harder exercise in style than to
write like Addison and call it writing well.

But, however much they differ individually, the Victorian essayists
yet had something in common. They wrote at greater length than is
now usual, and they wrote for a public which had not only time to sit
down to its magazine seriously, but a high, if peculiarly Victorian, standard of culture by which to judge it. It was worth while to speak out
upon serious matters in an essay; and there was nothing absurd in writing as well as one possibly could when, in a month or two, the same
public which had welcomed the essay in a magazine would carefully
read it once more in a book. But a change came from a small audience
of cultivated people to a larger audience of people who were not quite
so cultivated. The change was not altogether for the worse. In volume
III we find Mr. Birrell and Mr. Beerbohm. It might even be said that
there was a reversion to the classic type, and that the essay by losing its
size and something of its sonority was approaching more nearly the
essay of Addison and Lamb. At any rate, there is a great gulf between
Mr. Birrell on Carlyle and the essay which one may suppose that Carlyle would have written upon Mr. Birrell. There is little similarity between *A Cloud of Pinafores,* by Max Beerbohm, and *A Cynic's Apology,*
by Leslie Stephen. But the essay is alive; there is no reason to despair.
As the conditions change so the essayist, most sensitive of all plants to
public opinion, adapts himself, and if he is good makes the best of the
change, and if he is bad the worst. Mr. Birrell is certainly good; and so
we find that, though he has dropped a considerable amount of weight,
his attack is much more direct and his movement more supple. But

what did Mr. Beerbohm give to the essay and what did he take from it? That is a much more complicated question, for here we have an essayist who has concentrated on the work and is without doubt the prince of his profession.

What Mr. Beerbohm gave was, of course, himself. This presence, which has haunted the essay fitfully from the time of Montaigne, had been in exile since the death of Charles Lamb. Matthew Arnold was never to his readers Matt, nor Walter Pater affectionately abbreviated in a thousand homes to Wat. They gave us much, but that they did not give. Thus, some time in the 'nineties, it must have surprised readers accustomed to exhortation, information, and denunciation to find themselves familiarly addressed by a voice which seemed to belong to a man no larger than themselves. He was affected by private joys and sorrows, and had no gospel to preach and no learning to impart. He was himself, simply and directly, and himself he has remained. Once again we have an essayist capable of using the essayist's most proper but most dangerous and delicate tool. He has brought personality into literature, not unconsciously and impurely, but so consciously and purely that we do not know whether there is any relation between Max the essayist and Mr. Beerbohm the man. We only know that the spirit of personality permeates every word that he writes. The triumph is the triumph of style. For it is only by knowing how to write that you can make use in literature of your self; that self which, while it is essential to literature, is also its most dangerous antagonist. Never to be yourself and yet always—that is the problem. Some of the essayists in Mr. Rhys' collection, to be frank, have not altogether succeeded in solving it. We are nauseated by the sight of trivial personalities decomposing in the eternity of print. As talk, no doubt, it was charming, and certainly the writer is a good fellow to meet over a bottle of beer. But literature is stern; it is no use being charming, virtuous, or even learned and brilliant into the bargain, unless, she seems to reiterate, you fulfil her first condition—to know how to write.

This art is possessed to perfection by Mr. Beerbohm. But he has not searched the dictionary for polysyllables. He has not moulded firm periods or seduced our ears with intricate cadences and strange melodies. Some of his companions—Henley and Stevenson, for example— are momentarily more impressive. But A Cloud of Pinafores had in it that indescribable inequality, stir, and final expressiveness which belong to life and to life alone. You have not finished with it because you have read it, any more than friendship is ended because it is time to part. Life wells up and alters and adds. Even things in a book-case change if they are alive; we find ourselves wanting to meet them again; we find them altered. So we look back upon essay after essay by Mr. Beerbohm, knowing that, come September or May, we shall sit down with them and talk. Yet it is true that the essayist is the most sensitive of all writers to public opinion. The drawing-room is the place where a great deal of reading is done nowadays, and the essays of Mr. Beerbohm lie, with an exquisite appreciation of all that the position exacts, upon the drawing-room table. There is no gin about; no strong tobacco; no puns, drunkenness, or insanity. Ladies and gentlemen talk together, and some things, of course, are not said.

But if it would be foolish to attempt to confine Mr. Beerbohm to   10
one room, it would be still more foolish, unhappily, to make him, the artist, the man who gives us only his best, the representative of our age. There are no essays by Mr. Beerbohm in the fourth or fifth volumes of the present collection. His age seems already a little distant, and the drawing-room table, as it recedes, begins to look rather like an altar where, once upon a time, people deposited offerings—fruit from their own orchards, gifts carved with their own hands. Now once more the conditions have changed. The public needs essays as much as ever, and perhaps even more. The demand for the light middle not exceeding fifteen hundred words, or in special cases seventeen hundred and fifty, much exceeds the supply. Where Lamb wrote one essay and Max perhaps writes two, Mr. Belloc at a rough computation produces three hundred and sixty-five. They are very short, it is true. Yet with what dexterity the practised essayist will utilise his space—beginning as close to the top of the sheet as possible, judging precisely how far to go, when to turn, and how, without sacrificing a hair's breadth of paper, to wheel about and alight accurately upon the last word his editor allows! As a feat of skill it is well worth watching. But the personality upon which Mr. Belloc, like Mr. Beerbohm, depends suffers in the process. It comes to us not with the natural richness of the speaking voice, but strained and thin and full of mannerisms and affectations, like the voice of a man shouting through a megaphone to a crowd on a windy day. "Little friends, my readers," he says in the essay called "An Unknown Country," and he goes on to tell us how—

> There was a shepherd the other day at Findon Fair who had come from the east by Lewes with sheep, and who had in his eyes that reminiscence of horizons which makes the eyes of shepherds and of mountaineers different from the eyes of other men. . . . I went with him to hear what he had to say, for shepherds talk quite differently from other men.

Happily this shepherd had little to say, even under the stimulus of the inevitable mug of beer, about the Unknown Country, for the only remark that he did make proves him either a minor poet, unfit for the care of sheep, or Mr. Belloc himself masquerading with a fountain pen. That is the penalty which the habitual essayist must now be prepared to face. He must masquerade. He cannot afford the time either to be himself or to be other people. He must skim the surface of thought and dilute the strength of personality. He must give us a worn weekly halfpenny instead of a solid sovereign once a year.

But it is not Mr. Belloc only who has suffered from the prevailing conditions. The essays which bring the collection to the year 1920 may not be the best of their authors' work, but, if we except writers like Mr. Conrad and Mr. Hudson, who have strayed into essay writing accidentally, and concentrate upon those who write essays habitually, we shall find them a good deal affected by the change in their circumstances. To write weekly, to write daily, to write shortly, to write for busy people catching trains in the morning or for tired people coming home in the evening, is a heartbreaking task for men who know good writing from bad. They do it, but instinctively draw out of harm's way anything precious that might be damaged by contact with the public, or anything sharp that might irritate its skin. And so, if one reads Mr. Lucas, Mr. Lynd, or Mr. Squire in the bulk, one feels that a common greyness silvers everything. They are as far removed from the extravagant beauty of Walter Pater as they are from the intemperate candour of Leslie Stephen. Beauty and courage are dangerous spirits to battle in a column and a half; and thought, like a brown paper parcel in a waistcoat pocket, has a way of spoiling the symmetry of an article. It is a kind, tired, apathetic world for which they write, and the marvel is that they never cease to attempt, at least, to write well.

But there is no need to pity Mr. Clutton Brock for this change in the essayist's conditions. He has clearly made the best of his circumstances and not the worst. One hesitates even to say that he has had to make any conscious effort in the matter, so naturally has he effected the transition from the private essayist to the public, from the drawing-room to the Albert Hall. Paradoxically enough, the shrinkage in size has brought about a corresponding expansion of individuality. We have no longer the "I" of Max and of Lamb, but the "we" of public bodies and other sublime personages. It is "we" who go to hear the *Magic Flute;* "we" who ought to profit by it; "we," in some mysterious way, who, in our corporate capacity, once upon a time actually wrote it. For music and literature and art must submit to the same generalisation or they will not carry to the farthest recesses of the Albert Hall. That the voice of Mr. Clutton Brock, so sincere and so disinterested, carries such a distance and reaches so many without pandering to the weakness of the mass or its passions must be a matter of legitimate satisfaction to us all. But while "we" are gratified, "I," that unruly partner in the human fellowship, is reduced to despair. "I" must always think things for himself, and feel things for himself. To share them in a diluted form with the majority of well-educated and well-intentioned men and women is for him sheer agony; and while the rest of us listen intently and profit profoundly, "I" slips off to the woods and the fields and rejoices in a single blade of grass or a solitary potato.

In the fifth volume of modern essays, it seems, we have got some way from pleasure and the art of writing. But in justice to the essayists of 1920 we must be sure that we are not praising the famous because they have been praised already and the dead because we shall never meet them wearing spats in Piccadilly. We must know what we mean when we say that they can write and give us pleasure. We must compare them; we must bring out the quality. We must point to this and say it is good because it is exact, truthful, and imaginative:

> Nay, retire men cannot when they would; neither will they, when it were Reason; but are impatient of Privateness, even in age and sickness, which require the shadow: like old Townsmen: that will still be sitting at their street door, though thereby they offer Age to Scorn . . .

and to this, and say it is bad because it is loose, plausible, and commonplace:

> With courteous and precise cynicism on his lips, he thought of quiet virginal chambers, of waters singing under the moon, of terraces where taintless music sobbed into the open night, of pure maternal mistresses with protecting arms and vigilant eyes, of fields slumbering in the sunlight, of leagues of ocean heaving under warm tremulous heavens, of hot ports, gorgeous and perfumed. . . .

It goes on, but already we are bemused with sound and neither feel nor hear. The comparison makes us suspect that the art of writing has for backbone some fierce attachment to an idea. It is on the back of an idea, something believed in with conviction or seen with precision and thus compelling words to its shape, that the diverse company which included Lamb and Bacon, and Mr. Beerbohm and Hudson, and Vernon Lee and Mr. Conrad, and Leslie Stephen and Butler and Walter Pater reaches the farther shore. Very various talents have helped or hindered the passage of the idea into words. Some scrape through painfully; others fly with every wind favouring. But Mr. Belloc and Mr. Lucas and Mr. Lynd and Mr. Squire are not fiercely attached to anything in itself. They share the contemporary dilemma—that lack of an obstinate conviction which lifts ephemeral sounds through the misty sphere of anybody's language to the land where there is a perpetual marriage, a perpetual union. Vague as all definitions are, a good essay must have this permanent quality about it; it must draw its curtain round us, but it must be a curtain that shuts us in, not out.

LINES OF INQUIRY
"The Modern Essay"

As indicated in the first footnote, this essay is a review of a five-volume collection of essays that appeared in 1920; but as indicated by the title, it is also a set of reflections on the modern essay; and as the piece itself makes clear, it is also an attempt by Woolf to define her idea of the essay. How does Woolf organize her essay to deal with all of these purposes in a clear, coherent, and developed way? Given the organization, proportioning, and detailing of her essay, which of these purposes do you think is most important to Woolf?

In paragraph 2, Woolf asserts that "the principle which controls" the essay "is simply that it should give pleasure"? What kind of pleasure do you think she has in mind? Why does Woolf think that knowing "how to write" is so important to producing this sense of pleasure? What does knowing how to write have to do with evoking "the spirit of personality," which Woolf refers to in paragraph 8 as the essayist's "most proper but most dangerous and delicate tool"? Given her emphasis on the pleasure of the essay, as well as on the proper style and personality of the essayist, how do you account for Woolf's statement in her final paragraph that "the art of writing has for backbone some fierce attachment to an idea"? Exactly what idea of the essay is Woolf most fiercely attached to in this essay?

Which of Woolf's essays in this collection do you believe most effectively exemplifies her ideas about the essay? Which least effectively? What specific aspects of each essay account for your ratings?

ACKNOWLEDGMENTS OF PERMISSION

RHETORICAL INDEX

*TITLES UNDER EACH CATEGORY REFER TO ESSAYS THAT EX-
HIBIT THE RHETORICAL FEATURE IN WHOLE OR IN SIGNIFI-
CANT PART*

DESCRIPTION

EXPLANATION

NARRATION

AUTHOR-TITLE INDEX

Phone list

Robin Brankle	362-4808
Michelle Campanello	262-3731
Kelly Danielson	234-0899
Michelle Forgey	293-3137
Katrina Kemble	233-4982
Er-Hsun Khoo	255-8828
Stephanie McGwin	616-684-9895
Jeff McKinley	288-2520
Dawn Rose	271-8204
Corey Tankerslay	616-445-2540
Karl Trautman	289-1214
Renee Willis	287-9193
Shawn Rohde	277-0920
Vicky Stultz	237-0401
Ken Smith	237-4173